MARTIN LUTHER

REBEL IN AN AGE OF UPHEAVAL

HEINZ SCHILLING

translated by
RONA JOHNSTON

OXFORD
UNIVERSITY PRESS

OXFORD
UNIVERSITY PRESS

Great Clarendon Street, Oxford, OX2 6DP,
United Kingdom

Oxford University Press is a department of the University of Oxford.
It furthers the University's objective of excellence in research, scholarship,
and education by publishing worldwide. Oxford is a registered trade mark of
Oxford University Press in the UK and in certain other countries

German edition:
© Verlag C. H. Beck oHG, München, 2013. This translation
© Oxford University Press 2017

The moral rights of the authors have been asserted

First Edition published in 2017

Impression: 1

Published in the United States of America by Oxford University Press
198 Madison Avenue, New York, NY 10016, United States of America

British Library Cataloguing in Publication Data
Data available

Library of Congress Control Number: 2016958734

ISBN 978-0-19-872281-6

Printed in Great Britain by
Clays Ltd, St Ives plc

Palma sub pondere crescit
For Ursula et cetera familia

Acknowledgements

Looking back now this book is complete, I recognize above all my debt of gratitude to Detlef Felken, who years ago first tempted me to tackle a biography of Luther and then became an enthusiastic and a knowledgeable reader who unfailingly supported the project and provided his counsel. Without him, this book would not exist. In another way this statement is equally valid for my colleagues on the board of the Verein für Reformationsgeschichte (Society for Reformation History), of which I have been a member throughout a lifetime of research—first deputizing for Bernd Moeller, whose influence as president was so formative, then from 2001 to 2011 as president, and now again as an ordinary member. Without the interdisciplinary discussions that they encouraged, I would not have found my way from my initial home in structural history at Freiburg and Bielefeld to a biography of Luther, and to its theological component in particular. I am also grateful for fruitful contact with Reformation historians in Europe beyond Germany and in North America, facilitated in particular by more than a decade and a half as European editor of the journal *Archiv für Reformationsgeschichte / Archive for Reformation History*.

Following on from many generations of research on Luther and on the Reformation, today's biographer of Luther can draw on outstanding source editions and hundreds of articles and monographs—an obvious legacy, perhaps, but still deserving of grateful acknowledgement. Two contributions stand out, that of the editors of the Weimar Edition (*Weimarer Werkausgabe*) of Luther's works and that of Martin Brecht, author of the three-volume biography of Luther. Responsibility for this interpretation of Luther in the context of his own age and as he figures for us today is, however, entirely mine. I hope that this book will inspire interconfessional and interdisciplinary debate about Luther's historical significance and the worldwide impact of the Reformation, much as Brecht's work stimulated discussion of the loss of the Reformation, crushed historiographically between research on the late Middle Ages, on one hand, and on confessionalization, on the other. This debate could provide a scholarly platform for the political commemoration of the 500th anniversary of the Reformation, in 2017.

I thank Karin Heilmann for producing a typescript of the first chapter and for subsequent technical assistance in moving from manuscript to computer. Ruth Slenczka made her expertise available when it came to selecting the images. I wish also to thank Anja Wagner and Claudia Häßler, who as they tracked down literature and checked the citations, developed their own enthusiasm for Luther.

My wife read this book closely and critically and in debating how the text should be formulated embodied most effectively the role of a 'Mr Käthe'.

Berlin, early summer 2012

Contents

List of Figures and Maps

Figures

Maps

Abbreviations

LW   *Luther's Works.* Edited by Jaroslav Pelikan, Helmut T. Lehmann, and Christopher Boyd Brown. 75 vols. Philadelphia and St. Louis, 1955–.

WB   *D. Martin Luthers Werke. Kritische Gesamtausgabe. Briefwechsel* [Correspondence]. 18 vols. Weimar, 1930–1985.

WDB   *D. Martin Luthers Werke. Kritische Gesamtausgabe. Die Deutsche Bibel* [German Bible]. 12 vols. Weimar, 1906–1961.

Wrede, RTA II *Deutsche Reichstagsakten unter Kaiser Karl V.* Edited by Adolf Wrede. New series, vol. 2. *Der Reichstag zu Worms 1521.* Gotha 1896; reprint 1962.

WT   *D. Martin Luthers Werke. Kritische Gesamtausgabe. Tischreden* [Table Talk]. 6 vols. Weimar, 1912–1921.

WW   *D. Martin Luthers Werke. Kritische Gesamtausgabe (Weimarer Ausgabe) Schriften* [Writings]. 73 vols. Weimar, 1883–2009.

Translator's Note

My goal as translator has been to provide a text fully accessible to a reader who has no German. On a similar note Heinz Schilling resolved that this version of his text should carry a pared-down scholarly apparatus. Readers can turn to the original German edition (*Martin Luther: Rebell in einer Zeit des Umbruchs*, C. H. Beck, 2012; 4th ed., 2016) for more substantial notes containing additional references to works in German and for a twenty-four-page, mainly German-language bibliography.

Schilling has used Luther's own words throughout his text to provide a 'direct route' to the 'uncontaminated' reformer. When possible I have drawn on existing English translations of Luther, primarily the original fifty-five volumes of *Luther's Works* along with additional volumes in that series published more recently (see 'abbreviations'). If the endnote associated with a quotation references a work in German, then the translation is my own; an endnote that cites a work in English also acknowledges the quotation's translation.

Unless otherwise noted, all citations of Scripture are from the New Revised Standard Version.

Luther insisted, 'Interpreters and translators should not work alone.' I am very grateful to Bruce Gordon and Christian Moser for their support, both scholarly and good-humoured, for my translation of this book. And I am grateful, too, to Yale Divinity School Library for providing a convivial setting and undaunted assistance for this undertaking.

RONA JOHNSTON

New Haven, Connecticut, June 2016

Prologue

All the epochs when faith rules, in whatever form, are splendid, heartening, and fertile for contemporaries and posterity.

Johann Wolfgang von Goethe,
The West-East Divan, Notes and Essays,
'Israel in the Desert'[1]

Living in an Age of Faith and an Age in Transition

Martin Luther, the Wittenberg reformer, lived in 'an age ruled by faith', as Goethe would have it. Indeed, thanks to Luther, as the medieval period gave way to the modern age, for more than a century religion dictated the path taken by Germany and Europe. Those years proved 'splendid, heartening, and fertile', but they could also be dark, disheartening, and destructive. The contradictions of his age were also Luther's own: he experienced lofty hours of triumph, hopeful that all the world could be convinced, and bitter weeks in which Satan and his dark forces attacked both the reformer and his achievements. But Luther never doubted that God had called him to be his prophet.

Not that religion was lacking in the world into which Luther (or rather Luder, his surname for the first decades of his life) was born, on 10 November 1483 in Eisleben, in the county of Mansfeld, in central Germany. The final decades of the fifteenth century were consumed with concerns about belief and the church. That preoccupation was an expression of the unsettling tension created by the juxtaposition of the bold and worldly Roman papacy and the needs of a laity that no longer believed the clergy's promises about salvation and struggled to find a way to truth and redemption. Luther would provide that troubled laity with reassurance in the form of a well-anchored religion that each individual could grasp as his or her very own.

The Roman Catholic Church owes its own debt to Luther. Without the challenges from the Wittenberg reformer, the Church would surely not have freed itself so decisively from the worldliness of the Renaissance papacy and found its way into an age in which faith came first. New attitudes were already stirring within the Roman Church, but only the rebellion of the Augustinian monk inscribed faith and religion into the coming age and made them dynamic, world-changing forces.[2] While for many people this innovation meant freedom and salvation, for many others it meant devastation and damnation. Relentless confessional intolerance characterized the period after the Reformation for several generations, producing internal social tensions that erupted in bloody persecution and not infrequently even in the chaos of civil war. Externally, too, irreconcilable interpretations of the church and the world contributed decisively to the outbreak of the self-destructive wars in which competition between the European powers climaxed at the end of the Reformation century.

Goethe's enthusiasm for ages ruled by faith and, even more, his complementary want of enthusiasm for 'all ages in which lack of faith claims a paltry victory', characterized by 'illusionary lustre . . . and unfruitfulness', are hardly plausible to our secular world today. But that discomfort serves us well as we explore Martin Luther's biography a full 500 years after his Ninety-Five Theses were made public, on 31 October 1517. Only when we recognize that Luther and his contemporaries did not understand 'religion' and 'church' as part of the private sphere, as we do today, but as forces that completely embraced private as well as public life—both society and politics—will we be able to wrap our minds around why his theology presented such a challenge to the rulers of his day and why millions of people received that theology—which is hardly easy—with such great rejoicing. A risky comparison perhaps, but one worth making: the fear experienced in Luther's day because faith did not bring certainty is not unlike the fear we face today in the face of uncertainty about the direction financial markets will take and whether world peace is possible.

For centuries authors depicted Luther as the forerunner of their own age and as a trailblazer for the modern period. As each centenary came round, a new generation found its own Luther: in 1617, on the eve of the Thirty Years War, he was Luther the warrior, who would defend the Protestant world from the counter-revolutionary threat of those in thrall to Rome; in 1717, against the background of the early glimmerings of the tolerance and secularism of the Enlightenment, he was a more peaceable and open-minded

Luther; in 1817 and 1917, he was Luther the nationalist, hero of the religious profundity of the Germans and a protective shield against infiltration from the west by a Romance civilization that was vilified as superficial and light-weight. None of these Luthers had much to do with the historical Luther. Each time the relevant national or local centenary committee celebrated, to quote Goethe again, 'the spirit of the good men themselves'.

Now is the time to break away from the cult of remembrance and present Luther and his thoughts and actions, and the thoughts and actions of his contemporaries, as what they truly are for us today—witnesses to a 'world we have lost' or, rather, a world that is no longer ours and that therefore forces us to confront something very different. Luther thought and acted as a 'man between God and the devil', but we are seeking to understand that man from a world that no longer knows the devil, and if it knows God at all, then only in ways that would have been incomprehensible to Luther.[3]

History can emancipate us. Where we too readily accept the present as it is, history holds up a mirror and forces us to look at a different world of thoughts and actions. History relativizes today's impulses, just when we seem willing to believe there are no alternatives. If we confront what is very different in our own past, then we will recognize that not only our material circumstances but also human thought and emotions are essentially mutable. This book is not about a Luther in whom we can find the spirit of our own time; this book is about a Luther who was different, a Luther whose thoughts and actions are out of kilter with the interests of later generations, no matter how often they have been employed to legitimize actions in the present, and will continue to be employed to that end.

Luther's world is not our world, but that distinction does not mean that these worlds are unconnected. As we look for lines that run from Luther and the era of the Reformation through the modern age and up to today, we must be careful to ensure, however, that we do not try to make Luther one of us. We must also differentiate between intended and unintended outcomes. Luther's impact on his own age is to be held distinct from his historical impact through the ages. Over the centuries the reformer and his work have been interpreted in light of the perceptions and with the terminology of each new age. These accumulated layers of reception must be removed with all the care of an archaeologist in order to be able to read the original artefact.

The uncontaminated Luther can be discovered above all in his own words. We find our subject's thoughts and actions relayed to us in his writings to an extent that few other biographers can enjoy. Luther's influence came from his words, both written—in letters, manifestoes, pamphlets, and theological treatises, for example—and oral—in sermons, lectures, and discussions that have largely come down to us in transcripts made by members of his audience. This book therefore frequently cites Luther, translated for accessibility into modern English.[4] Luther's writing was colourful and imaginative, even earthy, with an unbridled energy. By taking this direct route to Luther, we can circumvent a dense forest of later writings to get straight to the positions he adopted in the ecclesiastical and political debates of his own time. We can then avoid the risk of being distracted by those who over the years have sought to defend or attack our subject—only a few decades ago, for example, it was suggested that Luther entered the monastery because he had committed a murder.

A focus on Luther's writings is not without its complications. Not because they are hard to comprehend or because the accuracy of the available texts is in question—the great Weimar Edition offers a very dependable go-to resource for Luther's works, and can be consulted along with other part editions and translations, especially into English. Additionally, since the mid-twentieth century church history has been more broadly framed, ensuring that engagement with Luther's theology is now far less likely to risk losing sight of Luther the man. The problem lies rather in the sources themselves, particularly the works that appear to contain personal testimony, where it is all too easy for the reader to feel he or she is in the presence of the real Luther. Ten or twenty years often lay between, at one end, the emergence and development of Luther's theology and the associated key episodes in the Reformation and, at the other, Luther's recorded narrative of these events. As recent research into the human memory has highlighted, Luther's accounts would have been conditioned by that time delay. Above all, his perceptions were shaped by a post-Reformation self-consciousness and adopted a deliberate self-stylization that the Augustinian monk of 1520 would not have recognized. This later Luther was the author of his principal personal testimony, written in 1545 and found in the preface to the first volume of his works in Latin, but he also constructed the earlier narrative that appears in the preface to his commentary on the Book of Daniel, published in 1530.[5] Even greater is the challenge presented by Luther's 'Table Talk', which has profoundly influenced the popular image of Luther for centuries. Luther did not compose these works himself or even authorize the versions that appeared. They contain transcriptions of his words made by his pupils—sometimes recorded as he spoke, but sometimes written down subsequently—and they present, in exaggerated form, Luther as his acolytes perceived him: here we find Luther the theologian and pastor whose evangelical teachings and words of pious edification were to be preserved for future generations, or Luther the rebel against the papacy and scholasticism, an image in accord with the interpretation of Johannes Aurifaber, the last of his secretaries who in 1566 published the first collection of Luther's Table Talk.

In order to explain Luther in the context of his own time and, vice versa, his times through his biography, this work draws more heavily on Luther's contemporaries than is usual in biographies of Luther written as church history. Without doubt Luther made a defining contribution to the secularizing tendencies that emerged in Germany and Europe in the sixteenth century, yet equally certain is that Luther was himself a product of a long-term process of transition. For as historians are increasingly aware, this 'new age' did not come into being somewhere around 1500; it had roots that reached back well into the late medieval period. Each historical personage, including Luther, has a double character, formed by his own context and formative of his own context. The chronological perspective on Luther's life and actions can be broad, stretching from the late Middle Ages up to and into the Confessional Age, which followed on from the Reformation. And as the work of an early modern historian, this account of Luther will not depict the institutions and individuals who refused to fall into line with him as adversaries simply unwilling or unable to recognize truth. Individuals who opted for the old church—Emperor, popes, and Catholic reformers; princes, theologians, and humanists, especially Erasmus of Rotterdam—must be understood on their own terms, with respect for their intellectual, cultural, political, and social worlds.

With prophetic authority Luther the rebel forced his age to act on fundamental existential questions about religion and faith. For Protestants both then and now, he was and continues to be a hero who shaped the course of history, opposing the great and the powerful and expecting them to follow him. He was the man of his own defiant words 'Here I stand; I cannot do otherwise, God help me, Amen', words spoken before the Emperor at Worms in 1521 and immediately sent out into the world as Reformation propaganda. But now is the time to recognize that his opponents too, and in particular Charles V, the young Habsburg Emperor had their own truths, which held them similarly captive and by which they, like Luther, had to abide. Only when we do historical justice to the alternatives to Luther's Reformation will we be able to understand the age of the Reformation, which was so much the work of Luther, as an era of 'splendid, heartening, and fertile' wrestling to ensure that true faith could rule.

PART ONE

Childhood, Education, and First Years as a Monk, 1483–1511

I

1483—New Departures for Christendom

The eleventh of November is the feast day of Martin of Tours. Legend tells us that in deepest winter Martin of Tours, a Roman cavalry officer, encountered a beggar at the gates of the town known today as Amiens; Martin split his cloak and gave one half to the poor man before him. Since ancient times Latin Christianity has marked the saint's day with Masses and pious contemplation. Children would sing, receiving in return tasty treats that included a crescent-shaped sweet pastry named after Saint Martin; adults marked the day by eating goose. At the end of the nineteenth century it became common to hold an evening procession, with Martin, mounted on his horse, leading a lantern-lit parade.

Their contemporaries would not have been surprised to learn that when mining entrepreneur Hans Luder and his wife, Margarete, had their son baptized on 11 November—the baby had been born the previous day—they followed established practice and had the child named after the saint fêted that day. Their son was now Martin Luder. Luder was the original family name, employed at various significant moments in the young man's life before being emphatically changed to 'Luther' in the course of the Reformation.[1] Martin was baptized in the Church of Saint Peter and Saint Paul in the Bridge District of Eisleben, a mining town in the county of Mansfeld. Having moved to Eisleben from Thuringia, Hans Luder and his wife (Figures 1 and 2) had recently acquired a modest home in this part of the city, which was largely populated by poorer and middling artisans.

With no parish record book or account from either Luther or his parents to tell us otherwise, we can assume that the baptism would have been carried out by the local parish priest, Bartholomäus Rennebecher. Luther's godparents were likely drawn from relatives who lived locally—including his uncle on his

Figures 1 and 2. Hans Luther (1459–1530) and Margarete Luther (1460–1531), parents of Martin Luther, by Lucas Cranach the Elder (1472–1553), oil on panel, 1527.

mother's side, Anton Lindemann, who was *Bergrat* in the county of Mansfeld, an administrative official for mining appointed by the ruler—and possibly also neighbours with whom his parents were friendly. The year of Luther's birth is not certain, however. When Luther's leadership of the Reformation brought him fame and the German public became eager to know more about the reformer's background, Luther's mother, already in her sixties, recalled that her son had been born shortly before midnight on 10 November. She was unable to specify the year, which was not at all remarkable for a time in which birth and baptismal records or documented family trees were still largely unknown. Luther was much more definite: 'I was born in Mansfeld in 1484', he wrote, 'that is certain', but he had no official record to back up his statement. Philip Melanchthon, his colleague in Wittenberg and his first biographer, proposed 1483 as the year of Luther's birth, and his suggestion quickly became accepted fact.

New Empires

In 1483 Christendom was changing. (Europeans used the term 'Christendom' in identifying themselves both then and for generations to come.) In the west, for decades Portuguese and Castilian caravels had been setting sail in hope of finding new routes to the spice-filled lands of India. The old routes, via the eastern Mediterranean and then by land through the Levant, had become increasingly risky as the Ottomans advanced into Asia Minor and the Near East. Iberian expansion to new shores was accompanied by a sense of mission, for as the treasures of those who lived in these new lands were acquired, their souls too would be saved.

Under the leadership of the Infante Henry the Navigator (1394–1460), who was also one of the foremost mathematicians and astronomers of his time, the Portuguese first went south, sailing along the coast of Africa. In the 1480s Christopher Columbus turned his gaze west, looking beyond the Azores and the Cape Verde islands, which had been known of for over a generation. Columbus was in no doubt that the world was round, and therefore at the beginning of 1484, only a few months after the birth of the later reformer, he laid out for John II, king of Portugal, his plan to search for a sea route to India by sailing west, across the completely unknown Atlantic. If the Portuguese had not been so committed to continuing their exploration of the coast of Africa and if deaf ears had not been turned on Columbus at the Castilian court, then America might well have been discovered very soon after the birth of Martin Luder.

We cannot easily evaluate what of these new worlds would have reached the circles in which the young Martin was growing up. Certainly educated Germans were very well informed. Martin Behaim, a merchant from Nuremberg, even made his way to the Portuguese court and took part in an expedition that in the early 1480s travelled south along the African coast as far as the mouth of the River Congo. During a stay in Nuremberg attending to personal affairs, Behaim fed his geographical knowledge into the creation of the famous Behaim Globe, one of the first spherical representations of the world and now in the German National Museum in Nuremberg. Yet the home in which Martin grew up appears to have known little, if anything, of the newly discovered worlds and to have had very limited contact with the colonial wares that were soon streaming back to Europe. Archaeologists recently carried out a highly productive excavation alongside the house in Eisleben owned by Luther's parents. Not a single household object, textile remnant, or food-related remain that had originated outside Europe and was contemporary with the Luders was found. A similar absence also characterized Luther's own household at the Augustinian monastery in Wittenberg a quarter-century later.

In the seafaring nations of south-western and western Europe, interest in overseas worlds, including their religious and political make-up, was not limited to intellectuals such as theologians, humanists, geographers, and biologists, for the broader public also proved eager for information. Yet right up until his death, Luther's sense of the world remained focused on the European continent, with remarkably little engagement with these new worlds. In the 1520s, in an epistle and a sermon he addressed an apparent contradiction, noting, 'many a heathen island has since been discovered, where the Gospel has never been preached. Yet the Scriptures say: "Their sound went out into all the earth."'[2] In *Supputatio annorum mundi*, a chronological table published in the 1540s, Luther interpreted illnesses that had reached Europe from newly discovered islands as a sign of the end of the world.[3] As Europe grasped at other continents, only the missionary and eschatological implications were of interest to Luther.

Martin Luther was not alone in wrestling with the world's religious and ethical foundations, and the public debate unleashed by his Ninety-Five Theses and by his appearance before the Imperial diet was also not unique. In Spain, too, theologians felt challenged to adapt ecclesiastical institutions and Christian spirituality to the new, game-changing circumstances. In a manner very similar to that of Luther for Germany, in Spain two Dominican monks, Antonio de Montesinos (*c*.1475–1540) and, in particular, Bartolomé de Las Casas (1474–1566), forced political figures and the public to participate in a fundamental debate about the very nature of Christendom and its presence in the world. Yet the impulses in each location differed: in Germany, Luther the monk from Saxony responded to an inner tormenting of his soul; in Spain, Las Casas and his supporters were outraged at the dishonourable reality of missionary and colonial activities, which included, at their most extreme, the enslaving of Black Africans.

Building on attempts by Pope Alexander VI to umpire, in 1494 the Treaty of Tordesillas had divided up the newly discovered worlds between the Portuguese and the Castilians. For many generations to come, the people of the Iberian Peninsula would carry the weight of European expansionism and the extension of Christendom. These societies provide strong evidence that powerful creative and transformative forces were at work also within Latin Christendom. The upheaval that from a German Protestant point of view is all too often ascribed only to Luther and the Reformation was also experienced elsewhere, and it pre-dated the Reformation. Since the death of John II of Aragon in 1479, Isabella of Castile and Ferdinand of Aragon, who had married in 1469, had ruled together over their united kingdoms, which would eventually come to be known simply as 'Spain'. Isabella and Ferdinand were 'the Catholic Kings' (*Los Reyes Cathólicos*), a title given to them by Pope Alexander VI. In January 1492 their army conquered Granada and with it the last bastion of the Arabs and Islam on the Iberian Peninsula. Within little more than a decade the Catholic Kings had completed the Reconquista begun centuries earlier. Spain was now again entirely under Catholic rule. At the same time Ferdinand cemented his family's claims to the kingdom of Naples-Sicily, not least through a marriage alliance with the rulers of Austria that would have a profound long-term bearing on the history of Europe.

The upheaval in the Iberian Peninsula extended to religion and the church. Just as individual lands were brought together into the new Castilian-Aragonese political unit that made up Spain, so too the church, spirituality, and learning also were reconfigured. Reform of religion and culture was part of the invigoration of the society of the new state. Improvements introduced by three archbishops, Hernando de Talavera, Pascual de Ampudia, and Francisco Jiménez de Cisneros, in the course of the first two decades of the sixteenth century were designed to renew religion and reform the church. Their innovations launched the national church of Spain of the modern age. While for Luther and the German Reformation reform meant confrontation with the papacy, in Spain reform came in deliberate partnership with Rome. This renewal made a Protestant Reformation of the kind advocated by Luther superfluous in Spain. The Spanish proved immune to Luther and his Reformation, which they viewed unsympathetically, even with abhorrence, as 'the German plague'.

Luther's world view was also distinguished from the Iberian experience of transition into the modern era in that his conception of Christendom was entirely focused on Europe. While for Spain Christendom now embraced the practical political experiences of a global project, for Luther mission remained a far more abstract theological problem. As a result, 'world mission' and the closely associated experience of globalization in early modern terms would long remain Catholic phenomena. This situation changed only when English and Dutch expansionist maritime interests, which were associated not with Lutheranism but with the Reformed version of the Reformation, entered the fray. The Spanish also expressed their religious self-assurance in their renewed piety, its heavens filled with baroque saints, as they expanded into new worlds. In the first half of the sixteenth century the overseas merchants of Seville donated an image for the altar at the Casa de Contratación, the administrative headquarters and principal cultural and religious institution for the Spanish overseas empire. The image (Figure 3) depicted the Virgin Mary spreading her

Figure 3. *The Virgin of the Navigators*, by Alejo Fernández, altarpiece painted for the chapel of the Casa de Contratación, Seville, 1531–1536.

cloak to give shelter, a representation that could be found throughout Europe at the end of the medieval period. The fearful evidently found great comfort in the idea that the broad cloak of the Mother of God could shield them from very real physical threats and protect their souls from harm.

Much like the Spanish conquistadors and traders, the mining entrepreneurs and mineworkers of central Europe were eager to believe themselves under the protection of the Virgin Mary and her sheltering cloak. That image could also be found—and was found particularly often—in the

Erzgebirge and the Harz mountains, where Luder would have seen the depiction as a child. He would also have been well aware of the intercessory powers of Anne, mother of the Virgin Mary, who was a saint called upon particularly by mineworkers. On finding himself without shelter from a severe storm and greatly fearing for his life, Luder then a student, had every reason to call out to Anne for help; in return he promised that he would turn to a godly life in a monastery. The path that he subsequently took to fulfil his side of this bargain led Luther, and that part of Christendom that was prepared, or forced, to follow him, in a radical and new direction. They turned their backs on traditional forms of piety, forms that in Spain and in other European countries that remained Catholic safeguarded the transition into the modern age and into new worlds. For Luther neither the protective cloak of the Virgin Mary nor the intercession of any of the other saints provided an answer; he believed that each individual should encounter God directly and find personal reassurance in God's promise of grace.

The developments in south-western Europe were not the only upheavals to take place during Martin Luder's early years. Enormous changes were also afoot in the south-east. The fall of the ancient and revered imperial city of Byzantium/Constantinople to an army of Muslim Ottoman Turks created a new threat that haunted Europe for centuries to come, both militarily and emotionally. Over the next century and a half the Ottoman Empire advanced ever farther through the Balkans and into the European continent, with large areas of the Mediterranean and its African coast also soon under Ottoman control. Initially only Greek Orthodox were affected, but by the early sixteenth century Latin Christendom was also bearing the brunt of Ottoman expansion. During the reign of the highly energetic Sultan Suleiman the Magnificent (1520–1566), both Venice and Hungary were threatened by the Ottomans. With victory over a Hungarian army at the Battle of Mohács in 1526, the Ottoman army had cleared the way into the plains of the Rivers Danube and Tisza from where the Ottomans could advance towards Carniola (Slovenia today), Styria, Carinthia, and Austria. In 1529 for the first time an Ottoman army laid siege to the Imperial city of Vienna, causing a psychological angst that would traumatize the German collective memory for centuries. With the fall of Rhodes in 1522, the eastern Mediterranean became to all intents and purposes a *mare clausum* of the Ottoman Empire. The Ottomans then used their bases on the North African coast as far as Tripoli as jumping-off points for an advance farther into the western Mediterranean, which led to direct confrontation with the Spanish Empire and the rulers of Sicily and Naples, Spain's allies.

While events in the Iberian Peninsula and overseas hardly touched the central European world of Martin Luther, the Turkish threat in the south-east of the Holy Roman Empire was very present, even where no Turk was ever to be seen. We have good reason to assume that while still young, Luder would have heard of the 'scourge of Christendom'—in sermons, in discussions amongst friends and family, from one of many publications containing anti-Turkish propaganda. Unlike the newly discovered overseas worlds on the other side of the Atlantic, 'the Turk'—a simplistic and inflammatory term used by the reformer in describing the military and religious threat facing Christians—would eventually become a substantial theme of Reformation theology.

Devotional Innovation and a Modernized Papacy

When Martin Luder was born, religion and church were in transition. New social groupings were emerging, both within religious orders and as a result of semi-religious lifestyles now available to the laity. And while the external appearance and behaviour of the Roman Papacy told a very differ-ent story, devotional forms were being transformed through a novel emphasis on interiority, the private, and individuality. Humanism and the *devotio moderna*, movements that put emphasis on reading by the individual and stimulated new devotional ideals, had been well received, in particular in highly urbanized north-western Europe and the coastal Low Countries, from where they had spread into the heart of Europe. Both women and men were encouraged to retreat into a corner with a good book and come to their own conclusions about the text by means of a spiritually framed reading that they were to conduct at their own pace. The Brethren of the Common Life, groups of men and women who lived together, have been placed on a scale somewhere between the medieval religious orders and the communal Christianity of the Reformation. Through such communities, new devo-tional forms and new reading practices also made their way into priestly circles, for their membership was both lay and clerical. A piety and spirituality shared by both laity and priest thus emerged in many locations, a precursor of the concept of the priesthood of all believers for which Martin Luther would soon advocate. Similar evidence can be found of other far-reaching innovations out of which historians believe the modern age developed, yet their origins have often been ascribed to the Reformation. Come the Reformation, neither Max Weber's 'inner-worldly asceticism' nor his related 'Protestant work ethic' was entirely innovative. Similarly, interpretative theories characterized as the 'civilizing process' and 'social discipline' have roots in urban and ecclesiastical communities at the end of the medieval period.

The relationship between church and state had also seen legal, organizational, and institutional innovation, and here, too, changes anticipated the Protestants' later reorganization of the church. Diversity and particularism within Latin Christendom did not begin with Luther and his Reformation. As early as the fifteenth century, the revolutionary movement in Bohemia named after Jan Hus had broken away to found its own church, but in the Hussite church we have only the most dramatic expression of a widespread development that in the rest of Europe often followed a peaceful course. In fourteenth-century Germany, the duke of Cleves was already deemed, as one description had it, pope in his own lands.[4] In the fifteenth century the process that saw the universal church turned into territorial churches was driven on by 'concordats', treaties drawn up between the ruler of a territory and the Roman curia that conceded to the temporal ruler particular rights over the church in the ruler's own lands. The pre-Reformation national and territorial churches were boosted by the papacy's confrontation with the conciliar movement and with the oligarchy of bishops that bore the weight of that challenge to the papacy. Facing opposition from the bishops at the Council of Basel, Pope Eugene IV (1431–1447) turned to the temporal rulers, but in exchange for assistance in thwarting the bishops' demands, he had to renounce significant rights over the church in each of their territories. From the mid-fifteenth century, one concordat followed another—in 1448 the Concordat of Vienna with the Emperor, which was then expanded in the *Concordata Nationis Germanicae* to cover the German princes and their territories; in 1472 a concordat with France, which was expanded in 1516; in 1482 with Castile and Aragon; and commas around finally in the sixteenth century with Poland and Hungary and with the Scandinavian empires. On the eve of the Reformation the unitary church of Latin Christendom existed as an idea only. The reality was found in regional churches—created by concordat, distinct from one another, and largely independent—whether in the form of national churches, as in France, identified with Gallicanism, and Spain, or in the form of territorial churches, as in the German lands.

Above all, at the very apex of Christendom, changes were afoot that caused consternation and estrangement south of the Alps too. As early as the twelfth and thirteenth centuries, rationalization, bureaucratization, and institutionalization had begun within the curia and the Roman Church. Some historians have identified in these processes a 'crisis of modernization' that provoked deep anxiety in Germany in particular. An enduring interpretation developed in the nineteenth century and associated in particular with the religious sociologist Max Weber proposed that the rebellion of an Augustinian monk in Saxony enabled the breakthrough of modernity; yet that same rebellion can also be interpreted as a reaction *against* modernizing impulses emanating from Rome.

The papacy's hard-fought victory over the conciliar movement achieved after the mid-fifteenth century told a similar tale. The pope, *pontifex maximus* and sovereign prince for he was spiritual head of the church and temporal head of the Papal States, was now liberated from conciliar participation in decision-making and became in effect the first quasi-absolutist ruler in Europe. This development, too, was the cause of great alarm and aroused great hostility. The pious could see, and indeed could not help but see, the extensive political authority of the bishop of Rome as an unscriptural despotism. With the occupants of Saint Peter's throne showing no sign that they intended to allay the distrust they had aroused—instead they appeared to take every opportunity to tell of their singular papal authority both in Rome and over Christendom—apprehensions about Rome and the curia grew rapidly, especially north of the Alps in the lands of the Holy Roman Empire of the German Nation. Assessing objectively, we can identify such discontent as a reaction not to the inactivity of popes who clung to tradition but to overly hasty papal attempts to respond to the demands of a new age. Such innovation could be found above all in the methods adopted to finance the increasingly colossal plans of the Papal States and the political and cultural representations of papal authority. The curia had been receptive to the ideas of Italian mercantile capitalism at an early date and proved something of a wizard at employing such modern financial methods.

By such means, by the end of the fifteenth century, Rome and the Papal States had become one of the leading centres of the Renaissance, with learning and the arts flourishing as almost nowhere else. Roman dominance was in part a result of the Turkish conquest of Byzantium in 1453, which had forced many leading artists and thinkers to flee to Italy, and to Naples and Rome in particular. For Luther, however, the 'Renaissance Popes' as they became known, who were so enthusiastic about new scholarship and artistic creativity, were responsible for the rotten state of the church. The Augustinian monk from Wittenberg could make sense of their errors and sins and even their crimes only as the work of Antichrist. This judgement would seem to miss the mark with Enea Silvio Piccolomini, who became Pius II (1458–1464) and was profoundly influenced by humanism, but Luther had a point when it came to the line begun by Sixtus IV (1471–1484), with a run of popes dedicated to the exercise of power and the wholehearted enjoyment of life. For Alexander VI (1492–1503), of the Borgia family and the most decadent of all, even the most kind-hearted of Catholic theologians and historians can only find somewhat questionable comfort in the argument that the Roman Church's ability to survive such a man is surely evidence of its godly origins. Contemporaries knew his successor, Julius II, Giuliano della Rovere (1503–1513), primarily as a figure in full armour. In his biting satire 'Julius Excluded from Heaven', Erasmus of Rotterdam had Julius II rejected at the gates of heaven because Peter wished to keep his heaven free of such people. Leo X (1513–1521), Luther's opponent in the years in which the Reformation broke through, was a very different proposition. A member of the Medici family, bankers and entrepreneurs in Florence, and therefore the personification of the Roman alliance with merchant capitalism, Leo X was highly educated and had fine taste. With cheerful equanimity, Leo X brought Rome and Christendom to an apex of aesthetic representation—betraying in the process, in Luther's eyes, the salvific message of the Gospel.

Particularism and the Early Modern State

The institutional and bureaucratic 'modernity' of the curia and the magnificent displays of art and power by the Renaissance papacy could not disguise that in the years before the Reformation, neither Christendom nor Europe was one single, undivided unit. Diversity was a hallmark of devotional practices and ecclesiastical institutions, but particularism and the favouring of individual interests were also characteristic of both rulers and peoples as they sought to assert their power and pre-eminence. 'Nation battles with nation, city with city, faction with faction, prince against prince,' wrote Erasmus of Rotterdam in the first quarter of the Reformation century, continuing, 'the English are hostile to the French, for no other reason than that they are French. The Scots are disliked by the British, solely for being Scots. Germans don't agree with French, Spaniards don't agree with either.'[5]

The political world was undoubtedly in transition. Political dynamics within individual territories were in flux, but externally too, in the relationships of these individual territories with each other and with the two universal powers, the pope and the Emperor, change was underway. The political and dynastic constellations that would be so critical for Europe at the moment of Reformation were already taking shape during Martin Luder's youth. Political theory which provided guidance, and potentially also discipline, for novel and exuberant political forces was also treading new ground, above all in Italy, where Niccolò Machiavelli laid the foundations for an innovative approach to politics that was freed from the constraints of Christian ethics. Just as new overseas worlds left no mark on Luther, so too such new political trends passed him by. Luther's political thinking was drawn in its entirety from Scripture—from the Old Testament in particular—and from Christian tradition, or at least those elements of Christian tradition that he accepted. In his political understanding, indeed particularly in his political understanding, we find Luther again an outsider, a man not of his own times.

From today's perspective we can distinguish causes and consequences of the many political innovations of the late medieval and early modern ages that would have been lost on their contemporaries. This advantage enables us to identify two overarching secular developments in particular: internally, within individual European territories, the early modern state began to take shape, while externally, within Europe more widely, transregional powers formed. Developments in Germany determined both Luther's personal experiences and his impact. Here the early modern state came to be identified not with the Empire as a whole, but with the individual territories of the Empire, with an additional distinctive form for the Imperial cities. As a result, for Luther, Electoral Saxony was key, and its rulers, the electors Frederick the Wise, John the Constant, and John Frederick, were the most significant political players. The struggle between the princes and the Imperial crown, represented by the Emperor and the German King, over how to accommodate these new political conditions and, in particular, the search for a balance between territorial interests and the interests of the Empire, would dictate both Luther's own fate and the fate of his Reformation.

The consolidation of the state internally and the development of broader European power constellations were closely linked. The situation for

Germany and its princes was unusual, for it involved an empire that did not function as a single state and the ambitions of an imperial ruler that played out on the broader European stage, well beyond the boundaries of the Empire. To join in the political power games of Europe and within the Empire, each player needed a territory or early 'nation state' at his back, yet at the same time success or failure in the European arena could advance or halt the internal consolidation of that state. As both internal state building and the elaboration of power constellations required clout and muscle, at the end of the medieval age the mood in Europe was distinctly bellicose, an atmosphere that was only intensified by the advent and impact of Luther's movement.

Around 1500 the pentarchy composed of the five powers at the heart of Italy—Naples, the Papal States Florence, Venice, and Milan—which had ensured an equilibrium and relative peace, collapsed. Its downfall can be attributed in part to the Ottomans and in part to the Spanish and French. In 1494 the French king, Charles VIII (1483–1498), had crossed the Alps in order to secure the throne of the Kingdom of Naples for his own line in the face of competing claims from Spain, initiating a long period in which the battle for pre-eminence in Europe was fought out on Italian soil, and the Italian rulers, above all the pope and his Papal States had to fight their own corner both militarily and diplomatically. For Europe as a whole, the outcome was a rivalry between France and Habsburg Spain that would last for centuries. In 1495, in response to France's aggressive intervention in their own sphere of influence in Italy, Ferdinand of Aragon and the Habsburg Emperor, Maximilian I, agreed to a political alliance, which, as was usual, was to be sealed by a marriage involving the two families. The wedding the following year of Philip the Handsome, son of Maximilian, and the Infanta Joanna, daughter of Ferdinand of Aragon and Isabella of Castile, laid the dynastic foundations for the Habsburg–Spanish empire that a generation later, under Emperor Charles V (1500–1556), the oldest child of this marriage, would make every other ruler in Europe a lesser, or minor, power. With the Castilian possessions in the Americas and Asia in mind, Charles V could justifiably claim that the sun never went down on his empire. Back in Europe, however, the supremacy of the Habsburgs was never recognized. The principal challenge came from France: Charles V fought five wars with Francis I and Henry II and in the end had to admit defeat.

The European power constellation that came into being during the first decades of Martin Luder's life was dominated by the Ottoman and

Habsburg–Spanish empires, with all their alliances and rivalries, and would significantly influence the course of the Reformation. In the 1520s and 1530s the Emperor's attention was repeatedly redirected away from the Empire as he dealt not only with his kingly responsibilities within Spain but also with wars against the Turks and against his European rivals, in particular the kings of France and the pope, leaving him without the time to deal with the 'Luther affair'. The battles and diplomatic manoeuvrings of these decades are still etched on the historical consciousness of Europe. The Battle of Pavia in 1525 left a clear mark, as with his victory over Francis I, Charles V became, for a time, ruler of Milan; a similar mark was left by the Treaty of Madrid, which Charles forced on his prisoner Francis I, captured at Pavia in January 1526, and which very soon would be broken by France, with the agreement and absolution of the papacy.

The deepest scar was left by the famous, and notorious, Sack of Rome of May 1527. While at war against the League of Cognac (an anti-Habsburg alliance composed of France, the pope, Milan, Florence, and Venice), Habsburg troops, both German and Spanish, stormed the Holy City, to the horror of all Christendom. With Pope Clement VII besieged in the Castel Sant'Angelo, the troops plundered the defenceless city like barbarians. Nothing can portray the brokenness of the Christian world and the crisis of the medieval order more effectively than the self-destruction of the two universal powers, who had been tasked not with war and terror but with peace and reconciliation. Two decades later, a similar process played out for Germany and the Protestants: only a few months after Luther's death, the Emperor's victory in the Schmalkaldic War opened the way for Imperial troops to enter Wittenberg and for the elector of Saxony, John Frederick, to fall into the hands of the Habsburgs.

Population Growth and Mercantile Capitalism

The economy, too, was in transition and, figuratively, so also was the population. Economic historians talk of the 'long sixteenth century', which began everywhere at some point towards the end of the fifteenth century, although in different regions of Europe at different times, and extended into the first third of the seventeenth century. Although population growth occurred throughout this period, during the early phase this increase was fast, even explosive, while by the second half of the Reformation century it had slowed

markedly. The increase in population brought new impulses to manufacturing and trade. Demand for food leapt, as did demand for items in daily
use, especially cloth and household goods. At the same time a market for
luxury produce sprang up and expanded, with greater consumption of
expensive food and drink. The princely rulers with their courts and the
nobility in their rural landholdings were the principal consumers of such
luxury goods, but they were joined by a smaller number from the upper
social strata in the towns and even, in regions such as Friesland and Tyrol, by
gentleman farmers.

'Princes who drink and princes who play'—this caricature of sixteenth-
century rulers has a good portion of truth to it. Some literally drank
themselves to death. The extant lists of food and drink consumed at ban-
quets that might last days, even weeks, provide a sense of the vitality and lust
for life associated with a Renaissance spirit that could also be found in
Germany. Such indulgence is hardly imaginable today. The vast majority
of the population, however, lived in far more modest circumstances, many
even in poverty. They could make little sense of economic pressures that
posed a very real threat: at the beginning of the 1530s, only a few years after
thousands had died in the Knights' Revolt and Peasants' War, commentator
Sebastian Franck (1499–1543) would describe the towns as being 'so full of
people that no one can make a living'.[6]

We have little precise data for this pre-statistical era, and certainly none for
Europe as a whole. Estimates suggest that in the course of the sixteenth
century the population of Europe increased by more than 25 per cent, from
around 82 million to 107 million, but with very marked regional variation.
The more heavily populated areas grew more quickly and the concentration
of trade and manufacturing continued. Both the scale of the growth of the
population and contemporaries' experience of that upward trend therefore
depended upon location.

Undoubtedly, such marked population expansion had a social impact and
influenced attitudes. No longer were adequate food supplies guaranteed.
A failed harvest could mean famine; famine could mean malnutrition;
malnutrition could leave the population exposed to illness and epidemics.
Also part of the mix were price increases, a fall in the value of coinage—
owing not least to the much greater supply of silver from South America
from the middle of the century on—and, finally, a lack of employment in
urban centres. By the end of the Reformation century, society throughout
Europe was more polarized: the small group of the rich were becoming

richer and were eager to display their wealth, while the army of the poor
grew rapidly in size, with their very survival now regularly in doubt. If some
form of class structure developed at all before the emergence of the industrial
society of the nineteenth century, then it was in the long sixteenth century.
In light of the impact of economic conditions, good grounds exist for the
frequent identification of this period as early bourgeois. Albrecht Dürer's
woodcut 'The Four Horsemen of the Apocalypse' (Figure 4) tells us that
economic problems and the concomitant fear of starvation, epidemics, war,
and mass death could already be found at the beginning of the century.

Concurrently and in close connection to these economic conditions,
something not unlike a Europe-wide economic system came into being
for the first time. Individual regional economies, which had previously
been largely independent, became increasingly interdependent, although
Immanuel Wallerstein's identification of a tightly interwoven 'Atlantic
world economy' for this period may be a step too far.[7] The Mediterranean
and northern Italy had been the economic powerhouses of Europe, but this
role was gradually taken up instead by the Atlantic communities of north-
western Europe. This relocation of Europe's economic heartland, which
would prove of profound historical significance, was already apparent in
Luther's lifetime, and from the mid-sixteenth century a more modern
economic triangle formed by the Netherlands, northern France, and
England took shape. Economic historians have identified in the growth of
shipping in the North Sea and the Baltic the first transport revolution of the
modern age. The impetus was provided only in part by the discovery
of the Americas; far more significant were the growth in the population of
western and central Europe and the increased demand for food and goods.
Additionally, the advance of the Ottomans had disrupted trade in the Levant.

The exchange of goods between western Europe and the Baltic grew
dramatically, primarily as the work of Dutch merchants, whose ships sailed
through the Danish Straits in their hundreds each year, transporting
eastwards tapestries, altar pieces carved in Antwerp, and other high-value
products of the workshops of western Europe, and carrying back the raw
materials of the Scandinavian and Baltic lands that were in such high demand
in the highly populated and economically active areas of central and western
Europe—timber and pitch for the rapidly expanding shipbuilding industry, as
well as honey, wax, and amber, but above all grain from the broad plain of the
river Vistula. At the beginning of the seventeenth century, this 'mother trade',
as the Dutch termed their exchange with the Baltic, was supplemented by

Figure 4. *The Four Horsemen*, from *The Apocalypse* by Albrecht Dürer (1471–1528), woodcut, 1498.

trade that reached west, to the New World via Seville and the Atlantic. The medieval trading axis that ran north–south through the principal trading stations and trading routes of Europe was very evidently being replaced by a new axis that ran east–west, through northern and north-western Europe and across the Atlantic, with its most important transit points, where goods were exchanged and reshipped, in the Netherlands, northern France, and England.

Contemporaries could not have been aware of the origins and long-term implications of such shifts. And in any case, the old economic centres did not suddenly cease to exist: Venice remained an important trading hub into the seventeenth century. The early mercantile capitalism of southern Germany and the closely associated mining industry of the Harz and Erzgebirge regions and the Alps emerged only at the end of the fifteenth century. For four or five decades around 1500 the European economy was much influenced by the southern and central German lands, largely under the sway of the trading houses of southern Germany. The greatest and most renowned of these was run by the Fugger family, who in the first third of the sixteenth century under Jakob Fugger the Rich spread their business interests throughout Europe and developed close ties with the princely rulers of their age, including both popes and Emperors The success of such trading houses rested on four pillars: long-distance trade, mining in the Alps and the Carpathians, banking on a grand scale, and distribution, which involved the decentralized organization of commercial mass production, mainly in textiles. Sitting in his grand townhouse on the Wine Market in Augsburg, Jakob Fugger directed a global enterprise that included mines in the Carpathians, the Erzgebirge, and the Alps as well as a European monopoly of alum and quicksilver, and a trading network that at times reached even to the New World. Increasingly frequently the Fuggers acted as bankers for the rulers, courts, and states of Germany and Europe, and for the Habsburgs in particular, for whom in one decisive moment they were able to secure the Imperial crown. In 1519, following the death of Emperor Maximilian, the Habsburgs turned to the Fuggers when they needed to raise funds to entice the German electors away from the candidacy of the French king, Francis I, and ensure that they voted instead for Charles, king of Spain and a Habsburg grandson of Maximilian.

The politics and culture of the Empire in the first third of the sixteenth century were largely powered by the strong economy. Even the success of the Reformation is hard to imagine without the riches and political weight of Luther's princely ruler, Elector Frederick the Wise, which in turn were a product of mining and flourishing trade and manufacturing in his territory. Only in the middle decades of the sixteenth century, as trade with Italy declined markedly and the first great state bankruptcies occurred, in particular in Spain and France, shocking the financial world, did the age of the early capitalist family enterprises of southern Germany reach its end. With whole fleets now sailing to Europe laden with South American silver, silver mining in Germany became unprofitable and the mining boom was halted, not only in Saxony but also in Bohemia, the Harz mountains, and the Alpine lands. During the last weeks of his life, Luther would be preoccupied with the repercussions of this downturn in Mansfeld, the territory in which he had been born.

A Century of Learning and the Arts

The intellectual world, the cultural world, the world of learning—they, too, all waxed and waned. The invention of printing in Mainz around 1450, when Johannes Gutenberg was the first to use moveable metal type, would prove to have been revolutionary but had not reached its full potential before the Reformation. That world-changing event was still in its infancy—it was the age of incunabula, of expensive single-page printings and unique editions such as the renowned forty-two-line Gutenberg Bible of 1454. The mass production of books arrived only with the Reformation, and with the pamphlet wars and publication of Luther's bestsellers, above all his renowned Luther Bible.

Humanism and the Renaissance advanced through Europe, impelled on to almost dizzying heights by the relocation of Byzantine learning to Italy and by the Renaissance court of King Matthias Corvinus in Hungary. North of the Alps such innovation initially took only baby steps, and sometimes made no progress at all: for example, the medieval Gothic style remained de rigueur for more upscale homes, council chambers, and churches. In 1499 the Sforza dukes of Milan, relatives of Emperor Maximilian I through his second wife, Bianca Maria, sent sculptors from Lombardy to the Emperor. Together with Jacopo de Barbari, from Venice, and Adriano Fiorentino, from Florence, these new arrivals planted in central Europe the seeds that would bloom as the art of the Northern Renaissance. Nevertheless, Maximilian's court was no Renaissance court. His style has been aptly summarized as an amalgam of the imagery of medieval Germany and the costumes and staging of ancient Rome.[8] The Fuggers saw things differently, however, and they had both the courage to adopt the visual language of the Renaissance and the money to realize their building conceits. At the beginning of the sixteenth century, they had a triumphal private chapel in the style of the Florentine Renaissance erected in the chancel at the west end of the church of Saint Anne in Augsburg. The chapel was decorated with individual sculptures of the directors of the family firm, Ulrich and Jakob, from models provided by no less a figure than Albrecht Dürer, who during these decades emerged as the leading artistic personality north of the Alps. First in line behind Emperor Maximilian in bringing Renaissance architects and artists to Germany was Luther's own ruler, Elector Frederick the Wise, who sought to endow his court with something of the most up-to-date lustre and prestige of the Italian courts.

Philosophy, literature, and education were also in transition. The conflict amongst theologians over the primacy of the *via antiqua* or the *via moderna*, which gave precedence to experience and promoted empiricism, had been put to rest, with universities usually offering courses based on both the old and new methods. Wittenberg was, however, an exception, for here instruction was restricted to the *via antiqua*. Humanism, which called for a return *ad fontes*, 'to the sources', and challenged all authority that was only assumed, was also on the advance. In Cologne, however, the Dominicans ruled, holding high the scholasticism of Thomas Aquinas and, as men of the Roman Inquisition, denouncing any deviation from Christian orthodoxy. They faced a new front composed of German humanists, some of whom were members of ecclesiastical institutions, but some of whom were not. With biting satire, humanists pilloried the empty babbling of stale scholasticism and the stubbornness of the Dominicans at Cologne, who refused to engage the new spirit of unbounded questioning and investigation. For the humanists the imperatives of this new age were to be met not by increasingly incomprehensible sophistic interpretations of tradition but rather by renewed and expanded knowledge that would come from unbiased examination of the sources.

At the beginning of the new century, Johannes Reuchlin, a humanist, was attacked for his study of Hebrew and his support for the publication of Jewish sources. Ulrich von Hutten and Crotus Rubeanus, a fellow humanist, sprang to his defence with their text *Epistolae obscurorum virorum*, which they published anonymously. The 'men of darkness' of the title would become proverbial in Germany for any enemy of progress. Overnight the work aroused a public debate in the Empire, as argument and counterargument—often finding their audience through printed pamphlets—highlighted the backlog of reform in education, the church, the state, and society and suggested how it might be tackled.

Although European humanism was undoubtedly an international movement, its early nationalistic emphasis served to intensify intellectual and cultural tensions. Examples can be found in the rediscovery of Tacitus' *Germania* and in the Celtic, Batavian, and Gothic origin myths that proved so popular in these very decades. Disputes such as that involving the Dominicans in Cologne could be packaged as an attempt by the German peoples to free themselves from infiltration by Rome and exploitation by the curia. Today we know such claims to have been largely groundless, and the relationship between curia and Empire in the fifteenth century has been characterized as 'unmistakably loose'.[9] Amongst all the peoples of Christendom, the Germans had perhaps least reason to complain that their wealth was flowing to Rome, yet contemporaries remained convinced, and the next generation would celebrate Luther as the German Hercules who, as depicted on a well-known woodcut by Hans Holbein the Younger (Figure 5), with a cudgel cut from ancient German forests, took out the Dominicans of Cologne and Jakob von Hoogstraten, papal inquisitor and the greatest of all enemies of progress, thus freeing the German church with a single blow from the bloodthirsty toadies of Rome.

The humanists lacked for neither drive nor optimism. That spirit is relayed in a much-cited celebratory cry by Ulrich von Hutten from 1518: 'Oh this age! Oh these letters! It is such joy to be alive!'[10] This new generation of intellectuals and writers embodied more than any other grouping the upsurge of a new age. What they lacked in numbers, they made up for in industry, and their contribution as propagandists can hardly be overstated. They threw their weight behind the theological and ecclesiastical rebellion initiated by Luther, adding greatly to the momentum carried by the movement. The self-confidence of the early modern individual, seen a century earlier in architects such as Peter Parler or painters such as Jan van Eyck, reached its first high point. In Germany that self-confidence also had religious connotations—as can be read from the similarities with images of Christ in Dürer's famous self-portrait of 1500 (Figure 6). Luther's grandiose entry with his self-identification as prophetic restorer of the church was

Figure 5. Martin Luther as Hercules Germanicus, by Hans Holbein the Younger (1497/8–1543), woodcut, *c*.1519. Luther has the pope suspended from his teeth as he holds inquisitor Jakob von Hoogstraten by the neck.

Figure 6. Christ-like self-portrait with fur-trimmed robe, by Albrecht Dürer, 1500.

another example of this prevailing attitude, even though the Luther cult would subsequently give much energy to endowing the momentous 'Here I stand' moment with an air of exceptionality.

Upturn in Germany

News of events overseas, in the Balkans or in Rome, would certainly have reached Germany. Educated individuals such as Martin Behaim, whom we have already encountered, and south German merchant families such as the Welsers or the Fuggers took part in new discoveries and sought to exploit the opportunities they presented. The magnificence and excesses of Rome were as well known as the brutality of the Turkish army. Initially, however, the direct impact on central Europe was very limited. The Renaissance advanced only slowly beyond the Alps and to the north— carried first into the towns of southern Germany on the back of trade with northern Italy and only arriving in central Germany a generation later. Martin Luder grew up surrounded by the Gothic and later, in Erfurt and Wittenberg, his environment was entirely that of an earlier age. Even the new castle at Wittenberg that Elector Frederick had begun building at great expense in the 1490s, employing the most sought-after craftsmen and artists, was at heart late Gothic; only here and there could signs of the early Renaissance be detected. Luther's first personal encounter with the Renaissance came on his visit to Rome in late 1510 and early 1511, charged with carrying out business for his religious order. However, he only became aware of the threat that Rome and the Renaissance papacy posed to Germany some years later, when Leo X and Cardinal Albrecht of Brandenburg looked to finance both their building projects and their accumulation of power in part by the sale of an indulgence in Germany, with the collection of the Peter's Pence.

Innovation was not a foreign import that arrived in Germany in the decades around 1500. Change came from within, admittedly less spectacular than elsewhere, but all the more sustainable and with all the greater impact on the everyday lives of the population. A new dynamism, previously unknown, took hold of the economy, politics, and education. Luther and his evangelical teachings were without doubt original, but they were also a product of this upsurge. The rapid spread of these new ideas was only possible because of the printed book, still in its youthful phase. Today this period of intensified communication is often termed the first media revolution. Yet it is unlikely that Luther would have held his own before the leading figures of the Empire or set the wheels of Reformation turning if the German economy had not been flourishing—above all the mining industry in the Harz and Erzgebirge mountains—and his success was only possible because just a few decades earlier the early modern territorial state had begun to take shape. In the critical moment at the Imperial diet at Worms in 1521 when Luther refused to recant, and afterwards, condemned and no longer protected by the law, everything depended on the protection provided by his Saxon prince, whose authority in turn stemmed from his well-financed early modern state.

During Luther's lifetime, Italy's economic dominance would be succeeded by a 'German age' in the economic history of Europe, with three particular centres of growth: southern Germany with its family firms involved on a worldwide scale in banking, textile supply, and mining; the North Sea and Baltic, with a marked increase in shipping as well as in cultural exchanges; and central Germany and Saxony, where the focus was on mining but which also profited from the increase in long-distance transport by land. While transportation hubs such as Erfurt and Zwickau blossomed, the advantage was felt most in the mountainous areas of the Harz, Thuringia, and Saxony, where older towns expanded rapidly and new settlements such as Annaberg, Marienberg, and Schneeberg sprang up.

As a result the population in central Germany increased and became more concentrated on particular locations. Village records indicate that the rural population grew especially quickly. In 1445 there were 1,143 peasant families in the 107 villages in the region of Dresden, but by 1550 there were 1,851; in Pirna and Frauenstein the population had grown from 125 to 201 and from 383 to 597 respectively. The actual rate of growth was much higher than these figures alone suggest, for a large number of villagers moved to towns. The percentage of the population that was urban also grew greatly, and in the mining areas of the western Erzgebirge over half the population lived in towns.

The primary beneficiaries of the wealth generated by mining and related industries and by long-distance trade were the local rulers—the electors and dukes of Saxony and, to a lesser extent, the counts of Mansfeld, whose lands were small and divided amongst family members. Although the Saxon lands were ruled by two branches of one family—the principal towns of the electoral Ernestine branch were Wittenberg and Torgau and the principal towns of the ducal Albertine branch were Meissen and Dresden—both parties benefited from the mining wealth, on the basis of which they constructed early modern territorial states that soon proved to be the most modern and most efficient in the Empire. The Saxon rulers had already claimed significant authority over the affairs of the church in their own lands, and they threw themselves into the intellectual and spiritual renewal of religious life. Indeed, the competition between the two lines of the family was most marked when it came to ecclesiastical matters: Elector Frederick, Luther's ruler, assembled a collection of relics that made Wittenberg a centre of the sacred and subsequently offered his protection to the Reformation that had come into being at his own university; Duke Georg was equally engaged with reform of the church and devotional life in his own lands, but he decided against the new theology that emerged from Wittenberg and became a bitter opponent of Luther, not because he was personally less interested in religion than his electoral cousin or because he believed reform of the church to be unnecessary—rather because he did not believe the radical transformations advocated in Wittenberg to be the correct way forward. In some ways his piety was more 'modern' and closer to Luther than that of his relic-collecting cousin, for Duke Georg favoured a Christ-focused religious experience and distanced himself from devotional practices that spilled over into pilgrimages and relics. His advocacy of lay education has drawn comparisons with Erasmus and he sought a growth of lay piety and a greater sense of the Christian in everyday life, in particular within the booming towns of the Erzgebirge, where social pressures were especially acute.

Unease and Insecurity

No other generation in Germany has likely been so preoccupied with death and salvation as was that of the late fifteenth and early sixteenth centuries. We can learn of its anxiety from personal testimonials and church endowments, but we can also see it in paintings and sculptures and read of it in theological and philosophical texts. For the large majority of Luther's contemporaries, the mood was set not by the secular optimism about the future that was typical of humanists but by a deeply rooted religiosity out of which emerged uncertainty about the very nature of life after death. Almost everyone believed that there *would* be a continued existence after death; at issue was the form that this existence would take. Where today people might focus their anxieties on currency markets or stock prices or on the worldwide economy and global politics, on which they believe their well-being to depend, at the beginning of the sixteenth century many people, intellectuals as well as the so-called simple folk, thought much about the transience of earthly existence and about life after death. In the visual arts and in literature these concerns found new introspective expression in, for example, the great Dances of Death on the walls of churches, monasteries, and cemeteries, but above all in a personal and private sense of the omnipresence of death, as seen in the moving boxwood relief entitled 'Death and the Maiden' by Hans Schwarz (Figure 7). The fears of the age made an appearance in grotesque form too, in what we might term the surrealist paintings of the Dutchman Hieronymus Bosch. Behind this agonizing engagement with death lay not fear of a cold and empty nihilistic hereafter but persistent uncertainty about what would come after physical death—reconciliation with God or the never-ending torments of the abyss of hell?

How can I receive the grace of God? What about my personal salvation? Such questions appear to have preoccupied many people living north of the Alps, and those living in Germany in particular. Luther's answers would set history on a new course. Italy, however, seems to have been little touched by such transcendental musings. In Italy the search for stability, security, and order was understood primarily in secular terms. At this time Machiavelli of

Figure 7. *Death and the Maiden,* by Hans Schwarz (*c.*1492/93–after 1532?), boxwood, Augsburg, *c.*1520.

Florence, the most committed of all secular advocates, developed his own political model, free of all moral considerations, which showed no interest in the world to come. North of the Alps, however, people had access to a well-stocked arsenal of devotional and redemptive activities as they sought to combat both their uncertainty and their fears. For protection they turned above all to the Mother of God, whom they thought most likely to be able to plead their case successfully in the heavenly court. The image of the Madonna with her protective cloak was one of the most loved motifs of the age, along with the Dance of Death. At the same time as the cult of saints bloomed, endowments and confraternities also proved very popular. Both provided a form of life insurance, although, admittedly, for life *after* death.

An endowment was made to ensure that after death Masses would be said for the soul of the individual who had made the endowment; confraternities had similar purpose but in communal form, with intercessions made by the living for the deceased members. The age of the pilgrimage had reached a high point, with thousands of the faithful taking part every year. They went, for example, to the 'Beautiful Virgin' (*Schöne Maria*) in Regensburg, a votive image that had proved its miraculous power in 1519, when a Regensburg craftsman made a wondrous recovery after a very serious accident. A contemporary chronicle tells of the pilgrimages that quickly followed:

> In the first three years after the chapel was founded 25,374 Masses were read. Whole parishes joined together and came from ten, twenty, or even more

Figure 8. *The Beautiful Virgin of Regensburg (Schöne Maria von Regensburg)*, by Albrecht Altdorfer (1480 or earlier–1538), painted following the miracle of 1519.

miles away in order to make an offering to the Mother of God and to ask for her intercession. As a pilgrimage procession made its way during the night through villages, accompanied by singing and much noise, women jumped up and joined the procession and not infrequently they were still dressed only in their nightclothes.[11]

The image of the 'Beautiful Virgin' was copied by Albrecht Altdorfer soon after the miracle (Figure 8) and sold in its thousands as a woodcut that decorated the homes of pilgrims.

The mass hysteria of this age could also have a dark side, as the Regensburg pilgrimage also illustrates. The origins of this pilgrimage site are found in a Jewish pogrom, and the man so miraculously healed had been injured while at work destroying a synagogue. The pogrom had begun immediately after the death of Emperor Maximilian I, when the Imperial protection afforded the Jews of the Imperial towns and cities, in exchange for a payment, was lifted. In this situation the Jews became scapegoats for Christian fears and uncertainties, both material—a particular reality in the Imperial city of Regensburg in light of its stagnant economy—and, especially, spiritual. In other areas of Europe too—in Trent, for example, in 1474/75—in the decades around 1500, Jews fell victim to the eschatological pursuit of salvation by their Christian neighbours, who accused Jews of desecration of the host or even the ritual murder of Christian children to give grounds for their gruesome punishment. The belief that the end of the world was near was heightened by the apparently unstoppable advance of the Turks. For most contemporaries the attempt by the Christian states to keep the Turks at bay was only superficially a contest over political power and economic dominance, for in their eyes it was the End Times fight to the death between Christ and Antichrist, between the heavenly hordes and the forces of darkness.

Anxieties about salvation also caused tensions within the church. The decades around 1500 saw strong anticlericalism, in particular within aspirational urban society, where it flourished amongst humanist thinkers, writers, and artists. They found endless opportunity to poke fun at, and pour scorn on, poorly educated Mass-reading priests and their pointless magical incantations, and on avaricious prelates, lecherous monks, and all-too-willing nuns. They relayed their contempt to a broader public in mocking treatises, woodcuts, and paintings that were both detailed and barbed. Criticism of Rome and of the carryings-on at the court in Rome was pronounced in Germany, especially amongst those with political influence, and the Imperial estates for years had been drawing up a catalogue of grievances about unwarranted practices within the church. The 'Complaints of the German Nation' (*Gravamina nationis germanicae*) were much debated at Imperial diets, and everyone looked to the Emperor, as the temporal head of Christendom, to remedy the situation. This anticlericalism was not in any way like the essentially modern and even atheistic anticlericalism that rejects wholesale the salvific claims of the church. The opposite is very much the case: wretchedly educated and morally bankrupt clergy were disparaged precisely because they were so far from the model of the honourable and conscientious priest. The anticlericalism of the age of the Reformation was an expression of the desire for a better church and for a safe path to eternal salvation tended by capable clergy.

The circumstances of his own age tell us little about the essentials of Luther's theology. His thoughts emerged from, and would be shaped by, that context, however, and that context also provided the social and political scaffolding of his Reformation. Above all, these circumstances help us make sense of Luther's life and work, for they show us that the reformer not only brought about change but was himself also a product of transition.

II

Childhood and Youth

Son of a 'Poor Hewer'?

Bathed in the spotlight of national and international attention, Luther's later life was revealingly exposed. By contrast, his early years in the midst of his family in Mansfeld and subsequently at school in Magdeburg and Eisenach remained largely in shadow. The reformer's account of his childhood, found primarily in his Table Talk, was subject not only to not-unexpected memory lapses, but also to a desire for self-representation often found in individuals who believe they have a starring role to play in history itself, which for Luther meant a leading part in the narrative of salvation. All the more welcome, then, is the contribution of archaeologists employed by the state of Sachsen-Anhalt who recently have made valuable discoveries about the daily life of the Luder family in Eisleben and Mansfeld. We can also be grateful that economic and social historians are now able to paint a far more accurate picture of the agriculture and mining in the district from which the reformer came.

The first decade and a half of Martin Luder's life was spent in the midst of the mining boom in the Harz mountains. His childhood was shaped by the everyday experiences of a young entrepreneurial family absorbed in making the most of the economic opportunities and in attending to the needs of a growing family. Later Luther would delight in framing his account of his birth and ancestry in traditional language. He would relate that he was the son of a 'poor hewer', himself 'the son of a peasant', who had moved to Mansfeld, where he had become involved in mining.[1] The reality was rather different. On his father's side, Luther's family had been settled in the Thuringian village of Möhra, south of Eisenach, for generations. His grandfather Heiner Luder counted among the more privileged peasants within the village; these men had no local feudal superior but rather, as free peasants, paid their dues directly to the elector of Saxony, their territorial lord. With their enhanced legal and social status, these Thuringian peasant farmers were not like unfree peasants in other parts of Germany who were closely tied to the land and to a local feudal lord. The Luders were not especially wealthy, but we can trace their ties to a good number of substantial and productive landholdings in and around Möhra. When resident at the Wartburg in 1521, Luther would roam through the neighbouring Thuringian Forest and came away with the impression that his extended family were to be found everywhere. Their legal standing entitled these Möhra peasants to pass on their landholdings freely, and traditionally those possessions were inherited, undivided, by the youngest son. The territorial ruler and his administration were some distance away, in Torgau, Weimar, or Wittenberg. Before 1513 there were no official regulations in place for the Wettin's south-western possessions. As a result the peasants of Möhra were well used to extensive communal self-government. Financial matters, village business, and local agricultural affairs such as the use of common lands were regulated in the interests of the more substantial peasantry, with no regard for the lowest levels of the peasantry who did not own their tenantry.

As the oldest of four sons, Hans Luder (1459–1530), father of the reformer, was not in line to inherit his father's landholding. Unless he was prepared to remain unmarried and work for his youngest brother, who would inherit from their father, he would have to move elsewhere and find a means of support other than farming. In 1479, aged twenty, Hans Luder married Margarete Lindemann (1460–1531), who was of a similar age; evidently he had resolved to follow the path of independence. The challenges of a new beginning and years of uncertainty lay before Luder and his wife, but they did not have to face these early years without either means or assistance. Substantial evidence suggests that the flourishing of the agricultural economy in the late fifteenth century meant that the eldest son of this Möhra family could be provided with a certain capital. Hans Luder's father's interests may have reached beyond farming, and it is possible that he also operated a copper mine, perhaps even on his own land, for Möhra lay in the area around Suhl where copper shale could be found. In that case, Hans Luder could have arrived in Eisleben with not just capital to invest but also personal experience in mining.

Additionally, Margarete's relatives reached out a helping hand to the young couple. Through his mother, Martin Luder belonged to a socially ambitious family, a connection that is often overlooked by historians and genealogists who traditionally have paid little attention to the maternal line within the reformer's family tree, concentrating instead on his paternal ancestry. Luther's maternal grandfather, Johann Lindemann, was a member of the citizenry of Eisenach entitled to sit on the town council, a grouping in the agrarian and manufacturing region of the western Thuringian Forest with many ties to the substantial peasantry who made up the rural elite. The marriage between Hans Luder, son of a peasant, and Margarete Lindemann, daughter of a burgher, was in no way out of the ordinary. It was equally unremarkable that the wife's family would have a hand in the lives of the young couple and their children. Margarete's older brother, Anton Lindemann, played a particularly significant role, for through his appointment by the counts as *Bergrat*, Lindemann was involved in the administration of the prosperous mining industry in the Harz county of Mansfeld, and he even ran his own smelting works. Copper mining closer to home in Eisenach-Möhra did not offer the young couple a secure long-term income, for the poor-quality copper was not a promising prospect. By contrast Mansfeld copper, centred on Mansfeld and Hettstedt, was of the highest quality. Making all possible efforts to promote their lands, the counts issued a manufacturer-friendly mining ordinance and arranged for the introduction of the most modern technologies, such as a process involving the use of lead as a catalyst that allowed silver to be separated out from the raw copper. Wishing to be sure that their potential ventures were legally sound, investors required an agreement be in place with the electors of Saxony, who were of long-standing influence in the Harz region. On 6 May 1484, after negotiations lasting several months, a settlement was reached in Leipzig. We have good reason to believe that in summer 1483, as *Bergrat* at Mansfeld, Hans Luder's brother-in-law Anton Lindemann would have known of the imminent agreement and could have informed his relatives in Möhra of both that settlement and the opportunities it represented for someone minded to invest; he had, we would say today, an insider tip. And indeed, in summer 1483 his sister and brother-in-law moved to the county of Mansfeld, followed soon after by Klein-Hans (Small Hans) Luder, a younger brother of Hans' who was similarly excluded from inheriting from their father.

With Margarete's pregnancy well advanced, the Luders moved into a house in Eisleben in the Bridge District, the home of many artisans. With some 4,000 inhabitants, Eisleben would not have seemed so alien to the young couple from Eisenach, who would surely quickly have felt at home in their new surroundings. Yet while the solid leading citizens of the former

Thuringian residence town of Eisenach looked to the past, Eisleben looked to the future, with expansive construction enlarging the footprint of the town, growing engagement in mining itself and in the manufacturing associated with mining, and mining and foundry workers who brought new life, and also unrest and danger, to the towns of Mansfeld county. Smelting masters were prepared to assume the risks of investment in capital projects, and while they might make speedy returns, they not infrequently quickly found they had lost everything. Hans Luder was not going to miss out on the opportunities available to him and soon established the necessary business connections. In Hans Lüttich, who came from an established local family of foundry masters, he found a suitable partner and joint investor.

It soon became evident that mining in Eisleben itself offered no opportunities for new investors: the *Erbfeuer* mining rights were privately owned, and the *Herrenfeuer* rights, which were leased by the counts of Mansfeld, were all also securely held by existing businesses. In spring 1484 Hans Luder and his partner leased from the ruler mining rights, as *Herrenfeuer*, in the nearby town of Mansfeld. With 3,000 inhabitants Mansfeld was only three-quarters the size of Eisleben, but it was more strongly associated with mining and agriculture. With the ruling counts' imposing castle of Mansfeld towering over the town, Mansfeld was strongly influenced by the court and administration of the small territory. The main street ran from the church square to the lower town gate, from where it led up to the castle and to the copper shale deposits. In the immediate vicinity of the main street lived court administrators and families involved in mining. The Luder family occupied a substantial property with more elegant buildings to the front and stabling and other outbuildings behind, and with an extensive kitchen garden with vegetables, fruit, and even grapevines.

The extensive and utilitarian character of the Luders' physical footprint in Mansfeld tells its own story. Supplies for mining and smelting had to be stored and the horses needed for the process of drying out the mineshafts stabled. The family's business interests also rested heavily, however, on agriculture and livestock, which provided a reliable income and therefore also some protection against the risks of mining. Finally, Hans Luder also made good use of the possibilities offered by the capital market, which expanded rapidly in the early sixteenth century. He lent out his surplus funds at interest, with the counts of Stolberg-Wernigerode and various ecclesiastical institutions amongst his debtors. As is always the case in an overheated economy, the remarkable possible profits came with substantial risk, a reality Hans Luder would eventually discover, although only towards the end of his working life, and his heirs still inherited the property he owned and 1,250 gulden in cash. But Martin's younger brother Jakob, who took on his father's business and the parental home, would be overwhelmed by the crisis in the Mansfeld mining industry and landed in severe financial difficulty.

Martin's childhood in Mansfeld was shaped by his father's success in business and by the rapid improvement in the family's social status that accompanied that economic achievement. Hans Luder became a significant presence in Mansfeld and, as was typical in late medieval towns, his standing brought with it public office. As early as 1491 he was one of the four *Vierherr*, representatives of the local citizenry responsible for the administration of the town together with the town council. As a matter of course this position would have brought Luder into contact with the nearby court and territorial administration. The office of *Vierherr* included ecclesiastical responsibilities, in particular at the town church of Saint George, located very close to the family property. There Luder would have represented the citizens of the town at the dedication of altars, in events related to the fabric of the church, including the building itself, and in the trade in indulgences that was already flourishing in the 1490s.

Luther later recorded that his father had avoided one cleric's insistent urging that he make financial contributions to the church by pointing to his responsibility for his large family.[2] That response is in keeping with the character of a hard-working and thrifty mining entrepreneur with his feet firmly on the ground at a time when secular and secularizing trends were developing precisely in economic and financial affairs. A possible anticleric- alism can also be read from Luther's account. Hans Luder was certainly, however, neither anti-religion nor anti-church. He located himself fully within the new religious impulses when he joined a fraternity, Unserer Leiben Frauen Gezeiten im Thal Mansfeldt founded in 1502 and made up of local dignitaries and when he took part in the activities, largely involving social welfare, of the fraternity of Saint George at the town church.

There was also nothing unusual in Luder's plan to ensure the improved status of his family by having his oldest son study law. Legal study ranked alongside a career in the church as a prime means to social advancement. With princely rulers and town magistrates requiring increasing numbers of legal scholars and administrative personnel, law studies could be a first step up the social ladder and might take the climber even as far as ennoblement. Very soon after, in the 1520s and 1530s, during the period of unrest that accompanied the Reformation, lawyers were increasingly likely to be among the families that dominated the councils of north and central German towns, and in subsequent generations they formed the core of early modern territorial bureaucracies. For Luder, a mining and metalworking entrepreneur with no family tradition of education, the conviction that his oldest son should study law would also have been fostered by the university attendance of members of the Lindemann family, a path they had followed as a matter of course: Johann and Kaspar Lindemann, sons of an elder brother of Margarete and therefore cousins of Martin, had studied law and medicine respectively and both entered princely service, as a councillor and as personal physician to the Saxon elector. The closeness of the family ties is evident in the presence of Kaspar Lindemann at the first and most challenging of the disputations that Luther the reformer faced, against Johannes Eck at Leipzig in 1519. A similar model was also provided by the Drachstedt family, friends of the Luders' in Eisleben who also ran a smelting works. The Drachstedts' son Philip held a doctorate in law and rose high, becoming a princely councillor and assessor at the Imperial Chamber Court. Well aware of the lack of security provided by his own business, Hans Luder the Mansfeld master smelter would have taken note of such careers and wished his own oldest son to follow a similar path. This makes all the more understandable his deep disappointment and anger when Martin ended his law studies, extinguishing his family's hopes of further social advancement.

Strict and Uncompromising: Everyday Life in Mansfeld

House and home were the domain of Luder's mother, who was therefore the dominant influence on the everyday experiences of her children and family. In the early years, when the young family was still unable to afford servants, she also shouldered the physical responsibilities of the household. While we have good reason to correct the romanticized picture of Luther's father's having pulled himself up from nothing, we have no reason to doubt Luther's memory of his mother's collecting wood in the forest and carrying it home on her back.[3] Money would have been short in the Luder family, for all resources were to be invested in the family's business interests, which is not to say that Martin's childhood was scarred by poverty, but it was marked by thriftiness and a certain meagreness. Later too, as business flourished, Luder's mother's contribution remained vital to the growing family. Again the picture is a little blurry, for we do not have an exact headcount for Martin Luder's siblings. We do know for certain that he had one brother, Jakob, and three sisters who reached adulthood, but we also have references to other siblings who died as children. Luder's mother would have introduced the children to religion. We know little of her own piety and spirituality other than a brief comment by Martin Luther in which he stated that his mother was superstitious and feared witches and demons. We are therefore left to conclude that Martin Luther's religious upbringing was likely much as was standard for the time, dominated by popular religion and focused on the veneration of the saints and the omnipresent works-based devotional practice.

Ignoring the lack of evidence to support their theories, psychologists have felt drawn, and still feel drawn, to interpreting the childhood experiences of the reformer and arguing for their significance for his subsequent thoughts and actions. Erik H. Erikson, an American psychoanalyst, explained the Reformation as an anti-authoritarian protest by the 'Young Man Luther'[4] against his father, basing his psychoanalysis on the reformer's own words, and in particular on memories of his childhood voiced twenty years later. One of these statements concerned his relationship with his father: 'My father once whipped me so severely that I ran away from him, and he was worried that he might not win me back again'; the other, his relationship with his mother: 'For the sake of a mere nut my mother beat me until the blood flowed. By such strict discipline they finally forced me into the monastery; though they meant it heartily well, I was only made timid by it.'[5] Even if Luther himself saw a connection between his experience of parental disciplining and the merciless image of God that led him to flee to the monastery, we must be wary of finding methodological equivalence between a reminiscence recounted at the dinner table and the utterances of today's middle classes on the psychoanalyst's couch. The circumstances in which Luther and his contemporaries lived and the well-being of their souls were determined by needs and fears and expressed in images and imaginings that were all foreign to the nineteenth and twentieth centuries, and to the individuals on whom Freud and his successors developed their interpretative tools and models. Luder did not grow up in a society characterized by excess and consumption, let alone in a permissive society. Due to the harsh climate few walnut trees grew in the east of Germany, and those few trees bore little fruit. A walnut was therefore valuable, and its allocation, as for other foodstuffs, fell to the parents. The father and mother who headed the household were also the master and mistress of the house, with an authority that they wielded over their children as well as their servants. Children of that era were hardly in a position to develop a psychosis about a dominant mother or father figure.

If Luther became a reformer because of his childhood, then almost every one of his contemporaries also had the stuff of a rebel and reformer. A possible derivation of his image of a God who judged without mercy— an image that continued to torment the Augustinian monk in his monastery cell—from his punitive father and his beatings becomes less plausible when comparisons are made with other reforming careers. Socially John Calvin was a product of the educated class of French public servants, and his childhood experiences were very different from those of Martin Luther, yet Calvin developed a sense of an almighty and sovereign God that was fully the equal of Luther's terrifying fantasies. Additionally, Calvin the reformer taught of a God of predestination, of an unfathomable God with unlimited power over the salvation and damnation of humankind who bestowed on everyone a lifelong anxiety about their election. By contrast, Martin Luther was eventually able to move beyond his menacing God and located a merciful God at the heart of his theology. If Luther really did have a father complex, then he successfully worked it through in his theology, where he found the Protestant God of eternal mercy who freed both Luther and millions of his contemporaries from their fear of eternal damnation. Anyone who still wishes to find the roots of Luther's early despair about a judging God in the reformer's relationship with his father will have to use the same psychological tools to explain how, unlike the reformer of Geneva, the Wittenberg reformer was able to rework his image of a menacing God into an image of a God of mercy.

There is every reason to suppose that from his birth in 1483 until he left the parental home in Mansfeld, probably in 1497, but perhaps in 1496, Martin Luder was a child like any other child in his social circle, with whom he shared material, social, cultural, and emotional experiences. Just as his father was very much part of the circle of dignitaries of Mansfeld, Martin was very much part of the next generation, in particular the element that was made up of boys such as Nicolaus Oemler and Hans Reinicke, both sons of master smelters, who were also preparing to study at university and attended the town school in Mansfeld along with Luder. We know of no events or behaviour that might serve as early indications that Luder was on the path to becoming a reformer. No points of reference emerge for the saintly vita on which his supporters would soon be working, nor do we see signs of a pathological evildoer, obsessed with the destruction of the established ecclesiastical and earthly order, as he was portrayed by his Roman opponents. We can identify, however, a number of attributes that would likely have given the young Martin Luder a distinctive personality.

For example, as an oldest child with many siblings, while still young Martin Luder would have been taught both responsibility and independence, skills that would have been honed when he left home and homeland aged thirteen to continue his education. Despite her strictness, Martin's mother was for her eldest son throughout his life the model homemaker who worked ceaselessly and with great dedication. Later, when he spoke so highly of the prudent housekeeping of his wife, Katharina, and of her care for the financial welfare of his own family, consciously or unconsciously Luther must have seen in Katharina's achievements a reflection of his mother's role in his parental home. Similarly, the professional and social status of his father and the milieu created by the young and dynamic mining-based society of his home town left their marks on Luther's understanding of vocation and of Christian activity in the world. His involvement in mining would have made Luther's father as used to hazardous ventures, decision-making under pressure, and necessary risk-taking as to presenting and asserting his own interests in more public arenas, whether in his business dealings or in civic affairs, or in relation to the territorial ruler and his councillors, who were so close at hand. He who hesitated or was distracted by the obstacles in his path was lost. As a reformer Martin Luther advanced unflinchingly and with courage and determination, his energies repeatedly called upon but never drying up. In entering the monastery in the face of strong opposition from his father; in developing his theology not only without being shaken by the animosity it aroused but even stimulated by that hostility into constantly reformulating his ideas more clearly; and in single-mindedly making his way to Worms, ignoring all warnings, Luther was simply following the rules of the game he had learned in childhood. We can likely see marks of his childhood in the self-confidence that led him to reject support and protection, even from his ruler, when it seemed such assistance might restrict him: 'Not so, Elector,' he shot out at Frederick the Wise when the elector sent Spalatin to urge him not to write against the relic collection of the elector-archbishop of Mainz, 'I would rather lose you [Spalatin], the Sovereign himself, and the world', than for the sake of 'public peace' renounce his pronouncement of what he believed true and surely necessary for the eternal salvation of the soul.[6]

The unwillingness to compromise and verbal rage that Luther later exhibited in his correspondence, employing even greater vehemence in his treatises and pamphlets—for example in 'Against the Papacy in Rome, Founded by the Devil' (*Wider das Papsttum zu Rom, vom Teufel gestiftet*)[7]— were a reflection of a social excitability and an impulsiveness that could extend even to the use of force that were characteristic of the milieu in which he had grown up. Such impulsivity had found its way into the inner reaches of Martin Luder's immediate family. His uncle Klein-Hans (Small Hans), who had followed his older brother Gross-Hans (Large Hans), Martin's father, to Mansfeld, had to answer repeatedly before the court in Mansfeld for fighting and violent behaviour, and he died in a pub brawl. As linguistic capacities in both one's mother tongue and learned languages are acquired in childhood, we can assume that while still a child Luther already 'looked into the mouths of the people'. The foundations for Luther's powerful use of language and for his contribution to the development of the German language were thus laid during his childhood in Mansfeld.

School and Studies

The educational path taken by Martin Luder, grandson of a farmer and son of a mining entrepreneur, was completely conventional. It led from the elementary school in Mansfeld, via Latin schools in Magdeburg and Eisenach, to university studies in Erfurt. At the end of the fifteenth century, the world of education in Germany, as throughout Europe, was changing. The days in which sons had little choice but to follow their fathers into certain occupations and thus a predetermined social status were long gone. The expansion of schools and universities, along with the existence of other forms of schooling, for example as a member of a religious order, meant that education could fuel mobility. This opportunity was seized above all by those who, like Hans Luder and his wife, had emerged from a peasant or urban background and had worked their way to economic success. Humanism had opened the door to various forms of schooling and university study, but in central Germany access was also fostered by the pragmatic administrative and political interests of princely rulers, urban magistrates, and ecclesiastical institutions. A wave of new late medieval and early modern territorial foundations meant that the number of universities was growing rapidly, with, for example, the establishment of universities at Wittenberg in 1502 and at Frankfurt an der Oder in 1506. Theology still reigned supreme at the universities, and study of the divine remained the noblest goal. Humanist inquiry, which explored the whole cosmos of classical and medieval learning, had long since separated itself from theology, even if theology still liked to term the humanities its *ancilla*, or maid.

Above all, however, having proven themselves an indispensable presence in daily life, lawyers and medical doctors were now seen by society as the equals of the theologians. In light of the growing importance of natural philosophy and practical economic and political knowledge, above all when it came to waging war, applied study had gained new respect. Such was especially the case in the mining region that covered Saxony, the Harz mountains, and Thuringia, where Georg Agricola (1494–1555), humanist and town doctor in Chemnitz, laid out the basics of metallurgy and mining in his 'On the Nature of Metals' (*De re metallica*), published posthumously in 1556; with other publications he became a pioneer in the earth sciences. Similar advances were made in ballistics and fortifications, and in agronomy, with humanist and ducal councillor Konrad von Heresbach, who was from the Lower Rhine region, setting out this new knowledge in his work entitled 'Four Books on Agriculture' (*Vier Bücher zur Landwirtschaft*).

The network of highly respected schools, both town schools and Latin schools, which extended through central Germany was integral to Hans Luder's plan to secure the social advancement of his family through the education of his eldest son. Luder's elementary education was acquired in Mansfeld itself, where, aged six, he began attending a school that stood only a stone's throw from his home and was accommodated in a small one-storey house in the shadow of the parish church. There Luder learned to read and write and to count a little, and he also learned the basics of Latin. Later the reformer would complain about frequent switching between Latin and German, which meant, he claimed, that pupils never really mastered either language. While his point was certainly valid, by the time he made his comment Luther had long demonstrated a matchless ability in German, and his Latin, while not necessarily elegant, was very reliable.

As was absolutely usual, school and church were closely intertwined, with religion included in the children's instruction. What religious knowledge Martin did not learn from his mother at home, he acquired at school, largely through daily prayer and singing. His own experiences later formed the foundations of a Protestant religious pedagogy still found today: 'God has preserved the church through schools. They are the preservers of the church,' he informed those sitting alongside him at the dinner table in Wittenberg, doubtless envisioning his own schooldays as he spoke.[8] Largely unintentionally, the performance of religious songs at school each day and during church services provided basic instruction in music, awakening in Luther a love of singing and music-making that he transferred into a commitment to Protestant songs and hymns, heard both inside and outside the church.

The children of Mansfeld had to leave their home town if they were to pursue their education beyond the elementary level. At age thirteen, Martin was therefore sent to Magdeburg, an episcopal city some seventy kilometres from Mansfeld. He was accompanied by his friend Hans Reinicke, also the son of a mining entrepreneur. Martin lived with the Brothers of the Common Life, a religious community strongly influenced by Dutch humanism that decisively shaped late medieval and early modern transitions in devotional practice and education in north-west Germany. The Brothers did not usually run schools themselves, but instead provided accommodation for pupils. As this practice appears to have been copied in Magdeburg, we can assume that Martin attended the cathedral school that lay very close to the community's house

After only one year, Martin moved to Eisenach, his mother's home town, where he lived with and was supported by relatives and friends. He continued his education by attending the Latin school that was part of the parish of Saint George, but while he was acquiring more advanced skills as a scholar, these years in Eisenach also brought Luder new spiritual experiences, in Franciscan circles and at the home of secular priest Johannes Braun, where pupils at the Saint George school met to pray together, to make music, and to discuss texts. The works they read were mainly spiritual, but the young men also discussed Petrarch, the secular father of humanism. Martin would also have breathed humanist air in the homes of the Schalbe and Cotta families, with whom he lodged, both of which included members of the town council.

Despite all the support they received from their wider families and from those around them, the years of schooling for students such as Martin Luder were hard and often scarred by deprivation. Unlike their fellow students who had noble or patrician origins, Luder and his peers were very much on their own, with no retinue, let alone their own household. As in Eisenach, in

Magdeburg too, Martin had in part to 'sing for his bread', in other words, to 'beg' for support for his basic needs. While such begging was no cause for contempt in a society that had a strong culture of supplication, it did add a time-consuming onus to Martin's existence that some of his fellow students avoided. Thriftiness and frugality, characteristics that led to a lifelong lack of dependence on material possessions, did not become prominent personality traits for Luder only as a result of the Augustinian vow of poverty he took on entering the monastery. His parents also had to do without. Their enterprises in Mansfeld had to bear the costs of Luder's board and lodging as well as the significant fees at the institutions he attended. At the University of Erfurt, matriculation alone cost a third of a gulden, a considerable outlay when a miner, one of the best remunerated skilled trades of the time, earned 30 gulden annually and when the average net worth of a citizen of Erfurt lay well below 100 gulden.

Martin Luder matriculated at the University of Erfurt in spring 1501. In Erfurt he found support in the social networks among the general population and at the university to which he had access via both the Latin school in Eisenach and his mentor Braun. At the same time, however, with matriculation came a transition far greater than a move of forty kilometres or relocation from Latin school to university. Both intellectually and politically, the young man—Luder was now seventeen years old—was entering a new world. Erfurt was not just a university town but also the capital of the central German possessions of the bishopric of Mainz. It was also a prime economic centre, a status built on the highly profitable long-distance trade in woad, which was used as a dye for the colour blue. The citizens of Erfurt were politically self-confident and as a result of the long distance between Erfurt and the territorial prince in Mainz, the magistrates of Erfurt had greater political scope than the councils of many Imperial cities. With its extensive rural territory, covering more than eighty villages, and a population of some 16,000 people, Erfurt was on a par in terms of size with Augsburg, and the city dominated the region both economically and in cultural and intellectual terms. If we pass over Luder's earlier short stay in Magdeburg, Erfurt was the only metropole in which the reformer ever lived for a substantial period.

The University of Erfurt founded at the end of the fourteenth century, was one of only two universities (the other was at Leipzig) in central Germany. Having embraced both nominalism—the 'modern' approach to philosophy and theology that stood counter to the realism of the Thomists—and humanism, the University of Erfurt was on its way to becoming a leading force in the intellectual life of the Empire. The faculty of arts, through which Luder had to pass before selecting to study in one of the higher faculties of theology, medicine, or law, was particularly modern in its teaching of philosophy and philology, in terms of both methodology and content. The theological faculty was less innovative, largely content with the 'repeating of old commentaries on scripture' and with 'internally emaciated scholastic methods'.[9] For the more thoughtful students who, like Martin Luder, sought real understanding, the divisions produced by these different affiliations could only be stimulating, for they found themselves in the midst of fundamental disputes over method and forced to adopt and defend their own positions.

Martin's father appears to have covered his son's basic living expenses during his studies in Erfurt. Luder was not forced to live in one of the less respectable private student hostels run by the poorer masters, but became instead a member of the highly regarded 'George Fraternity', whose ordinances set a strict code of behaviour that guaranteed a well-regulated progression through the university. Having taken his bachelor's exams on 29 September 1502, Luder completed his liberal arts studies without any problem, receiving his Master of Arts degree in January 1505. He then began to study law, just as his father had intended.

Intellectual Profile

The attempt to characterize Luder's education only makes all the more evident our lack of concrete detail. Above all, we simply cannot know how deeply he was influenced by the *devotio moderna*, which brought new ideas about education and piety from the Low Countries, or by humanism, although we do know that he came in contact with both movements while at school in Magdeburg and Eisenach. Humanism would have left a significant mark on his study of the liberal arts in Erfurt—from his reading of classical authors, including poets; from his humanistically inclined teachers and fellow students; and, last but not least, from awareness of method and critical distancing from scholastic approaches that he encountered in his studies. Even though Luder would not have declared himself free of scholasticism, the way had been paved for the contempt with which the reformer would later denounce scholastics as hollow-ringing sophists. In 1520 he declared his affinity with William of Ockham and the modernists within medieval philosophy who, unlike the Thomists who still dominated at most universities, separated reason from belief, with reason being of this world and belief a thing of the next.[10]

The humanist influences that Luder experienced while still young stayed with him throughout his life. They could be found in his great esteem for the word, in his decisive turn to the sources, in the rhetoric found above all in his letters, in his interest in classical authors such as the Greek fable-teller Aesop, and even in his love of music, which was sent in a new direction by the humanists. That he never embraced humanist anthropology, however, which he also encountered later in the optimistic writings of Erasmus of Rotterdam, with their emphasis on the autonomous capability of human-kind, would be highly significant not just for the next steps taken by Martin Luder, student in Erfurt, but also for the evangelical theology of Martin Luther, reformer.

Examined closely, Luder's intellectual identity appears to have been shaped far more existentially than academically. He gave great weight to his personal experiences as lived knowledge. It is hardly surprising that religion featured strongly, in light of the strong devotional culture of central Germany and Luder's close contact with the religious groupings in the various locations where he lived. Also typical is his strong interest in music, which Luder fostered while a student in Erfurt by playing the lute.

Figure 9. Philip Melanchthon, by Albrecht Dürer, copperplate, 1526.

Luther later attributed his existential decisiveness directly to his birth and his origins. At the high point of the conflict over the freedom of the will, a dispute in which he engaged with uncompromising severity, he provided this self-characterization:

> To this end I am born: to wage war against hordes and devils and go out to battle. For this reason, my books are very stormy and more warlike. I have to dig out the roots and stumps, chop out the thorns and underbush, and fill in the potholes. Thus I am the rough woodsman, who has to clear and straighten the path.

The character and temperament of his friend and colleague Philip Melanchthon (Figure 9) were very different, he acknowledged, and tellingly Melanchthon was a product of the south German-educated burgher class and had been educated by studious humanists: 'But Master Philip follows carefully and quietly and enjoys building and planting, sowing and watering, according to the gifts that God has richly given to him.'[11]

III

Crisis and Flight to the Monastery

A Student in Crisis and His Conversion at Stotternheim

Luder's legal studies lasted only a few weeks. The semester began in Erfurt on 19 May, the day of Saint Ivo, patron saint of the legal faculty. On 17 July, only two months later, the law student entered the Erfurt monastery of the Augustinian Hermits and became Brother Martin. What had happened?

Martin Luder, now twenty-one years old, had evidently begun to study civil law, for we know he owned a copy of the Corpus Iuris Civilis that he sold before entering the monastery. He also seems to have started to work with the glossators, the northern Italian legal experts of the twelfth and thirteenth centuries whose commentaries on Roman civil law had much the same authority as the law itself and therefore formed the core of legal studies. More specifically, he seems to have used the *Glossa ordinaria* by Accursius, glossator from Bologna, an indispensable textbook written around the middle of the thirteenth century that provided almost 100,000 explanatory glosses on the whole Corpus Iuris Civilis. Later, long after he had switched to theology, Luther would repeatedly criticize Accursius, deeming his method for judging legal issues utterly arbitrary. These were not the words of a law student, however; here we have the retrospective judgement of a reformer who demanded unambiguity and clarity, not interpretative possibilities. Where legal minds disputed reality and relativity, the theologian sought complete insight into the indivisible and immutable truth.

Behind this assertion and other such pronouncements—made by Luther largely as he sat around the table with his friends—stood the experiences of a reformer who had found his life's purpose in the rediscovery of a truth that was for him absolute and uninvincible. This retrospective perspective explains

Luther's reproaching of lawyers for their concern with earthly matters and 'not with the conscience'. Lawyers, he claimed, could not withstand the devil, whatever the merits of Bartolus and Baldus and all the other scribes.[1] The office of the theologian was, therefore, far superior to that of the lawyer:

> A jurist can be a scoundrel but a theologian ought to be a godly man. The reason is that a jurist has power over the bodily things with which he deals, but it requires a godly man to be a theologian because God himself, his heaven and all his gifts, righteousness, the forgiveness of sin, and everything else are entrusted to him. God himself relies upon him, for it is written, 'If you forgive the sins of any, they are forgiven.'[2]

The self-possession of these words was not the self-possession of Luder the student in 1505, when he was uncertain about where life would take him. Even if the legal manuals of the educated glossators seemed hollow and empty, as a student in the first semester of his law studies Luder would hardly have been in a position to condemn and dismiss all legal learning. The crisis that he experienced soon after beginning his legal studies was not the break-through event that made him a reformer. It was also not the crisis of an individual who could see a clear alternative to his current prospects and felt bound to chase that alternative no matter what resistance he faced. Emerging from the relatively sheltered world of school and a first degree in the arts, Luder now wavered as he considered the adult life for which his studies were to prepare him. Alienated from the world of his father, he had lost the anchor that tied him to the study of law as a first step towards a significant position in politics or commerce.

The contemporary setting determined how that crisis escalated and how it would be resolved. Luder was the child of an age that despite all its economic and political innovations, all its many church institutions with their redemptive offerings, all its intensity of lived religiosity, and all its investment in sensual pleasures and the joys of life, was characterized by deep uncertainty and a search for security. In the preaching they heard and the pastoral care they received and in the many depictions of the Dance of Death and other allegories of the *memento mori* they encountered, individuals were confronted almost daily with the transience of their lives on earth.

The extent of their uncertainty varied from person to person, as did their trust in the path to salvation laid out for them. Luder's requirements were evidently high, and he was not content with the usual forms of consolation. Studying law would likely guarantee him a secure future, but for him that was insufficient. His crisis at this time of transition appears to have been brought to a head by immediate encounters with death. During his early years of study at Erfurt, three law professors died, and the students were required to attend their requiem masses and interments. In 1504/1505 plague hit the city. While still studying for his first degree Luder had come very close to death himself when he sliced open an artery on his thigh with the dagger that as a student he was entitled to carry; he had nearly bled to death. His response to that life-threatening wound suggests that death as such was not the cause of his unease—he used his recuperation as an opportunity to learn to play the lute. The confrontation with death did lead him to wonder, however, whether he was sensible to design his life around a profession that was concerned only and entirely with the problems and values of this world. These doubts appeared to be shared even by the great men in his field, for it was rumoured that on their deathbeds two of the professors who had recently died had strongly rued their choice of career, for as doctors of law they believed themselves denied the confident and contented deaths of monks and clergy.[3]

The religious dimensions of Luder's personal crisis, its focus on God and the hereafter, came fully to the fore at the beginning of July 1505 on the open road near Stotternheim, a village that lay a few kilometres north of Erfurt. At the end of June, Martin had returned home. Only for a very weighty reason would he have been absent during the semester, and perhaps his visit was impelled by his father's determination to see his student son, who had now reached adulthood, wed, or, according to Luther's words of 1521, 'to tie me down with an honorable and wealthy marriage'.[4] Luder certainly used the opportunity to convey to his father his dissatisfaction with his legal studies, although the possibility of his entering a monastery was not part of their discussion. As was usual, Luder's return journey was undertaken largely or completely on foot. While passing through the open countryside on Wednesday, 2 July, he was overtaken by a violent summer thunderstorm that left him fearing for his life. The details of this event come to us only from personal accounts given much later, in which the reality was overlaid by memories moulded by the Reformation. This recasting is particularly evident in a Table Talk from 16 July 1539, our principal source for the events at Stotternheim:

> 'Today is the anniversary of my entering the monastery in Erfurt, and therefore I should mark that new start', with those words he began to tell the story of how . . . prostrated by a flash of lightning in fear and terror he had said, 'If you help, Saint Anna, I will become a monk.'[5]

We see reality and self-projection similarly entwined in an earlier work, a Latin dedication from November 1521 that Luther attached to his work 'The Judgement of Martin Luther on Monastic Vows' (*De votis monasticis Martini Lutheri iudicium*), written while he was at the Wartburg. The dedication is to his father and asks him to forgive his son for abandoning his study of law and entering the monastery.[6] Hans Luder had no Latin, and we can assume that his son's words were intended for much broader consumption. Following the events at Worms, the Reformation public had grown rapidly, and Luther found himself required to provide a plausible explanation, not just theological but also personal, of his progress into the monastery and then out again. The events of 1505 had been inevitably swept up by the recent flood of Reformation ideas, which included rejection of monastic life. His father would seem to have been right, and Luther's refusal to listen to him was an act of disobedience that now needed theological legitimation. Viewed from this new present, Luther had taken a wrong turn when he entered the monastery, for, polluted by evil, the Roman Church had given not just Luther but also thousands of other Christians a false sense of security about their salvation.

We must be wary of using post-Reformation reflections to understand the pre-Reformation conversion of 1505. The young law student was not forced to adopt a new life under pressure from the Roman Church; he went willingly, motivated by an inner desire to find meaning for his life beyond a future determined by worldly and material concerns. Although his vow came spontaneously—like a bolt of lightning, we might say—it was also something of a rational and considered decision, for it provided a way out of the crisis in his university career that Luder was already facing as he transferred from study of the arts to the study of law. While his parents were greatly exasperated by the decision of this cosmopolitan young man to spend his life in a monastery, that decision was hardly unusual for his age. Additionally, while at school in Magdeburg and Eisenach, Luder had encountered and learned to value the spirituality of the mendicant orders. The lasting impact of that experience even after he moved to Erfurt is evident in the letters in which Luder informed his friends in Eisenach of his decision to seek ordination as a priest.

We cannot reconstruct unequivocally all the circumstances surrounding Luder's entry into the monastery. His decision certainly came in a moment of mortal fear and resulted in a conversion that took the form of a radical change in lifestyle. Compulsion was part of that reality, as Luder explained to his father two years after the events themselves, on the occasion of his celebration of his first Mass: he had become a monk not of his own free will, but because he had been called by heaven to take holy orders; he had entered the monastery not because it seemed to offer an easy life, but because his fear and terror of a sudden death (*terrore et agone mortis subitae*) had compelled him.[7] This explanation was recorded in 1521, in the dedication of 'On Monastic Vows', but as Luther's father was still living at that date and therefore would have been able to testify to the truth of his son's account, we can assume that such a sentiment expressed in much these terms had indeed been relayed to him in 1507.

The allusion to Saint Anne, who is not to be found in Scripture but emerged in later tradition as the mother of Mary and grandmother of Christ, can be tested against the sources. The reference appears for the first time in the Table Talk of 1539, so more than three decades after the event and at a time when Luther had long been involved in the consolidation of the Reformation through interpretation of both its history and his own. Yet almost all of Luther's biographers have adopted his account without question, for it is entirely in accord with how individuals at the beginning of the sixteenth century would most likely have behaved in such a situation—in times of crisis they might well have called upon one of the numerous saints offered by the late medieval church for assistance. And that someone in fear of his or her life would turn to Saint Anne also makes historical sense. The cult of Saint Anne had emerged when Martin Luder was around fifteen years old. In Germany Anne had quickly become something of a saint of choice, especially in the mining regions of the Harz mountains, Thuringia, and above all Saxony, with its flourishing mining town of Annaberg, where miners called on Anne for protection from sudden death. Martin may have become acquainted with Anne in Mansfeld, with its strong ties to mining, and he would certainly have encountered her cult in Eisenach, where by the 1490s at the latest, prayers were being offered to Saint Anne in the church of Saint George. Anne would soon also become a subject for leading artists. Lucas Cranach the Elder painted a large altar to Anne (Figure 10) for the church of the Teutonic Order in Buro, which lay on the Elbe a little upstream of Wittenberg, between Coswig and Rosslau.

The law student would have been well acquainted with Anne as a saint who could protect against a sudden and untimely death. Untimely death should not be understood as dying before one's time, while still young, but rather as dying without time to prepare for the Last Judgement, on which day each individual would be required to account for his or her life on earth. The historical context makes it very plausible that many years after the event

Figure 10. Two altarpieces to Saint Anne, by Lucas Cranach the Elder, 1510–15, now in the village church of Klieken, by Coswig.

itself, Saint Anne was the saint to whom Luther recalled making his vow and the saint he repeatedly named as his idol.[8] Their relationship is not contradicted by the reformer's sharp criticism of the cult of Saint Anne. For Luther the mother of Mary was an especially dangerous invention of the papacy. In portraying Anne as able to save from mortal danger, the church directed attention away from Christ, the true source of God's grace. Luther's concern was not with secular history; the role that he retrospectively attributed to Anne in his taking of holy orders—which he now deemed false—provided her with a part in sacred history. She had participated in God's redirection of his life into becoming a reformer: 'But,' he continued in the Table Talk of 1539, after the description of the events at Stotternheim, 'God understood my vow in terms of the Hebrew: Anna means grace'[9]—Luther was drawing on the Hebrew name Hanna/Channah, which he sought to associate with *chen*, or grace. Even the flight of this errant student to the false idols of the saints was predetermined. God had led him through error onto the true path to acknowledgement of the grace of God, and in so doing had made him a prophet of God's pure word.

That Luder's plea for help from the saint contained a promise to become a monk was perfectly typical of responses to mortal danger. Such circumstances were even covered by church law, which declared commitments made *in extremis* to be not binding. Of greater biographical interest than the vow itself is Luder's determination not to be diverted from his original intent even though he could have used this legal loophole and faced pressure from his university friends. As was typical of Luther throughout his life, the religious and transcendental were readily combined with the practical and rational, and in just two weeks he had set his affairs in order, given up his student quarters, sold or given away his belongings, and informed his friends of his intention—his parents he told only after the fact. With an evening of celebration to mark his departure, he drew a line under his student life. His friends accompanied him 'to the monastery at daybreak', and Luder carried with him only his copies of Plautus and Virgil, for the pillars of his study of the arts carried more weight for him than any sophisticated legal text. He also abandoned his lute playing, having performed with both pleasure and evident talent at his farewell party, because, again according to later reminiscence, 'no other study pleased me so much as sacred literature'.[10]

In addition to the details they provide, the accounts of Luder's personal crisis in summer 1505 highlight an enduring theme that gave cohesion and stability to both his biography and the Reformation: the eschatological significance of the task he had been given and of events on earth as a whole. On the open road outside Erfurt he had felt himself touched by a power that came from beyond his earthly existence and controlled his soul and whose eternal nature he did not doubt. Amongst those to whom he recounted his experience and his decision, no one doubted that divine presence, neither his fellow students nor his fellow monks, who saw in him 'a second Paul, who had been miraculously converted by Christ'.[11] Even his father was convinced that powers not of this earth were at work, although for Hans Luder those powers were not of God but of the devil, who through deception and magic (*illusio et praestigium*) had forced his son from the path to a fulfilling life on earth.[12]

A decade and a half later, in 'On Monastic Vows', this judgement was turned on its head and the roles reversed. The student's resolution in maintaining his vow was now deemed disobedience to his father and an offence against God's order; his father's warning had become the voice of God. The sacred significance of the events was retained, however, and even intensified:

I think that from (the days of) my childhood Satan must have foreseen something in me (which is the cause) of his present [i.e. through the Reformation] suffering. He has therefore raged against me with incredible contrivings to destroy or hinder me, so that I have often wondered whether I was the only man in the whole world whom he was seeking. But it was the Lord's will, as I now see, that . . . the monasteries should become known to me by my own actual experience, that is, through many sins and impieties.[13]

Only by travelling this false path, Luther wrote, was he able to recognize the errors of the papal church, with their implications for salvation, and to experience release through the grace of God. Additionally, he continued, his opponents could hardly complain that he knew nothing of what he talked about.

Luther's retrospective interpretation of his vow to Saint Anne became part of his account of his role in sacred history. Whether in 1505 Luder the student really did turn to Saint Anne or whether thirty-four years later Luther the reformer saw in Anne only a concrete expression of his earlier pernicious trust in the intervention of the saints, Luther certainly had an unwavering confidence in his Reformation and in the path that had led him to that Reformation. He relayed that message to succeeding generations, who were undoubtedly also addressed in this Table Talk. His own renaming from Luder to Luther/Eleutherius, the one set free by recognition of the grace of God, took place just as the Reformation became a reality. Similarly, the etymological interpretation of the link between Anna/Hanna and grace shows that he understood himself as chosen and guided by God at the very moment when, with his decision to become a monk, he had strayed, to Reformation eyes, farthest from the path to salvation. For both Luther and the form of Protestantism he founded, the events of 1505 were given a certain dignity by the eschatological dimension of the struggles, both worldly and redemptive, that beset the soul of Martin Luder as both student and monk. That turmoil was understood as the conflict between Satan, who sought to prevent the rediscovery of the pure teachings and therefore supported the false Roman Church, and God, who had chosen Luther to be his instrument in the necessary renewal of the Christian church. Their battle was over salvation and damnation, and not simply for Luther and his contemporaries but for all generations to come.

On earth this battle played out as a son's rejection of the plans laid out for him by his father in favour of his own determination of what he might become. Theirs was a generational conflict that might almost seem modern had only the roles been reversed: according to Protestant church historian Heinrich Bornkamm, the father was 'typical of the early modern successful individual for whom the social advance of his family meant more than any sacrifice that could possibly be made to God'. His son, by contrast:

> took a step backwards, into monastic life and a world that had long ago lost its prestige and continued to be little valued. His future significance would be decided by his withdrawal from the latent secularism that was beginning to affect his age and, against all reason and despite the warnings of his father, his taking up a path that led away from the world.[14]

This volte-face could hardly have been more radical—from now on Martin's life was directed not at a successful career but at nearness to God; the core of his life was not the world but salvation. The severity of the break is particularly evident in his leave-taking from his friends. Luder appears to have enjoyed a typical student life, and the farewell event on the evening of 16 July to which he invited his friends proved a happy gathering that no one wanted to believe could really mark the end of their time together. The following morning when it was apparent that Luder was entirely serious, some of his friends wept and were unable to accompany him. That Luder became a monk was not really so remarkable. For all the criticism of the poor behaviour of monks and the excesses of monastic life, the existence of monasticism and its status within Christianity largely remained unquestioned. What *was* remarkable was the all-encompassing religiosity with which Luder made his decision. His original genius, as we might term it, was not at all in keeping with the spirit of the Renaissance that was now making its way from Italy into Germany. Religion was threatening to pale into little more than an attitude and a lifestyle, as typified by art-loving popes, cardinals, and church diplomats on the model of Leo X, Albrecht of Brandenburg, and Girolamo Aleander, a scholar and diplomat and the papal nuncio of 1520/21, tasked with defeating the German heresy facing Emperor and Empire. The essential unwieldiness and unconventionality in Luder/Luther's character, which grew over the decades, would place that new turn at Stotternheim amongst 'the greatest and more consequential conversion experiences in the history of the church'.[15]

'Dead to the World'?

The image that depicts Luder exiting the world on the morning of 17 July 1505 as the door of the Augustinian monastery in Erfurt closed behind him says more about Luther's later representation of events than about the realities of the moment. Luther declared, 'I was dead to the world, until God thought it time',[16] but his description is only really accurate in that the novice's first step within the isolation of the cloister was to dedicate himself to devotional practices and to learn the ways of monastic life. In joining the Hermits of Saint Augustine, Luder had selected the 'humanistic mendicant order *par excellence*'.[17] The Black Monastery in Erfurt was one of strict observance, for it belonged to a group of reformed Augustinian monasteries that sought to cure monastic life of the low standards so criticized by contemporaries by following the strict original rule of their order. The works of Saint Augustine of Hippo, for whom the order was named, continued to be read, as was established practice, but under the influence of Johannes von Staupitz, vicar general of the German Augustinian province and soon-to-be principal mentor of the novice Luder, and in accord with the humanist call for a return to the sources, the Bible was now given a place at the heart of monastic life. Although during his studies for his Master of Arts degree some years earlier Martin Luder would have come into contact with the Bible in the library of the university at Erfurt, his familiarity with Scripture came from his years as an Augustinian monk. Staupitz met the young novice during a visitation of the monastery in Erfurt in 1507 and immediately took on responsibility for his spiritual formation. In the final letter he wrote to his paternalistic friend and mentor in September 1523, Luther recorded, 'it was through you that the light of the gospel first began to shine out of the darkness into my heart'.[18]

While members of the Carthusian order were required to dedicate themselves to silent contemplation, being an Augustinian did not mean complete separation from the outside world. With their monastery located within the city walls, the Augustinians of Erfurt were an active presence amongst the residents of that town, with a role in civic cultural, social, and political life, which in the decades around 1500 was particularly lively. In neighbouring Saxony, Augustinians had even been much involved in the foundation of the university at Wittenberg, as participants in the political and intellectual movements of the age. The monastery in Erfurt had close ties with the humanist-inclined scholarly circles associated with the local university and with the residents of the town. In the monastery, clergy and citizens had a forum where they could express their views on literary and theological questions and even on political and social issues, which were particularly heated in these years both in the Empire more broadly and in Erfurt itself.

Luder's leaving the world behind him by entering the monastery should not in any way be understood as Luder's removing himself from contemporary concerns. The reverse is very much the case. Luder modelled the concept of the monk that had emerged in the Western church whereby each member of a monastery renounced this world and directed his mind only to the next, taking on tasks and problems that were beyond the abilities of the common man. Reduced to its core, his responsibility as a monk—initially as a simple brother in his monastery and later, after 1512, alone in his study as Wittenberg professor of biblical exegesis—was to act as a surrogate for his contemporaries by experiencing the fears and shouldering the problems that arose from their lack of certainty about their salvation. As a monk in the Augustinian monastery in Erfurt, Luder threw himself into the works-based piety of the late medieval church. Like his contemporaries, Luder was convinced that eternal salvation could be achieved through individual action—by performing good works and by adopting the strict lifestyle that was believed pleasing to God, with prayer, penitence, and self-flagellation. With his entry into the monastery, Luder committed himself to this active popular piety. But even as he excelled in performing devotional act upon devotional act, he gained no confidence that salvation would be his. His experience prepared the way for a paradigm shift in the anthropology of devotion that would have profound historical consequences, as the performance-based medieval understanding of piety was replaced by the grace-focused piety of early modern Protestantism.

Martin Luder's life in the monastery at Erfurt, like the lives of the fifty or so other members of that monastery, was dictated by the strict interpretation of the Augustinian rule that had been decreed for the reformed German monasteries of the Augustinian Hermits in 1504. He would have been admitted to the monastery in a formal ritual led by the prior, in which the candidate, already identified by the distinctive tonsure of the monk, first heard the rule of the order explained and then was dressed in the habit of the order; next he made a general confession about his previous life and received the kiss of peace from the prior and from the monks, as a sign of his membership of the fraternal community. A probationary period of one year and one day followed, in order to ensure that the desire to become a monk remained even when the candidate faced the often hard reality of life in the monastery. During this period either candidate or convent could decide that the former should not remain in the monastery. With that eventuality in mind, the personal belongings that the candidate brought with him to the monastery were carefully noted and stored. No doubts were expressed in Luder's case and when his novitiate was over, he took his final vows, making an eternal declaration before God that he would be a monk and abide by the ideals of obedience, poverty, and chastity. Formal ceremonial accompanied this stage, paced by symbolic moments: the novice knelt before the altar, prayed, called upon the saints, and requested that he be accepted into the community. Blessed by the prior and having received the kiss of peace from the other members of the monastery, he was then led to his place on the monks' bench in the choir of the church, a seat to which, as a fully fledged brother, he was now entitled.

The years that followed also appeared to take a standard course, and Luder's monastic career can be deemed very successful. He did not experience the late medieval church as a stale, let alone corrupt, institution. The Augustinians he had joined were very dynamic and in the midst of a transition to a new piety and new organization. Brother Martin was fully involved in the services that the Augustinians provided in the church and farther afield, in both town and countryside. His talents were recognized by his superiors within the order, by Winand von Diedenhofen, prior at Erfurt, and particularly by Johannes von Staupitz, vicar general, and both men became his staunch supporters. Their first step was to ensure that Luder became a priest and was therefore able to help fulfil the monastery's responsibilities in saying Mass for the citizens of Erfurt and tending to their spiritual needs. With characteristic seriousness, Luder prepared himself for the priestly office by studying the most up-to-date handbook on the duties of the priest, 'Exposition of the Canon of the Mass' (*Auslegung des Messkanons*) by Gabriel Biel, theologian at Tübingen. As a result, Luder was far better acquainted with the theological meaning and correct performance of the rituals of the Mass than were the majority of his contemporary Mass-saying priests, who often allowed the sacrifice of the Mass to appear little more than a magical trick. Having been consecrated as subdeacon at the end of 1506 and soon after as deacon, Brother Martin was finally ordained as a priest by the suffragan bishop of Erfurt in April 1507. On Cantate Sunday, 2 May, he celebrated his first Mass, for which his family and friends travelled to Erfurt from Eisenach and Mansfeld. At the head of the large company was Luder's father, with whom he had in the meantime been reconciled, who gave a not-inconsiderable gift of twenty gulden to the monastery.

With an eye to the spiritual needs of the residents of the town, the order was keen to find well-trained priests with a solid grasp of theology.

Immediately after his ordination, Luder was therefore directed to study theology. Brother Martin returned to life as a student, but the everyday experiences of this course of study were very different from when he had been studying the arts three years earlier. The monastery remained his home and his teachers were members of the order. Luder did not make it easy for himself as a student of theology: while assiduously following the set course of study, which required extensive engagement with scholastic philosophy and theology, he also remained true to humanist methods and their critical approach to the sources that he had learned while studying the arts. From the midst of this confrontation between traditional learning and the detached investigative methods of the humanists, carried out with their new philological tools, layer by layer Luder was able to peel away the philosophical, religious, and juristic overlay from the Gospel until he reached the Scriptural basics. Helmar Junghans, a Protestant church historian, suggested that it was precisely because Luther's approach was essentially conservative and because he only gradually and with much hesitation rejected both scholastic teachings on philosophy and theology and the legal authority of the papacy that he did not simply turn his back on tradition but instead destroyed it from within.[19]

As early as the winter semester of 1508, Brother Martin had stepped in as a temporary replacement for a professor of philosophy at the newly founded university at Wittenberg, most likely at the insistence of his mentor Staupitz, the dominant personality in the politics of that university, where he was also professor of Bible. As was not uncommon, Luder was therefore simultaneously student and professor, teaching first philosophy and then, after receiving his baccalaureus biblicus degree in March 1509, theology too. At the end of 1509 the monastery in Erfurt insisted that Luder return from Wittenberg—a decision that may have been influenced by a desire to remove him from the influence of its Saxon competition and to supervise his studies more closely. On his return to Erfurt Luder must have been aware of the resentments of the older university at the newer institution (a tension that will be all too familiar to those involved in academic life today): the faculty at Erfurt were not willing to recognize the course of study that Luder had successfully followed in Wittenberg, and it was only with some difficulty that he gained permission to teach foundation courses in Erfurt. Luder did eventually receive his doctorate in theology at Wittenberg, in October 1512, after his transfer from Erfurt to Wittenberg had been made necessary by circumstances that we will discuss shortly. By that date, he had already given lectures on theology in Erfurt, in the theological faculty's *auditorium coelium*, or heavenly lecture hall, which was located above the cathedral cloisters. A novice teacher will often stay close to the textbook, and in Luder's case that standard text was Peter Lombard's 'Sentences', the classic dogmatic work of his age. Fortunately, thanks to its transfer to the library of Zwickau town council's school, Luder's personal copy of that text survives, providing us with the earliest record of his theological work. The marginal glosses that it contains were in effect Luder's lecture notes, added to help him explain the text to the students during class. They suggest he was a careful reader and painstaking interpreter who abided by traditional methods and teachings but at the same time employed new humanist standards for source criticism and textual analysis. Around this time Luder also began to study Greek, with Johannes Lang, a fellow monk, as his instructor.

Works Righteousness and a Tormented Soul

Externally, then, the principal features of Luder's life as a monk were in no way so very different from the experiences of his fellow monks. However, when it came to the well-being of his soul and his inner emotional and religious development, the story was very different and very much his own. Johann Greffenstein, the elderly and experienced master of the novices in Erfurt—Luther would recall him as a 'learned and pious' man[20]—recognized immediately that the novice Martin Luder was very serious about his new status and wrestled with the purpose of monastic life in near to existential terms. Luder made every possible effort to live up to his spiritual and temporal responsibilities. His concerns about his eternal salvation and his fear of a death that would call him before the heavenly judge unprepared had not left him when he entered the monastery. To the contrary, the devotional exercises into which he threw himself with such great fervour—in the monastery it was said that he wanted to knock down twelve pins where there were only nine[21]—appear to have heightened his anxiety that when his time came, he would still have failed in the eyes of Christ, judge of the world. He was held prisoner by his fears of the abyss of hell and the eternal torment of the damned, an image so dramatically depicted by his contemporary the Netherlandish painter Hieronymus Bosch (Figure 11). Luder tried to banish his frightful visions with new and increasingly onerous acts of penance, for the church promised that pious works would give entry to the kingdom of heaven. Year after year Luder remained trapped in this

Figure 11. The eternal agonies of the damned in Hell, right panel of *The Garden of Earthly Delights*, by Hieronymus Bosch (*c.*1450–1516), painted between 1490 and 1510.

endless circle of fear and the need to act: he meditated, prayed the rosary, and sang psalms to the point of exhaustion and until plagued by chronic lack of sleep. Yet all that he did only led him further into doubt, for he believed that his actions would always be inadequate and that at judgement he must therefore expect not reconciliation but the wrath of God.[22]

Luder seemed almost possessed by a need to confess the sins he believed he had committed—he confessed regularly and his confessions would last for hours and be so full of minutiae that on one occasion even Staupitz, his well-meaning mentor and confessor, lost his patience and interrupted him with incomprehension, warning him, 'I don't understand you.' According to an account provided later by Luther, 'Afterward when I went to another confessor I had the same experience.... Then I thought, "Nobody has this temptation except you," and I became as dead as a corpse',[23] in other words, spiritually deader than dead. Luder/Luther would explicitly emphasize that his despairing sense of sinfulness was not about sexual misconduct, it had nothing to do with '*mulieres*', or women, but stemmed rather from 'real knots', which his explanation suggests should be understood as a sense of distance from God. He was remembered as being 'very pious' and, at the same time, '*tristiz*', a term that suggests an unhappiness that went beyond simple sadness caused by worldly concerns. Prayer, vigils, feasting, and self-mortification gave him no relief from the burden of his sins and brought him so close to collapse that he ended up in the monastery infirmary.[24] No matter what devotions he performed and no matter how wholeheartedly he threw himself into his later responsibilities as an official in his order or as professor of Bible at the Augustinian university at Wittenberg, his life as a monk brought him no peace. No effort was sufficient to end his over-whelming sense of distance from God.

In Wittenberg almost ten years later, Luder remained in the grip of the idea of a merciless judging God, whom he encountered every day on a sandstone relief in the nearby graveyard, where Christ was portrayed as judge of the world, sitting on a rainbow and holding a sword and with a lily in his mouth. He described these years retrospectively as a time of remoteness from Christ, of shrinking from Christ: 'For I did not believe in Christ; I regarded Him only as a severe and terrible Judge, portrayed as seated on a rainbow.' He recounted that each time he looked at Christ, he saw behind him the devil—in other words, the jaws of hell into which his soul would inevitably plummet, as human inadequacy and sinfulness meant that no other verdict from the judge of the world was possible. He sought relief in acts of penance and devotion, constantly forcing on his body to greater feats—much like a modern-day athlete, but in his case with no hope of acknowledgement or reward. With Christ distant, he looked for 'other intercessors, Mary and various other saints, also my own works and merits of my order'.[25]

In late medieval Germany devotional practices were not infrequently carried out with marked enthusiasm and dedication, but even in that context the actions of this Augustinian monk in Erfurt were remarkable. Just as the iconoclasts of the Reformation were the very people who had endowed images in the late Middle Ages, Martin Luther the reformer had begun his religious journey as a particularly dutiful member of the late medieval church. Its active piety and cult of the saints were no obstacles to him, just as he had no qualms about the papacy and the various branches of the hierarchy over which the Roman pontiff ruled like an absolute monarch. His problem was much the reverse: he took the various demands of the church very seriously and therefore was all the more distressed when they did not bring him the existential relief he sought, providing little more than a bandage for his wounds.

His priesthood also did not provide Luder with any reassurance about his salvation, even though the church taught that a priest had a special relationship with God and was an intermediary between God and laity. Certainly the promises of salvation the Roman Church gave to its priests and the priest's function as an intermediary seem to have moved Luder initially, when he was still a novice in Erfurt, just as over five hundred years later they would inspire the maid Tata Linek, a character in Franz Werfel's novel *Embezzled Heaven* (*Der veruntreute Himmel*), to invest all her hopes, and her savings, in her unworthy nephew Mojmir's becoming a priest. When Luder invited Johannes Braun to attend his first Mass, he informed his mentor from Eisenach, 'God, who is glorious and holy in all his works, has deigned to exalt me magnificently . . . by calling me into his supreme ministry.'[26]

But for Luder to have rested content with the change in his ecclesiastical status and to have given himself over unquestioningly to the teachings of the church would have been uncharacteristic. The Mass and the priesthood were holy institutions, of that he was clear, but becoming a priest did not signal the final round in his existential wrestling over the correct relationship with God. As a layperson, Luder had encountered God during the celebration of Mass only through an intermediary, the priest, but now his encounter with God was unmediated, coming at the moment in which the bread in the hands of the priest became the body of Christ. This moment repeatedly reopened the wound caused by self-doubt and fear of the merciless judgement of God. At his very first celebration of the Mass, this distress had gripped him. In 1532, long after the Mass had been abolished in his evangelical church, he recalled the experience:

> When at length I stood before the altar and was to consecrate [i.e. to change the bread and wine into the body and blood of Christ], I thought of running away from the altar and said to my prior [the prior would usually assist when a newly ordained priest celebrated Mass for the first time] 'Reverend Father, I'm afraid I must leave the altar.'

Only the prior's robust encouragement to continue without showing any signs of indecision—'Go ahead, go faster'—meant that Luder's celebratory first Mass did not prove a catastrophe, which would surely have left his father, who had travelled to Erfurt especially for the occasion, all the more aggrieved.[27]

Luder was not alone in being troubled by the priestly encounter with God in the celebration of the Mass, for his friend Wenzeslaus Linck and even Staupitz himself faced their own problems. Yet Luder's response was distinctive. Familiarity and priestly confidence stemming from the routine of ritual did not satisfy his search for God; his answer was to be gleaned by personal investigation. That quest did not lead towards the altar where Mass was celebrated; it led in the opposite direction, towards a redefinition of altar and church that came from restructuring the relationship of God and humankind, with the course of history changed as a result. For Luder and the Protestants the altar was no longer the locus of the Mass and the site of transubstantiation; now it was where those celebrating the Lord's Supper came together. The Church of Rome became the church of the community, in which all Christians were called to be priests.

The unconditional lack of compromise by this monk and priest in Erfurt is evident in his unwillingness to allow tried and tested methods to resolve his spiritual crisis, or his emotional crisis, as we might term it today. Neither devotional practices nor the promises of salvation received by priests from the church were the cure. Luder wanted a complete answer, and once he had that response, and judged it sufficient, he proclaimed it to his contemporaries and to generations to come as the universal answer to the problem of salvation.

Life in the monastery and the redemptive offerings of the medieval church available to him there did not free the young monk from the torments of his struggles to find a merciful God. The renewed evangelical theology he encountered via the Augustinian Hermits, first in Erfurt and later in Wittenberg, provided him, however, with a decisive means to overcome his anguish. A key role was played by Staupitz (Figure 12)—one generation older than his pupil and a member of a Saxon noble family, Staupitz had known the reigning Saxon elector as a friend since childhood. Along with Martin Pollich, a medical doctor and the first rector of the university at Wittenberg, Staupitz had been one of the elector's principal advisers in the establishment of that institution, where he became professor of Bible and head of the theology faculty. Luder and his talents quickly caught the ear of Staupitz, probably at an Augustinian chapter meeting held in summer 1505. As Luder's confessor and spiritual adviser, Staupitz played a decisive part in

Figure 12. Johannes von Staupitz, after 1521.

the monk's decision to become a priest and also in his receipt of a doctoral degree, which according to Luther's later reminiscences, he was given against his will.[28] Luder and Staupitz became equals in their discussions of theological issues, which continued into the early months of the Reformation. By this time, however, Augustinian politics had caused Staupitz to leave his original order to become a Benedictine monk, and in 1521 he became the abbot of the monastery of Saint Peter in far-off Salzburg. Staupitz followed the course of the Reformation at a distance, sympathetic to the cause without adopting it personally, and as Luther sought to clarify his positions in their extensive correspondence, Staupitz became in effect the theological conscience of his former pupil.

In the early years of their relationship, the vicar general accompanied the young monk through his spiritual turmoil with paternal concern, but he could make little sense of Luder's self-doubts. The cultured and pragmatic theologian had no personal experience of the elementary and radical character of Luder's quest for salvation and the doubts it generated. He did provide his young fellow Augustinian with the optimistic image of the Christ of reconciliation that would begin to propel Luder out of his fears. Staupitz's Christology had at its core not the Christ who judged but the Christ who suffered, and who through that suffering had brought redemption to the world. His image of Christ could be found in the crucifixion of the Isenheim altar and in the lamentation of Christ in the collegiate church in Aschaffenburg (Figure 13), both painted by Matthias Grünewald in precisely these years. The image in Aschaffenburg was a commission from Cardinal Albrecht of Brandenburg, archbishop of Mainz, and suggests an emotional bond between

Figure 13. *The Lamentation of Christ*, by Matthias Grünewald (1470–1528), oil on wood, commissioned *c.*1525 by Cardinal Albrecht of Brandenburg, archbishop of Mainz.

reformer and archbishop in their devotion to Christ that is all the more moving in light of their subsequent deep animosity.

As vicar general, Staupitz sought to bring his sense of Christ as redeemer to his fellow Augustinians: 'Your fearful image,' he told them in the context of a discussion of confession, 'is not Christ.' The true Christ, he continued, does not force the sinner into doubt and ruin, but is the redeemer 'who offered himself to mankind for forgiveness of sins'. These words were pronounced in Eisleben at the conclusion of a procession in which his pupil had participated, wearing the 'dress of a priest', as Luder expressly noted. Viewing the sacrament carried aloft at the head of the procession, Luder later recounted, he had again been wracked by existential doubts. The procession probably took place when the new Augustinian monastery in Eisleben was consecrated, in 1516, and therefore at a time when Luder was already well established as a professor and held significant office within his order.

Very soon this pastoral reassurance would bear remarkable fruit. Sitting in his Wittenberg study Luder alighted on the decisive passage in Scripture that opened his eyes to the redeemer God who brought salvation and that banished his fears of God as judge without mercy. Less than a year before his death, Luther recorded that he was clear that the seed of this new image of Christ, from which the doctrine of a merciful God had grown, had been sown by Staupitz, who had 'given birth to him in Christ', placing his own life and the life of Christendom on a new foundation.[29]

The second decisive precondition for the Reformation, Luther's close engagement with Scripture, can also be laid at Staupitz's door. The generations who came after the Reformation would have been hard-pressed to imagine a world from which the Bible was absent, but knowledge and study of Scripture were far from usual in the late Middle Ages. Even students of theology and the higher ranks within the church including clergy, monks, and the semi-clerical religious were rarely well versed. Certainly Holy Scripture was everywhere present, but not as an autonomous text, for it had been overlaid with explanation and interpretation, primarily the work of scholastics and a product of their Aristotelianism. It was hardly unusual for a doctor of theology such as Luder's Wittenberg colleague Karlstadt neither to own a Bible nor to have any detailed Scriptural knowledge. In the 1504 constitution for the Augustinian Hermits completed under Staupitz's leadership, Luder's mentor had included a statement that all novices in the observant monasteries were 'to read Holy Scripture enthusiastically, to listen to the scriptures reverently, and to learn from them with burning desire'.[30] Later Luther thought he could recall that Staupitz had required all reading in the monasteries to come from the Bible.[31]

As Luder would have discovered, these instructions did not profoundly reshape everyday monastic life. Even in the scholarly work undertaken within the reformed order of the Augustinian Hermits, reading the works of philosophers and theologians—what today we would call the secondary literature—was considered more important and more worthy than examination of the primary source, the Bible. Luther recalled that after his ordination as a priest, his professors had effectively taken away the Bible, which in accordance with Staupitz's reforms had been his constant companion through his time as a novice, in order that he work only with scholastic theological texts. He claimed that he had to creep into the library to continue to study the Bible.[32]

The incomprehension and scepticism amongst some of Luder's fellow Augustinian monks should not lead us to believe, however, that Luder's love of Scripture was novel and revolutionary. The Waldensians of the late twelfth century had placed reading of the Bible at the heart of their devotional practices, one reason they were condemned as heretics. The fate of the Waldensians did not extinguish the centrality of Scripture. In the flourishing towns of the late Middle Ages a form of lay piety developed that had at its core the individual's reading of devotional writings, in particular the Bible, which produced a first wave of translation of Scripture into the relevant vernacular. The exposure of the faithful to Holy Scripture was not the work of the ecclesiastical hierarchy in pastoral mode; the church remained highly suspicious of those who read the Bible for themselves.

As we have noted, however, by 1500 there had already existed for some years an educated laity that was determined to make its own decisions about its devotional experiences and would not be deterred by orders to the contrary from the official church. In Magdeburg and Eisleben, the young Augustinian monk had encountered, and come to value, this new 'modern' piety.[33]

Reading the Bible became central to his existence. He lived through the Bible and viewed the world through a biblical lens. In Scripture he found the guiding principles for all his thought and action. While other text-based religions believed in unmediated dependence on the word as written, for Luther the centrality of the word meant that the text itself had to be analysed and interpreted. The final note he wrote, found on his writing desk after his death, spoke of this unending task of interpretation: 'I do not think anyone has had sufficient taste of the Holy Scriptures if he has not led the community with the prophets and the apostles for a hundred years.'[34]

With his university teachers very doubtful about autonomous reading of the Bible, Luder's ability to cite Staupitz and the official position of the leadership of his order in defence of his desire to place Scripture at the centre of his theological work was all the more significant. Staupitz helped set the course that would eventually take this new Scriptural theology out of the monk's study cell and into the world, for even while Luder continued to be wracked by self-doubt, he received his doctorate in theology and subsequently became Staupitz's successor as professor of Bible at Wittenberg.

Brother Martin's approach to the Bible was also in accord with the intellectual spirit of his age in that the radical demands of the humanists for a return *ad fontes*, to the sources of antiquity, naturally also touched on the sources on which Christianity was founded. While in Erfurt and Wittenberg the Augustinian monk was looking to the Bible for a cure for his tormented soul, Erasmus of Rotterdam was working on his reconstruction of the original text and in so doing made the study of the Bible a respectable endeavour in intellectual and scholarly circles. As a result of the humanistic character of his early studies, Luder was in a position to bring the philological and grammatical tools of the humanists to his exploration of the biblical text.

The essence of Luder's interest in Scripture did not lie, however, in history or philology or grammar. He understood the Bible in existential terms, the only way he could make sense of his devotional predicament, his crisis about life itself. The Bible provided the guiding principles for life, and for Luther that life led either to or away from eternal salvation. Far beyond all humanist engagement with the text, Luther viewed the apparently foundering world and identified the Bible as the single anchor that might save humankind, both individuals and Christendom as a whole, that might, in today's language, rescue society. In and of itself Luder's work on the Bible did not make him stand out, either as a student in Erfurt or as a professor in Wittenberg; his uniqueness stemmed from the existential radicality with which the Bible was heard and given context, its *Sitz im Leben*. Religion and what religion meant for humankind now had new meanings that proved typically early modern. Emerging from Luder's years of anguish and 'tribulation' (*Anfechtung*), the theology of this new era revolved around the postulation of the freedom of the Christian, who can find his or her way to God without need of intermediaries or authorities. With religion and the world so closely interwoven in this age, a structural entwining that the reformer did not challenge, this new theological paradigm could only herald revolutionary change for church, state, and society.

To Rome in the Service of His Order

If we were to imagine Luder a moralistic misfit who struggled to come to terms with his life in the monastery, let alone in the world, we would be on the wrong track. His doubts about a merciful God did not paralyse him. He was not one to resign himself to distance from God. The torments of his soul provided the impetus for his determination to understand what lay at the heart of human existence and the relationship between humankind and God. He also had no doubt that he must practise obedience and humility, submitting himself willingly to the requirements of his order. He fell into line with the insistence of his fellow Augustinians in Erfurt that uneducated and educated were fully equal, which meant that while he studied he was still required to supplicate, which was integral to the mendicant orders, and to clean out the latrines.[35] When it came to the crucial issues of belief, however, as a monk Luder already demonstrated the resolution and stubbornness that would later characterize him as a reformer, qualities that enabled him to resist unconditionally anyone and anything that might bring him from the truth he had now identified, resistance that reached as far as pope and Emperor.

The authorities within his order, and the vicar general in particular, were quick to recognize the strength and assertiveness of this new member, whatever his self-doubts, and enabled his rapid rise to the upper ranks of the monastery community in Erfurt. In late 1510 Luder undertook a political task for his order that would take him far from central Germany, not just geographically. He travelled to Rome 'on the business of his order', as scholars of the Reformation will often write, yet that description hardly does justice to the sensitivity of his task. Again we lack specific detail, especially direct evidence, with little information available on the occasion for his journey. Although we can attempt to reconstruct the circumstances from other sources, much remains unclear, including even when he travelled to Rome—was it 1510/11 or 1511/12?—and the interests he was to represent when he arrived—was he to make Staupitz's case or to speak on behalf of his mentor's opponents within the order? According to the reading of the sources that currently seems most plausible, and which is adopted for our discussion here, the journey took place in 1510/11 and was the result of a moment of rebellion in which Luder himself was much involved. His participation is all the more remarkable as it seems that the antagonism was directed both against his pastoral mentor and supporter and against Staupitz's activities as vicar general of the observant Augustinian monasteries in Germany. The dispute concerned the reform of the order and therefore also the reform of the church, which had been under discussion for generations and not only within the institution itself. Even the Imperial diet had addressed ecclesiastical reform, assembling complaints raised in Germany in the text entitled 'Grievances of the German Nation' (*Gravamina nationis germanicae*), which had caused something of a furore.

The Observants formed a distinct grouping within the German Augustinian monasteries. Along with Erfurt, some dozen similarly minded monasteries could be found in the four German provinces of the order: Saxony-Thuringia, Cologne, Rhineland-Swabia, and Bavaria. They had accepted the need for reform and were largely supported by the relevant princely power or city magistracy. They either kept their distance from the conventual, or unre-formed, monasteries of the order or sought to impose their reforms on these other institutions too. Their institutional and legal situation was also distinct, for they had their own vicar general, Johannes von Staupitz, and their own constitution. Additionally, however, they also sought a far broader exemption, from the administrative and judicial authority of the headquarters of the order in Rome, and an alliance with the province of Lombardy, which already possessed a papal privilege of this sort. In order to prevent the division of the order in Germany that appeared to be in the offing, Staupitz favoured union, proposing a polity that would bring the two branches together again, and he sought the agreement of Giles of Viterbo (Egidio da Viterbo), the new prior general of the order, who resided in Rome. The plan was designed around Staupitz himself, who would become provincial vicar for Saxony-Thuringia and in that position would be both head of the unreformed monasteries in the province of Saxony-Thuringia and vicar general of all reformed German Augustinian monasteries.

That model may sound complicated today, but it was typical of the late medieval church, where the forces of reform and the forces of continuity were just about balanced, and, taking matters into its own hands, Rome blocked revolutionary change in either the structures of the church or the spiritual and devotional experiences it delivered. Seeing the threat clearly, the German reform monasteries raised a storm of protest against the projected union. Their response was equally typical of an age in which the desire for communal self-determination in both ecclesiastical and temporal matters, and the associated protest movements, had not yet lost out to rule from above. In the monasteries the conciliarist principle 'the convent is superior to the abbot'—today we might identify a form of grass-roots democracy—remained very much alive. Thus the Reformation concept of the communal church also had roots in the late medieval church.

In summer 1510 Staupitz sought to present his ideas at a meeting of the reform congregation held at Neustadt an der Orla, but he encountered substantial resistance. A core group of seven monasteries—Nuremberg, Kulmbach, Erfurt, Nordhausen, Sangerhausen, Himmelpforte, and Sternberg—viewed him as a traitor to the cause of reform and refused to continue to submit to his authority, electing as vicar general in his place Simon Kayser, prior at Kulmbach. At the forefront of the opposition alongside the monastery in Nuremberg, whose advocacy of reform was actively supported by the magistrates of that Imperial city, was the monastery in Erfurt, led by Johann Nathin, professor of theology at Erfurt and an early teacher of Luder during his studies at Erfurt, and by Luder himself. We should recall that a year earlier Luder had been ordered to return from Wittenberg to Erfurt and we can speculate that his recall might have been related in some way to the tension over Staupitz's plan for union, with Luder thus perhaps deliberately physically distanced from the vicar general. Nathin and Luder seized the initiative by advocating in Rome against Staupitz and his unpopular union. The impact of Luder's involvement is apparent in the nature of that task, for they would appeal not directly to the pope, as Nathin had wanted, but to the head of the order, Giles of Viterbo. The young monk also left his mark on the content of their commission: they were not to raise legalistic concerns about the union; their mission was to ensure the prior general could envision the danger that such a union would pose for the devotional life and moral values of the reform monasteries.

On account of his age, Nathin was unable to undertake the journey, and the responsibility fell instead to Brother Martin. Luder left Erfurt in November 1510, accompanied by a second monk, as was required by his order. Much of their travel was on foot and with the challenges of their route, which led across the Alps, compounded by travelling in winter, this journey would surely have been stressful. On occasion they would have had to sleep out of doors. At this stage in his life, Luder's constitution appears to have been robust. His physical ability to undertake this journey suggests that the fainting attacks from which he had suffered during his early years in the monastery were not symptoms of physical problems but rather visible manifestations of his restless soul. The journey to Rome and back took the two monks away from Erfurt for five months: two months each for the journeys to and from Rome, stopping off along the way at other Augustinian monasteries, and one month to conduct their business in Rome itself. The trip was the longest Luder ever undertook and the only time he left German soil. It took him to a metropole which, although not amongst the largest in Europe at the time, in terms of its culture and the size of its population—around 50,000—was completely unlike anything Luder was used to. Along the way he had passed through a number of large cities, including not only Nuremberg but also Milan, with a population of well over 100,000, and Florence, with a populace just short of 100,000. Even in comparison with these cities, the atmosphere of Rome was remarkable, partly because the city attracted a never-ending stream of pilgrims and penitents who sought to visit relics in search of relief from their sins or to attend the papal courts in search of a judgement in temporal matters, but partly, and principally, because the eternal city was clad in the scaffolding whose removal would reveal all the radiance of the Renaissance.

City life seems to have left as little impression on Luder as did the magnificent scenery through which the two monks travelled. The journey to Rome was not formative for Luder; it left no lasting mark on his character or thought. The experience was hardly untypical of his age, however; only for later generations did travel and the impressions gained while travelling come to be seen as educational experiences in their own right. We do have evidence, however, that during the Renaissance some travellers observed nature and the world around them very closely, individuals such as Enea Silvio Piccolomini, humanist and later Pope Pius II, who reported on the German cities he visited in 1457/58. There was also a possibility that travel could influence the personality of the traveller, as we can read in the diary of Thomas Platter, a medical doctor from Basel, kept in the latter sixteenth century. The lack of anything similar for Luder is indicative of a personality that was little affected by external worlds and was concerned instead entirely with existential matters. When he recalled the trip, Luther talked primarily of religious and ecclesiastical concerns—that the large cathedral in Ulm was unsuitable for preaching, that in Milan he had not been permitted to say Mass as he did not know the Ambrosian rite, that Florence was rich with hospitals and orphanages. He responded to nature as a practical son of the land, commenting on the unproductiveness of Swiss soil, but he also found in nature, in olive trees or lemon trees, for example, symbols of the spiritual and references to biblical events.

We also have no personal testimony from Luder about his stay in Rome. The only ego-documents we can access on the subject are very fragmentary recollections found in letters and his Table Talk. All were recorded after the Reformation and therefore have a potential bias that means they cannot be used as authentic sources to reconstruct his actual experiences and his emotional engagement with those experiences. We do not even know for certain where he resided in Rome. Two locations seem possible: at the northern city gate was the monastery of the Lombardian Congregation of Santa Maria del Popolo, which had an approach to the spiritual that was not so unlike that of the reform monasteries of Germany, while close to today's Piazza Navona was the monastery of Sant'Agostino in Campo Marzio, the residence of the prior general. The whole purpose of Luder's visit to Rome was to win the support of the prior general, which provides us with good reason to favour the latter as Luder's lodgings. The relationship between the Lombardians and the administration of the Augustinian order was extremely tense, and taking up quarters in the monastery of Santa Maria del Popolo could have reduced the chances of success from the outset. Even appearing before the prior general and his chancellery was risky, for Giles of Viterbo supported Staupitz's plans for union and saw Staupitz's opponents as rebels.[36] In Rome especially, disobedience could lead an Augustinian monk straight to the order's prison. In undertaking his daring deed in Rome, Luder demonstrated an early willingness to take risks. That temperament often came across to outsiders as naivety, but it made his actions as a reformer possible. The suggestion that he would have been unaware of the danger because of his youth—he was already twenty-seven years old—or inexperience does not hold water.

The proceedings seem to have taken place in an objective atmosphere. Luder would later praise Giles of Viterbo as a serious monk and preacher who was concerned that the church be reformed. We do not know if Luder either saw or spoke directly to Giles, but we do know that he did not achieve the goals of the radical opposition to Staupitz. The register of the chancellery of the Augustinian order succinctly records for January 1511, 'Because of the law the Germans are forbidden from appealing (to the Pope)', making evident that the prior general remained by his support for the Staupitz Augustinian republic. The intervention does not appear to have been entirely fruitless, however, for that same month the prior general sent a personal note to Staupitz urging him to demonstrate 'love and full obedience' in resolving the matter.[37]

The execution of such tasks usually involved extended periods of waiting, and the German monk would have had plenty of time to get to know the city of Rome itself. Pope Julius II and his court were absent from the Holy City, involved in campaigning in northern Italy. Even without the papal court, the city had much to enthral a visitor from the comparatively sedate world of central Germany. With the victory of the pope and the Roman curia over the conciliar opposition, their authority in Rome and the Papal States was now unlimited, and at the beginning of the sixteenth century Rome was beginning to exhibit a newfound splendour that in many ways looked back to the classical glory of the Augustan age. The life that pulsed right outside Luder's door was remarkable even for Rome. Populated by artisans, merchants, and dockworkers, the Campo Marzio, in which both of Luder's possible quarters lay, was being extensively renovated and rebuilt, both the docks where goods were transferred and stored and the narrow streets with their workshops and living quarters. Farther upstream the great patrician families from which both cardinals and popes came were tearing down whole neighbourhoods to make space for their new palaces. Even the titular church of San Lorenzo in Damaso had to make way for the first Renaissance palazzo, built by Raffaello Riario, cardinal nephew of Pope Sixtus IV, which became the Palazzo della Cancelleria, home of the papal chancellery. The first new villas could also be admired, such as the home built by banker Agostino Chigi outside the city on the right bank of the Tiber—today the residence is known as the Farnesina, after its later owners—with its garden loggia that Raphael turned into a jewel of the early Renaissance.

Further upstream, in the papal palace in the Vatican, Michelangelo was at work, commissioned by Julius II to repaint the chapel erected by his predecessor Sixtus IV. The frescos of the creation and the prophets on the ceiling were already complete, and Christ's ancestors on the fanlights of the arches around the windows were being worked on. The medieval church of Saint Peter that had stood in front of the palace had been torn down, for in neither scale nor decoration did it satisfy the taste of the Renaissance popes or make the statement they required. The new church had not yet been erected even in skeleton, and the altar remained open to the skies. The situation was very different for the 'Teutonic Cemetery', founded at the time of the Franks, which lay directly alongside the site of Saint Peter's. By the beginning of the sixteenth century the German and Flemish Confraternity of Our Lady of the Teutonic Cemetery had already completed the Renaissance reconstruction of their church building. The church of Santa Maria della Pietà soon flourished as a spiritual and cultural meeting place for all those who had travelled from Germany to Rome, whether their stay in the city was lengthy or only brief. Additionally, not far distant, at the initiative of Johannes Burghard, a German prelate and member of the curia, a parish church was being constructed in the old town specifically for members of the 'German nation' who were in Rome. The choir of that church, Santa Maria dell'Anima, was consecrated just as Luder arrived in the papal city from Saxony. Taken altogether, the evidence tells of an active solidarity and lively intellectual exchange amongst Germans living in Rome, into which Luder could immediately have entered had he been so minded.

But the Augustinian monk was in no mood for art or intellectual debate. He focused entirely on Rome as a kind of world market for salvation, ignoring the Renaissance fever that gripped the eternal city and concentrating instead on its role at the heart of traditional medieval works righteousness. He threw himself into pilgrimages, fasting, acts of contrition, and the saying of Masses in order that he might acquire all the redemption that was on offer. He spent one day on a pilgrimage to the seven principal churches of Rome (see Figure 14) while fasting, ending his tour by saying Mass at Saint Peter's; he made his way to the catacombs and to other locations associated with the early Christian saints of Rome; at the Lateran Palace he ascended on his

Figure 14. *Speculum Romanae Magnificentiae: The Seven Churches of Rome (Le Sette Chiese di Roma)*, attributed to Giovanni Ambrogio Brambilla (active 1575–1599), etching and engraving, 1575.

knees the stairs that had supposedly been brought to Rome from Pilate's Jerusalem residence, reciting the Lord's Prayer on each step. He hoped that his pious acts could be exchanged for the relief of souls in purgatory, and in particular that of his grandfather Heiner from Möhra, noting that he 'was almost prostrated by the thought that my mother and father were still alive, because I should gladly have redeemed them from purgatory with my Masses and other excellent works and prayers'.[38] The sheer number of priests on pilgrimage, their presence overwhelming even in winter, prevented Luder from saying Saturday Mass at Saint John Lateran, the cathedral of the bishop of Rome and the oldest and most venerable papal church in Rome. Luder deeply regretted this missed opportunity, by which, as a priest, he could have ensured the salvation of his mother.[39]

Retrospectively Luther would reproach himself for his blindness and for his entanglement in the empty rituals of such devotion, but he did not become a reformer when he was in Rome. His experiences in Rome only influenced his thought and actions later, after his theological work on the Bible had revealed to him a new understanding of God and church. Only then did the papal church appear an unscriptural institution made by humans, and even by the devil, whose machinations were intended to lead Christians not to salvation but to damnation. Earthly realities did not determine Luder's judgement on Rome, shaping his thoughts and actions and leading him to develop a counter-model. His starting point was intellectual engagement with the spiritual foundations, always primarily in light of salvation. When the reality was measured against the insights that could be won or, rather, as Luther understood it, were revealed by God, Rome and the papal church emerged as utterly inadequate.

The decisive rejection of the Observants' demands for independence also appears to have had very little personal effect on Luder. Evidently he saw his order's reform programme as largely an external matter and therefore open to compromise. In a way Brother Martin appears to have returned home from Rome more conservative and more in accord with the church than when he left. In the Eternal City he had encountered the significant shortcomings and abuses highlighted by critics of the church, especially in Germany—the hedonism and moral failings of the Renaissance church, papacy, curia, and cardinals; the devotional mill that churned out piety for sale; the lack of education among the lower clergy and rank and file of monks; and above all the apathy and superficiality with which priests in Rome said Mass, at a time when that holy act still shook him to his very soul. All that he saw and experienced, however, could not alter his faith in the redemptive purpose of the church as it existed on earth. Rome and the papacy remained holy in his eyes because they were built on the blood and graves of the apostles Peter and Paul and of Christian martyrs. Separation from this church or the overthrow of the papacy and its corrupt papal court did not even cross his mind. Much the opposite was instead the case, as he told himself that improvement would come only with increased efforts by all Christians on behalf of the Roman Church.[40]

Luder seems to have concluded that his own contribution would be to live out the obedience he had sworn, rather than rebel against his superiors, for on his return from Rome he immediately began to toe the Staupitz line again. In the remaining years before his new theology came to fruition, a theology whose foundations were very different from those of the reform movements of the medieval church, Luder's monastic life and

political-ecclesiastical activities were shaped principally by the traditional
monastic principle of unconditional obedience. He even first delivered his
Reformation ideas in letters to his ecclesiastical superiors, evidence of the high
esteem in which he held the model of monastic obedience.

His former fellow rebels amongst the Observants were not ready to
follow him into Staupitz's camp. The majority were unwilling to accept
the response in the negative with which their emissaries had returned across
the Alps. Staupitz's hope that further discussions would defuse the tension
between the two parties came to nothing, and the conflict therefore continued. Luder found himself in a very difficult position. Only a minority of
the members of the Erfurt monastery were in favour of joining him in
reconciliation with the official stance of the leadership of their order. The
majority responded very badly to Luder's shift from leader of reform to
supporter of union, which they saw as the death knell of reform, and they
fell out with him personally. His relationship with Nathin, who so recently
had praised Luder as a rising star of the order,[41] suffered particularly badly.
Nathin's opposition to Luder would prove both profound and lasting, and it
overshadowed the granting of Luder's doctorate in Wittenberg in October
1512 and caused Luder difficulties as he gave his first lectures at the university
in Erfurt. The very unpriestly circumstances in Erfurt were brought to an
end only when Luder and his like-minded friend Johannes Lang were
transferred to Wittenberg in summer 1511.

The conflicts over union were resolved in May 1512, at a chapter meeting
held in Cologne with Luder in attendance. Staupitz had to abandon his
project—further evidence that the medieval church was far from a purely
hierarchical institution. As compensation, he was given a free hand in
appointing a number of positions within the order, and he used this opportunity to bring Luder to Wittenberg as subprior.[42] The path was being
cleared for Luder's progression to professor of Bible. In retrospect the failure
of Staupitz's plans for union seems of little significance—within a decade the
German province of the Augustinian Hermits would have been effectively
disbanded, devoured by the firestorm lit in Wittenberg in 1517 by its newly
most prominent member. How we interpret its demise depends largely on
our standpoint: a Catholic perspective[43] will likely identify its collapse as a
result of the failure of Staupitz's plans as vicar general, but its disappearance
can also be seen as evidence of the strength of the ideals of Augustinian
reform, which found a home in a new form in the Lutheran Reformation.
Certainly the earlier resentment of the members of the Erfurt monastery

against their former fellow monk had evaporated by the time Luther passed through the city on his way to the Imperial diet at Worms in 1521—they proved just as keen as the great crowd of residents of Erfurt to hear their now-famous Wittenberg brother preach.

Seen in light of the Reformation, Luder's work on and with the Bible as professor of theology is the defining aspect of his first years in Wittenberg, but his activities were not limited to the university, for he also had a leading role in the Augustinian monastery, first as subprior and subsequently, from 1515 to 1518, as district vicar and provincial vicar of Saxony-Thuringia. During those three years, which were so decisive for the development of his new theology, he was therefore not only carrying out his duties at the university but also coping with his responsibilities as head of the province. In that latter position he exercised oversight of ten monasteries, with an eleventh, Eisleben, added in 1515/16; a number of Saxon Augustinian monasteries, Grimma for example, were exempt and therefore answered not to Luder as provincial vicar but directly to Staupitz as vicar general.

Two particular events dominated Luder's responsibilities as provincial vicar and also, although in different ways, influenced his later activities as a reformer—the foundation of the Augustinian monastery in Eisleben, the town in which he had been born, and an extended visitation lasting several weeks carried out in April/May 1516. The journey he undertook to carry out that visitation led him through Saxony and Thuringia: he started out from Wittenberg, then travelled via the monastery of Herzberg to Dresden, Gotha, Langensalza, Nordhausen, Sangerhausen, Erfurt, and Eisleben; he also visited the convent of Neustadt an der Orla, which lay somewhat apart, in the far south of the Thuringian Forest, and, at the beginning of June, the monastery in Magdeburg, which lay on the northern edge of the province. The visitation gave Luder a far better understanding of the land and its people, and his eyes were opened to the strengths and weaknesses of the individual monasteries. Sometimes, as at Gotha and Langensalza, he stayed only a few hours, for he found their income and finances in as good shape as their discipline and spirituality. Larger institutions such as Magdeburg and his mother house at Erfurt required more time and more attention, as did the monastery at Neustadt an der Orla, which was internally divided and demanded all the visitor's skills in restoring order and enabling reconciliation.[44]

The establishment of the monastery at Eisleben was a very different experience. Luder's home town had grown, and a new place of worship for the recently founded 'new town' was required. The counts of Mansfeld, rulers of both the town and the territory, tackled that problem by resolving that a church dedicated to Saint Anne be erected and a monastery of the Augustinian Hermits established, its members required to carry out the parish responsibilities at the new church. As provincial vicar, Martin Luder represented the Augustinians, together with Vicar General Staupitz, both when the endowment was formally established in summer 1515 and when the buildings of the new institution were consecrated the following May. Luder took his place alongside Staupitz, standing firmly in the middle way that represented the reconciliation of Augustinian reform and conventual traditions. The radical reform politics of five years earlier were now firmly behind him and his former fellow conspirators bluntly deemed arrogant and disobedient.

Luder's engagement in Augustinian politics as provincial vicar, which meant he was actively involved in the foundation of the Augustinian monastery in his home town, is all the more fascinating when viewed retrospectively. Eisleben was the last Augustinian monastery to be founded within the Augustinian Saxon province. Only a few years later the provincial vicar who had consecrated that new monastery would be toppling monasteries, bringing down the whole way of life of the monk, and not just in his home province. One other feature of the consecration of the monastery at Eisleben is also noteworthy. That pastoral discussion in which Staupitz, the vicar general, talked Luder, his fellow monk, out of his fixation with God as judge and redirected him towards Christ as the redeemer who reconciled humankind with God took place on the margins of the festivities that marked the consecration of the monastery at Eisleben.[45] The theology of grace that emerged from the study of Martin Luder the Wittenberg professor of Bible was the product of a seed planted in the soul of Martin Luder the monk as he went about his official duties. In 1516 neither vicar general nor provincial vicar had any thought of such consequences.

PART
TWO

Wittenberg and the
Beginnings of the
Reformation, 1511–1525

I

Wittenberg—'On the Edge of Civilization'

In summer 1511 the conflicts amongst German Augustinians over what reforms of their order were needed and how they might be achieved led to Martin Luder's return to Wittenberg, this time permanently. His transfer was designed to restore peace at the Erfurt monastery, but it also gave Vicar General Staupitz the opportunity to install an able teacher at the university at Wittenberg, which he had helped establish. Shortly after Luder's move to Wittenberg, Staupitz himself left Saxony. Although he returned only occasionally, in this age of humanist letter writing he remained in close contact with his former institution, and with Brother Martin in particular, his successor as professor of Bible. With Luder's move to Wittenberg, the scene was set for a symbiosis of individual and location that had historic significance comparable only with the later union of Goethe and Weimar. Kant's relationship with Königsberg rested on very different foundations, for in the East Prussian city the philosopher lacked the congenial colleagues-in-arms found by Luther in Wittenberg.

Religious sociologists might judge the harvest reaped from that relationship in the second decade of the sixteenth century to be the product of previously untilled land, distant from the urban centres in the south and west of the Empire with their rich cultural traditions. The reformer understood the situation very similarly, for having left behind the large central German town of Erfurt, he felt he had arrived at the very edge of civilization, *in termino civilitatis*.[1] In the 1540s Melanchthon, who in summer 1518 had moved to Wittenberg from highly urbanized southern Germany, was very understanding of Justus Jonas' acceptance of a call to Halle, where, Melanchthon noted, he would live in a town and not in the countryside as in Wittenberg.[2] Size alone can explain that verdict—Halle had a population of a good 10,000, while Wittenberg had only around 2,000 inhabitants and along with Meissen was the smallest of the towns of Saxony-Thuringia. The population of Eisleben, the town in which Luder had been born, was more than double that of Wittenberg. Additionally, like all large- and medium-sized towns, Halle had a very rich and varied ecclesiastical landscape, with four parish churches, dozens of monasteries, and many additional ecclesiastical institutions; its recently founded collegiate church was a cathedral in all but name. Wittenberg, by contrast, had just a single parish church and three small monasteries of mendicant orders with largely unremarkable chapels. Only the princely castle church with its All Saints' Foundation was particularly notable, and that building was part of as-yet-incomplete expansion plans. When travellers from other countries such as the humanist Enea Silvio Piccolomini sang the praises of Germany's towns, they had in mind the numerous large and wealthy Imperial cities of the south, not the minor towns in the east, which with their small, thatched wooden and half-timbered buildings would more likely have registered to an Italian as large villages.

Yet up until the nineteenth century, the Empire benefitted greatly from precisely this extensive network of medium-sized and small towns, where the economic and cultural achievements of the urban burgher class were just as likely to have roots as in the large Imperial cities and trading centres. Early modern urbanization in Germany was not based on the rapid and disproportionate growth of a metropole on the model of Naples, Paris, and, a little later, Amsterdam and London, but rather on the strengthening of this network of towns. Around 1500, Saxony experienced a quite remarkable increase in urbanization. Luther and the Reformation were part of this process, both its product and its motor, which brought the reinforcement of communal structures and institutions and the expansion of the social welfare system, schools and higher education, and additional civic institutions. Evidence of such developments can still be seen today: the town of Grimma, for example, is dominated by the former princely school. In Mansfeld, Luder's home territory, the boom in mining had enabled the towns to flourish, not least Eisleben, the city of Luder's birth, where Count Albrecht IV had founded a 'new town'. With their new monastery, dedicated in May 1516, the Augustinians and their provincial vicar Luder were part of this process of urbanization in Eisleben. For contemporaries the church was just as much part of the developing civic landscape as were the street layout and the water supply. Urbanization in the Saxon Erzgebirge progressed at an even greater pace, where wasteland and wilderness were to be tamed by a run of new mining towns that reached from Marienberg and Schneeberg via Annaberg and Buchholz to Joachimsthal, which lay in Bohemian territory. In these new towns, too, material and spiritual interests, the secular and the ecclesiastical, were closely bound together, as is still evident today in the mighty and disproportionately large churches found in these towns, and perhaps even more impressively in the mines of Joachimsthal, where shafts with names such as Eve, Adam, and Maria bring half the Bible to life. Tradition and innovation came together in such towns, in their layout, for example, which for Marienberg followed the most recent Italian archetypes, and in their churches, where the previously dominant High Gothic now gave way to a Renaissance vocabulary. In Annaberg that substitution came at the behest of local ruler Duke George after he had viewed the Fuggers' Renaissance chapel in the church of Saint Anne in Augsburg.

Reconstruction as an Electoral Residence and University Town

Although Wittenberg was not one of the mining towns of Saxony, it profited from the wealth that mining brought to the territory and its rulers. Significant changes were afoot as Wittenberg came to typify the processes that saw medieval society take on its early modern form. Where the medieval town and its citizens had flourished from trade and manufacturing, the dynamics of the urbanization associated with the early modern state focused on the ruler's residence and his administrative centres. Wittenberg had grown as a result of long-distance trade, with a very significant hub developing at this crossing point on the River Elbe. Trade and manufacture would remain important, and the wealthiest citizens of Wittenberg were always involved in commerce, as was the case for Lucas Cranach, who settled in Wittenberg in 1505, and was soon its wealthiest resident. The success of this artistic entrepreneur makes evident, however, that Wittenberg flourished at the beginning of the sixteenth century entirely as a result of its role as a princely residence and university town. The opportunities offered by the Wettin court and the new academic enterprise gave Cranach reason to move from thriving Vienna, the home of the Habsburg court, to the town on the Elbe. With the Reformation, Wittenberg subsequently also became an ecclesiastical centre of Europe-wide significance on a par with Rome and Geneva.

The emergence of Wittenberg can be laid at the door of Frederick the Wise, the Saxon elector, who in the decades around 1500 was one of the more significant and most powerful of the rulers within the Empire. Self-assured and open to scholarly and artistic innovation, he was second only to Emperor Maximilian in embodying the ideal of an energetic Renaissance prince, not least in his commissioned portraiture, for which he employed the most famous artists of his time—Albrecht Dürer for a version in paint and, even more impressively, Italian master Adriano Fiorentino for a life-size bronze bust (Figure 15). In 1485 the Saxon lands had been divided in two: the capital of the Albertine dukedom was Dresden; in 1486, on becoming ruler of the Ernestine electorate, Frederick the Wise immediately made Wittenberg his residence. The new elector's decision was somewhat surprising, for Wittenberg was rather unfavourably situated in the north-eastern corner of the newly created and still very fragile territory, with its lands in the south interlocking, even blended together, with those of the Dresden ducal line. Torgau, Weimar, Gotha, or Coburg must have seemed far more likely choices as residences, with decent palaces ready and waiting and in some instances a more central location. But Frederick surely found Wittenberg's lack of pretension appealing, for relatively untouched by political or cultural influences, the town was open to his highly personal vision of a modern princely seat, including all that came with a court and territorial administration. The existing but long-insignificant castle, which had belonged to the Ascania line, was torn down to make way for a new building. In Wittenberg Frederick identified an opportunity to underscore his electoral status, tied to the electoral lands that surrounded Wittenberg, particularly in light of

Figure 15. Life-size bronze bust of Frederick the Wise, elector of Saxony, by Adriano Fiorentino (c.1450–1499), 1498.

the need to reinforce his position in areas that bordered the archbishopric of Magdeburg and electoral Brandenburg, the elector's rivals to the west and north.

The renovation and expansion of Wittenberg were not designed to produce the model Renaissance town advocated by Italian theorists and architects, unlike the layout of the new Saxon mining town of Marienberg. Elements of that ideal were adopted, however, facilitated by the clarity and simplicity of the existing triangular layout of the town. Three institutions were particularly close to Frederick's heart: the castle, whose design would make a physical statement about his court and government; the university, a new creation; and the All Saints' Foundation, which was to be expanded. In order that his residence might be the equal of the mighty Albrechtsburg, the castle in Meissen belonging to the rival Albertine line, Frederick appointed leading architects and painters to provide the building with allusions to noble sentiment found in biblical and Graeco-Roman allegories and in depictions of principled heroic acts. In addition to a Dutchman and the Italian Jacopo de' Barbari, Dürer, Riemenschneider, and Hans Burgkmair were all engaged to work on the project. In 1504 Lucas Cranach the Elder was appointed court painter and the following year took up permanent residence in the town, where he set up a painting workshop that soon enjoyed an extensive reputation. Within the Empire, only the Emperor himself could also boast of having in his employ such an elite team of architects, artists, and artisans.

Elector Frederick dedicated just as much energy to the establishment, in 1502, of the university at Wittenberg, which was given the name 'Leucorea', the Greek translation of Wittenberg/Weissenberg/White Mountain. While imposing palace buildings were a must for a residence town in this age, a university was far less common. In the central and northern Empire the large Hanseatic towns and free towns were traditionally home to universities—Greifswald, Rostock, Erfurt, and Cologne, for example. In neighbouring Brandenburg the first territorial university, founded in 1506, followed that traditional pattern, for it was located not in the ruler's residence town of Berlin, but in the merchant town of Frankfurt an der Oder and was established on the initiative not of the elector but of the city council. The links between residence and university in Wittenberg made evident that Frederick planned to display his territorial power through education and scholarship as well as in his palace and court. One generation later Landgrave Philip of Hesse adopted this same model for, now influenced by the Reformation, he too founded a university in his residence town, in Marburg.

The new foundation in Wittenberg rapidly gained a certain eminence, for the Electoral Saxon government appointed professors of significant repute, initially to the law faculty in particular, and swiftly put in place the necessary infrastructure. The palace library, for example, was expanded and turned into a university library accessible to both professors and students and placed by the elector in the expert hands of his private secretary, Georg Spalatin. Printing was still in its youth, but its significance for scholarship was not overlooked, and systematic steps were taken to bring print shops and publishing businesses to Wittenberg—between 1503 and 1508 no fewer than three were already active in this small, somewhat remote town.

Contemporaries would have been in no doubt that any town that became a ruler's residence must host an eminent ecclesiastical institution with a correspondingly distinguished church. To that end Frederick reinvigorated the All Saints' Foundation established by his forefathers and had built an impressive new church for the foundation, which in light of its location directly alongside his residence would subsequently become known as the 'castle church'. Foundation and church were established to a particular end—they were tasked with housing and caring for the elector's remarkably rich collection of relics, rich both in the number and nature of its relics and in the assurances of salvation and indulgences (time remitted from purgatory for the soul of the sinner) it offered. It would be anachronistic to pit the Saxon elector's faith in relics and enthusiasm for their collection against his humanist outlook or to suggest that Frederick lacked the true spirit of the Renaissance. Humanist outlook and Renaissance spirit went hand in hand with a profound late medieval spirituality and with the veneration of the saints, or at least such was the case in Germany. The richness of a relic collection was just as much a form of self-representation for a ruler as was the magnificence of a palace or the splendour of a court. The collection also had useful political purpose, for its sacral capital could be employed to support the construction of the electoral Saxon state and to ensure God's protection of both the territory and its people. The relic collection at Wittenberg had added import because the archbishop of Mainz and Magdeburg, a member of the ruling family in neighbouring Brandenburg, had established a collection of relics in his residence town of Halle that was similar in size but markedly less significant.

When Martin Luder arrived in Wittenberg from the monastery in Erfurt, much of this 'Renaissance project'—a term that is certainly apposite—had already been realized. A 'city of marble' had come into being on the banks of the Elbe, announced Christoph Scheurl, a humanist from Nuremberg and adviser to Elector Frederick, with panegyric exuberance.[3] Anyone who approached the River Elbe from the south—as would have been the case for the Augustinian monk, who had travelled from Thuringia—would have viewed the silhouette of the town much as it still appears today (see Figure 16). The town's frontage on the River Elbe ran for just under one and a half kilometres. On the western end, to our traveller's left, immediately beside the Coswig Gate, the castle rose mightily out of the low river meadows into a wide and otherwise empty sky, and the observer would have been able to see its round corner towers, a lofty white, two-storey south wing, and the mighty pitched roof of the castle church, whose tower formed one of the towers of the castle. Turning his gaze away from this district at the western end of the town, which contained the princely courtly, administrative, and ecclesiastical buildings, and looking instead along the Elbe to the eastern end of the town, the traveller would have spied, at the Elster Gate, the university and monastery district, which despite this combination was distinctly more modest than the castle buildings. Farthest east and directly behind the city wall were the buildings of the monastery of the Augustinian Hermits, where Luther would live for the remaining three and a half decades of his life. To the west followed the gables of the university's Old College, built in 1503, and New College,

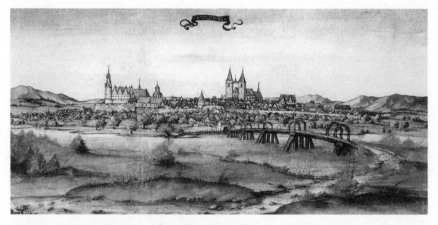

Figure 16. Wittenberg seen from the River Elbe, sketch from the travel album of Count Palatine Otto Heinrich, 1536, now in the library of the University of Würzburg.

completed in 1509. In between the worlds of the court, in the west, and the academy, in the east, lay the domain of the citizens of Wittenberg, distinguished by the highest building in the town, the town and parish church of Saint Mary, with its soaring double tower and pitched roof, and, a little west of the church, by the distinctly lower town hall. Although the town hall initially retained its medieval restraint, in a demonstration of early modern urban confidence, in 1521, and therefore during the Reformation, the citizens of Wittenberg began a reconstruction that lasted some fifteen years. In front of the town hall lay the marketplace, the centre of trade and commerce. The marketplace could be reached easily from the river via the Elbe Gate, which lay slightly to the west of the centre point of the town's frontage on the river. The oak bridge that crossed the River Elbe at the Elbe Gate was an essential element of the Renaissance reconstruction of Wittenberg for it bound the town directly to the traffic routes on the south side of the Elbe.

With much scaffolding still standing, change was very evidently afoot, although with innovation came uncertainty. The castle was still incomplete: to the east, where a visitor might expect to see a fourth wing of the castle, an outer ward with offices and storerooms was to be built, but its construction had recently been halted without any clear sense of when it would be resumed. As most of those employed on the project remained trapped in medieval tradition and spoke the language of cell vaults and curtain arches, the building struggled to convince the onlooker that it was, in fact, a Renaissance palace. All the more concerning would have been the situation in that middle district, the heart of the daily life of the town's residents, for the marketplace was far from complete, with both the reconstruction of the town hall and the development of neighbouring properties belonging to merchants and more prosperous artisans yet to come. The character of the Wittenberg we see today is largely formed by the cohesive development that surrounds this central district, with its impressive residential, manufacturing, and commercial properties, including the home, workshops, and sales offices of Lucas Cranach, court painter, publisher, and apothecary, in particular, but those buildings were completed only some years later, during the Reformation.

At the eastern end of the silhouette of the town was a new structure that had been quickly erected for the Augustinian monastery during the first phase of building, after 1504, on the property of the abandoned Hospital of the Holy Spirit. Somewhat primitive, or perhaps simply utilitarian, it could hardly hold a candle to the great medieval monastic buildings with which the newly arrived monk from Erfurt would have been familiar. It included only an approximation of a cloister, and for the convent itself, instead of the usual four-part rectangular structure, a single towering building had been constructed, with three floors, a mighty gabled roof, and a stair tower on the courtyard side. The top floor housed around forty cells in which the monks slept, while the main floor included their library as well as study and lecture space for the theology faculty, whose members were associated with the monastery. At ground level were the kitchen and refectory, and also for a time the office and print shop of Johannes Rhau-Grunenberg, another sign that the monastery's focus was on serving the university and the academic world more broadly.

One study was set aside for the professor of Bible, a room that later the reformer would repeatedly term his 'tower' and that would go down in history as the setting for his momentous 'tower experience'. The room no longer exists, and we do not know precisely where it was located within the building. For many years Reformation historians believed it was in the second floor of a tower that bordered the monastery buildings to the west and had originally been part of the medieval city walls. Recent archaeological excavations on the south side of the monastery, closest to the Elbe, have revealed that around 1515/16 an addition to the monastery was made in the form of a square tower of noteworthy design and layout. A number of factors suggest that Luder's study would have been located in this tower. At this date, as provincial vicar Luder was, along with the prior, the most senior member of the monastic community. Additionally, while we know that the extension to the south included a latrine, we have no evidence that such a room was included in the narrower and smaller tower to the west that had been part of the city walls. If we are to take the reformer at his word and accept that his revolutionary breakthrough came to him as he sat on the toilet, then only the southern structure fits our requirements.

In 1512 the Augustinians in Wittenberg did not as yet have their own monastery church. There were plans to build a place of worship opposite the monastery, on the side facing the street, where the northern wing of a more traditional monastic layout would have been found. In the meantime, the monks held their services in a small half-timbered chapel on land that had been part of the now-defunct Hospital of the Holy Spirit, whose properties had passed to the Augustinians. No start was even made on the church building and when the Reformation redirected the focus of ecclesiastical life onto the community and the parish church, even the chapel became redundant; it was torn down in 1540.

The university, too, was still under construction. For Frederick the Wise, providing a home for flourishing scholarship in his Wittenberg residence town was also a prestige cause. The presence of the university would remove a stain on the character of the electorate of Saxony, for amongst all the electorates only Saxony and Brandenburg lacked a territorial university. The university at Leipzig had passed to the ducal Meissen-Dresden line when the Wettin family lands were divided in 1485. In 1502 an Imperial privilege was granted for the establishment of a university at Wittenberg, with papal approval following the next year. The sequence of these events should not be read as an early pointer towards the Reformation, as traditionally receipt of a papal privilege was the first step in the founding of a new university, but it does suggest a shift in emphasis in which Frederick the Wise played a significant part.

With all four traditional faculties—theology, law, medicine, and the arts—and with forty-four professors by 1513, the Leucorea quickly attracted some 400 students. Before the university had its own space, in the Old College and New College, teaching took place at a number of locations throughout the town, including the town hall and town church. The theologians, who taught both for the university and for the Augustinians, held their lectures primarily in the auditorium at the Black Monastery. The castle church served as university church and university auditorium, and it was here that public disputations were held. The north door's function as a noticeboard for advertisements and notifications would later provide it with a starring role in the Reformation. Although designated space was available for students in two hostels and on the top floor of the Augustinian monastery, students who studied at Wittenberg often preferred more comfortable lodgings in the homes of their professors or citizens of the town, or in neighbouring villages. In the wake of the Reformation, Wittenberg would be the most desirable university in the Empire for a generation, with numbers matriculating at their highest between 1535 and 1545, with a peak reached in 1544, two years before Luther's death, when 814 students matriculated. The number of students and the number of citizens were roughly equal, which led repeatedly to clashes, even though many students lived outside the town.

The university was financed in part by funds from the elector, so in effect by the state, and in part by funds from the church, which paid, for example, the salaries of professors who were members of the All Saints' Foundation. Professors who were also monks, as was the case for Luder, received no salary, for they lived according to their vow of poverty in the monastery,

concern for Luder's personal needs, as we saw with the example of the cloth he had sent to the monk for a new habit. The relationship was not completely one-sided, for Luder was drawn into the concerns of the court and the elector, including possible additions to Frederick's relic collection.[12] When the storm over Luder's Ninety-Five Theses erupted and he found himself branded a heretic, this close relationship, crafted during the monk's early years in Wittenberg, guaranteed him the support and protection of the elector as he faced opposition within the Empire and clashed with Rome.

Yet the elector never received his professor/reformer in person, which is all the more remarkable in light of the relative simplicity of arrangements in Wittenberg and Electoral Saxony. For the early years the lack of personal contact can be explained in part by the character of Martin Luder, who was not one to force himself into proximity with power, not least because he sought to embrace the monastic ideals of humility and self-discipline. Subsequently, distance from his reformer was a sensible precaution adopted by the elector himself, who had laid aside the impetuosity of his youth and now lived up to his new nomenclature as 'the Wise'. Even during the diet at Worms, an episode so dramatic for him personally and for his Saxon government, he avoided any direct contact beyond the public setting of the Imperial diet, perhaps also somewhat nervous of contact with unorthodox teachings that might jeopardize his salvation. This personal distance did not mean the reformer was unable to write to his ruler and express his opinions frankly. In one letter, for example, he criticized the introduction of a new tax that 'has reduced Your Grace's reputation, name, and good will'.[13] When it came to the radicalism and dynamism of his own views, Luther spoke out without any hesitation against all requests to tone down or reconsider his position.[14]

For many years the principal intermediary between ruler and reformer was Georg Spalatin (Figure 17), a humanist both theologically and legally trained. At court Spalatin rose to become one of the closest confidantes of the elector and his family. His first role was as tutor in Wittenberg to next-in-line John Frederick and other close relatives of the ruler, whose studies he oversaw from 1511; he subsequently was the first historiographer of the Wettin family and librarian at the castle and university library, and finally became private secretary to Frederick the Wise, whose ear he had, ahead of all others, from 1516 for both secular and spiritual matters. Spalatin's early personal contact with Luder was more or less unavoidable, partly because Spalatin, only a few months younger than Luder, had grown up in Erfurt in

Figure 17. Georg Spalatin aged twenty-six, by Lucas Cranach the Elder, 1509.

the same intellectual and academic circles as Luder and was in close contact with Johannes Lang, Luder's fellow Augustinian monk and friend in that city, and partly as a result of his role as tutor to Frederick's family and councillor to the elector himself. When the Reuchlin dispute flared up and the Saxon court needed to take a stand on the value that should be attached to Jewish texts, it was very natural for Spalatin, who had been asked to provide an assessment of the issue, to turn to the Wittenberg professor of Bible, whom he approached in 1513 via their mutual friend Lang with a request for his opinion. In February 1514 Luder responded with a first extensive written account that focused on humanist scholarly freedom and energetically demanded that evaluations and opinions such as those given by Reuchlin, a Hebraist, must be 'free from danger'. Otherwise, Luder warned, 'these inquisitors would act at will . . . and declare the orthodox to be heretics'.[15]

A short time later, during the Luther Affair, when the Saxon government so forcefully supported the fundamental idea that scholarly investigation into matters of faith should not be constrained, this position had its roots in Luder's earlier counsel. The role of experts as political advisers, so debated today, was evidently a matter of course in Wittenberg. In accord with the humanist model, the bond between electoral councillor and Augustinian monk, forged well before the Reformation, was exercised in a correspondence that amounted to hundreds of letters. These letters lay bare a close and trusting bond that went beyond the conventions of humanist friendship or the practicalities of the interaction of court and university. As early as 1516 we can discern in Spalatin's tentative attempts to explain the relationship between law, justice, and faith a theological interlocutor and learned companion sought out by Luder for an intellectual exchange that would help him sharpen his own thinking. We see that process in action in the correspondence between the two men from October 1516 that accompanied Luder's disagreement with Erasmus of Rotterdam, the prince of humanists, who was held in such high regard by both men, for through his decisive rejection of Erasmus' interpretation of Paul and theological valorization of Jerome at the expense of Augustine, Luder found himself setting out his own teaching on justification. We see it again with the issue of the veneration of the saints, which in September 1516 in the course of an academic disputation led by Luder had been redefined in a way very disconcerting to scholastic minds.[16]

At the time of the dispute over indulgences, their exchange became primarily an opportunity for Luder to test out his stance. Yet although Spalatin functioned principally as a sounding board, the penetrating questions he posed in his letters were of significant help to Luder. 'You again add two small questions,' Luder noted in a letter of 15 February 1518, and elaborated his answer over several pages that followed. Within the week he found himself again facing a crucial question, when he was asked whether scholastic dialectic and the church fathers should be employed to enable a correct interpretation of the Bible; this time there would be no debate— Luder replied with an unconditional 'no'. Luder thus revealed to his friend the fundamental principle of the Reformation, which, he believed, could be recognized personally and 'practically'.[17] This close communication, which drew the elector's private secretary into the inner workings of emerging Reformation theology, made it possible for Spalatin to bring Luder's teachings to the Saxon court and to present the views of the professor of Bible and reformer to the elector accurately and in person. Spalatin's familiarity with the Saxon court and its manner of governing also enabled him to employ tactics that safeguarded the Reformation. Spalatin's contribution was all the more important because of Luder's utter refusal to contemplate any compromise, which meant that the reformer could never be persuaded to take into account the political calculations required of the temporal authorities.

The University and Reform of its Academic Programme

Although his responsibilities as Augustinian provincial vicar would often take Luder away from Wittenberg, even as a newly appointed professor he was rapidly drawn into university politics. He built up a network of academic connections in his new home town that would support him in the conflicts unleashed by the Ninety-Five Theses, and from this network he subsequently drew colleagues and collaborators for the work that accompanied the institutionalization of the Reformation, above all for the mammoth task of translating the Bible. Luder's reforming theology was incubated by a group of reform-minded individuals, a debate club in effect, composed of Wittenberg professors.

Immediately on his arrival at Wittenberg, the new professor was brought into the circle of his fellow Augustinian professors. He had close contact with Wenzeslaus Linck, Augustinian prior and professor of theology, who was of an age with Luder; even after his transfer to the monastery in Nuremberg in 1517, Linck remained in touch with Wittenberg and with the reformer. From 1515/16 Luder also developed closer relationships with professors who were not members of his monastic community. Since receiving his doctorate in autumn 1512, Luder had had ties to Andreas Bodenstein, known as Karlstadt, who from 1505 had advanced his career quickly as professor of theology at the University of Wittenberg and as archdeacon of the All Saints' Foundation. Although some three years younger than Luder, Karlstadt was well established at the university and had overseen the award of Luder's doctorate, which he deemed commensurate with the quality of Luder's scholarship to date. As colleagues in the theology faculty, the two men initially worked independently, but Karlstadt's conclusions, reached via Neoplatonism, mysticism, and humanism, corresponded very largely with Luder's. With the church father Augustine now a common focus of their work, their relationship became much closer in summer 1516, by which date Karlstadt had received the degree of doctor of canon and civil law in Rome. Around the same time Nikolaus von Amsdorff, nephew of Luder's mentor Staupitz and a member of a noble family from Meissen, developed a closer bond with the Augustinian monk; only a few years later the reformer dedicated his tract 'To the Christian Nobility of the German Nation' to Amsdorff. Amsdorff held an endowed position in the philosophy faculty and like Karlstadt was therefore a member of the Wittenberg theology faculty although not a monk. Via Luder's lectures on the Letter to the Romans, he was drawn into discussions of the new Wittenberg theology. When the controversy over the Ninety-Five Theses erupted, Amsdorff, Luder's more worldly wise near contemporary, stood at his friend's side. He accompanied Luder to the disputation held at Leipzig in 1519 and to the Imperial diet held at Worms in 1521 and was with him on the return journey from Worms, which ended so dramatically outside Eisenach.

As we might expect of a new and still relatively uncomplicated institution, at the university in Wittenberg bonds were forged across faculties. Luder had close ties to Christoph Scheurl, a lawyer, a friendship that continued even after Scheurl became syndic in Nuremberg. Evidently equally collegial was Luder's relationship with Hieronymus Schurf, doctor of canon and civil law and several times rector of the university, with whom Luder had private discussions as the two men travelled to Kemberg, a small town twenty kilometres south of Wittenberg, shortly before the controversy over the Ninety-Five Theses broke out.[18] That collegial contact was intensified by the visitation—or 'review' we might say today—of the university undertaken from September 1517 and the reform of the programme of study that resulted. The visitation followed complaints about the poor quality of teaching in the law faculty, protests that had alarmed the elector and given cause for a university-wide review. Fifteen years after the foundation of the university, the elector believed it was time for his favourite project to present a balance sheet that named its successes and failures.

The guiding spirit behind the visitation was Spalatin, the elector's private secretary, who in keeping with his humanist credentials immediately began to draft a reform plan. Luder's existing close intellectual exchange with Spalatin—in their discussions of Erasmus they had already touched directly upon what students should be studying—helps explain why Luder, along with Karlstadt as dean, was drawn into Spalatin's reform project.

At gatherings held at Karlstadt's home during winter semester 1517/18, proposals for the improvement of the student experience at Wittenberg were hammered out. A catalogue of requests to be put to the ruler was drawn up. Then as today, improvements to the programme of study were deemed impossible without the appointment of additional professors. Tellingly, it was Luder who sent the faculty proposal on to Spalatin, although only on 11 March 1518.[19] Luder enjoined Spalatin now to do his bit at court. Although he commented on the delay by explaining that the professors had been wary of confronting the elector with new and costly demands, their reluctance can also be explained by the recent outbreak of the indulgence controversy.

One-sided fixation on the reformer and his spiritual and theological progress will often bring failure to recognize that in these decisive months, reform of the university and the Reformation were closely intertwined. We can assume that in autumn 1517 notes, drafts, and proposals on both indulgences and university reform would have lain side-by-side, as it were, on Luder's desk in his study in the tower at the Augustinian monastery. In these weeks he also addressed both topics with his colleagues and friends in his correspondence and in person. That academic reform and Reformation theology unfolded in parallel underlines the scholarly character of the indulgence controversy that erupted in these very weeks. The roots of the Reformation were nurtured by the university.

The principal impact of the academic reform on Luder's work environment—Spalatin had quickly and without great difficulty convinced the elector to finance the reform plans—was that teaching of philosophy and philology was expanded and two new professorial chairs were created, one for Greek and one for Hebrew. The appointment in August 1518 of twenty-one-year-old Philipp Schwarzert from Tübingen, who had not yet received his doctorate, to the chair of Greek improved the professor of Bible's work situation at a single stroke and also reinforced his circle of friends with a new pivotal relationship. Using the Graecized version of his name, Melanchthon quickly rose to be an undisputed authority in his field. Melanchthon did not initiate the reform of the university at Wittenberg, as too often has been asserted by those with only a superficial grasp of events. His call to Wittenberg was part of a vision of reform that had already been developed by Luder and his colleagues. Subsequently held in great esteem as the 'teacher of Germany' (*Praeceptor Germaniae*), Melanchthon was just as much a product of academic reform at Wittenberg as he was, a little later, its motor.

Although he was a pupil of the famous humanist Johannes Reuchlin and had something of a reputation as a humanist wunderkind as a result of his teaching at Tübingen, Melanchthon initially did not make a particularly strong impression. Not a tall man, he was remarkably young to be called to a professorial chair. A number of leading lights at Wittenberg, including Luder himself, would have preferred to see Petrus Mosellanus, the eminent Greek scholar at Leipzig, appointed to the chair at their university. On 28 August 1518, however, only three days after his arrival, Melanchthon stood at the lectern to give an inaugural lecture that would soon be much vaunted by humanists. His fierce plea for the study of Greek and for a concomitant modernization of academic teaching convinced his audience that he was the right choice for Wittenberg. Luder immediately rejoiced, 'Our Philip Melanchthon is a wonderful person, one who is superhuman in almost all respects. And yet he is still my confidant and my friend,' and a year later remarked, 'that little Greek scholar outdoes me even in theology itself'.[20] For his part Melanchthon was utterly committed to his older colleague and to his mission: in 1521, while

Luther was at the Wartburg and therefore absent from Wittenberg, Melanchthon recorded, 'I would rather die than be parted from this man.' From their scholarly symbiosis and lifelong personal bond grew a shared achievement that changed the world. Their different characters, of which no one was more aware than Luther himself, and the scale and risks of the task to which they set their shoulders, repeatedly put their relationship under strain. It was principally the younger party who had to bear that burden. In spring 1548, after Luther's death and in the dark weeks after Charles V's triumph over the Protestants who had united to form the Schmalkaldic League, Melanchthon complained to a trusted friend, 'I bore an almost dishonourable servitude, for Luther more often allowed his temperament to rule, which contained a not insignificant pugnacity and bossiness, than he would have done if he had paid attention to his reputation and to the common good.'[21] Yet despite the pressures on their relationship, the two men never fundamentally parted ways.

Filling the new chair of Hebrew proved a lengthy and far harder business. Even as he faced all the anxieties and pressures of his examination by Cajetan at Augsburg, Luder sought to ensure that the eminent Hebraist Johann Böschenstein would receive a financially sound and friendly reception in Wittenberg, even though he thought Böschenstein somewhat timid and mistrustful. In the end Böschenstein remained at the Leucorea for three months, from November 1518 to January 1519, and left Wittenberg as the result of a profound difference of opinion. Differences in character and outlook may have played their part, with Melanchthon speaking out sharply against 'vagabond doctors who move from place to place', neglecting their students, but the decisive issue was certainly objective academic differences. Luder and his colleges saw Hebrew as the servant of theology, employed for a better understanding of Scripture. Their attitude towards the Jewish and rabbinic content of works in Hebrew went beyond simple indifference, for they believed such texts to be harmful, even downright dangerous. They were similarly dismissive of the philological or rhetorical in Böschenstein's teaching. With their specific goals for the reform of their university in mind, the existing Wittenberg faculty quickly recognized that they had taken a wrong turn with Böschenstein and did everything to find their way back. Böschenstein had to leave Wittenberg deeply disappointed, as he made evident with some bitterness. He recorded that he had invested his hopes for his future life and salvation in the new theology of his colleagues, and that the Augustinian monk's refusal to express any form of gratitude for his faithfulness was a product of that monk's weakness of character, of the tyranny of his ambition, and his conceited thirst for glory.[22]

We should not dismiss Böschenstein's harsh assessment of the self-confident reformer as the unjustified retort of an injured party. Here, rather, is another example of the unconditional commitment that Luther demanded of both himself and others, in order that he might perform the task to which he had been called. We must also remember that their vulnerability during these years meant that the Wittenbergers could not run the risk of internal tension or dissent. Everything hinged on the maintenance of a common purpose and common will, and the chair of Hebrew had to be a member of that united front, for that position was no less important for the correct interpretation of Scripture, or for its translation, than was the chair of Greek. The appointment of Matthäus Goldhahn, Latinized as Aurogallus, to the chair of Hebrew proved a godsend. Aurogallus, who took up his new post in February 1521, two and a half years after Melanchthon's appointment to the chair of Greek, was a leading figure in his field, and he remained loyal to the Leucorea until his death in 1543.[23] With his appointment, the faculty at Wittenberg now comprised scholars of outstanding intellect, exceptional individuals who believed they had been called to dedicate themselves, with fresh intensity and a common resolve, to the renewal of theology and church. The existence of that community would prove vital to the success of the Reformation, providing polemical vindication and explanation of Protestant teachings and the Protestant church.

All in all, it seems unlikely that Luder would have found in any other university conditions so well suited to, first, the creation of his theology and, then, the construction of the theological and organizational foundations of the evangelical church.

A Network of Friends and Acquaintances

In his secondary appointment as preacher at the town church, a position that he would have assumed in 1513, Luder had direct contact with the clergy and community at that church, particularly when Simon Heins, his colleague at the university, was called to the church as its pastor. His ties to the parish community became even stronger in 1523 when, following the death of Heins, the position of town pastor passed to Johannes Bugenhagen, who had left his Pomeranian homeland to study the new theology in its birthplace.

Luder's circle also included a good number of citizens of Wittenberg, drawn particularly from the town's printers and publishers, who issued his teaching materials and early writings, and from members of the town council and resident merchants. In 1520 Lucas Cranach, business entrepreneur and council member, asked Luther to be godfather to his daughter Anna. Five years later Cranach would be best man at Luther's wedding and subsequently stand as godfather, in turn, for Luther's son Hans.

Exploration of Luder's world reveals very clearly that in his earlier incarnation the man who later became the reformer was no solitary monk or bookish recluse holed up in an ivory tower. Luder was in constant contact with members of all social groupings in Wittenberg, with whom he was involved in regular intellectual exchange. Such relationships were made possible by the particular social character of the town—open, inquiring, and adaptable—which was a product not only of the university and the town itself but also of the court. The Augustinian monk and professor was quickly drawn into the new milieu produced by the castle and university, a context that proved attractive to artists, scholars, and intellectuals. Like Luder, almost all members of his circle were recent arrivals in Wittenberg. With the exception of nobleman Nikolaus von Amsdorff, all were also members of the aspiring burgher class. All were humanistically educated. And with the exception of Cranach, who was ten years older than Luder, all belonged to the generation born in the early 1480s.

This network of individuals provided the social prerequisite for the symbiosis of Wittenberg and Luther. Their relationship reached far beyond Wittenberg itself, and it contained a history-defining dynamic that contributed crucially to the creation of the early modern age in Europe and to the emergence of modernity. For the members of this circle, Luder, already in his thirties, was a valued partner whose voice carried particular weight. They were intrigued by his scholarly ideas, not least because they were based on a profound Scriptural knowledge highly impressive to his contemporaries. But as Luther advanced down the path of Reformation, he encountered others in both university and town who believed he had chosen the wrong route. He found himself in conflict with his university colleague Karlstadt and with his fellow monk Gabriel Zwilling over the course and the character of the Reformation, and his disagreement with Hieronymus Schurf, his colleague from the law faculty, about the value of the Corpus Iuris Canonici, became even more heated when, in 1520, Luther had that collection of canon law join the papal bull threatening his excommunication on the pyre before the Elster Gate.

On one occasion Luther became embroiled in a potentially dangerous conflict with his students. The dispute was sparked not by his theology, but by student privilege, specifically, the right to carry a weapon. Believing they alone were legally entitled to be armed, the students felt threatened by the painters at Cranach's studio who also wanted to carry daggers. In a sermon given on 15 July 1520, Luther spoke out against the unrest generated by this still-unresolved quarrel, which he declared the work of the devil. Incensed, the students warned 'this little monk' that should he ever give such a sermon again, they would 'polish his bald pate with a stone', or, in other words, smash in his tonsured head.[24] Theirs were strong words, especially as by this date their 'little monk' had gained renown as a hero of free speech and free thinking, a status bolstered by pamphlets, disputations, and the heresy verdicts of leading universities such as Cologne and Louvain. The students' belligerence was short-lived, however, and soon they were again protectively gathered around their professor, ready to defend him whatever the threat.

Luther's experiences with his colleagues at the theology faculty had certain similarities with his experiences with the students. At the end of 1518, while all was balanced on a knife-edge—would the elector give in to pressure from Rome and deliver up the accused heretic?—the faculty's members rallied to Luder's defence with an extensive expert assessment of his teachings.[25] Townspeople, court, and town church also had his back as he dared to attack the traditional ordering of church and world. Even for a man with Luder's self-confidence, their encouragement was far from insignificant. Unlike in the Bible, in Luder's time it seemed the prophet could have honour in his own land. No signs were yet visible of the oppressive sense of superiority that on occasion would later threaten to turn Luther's colleagues and friends into little more than his pupils. Much to the contrary, these relationships flourished as exchanges between equals. And for many of his colleagues—Johannes Lang, Georg Spalatin, and Cranach the Elder, for example—Luther was also an unconditional friend. That equality would crumble only as Luther sought to assert his teachings, a storm that, even though he was supported by the Wittenbergers, Luther had to ride out on his own.

The verdict that a man like Luther could never be a friend in the fullest sense of the word, as proposed by Martin Brecht, for example, must be treated with some caution. In the early years it was precisely his skills at friendship that opened up for him the world of intellectual exchange, a world in which he participated fully despite his spiritual and scholarly hankerings and despite his assimilation into monastic life. If we think of Luther as simply a fellow human being, something almost tragic emerges from the fundamental changes to his relationships within this circle wrought by the potency of his mission. Not that he lost or pushed away his friends. Rather these relationships, formed as a meeting of minds, became asymmetrical. That tragedy was not experienced to the same extent by the reformer himself, who became increasingly consumed by, even obsessed with, his mission, and who from 1525 had the additional support of a family, but the distress was felt by his friends, who now stood in his potent shadow. No longer partners, they had become in effect Luther's support team, required to position and elucidate their thoughts and actions as part of the reformer's mission.

Melanchthon tolerated the proximity of the Reformation giant right up until Luther's death, but we know that the burden caused him pain, and not only at the Imperial diet of 1530. Harder still was the new dynamic for Georg Spalatin, who had had such close theological ties to the initial success of the Reformation and had so cleverly brought on board such powerful support. Even when the Reformation no longer required his mediation and Spalatin became pastor and superintendent of the church in distant Altenburg, Luther still felt bound to his former comrade in arms. In summer 1544, Spalatin's wife wrote to Luther to inform him that her husband was suffering from severe depression. Luther immediately replied with a remarkable letter of consolation, for which he gained praise as '*medicus conscientiarum morbidarum*', a doctor of the troubled mind.[26] But that communication brought little relief to his sick friend, who died only a few months later. Spalatin was well aware that with Luther now more a monument than a man, an exchange between equals was no longer possible. To a significant degree his depression had been caused by the fear that he was unable to perform the duties of his office consistently in accord with the fundamental principles of Luther's theology. This final mental collapse had been triggered by Luther's harsh criticism of his pastoral decision to allow a widowed pastor within his superintendency to marry the stepmother of his dead wife, a decision that Luther saw as sanctioning incest and sharply condemned.

II

Eleutherios—The Birth of a Free Man

The Long Road to Reformation Theology

Wittenberg—its court and university—formed only the Augustinian monk's outward world; his internal world was still generated by his unresolved questions about God. His questioning had taken on a new dimension, however, for his existential search had become an objectified scholarly pursuit. His ability to combine those two endeavours so happily can principally be credited to Wittenberg. The Reformation, with all its profound historical implications, emerged from the fertile cultural soil of that city, and specifically from the recently founded university, ready to embrace new questions and new answers. Unburdened by the exegetical traditions that tied theological learning at the old universities to compendia such as the 'Sentences' of Peter Lombard, at the Leucorea Luder had a scholarly freedom that seems almost modern in character. At the centre of his life he placed the Bible, and only the Bible. He was very ready to pay little attention to traditional medieval commentary; instead, as he stated concisely and clearly: 'One must know that Scripture without any glosses [i.e. without the glosses of centuries of exegetical sophistry] is the sun and the whole light from which all teachers receive their light, and not vice versa.'[1] To the delight of his students, who were weary of the routine of scholastic exegesis, he began with the Psalms, something of an obvious choice for a monk, whose daily existence would have been shaped by their singing or praying. He taught on the Psalms from 1513/14 until winter semester 1514/15 and perhaps even into summer semester 1515; the Letter to the Romans followed, until the summer semester of 1516, and was succeeded in turn by the letters to the Galatians and the Hebrews. In summer semester 1520 he gave a second series of lectures on the Psalms.

Texts of Luder's early lectures rediscovered in the late nineteenth and early twentieth centuries have been closely examined with an eye to Luther's exegesis. Yet even today no consensus has been reached on whether, or to what extent, they contain elements of his later Reformation theology. Later Luther himself frequently stressed the significance of the Psalms and Paul's letters as key texts that had brought him back repeatedly to his fundamental concerns, the righteousness of God and the role of penance as atonement for human sinfulness.[2]

In their outward appearance, Luder's lectures would have been typical of lectures held throughout the universities of Europe at the time. He lectured every day for two hours. Initially the daily lecture was held in summer at 6 a.m. and in winter at 7 a.m., but from summer semester 1516 it was shifted to the afternoon, at 1 p.m. The biblical text formed the core of the lecture. The professor explained the terms found in the text and stated what the passage meant, information that his students recorded either between the lines—as an interlinear glossary—or in the margins. Explanation and interpretation followed line by line, word by word. To ease the task for both professor and students, the Augustinian monk employed the most modern technology of his own day. He commissioned the Wittenberg printers—one of whom had his print shop in the monastery itself—to set the relevant text with a good distance between the lines and a broad margin, to make it easier for his audience to record his explanations (Figure 18). More significantly, he employed the most recent tools of humanist philology: a compendium of the Psalms by the French humanist Lefèvre d'Étaples; Reuchlin's introduction to Hebrew, *De rudimentis hebraicis*, of 1506; and naturally, immediately on its publication in 1516, Erasmus' edition of the New Testament, with critical annotations, in which the original Greek text appeared alongside the Latin translation. While Luder did turn to the standard commentaries and interpretation by the church fathers and scholastics, he did not deem these works authoritative, but rather regarded scholastic philosophy with the critical scepticism that he had imbibed during his early university studies at Erfurt. Although his engagement with the church fathers was largely limited to Augustine, he made extensive use of this one theologian, in particular for his reading of the Letter to the Romans. Further influences came from the mystical tradition, in writings where empathetic immersion in the meaning of the text complemented scholastic learning, with emotional responses, and

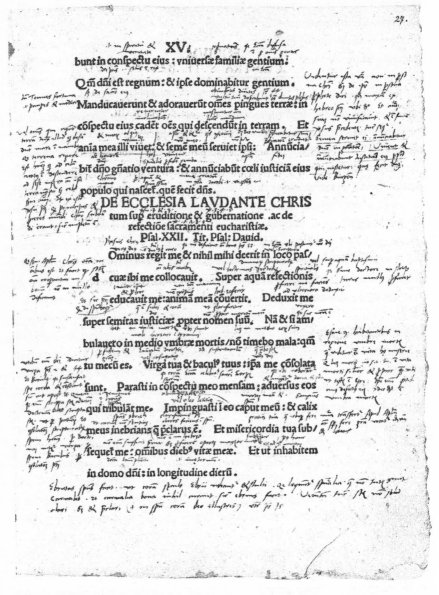

Figure 18. Manuscript of a lecture by Luther on the Psalms, 1513/15, in a Psalter printed with widely spaced lines.

not just reason, guiding interpretation. Luder followed such practices in his meditative contemplation of individual passages of Scripture. This approach allowed him to engage his emotions as he advanced through the text, and the understanding that he achieved through this unity of philological learning and meditative experience appeared to him both inspired and revelatory. And it bolstered his prophetic role, in which he was directly inspired by God.

The distinctive character of Luder's teaching came not just from his interpretative method but also from his selection of texts and the questions he asked of them. As he brought his own existential problems with God to the passages he interpreted, and with them his tormenting uncertainty about humankind's salvation from sinfulness, step by step both he and his audience acquired a new understanding of Scripture that created a paradigm shift in the sociology of knowledge. Subsequent generations would identify that experience as a revolutionary breakthrough into a new era, even into the modern age and modernity. For Luder himself the distinctive character of his achievement was very different—he looked back, to the past and to the original Christian and evangelical meaning of the word of God.

The sources do not enable us to reconstruct exactly when and how Luder's discovery, or rather rediscovery, took place. Suggestions in the literature vary greatly—from a sudden breakthrough or inspired moment of recognition before 1517 to a long-drawn-out process across the years, with the definitive turn to the Reformation coming only during the conflicts that followed the publication of the Ninety-Five Theses, so only after 1517. Since this issue lies at the very core of the Protestant identity, narratives of a mythical birth and other symbolic interpretations seem unavoidable. Launched by the reformer's stylized self-identification as a prophet of God who unmasked monks and popes as creatures of the devil, such accounts were part of the great mythical narratives of the nineteenth and twentieth centuries that celebrated Luder's breakthrough in terms of national or revolutionary progress and are found today in formulations of a modern theology of freedom.

For the historian, then, the question remains: when did Luder, as a monk in Wittenberg, become aware of how his thinking had shifted and of the fundamental break with traditional theology and the traditional church legitimized by that shift? Here again the sources provide us with no simple answer. We have no records—a diary, for example—to provide us with an *histoire intellectuelle*. Not that we have reason to expect that Luder would have recorded such self-reflection when located in the spiritual and intellectual context in which he found himself, as a monk, in his early years at Wittenberg. Luther's first substantial published personal reflection, provided in the preface to the first volume of his collected Latin works, is dated March 1545, only a year before his death; otherwise, we have only scattered comments found in his letters and his Table Talk, most of which also come from the later years of his life. Much attention has been given to Luther's accounts of a sudden moment of awareness that struck him like a flash of lightning as he was immersed in contemplation of Paul's words in Romans 1:17 on the justification of God. That moment, relayed to us second-hand by Luther's companions around the table, has dominated interpretation up to the present day. The setting is variously described in the Table Talk as the tower or the toilet, and sometimes both, so for example, 'The Holy Spirit gave me this realization in the cloaca'; 'The Holy Spirit unveiled the Scriptures for me in this tower.'[3] Both opponents and supporters eagerly seized upon the description: where the former ridiculed the Reformation as 'toilet theology', the latter revered the 'tower experience'.

The preface of 1545 contained Luther's authoritative version of an event that now lay over twenty-five years in the past. Luther no longer made specific reference to a definitive experience in the tower or on the toilet. There is reason, then, to chalk up his earlier comments in convivial company to the earthy language and coarse humour so loved by the Wittenberg patriarch, a mode of speech that only grew more common as he came to see himself as the founding father of the new church. The account provided by the preface was intended not for his immediate friends but for the contemporary public and for posterity. In place of a sudden revelatory experience, it described a difficult process during which Luder had freed himself from established ways and ingrained errors. According to Luther's account:

> I had then already read and taught the sacred Scriptures most diligently privately and publicly for seven years, so that I knew them nearly all by memory. I had also acquired the beginnings of the knowledge of Christ and faith in him, i.e. not by works but by faith in Christ are we made righteous and saved. Finally . . . I had already defended the proposition publicly that the pope is not the head of the church by divine right. Nevertheless, I did not draw the conclusion, namely, that the pope must be of the devil.

In Luder's account this internal maturation with its new understanding of God and Christ continued up until at least 1520, suggesting that his Reformation theology was also a later development: in 1520, he wrote, armed by his work for his earlier lectures, 'I began a second time to interpret the

Psalter. And the work would have grown into a large commentary, if I had not again been compelled to leave the work begun, because Emperor Charles V in the following year convened the diet at Worms', thus breaking off in response to his citation to appear at Worms.[4] The conflict over indulgences and the clashes with the sacramentarians and with other dissenters in his own camp that rapidly followed occupied Luther so greatly that the Reformation no longer look shape in his professor's study but was crafted instead in public debate.

A careful reading of the preface reveals that the aging reformer made no direct link between the Ninety-Five Theses and the breakthrough of Reformation theology, with its new image of God and humankind, a link that is also absent from a very early explanatory account addressed to Staupitz in May 1518.[5] We have reason to think, indeed, that the indulgence controversy was entirely a product of late medieval theology. Retrospectively, too, when Luther explained his role in light of historical and contemporary theology in his preface to his commentary on Daniel published in 1530, the reformer distanced himself from any idea that the Ninety-Five Theses marked a sudden breakthrough:

> We all reached that point gauchely and awkwardly . . . for I too had even been looking for something different and when I began to write I thought namely only of the misuse of the indulgence, not of the indulgence itself, let alone the pope or any hair of the pope. I understood neither Christendom nor the pope correctly . . . for we were ourselves at that time papists and antichrists.[6]

The 'tower experience'—should we choose to retain an image so beloved by Protestants—must then be placed somewhat later, in spring 1518 before the composition of that letter to Staupitz. To celebrate 31 October 1517 as Reformation Day is to use an external event rather than the internal logic of emerging Lutheran theology as a benchmark, certainly if we go by Luther's own account of his self-realization.

Protestant historians of theology who, despite Luther's later witness, date the decisive Reformation turn much earlier, to the first years in which he taught at Wittenberg, do so on the basis of what we know of his early lectures and of sermon drafts by the professor-monk, where elements of his Reformation thinking can be found. While such detailed analysis of the sources after the fact is welcome, we must be wary of jumping to conclusions about an early theological breakthrough. In May 1516, in his role as provincial vicar Luder attended the consecration of the new Augustinian monastery in Eisleben, the town of his birth. On that occasion he responded to God's presence and to what he took to be God's irresistible justice for the sinner with fear and terror. It seems that over the years, as he studied Scripture, lectured, and provided pastoral care, Luder felt his way cautiously towards a new awareness, until suddenly, in spring 1518, the implications for his search for God became clear.

Two key texts document this moment of realization: it is expressed theologically in his sermon on double justification[7] apparently given on Palm Sunday, 28 March 1518, in the town church at Wittenberg; and it is documented biographically in the letter to Staupitz of May 1518 noted above. From the midst of all the turbulence surrounding his Ninety-Five Theses, the reformer gave account of his recognition of the paradigm shift within his own theology and therefore—he was already clear about the connection—for Christian theology more generally. According to Luther, the realization that brought existential freedom stemmed from his work on the Psalms and as he 'beat importunately upon Paul'.[8]

Luder published his letter to Staupitz as the preface to one of his works explicating the Ninety-Five Theses.[9] In that letter he reminded his mentor and spiritual director of a pastoral conversation they had had—it is possible that Luder was referring to an event that occurred at the time of the consecration of the Eisleben monastery in 1516—in which Staupitz had encouraged him to understand the essential meaning of penance as 'love for justice and for God'. That thought, Luther wrote, had planted within him an idea or a word that stuck to him 'like the sharp arrow of the Mighty'.[10] The systematic search for passages on 'penance' initiated by that exchange had produced new insight into the relationship between personal imperfection, penance, and the justice of God, which when understood as the 'transform-ation of one's mind and disposition' enabled him to recognize that contri-tion about one's sinfulness was less 'an action than a change in disposition'. When exactly that thought came to him, and with it the related recognition of God's righteousness in Christ, the text does not reveal. His attack on indulgences, however, was evidently a product of this fundamental rework-ing of his theological categories:

> While this thought was still agitating me, behold, suddenly around us the new war trumpets of indulgences and the bugles of pardon started to sound, even to blast...In short, while the doctrine of the true poenitentia was neglected, they even dared to magnify not poenitentia—not even its least important part, which is called satisfaction—but only the remission of this least important part.

Since his youth Luder had been haunted by the nature of God's righteousness. As he wrestled with Romans 1:17, Luder now found assurance in an explanation that was closely related to his new understanding of penance: 'for there the righteousness of God is revealed, which comes from faith in faith, as is written, the righteous will live by faith'.[11] In his sermon on double justification, Luder now defined justification as justification through Christ, an idea that had developed out of Staupitz's pointing to the suffering Christ. Through faith in Christ, the righteousness of God becomes the righteousness that saves humankind, for faith and faith alone—*sola fide*—justifies humankind. Luder's despair had been deluded. God's justice does not doom humankind; God's justice saves humankind, despite, and even especially in view of, its sinfulness.

In spring 1518 the reformer recognized that he had uncovered the only sure path to salvation for himself and for all Christians. He immediately shared his discovery with his audience and with his readers, clearly and lucidly naming for the first time the spiritual essence of what would eventually be identified as Reformation: 'the knowledge of Christ and faith in him ... i.e. not by works but by faith in Christ are we made righteous and saved'—Luther's own words as he looked back from 1545.[12] A modern theologian might write of the Reformation's belief that in Christ, the Son of God, both human and divine, God has granted humankind unconditional justice, truth, and strength. In dialogue with the medieval theology of penance and theology of Christ as represented by Staupitz, and possibly influenced—here we can only speculate—by intense late medieval discussions of adjudication based on mercy rather than in accord with harsh legal strictures,[13] something qualitatively new had emerged from Luder's wrestling with human sinfulness. A fundamental transformation began to take shape not just for Christian devotion but for Christian culture as a whole and that process would have profound implications for the character of the modern era in Europe. Works-based spirituality and the devotional marketplace gave way to a piety based solely on faith and grace, with all the offerings of the late medieval church now appearing little more than salvific sticking plasters. For Luther and his supporters the certainty of salvation was found solely and freely in faith in Christ.

An Alternative Roman Reform

This fundamental shift was not a product of medieval calls for renewal or of a restoration of the Augustinian order that had run amuck. Precisely that distance from the in-house reform of the old system enabled the Augustinian monk in Wittenberg to establish the essential premises of a reformulated relationship between God and humankind that produced the Reformation's systemic change of church and world.

This qualitative difference—and where Luther broke with medieval reform—can be illustrated by turning our attention to the reform initiated in Rome in the same years. Rome's actions show that Luther's Reformation was not the only path that reform could take, for late medieval approaches to reform were concrete and innovative. This form of renewal did not split from the existing Roman system but instead provided both doctrine and ecclesiastical organization with a modern character. The reforms of the Roman Church were not nearly as fruitless and as empty as historians of the Reformation, so often confessionally Protestant, have frequently suggested. We need to acknowledge the existence of two distinct forms of religious and ecclesiastical transformation in the modern age—the radical break of the Wittenberg Reformation and the internal and system-loyal innovation of the Roman Church.

As the Augustinian monk in Wittenberg pondered the words of Paul, a group of clerics and highly educated laity in Rome came together to look for new, dynamic, and sincere forms of Christian expression, inspired, much like Luder, by discontent with the faith and piety of their age, as illustrated, for example, by the creation of the reformed Theatine Order. Unlike the German monk, however, these Italians had grown up in the embrace of the Roman curia, and thought of overturning the papal church would never have crossed their minds. Their vision was not of revolution but of a new stability, to be achieved by eliminating abuses and returning to the apostolic way of life. By the end of the fifteenth century a new push to make the Gospel the guiding principle for all of life was evident on the Apennine peninsula amongst both clergy and associated lay elites, who formed a grouping that has been termed, using the Italian, the *evangelismo*, or evangelicals. Unlike Luther a little later and Girolamo Savonarola, the Dominican monk who had preached repentance in Florence a little earlier, in the 1490s, the members of this grouping did not find in the Gospel grounds for overthrowing existing forms of church and society. Their concern was to ensure that the knowledge they gleaned from the Bible and the new spirituality that they then constructed were fully in accord with the teachings of the Roman Church.

The Oratory of Divine Love was a central component, in terms of personnel and institutionally, of this new reform phase at the beginning of the sixteenth century, as in Genoa and Rome clerics and laity came together to lead an apostolic life of brotherly love in Christ, reaching out to the poor and the oppressed. The statutes of the Oratory spoke not of pious works to be performed for the sake of the soul of the benefactor but of lived charity as an expression of God-given grace. In distancing themselves from the prevalent conception of the pious life, which valued good works above all else, this grouping had much in common with the early reforming impulses developed by Luther in distant Saxony.

Yet it would be misleading to speak of 'Opinions analogous to those of the Protestants entertained in Italy', the heading in the relevant chapter of Leopold von Ranke's *The History of the Popes during the Last Four Centuries* (in German, 1834–36). The fundamental difference is palpable: at the heart of the Italian reforms were the clergy themselves, whose spirituality, lifestyle, and education were all to be improved. When that core of the Roman Church was healed, when the priests themselves were transformed, then organically and immediately the healing of the laity would follow. Luther's concept was entirely different, for, as we will see, the reformer's understanding of grace meant that all the baptized were priests and there was no longer a distinct priestly estate or church.

The Theatines, founded in Rome in 1524 under the spiritual leadership of Venetian prelate Gaetano di Thiene and the strict disciplinary leadership of Gian Pietro Carafa, bishop of Chieti, and approved by the pope that same year, was a congregation of clerics regular, a community of religious who lived according to an established rule, in this case that of the Augustinians. The fundamental differences between their sense of self and their ecclesiastical-political goals and those of the Augustinian monk in Wittenberg are clearly evident in the exclusivity of the events that celebrated the formation of the order. Early on 24 September 1524 four priests entered the Basilica of Saint Peter in Rome: Gian Pietro Carafa of Naples, Gaetano di Thiene of Vicenza, Bonifacio de Colle of Alessandria, and Paolo Consiglieri of Rome. The four men celebrated Mass with Gian Battista Bonciano, the papal commissioner, in a side chapel, away from the crowds (!), and received communion. Together with the members of the cathedral chapter, they then moved to the high altar, where the papal commissioner knelt and was presented by Carafa with a papal bull, whose contents were read out. One after another, Carafa and the other three men declared publicly their obedience to the pope and his apostolic successors and took vows of poverty, chastity, and obedience. They had entered the basilica as secular clergy; having taken the most solemn vows, they left as 'regular', rule-following clergy.

Much like Luther's Reformation in Germany, this model of church reform also seemed highly plausible. Despite the adverse circumstances of its early years, in particular the Sack of Rome of 1527, when the Holy City was pillaged by the troops of Emperor Charles V, the new community grew quickly and developed its own reform dynamic within Italy and soon also farther afield. Although its activities were originally entirely independent of Luther, the order found that in addition to efforts on behalf of internal renewal, one of its principal tasks was participation in the dispute with the German Reformation as it sought to contain that movement. The Theatines—the name comes from 'Theate', the classical name of Carafa's bishop's see, Chieti—were qualified for this task not least by their very close ties since their foundation with the lay elite, from which spread their remarkable charismatic appeal to the laity of the church more broadly. That attractiveness to the laity was even greater for the second reform order, established in 1534 on similar theological foundations and according to similar ecclesiastical regulation—the Jesuits immediately stood at the forefront of internal reform.

In the long run the internal reform launched by the Theatines and the Jesuits would be no less successful than the Protestantism that originated with Luther and was moulded in their own distinct ways by other reformers, Calvin in particular. Both internal Catholic reform and Protestantism were formative for the confessional culture of early modern Europe. Ignatius of Loyola, the founder of the Jesuits, who left the greatest mark on his order and, as a result, on Catholic reform, can be placed alongside Luther and Calvin as the third reformer. In the decrees of the Council of Trent (1545–1563), which gave reform its dogmatic and organizational character, the Roman confessional church took shape, a church that just like Lutheranism and Calvinism should be understood historically as a new and early modern church.

This success story is bound up with a tale of enmity, power, damaging rejection, and even dictatorial arrogance. It would not be long before the pope became Antichrist for Luther and his followers, and Rome the Gomorrah of sacred history. In turn, the Roman reformers soon saw the Protestants as little more than heretics who were to be exterminated and even today are still denied recognition as a church. The personification of this perversion of the original character of reform was none other than Gian Pietro Carafa himself: three decades after he had launched a process of reform that had many parallels with that of Luther, as Pope Paul IV (1555–1559) he had become the merciless enemy of the Protestants; as pope he established the Index listing forbidden books and sharpened the sword of the Inquisition. 'And if my own father was a heretic', he is said to have declared, 'I would still gather the wood needed that he might be burned.'[14] His regime of terror was too great even for Romans now so used to their Renaissance popes: after his death they damned his memory, tore down his statues, and set fire to the building that had housed his inquisition.

The Ninety-Five Theses—Myth and Reality

We return to Wittenberg. Confronted with the light documentation of the course of events, Luther's subsequent interpretation, and the Reformation remembrances of later centuries, the biographer must distinguish between external events, internal developments, and growing awareness of the revolutionary character of Reformation ideas. Generations of research on Luther and on the Reformation have left little reason to doubt that at different times these three elements were bound together in complex ways and that they did not generate one definitive moment of reformation.

For the progression of external events, the indulgence issue faced by Luder in late summer 1517 as both professor of Bible and parish priest in Wittenberg has always been deemed decisive. Indulgences, part of the church's penitential system, had been developed theologically and canonically in the high Middle Ages. Humankind was separated from God by its sins, and each individual should expect to receive punishment for those sins, punishment that was described in sermons and stories and depicted in the great frescos of the Gothic cathedrals, as at Albi, with its terrifying hellish abyss into which plummeted those who had not been relieved of their sins. The church mitigated some of the existential fears generated by such images when it held out to the faithful the possibility of working off in this life, through pious acts of penance, time that would need to be spent in the torments of hell in order for the soul to be purified. Comfort could also be gained from the performance of penance for the remission of the sins of someone who had already died. Luder had been eager to acquire indulgences for dead relatives when he was in Rome.

For Luder, as for many others at the start of the sixteenth century, much consolation was found in indulgences, with their simple and dependable guarantee of relief from overwhelming anxiety about the salvation of the living and of those who had already died. While the church's offer of grace was therefore accepted eagerly, its very popularity encouraged a much-simplified understanding of the theologically challenging teaching on indulgences. Just as the indulgence was becoming banal, demonstrations of status by the ruling elites—and not just the secular elite, but also the elite of the church, above all the Renaissance popes in Rome—were becoming characteristic of the age. Early capitalism in the form of the mercantile capitalism born in Italy was not at all reticent about designing fiscal tools that could be used to raise the funds needed to build up ecclesiastical centres, both Rome itself and within the Empire. An unholy alliance was formed between early modern financial wizardry and the pastoral needs of the people. Inevitably the indulgence was tainted by association. This apparently God-given gift to the Renaissance popes, which would feed their hunger for works of art and new buildings and answer all their financial worries, proved to be an explosive charge laid in the heart of the Roman Church.

As we know—staying with our analogy for the moment—the fuse was lit in Wittenberg and the blast that followed blew apart the medieval indulgence system within only a few months, at least in Germany. That explosion was without doubt a result of the Ninety-Five Theses, published in autumn 1517. Luder's attack on indulgences was by no means as original as the memorialization of Luther and Protestant church histories would soon pronounce. A receptive audience for the Ninety-Five Theses was waiting, making possible the rapid spread of Luder's ideas. Amongst the more educated, both clerical and lay, the indulgence had already lost much of its appeal. In some places the population was already exhibiting what has been termed an increasing disdain for the indulgence, although not in Brandenburg and Saxony in central Germany.[15] Hard financial data brings that picture greater detail: in the lands of the Lower Rhine and in the Low Countries, where the Reformation enthusiasm that followed the publication of the Ninety-Five Theses made little headway, even before Luder entered the scene, great ecclesiastical construction projects had been financed no longer by indulgences but by charitable offerings instead.

The theological protest by the Augustinian monk in Wittenberg, which was largely independent of his contemporaries' criticism of indulgences, was a sign of solidarity with the church and highly traditional views; it was not evidence of the revolutionary mentality attributed to Luther by later followers and by many scholars of the Reformation. In spring 1517 Luder had suddenly encountered the indulgence issue in concrete form. His concern was not with the teaching on indulgence, but with how it was being applied. Specifically, he was exasperated by the indulgence campaign being run near Wittenberg by Johannes Tetzel, a Dominican monk, and his colleagues. They were not permitted to preach the indulgence in Wittenberg itself, for Elector Frederick feared a substantial drain of cash and summarily prohibited them from entering his lands, but Wittenberg lay on the edge of his Saxon territory, and the residents of the town could easily make their way instead to neighbouring Brandenburg or into the bishopric of Magdeburg, to Jüterbog, for example, to hear the indulgence preached and acquire an indulgence certificate. Many were all the more willing to make the trip when Tetzel and his agents drummed up business by simplifying the complex teaching on indulgences, claiming that the certificate of indulgence gave direct access to heaven; officially the church spoke only of remission of part of the time that was to be spent in purgatory as punishment for sin. Some preachers were said to have made the audacious claim that armed with the indulgence, individuals could sin to their heart's content.

The immediate controversy over the indulgence was a product of the preaching of those selling indulgences and the contradiction between the church's financial needs and its pastoral responsibilities. Those who preached the indulgence were Dominicans; their critics were Augustinian Hermits—it seemed that at the end of 1517 another of those internal conflicts was looming that had so often shaken the medieval church with its colourful array of priests, monks, and innumerable roles somewhere between church and world, conflicts that had always somehow been resolved in the end. An additional twist in this case stemmed from the political enmity of Electoral Saxony, on one hand, and Brandenburg and Magdeburg, on the other, but such rivalry was hardly remarkable in central Germany and bore no clue that the church in its present form might be overthrown. The novelty of the situation that meant that the 'squabbling of monks at the ends of civilization' shook the Latin church and the world it wrought to their foundations was a result—in retrospect we might say an inevitable result—of two idiosyncrasies of the events of 1517: Luder's personality and the advanced financial economy of the curia and the church hierarchy in the Empire.

Our earliest detailed account of how Martin Luder was confronted by Tetzel's indulgence-selling operation comes from a history of the Reformation written in 1541 by Friedrich Myconius, superintendent of the church in Gotha.[16] The hero of this narrative, still found today in accounts of the Reformation attack on indulgences, is neither the university theologian of Luder's early years in Wittenberg nor the preacher who had already been active for some years at the town church; its chief protagonist is Luder the pastor, of whom we find very little trace in contemporary sources. While hearing confession, Myconius relates, the Augustinian monk learned of Tetzel's crass distortion of the indulgence and, believing the salvation of the members of his community entrusted to his care under threat, reacted immediately. According to the 1541 account, penitents who had acquired a letter of indulgence outside Saxony had demanded absolution from Luder without showing any contrition and without performing the required penance.

This episode is a central feature of the image of their own 'church father' that mid-sixteenth-century Protestants sought to paint: Luther was depicted as an engaged pastor protective of the souls entrusted to him who was pierced to the core by this defiant refusal to do penance because precisely in these weeks he had been contemplating the nature of penance and its role in his own salvation and in the salvation of every Christian. As he sought in heartfelt inner atonement relief from his fears of the unrelenting God of judgement, he encountered a flippant lack of respect for penance amongst the preachers of this indulgence, which put at risk the sinner's access to the God of grace. Luder's problem was not that money was being spent on a worthless piece of paper; his distress was a result of discovering that individuals under his pastoral care had been tempted away from true repentance and therefore from the only secure route to salvation, and that the culprits were representatives of the church, complicit in exploiting as a marketing ploy the sinner's unwillingness to do penance. As sinners came to believe in a false certainty of salvation, the real certainty of their eternal damnation became all the greater. The Augustinian monk's involvement was twofold—as an individual already wrestling with his own salvation and as pastor at the parish church in Wittenberg.

But we must pause. If we return again to the sources, and in particular to the reformer's own statements, we find that his argument with indulgences was a product not of his pastoral responsibilities—carried out only exceptionally and infrequently by Luder in these years—but of his theological labours. The Ninety-Five Theses were the work of a university professor whose principal concern was not with practical theology but with the teachings of Scripture. His uncompromising approach and ability to disregard the interests or sensitivities of others can be seen in the biographical context of the break that he brought about. A long decade of serious and uncompromising searching for God had left him decisively hot or cold, with no tolerance for the lukewarm; here were the roots of his famous declaration, soon to follow, 'Here I stand, I can do no differently.' Such categorical thinking and action undoubtedly stemmed from Luder's background and circumstances, but above all they were products of his training as an academic theologian, specifically his great familiarity with Scripture, largely acquired through self-study outwith the academic curriculum.

Luder's own account, recorded in a Table Talk, relates that when the monk heard of Tetzel's 'heinous claim' that the indulgence he was offering would even free from the fires of purgatory someone who had seduced the Virgin Mary and made her pregnant, his response took two forms: he sought to discourage the acquisition of the indulgence, and he began intensive research in order to establish a clearer picture of the church's teaching on indulgences and its Scriptural foundations.[17] Luder thus gathered up the indulgence issue, at first glance a matter of practical theology, and transported it into his study for examination under his scholarly microscope. His first step had to be to turn to Scripture. The Wittenberg community were the first to learn of the discoveries he had made in his study, announced from the pulpit, but in summer 1517 Luder addressed a broader academic audience through the publication of his 'Treatise on Indulgences' (*Tractatus de indulgentiis*), a copy of which could be found in the library of the archbishop of Mainz. Soon after, in October 1517, he believed his scholarly grasp of the issues surrounding indulgences to be sufficiently firm to be set out in a run of ninety-five theses. He was so certain of his findings that he immediately had his comprehensive examination of current indulgence practice printed in poster form. The first of these theses makes evident that his concerns were rooted in the theology of penance: 'When our Lord and Master Jesus Christ said "Repent", he willed the entire life of believers to be one of repentance.'

In his theses, Brother Martin made no mention of the fiscal implications of Tetzel's indulgence-selling business or of its ties to the politics of the church—the second idiosyncrasy of the constellation formed in 1517. Luder paid them no attention, but he also could not have paid them any attention because they were known to only a very small circle. The Jubilee Indulgence announced by Pope Julius II at the beginning of the new century and recently, in March 1515, renewed by his successor Leo X bore all the marks of its age—profit maximization, cash payments as penance, and a rational, strategically planned campaign. Every individual who got on board could expect to profit—the simple preacher, indulgence-selling strategists Johannes Tetzel and his colleagues, the primate of Germany and his bankers in Augsburg, and the pope himself. As the profits would be spread so thinly, however, it was all the more necessary that those profits be substantial, for otherwise there would be little left to make its way up the chain to Rome.

The curia needed the funds to finance the modernization of Rome, the papal residence city, and for the modification and new construction at the Vatican of Saint Peter's in particular, which was to be turned into a triumphalist basilica that would broadcast the eminence of the papal church. Cardinal Albrecht of Brandenburg, archbishop of Mainz and as primate of Germany another leading authority within Christendom, was also interested in the fundraising potential of the indulgence. Albrecht owed a huge debt of some 50,000 gulden to the Fuggers, bankers in Augsburg, a figure more than a hundred times greater than the annual salary of a respected professor. The archbishop, a member of the Hohenzollern family, had paid the curia 24,000 gold ducats when he was appointed archbishop of Mainz. In part that sum was the *pallium*, paid on taking up office by every archbishop and named after the broad white woollen band decorated with black embroidered crosses, blessed by the pope, that they received as a sign of their new status, but in part that sum was also payment for exemption from the ban in church law on the accumulation of offices. Albrecht was already archbishop of Magdeburg. Although canon law prohibited one individual from holding two archbishop's seats simultaneously, that rule might be set aside by a pricey papal dispensation.

In the indulgence that would finance the rebuilding of Saint Peter's, Albrecht identified an opportunity to pay off at a stroke all the debts he had accumulated in order to acquire the Mainz archbishopric. In exchange for permitting the sale of the indulgence in his two dioceses, Albrecht received from the curia the right to retain one half of all the funds the indulgence raised. In January 1517 he placed the practical organization of the sale in the hands of Johannes Tetzel, a Dominican monk much experienced in such matters. With the support of a band of colleagues, over the following months Tetzel sold the indulgence in the Hohenzollern territories in central Germany, so in the archbishopric of Magdeburg and in electoral Brandenburg, ruled by Albrecht's brother Joachim I. If we were to set aside the religious implications, we could speak of a fiscally impressive undertaking, with both curia and archbishop full of the spirit of early mercantile capitalism. But the flow of cash was tied in with Christian salvation, bringing a religious component to the whole affair that had marked parallels with the *montes pietatis*, the money-lending institutions of the north Italian states, which united Christian compassion and capitalist business acumen. This overlapping of religion and revenue would be shattered by Luder when he insisted on the autonomy of salvation and of religion more generally, establishing in the process new and modern foundations for both religion and economic affairs.

The fiscal and political connections to the sale of the indulgence had largely been kept secret, known to few contemporaries and certainly not to a monk in a remote provincial university. Yet Luder would hardly have acted differently had that link been known to him. Worldly tactical thinking was completely alien to him, and the penitence issue too serious. Still, his ignorance enabled him to think and act with a guileless vehemence and openness that would impress an impartial observer today. Later, once he had broken with Rome, he saw in the capitalist finances of the curia only the work of Satan, while his background and the monastic ideals to which he had subscribed predisposed him to reject the mercantile capitalism that developed in southern Germany and from there reached out across the Empire.

In late summer 1517, as Luder was working on his theses against Dominican Johannes Tetzel's preaching of the indulgence, the idea that he might be taking on the authority of the pope would not even have crossed his mind. The theses were drawn up in the service of a search for truth undertaken within academe and within the church. The display of the theses was not the revolutionary act envisaged by posterity by the time of the first centenary in 1617 and above all in the revolution-obsessed nineteenth century. Whether the theses really were made public, let alone nailed up, on 31 October 1517, All Saints' Eve in Wittenberg, was long in doubt. The reformer never spoke of such an act. Only much later did reports of the nailing up of the theses emerge, and they came from individuals who had not even been in Wittenberg in 1517. Recent discoveries in the sources have revealed it to be more likely that the Ninety-Five Theses were indeed posted on the door of the castle church, but even then, the context was very different from that constructed by the rhetoric of a Protestant revolution, with its hammer-swinging monk. The display of the theses was intended to disseminate information and initiate discussion in a form common across the universities of Europe, where an academic disputation would be announced along with a call to debate specific theses with their author. The professor himself would have been highly unlikely to have taken hold of a hammer to nail up his theses on the church door; that was rather the task of the beadle, who would have posted the announcement at a spot already designated for such communications. The process was so standard that the reformer never saw the need to make any great fuss about it.

Luder intended his theses to be read by colleagues and acquaintances, an audience comprising humanistically educated monks, clerics, students, and laypersons who were interested in theology, a leading intellectual activity of their time, and were looking for new ways to develop education, art, and learning. Luder turned penance and its false portrayal in the preaching of the indulgence into an intellectual problem and a topic for the educated elite to tackle. He covered no new ground in his theses, for his correspondence with Staupitz and Johannes Lang and with Georg Spalatin in particular had repeatedly addressed and examined in detail pivotal theological themes such as penance, righteousness, the grace of God, and the conditions for salvation. That the indulgence issue reached a wider audience and was the catalyst for the events that followed had little to do with the content of the theses and much to do with the way in which that content was communicated. Luder had one of the printers in Wittenberg—probably via the print shop run on the ground floor of the Augustinian monastery—produce what was in effect a poster depicting the Ninety-Five Theses, intended to publicize an upcoming disputation, which never took place. Long before the printing storm unleashed by the Reformation, the Wittenberg professor of Bible, now thirty-four years old, was evidently well aware of how to make use of modern media.

That the theses were sent out from Wittenberg to other locations was also not uncommon. The previous year Luder had had distributed a series of theses for a debate at the University of Wittenberg over which he had presided, sending them, for example, to his friend Johannes Lang in Erfurt.[18] When the indulgence theses of October 1517 were distributed and discussed throughout the Empire without Luder's direct involvement, Christoph Scheurl, a humanist in Nuremberg, expressed his disappointment that his Wittenberg friend had not sent him a copy.[19]

In the specific instance of the planned disputation on indulgences, Luder seems to have foregone sending out the published theses, because—according to his answer to a question Scheurl had put to him in the letter mentioned above—he did not deem the academic theses suitable for teaching the people. He noted he had 'my doubts myself about some things'; had he reckoned on publication by a third party, he 'would have put other things very differently or claimed them more strongly or left them out altogether'.[20]

Somehow the text produced in Wittenberg arrived in the hands of printers elsewhere. They sensed an opportunity and their reprints were soon to be found throughout the Empire. The rest was the work of a communication network made up of humanist and other educated circles, independent of the church, whose members eagerly took up the published text and made it part of public debate. For as yet unexplained reasons, Luder's call for a debate gained no traction at the university in Wittenberg, but his theses had left the narrow academic confines to be taken up in Christendom more broadly. Just one or two generations earlier, this material, disseminated slowly but surely, would have fed only academic discussion; now, conveyed in print and through humanist correspondence, in just a matter of weeks that same material generated a public event. A mighty debate over the cultural and intellectual foundations of a whole civilization had been launched.

Luder had passed on the theses only within the relevant church hierarchy, sending letters dated 31 October 1517 to Bishop Hieronymus Schulz in Brandenburg, in whose diocese Wittenberg lay, and to Schulz's superior, the archbishop of Magdeburg, Albrecht of Brandenburg.[21] He could do so without inhibition and in all innocence, for he knew nothing of the double archbishop's personal stake in the sale of the indulgence.

According to the memorialization of the Reformation initiated during Luther's lifetime and for modern historians, too, the Ninety-Five Theses changed the world. There is therefore good reason to mark 31 October as Reformation Day. Looking back, Luther repeatedly stressed that his theses on the indulgence were not a trumpet blast that brought down the walls of the papacy. As we have seen, essential components of his innovative theology were developed only in the months that followed. This theological radicalization was built in, however, to his position on indulgences. He had initiated a chain reaction that could not be halted—the dominoes were now falling, one after another: the inevitable entry onto the public stage of Germany and Christendom of a monk who had previously had only a local or regional presence; that monk's condemnation by the curia as a heretic; his progression, made inevitable by the curia's verdict, to reformer and founder of an anti-Roman evangelical church. Yet these falling dominoes were the product of an elastic historical constellation that embraced personal and political interests and concerns.

'Thrashing Alone at the Papists'

Only in late November 1517 did Albrecht of Brandenburg, the most important of those who had been sent Luder's letter and Ninety-Five Theses, turn his attention to that material. He was staying in Aschaffenburg, a secondary residence for the Mainz archbishopric. It would never have crossed Albrecht's mind to respond to the theological content, partly because, although he had received a humanist education, he was no theologian, and partly because he was not willing to put the restoration of his financial well-being at risk. Additionally, as a Hohenzollern he was automatically bound into the dynastic rivalry with the Saxon Wettins and was therefore little inclined to give that family's new university the academic seal of approval by deigning to enter into a dispute with one of its professors. He did not respond directly to the material he had been sent by Luder, but he did do all he could to put a stop to the monk's activities. The first step was to acquire a negative assessment from his own university in Mainz, and he ordered his councillors to launch a *processus inhibitorius*, in effect a cease-and-desist order. At the same time he sent the printed text on the indulgence to Rome in order that the curia be kept informed. The curia in turn did not appear particularly alarmed; their only concern was that any disagreement might turn into one of the numerous perilous clashes between religious orders. The vicar general of the Augustinian Hermits was instructed to ensure the German monk returned to his senses as quickly as possible and to order him to keep silent, reminding him of his vow of obedience.

The first reaction Luder faced came not from Mainz, then, but from Frankfurt an der Oder, in Brandenburg territory, and was a matter for the academy, not the church. Initially the Dominicans were also keen to avoid direct confrontation and discouraged Tetzel from pursuing a legal case against the Augustinian monk in Wittenberg for his slanderous misrepresentation of Tetzel's preaching of the indulgence. The disagreement was formulated instead as a falling out between scholars, and therefore in early 1518 Tetzel used a disputation at the university in Frankfurt, which had strong ties to the Hohenzollern family, as the opportunity to prove that the sale of the indulgence was justified. The theses for this disputation, immediately printed on a single sheet and distributed throughout Germany, were formulated not by the Dominican monk but by a theologian at Frankfurt, Konrad Wimpina (Koch), an old opponent of Martin Pollich's, first rector of the university at Wittenberg. The rivalry between these two young institutions had become intermingled with a scholarly debate over the theological significance of the indulgence.

If those in Frankfurt had hoped that their theses would isolate the rebel monk in Wittenberg, they were soon sorely disappointed. Their refutation blew wind into the sails of the dispute, especially in Wittenberg, where, in mid-March 1518, students ripped the opposing theses out of the hands of the sellers and burned the sheets of paper—reportedly no fewer than 800 copies—in the market square. Although their action was a remarkable demonstration of support, Luder was not overly happy, as the students' response smacked of rioting, in which he might be implicated.[22] Tetzel's Dominican order kept the ball rolling, and in September 1518 the Roman curia's procurator fiscal launched heresy proceedings against the Augustinian monk in Wittenberg.

Initially that method seemed a dead letter, for with the death of Emperor Maximilian in January 1519 proceedings ground to a halt. The curia was concerned to ensure that Maximilian's successor in the highest temporal office in Christendom would be sympathetic to the interests of Rome, and their candidate was none other than the Saxon elector himself, Frederick the Wise, Luder's ruler. It hardly seemed the right moment to antagonize their desired candidate with a peremptory process against his own Wittenberg professor. Whether Martin Luder was a heretic remained unresolved, and in the meantime his Reformation had the time it needed to put down roots and begin to grow.

Luder's indulgence theses set off a chain reaction with a run of remarkable events that changed the church and the world. The theses also forced their author into a new existence in new circumstances. He was transformed personally, in a process that Luder celebrated as the birth of a new man: while the church hierarchy remained silent and Luder could only speculate on where his letter might lead, the Augustinian monk became famous, first in Germany and soon even farther afield. The days of self-referentiality, the days in which his attention was focused above all on his own salvation, those days were now over. Or rather his personal fears and his spiritual and intellectual strategies for overcoming and resolving those fears were now out in the world as models for millions of his fellow Christians. His activities were no longer contained within the lecture hall and his study, although those locations remained the setting for his intellectual endeavours and his writing. At the forefront now were his public debates with the most sophisticated scholars of his day and the pre-eminent political figures in the church. He would need to draw on all his talents as a shrewd and confident debater and writer, and he would have to prove his determination and self-confidence in situations that were both dangerous and highly political, even to the extent of appearing before his Emperor and the Empire. The Wittenberg monk advanced the theology of the Reformation through public debates, and his participation made him a celebrity in Germany and soon also beyond the bounds of the Empire. In the course of these debates he developed a style and an originality of expression that he retained until the end of his life.

Initially this new phase in Luder's life was as far from triumphal as could be. 'Everyone left me to thrash at the papists on my own,' he would recall later, not without bitterness.[23] He did receive enthusiastic encouragement from some quarters: Albrecht Dürer for one, who had informed Luder via Spalatin that he felt a strong urge 'to come to Dr Martinus and assiduously portray him in a copper engraving, to create a lasting memory of this Christian man who has helped me escape great fears'.[24] But endorsement throughout the Empire and at all social levels only increased Luder's burden. He alone would determine whether his criticisms would lead to the redefinition of the Christian experience for which so many people longed or whether his challenge would run into the sand, as had been the case for so many earlier attempts at reform. During these days he was not at all certain that he would be able to finish what he had begun. He feared he had overextended himself, for now all the world wanted a clear statement in the indulgence debate on precisely those points where, he had written, 'some things remain doubtful to me', thereby 'expecting something greater of me than I can achieve'.[25]

Despite all his activity, these were months of great loneliness, perhaps the loneliest of Luder's life. Step by step he left behind the spiritual and material security afforded him by the teachings of the Roman Church and membership of the Augustinian order, security that had always been there, whatever doubts and crises he had faced. Additionally, he increasingly no longer felt sustained by the proven theological and pastoral support of his mentor Staupitz, on which he had long depended. It would be some years before he would find such support again, in the secular environment formed by his colleagues and family.

Yet precisely in those unsettling and menacing weeks and months of the indulgence controversy, Luder became aware of the breakthrough he had achieved. He developed a different sense of self as he grasped the life's task that had fallen to him. His newly recognized relationship with God had made him a new person, a man who felt himself emphatically free. He gave expression to this new self-consciousness in a new name. Between November 1517 and January 1519 he signed letters to close friends such as Johannes Lang, prior in Erfurt, and Melanchthon, his colleague in Wittenberg, with the designation 'Eleutherios'.[26] Ostensibly Luder had adopted a Greek form of his existing name, as was common amongst humanists, to produce a scholarly pseudonym. But the new name carried a distinct message, for it expressed the mission of its bearer: 'Eleutherios', the free one—the one who had been liberated and, at the same time, the one who would liberate. As it became clear that Luder would not remain simply a scholar or a man of the church, but had been sent, as it were, for the salvation of all mankind, the liberator abandoned the Greek form of his name, incomprehensible to most people. He preserved, however, a reminder of the freedom that was at the heart of reformed theology: the central *th* in the Greek form of his name was carried over into his family name. Martin Luder became Martin Luther, the name with which he became famous.

For historians the change in name is all the more significant because it provides one of the very few immediate signs of Luther's sense of self during the early years of the Reformation. His testimony about this period is very largely of a later date and often of a much later date and is therefore overlaid with retrospective meaning. The name change brings home to us that our subject had become a new person, for the man who had been Luder was now Luther.

First, this 'new' Luther was a publicist who spoke the language of the people. Up until 1517/18, Luder the professor of Bible in Wittenberg had to show for himself only what, even by the academic standards of his age, was a rather short list of publications. He was practically unknown as an author. In keeping with contemporary academic convention he had published largely in Latin. The few items he had already published in German—the 1516 preface for his edition of the *Theologia deutsch*; his 1517 exposition of the penitential psalms, in effect the first book he authored—were heavy-handed and did little to engage the reader. His personal crisis was precisely a *personal* crisis, and in keeping with the traditional practice of Western monasticism, he had dealt with it discreetly; it was not a matter for a wider public. His responsibilities as a professor were focused entirely on his students at Wittenberg. Even the Ninety-Five Theses themselves were a product of the narrow tradition of academic writing and were not intended for wider consumption. When news reached Luther that they could be found, and were being read, throughout Germany, he immediately insisted that he had intended his text only as material to be debated 'with a few people who live with and around us'.[27]

Once the theses had escaped their narrower academic and ecclesiastical confines, they developed their own dynamic amongst a different readership. Their author had little choice but to accept this new situation, and now, for the sake of his cause, Luther was forced to change his ways. No longer were his ideas formulated for his colleagues and his students; his primary audience had become a large and public readership. From now on his truth was not truth in a scholarly sense but the truth that would speak to the people 'alone and above all'—an approach that was very much in keeping with his new identity and its associations with freedom. For the sake of that truth he was ready, if necessary, to compromise the ingrained humility of his years as a monk—while humbleness remained a guiding principle, it was not evident in how he addressed and appeared to the broader public. He justified his attitude in a typically personal and revealing letter to his friend Johannes Lang in Erfurt: 'If I am presumptuous, the truth will not become worthless because of my presumption . . . Even if humility itself were to begin something new, then it would immediately be accused of arrogance by those who think differently.' It is no coincidence that this letter was the first he signed 'Martinus Eleutherius'. With a newfound assuredness, he insisted that humankind was inherently helpless, that God alone was the source of truth and his own actions, recording, 'It is not my intention that what I do should stem from human effort or counsel, but rather from that of God. For if the work comes from God, who will stand in its way? And if it is not of God, who can support it?'[28] During the weeks that followed the publication of his theses, he developed the existential anchoring of the truth and of his person that would enable him to hold firm even when challenged by Emperor and pope and buffeted by storms in his own camp involving fanatics, Anabaptists, and rebellious peasants.

Luther felt 'forced to demonstrate the proof of my theses' in order to bring the truth not just to small academic or ecclesiastical circles but also '*vulgo*', to the people.[29] Where at much the same time Erasmus the humanist spoke of the '*populus christianus*' as a supranational Christendom, for Luther that 'Christian people' was above all his own people, to whom he had been sent as a prophet. He believed he had been called to write in German, and specifically in the Saxon–southern German of his homeland and in a form intended for the general populace, a style that was therefore very different from that of his academic theses. Luther threw himself into this task in the first months of 1518, and from a standing start he very soon mastered this new art, an achievement that is all the more remarkable in light of his lack of experience as an author. This success served only to convince him all the more that he was God's mouthpiece. In early March he announced the publication of 'a small book in the German language about the value of the indulgence' in order to resolve 'all that is uncertain about the theses'.[30] The reference was to his 'Sermon on Indulgence and Grace' (*Sermon von Ablass und Gnade*), which soon appeared in German and did far more than the Ninety-Five Theses themselves to spread awareness amongst the faithful of his attack on the indulgence. Although the Latin text of his 'Resolutions of the Dispute Regarding the Efficacy of Indulgences' (*Resolutiones disputationum de indulgentiarum virtute*), which provided further explanation of his indulgence theses, was also already largely complete, that work was published only in August 1518, as permission to print from the bishop of Brandenburg, in whose diocese Wittenberg lay, was delayed. Significantly, as yet Luther was not prepared to act without authorization.

Secondly, this new Luther was Luther the polemist. To counter his opponents, but above all to illuminate the content of his new theology, he was prepared to use cutting and vulgar formulations, whether very deliberately or as a natural product of his temperament. In so doing he brought the crassness of the language of his time to a new high. Some have seen in his language evidence of 'his personality and experience', deeming it 'an expression of the fullness and emotional richness of his life united with a sober spirit and intellectual perspicuity that demonstrated a heightened sense of responsibility and inner tribulation'.[31] His language was certainly an unmistakable sign of an increasingly entrenched characteristic: his utter certainty that he spoke the truth of the Gospel and that as a prophet of God he was participating in the End Time battle with the devil and his allies.

The robust and popular style of the writings of the Augustinian monk in Wittenberg reached a first climax when deployed in the great Reformation treatises 'The Freedom of the Christian' (*Freiheit eines Christenmenschen*) and 'To the Christian Nobility of the German Nation' (*An den Christlichen Adel deutscher Nation*). That his style ran counter to the conventions of the age and attracted the attention of the scholarly world is evident from the response of Erasmus of Rotterdam, previously unchallenged as the leading voice amongst intellectuals. In May 1521 Erasmus addressed a letter to Justus Jonas, a colleague of Luther's in Wittenberg, which he intended for circulation amongst humanists within the Empire. He criticized Luther's indignity, for Luther, Erasmus wrote, 'has poured it all out at once, making everything public and giving even cobblers a share in what is normally handled by scholars as mysteries reserved for the initiated'.[32]

Thirdly, this new Luther was a radical opponent of pope and Roman Church. At the time he formulated his theses on the indulgence, Luther still believed that Christian freedom could be realized within the church and that the pope could undertake the necessary reforms. Looking back in 1545 the elderly reformer accused his younger self of having 'much...and important matters... conceded to the pope in my earlier writings', because he had not immediately drawn 'the conclusion, namely, that the pope must of necessity be of the devil. For what is not of God must of necessity be of the devil.'[33] In summer 1518 he had written confidently, 'This Christ is the judge whose verdict I am awaiting through the Roman See', and he had prefixed his 'Resolutions' with a personal dedication to Leo X (Figure 19).[34]

Luther was forced to reconceive the evangelical ordering of the church as Reformation only because of the actions of the German episcopacy, in the person of Albrecht of Brandenburg, archbishop of Mainz, and the Roman curia. These definitive years in the *causa Lutheri*, the 'Luther Affair', ran from 1517 to June 1520, when the papal bull threatening Luther with excommunication was issued. In October 1518, when he appeared in Augsburg before Thomas Cajetan, the cardinal legate, Luther had already challenged the papal authority of the keys. In 1520 he recorded the definitive and radical break: 'We here [in Wittenberg] are convinced that the papacy is the seat of the true and incarnate Antichrist, and we believe that for the sake of the salvation of souls we are permitted to do everything to counter its lies and deceptions.' This judgement was quickly adopted by his followers, so that in spring 1521 the reformer could report with evident satisfaction that 'our youth' had made fun of the pope and his cardinals, bishops, and attendants as carnival puppets in a 'very funny and ingenious play' performed on the streets.[35]

Figure 19. Pope Leo X with two cardinal-nephews, Giulio de' Medici (left, later Pope Clement VII) and Luigi de' Rossi (right), Raphael (1483–1520), c.1517.

The Reformation now also embraced ecclesiology, pronouncing that the pope had no place within an evangelically renewed church. It was not just that the papacy had no authority in divine law—Luther had already rejected those roots a year earlier, at his disputation at Leipzig with Johannes Eck. Now for Luther the pope was Antichrist himself and in light of his role in sacred history should be attacked by any means at hand, in a battle that was inevitable. Antichrist was evidently at work, for this unevangelical papacy was 'leading into sin and ruin', not to salvation but to eternal damnation. Even before his appearance at Worms, Luther was certain that popes were 'murderers of souls'[36] whose handiwork must be halted whatever the cost. From the beginning Luther's message had two components: proclamation of a new teaching on justification and criticism of the pope and his church.

In the course of the 1520s this double message led the new Luther to develop a fourth characteristic, and one that would determine his thoughts and actions right up to the end of his life—his sense of call as a prophet. The greater his recognition that the pope and his church were unevangelical and anti-Christian, the more clearly Luther could see his dual responsibilities as prophet—to bring word of his evangelical theology of grace and to warn that Antichrist was occupying the false throne of Peter and that its defilement of the church of Christ stood in the way of salvation. He believed himself confirmed in that role by the resonances his prophetic message struck among clerics, peasants, townsfolk, nobles, and even rulers. Looking back on the months in which his reformed theology took root, Luther saw his rediscovery of the pure Gospel and the true evangelical church of Christ not as the innovative and personal achievement of a scholar, but as a task given by God through divine revelation. He had launched his challenge to the indulgence 'gauchely', as an ignorant papist, and only because he was led by God was he able to recognize the correct path to redemption. Like Isaiah, the Old Testament prophet, Luther, too, had been 'afflicted' by God. God had said to Isaiah, 'I was ready to be sought out by those who did not ask, to be found by those who did not seek me' (Isaiah 65:1), for, Luther noted, 'the Gospel comes from above.' As prophet, Luther was tasked with repeating God's message, but he was also to call for a response to that message that was to take the form of the eschatological battle with the Antichrist in Rome. He was convinced that his Reformation marked the beginning of the end for Rome: 'We think that the end of the papacy has begun in large part.' Like Judas Maccabaeus, the biblical military leader and godly war hero whose sword purified the Temple and re-established true worship, Luther continued, 'now the Gospel is sweeping aside the idolatrousness . . . and as Christ said, his angels will clear away all that is offensive from his kingdom.' Luther believed he had been sent into battle by God as prophet and divine warrior to free Christendom from its entanglement with the papal Antichrist.[37]

From the early 1520s Luther exercised his prophetic office in new ways and with ever-stronger language in order to unmask the pope as Antichrist and to halt his satanic obstruction of salvation. Today Protestants have left such demonization far behind, but churches that have evangelical foundations or constitutions have retained his radical rejection of the papal office. This fundamental principle lay behind the ecclesiastical reform initiated by Luther, wrapped up in the rhetoric of his times, and in the long term has made impossible the reunification of the Protestant church and the Roman, papal, Church.

And finally, a fifth characteristic of the new Luther: his pessimistic and negative image of humanity. For the reformer, humankind had been both fundamentally and essentially corrupted by the Fall. Day by day all of humanity now had to struggle against the depravity of the 'old Adam'— even the new Luther, liberated through the grace of God, was not free of sin; he too remained an 'old' and sinful human, and therefore a 'bad' human. In the response to the question 'What then is the significance of such a baptism with water?', which he included in his Small Catechism of 1529, a text still used in the Lutheran church today to introduce children to Christian doctrine, Luther formulated this self-discovery with consummate vividness:

> It signifies that the old creature [lit. the Old Adam] in us with all sins and evil desires is to be drowned and die through daily contrition and repentance, and on the other hand that daily a new person is to come forth and rise up to live before God in righteousness and purity forever.[38]

And then despite his pessimism he added elsewhere with a typical reconciliatory and compassionate humour, 'but be careful for the beast can swim'.

For Luther the sinfulness of humankind was part of the order of creation. Sin was a way to God. The papal teaching 'that the commandments are fulfilled by works', the description given by Luther in his 'On the Freedom of a Christian' of 1520, could only lead the Christian astray, for 'the commandments must have been fulfilled previous to any good works, and good works follow their fulfilment'.[39] His Roman opponents, who taught that human self-perfection could be achieved through good works, saw Luther's position as frivolous, but acceptance of the essential depravity of human nature was at the heart of his anthropology and his doctrine of justification. In light of the human's fundamental inability to do good, Luther held, each human can only be saved if he or she relies utterly on the grace of God and not on the conditional nature of good works, a message all the more momentous for those drowning in the guilt of sin.

Luther's famous command 'sin boldly' (*pecca fortiter*) was not licence to do evil but rather pastoral advice. This expression is found in a letter Luther wrote in 1521 from the Wartburg to Melanchthon, where it appears as a personal theological exhortation at the end of a long report on the Lord's Supper and on the vow of chastity taken by priests and nuns. The greater the courage with which one sins, the sooner one will be ready to place all one's hopes in Christ alone. This encouragement to spirited sinning forms a call to look to Christ, in whom Melanchthon was to trust more courageously: 'Be a sinner and sin boldly, but believe and rejoice in Christ even more boldly, for he is victorious over sin, death, and the world.'[40] Without awareness of sin there can be no salvation, for without awareness of sin there is no knowledge of grace: 'If you do not feel any sin, you are assuredly completely dead in sins, yes, dead, and sin is reigning over you with might.'[41]

A complement to his unconditional trust in God, Luther's radical mistrust of human nature and of all utopias that stemmed only from the good in humankind informed his thoughts and actions throughout his life when it came to the necessary ordering of this world and the conditions for salvation in the next. Here was another fundamental variation from the Roman Church, which in placing such high value on human action had to count on humankind's ability to do good. These divergent principles ensure that today Catholic and Protestant theological understandings of human dignity also diverge. They also had implications, evident to Luther as early as 1524, that reached far beyond later confessional cultures. Erasmus of Rotterdam, who had already derided Luther privately to members of the curia and had little interest in theological quibbles, spoke out in his programmatic treatise 'On Free Will' (*De libero arbitrio*) against Luther's doctrine of the bondage of the human will and thus against his pessimistic view of humankind. Luther's anthropology also caused tensions amongst his followers, above all for Philip Melanchthon, his closest collaborator, who as a humanist and teacher put great hope in the positive possibilities of humankind. Luther's authority was always able to dampen these diverging viewpoints when they threatened to pull his movement apart. Immediately after his death, however, conflict broke out in full force between Melanchthon and the 'true' followers of Luther precisely over the nature of humanity, and Lutheranism faced its first existential crisis.

III

The Reformer—Standing His Ground before Church, Emperor, and Empire

Finding Clarity

Months of Uncertainty and Anxiety

Luther did not become a reformer overnight. The publication of his Ninety-Five Theses was only the opening act in a back and forth, rife with tension, involving his continuing intellectual and personal development as professor at the university in Wittenberg, on one hand, and complex external events that became part of that everyday existence, on the other. In a multi-faceted process for which he did not bear sole responsibly, events beyond the university turned the Augustinian monk into one of the most prominent figures of his age. He was borne through these months and years on a wave of approval and admiration, but he also faced biting criticism that challenged him to the core, even to the extent of being accused of heresy, which put his life on the line: 'In three weeks I will have the heretic in the fire and he will go to heaven in a bath cap,' Tetzel had sworn as early as 1517. Within a few weeks Tetzel's words reached Luther,[1] who now lived in the shadow of that all-too-real threat. Those who criticized the church could not easily shake off the memory of the bonfire lit in Constance some hundred years earlier to silence Jan Hus, the 'heretical' Czech reformer.

The situation seemed all the more dangerous as in October 1518, one year after Luther had published his Ninety-Five Theses, it was impossible to predict whether the electoral Saxon ruler would stand by him in the long run or whether Frederick would decide to distance himself from his criticized professor. When Luther learned that Karl von Miltitz, Rome's special legate, was on his way to the Saxon elector and had with him 'three papal letters in order to arrest me and hand me over to the pope', he prepared himself for the worst—for imprisonment, death, or, as the best of the worst, banishment to France, an idea that Cajetan, the papal legate, had thrown into the mix. Whatever the outcome, he was clear 'that in this matter and on other matters I must make haste', by which he meant that he had to give his newly discovered truth both written and organizational roots in order that it might not be stifled should he die or be imprisoned: 'In order that they don't kill me when I am unprepared or weigh down on me with punishments,' he recorded, 'I have organized everything and await God's decision.' As a precaution he had instructed his community in Wittenberg, 'Live well . . . should I not return', exhorting them 'not to be alarmed by the enraged papal punishments directed against me . . . but rather to leave this matter and similar things to God'.[2]

Before he was able to exclaim in Worms, 'I've made it through,' Luther had to live through a dramatic period during which he continued to work, undeterred, on the essentials of his new theology. In this existential crisis he acquired an inner strength that subsequently, from the mid-1520s, enabled him to promote the reorganization of church, state, and society with the authority of a prophet sent by God. The anxieties and exertions of all his travels, poorly equipped and undertaken largely on foot, unleashed a range of troubling physical complaints with emotional origins, above all stomach pains and agonizing constipation. Having suffered on his journey in 1518 to Augsburg, where he was questioned by Cajetan, the papal legate, Luther was tormented by the same ailments all the more when he travelled to Worms in spring 1521.[3]

Yet during these testing times Luther's theology assumed its definitive Reformation form while Luther's character acquired the steeliness that left the reformer equal to the demands and attacks of the following decades. Luther interpreted his physical pains as assaults by the devil and therefore as a sure sign that his truth was from God and could not be halted by a human hand, no matter what burdens his body might have to bear. In a letter written in late autumn 1518 to Spalatin and the Electoral Saxon government in which he informed them that the curia was about to take action against his freedom and perhaps even his life, he could still assure his friend, 'I am full of joy and peace and lecture and teach as before.'[4]

Explaining Himself to His Order and to the Papal Legate

First Luther had to defend himself in three ecclesiastical or academic fora, which in keeping with the contemporary character of Christendom, were in part commissioned by Rome and in part acted autonomously: he appeared first before the Augustinians and subsequently before the papal legate; only then did he receive the academic hearing he had wanted from the start, at Leipzig.

His first test was examination by the Chapter General of the Augustinian Hermits, which took place on 26 April 1518 at Heidelberg. The curia had commanded the leadership of his order silence their errant brother, but counter to the hopes of Rome, the outcome was not the disciplining of this single monk by his superiors, but an impressive rallying of forces amongst Augustinians in support of their maligned brother. Within a few years Martin Bucer and Johannes Brenz, who had been present at Luther's appearance before his order and were greatly impressed by his arguments, were themselves reformers in southern Germany.

The response at Luther's motherhouse in Erfurt is telling. The provincial vicar's appointment of his friend Johannes Lang as prior some years earlier now paid dividends—a further example of his knack for good investments. With Lang's return to Erfurt—we recall that he had been transferred to Wittenberg along with Luther—the most important of the Augustinian houses of central Germany was now led by a man who had ties to the Wittenberg innovations, which led to support from the influential and highly regarded monastery for the new philosophy and theology. Lang joined the fray on Luther's behalf, but older brothers such as Johann Nathin and Bartholomäus von Usingen would have none of it. Jodokus Trutfetter, who had taught Luther at the university at Erfurt and whose nominalism had left distinct traces in Luther's thought, refused to receive the rebellious Augustinian monk when Luther sought him out as he travelled back from Heidelberg; a second attempt the next day was successful but generated a deep rift between the two men. Enthused by his discoveries, the younger monk reproached the older brother for his stale methodology and hair-splitting approach and demanded that he abandon the nominalism he had taught and practised for decades, a method that was by no means antiquated. From now on, Luther insisted, Trutfetter should rely only on the Bible and the church fathers. The breakdown in their relationship was all too typical of Luther, as was also his subsequent deep regret. When Trutfetter died soon after, Luther was tormented by the thought that his vehemence had contributed to his death. Yet, thanks to his tenacity and the unconditional support of Lang, monastery, university, and soon also the citizens of Erfurt were won over to his cause. Three years later as he travelled to the Imperial diet at Worms, Luther returned to Erfurt, where this time he received a truly triumphal reception.[5]

Only a half year later the rebel monk faced a challenge far greater than explaining his actions to his own order in Heidelberg. In October 1518 he was called to Augsburg, where the Imperial diet was in session. On the periphery of the diet, from 12 to 14 October, he appeared before Cardinal Cajetan, the papal legate, to give account of himself in an interrogation full of legal and political traps set by the church. The true nature of the process was very clear to his contemporaries: Staupitz, vicar general of the Augustinian order, expressly relieved Luther of his duty of obedience, which provided Luther with room to argue his case, but at the same time also moved the order out of the sights of the curia. The principal task of Thomas Cajetan, a curial cardinal, at the diet was to seek financial and political support from Emperor Maximilian and the estates of the Empire for papal Turkish policy. Cajetan, however, was also a Dominican monk and therefore a member of the same order as Tetzel, the preacher of the indulgence originally attacked by Luther, and he was also one of the leading theological minds of his age and a highly skilled churchman. In his theology and philosophy he favoured a modernizing scholasticism that could embrace economic and fiscal innovation, along with the challenges of the new worlds overseas. When it came to the politics of the church, he backed the primacy of the papacy all the way, a position he had vindicated in two recent treatises that formed a defence against a budding new conciliarism. This was not a man from whom one might expect any sympathy for criticisms of pope or church, but he was also not a man who would be swept up in blind enthusiasm or condemn whatever the evidence. He had examined Luther's writings with great care and was eager to find a means for Luther to avoid the trial that seemed to await him.

For three days the two men discussed and debated—Cajetan tried to calm the maverick monk and persuade him to recant, while in turn Luther used all his biblical learning and all his ingenuity to try to persuade the cardinal, as a trained theologian, to accept his understanding of Scripture. Neither was successful. Luther was disappointed, even exasperated. In their discussions he sensed little of the 'good will' that the cardinal had promised him through intermediaries amongst the electoral Saxon representatives at the Imperial diet. To Luther it seemed evident that this emissary of the pope only wanted to ensure that the power of the keys claimed by the papacy was not put up for debate and that the troublemaker in the remote Saxon province was silenced. The prelate was not prepared to debate the content of Luther's claims, the real issue as far as Luther was concerned. When Luther learned of the existence of an 'apostolic, or rather, diabolic breve' in which the curia demanded that should he refuse to recant, he must immediately be arrested, he refused to admit to himself that the letter might really be the work of Leo X. But his suspicions had been awakened 'that the Romans are beginning to be afraid and to put little trust in their own case. Consequently they are painfully searching for loopholes.'[6]

In these circumstances it seemed highly prudent for the Augustinian monk to leave Augsburg secretly, slipping out under the cover of darkness on the evening of 20 October. The city gates were already locked; an ally had to open a small door to let him exit. With the support of his fellow Augustinian monks and likely in response to the advice of members of the Saxon delegation to the Imperial diet, before he left Luther had ensured his theological and church-political views had been officially recorded. With the help of a legal professional in Augsburg, he had drawn up a formal notarized appeal 'from the badly informed pope to the pope who is to be informed better'. Immediately after Luther's departure from Augsburg his fellow Augustinian Leonhard Beyer, who in keeping with the rules of their order had accompanied Luther on the journey to Augsburg, handed over the document before witnesses to the cardinal. At the same time, the appeal was displayed on the doors of the cathedral at Augsburg, a virtuoso public act that Luther extended on his return to Wittenberg with a further appeal. Now he called for a council of the church, looking to form an alliance with the University of Paris, which had also called for a council, although for a very different cause. The proposed creation of a momentous constellation that would cover far more than just the Empire suggested the spirit of conciliarism had been revived. The Renaissance papacy would have sensed something fiendish in the air. The hard-won papal victory over conciliarism achieved towards the end of the fifteenth century and the exclusive monarchical authority of pope and curia now seemed again at risk.

His two appeals insufficient, the restless Wittenberg monk propelled further information out into the public. At the beginning of December

Spalatin forbade him, in the name of the Saxon government, from publishing more; Luther replied immediately that 'the acts have already
appeared', referring to the 'Dealings of the Augustinian Friar Martin Luther
with the Lord Apostolic Legate at Augsburg' (*Acta Fratris Martini Lutheri
Augustiniani apud D Legatum Apostolicum Augustae*),[7] in which he had set out
his version of the events at Augsburg. Luther informed his friend, caught
unawares, that he had composed that text 'with much candour about the
truth, but despite that still not with complete boldness'.[8] For an individual
accused of heresy by the holy church to publish what was in effect the
minutes of the proceedings against him was unheard of, but scholars both
within and outside the church were now all the more eager to hear what
he had to say.

Immediately after Luther's examination at Augsburg the curia had
launched a new attempt to silence Luther and persuade him to back
down. Several months of secret diplomacy followed, but circumstances
suggest that these efforts were doomed to fail from the start. In their courtier
Karl von Miltitz, the curia certainly had a diplomat who as papal chamberlain
and a scion of an old Saxon noble family could not have been more suitable
for the role of intermediary between Pope Leo X and Elector Frederick. He
presented Frederick with the Golden Rose, the highest honour the pope
could bestow on a secular prince (and one that Henry VIII of England
would also soon receive). With the honour came a certain responsibility—in
the case of the Saxon elector that meant keeping the interests of Rome in
mind both when it came to the election of the next Emperor, already
anticipated and a reality only a few months later, and in the Luther Affair.
Miltitz whose motives and intent were hard to determine, also worked very
hard to win Luther over to the papal solution to the conflict. But no
agreement could be reached, not even through several meetings in person,
the most important of which was a discussion that took place at the
beginning of 1519 in the Wettin secondary residence of Altenburg.

Defeat by Johannes Eck

The Leipzig Disputation, held in July 1519, saw the battlefronts more
clearly, and more permanently, drawn. The event was in effect a double
disputation, for before and in between the days on which Luther and
Johannes Eck disputed, Eck was also involved in a disputation with Andreas
Karlstadt, one of Luther's colleagues in Wittenberg. Eck was a professor at

the university at Ingolstadt, where he taught not just theology but also logic, geography, and canon law. He saw in Luther a very personal challenge, for he had recently written a treatise on the doctrine of justification in which he had declared free will and good works to be decisive for the justification of humankind before God. He was one of the first to declare his interest in participating in a disputation with Luther, believing that his career at the great universities in Heidelberg, Cologne, and Freiburg and his academic experience would surely secure him an easy victory over a representative of a provincial university. The theses with which he challenged Luther and Karlstadt focused on the cornerstones of their attack on the church—on the relationship between grace and free will, penance, and papal primacy— and were therefore particularly well suited to draw out his Wittenberg opponents and even tempt them onto thin ice.

The disputation took place in Leipzig from the end of June until mid-July 1519 and was therefore held under ducal Saxon auspices. Like his cousin in Wittenberg, Duke George of Saxony was eager to see his territories turned into an early modern state, and he had a particular eye on reform of the church, even more so than Frederick. With a personal interest in clarification of the theological issues that were proving so controversial and flouting a prohibition issued by the bishop of Merseburg, George had forced the hesitant university in Leipzig to host the disputation. Immediately on his return from Leipzig, Luther wrote to Spalatin, and therefore to the electoral government, to inform him of what had happened, and he recorded that he believed George to be 'a wise and pious prince' but 'was grieved that... [he] was open to the influence of others and followed their opinions'.[9] Bickering over procedure broke out even before the disputation began, and there was disagreement, too, about who should receive the records of the debates that would be used to determine which party had won. Luther and his Wittenberg colleague Karlstadt believed themselves caught in a double bind: 'so that we should be confounded by both alternatives, whether we gave up the debate [which their opponents could exploit as a confession of error], or placed the outcome into the hand of unfair judges'. Eck was well able to use academic finesse to his own ends, securing, for example, the concluding remarks for his side. From the beginning Luther feared that 'Eck hoped that he might carry off the victory by his loud shouting and impressive delivery', in which—as Luther had to admit to Spalatin in retrospect— in his opening disputation with Karlstadt, on free will, Eck was largely successful.

But the new liberated Luther was certainly not a man who would readily capitulate in the face of 'such hatred . . . never more shameless or more impudent', as he described it in his report to the Saxon government. On 29 June, the feast of Saint Peter and Saint Paul, he had opportunity to preach in Leipzig. His audience was so large—campaigning by his supporters had surely played its part—that the sermon was given not in the castle chapel but in the Princes' Hall in Pleissenburg Castle. For Luther here was an opportunity to liberate his views from the confines of scholarly disputation and communicate them to a far greater public in Leipzig. With an air of innocence he justified his subject matter: the text on which he would preach, Matthew 16:13–19, 'includes all the materials of the whole disputation', and therefore he had every reason to use his sermon to canvass support for his theological positions. With his thesis 'It is true that the keys were given to St Peter; but not to him personally, but rather to the person of the Christian church. They were actually given to me and to you for the comfort of our consciences',[10] he even took a decisive step towards the concept of the priesthood of all believers, a position that he would present to a much wider public only a few months later when he published his 'Address to the Christian Nobility of the German Nation'.

In his sermon, Luther hammered in the nails on which he would hang his arguments in the disputation. For some time now, indulgences had no longer been the vital issue, and Luther could report, 'the indulgence toppled entirely, Eck agreed with me in almost everything and those who defended the indulgence were laughed at and mocked'. But indulgences had been replaced by a far more hotly disputed issue—ecclesiology, doctrine about the church and most concretely the papal primacy claimed by Rome. The first disputation between Eck and Luther took place on 4 July in the Knights' Hall at the castle; the audience was again large, but on this occasion it was limited to academics. Eck launched the first disputation by citing a series of passages from Scripture that in his opinion justified the claim of the papacy to supremacy, 'You are Peter', 'Tend my flock', 'Strengthen your brothers', 'Follow me'—all strong words, as Luther had to agree. Aware of the dangerous situation he faced, the Wittenberg monk fell back on the history of the church, which he had studied intensively in preparation for the disputation. He used arguments drawn from that history to prove that the pope had never been the supreme head of all Christianity. But, he insisted, he was not denying the papacy's 'primacy of honour'. He countered Eck's thesis that papal authority had been granted directly by God and therefore was in accord with divine law, *iure divino*, with the assertion that the popes' claim to be Christ's representatives on earth was founded only on human law, *iure humano*. The Renaissance papacy, which so recently had established its claim to absolute authority on the back of the defeat of conciliarism, could only condemn such relativization as heretical. With extraordinary debating skills, Eck drew precisely this conclusion and forced his sparring partner to adopt ever riskier positions, to the extent that Luther even found himself expressing solidarity with individual teachings of the Czech theologian Jan Hus, who had been burned as a heretic in 1415, and stating explicitly that councils could err and, indeed, had erred.

Having started badly, the whole Leipzig venture ended on an even worse note. Duke George of Saxony was now the intransigent foe of the Wittenbergers, and from now on did all he could to isolate the church reform that he had already launched in his own lands, independently of Luther, from any influences from Electoral Saxony. Most significantly, the heresy trap had been sprung. The official record of the disputation, which registered in detail every statement made by the debaters, was sent to the conservative theological faculties at Cologne and Louvain, whose judgement, in August 1519 and November 1519 respectively, was speedy and predictable.

Luther and his supporters had long since abandoned their earlier willingness to restrict themselves to a limited academic audience. The secret protocols of the meeting had hardly been launched on their journey when several pamphlets appeared in Erfurt with private transcriptions of the Leipzig Disputation—whether they were published with Luther's knowledge we cannot know. Whatever the case, Luther's outrageous provocation in denying the pope any claim to authority had now spread beyond narrow academic confines and was a matter of public knowledge. In terms of both process and argumentation, the '*Causa Luther*', or Luther Affair, as the official church termed the matter, had now been launched down two divergent paths on a search for truth—the official route, laid out by the church, led to a guilty verdict and excommunication; the second route, paved by the media and public opinion, saw the contentious issues submitted to each Christian, who would judge freely according to his or her abilities.

'The Time to Speak Has Come'—The Reformation Treatises of 1520

Despite his defeat at Leipzig Luther hardly faltered. He was unmoved by the abuse of his background and his parents by one of his opponents in Leipzig, and in January 1520 he informed Spalatin, purely with rhetorical intent, 'I only wish something would quickly happen to free me from the obligation to lecture and teach', for only then, he argued, would it be possible for him to hold his tongue.[11] His ultimate goal was to garner the full support of the Saxon government, whom he sought to convince that 'sacred theology' could not be taught honestly without 'offending the prelates' and without raising doubts about the doctrines of 'free will, grace, and the keys of the church'.[12] Certainly he would, he suggested, 'restrain my impetuosity', but he still 'was not able to dispel all dislike of them [his Leipzig opponents], for I am flesh and their hatred was very shameless and their injustice was very malicious in a matter so sacred and divine'.[13] He acknowledged he was not always able 'to curb the heat and the pen', and that if 'the dog is aggravated', then it will respond 'more fiercely than it should'.[14] A frank statement made to Spalatin in mid-February 1520—'In short we all are Hussites and did not know it. Even Paul and Augustine are in reality Hussites'—indicated a marked development in his thought.[15] Where in Leipzig he had professed only individual teachings of the Czech theologian who had been burned at the stake in Constance in 1415, now Luther placed himself unconditionally in a continuity that reached back to the notorious heretic and his radical criticism of the church, which could be found in his treatise 'The Church' (De ecclesia) of 1413, in which Hus denied tradition any role and recognized the Bible as the sole foundation of the Christian life and Christian institutions.

Although the Saxon government was unable to convince its professor, now accused of heresy, to demonstrate a more diplomatic reticence when it came to Rome, in February 1520 it emphatically demanded that Luther provide unambiguous explanation of the issues where his views were not in accord with established teachings. In response, by the middle of March Luther could announce that he had 'in hand and was penning the sermon on good works', which, he wrote, was turning into a veritable small book and promising to be the best thing he had written to date.[16] This treatise, published in June 1520, launched the career of a truly popular author, and at times polemicist, who had fully mastered the ability to make his case to his public. The superior skills of a man such as Eck within the academic arena counted for nothing in the face of Luther's ability to bring home an argument for all levels of society.

The great Reformation treatises followed blow upon blow, and 1520/21 proved Luther's 'golden year' as an author.[17] At times he wrote so quickly that the printers of Wittenberg struggled to keep up with him. The great treatises of 1520 took his fundamental criticism and proposed renewal of religion and church so far down a new path that there could be no going back. Under the motto 'The time for silence is past, and the time to speak has come',[18] in early summer Luther began to set down his demands for reform of the church, and by August this work, entitled 'To the Christian Nobility of the German Nation concerning the Reform of the Christian Estate' (*An den christlichen Adel deutscher Nation: Von des christlichen Standes Besserung*), could be read throughout the Empire. The first edition contained a remarkable 4,000 copies, but even then proved insufficient; a series of reprints also sold extremely well. Called to arms in the cause of reform, the laity ripped copies of the text out of the hands of its sellers. The Reformation was now a media event, and the reformer a best-selling author of an entirely new kind. Luther appears to have been under so much pressure that on occasion he had no opportunity to edit the final copy. It was evidently important to him to let his Erfurt friend Johannes Lang know that 'the publication was not in my hands. For it was printed, 4,000 copies made, and was sold. I can assume that our Lotter [Luther's publisher in Wittenberg] made no great loss. If I did something wrong, only prayer can help now.'[19]

By this date Luther already had his next programmatic text well in hand. With an audience amongst the clergy and the more educated in mind, this time he wrote in Latin, publishing 'On the Babylonian Captivity of the Church' (*De captivitate Babylonica ecclesiae*) in October 1520. Translated into the vernacular and repeatedly reprinted, its extreme and novel criticism of the dogmatic foundations of the Roman Church was soon making tremendous waves. Without flinching, Luther took aim at the seven sacraments, which formed the core of the Roman Church. With the organization and distribution of the holy sacraments reserved for the priestly caste, Luther proposed, the church's teaching on the holy sacraments had become a tool exploited by the Roman institutional church to exercise authority. Christians had been left powerless and chained to the pope. He countered that error with a bold act of simplification: of the seven sacraments of the medieval church, the purified evangelical church accepted only three—the Lord's Supper, baptism, and penance could be found in the New Testament and were to be liberated from their usurpation by the Roman priestly class. Marriage, Luther recorded, is of this world and not a sacrament, but the institution of marriage is protected by the benevolence of God. Priestly ordination, confirmation, and extreme unction were frauds perpetrated by the Roman Church, according to Luther, and had been created to buttress the fabricated necessity of the priestly class for salvation.

Luther's calling to account of the theological core of the Roman Church could hardly have been more radical. While some now supported him all the more, in other quarters enthusiasm waned. Erasmus had already mocked Luther for the popular tone of his appeal to the wider population. Now former supporters amongst the clergy and in humanist circles also distanced themselves from the reformer, for they were not prepared for such radical theological reformulations and were not willing to shoulder the changes in the ecclesiastical and social order that must necessarily follow. Luther repeatedly insisted that he was no innovator, that what he described was only a rediscovery of the original teachings of the church, but to no avail.

Mid-November 1520 saw the publication of the third and most famous of Luther's Reformation treatises, 'On the Freedom of the Christian', furnished with an open letter to Pope Leo X. With Luther's sharp censure of the papal church in 'On the Babylonian Captivity of the Church' still so fresh in their minds, contemporaries were not a little surprised by this approach. The surprising association of theological paradigm change as laid out in 'On the Freedom of the Christian' with a confident appeal to 'the most holy father in God' can be explained by the particular political situation of late 1520 and by Luther's position on ecclesiastical law. This third text, and especially the accompanying open letter, should be read against the backdrop of the heresy verdict recently issued by the Roman Church and the papal bull that followed, threatening Luther with excommunication. The bull, usually named after its opening words 'Exsurge Domine', begins: 'Arise, O Lord, and judge your own cause ... for foxes have arisen seeking to destroy the vineyard whose winepress you alone have trod.'

During the months in which the rebellious Augustinian monk in Wittenberg was preparing his first Reformation texts for publication, the theological faculties at the universities in Cologne and Louvain discussed his theses; in late August 1519 and November 1519 respectively they declared his views heretical, with the verdict published in February 1520 in Louvain. At the same time the heresy trial in Rome was revived and moved forward swiftly, for the election of Charles V in 1519 meant that the need to avoid alienating Luther's ruler, Frederick the Wise, had

disappeared. Luther, the person most affected by these various investiga-
tions, was given no opportunity to make his case to the faculties at Cologne
or Louvain or to appear before his judges in Rome. Additionally, the Bible
was not used to refute his claims. A vital contribution to the wording of the
Roman judgement was made by Luther's sparring partner at the Leipzig
disputation, Johannes Eck, who had been in Rome since the spring. The
close ties between the curia and Eck formed their own tragedy. Rome
relied on a theologian who, although certainly not second-rate, was utterly
conventional. While Eck could not escape the rut in which reality was the
only judge of legitimacy, Luther was reconceiving the theology of the
church from the ground up with a creativity that was incomprehensible to
men such as Eck. The latter was simply incapable of providing counsel that
was equal to the task.

The outcome was relayed in the consistory on 1 June 1520 and issued
on 15 June, in the papal bull *Exsurge Domine*, which threatened Luther
with excommunication. The judgement was then made public on 24 July
with the bull put on display at Saint Peter's and at the papal chancellery on
the Campo dei Fiori. Rome now also took its case to the public, but in a
manner very different to Wittenberg. Rome saw no need to convince
Christendom or to include Christendom in a search for the truth; for
Rome engaging the public was simply a matter of announcing its verdict,
which listed forty-one false teachings by Luther, declared him a heretic,
and demanded he recant within sixty days. Should he refuse to recant, he
would be deemed excommunicate, which came with a comprehensive loss
of all legal protections.

The bull became critical for Luther and the Saxon government at the end
of September 1520, when it was formally published in the central German
bishoprics—and by no other than Johannes Eck. Eck was not a clever choice
for the curia, for it bound the legal case in with old personal enmities and
their political ramifications, as was demonstratively confirmed by Duke
George of Saxony, who honoured the papal nuncio Eck with the gift of a
gold-filled chalice. Luther's response on learning of the publication of the
bull at the beginning of October similarly acknowledged Eck's involvement,
for he announced his intention to attack the bull as 'full of lies, godless, and
with the mark of Eck at every turn'.[20] When it came to the pope and the
curia, however, he indicated that he was prepared to trust the assurances of
Karl von Miltitz, the papal special envoy, who, continuing his role as
intermediary begun a year earlier, met with Luther on 12 October at the

Antonite foundation at Lichtenburg on the river Elbe to advise him on his response to the bull.[21] The prelate's aim was evidently to sidestep the personal quarrels of the German theologians and put Luther in direct contact with the pope. To this end, according to the version of events provided by Luther, Miltitz recommended 'that I should publish a letter in German and in Latin, addressed to the Pope, as a preface to some brief writing'. He continued, 'In this letter I am to relate my whole story and show that I never wanted to attack the Pope personally, and throw the whole blame on Eck.' Luther had all the more reason to fall into line with this proposed tactic because his attack on the papacy at Leipzig had indeed been provoked by Eck. He therefore offered 'as humbly as I can, to keep silent, provided that others keep silent too'. And so that 'I may not seem to omit anything in my power to make peace', he agreed that he would compose both texts, the letter to the pope and the explanatory booklet, 'at the earliest possible moment'.

By this time, however, Luther had already declared the pope to be the 'true and incarnate Antichrist',[22] and his only real hope was that he might be able to convince Leo X to undertake a fundamental redefinition of the papal office. That hope proved all the more illusionary when Luther, completely counter to the hopes of Miltitz, proved unwilling to submit to a process of truth-seeking that would take place entirely within the church. From the start Luther composed these works addressed to the pope with the German public very much in mind: both 'On the Freedom of a Christian' and his open letter to Leo X, which recommended this 'little treatise' to the pope, were written in the vernacular and then translated by Luther into Latin. Both versions, backdated to September 1520, so before Eck's publication of the papal bull, were published at the beginning of November by Johannes Rhau-Grunenberg in Wittenberg and quickly reprinted elsewhere in the Empire.[23]

By the time these texts arrived in the hands of Leo X, they were already well known not just to the educated elite but also to the general public. Today, so used to modern media and public debate, we would hardly be surprised by this dissemination of information, but many of Luther's contemporaries must have been astounded by an unprecedented situation. For those in Wittenberg a clear logic was evident, perhaps even a deliberate masterstroke, intended to force the pope into public debate, bringing the heresy proceedings conducted behind the closed doors of the church into a far larger forum at the last minute.

Whatever the specifics of the moment, 'On the Freedom of a Christian' provided the systematic foundations of a new evangelical church, its core formed by the freedom of the Christian, not by papal primacy and the priestly administration of the sacraments. The genesis of the text demonstrates, however, that Luther still had absolutely no intention of founding a rival church. 'On the Freedom of a Christian' and the open letter stood at a critical intersection of the two divergent paths laid after the Leipzig disputation: here was the point where Luther's entirely new strategy for establishing the truth, by appeal to the public, overlapped with the traditional procedures of the Roman Church, which also sought the truth, but in a process completely apart from the public, within purely academic or ecclesiastical structures and with an irrefutable final verdict enshrined as ecclesiastical law. In light of such fundamental differences about how theological debate should be conducted, the possibility that the crisis could be averted at the last moment was very slim.

Any chance of agreement was eliminated entirely by the content and argumentation of Luther's two texts. At the urging of papal emissary Miltitz, his Augustinian order, and the Electoral Saxon government, Luther, who still emphatically self-identified as an Augustinian monk, turned to the task of writing his response to the pope with an open mind and a will to find a solution. He had no intention, however, of lining himself up alongside the flatterers and yes-men of Rome. With all due deference to Leo X, in his open letter to the pope Luther drew an explicit picture of the appalling condition of the church without pulling any punches. For the church to be restored to its evangelical biblical origins, the pope would need to undertake drastic reform; specifically, Luther demanded nothing less than that the curia dissolve itself. For, Luther wrote to Leo, 'the Roman Curia . . . neither you nor anyone else can deny is more corrupt than any Babylon or Sodom ever was'. For Luther no words or deeds could help the curia. According to Luther, Leo was sitting 'like a lamb in the midst of wolves and like Daniel in the midst of lions'; everything now depended on his freeing himself from the influence of sycophants such as Johannes Eck and on his reading of this 'small book . . . [which] contains the whole of Christian Life in a brief form', whose contents he should verify and then put into practice.[24] Luther's propheticism had emerged strongly during these months, and in that vein he recorded, 'If it turns out the way we hope [with Leo seeing sense], it is well; if it turns out differently, it will also be well, because this is then the will of the Lord.'[25]

No Last-Minute Solution—Appeal to Leo X and an Admission of Guilt from Adrian VI

Influenced by his recognition that only the grace of God could liberate a sinner, the Wittenberg monk selected 'the freedom of a Christian' as the theme of what would be, as must have been clear to him, a last decisive attempt to win the pope over to his theology and to the fundamental reform of the church that would necessarily follow. From the midst of a publication frenzy, with his writings rushed off his desk into an avalanche of new publications and reprintings, Luther used just thirty short paragraphs and a highly engaging style to outline his new anthropology and with it his 'reformed' and 'evangelical' church. The order of this new church was based on the freedom of the Christian, found in the direct encounter of each individual with God and mediated by Christ as saviour, but without pope or priest as intermediary. The introductory essential definition of the individual, based on the words of Paul, would have roused any reader—or anyone who heard the work read out, a form of engagement with the text that was equally important for the spread of its content—'A Christian is a perfectly free lord of all, subject to none. A Christian is a perfectly dutiful servant of all, subject to all.'[26] As Germans of all social classes took these words to heart, hearing a call to change their world and with it Christian society focused on the church community, the church hierarchy looked on, fearful that the foundations of their church might fall. Luther was fully aware of the challenge his words contained, but the right decision was still possible as far as he was concerned: his wording 'as it pleases the Lord' suggested that God might yet open Pope Leo's eyes, as he had opened the eyes of Luther, a simple monk.

For the historian, who in seeking to establish historical processes cannot employ the direct intervention of God as explanation, it seems extremely unlikely that Leo X would have allowed himself to be swept up in Luther's theology of freedom and then led the way to reform of church and Christendom. Freedom was also a significant term for the Renaissance papacy, but it was not employed in an anthropological sense that saw every Christian directly responsible to God. For Rome freedom was about the freedom of the pope from the shackles of conciliar control, about the freedom of the papacy to assert its authority, as so recently and exemplarily demonstrated by the warrior-pope Julius II, and above all about the freedom

Figure 20. Pope Adrian VI, by Bernard van Orley (1487/91–1541), 1522.

to represent the papal church through art as epitomized by the project at Saint Peter's, against which the Wittenberg monk with his criticism of the indulgence had unknowingly rebelled.

Yet perhaps God had intervened at the last moment in order that such diametrically opposed understandings of freedom could be reconciled. Some eighteen months after the publication of Luther's 'On the Freedom of a Christian' Leo X died, and from the conclave that followed, in January 1522, emerged a surprising successor, aged humanist Adrian Florensz, teacher of Erasmus and the Emperor, who became Pope Adrian VI (Figure 20). Adrian VI began a process of reform, downsizing the papal court, halting the sale of offices, and ending nepotism. He even provided an admission of guilt, in the form of a statement read by his emissary before the German Imperial diet in January 1523, in which he declared:

> God permits this persecution of his church because of the sins of the priests and the prelates... for we well know that for some years already much that is detestable has happened at this Holy See: abuses in spiritual matters, violations of the commandments, yes, that everything has led into trouble.[27]

But in Rome his actions brought only hatred and ridicule that continued even after his death, which in September 1523 had released him from a hopeless situation. With power relationships and political interests in Rome what they were, from the start Adrian VI's programme of reform had been bound to fail. As Luther was also already well advanced in his criticism of the papal church and in his creation of a counter-model in an evangelical church, it is hard to speak of any real chance of last-minute reconciliation.

A Beacon of Hope against the Papal Antichrist

By late 1520 Rome had not even responded to Luther's open letter and 'On the Freedom of a Christian', let alone reconsidered the threat of excommunication. Luther was continuing to insist that only refutation based in Scripture was valid, and he therefore refused to recant. Additionally, at the very time he wrote to Leo X, he also attacked the papal bull as a fabrication by Eck and 'the bull of the Antichrist'.[28] The deadline set for his recanting passed, and Rome's threat became reality. Once again the hunted became the hunter. Further provoked by the announcement in Leipzig that his books were to be burned and by the book burnings that followed in Cologne and Mainz, in early December Luther sent word via Spalatin to the Saxon elector that as a countermove he intended to consign papal legal texts to the flames. The Saxon government appears not to have reacted, possibly because the plan remained somewhat vague. After discussion with his closest colleagues and friends, some of whom took an active part, on 10 December, exactly sixty days after the bull had been read publicly in Wittenberg, Luther put his plan into action unhindered.

Informed of the imminent event by an announcement drawn up by Melanchthon, students 'concerned for the evangelical truth'[29] gathered with a small number of their professors before the Elster Gate, and therefore outside the town, to stand with their teacher as he performed an act that while certainly spectacular was far from unique in the academic and ecclesiastical world of the Middle Ages. The location chosen for this burning of an opponent's writings was the site where the town's residents would rid themselves, or purge themselves, of anything that they believed brought them dishonour. For dishonour also to be associated with books was not uncommon, and such acts of cleansing did not have the negative associations of book burnings today. Unprecedented and sensational was not that books were burned, but *which* books were burned. Johann Agricola of Eisleben, a pupil and young colleague of Luther's at the theological faculty, lit the bonfire and consigned several editions of canon law to the flames, following with a guide to scholastic confessional practice and a number of short works by Luther's opponents Eck and Hieronymus Emser. The reformer would have been happy to add the works of the great scholastics Thomas Aquinas and Duns Scotus, but the theology librarian had refused to hand over his copies to

Luther for his bonfire, evidently unwilling to lose from his collection texts that were thought fundamental to the study of theology.

Only as these first works were already burning did Luther approach the fire himself and throw into the flames a copy of the papal bull threatening his excommunication. The words that accompanied his action appear to have been spoken only faintly, and we cannot be entirely certain of the accuracy of the version that has come down to us: 'As you have destroyed the truth of God, today the Lord destroys you. Get into the fire.' Soon after the event, Luther informed his mentor Staupitz that he had acted 'at first with trembling and praying', but, he continued, 'now I am more pleased with this than with any other action of my life for [these books] are worse than I had thought.'[30]

Only subsequently, reworked by the public and through memorialization, did Luther's action become a revolutionary repudiation of his threatened excommunication. Amongst Luther's contemporaries, including his colleagues in Wittenberg, the burning of the books of canon law aroused great passion, even with professors who had been sympathetic to his cause, especially members of the law faculty, opposed to and alienated by his actions. This academic 'happening' meant that Luther had broken completely with Rome—he had denied the pope any authority to adjudicate in matters of faith and, at the same time, had declared the centuries-old legal foundations of the Roman Church invalid. His protest was made known in Saxony and in Germany more widely through now well-established channels—first by way of a letter to Spalatin written soon after the event itself, in which Luther mentioned the whole business only in passing and along with another issue concerning the church in Saxony, evidently reckoning that the Saxon government could not be displeased;[31] then, the next day, with a sermon to the student body; and, finally, with a pamphlet entitled 'Why the Books of the Pope and His Disciples Were Burned by Dr. Martin Luther' (*Warum des Papstes und seiner Jünger Bücher von D. Martin Luther verbrannt sind*).[32]

The Road to Worms

Placing Hope in the Young King Charles

However spectacular Luther's first appearances had been and however many people had read and heard his great reform treatises, the universal claims of his new theology belonged on a universal stage. With no church council, neither universal nor German, on the horizon, such a forum could be found only in an Imperial diet, which as the most distinguished body within the Holy Roman Empire of the German Nation attracted notice throughout the Latin West. The Saxon court saw in the assembly of Emperor and Imperial estates an opportunity to find a solution to the Luther Affair that would satisfy all concerned, and independently of such political tactics, it was also in Luther's interests to appear before an Imperial public.

The appeal was all the greater as the Imperial gathering so greatly anticipated in late 1520 promised to be more dazzling than practically any before. It would be the first Imperial diet attended by Charles V, a Habsburg who had been elected German king the previous year *in absentia*. At the age of just nineteen, Charles had become the most powerful ruler in Christendom: on the death of his father, Philip, in 1506 he had become ruler of the lands of Lower Burgundy, since 1516 he had been king of the united Spanish empire, and in January 1519, on the death of his grandfather Maximilian, he had also inherited the Austrian hereditary lands. On 23 September 1520 Charles arrived in Antwerp from Spain in order to take up the reins of the Empire, which meant in concrete terms that he would be crowned German king and call his first Imperial diet. The coronation, held in the cathedral at Aachen on 23 October, was attended by many of the rulers of the Empire. The constitution of the Empire required that the new ruler's first Imperial diet be called soon after his coronation. As the new king would be present, making his first personal appearance in Germany, the diet would likely be attended by all the politically influential electors and rulers of the Empire, who were represented by their chancellors and councils at more 'normal' Imperial gatherings. Here was also an opportunity for papal diplomacy, in the guise of nuncio Marinus Caracciolo and special emissary Girolamo Aleander, whose proximity to the king might make it easier to win him over to papal ways of thinking. Rome held one particularly useful card in the title 'Elected Roman Emperor', which the pope conferred on Charles on 26 October 1520, after his coronation as king, enabling Charles' chancellery to use the Imperial title even before he had been crowned Emperor, an invaluable privilege in a world in which prestige and honour were so prized. The curia thereby also signalled that the pope was ready to anoint and crown in Rome the new German king as Emperor.

With the celebrations in Aachen surrounding the coronation over, Charles and his court moved on to Cologne. There he consulted extensively on urgent Imperial matters, dealing in particular with the electors, who according to the terms of the electoral capitulation, were to decide with the king on the date and location of the first Imperial diet. At all turns Elector Frederick the Wise of Saxony, politically powerful and highly regarded, played a key role. The Habsburg government, and especially the young king himself, valued Frederick's judgement and support. Advised by men such as his confessor and confidante Georg Spalatin and his Saxon chancellor Gregor Brück who were well-disposed to Luther, Frederick had decided to take the part of his Wittenberg professor against the curia's unjust verdict, just as some years earlier he had stood up for humanist and Judaist Johannes Reuchlin against the Cologne Dominican inquisitors in the commotion surrounding Jewish writings. Within the Empire the Luther Affair had become politically charged as the reformer continued to write his reform treatises in Wittenberg and pitched the bull threatening his excommunication into the flames before the Elster Gate. The decision that he would be allowed to defend his cause before Emperor and Empire still lay a long way off and would be reached only through delicate negotiation and much diplomatic and political skill on the part of the Saxon court.

The attempt to ensure that Luther was invited to appear before the Imperial diet had begun during the coronation celebrations in Aachen in October 1520, but no invitation had as yet been issued by the time of the ceremonial opening of the diet, which took place in Worms on 27 January 1521. Torn over the issue, the Emperor-Elect and his councillors found themselves in a difficult situation.

On one hand, Luther had been threatened with excommunication and the papal bull *Decet Romanum Pontificem*, issued on 3 January 1521 and known to Charles V since 18 January, had declared him to be a heretic according to the laws of the church. Raised in the intense religiosity of Burgundy, Charles knew to abhor a heretic, and he repeatedly and publicly showed his contempt for Luther—in February 1521, in a particularly dramatic act, he demonstratively tore up unread a personal letter from Luther.[33] He would have liked nothing better than to have adopted the recommendations of the papal special envoy Girolamo Aleander, who had been tasked with publishing the heresy verdict at the Imperial court, by declaring Luther, as a heretic, an outlaw of the Empire. Where his sovereign authority was unconditional—in Spain, the Netherlands, and the German Habsburg hereditary lands—he took action against Luther without hesitation. Spectacular book burnings took place at universities and ecclesiastical centres in the Netherlands and in western

Germany, but this time it was Luther's works that were consigned to the flames, on 17 October in Liège, on 28 October in Louvain, on 12 November in Cologne, and, finally, on 29 November in Mainz.[34]

On the other hand, Charles was in the delicate early stages of his reign, when much depended on his winning the sympathies and support of the Imperial estates and on his scrupulously observing the Imperial consti- tution. Such a significant decision could be made only after consultation with the estates. The pronounced anti-Rome feelings amongst the Imperial estates also had to be taken into account—those sentiments had been spelled out in the *Gravamina nationis germanicae*, the catalogue of complaints about the pope and the curia drawn up by earlier Imperial diets—and would likely, as indeed proved to be the case,[35] play a definitive role at the upcoming diet. The Luther Affair could only be tackled in close cooperation with the Imperial estates, and above all with the Saxon elector, especially as since Charles' election as king, popular support for Luther had grown enormously. The discussions of how to proceed were overshadowed by a fear that the appearance of the 'heretic' before the Imperial diet could prompt unrest amongst the 'common people' in both town and countryside, or even rebellion.[36]

For a hearing for Luther at the diet to be avoided, Frederick the Wise would need to be brought on board with the papal position that no court in Christendom had the authority to examine or even discuss a verdict of heresy passed in Rome and that therefore the Imperial bann should be issued without delay. In Aachen the Saxon elector had doggedly avoided the pope's emissaries, and in Cologne, Aleander, the papal legate, therefore turned to surprise tactics. On 4 November he unexpectedly appeared in Frederick's path during Sunday Mass at the Franciscan monastery, seeking the elector's commitment to the execution of the heresy verdict passed on his professor of Bible. In response the elector diplomatically distanced himself from the brash demands of the envoy and went on the offensive himself. First, he informed the envoy, Luther must be able to present his case before distinguished scholars, before pious and impartial judges. To date, Frederick declared, no one had convinced him that 'Luther's writings are so trounced that they deserve to be burned'. He could therefore continue to consider himself an 'obedient son of the church', faithful to traditional belief.[37]

The elector's strategy is very evident: both critics and supporters of the Augustinian monk were to recognize that for the Saxon government, here was a matter of procedure and the procedure to be followed should be as determined by the law and constitution of the Holy Roman Empire and the privileges of the German estates, not by Roman ecclesiastical law. To Saxon minds, unquestioning acceptance of the verdict passed in Rome followed by its execution through an automatic Imperial bann were incompatible with the Imperial constitution. The accused must first be called before the highest court in the Empire, where he would be heard by the king and the estates, brought together in the Imperial diet; only then could a decision be made, which would be binding on all the estates of the Empire.

Weeks of uncertainty and confusion followed. Charles summoned Luther, then, at the insistence of Aleander, withdrew the citation; Electoral Saxony questioned its participation in the diet on the grounds that during negotiations before the event itself, 'Luther's books without having been heard and without having been defeated by scripture were burned at Cologne, Mainz, and elsewhere';[38] and finally, at the end of January, with the Imperial court already in Worms and the Imperial diet about to be launched, under a Habsburg initiative over several days a round of secret talks involving Jean Glapion, Charles' confessor, and Gregor Brück, the Saxon chancellor, took place.[39] The Imperial government sought a forced reconciliation of the 'heretic' with Rome that would break the political impasse. This plan foundered as again Saxony stalled, continuing to insist that the differences be aired publicly. This final exchange did convince those who advised Charles during the month that followed that his political Imperial goals would be at risk if Saxony did not get its way, for in the meantime, on 19 February, the Imperial estates had passed a resolution adopting Saxon demands as their own.[40] Initially the Imperial court thought it might be possible for the invitation to Luther to be issued by Saxony, hoping thus to avoid associating the emperor with the 'activities and general clamour' that in the meantime had become so much part of the Luther Affair.[41] Only when Frederick understandably refused to fall into line, did Charles, on 6 March 1521, issue the citation for Luther to appear before the diet, and he also promised free and safe passage to a man whom the curia deemed to have been lawfully judged a heretic. Imperial herald Kaspar Sturm was commissioned to carry the citation and the assurance of safe passage to Wittenberg—he left Worms on 15 March and presented the Imperial mandate to Luther exactly two weeks later.

While the question of how to proceed had been resolved by adopting the Saxon plan, the details and legal status of Luther's appearance before the diet remained uncertain. Had he been called to appear before an arbitration tribunal composed of experts who could assess his case?—which was how Luther and the Saxon court understood the summons. Or was the heretic merely to be given the opportunity to distance himself publicly from his writings and to recant his teachings?—the view of the Imperial party and the curial emissaries. The papal diplomats were still refusing to admit defeat: acting together with Glapion, Charles' confessor, even as Luther was approaching Worms they attempted to prevent his appearance before the Imperial diet by redirecting him, citing security concerns, to the castle of Franz von Sickingen, an Imperial knight, at Ebernburg.

'In Spite of All the Gates of Hell and the Powers in the Air'

What of Luther himself during these months? During the dogged wrestling in the west of the Empire over how to proceed, undeterred Luther continued to debate with his opponents through his published works. He maintained close contact with the electoral Saxon court, which had travelled west, largely via Spalatin and on occasion with the ruler's family directly, as in January 1521 when Prince John Frederick sent him a message from his uncle Frederick.[42] Without limiting his freedom of action, Luther kept Spalatin, whom he knew to have the ear of the elector, informed of his most significant steps—for example, he informed Spalatin of the burning of the papal legal texts and the bull threatening him with excommunication on the day itself, although only after the act.[43] He also sent Spalatin copies of the proofs of the major polemical works that he wrote during these months, including his refutation of the papal bull, the *Assertio omnium articulorum*. Only when he sought to ensure that by dedicating one of his works to the ruling dynasty its contents would become semi-official did he ask for advice in advance.[44]

Luther adopted a similar role in the political wrangling over his appearance before the Imperial diet. In support of Saxon attempts to win over the newly elected German king to his being heard before the Imperial diet, Luther published his 'Offer', in both German, with the title *Erbieten*, and Latin, as *Oblatio*, having first coordinated its contents with the Saxon court.[45] This text took the form of a pamphlet addressed to Charles V in which the Augustinian monk announced his readiness to justify the teachings that had been found objectionable but also set out the conditions under which he was prepared to do so. On a highly personal note, on one hand he pointed out the 'provocations, insults, perils, and whatever evil the wicked can devise' that had been his lot for the last three years, while on the other hand, he apologized that he had 'previously at times ... written too seriously or too offensively'. When it came to the substance of his claims, he remained resolute, and he demanded that 'as an obedient son of the holy Christian church' explanation be given to him 'on the first basis of the holy scriptures'. In practice this 'Offer' was anything but a personal message for Charles V. Yes, the work was written in Latin, which the young king understood, but it appeared concurrently in German, and with the single-sheet 'Offer' published and sent out into the world, the Imperial government was forced into a public debate. For Luther the publication of this pamphlet also paid off in that Franz von Sickingen read a copy of the 'Offer' that had been put on public display in Cologne and immediately offered his enthusiastic noble support.[46]

In late 1520 Luther was delighted to learn that the Emperor seemed about to summon him to Worms, and he began to prepare for the journey. All the greater, then, was his disappointment when the Emperor retracted his consent.[47] In order to influence the restarted negotiations in his favour, at the beginning of 1521 Luther sent two copies of the 'Offer' to Worms: one was intended for the Saxon elector, but the second was addressed to the Emperor and included an extensive personal cover letter—this was the missive sent by Luther to Charles that, rather than read, the Emperor immediately ripped up.[48] Admittedly, Luther was not too hopeful that he had found in Charles a man who 'for Christ would attack this devil [the pope]', particularly when he heard that 'the imperial court is ruled by tyrannical mendicant monks'.[49] Yet he continued to insist that the Emperor-Elect was the person who should take on this 'case of God, of universal Christendom, and of the whole German nation—and not of a single man, much less my own'.[50] He had to persist with this line as in these very months he had declared the pope to be Antichrist, which left the Holy Roman Emperor the only universal institution with jurisdiction over a matter that concerned the whole of Christendom and with the authority to refute the Roman Antichrist. This dilemma remained with Luther for the rest of his life, preoccupying him even after his encounter with the Emperor in Worms had proved so deeply disappointing and even though Charles V's deep aversion to Luther's theology meant that it was pointless to pin any hope on the Emperor.

For Luther, the universal authority of the office of Emperor always ranked above any particular authority. This attitude encompassed even the Saxon elector, who had served him so well in preparing his path to the Imperial diet and to his appearance before the head of the Empire. Ten years later when, after the Imperial diet held at Augsburg of 1530, all seemed poised for war to break out between the Schmalkaldic League, led by the rulers of Saxony and Hesse, and the Emperor, who had just been crowned in Bologna, Luther still baulked at the advice of the so-reviled lawyers and long refused to agree that inferior powers had any right to rebel against the universal authority of the Emperor.[51] Neither during the early stormy years of the Reformation nor subsequently did he wish to see 'the battle for the gospel fought with force and deaths'.[52] Potential for unrest and a willingness to take action certainly existed, especially amongst the Imperial knights. On that count, the fears of the Habsburg court and the curia that Luther's appearance before the Imperial diet could spark insurrection were well grounded, but Luther was neither willing to use force in his own cause, or even that of the Gospel, nor eager to stoke unrest. He was no Savonarola, even if one of his opponents sought to hang that label on him literally: when Luther passed through Naumburg on his way to Worms he was handed a picture of the Dominican preacher of repentance who a quarter-century earlier had been the cause of such furore in Florence. The blending of religious reform with social upheaval was for Luther the work of the devil. He condemned and opposed figures such as Thomas Müntzer and the leaders of the Anabaptist Kingdom of Münster. Only 'through the word', it was evident to him in 1521, 'is the world overcome and the church preserved and through the word it will be made strong again. The antichrist will be ground down through the word without a hand even stirring itself.'[53]

Even though Luther had repeatedly stressed that even illness would not keep him away from the diet,[54] in Worms the Saxon court was not at all sure that the monk would risk the journey. Luther's thoughts certainly ran all too readily to the bonfire on which Jan Hus had been burned to death in Constance a century earlier despite promises of safe passage.[55] In the course of his journey he spied mandates displayed on public buildings in which the German king had already condemned his writings; on being asked by the herald if in these circumstances he still intended to continue on to Worms, Luther answered in the affirmative and with resolution, 'but trembling'.[56]

Fear did not deter the Wittenberg professor of Bible. He craved that moment in sacred history when he would stand before the highest body in Christendom to declare the truth of the pure word of God that he had so recently discovered and expose the devilish deceptions of Rome. 'Up to now one has only played around in this case', he assured his paternalistic mentor Johann von Staupitz, 'now something serious is at hand', but he continued, 'all these things are now completely in the hand of Almighty God. No one can deny this... There is such a tremendous turmoil that I think it cannot be quieted except by the arrival of the Last Day, so great is the animosity on both sides.' He ended the letter, 'Farewell, my Father; pray for the Word of God and for me. I am carried away and tossed about by the waves.'[57]

The certain knowledge that 'the pope is the Antichrist' had 'freed him in many ways'[58] and since late 1520 Luther had been determined to take up the struggle against the power of evil, and to do so openly: 'according to St. Paul's teaching, it is the time to accuse, ridicule, and punish publically all the obvious offenders before the whole world, so that the cause of the offense may be driven out of God's kingdom', he informed the primate of the church in the Empire.[59] He was adamant: 'If I am called only on account of a recantation, then I will not come.'[60] Instead he hoped that the Emperor would 'arrange that this case be turned over to devout, learned, understanding, trustworthy, and Christian men, both clergymen and laymen, who are well versed in the Bible and who understand and differentiate between divine and human laws and commands', who would then 'discuss the case carefully with me'; he would give account only to them.

On 14 April 1521, when he was already in Frankfurt and therefore close by, he announced to Spalatin with great cheer that he would 'enter Worms in spite of all the gates of hell and the powers in the air'. Like so many of his words, this statement became proverbial for Protestantism, reworked as a pointed image: 'there were as many devils in that city as there were tiles on the roofs'.[61] Luther's expression was to be taken literally, for ever since the church hierarchy had rebuffed the rediscovered pure Word and therefore had been unable to comprehend the revealed evangelical truth that it contained, the Wittenberg monk had believed that he was participating in an eschatological battle, required to defend himself from the machinations of hell and its creatures in this world. As they sang out the hymn 'A Mighty Fortress is Our God' (Ein feste Burg ist unser Gott), later generations of

Lutherans throughout the world understood Luther's message just as literally as had the founder of their church when in Worms in 1521:

> And did the world with devils swarm,
> All gaping to devour us,
> We fear not the smallest harm,
> Success is yet before us.
> This world's prince accurst,
> Let him rage his worst,
> No hurt brings about;
> His doom it is gone out,
> One word can overturn him.[62]

Processing in Triumph and Pain

After the summons arrived in Wittenberg on 29 March, the Augustinian monk left for Worms on 2 April. He travelled in a horse-drawn carriage that was far from comfortable—the town council had rented it for him from a master goldsmith and had at least added a roof as protection from the wind and weather. The university had equipped him with twenty gulden for his expenses on the journey. In effect he was on a work trip, financed by magistracy and university, to give account of his revolutionary research findings before the highest court of the Empire. As the regulations of his order required, Luther was again accompanied by another Augustinian monk. The naivety of Johann Petzensteiner, his travelling companion, repeatedly caused Luther trouble. For example, Petzensteiner chatted away blithely to Johann Cochläus, dean in Frankfurt, already one of Luther's most active adversaries and on the lookout for any unguarded utterances. In order to deflect any danger, Luther quick-wittedly parried with a joke: 'My brother Petzenstein believes himself to be more erudite than any of us, particularly when he has downed a good few drinks.'[63] His other companions on the journey were a different matter. Nikolaus von Amsdorff was a member of the Wittenberg theological faculty and had also accompanied Luther to the Leipzig Disputation in 1519. Justus Jonas, lawyer and theologian, joined the party in Erfurt. His inclusion was likely associated with the chair of ecclesiastical law at Wittenberg, which had recently been vacated with the death of his teacher Henning Göde, and to which Jonas was to be called formally by the ruler, who was currently in Worms. Pommeranian nobleman Peter von Suaven represented the student body. Thomas Blarer, later reformer of Constance, may also have been one of the party. Even though Philip Melanchthon, the young shining light of the faculty of arts, had not been able to fulfil his wish to accompany Luther, the group that did travel clearly and impressively documented the solidarity of the university at Wittenberg with its professor under fire. Once he reached Worms, Luther would have at his side the whole company of electoral councillors to provide him with both political and legal advice, above all Georg Spalatin, who remained the conduit between reformer and elector, and Wittenberg professor of law Hieronymus Schurf, who acted as Luther's legal representation. At the first hearing, for example, Schurf insisted that the title of each book under scrutiny by Emperor and Empire be specified.

At the time of his journey, Luther was already a famous figure, in today's terms a best-selling author and media star. His procession to Worms was a public event that brought people to take a stand in a dispute over principles that concerned the very core of Christendom. Some who disagreed were reserved, like the population of Leipzig, who paid little attention to Luther as he passed through their city; others used the opportunity to express their displeasure to the heretical monk, as did the cleric in Naumburg whom we encountered with his picture of Savonarola. The celebrations of his supporters were far from reserved. Luther and his companions were met at Erfurt by Crotus Rubeanus, the rector of the university, along with forty horsemen and together they made a celebratory entry into the city. When Luther preached the following day, the Augustinian church was full to bursting because so many people wanted to see the monk and hear him preach, an experience that was repeated everywhere he paused to preach during the journey to Worms.

As Luther understood his travelling to Worms as a mission in the cause of salvation, he saw the devil behind every and all misfortunes that occurred along the way—in the panic that broke out among those who had come to hear him preach in Erfurt; in the publication of the Imperial mandate against his writings, which he deemed a rush to judgement; in the illness that had plagued him since he had left Eisenach 'in a way', he wrote, 'which previously has been unknown to me'.[64] Luther experienced that struggle physically—this illness, which held him in its clutches both while he was in Worms and during his time at the Wartburg, brought him agonizing digestive problems: 'The Lord', so he informed his friends in Wittenberg in a direct language very much his own, 'has afflicted me with painful constipation. The elimination is so hard that I am forced to press with all my strength, even to the point of perspiration, and the longer I delay the worse it gets. Yesterday on the fourth day I could go once, but I did not sleep all night and still have no peace.'[65] These pains were at the same time an affliction of God, that 'I may not be without a relic of the cross'.[66]

Throughout his life the reformer continued to be beset by digestive problems—only a few days before his death he praised the effects of Naumburg beer to his wife, Katharina, beer that, he wrote, 'agrees with me and gives me about three bowel movements in three hours in the morning'.[67] While we can assume that these physical problems had physiological origins, the psychological strains undoubtedly also contributed to outbreaks at times of particular crisis, especially during the weeks before and after Luther's appearance in Worms before the good and the great of the Empire, when the burdens he bore required superhuman strength.

He did not lack for approval and encouragement during the fourteen days he travelled to Worms, and also in Worms itself. As the monk summoned to appear before Emperor and Empire approached the Imperial city in his horse-drawn carriage on the morning of 16 April, a Tuesday, trumpets announced his arrival from the tower of the cathedral. A cavalcade of Saxon nobles awaited him outside the city gate and accompanied him to his quarters, while the streets thronged with hundreds of people, overwhelmingly supporters, who greeted him tumultuously, much to the displeasure of Aleander, the papal legate, and the much smaller number of Luther's opponents.[68] In order to be able to keep an eye on Luther and to screen him from his supporters, the curia had wanted him housed with the Habsburg court. The Saxons insisted, however, that he stay in accommodation belonging to the Knights of Saint John, along with some of their own delegation. As the royal archmarshall was also resident there, Luther would still be under a watchful eye. With space at a premium, as was usual during Imperial diets, Luther had to share his sleeping quarters with two electoral Saxon officials, surely not happy circumstances for a man used to a solitary monastic cell and burdened with momentous decisions.[69]

Luther sought to preserve an air of normality in his cramped quarters. Early the next morning, still not knowing exactly when he was to appear before the diet, he carried out his standard pastoral responsibilities, visiting the seriously ill Saxon nobleman Hans von Minkwitz, whose confession he heard before celebrating communion.[70] In the late afternoon, on returning to his quarters after his first cross-examination, he sat down to write a letter he might have written on any day, on this occasion to the famous Viennese humanist Johannes Cuspinian, political adviser to the late Emperor Maximilian, requesting, as was standard practice amongst humanists, his friendship and admission into his circle—although evidently the impressions of his recent experience still lingered, for he informed Cuspinian that 'with Christ's help . . . I shall not in all eternity recant the least particle'.[71] Luther also had to pay the price of his fame, for alongside his principal purpose in travelling to Worms, he received an unending list of visitors, including members of the high nobility and many Imperial knights who had read his letter to the nobility with enthusiasm and now, in this moment of danger, wished to offer him their protection. Landgrave Philip of Hesse, just sixteen years old, who would soon become one of the most energetic of all the Imperial princes who supported the Reformation, took a different tack. In Worms Philip used a tricky question to try to break through Luther's reserve: Was it really God's will, he asked, that, as was stated in Scripture on the Babylonian captivity, a woman whose husband was proven impotent was allowed to take another husband?[72] Luther was smart enough to ensure this problem was not allowed to epitomize his Reformation, and he gave the count an evasive answer. Almost two decades later, when the theologians of Wittenberg found themselves facing the possibility of a bigamous marriage by the Landgrave, with its explosive implications both for the politics of the Empire and for the law of the church, that avenue of escape was closed.

Reformer and Emperor

Advancing the Holy Faith or Universal Evangelical Reform

On the morning of the day after his arrival in Worms, Luther was informed that he was to appear at 4 o'clock that afternoon at the bishop's palace at the cathedral to give account of his teachings. The two men and two worlds that faced each other at that session of the Imperial diet—and at a second session at the same time the next day—could hardly have been more different. Emperor-Elect Charles V was just twenty-one years old; the thirty-seven year-old professor of Bible, who regardless of his fundamental theological objections to the sacred role of the religious orders continued to wear the Augustinian habit, was a mature man. A two-week-long journey lay behind the monk and had brought him from remote Wittenberg in the central German electorate of Saxony, which has been described by historians as a 'colonial land' with little intellectual or cultural spark, to the west of the Empire and to the Rhineland specifically, which, with its ancient cultural associations, had retained an inherent Romanness and as a result tended to have closer ties to the pope in Rome than did the lands in the east of the Empire.[73] A product of this western and southern European world through and through, the young Emperor had been brought up in the cultural world of Burgundy, which while both religiously and politically innovative, deliberately bound such innovation in with tradition. To see in the juxtaposition of Charles and Luther the medieval lined up against the modern is simply wrong, evidence of a failure to fathom who and what the Habsburg Emperor was. Both men believed in the need for change; where they parted ways was on how that change might be achieved and the extent to which the traditional could be carried over into the innovative. The young Emperor had no doubt that the renewal of Imperial authority and the consolidation of his rule over an Imperium that stretched from the New World, via Spain and Burgundy, as far as the Balkans on the easternmost edge of Latin Christendom, could only succeed on the back of the universal Roman Church. He was prepared to see the church, with its flaws and deficiencies, reformed, but such renewal was not in any way to weaken the church at its core. Very much by contrast, Luther had come to believe that only the abolition of the papal church, with its unevangelical embellishments that had proliferated across the centuries, could restore the well-being of Christendom; any other possibility required a pact with Antichrist, which could lead only to eternal damnation.

For both Luther and Charles V the moment was decisive (Figure 21). Each man stood at a new beginning; each man had his own vision of the universal task he faced. For both men reform of Christianity was the issue, and in light of the interweaving of religion and politics in the Europe of this this earlier age, reform of Christianity meant change for both church *and* society. The professor of Bible began with the core Christian faith, which he believed could be freed of all human additions and returned to the original condition of the first Christian communities. The young Habsburg began with Imperial rule, which was equally secular and sacred. In the proposition with which the diet at Worms was opened, he stated that he had not sought to become Emperor on the death of his grandfather for the sake of the office itself, but 'for the restoration and rebuilding of the holy empire, and for the increase and uplifting of our holy faith, and in order that its enemies there will more readily be destroyed', a programmatic account that formed

Figure 21. Martin Luther confronts Emperor Charles V, a cardinal, and other clerics. Woodcut title page for a printed account of Luther's examination at the diet at Worms, printed in Augsburg, 1521.

in effect a policy statement. A reformed Empire, reinvigorated with the assistance of 'the power of his majesty's Hispanic kingdom',[74] was viewed as the foundation of a new order for Christianity or for Europe; Charles also sought the return to an original condition, but in his case to the original single Imperial entity that had been shattered by the rise of early modern states.

The extent of his lands and rule—from Austria in the east, via Naples and lower and upper Burgundy, and on to the Spanish empire and its overseas possessions in the west—meant that the heir of Emperor Maximilian and of the Catholic kings of Spain was the most powerful ruler in Europe. The ideal of universal Imperial authority would only be able to function as the European order in the long term, with the individual rulers assimilated under the *auctoritas* of the Empire, if the Emperor was able to bring the German princes on board with that model. One additional complication lay ahead—the pope in Rome could not be ignored, for the Imperial coronation and the anointing of the new Emperor fell traditionally to the *pontifex maximus*. Charles was doubly invested in the catholicity and universality of the church and of religious belief in—his political consideration of the pope, but above all in his universal understanding of the very concept of the Empire, which had no room for separation or particularity but depended entirely on a single faith and an indivisible universal church.

The expectations invested by the two protagonists in their encounter were not just very different; they were also irreconcilable. Charles expected nothing less than recantation, for only then could he turn as quickly as possible, free of such troublesome quarrelling amongst theologians, to his real task, the reordering of Empire and Europe in keeping with Habsburg intellectual and political ideals. With the medieval *societas christiana* now disintegrating into a plethora of early modern states and the Imperial dignity therefore in decline, Charles believed his prime responsibility lay in the realization of a new order in Europe, one that on one hand would encompass all the individual political entities and on the other hand would restore the status and effectiveness of the Imperial authority. Even in this changed world with its early modern state system, the Emperor, in this case Charles and his Habsburg dynasty, was to stand above the rulers of those individual states and as supreme head of Christendom have command over the continent.

By contrast, Luther and his supporters—who included members of the Imperial estates who may have been small in number but made up for any lack in quantity by their highly active engagement—had not yet given up hope that the young Habsburg Emperor could be brought over to their side, and that with Charles at their head they would be able to force Rome to undertake the desired reform. Both parties would soon see clearly that they had deluded themselves fundamentally. The Wittenberg monk was as little willing to consider recanting, as Charles, a Habsburg with an overwhelming sense of majesty, was willing to consider rebelling against the Roman Church.

'A Conscience Held Captive by the Word of God'

The extent of the public interest in the encounter between Emperor and monk is evident in the fact that we know in detail about almost every hour of Luther's stay in Worms. The information is found in minutes taken and letters written by some of those present, by Dr Konrad Peutinger, for example, Augsburg envoy to the diet, or Dr Hieronymus Vehus, councillor to the Margrave of Baden. The veritable flood of printed semi-official texts and the pamphlets based on them is an even more informative source. Each side was eager to see its own reading of events spread widely, not least because of the potential commotion they both feared. It was not the critical and somewhat derisive clerical and Roman reports of Aleander,

Cochläus, or their ilk, which tended to play down the impression that Luther had made, that found a sympathetic ear, but an anonymous depiction of events, which can be traced back to the Saxon court and perhaps even directly to Luther and Spalatin. The German version, which contained Luther's speech verbatim, was published immediately in Basel, Hagenau, and Strasburg, and naturally also by the printers back home in Wittenberg; soon those texts were enthusiastically being read and read out throughout town and countryside.[75]

According to this authentic, although certainly not neutral, account, right up until the moment when he entered the room in which the hearing was to take place, accompanied by Ulrich von Pappenheim, Imperial archmarshall, and Kaspar Sturm, Imperial herald, Luther still did not know exactly what he would face. The form of the proceedings had been agreed only that morning by Aleander and Glapion, without reference to the electoral Saxon party. The reformer expected, or at least hoped, that he would be given the opportunity to justify his teachings and to argue his case on the propositions faulted by Rome with men who were knowledgeable and objective. He was evidently taken by surprise, therefore, when the official of Electoral Trier, Johann von der Ecken, who spoke on behalf of the Emperor, simply asked whether the works lying on a table were by him and, after Luther had acknowledged that he was their author, demanded without ceremony that he recant. While Luther was ready to acknowledge his writings, after the titles, at the insistence of his legal counsel, Hieronymus Schurf, had been read out individually, he declared that he could not respond to the demand that he recant, for this 'matter concerns the word of God, which is the highest thing in heaven and on earth'. He did not want to run any danger, he replied, that Christ's judgement might come to pass—Christ 'had said, anyone who is ashamed of me on earth, that person will I be ashamed of before my heavenly father and his angels'.[76] After a short break for consultation, the Imperial spokesman remonstrated sternly with Luther for his presumption in suggesting that he alone spoke the truth and for thereby causing turmoil in both church and Empire. Although legally Luther was not entitled to any time for reflection, von der Ecken continued, as he should have known that he had been summoned to recant, the Emperor-Elect would graciously grant him that time, until the same hour the following afternoon.[77]

Although Luther had remained resolute, his first and short appearance before the Imperial diet had hardly made an overwhelming impression.

According to Aleander, on first setting eyes on Luther, the Emperor had stated, 'he won't make me into a heretic'.[78] Several of those present reported that Luther had spoken very quietly and with reserve—'in a low voice'[79]—and had therefore not been understood by many in the room. Even the Saxon elector, who had consistently refused to meet the rebellious monk in person and now in Worms saw him for the first time close up, was visibly disappointed. The elector and his councillors were anxious about the outcome of this public appearance by their professor of Bible, an event for which they had pushed. Other observers also mistakenly believed that the Wittenberg monk felt intimidated and was on the retreat. The members of the curia, and Aleander in particular, were openly pleased and believed that the outcome they desired was just around the corner. At the same time, his enemies were not unaware of the continuing threat Luther represented, and he was told that he should make his case the following day only orally and not in writing.[80]

Convinced that he had been commissioned by God, Luther was far from defeated. The continuing visits from many Imperial knights and their assurances that they would vigorously defend him from the machinations of Rome's devotees were for Luther simply an earthly demonstration of the grace of God, which he never doubted. When Konrad Peutinger, the Augsburg envoy, visited Luther in his quarters the following morning, he found a 'cheerful' man, who was 'in good spirits' and who asked earnestly after Peutinger's wife and children.[81]

Luther's second appearance before the diet, on the Thursday after his arrival in Worms, was that of a man steadfast and sovereign. His way to the diet was again lined by an excited crowd, and he had to wait a good hour while the diet completed its work on the previous item on the day's agenda. A great throng of people also attended the hearing itself, where the mood was tense, for part of the crowd had succeeded in forcing their way into the room in which the encounter was to take place. From the start of his speech, in which he responded in detail to the Imperial spokesman's repeated demand that he recant,[82] Luther demonstrated that he was master of the situation. That the circumstances of the previous day had likely contributed to his discomfiture, he acknowledged openly, stating that he was 'a man accustomed not to courts but to the cells of monks'.[83] In light of his lack of courtly experience and his interest only in 'the glory of God and the sound instruction of Christ's faithful' should he 'have ... not given the proper titles to some'—which according to a note made by Peutinger had indeed happened in the case of the ecclesiastical rulers and the non-princely estates—then, Luther insisted, he had not done so in order to offend, and he asked for forgiveness. Thus freed from any scruples, he was now ready to pronounce on the matter before him and did so with scholarly meticulousness and discrimination; he spoke first in German, and then, at the request of the Emperor-Elect, who understood very little German, repeated everything in Latin.

According to Luther, his writings—he again acknowledged his authorship with self-confidence and accepted sole responsibility for their content—were of three kinds. His preaching and exposition of the Bible for the Christian community were Scriptural, he noted, and his opponents would find nothing with which to object. There could be no question of recanting these works. The same was true, he continued, for the works he had composed that criticized the abuses of Rome and repeated grievances that were already widespread, for 'the experience of all and the complaints of everyone witness that through the decrees of the pope and the doctrines of men the consciences of the faithful have been most miserably entangled, tortured, and torn to pieces. Also, property and possessions, especially in this illustrious German nation, have been devoured by an unbelievable tyranny'—a clever allusion to the *Gravamina nationis germanicae,* which was being addressed by a commission of the Imperial diet alongside the Luther Affair. Any recantation, Luther thus established, could only be concerned with the third type of book that he had written, those small works in which he had 'been disputing... about the teaching of Christ'. He would follow the model of Christ for 'the Lord himself, who knew that he could not err, did not refuse to hear testimony against his teaching', and therefore he called on 'anyone who is able, either high or low, [to] bear witness, expose my errors, overthrowing them by the writings of the prophets and the evangelists'. Spokesman von der Ecken interjected that Luther's request for refutation was improper, as his teachings repeated heresies that had already long before been refuted by councils, above all by the Council of Constance when it passed its verdict on Jan Hus, but Luther only became all the more pointed: he believed neither pope nor councils for they had been proven to have erred and had contradicted themselves. He would allow himself to be convinced only 'by the testimony of the Scriptures or by clear reason'.

If the day before, as he stood before the leading figures of the Empire, Luther had doubted whether he really could be the only one to teach the truth, since then a solitary but critical inner struggle had brought him the certainty that was his fate. Luther was sure that he neither could control, nor wanted to control, the circumstances in which he lived. He concluded with a maxim that would become famous: 'I am bound by the Scriptures I have quoted and my conscience is captive to the Word of God. I cannot and I will not retract anything, since it is neither safe nor right to go against conscience. I cannot do otherwise, here I stand, may God help me, Amen.'

Today these words still imbue Protestants with self-confidence, although they also tie their hands, particularly when it comes to ecumenical discussions, and especially when these discussions concern the papacy. In the moment in which they were uttered, they left a tremendous impression on their audience. There was evidently no point in continuing the hearing before the full Imperial diet. The Imperial spokesman, who had so recently sought to derail Luther with his probing questions, now, after a skirmish on the role of councils, saw no possibility of forcing even the smallest of concessions from Luther. The gathered Imperial estates required time to consider the next step, as not just the Emperor-Elect, who had listened without any great display of emotion and without intervening, but also the estates paused to reflect. The only members of the audience who were not transfixed by Luther's words were those whose stance had already been determined at the outset by their political or other ties to Rome; in other words, almost every German who was not part of the church hierarchy was gripped by his response. Such was the case also for the crowds gathered outside the room in which the hearing was taking place, who received an account of the gist of Luther's words and immediately the hearing ended raised 'much loud noise'. The growing group of Luther backers amongst the estates believed their support validated, above all Frederick the Wise, who praised Luther's speech and showed his admiration in the qualifying addition, 'He is far too bold for me.'[84]

A wave of enthusiasm for Luther swept through the German public, powered in particular by editors at the Rhau-Grunenberg publishing house in Wittenberg, the press that Luther was currently using. They took the record of the words that Luther had spoken at Worms and ingeniously sharpened and extended its content, without any contribution from Luther, who by this date was holed up in the Wartburg. *I cannot act otherwise/here I stand/God help me/Amen*[85]—thus ran their account of Luther's concluding words. The Wittenberg pamphlet brought this formulation to the broader public, and this defiant version became indelibly associated with Luther, passed down through generations of German Protestants. Even today this version defines Protestant tradition—right up to the commercially successful 'Luther socks', which sport the words 'Here I stand'.

A Sovereign Held Captive by His Noble Ancestry

Luther's 'Amen' did not bring the Luther Affair to an end at the diet at Worms. Charles and the curial party had already decided that refusal to recant would be followed by declaration of the Imperial bann and that the Emperor was legally entitled to execute the mandate already formulated by Aleander without any further involvement by the Imperial estates. The appearance, however, of the monk from the remote Saxon province had touched the young Habsburg more than he gave to see and more than his court was willing to admit at the time or later. Not that what he had just experienced had unnerved or even fascinated the Emperor-Elect; rather, Charles' majesty had been challenged. He held it his responsibility to counter the heretical monk's individualistic—and in Charles' eyes subject-ive—assertions about faith with his own confession, with its very different foundations. He recorded that profession in writing the same day, and the following morning his words were read out before the Imperial estates.[86] As the foundation of his faith he brought into play his noble ancestry—the most Christian Emperors the Catholic kings of Spain, and the archdukes and dukes of Austria and Burgundy had always understood themselves to be 'defenders of the Catholic faith, the holy ceremonies, laws, instructions, and holy traditions'. He himself, Charles, had written:

> was prepared to live and to die according to their example ... For there is no doubt, that the views of a single member of a religious order are in error when they run counter to all of Christendom both for the previous thousand years and even longer and also in the present; according to those views the whole of this Christendom would have been in error always and would still be in error today.

And, he continued, he, just like the Imperial estates of 'the noble and renowned German Nation ... is called by privilege and unique standing to be the defender and protector of the Catholic faith'. Therefore, he confessed, he regretted that he 'had hesitated for so long to take action against this Luther and his false doctrine', continuing, 'I am firmly resolved no longer to hear him but instead to take action against him as against a notorious heretic.'[87]

The previous day Luther had looked only to his subjective conscience and had found there a bastion of 'blessedness' and religious self-assurance that he would never fundamentally question. The young Habsburg, by contrast, looked objectively to the institutions and traditions of his lineage, which he equated with the experiences of Christendom and its historic ability to assert itself when challenged both internally and externally. No less decisive for the Emperor than for Luther was the conviction that God was on his side, and Charles was sure of divine assistance in his battle against the German heresy, or the 'German plague' as it would soon be known in his Spanish milieu.

Luther's speech has been called the key text of Protestantism,[88] and for good reason. Equally significant, however, is the short text that Charles V recorded in his own hand. Unlike Luther's speech, which opened, and still opens, a window onto the collective identity of Protestantism, the Emperor's words allow us access only to his person and politics. With its roots in the Imperial office, in a personal majesty, and in the traditions of Charles' dynasty, the religiosity Charles displayed at Worms was the very personal religiosity of the Habsburgs. It could provide no direction for the internal reform of the papal church.

That distinction helps explain why Luther's words have been heard around the world and have always characterized the reformer, while Charles' words have been forgotten. Even the numerous and widely distributed pamphlets that were a product of Luther's appearance at Worms took very little note of the Emperor's speech. When historians quote Charles' text, they do so largely to provide evidence of what they see as a superficial traditionalism of Charles and his court when it came to religion and church politics. An unjaundiced view, however, can identify a sense of tradition that, just like Luther's rebellion against Rome, drew on personal religiosity and consciousness of personal salvation. The roots of Charles' distinct and pre-confessional piety lay with Erasmus and the *devotio moderna* of the Low Countries, which he would have encountered through his tutor Adrian of Utrecht and which, we should remember, Luther had also encountered as a schoolboy. Those roots lay also in the chivalric orders— in the Order of the Golden Fleece, so closely associated with the House of Burgundy, of which Charles had become a member while still a child, and in the Spanish chivalric orders of the Reconquista, with their patron saints Saint James and Saint George, the dragon killer. On a magnificent winged altar in Valencia (now part of the collection of the Victoria and Albert Museum in

Figure 22. Panel depicting Saint George fighting the Moors, from the Altarpiece of Saint George, formerly in Valencia Cathedral, c.1400.

London, see Figure 22), Charles would have seen the latter saint depicted as he intervened personally in the struggle against the Moriscos, bringing victory to the Christian armies. These chivalric orders, whose original religious purposes were still very evident to both members and onlookers, stoked Charles' burning desire to defend pure Catholic teachings, but he was aware that this battle could be won only if the church were renewed from within, a process he had seen initiated by the humanists and proponents of the *devotio moderna* in his Burgundian lands and by Archbishop Cisneros in Spain.

This traditionalism was both political and active and bore a clear sense that the world could not remain as it presently was. Looking to tradition, Charles unflaggingly insisted that the reluctant popes call a universal council to tackle abuses within the church. The secular ordering of Christendom, which the emergence of the early modern state had set in flux, was also to be rethought, through wide-ranging political and intellectual projects. Traditional thinking needed also to accommodate the persistent new challenges of the Habsburgs' global empire.

'Here I stand, I cannot act otherwise. God help me'—those defiant and existential words could have been assigned just as well to Charles as to Luther. For Charles their absolute certainty functioned on two levels: psychologically, as a product of his upbringing and the personal religiosity it engendered, formed entirely from the Catholicism of his ancestors; and politically, for Christendom would need to be securely bound together by Catholicism if Charles was to realize his political plans. Both the safeguarding and consolidation of Habsburg authority in the vast Habsburg lands and the implementation of the universal ideal for the reordering of the political make-up of Europe would require the unified ideological basis that, to Charles' mind, only the unified Catholic Church could provide.

Charles' audience would still have had the reformer's words from the previous day ringing in their ears, but they were deeply moved by the religious vision of the young Emperor, a response shared by Luther's own ruler, whose presence when the Emperor's text was read is specifically noted in reports. The Emperor seemed just as sure as Luther that he was following the will of God, and he was also just as adamant. After weeks of reticence and political manoeuvring, the Emperor had taken a very personal stand and had laid out the guiding principles for his religious and ecclesiastical politics. A number of princes who on hearing Luther's speech had begun to falter now re-established strong bonds with a traditional faith under the influence of the Emperor's exalted sense of majesty. Even after the Emperor had made his position known, however, the Imperial estates, political participants in the authority of the Imperial crown, were not prepared simply to accept the papal maxim '*Roma locuta, causa finita*'—Rome has spoken, the matter is at an end.

Subsequent Negotiations and Luther's Departure

The activities of the Imperial diet extended beyond the full sessions. Since the late fifteenth century, the Imperial assembly had been adopting greater routine, and early modern procedural forms allowed for particularly difficult problems to be transferred out of the plenary session and into committee, where the various estates—electors, princes, counts, and cities—were represented in proportion to their membership of the diet as a whole. This procedure had already been followed in February 1521 at Worms for the *Gravamina nationis germanicae*, the estates' anti-Rome catalogue of complaints, and the estates were now eager to deal with the Luther Affair in the same way. The next day, a Sunday, was reserved for worship and was to be kept clear of any political matters, but at the start of the following week's business, the Emperor declared that he was prepared to see the discussion transferred into committee, on condition that the committee met for not longer than three days, had Luther's recantation as its goal, and brought the whole business to a definitive end with an Imperial bann, which was to be issued at the moment Luther refused to recant.[89]

Luther initially knew very little of these subsequent discussions. With his second appearance before the Emperor behind him, he felt relieved of a great burden. Back in his quarters he raised his arms and called out triumphantly, 'I'm through! I'm through!', letting off steam in a gesture used by soldiers after battle in his own time and by sportspeople today. Yet while the Emperor and the Empire made no further claims on the monk for the moment, he was not granted any quiet. Some of the most powerful men in the Empire lined up at his door, including Philip of Hesse, Duke William of Brunswick and Count William of Henneberg; others sent refreshments to fortify him.[90] In the town at large, trouble was brewing: even as Luther left the diet, disturbances had broken out. The crowds waiting outside the bishop's palace for the conclusion of the proceedings had mistakenly believed that the two armed men who had been ordered to accompany Luther were in fact there to take him to prison. When a number of Spanish soldiers in Charles' entourage called out 'into the fire with him', both anxiety and discontent grew amongst the great crowd of people who had gathered in Worms, a throng typical of Imperial diets. Spontaneous declarations of support for Luther could be heard.[91]

The tension was heightened by two anonymous threats that surfaced after Luther had made his statement before the diet, one threatening the heretic and the other celebrating the reformer. The pro-Luther text, which has been preserved, was displayed on the town hall during the night and threatened that 400 members of the nobility with 8,000 cavalry and foot soldiers were ready to take action should the courageous monk be in danger. The curial party assumed that the reference was to an imminent assault led by Sickingen and Hutten, but Luther's supporters, including Hutten himself, believed the threat to be a forgery designed to smear Luther through association with sedition. With no further information available, the rumour mill continued to turn.[92]

From those who shared his quarters or from Saxon councillors, Luther would have learned of the disturbances on the streets, of Charles' speech, and of the estates' desire for a committee of the Imperial diet to be formed. He was therefore not surprised when the following Monday, 22 April, two priests, probably from the archdiocese of Trier, invited him to appear before that committee two days later, on Wednesday at 6 o'clock in the morning. The committee had been filled with high-ranking members of the diet: Trier and Brandenburg represented the first estate, which comprised the electors; Duke George of Saxony and the bishops of Augsburg and Brandenburg the second, princely, estate; the head of the Teutonic Order and Count George of Wertheim the third estate, whose members were counts and abbots of the Empire; and Dr Bock, envoy of Strasburg, and Dr Peutinger, envoy of Augsburg, the fourth, urban, estate. The discussions, which took place over the Wednesday and Thursday partly in the quarters occupied by Trier and partly in those occupied by Electoral Saxony, changed nothing.[93] The members of the committee, and Richard von Greiffenklau, archbishop of Trier, in particular, showed both respect and understanding for Luther and sought to find a way for him to come round. But rapprochement, let alone an escape from the impasse, was not possible, for, as the speaker of the committee, Dr Hieronymus Vehus, chancellor to the margrave of Baden, noted at the start of the proceedings, the committee had no mandate for a disputation, but had been created for 'gracious and fraternal' reasons to bring the rebellious monk to recant.[94]

All the committee could therefore do was to hear repeated statements from each party of already established positions: Vehus spoke of the unity of the church, which with a mind to Luther's biblicism he compared explicitly to the 'seamless garment' of Christ for which the soldiers at the cross threw dice and which must not be allowed to be 'ripped apart by his [Luther's] teachings and opinion'.[95] Luther countered by citing his conscience, which would not allow him to betray the revelation of salvation even for the sake of peace on earth, for Christ was the 'stumbling stone'.[96]

Also unsuccessful was the somewhat devious attempt by Johann Cochläus, dean in Frankfurt, to throw the reformer off his tracks at the last moment, although Cochläus was at least motivated by concern for the church. Cochläus, who would soon number among the most radical of Luther's opponents, offered Luther the very disputation for which the reformer had hoped, but under the condition that he surrender his free conduct. Eager for the opportunity to present his case in detail, the monk, still something of an amateur at this game, would have agreed, but the electoral Saxon lawyers protected him from Cochläus' ploy.[97]

By Thursday, 25 April, this last attempt at mediation, undertaken away from the main meeting of the diet, had failed. The archbishop of Trier, a capable reformer of church and bishopric and neither a member of Charles' party nor a supporter of Luther, provided the excommunicate monk, who unless a last-minute solution could be found was about to become an outlaw of the Empire, with a final noble gesture—Luther could himself 'suggest the means' whereby the judgement of the Empire could still be avoided. When as expected Luther could see no possible way forward, Greiffenklau guaranteed Luther an honourable departure, thereby ensuring that the promise of safe conduct was respected.[98] Luther was keen to set off immediately, but Spalatin insisted he wait until he had been formally dismissed. Official permission to depart was brought to Luther that afternoon by Maximilian von Zevenbergen, the Austrian Habsburg chancellor, representing the Emperor, and von der Ecken, the official of the archbishop of Trier, representing the Imperial estates. Luther was ordered to return home within twenty-one days and warned that during the journey he must not preach, write, or in any other way cause the people to become worked up. Each side employed a notary to record its legal position: the Emperor declared that with Luther's refusal to recant he was entitled, indeed required, to proceed as one appointed to protect the Christian faith and must therefore declare the Imperial bann; Luther again emphasized that he had not been given any opportunity to debate publicly and that he had not been disproved by God's own word. He expressly acknowledged the Imperial conditions for his departure, but reserved the right 'to confess and testify to the Word of the Lord',[99] in other words to preach, during his journey home.

With Luther's departure the next morning, on Friday, 26 April, one of the most momentous episodes in the history of Germany and of Latin Christianity was concluded. The composition and publication of the edict of condemnation was a simple bureaucratic matter. Noteworthy, however, is that the verdict, issued under Imperial prerogative, was delivered in the name of the Emperor and not in the name of the Imperial diet. Weeks earlier, the Habsburg court had commissioned Aleander, the papal legate, to draft the verdict that would be issued against Luther. All that remained was to settle the last details, check over the final version, and distribute that approved text throughout the Empire. The Imperial estates were informed of the edict merely as a courtesy. Relatively minor copyediting problems meant that although the Imperial edict was formally issued on 8 May, it received its first public reading on 24 May and was signed by Charles only on 26 May.[100] The Imperial bann placed on Luther by the 'edict of Worms'—the name the infamous text would soon acquire—was disliked by the vast majority of the Imperial estates, and their dissatisfaction was replicated by the great majority of Germans.[101]

With the issuing of the Imperial bann, Luther had become an outlaw of the Empire; he was now entirely without legal protection, whomever or whatever he faced. Yet he was in no danger, for by the time the edict was made public he had already been stowed away safely at the Wartburg, one of the most invincible strongholds of Electoral Saxony. That he had disappeared was already known in Worms by 11 May.[102] On 26 May, therefore, as Charles signed the edict, he was aware that in practice he was decreeing only the burning of Luther's books, and that his action posed no real threat to Luther's life. The Imperial court would also have had no illusions about steps that would be taken against Luther's supporters. We can go further, for it is highly possible that a secret or tacit agreement between the Habsburg government and Electoral Saxony had established that the most extreme implications of the edict would not be enforced. Certainly the edict was never formally delivered to the Saxon elector and therefore never went into legal effect in his territories. To Luther's surprise, the 'terrible edict', about which Spalatin had warned him at the beginning of May, had reached ducal Saxony by mid-June but not its electoral neighbour, Luther's home territory. The edict was not valid precisely in the place where its target lived.

The Historical Significance of the Events at Worms

That the decision in the Luther Affair was made just as a new ruler was finding his feet as German king and Emperor was of momentous significance for Luther and the Reformation and for Germany and the unresolved issues of the German constitution, as the events at Worms highlighted. As was usual during this delicate phase in a new reign, the young Charles V was looking to establish support, and additionally, as king of Spain, Charles found himself required to function in circumstances very different from those of his Imperial predecessors. At his first Imperial diet Charles had failed to dissuade the Wittenberg monk from his vision of a radical renewal of the church in light of his theology of salvation and freedom, and Luther's 'Away from Rome' (*Los von Rom*) movement even emerged from the diet both morally and politically strengthened. Luther and the religious issue would continue to keep Germany, the Empire, and indeed all of Latin Europe in suspense for the foreseeable future. Luther's speech at Worms launched a powerful wave of enthusiastic support that propelled on the rapid spread of the Reformation and provided the impetus for its institutional establishment. Months earlier Aleander, the papal nuncio, had already reported to Rome with great annoyance that 'the whole of Germany is in uproar. Nine tenths are calling out the battle cry "Luther" and for the remaining tenth, even if they are indifferent about Luther, the solution is at least "death to the Roman court." '[103]

For German history the entanglement of ecclesiastical and religious renewal with early modern politics, constitutional affairs, and society would be decisive for centuries to come. Evidence of that intertwining can be seen clearly in the diet at Worms itself, for through its role in the debates over the Reformation the Imperial diet consolidated its position as the representative organ of the German estates and their liberties, secular but especially religious–ecclesiastical, which were practically unique in Europe. The age of the Reformation became the great age of the German diets and of the estates represented at such diets. Additionally, the association between the Reformation and the liberties of the estates helped pave the way towards subsequent German federalism. The territorial ecclesiastical structures laid down and expanded in the Middle Ages were decisively strengthened in the Protestant territories by the establishment of autonomous territorial churches. Electoral Saxony was at the forefront of this movement, led by the Wittenberg reformers, but it was followed by numerous other territories and towns that also decided in favour of Luther. They were followed in turn by territories that had rejected the Reformation but created similar territorial church organizations within the bounds of the old church. The diet of Augsburg of 1555 produced a widely acclaimed religious peace, but it also generated a new constitutional framework that had even greater impact, for it provided the legal foundations for both multiconfessionality—initially involving only Catholic and Lutheran territories, but with Reformed Calvinist churches included from 1648—and the Imperial constitution that formed the basis for modern federalism.

For both Luther and the Emperor their encounter at Worms in 1521 proved fateful, even though their paths diverged and their domains no longer overlapped. Over the months and years that followed they went about the tasks that fell to them independently of each other, but how they thought and acted was determined by the divergent stances they had adopted in front of the Imperial diet at Worms. From the Imperial castle of Friedberg, north of Frankfurt, Luther addressed Charles again. The personal letter he sent to the Emperor (Figure 23) was a political text, required of him by the Saxon government and immediately communicated in a German translation to the Imperial estates who remained in Worms, but the exceptionally long letter is very much in Luther's own style and expresses his own perceptions and aspirations. He places before the Habsburg Emperor two elements of his position: he restates, first, that his 'conscience is bound by ... Scripture', which makes his recantation impossible unless on the basis of Scriptural evidence and, secondly, that he is loyal to 'all native Germany', with the Emperor at its head, for which he begs God's blessing with 'joy and trust'. He again calls upon Charles specifically as his protector 'not to allow me to be crushed by [my] enemies, to suffer violence and be condemned', but instead to ensure that he is given the right to make his case 'before trustworthy, learned, free, secular as well as ecclesiastical judges', who must be without ties to specific interests, for 'the Word of God ... ought to remain above everything, and be the judge of all men'.[104]

If Charles was to remain true to the essence of the religiosity he had displayed at Worms, then it was simply impossible for him to act as Luther desired. For two decades, as Charles manoeuvred his way through all the Imperial and European political interests of his dynasty, he remained unwavering in his aversion to Luther and in his determination, when the time was ripe, to eliminate the German plague that Luther had spread through Christendom. Luther was not unaware of the anti-Reformation principles that dictated the positions the Emperor adopted, and over the

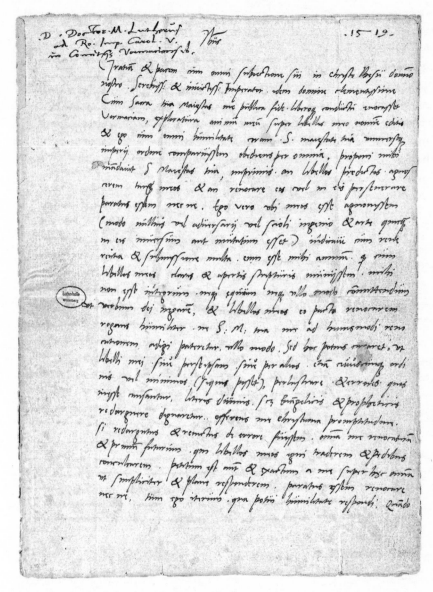

Figure 23. Luther's letter to Emperor Charles V written on 28 April 1521 as the reformer travelled back from the diet at Worms.

years his picture of Charles became ever darker until it reached the point where he could no longer place any hope in the Emperor or those around him. But while Luther held the popes in Rome to be non-Christians and therefore also, in keeping with attitudes of the age, non-human, he never placed the Emperor in the same category. To the contrary, even as an old man, Luther spoke repeatedly and with compassion of 'the pious Charles, who has many adversaries and for that reason must be wished luck'.[105] In turn, Charles, too, ran shy of the ultimate debasement of Luther as a human being. As we will see, we cannot be entirely certain that in the moment of his death he did not move in the direction of Luther's theology.

IV

Beginning to Labour for the Cause

Transported to a Mighty Fortress and Hero of the Uprising

At a Crossroads in History

Unlike so many of the texts Luther dashed off in haste, the letter he wrote at Friedberg has a calm argumentation and almost classical style, indicative of how its author had matured through the conflicts of recent years.[1] Despite all his apprehensions, Luther had been able to hold his ground before the most eminent of world figures, and as a result he acquired a new confidence and greater self-assurance. As he wrestled with his thoughts between the first and second hearings at Worms, he may have recognized that it was both logically and psychologically impossible for him to act counter to the word of God as he understood it. That realization brought a clarity that fortified him and gave his reasoning an inner consistency, but above all it immunized him against external pressure. Not that he believed himself out of danger—very much to the contrary, he had adjusted to the idea of suffering and even to the possibility of a violent death, as he candidly acknowledged to the archbishop of Trier.[2] He was little concerned with his fate on earth, for his self-assertion at Worms had strengthened his conviction that God would ensure the victory of his word in the pure form that he, Eleutherius-Luther, had rediscovered. Soon after his arrival at the Wartburg, he wrote to Melanchthon, 'I desire nothing more than to meet the fury of my enemies head on.'[3] His supporters also became attuned to the idea of his suffering—the pamphlet entitled 'The Passion of Doctor Martin Luther' (*Passio Doctoris Martini Lutheri*) even drew a direct analogy with the suffering of Christ.

Luther's experiences at Worms had taught him something more: yes, the Electoral Saxon government could protect him and steer him around the many legal pitfalls, and yes, the public support he had experienced on the streets of the Imperial city was remarkable, but in the end everything came back to him, everything depended on his own powers of reasoning. Right up until the end of his life all that he thought and did was shaped by two factors: absolute certainty that he had uncovered the truth, which exempted him from pressure from his opponents; and unwavering self-confidence, which gave him freedom to act independently, even of his supporters. Nothing was more important for him than:

> that I can take pride as could St Paul, even if I am also overly hard, that I have always spoken the truth and no one can accuse me of having dissembled. If I should have a flaw, then I would prefer that I speak too harshly and declare the truth too brutally, than that I should have anytime dissembled and held back the truth.[4]

Luther's greatness rested on a directness and a ruthlessness that together ensured the Reformation set history on a new course. Yet these characteristics also defined the limits of the Reformation. Luther's utter refusal to countenance any possibility of compromise when it came to God's truth anchored his teachings and thereby ensured the cultural and intellectual differentiation of Christendom in Europe, but it also meant that Luther believed any form of mediation pointless as long as his opponents also insisted on their own understanding of the truth. Luther's stature and resolution therefore went hand in hand with fundamental differences over the nature of religious truth and with conflict that at points brought Christendom and Europe to the verge of chaos. Such unflinching certainty—typical, admittedly, not only of Luther but also of all the great religious leaders of his age and a cause of great enmities—may have been historically unavoidable. How else could the symbiosis of religion and culture, or church and state, that had ruled Latin Christian Europe for centuries have erupted, preparing the way for early modern multiconfessionality and modern pluralism?

'Is He Still Alive or Have You Murdered Him?'

Luther had become the hero of the Reformation. The length and breadth of the Empire there was now an expectation that he would do no less than bring about the '*reformatio*' of church and society announced in the famous *Reformatio Sigismundi* text, composed in 1439. For the moment, however, the hero was in seclusion, marooned from May 1521 until February 1522 in the Wartburg, above the town of Eisenach. We cannot know for certain whether the Imperial outlaw was surprised to be forced by his elector to accept asylum. The security demands of such a secretive operation meant that he would have known few details of what awaited him, although clearly a number of those who were accompanying him were at least partially aware of the plans, including Nikolaus von Amsdorff. The Electoral Saxon government appears to have avoided putting anything in writing. Luther was not entirely unsuspecting. On leaving Worms he had written to Lucas Cranach from Frankfurt, 'I shall submit to being "imprisoned" and hidden away, though as yet I do not know where', continuing with a play on Christ's own words, 'For a little while you will not see me, and again in a little while you will see me.'[5] The following day, while at the Imperial castle of Friedberg he had parted ways with Kaspar Sturm, the Imperial herald, who was responsible for ensuring Luther's safe passage, and had given Sturm a formal letter of dismissal. There were to be no official witnesses to the Saxon enterprise, and the Imperial party would have had no desire to know or see too much.

Initially there was nothing out of the ordinary about Luther's journey home—if we set aside the previously unheard-of celebration of an outlaw as a hero everywhere he went and ignore his hugely popular preaching, undertaken despite the Emperor's prohibition. The trickery began as soon as Luther passed into Thuringia, and the monk and his entourage found themselves in Electoral Saxon territory. After Luther had preached in Eisenach and had greeted acquaintances of his youth, he separated himself from his travelling companions and began a detour that led to the south-east. He planned to visit a good number of members of his family who lived in the region, and he was accompanied now only by the coachman, the obligatory fellow Augustinian monk, who was in this case Johannes Petzensteiner, and Amsdorff, who as an Electoral Saxon official had evidently been commissioned by those pulling the strings to exercise some oversight. On 4 May, after the small group had concluded a visit to some of Luther's relatives, they turned north-east, heading in the direction of Waltershausen, where they would pick up the main route to Electoral Saxony again. As they passed by the castle of Altenstein in the Thuringian Forest, they were brought to a halt by a number of armed horsemen.

Luther was forced out of the carriage and had to walk—although only as far as the next turn in the road, where a horse had been left ready for him. Luther mounted and took off into the unknown.

The pretence had been successful: it looked as if the opponents of the Reformation had failed to keep the guarantee of safe passage. In on the ploy, Amsdorff pretended to be utterly surprised, while uninitiated Petzensteiner remonstrated at the top of his voice and fled for Waltershausen, where he provided the news of the violent ambush of his Augustinian brother. Word spread swiftly throughout the Empire. Only two weeks later, Albrecht Dürer recorded in his diary:

> On Friday before Whitsun in 1521 I received news at Antwerp that Martin Luther had been so treacherously taken prisoner. For although he had been given Imperial escort by Emperor Charles' herald, as soon as he had been brought by the herald to an unfriendly location near Eisenach, the herald said he was no longer allowed to be his and rode off. Immediately ten horse [men] were there who deceitfully led off the betrayed pious man, filled with the holy Spirit, for there was a follower of Christ and of the true Christian faith. And whether he still lives or whether they have murdered him, I do not know.... Oh God in heaven, that we should lose this man who has written more clearly than ever any other, to whom you have given such an evangelical spirit, we ask you, oh heavenly father, to give again your holy spirit to another who will again gather together your holy Christian church.... Oh God, if Luther is dead, who will in future explain the holy Gospel to us so clearly! Oh God, what might he have written for us over the next ten or twenty years! Oh all you pious Christians help me to bewail this man filled with the divine spirit and ask God that he will send us another man who can illuminate us.[6]

Present in Word and Image

Dürer's words echoed the thinking of many in the Empire, who were similarly determined not to allow themselves to be turned away 'by the un-Christian papacy that strives against Christ's liberation by burdening with human laws' from the rediscovered Gospel and the doctrine of grace, which according to Luther was the only path to salvation. The reformer might be imprisoned, he might even be dead, but his teachings were here to stay, found the length and breadth of the Empire. No number of bonfires would be sufficient to burn all those books and pamphlets. That message is confirmed by statistics calculated more recently: with Luther's appearance, book production had rocketed and the book market exploded, from 200 works produced each year to nearly 900. Once a publisher got hold of one of Luther's texts, he would quickly republish the work. As early as 1519 Erasmus' publisher Johannes Froben, who had a Europe-wide reputation, had written to Wittenberg:

> We sent six hundred copies to Frankfurt and to Spain. And now they are also being sold in Paris... And Calvus, a book merchant from Pavia and a very well educated and knowledgeable man, has had a good part of such small books brought to Italy and wishes to distribute them in all the towns... All but ten copies of those I printed are now sold, and I have never had any other book sell so well.[7]

These were still only the early days of Luther's total output. The three great reform treatises did not appear until the following year, when they were immediately printed by the thousand, with numerous reprintings following. At the same time a flood of largely polemical, attention-grabbing illustrated flyers poured forth and were eagerly torn from the hands of travelling newssellers at annual markets, outside churches, and on the streets. These pamphlets were single-page printings much like newspapers that reached a broad public with their accounts of current events. Lutheran propaganda took the lead, but Luther's opponents were close behind.

Luther's publishing success is all the more remarkable given that the often-extensive pamphlets were expensive, and even the flyers that would soon appear on the market in their thousands, even their hundred thousands, cost at least the hourly wage of an artisan. Their message reached the great majority of the population who were illiterate—partly through their humorous illustrations, whose polemical point was unmistakable, and partly via individuals who read out the most telling passages to audiences at markets or in public houses.

Printing was not solely responsible for this success. Luther and his supporters made full use of all the media of their age, not just print media but also other literary, oral, and above all visual forms. Luther's likeness was spread in its thousands in engravings and woodcuts. Anyone who wanted to—and that meant pretty much every German—could gain a sense of just what this hero of the people looked like. Luther was not particularly concerned with the specifics of his image. On one hand, the impetus was commercial, as in the case of the earliest depiction of the reformer, which was a by-product of his 1519 disputation with Eck and appeared on the title page of the publication of his Leipzig sermon. On the other hand, some portraits reflected a creative impulse that found in the rebellious monk a particularly congenial subject, as can be identified in the work of Lucas Cranach, whose portraits of the reformer are an integral part of today's memorialization of Luther (see, for example, Figure 24). Some art historians have argued that Cranach's portraits were commissioned by the Wittenberg court and depicted a range of Luthers who could be deployed as the political situation demanded, but that thesis seems hardly plausible.[8] We have no evidence that Georg Spalatin or any other Saxon statesman guided Cranach's hand from a distance in light of Electoral Saxon politics.

What really motivated Cranach—alongside the commercial interests of his workshop—was a Renaissance artist's fascination with the individual essence of a notable figure, and in this instance of a man who was also the artist's friend. Cranach's great model Albrecht Dürer, from whom we have already heard, was also very keen 'to give great effort to making a likeness of Dr. Martin Luther and to engrave it in copper, to create a lasting memorial of this Christian man'.[9] Personally acquainted with Luther and with the particular atmosphere of Wittenberg, Cranach created a likeness of the Augustinian monk as professor, as he taught holding the Bible in his right hand and gesticulating with his left. This is no mild-mannered Luther ready for discussion, the image of Luther that art historians tell us the Saxon court wanted for the diet at Worms. The sources say nothing of such a commission, made with the court's political purposes in mind. The image we see here, created with Cranach's subtle psychological empathy, is of a pious,

Figure 24. *Martin Luther as an Augustinian Monk*, by Lucas Cranach the Elder, engraving, 1520.

biblically learned figure determined to challenge the great men of the church and the Empire.

Luther valued highly the work of his Wittenberg 'godfather', the term he used for Cranach after he had stood as godfather for Cranach's daughter Anna in 1520. He thought himself and his 'mission' well depicted in the engravings of 1519/20, and he also approved of Cranach's later paintings of him as Junker Jörg—from a sketch Cranach had drawn during one of Luther's incognito visits to Wittenberg—and as a husband, on a double portrait where he appeared alongside his wife, Katharina. He saw depictions of himself and images within the church, which he prized without endowing them with inherent salvific properties, in a similar light. Both had practical purpose. The portraits were another weapon in the battle to ensure his Reformation teachings were broadcast; they were not to be used to promote his own image or to market himself. For Luther, the word spoken or printed was far more important than any image, a point that should not get lost in our present enthusiasm for all that is visual. Luther believed himself fully present, body and soul, in his preaching and in his writings, but not in a portrait.

Reform by the Sword of the Nobility and the Might of the People?

The simmering unrest that had spread throughout Germany immediately after Luther's appearance in Worms was stoked by news of the disappearance of this highly esteemed and much-loved spiritual hero. First to the barriers were the Imperial knights. Their leaders, Silvester von Schaumburg-Münnerstedt and Franz von Sickingen, had already offered Luther the protection of the nobility of Main-Franconia and the middle Rhine in 1520 and continued to have his back while he was in Worms. Ulrich von Hutten, highly animated knight-humanist, had urged Luther on in 1520: 'Let us fight for the common cause of liberty; let us free the oppressed Fatherland!'[10] In the year of the Imperial diet at Worms he leapt to Luther's defence brandishing his literary sword, opening his highly regarded dialogue entitled 'Vadiscus or the Roman Trinity' (*Vadiscus oder die römische Dreifaltigkeit*) with a nationalist fanfare against the foreign curia, while at the conclusion came an explicit call for the reform of the church by force.[11] Luther was very taken with his fellow German's resolute condemnation of the 'Roman fury', but he was in turn resolute in his rejection of the use of force in matters of faith: 'But I do not wish the battle for the Gospel to be fought with coercion and death . . . The world and the church are saved by the Word and they will also be reformed by the Word.'[12]

While the knights were certainly eager to turn the tables on the clergy, they also demonstrated a genuine evangelical enthusiasm for the word and for the renewal of the church. In 1521, the year the Imperial diet met at Worms, Sickingen halted the daily celebration of Mass in the chapel at Ebernburg, introduced community worship on Saturdays, and had the Lord's Supper celebrated without the elevation of the host. He was ahead even of the Wittenbergers and prided himself in having organized one of the earliest evangelical communities. A tempestuous wave of reform followed in Sickingen's other possessions and in other lands belonging to Imperial knights.

The rebellion of the Imperial knights did not stop at the word of God and the evangelical cleansing of their churches that the word appeared to require. Via the freedom of the Christian they arrived at the freedom of their Imperial estate, which meant as a first step that they should throw off the economic and political oppression of the ruling princes and their territorial states. The theological notion of the Christian community, taken from Luther, and demands for communal self-determination in secular matters proved a highly explosive combination. Their struggle, spiritual and ecclesiastical, to prevent the Roman hierarchy from intervening in the communal church was for the knights also a declaration of war on their political and social subjugation to the princes, especially the ecclesiastical rulers, and their early modern territorial state. The nobility of the Wetterau and Swabia formed an early alliance, and in August 1522 600 knights meeting at Landau formed a 'fraternal union' that was to last six years. This union was both a religious alliance in the cause of the Reformation and a political alliance, defensive and offensive, directed against the emerging new form of territorial state.

In south and south-west Germany, where many of the Imperial knights had their lands, the knights were being deprived of oxygen by the political ambitions of bishops and abbots, and their activities in the name of freedom in 1522/23 were therefore largely directed against the ecclesiastical authorities in Franconia and the Middle Rhine. For the first time force was used to attempt to realize Luther's teachings, as they were understood by the knights, with political and social, and not just ecclesiastical, implications. Sickingen's campaign against the elector of Trier, his principal hate figure, misfired, and the Imperial knight was placed under Imperial bann. He was forced to take refuge in his castle at Landstuhl from the combined forces of the electors of

Trier, the Palatinate, and Hesse, but his knightly fortifications proved unable to withstand the rulers' modern artillery. Sickingen died in the ruins of his ancestral seat. Ulrich von Hutten's end was all the more miserable. The voice of Sickingen and all anti-Roman forces, Hutten discredited himself both politically and morally with a banditry that today we might well term 'terrorism', directed in particular against the town and prince-bishopric of Strasburg. When he immoderately, if with some justification, attacked Erasmus of Rotterdam for his timidity and unreliability, he forfeited the sympathy of humanists. Already dying, he fled to Zurich and the protection of Huldrych Zwingli, and died soon after on the island of Ufenau in the Lake of Zurich—where he was cared for and comforted by monks from the monastery of Einsiedeln, members of the very estate that he had despised and persecuted all his life.

The Imperial knights had thought that together with the Emperor they would be able to hold territorialization within the Empire in check and at the same time realize reform of the church. Their plan had proved misguided. Luther had demonstrated political acumen in maintaining his distance from Sickingen and from the knights' cause. Charles V had left Germany as soon as the Imperial diet was concluded and over the next years would be principally engaged in securing Habsburg interests in Spain and against the Habsburgs' French rivals. Even if he had had the time and had been willing to proceed against the princes in conjunction with the knights, he would never have consented to make joint cause with a man he deemed a heretic. In these circumstances, it was left to the princes of the Empire to set the tone, particularly when it came to ecclesiastical politics. Protected by his ruler, Elector Frederick, Luther was therefore also protected by a pivotal force within the Empire. In upholding the legitimacy and authority of the princes and their territorial states despite his bann by Emperor and Empire, Luther proved very wise.

Long before any ruler took action for his territorial church, roused by the new teachings the citizens of the Imperial, Hanseatic, and territorial towns forced priests responsible for saying Mass out of the church and together with Luther's supporters amongst the clergy insisted that the magistrates, whose hesitation was often tied to political concerns about the response of the Emperor or a local ruler, accept the Reformation. They could build on new forms of civic spiritual life that had developed in the Middle Ages and left the towns particularly receptive to Luther's teachings. The creation of the civic preaching office in the late Middle Ages meant that citizens had grown used to quality preaching and biblical exegesis. Groupings within the ecclesiastical and political elites had long demanded reform of the church and improvements in pastoral care. These preconditions did not guarantee that a town would immediately side with Luther: in Cologne, for example, the presence of reform-minded groups at the university and amongst the Carthusian monks and the political elite of the city instead immunized the Imperial city, which proudly bore the crowns of the Three Kings of the Orient on its coat of arms, from the Reformation. Other than in a handful of cases, however, during the 1520s all the towns of the Empire, both Imperial and territorial, embraced the Reformation, and its communal ideals in particular.

Nuremberg was one of the first towns to adopt the Reformation. While in Wittenberg Luther was taking decisive steps in developing his theology, in Nuremberg, a group of individuals with a burning concern for theology and the politics of the church began to meet at the Augustinian monastery under the leadership of Staupitz, who was joined from early 1517 by Luther's friend Wenzeslaus Linck. Amongst the members of this circle were leading citizens of Nuremberg, including several members of the town council, syndic Christoph Scheurl, town secretary Lazarus Spengler and also Albrecht Dürer, undisputed master of Renaissance art in Germany. Guild members in Nuremberg also adopted Luther's teachings with enthusiasm. By 1521 master cobbler and master singer Hans Sachs already owned forty Reformation texts. In 1523 he declaimed his fervent support for Luther, a product of his passion for the written word, in his 700-verse text entitled 'The Wittenberg Nightingale, Now Heard Everywhere' (*Die Wittenbergisch Nachtigall, die man jetzt höret überall*). Sachs provided a humanist declaration of the joy of life that can be compared with Hutten's jubilant 'Oh this age! Oh these letters! It is such joy to be alive!' Above all, Sachs had written in praise of the evangelical torches now burning in the east and to warn Christian sheep about the 'lion', Pope Leo.[13]

With enthusiastic support for Luther found amongst all layers of society, it is not surprising that in the early 1520s Reformation-minded clerics already held posts within Nuremberg. Political concerns—the city was custodian of the Imperial crown regalia, had been home since 1521 to the Imperial council, and on three occasions had hosted the Imperial diet—meant that the magistracy initially refused to alter the church order and introduce the Reformation, but with the residents of Nuremberg becoming increasingly evangelically minded, in spring 1525 the council, concerned to maintain religious unity, resolved to oversee the introduction of the Reformation.

The course of events varied from town to town. Often initiated by spontaneous communal singing during worship, the impetus frequently came from residents of the town who forced out the Roman priests and compelled the town council to install Lutheran pastors in their place. With long-standing experience as a dynamic communal force, citizen groups within the towns of Germany were able to act independently of, even counter to, the magistracy in articulating and realizing their ecclesiastical and religious interests. The Reformation really was 'an urban event' in Germany,[14] and not just in the west and south, which had been highly urbanized since the classical period or the high Middle Ages, but also in central, eastern, and northern Germany. This revolutionary movement also gripped Wittenberg, and it did so with such intensity—as we will see shortly—that Luther threw caution to the winds and left the security offered by the Wartburg to return directly to the town on the Elbe.

At the time of the Imperial diet of 1521 peasants also appeared as Luther's partners and as trailblazers of the Reformation, but these peasants were not flesh and blood; they were literary creations, typified by the figure of Hoeing Hans (*Karst-Hans*), the hoe-carrying tiller of the land who earned his daily bread by the sweat of his brow. In 1521 two German-language pamphlets entitled 'Hoeing Hans' (*Karsthans*) and 'New Hoeing Hans' (*Neuer-Karsthans*) depicted peasants as supporters of the Reformation calling for revolt against the self-seeking Roman clergy. The following year Hans Maurer, known as Zündauf, a medical doctor, became a real-life Karsthans for Strasburg, Freiburg, and Tübingen—an area of Germany in which the peasants were strongly oppressed and therefore all the more ready to resist—when his preaching against clergy and church adopted a strong social-revolutionary bent. The peasants only appeared in person on the Reformation stage four years later, when they grounded their Empire-wide revolt, by which they hoped to achieve freedom and self-determination in both eccle-siastical and secular affairs, in Luther's preaching of the inalienable authority of the law of God and of the freedom of all Christians.

'The Gospel is a Law for Those Who Are Willing and Free'

Having opened the floodgates, Luther now observed and commented on events from the Wartburg. Understandably for someone who had been declared an outlaw and faced physical danger, his first concern was about his opponents' use of force as they sought to master the demands seething through all layers of the population. The potential outcome was clear to Luther: 'If the Pope will take steps against all who think as I do, then Germany will not be without uproar.' But he was equally certain that in the long run Rome would not succeed, for, he wrote, 'God is arousing the spirits of many, especially the hearts of the common people. It does not seem to me likely that this affair can be checked with force; if [the Pope] begins to put it down, it will become ten times bigger. Germany has very many Karsthansen.'[15] This reference to 'Hoeing Hans' as the personification of the peasant unhappy with the social and ecclesiastical circumstances of his rural existence and ready to resort to violence is evidence that Luther was very aware the protest against the church could become a social protest. He was also well aware that were he to issue a call to arms in support of his demands, half of Germany would stand with him.

The thought of leading a popular movement or even justifying the use of force in the cause of reform would not have crossed Luther's mind. During these months Luther became 'Junker Jörg', but that knightly and soldierly persona was no more than necessary camouflage. While at the Wartburg, he continued to think and act as a monk and professor of Bible, countering his own invocation of Hoeing Hans with the comment that 'God must do what is good in his eyes'.[16] His fundamental position, iterated as early as the Ninety-Five Theses, would not change: the pure word of God must prevail, and the pure word of God would prevail without the use of force. He maintained his resolve, despite his disappointment that Emperor and Empire had refused to provide the anticipated help to counter the machinations of the creature of Rome; instead they had placed the reformer himself under Imperial bann. He was not tempted to tackle the Gordian knot by inciting, as he easily could have done, a rebellion by knights, townsfolk, or peasants. Revolutionary tumult was not part of his salvation theology or his historical theology.

Luther was aware that the concept of justification by faith alone and the notion of freedom that it engendered meant deep-reaching changes for church and society, but he decisively rejected revolutionary action, which he believed could only harm God's cause. When four years later the peasants grounded their revolt against their social and political subjugation in Luther's concept of the freedom of the Christian, they were under a tragic misapprehension that cost many of them their lives and Luther much sympathy. Luther was not the revolutionary figure celebrated throughout the land in 1521, as would have been readily apparent to anyone with a sober appreciation of his writings and his actions. Despite the Imperial bann and despite having been declared an outlaw of the Empire, he had refused to be drawn into the oppositional movement of the Imperial knights. Where he seemed to adopt a revolutionary tone, he did so in the context of sacred history, not as an exhortation to political action. Thus, for example, when fearing diplomatic repercussions, Hans von der Planitz, the Electoral Saxon representative to the Imperial administration in Nuremberg, reproached Luther for his sharp outbursts against his arch-enemy Duke George of Saxony, Luther responded defiantly, 'A different age has dawned when today one encroaches upon the great, which previously was not usually done', but he immediately removed the revolutionary sting, continuing, 'God will show us what he intends when God so wills.'[17]

Luther looked not to insurrection but to his ruler, and he continued to put his trust in the protection and ordered authority of the territorial state. The months he spent at the Wartburg served only to confirm that decision. During his stay he became an even-more cautious reformer of church and society and remained averse to impulsiveness. With church hierarchy and Emperor evidently unwilling to engage in reform, he banked instead on the authority of the territorial rulers and on the early modern state, which he identified, correctly, as the real political power of his age. In autumn 1521, when he received reports of violence incited by his impatient comrades that had broken out even in Wittenberg, Luther only became all the more averse to rebellion and all the more decisive in condemning force from below as illegitimate and ungodly. When Melanchthon briefly flirted with the idea of 'the law of the sword', Luther immediately alerted him, 'no such law is found in the gospel, either as commandment or as counsel; nor would it be at all appropriate, since the gospel is a law for those who are willing and free, those who have nothing to do with the sword or the law of the sword.'[18] Yet even though Luther sat in princely protection in the Thuringian castle, he was not at home in those surroundings. He would never have a comfortable relationship with the Electoral Saxon authority, nor indeed with any other political power.

Time for Reflection and Work

Daily Routine at the Wartburg

After his 'kidnapping', Luther rode for several hours to reach his new lodgings. An inexperienced rider, he wrote to Amsdorff a few days later that he had arrived in the middle of the night shaken to his bones. His description of his new location was very vague, not because he was uncertain where he was, but because he was bound to maintain secrecy.[19] He ceased wearing his monk's habit and allowed his thick hair to grow over his tonsure. The addition of a beard, he wrote, meant that even friends 'would hardly know me; I can't even recognize myself any longer'.[20] No longer easily identified, the Augustinian monk, who adopted the alias Junker Jörg, could move around with relative ease within the castle and in the town of Eisenach, which lay below the castle—'a free man amongst captives', as he gladly noted.[21]

In early summer 1521 new material by Luther was published in Wittenberg and distributed throughout the Empire—both supporters and opponents now knew that the reformer was still alive. Where he was living remained, however, an Electoral Saxon state secret. During his forays beyond the Wartburg, Junker Jörg was always ready to take off again whenever his cover was threatened. Even the Saxon ruler followed the rules of this game, not least because he could not then be accused of having had direct contact with a man who had been placed under ecclesiastical and Imperial bann. Duke John, brother and co-regent of the elector, corresponded regularly with Luther, but when he visited the Wartburg in September 1521, he avoided all contact with Junker Jörg.

By contrast, Luther did have close contact with the captain of the castle, Hans von Berlepsch, who was in effect Luther's host. He ensured his guest received all the most recent publications—by Karlstadt, for example[22]—and he wined and dined Luther so extravagantly that the frugal monk was embarrassed. Spalatin had to assure Luther that the elector was covering the costs of his stay, otherwise, Luther wrote, 'I would not remain one hour, if I thought that I were consuming the property of this man here, although he serves me cheerfully and freely in all things.' Almost apologetically, Luther added, 'it is my nature to fear being a burden where perhaps I am not a burden; but an honorable man ought to have such scruples.'[23] The reformer was even invited to participate in hunts that lasted several days. Luther was more concerned for the well-being of a hare that had been caught alive than for the replenishment of supplies with the game that had been hunted, and he recorded, 'I theologized even among the snares and dogs ... for what else does this picture [of a hunt] signify if not the devil who hunts innocent little creatures with his ambushes and his dogs – that is, with the ungodly teachers, bishops, and theologians?' Luther jokingly threatened

Spalatin, to whom he wrote these words, 'in paradise you courtiers who are lovers of game will also be game which Christ, who is the best hunter, can hardly catch and save in spite of all his great efforts.'[24]

During his first days at the Wartburg, the 'prisoner' complained that he was 'sitting here, drunk with leisure'.[25] That lack of movement may have contributed to the reoccurrence, sometimes for weeks on end, of the digestive problems that had beset him for years; constant emotional stress was undoubtedly also a factor. By the summer he felt he could bear the pain no longer and was considering that he might 'go to Erfurt and not incognito' to seek the advice of doctors or surgeons.[26] Medication sent by Spalatin brought no lasting relief. His physical troubles were compounded by mental anguish that left him depressed and even longing for death. He had an explanation for both his physical and emotional pains—the hurt he felt was the work of the devil, designed by God's adversary to divert him from his proclamation of pure teachings. All the torments he suffered only convinced him all the more that he was on the right path. The most harmless rustles and thumps in the old walls and cellars of the castle were signs of the devil at work and evidence of his bitter resistance to the renewal of the Gospel, as were also the ravens with their crowing and the black dog that he had to chase out of his bed in the evening. Luther's throwing of an inkwell at the devil is, however, a later invention. The ink stain on the wall that so awed Luther pilgrims of the nineteenth and twentieth centuries made its first recorded appearance in the *Topographia Germaniae* of Matthias Merian, a work of the mid-seventeenth century.

The 'tribulations of the flesh' (*Anfechtungen des Fleisches*) did not lead Luther to lose sight of what needed to be done in concrete terms for God's cause. Building on his self-assertion before the Imperial diet and on the public movement against Rome that his actions had aroused, he could not now hesitate to develop his positions and make them known to Christians in Germany and farther afield. He was eager for Junker Jörg to pick up the work that Dr Martinus had begun in Wittenberg. Just ten days after his capture, he informed Georg Spalatin, and thus also the Electoral Saxon court, 'I shall write a German tract on the freedom of auricular confession. I shall also continue working on the Psalms and the "Postil" as soon as I have received the necessary things from Wittenberg—among which I also expect the unfinished "Magnificat"'.[27] He sought scholarly clarity and hoped that through Scriptural evidence and theological argumentation he would be able to convince the people that change was essential. More specifically, he sought to improve his intellectual tools: 'I am studying Hebrew and Greek, and am writing without interruption',[28] he reported in a letter of 10 June to Spalatin.

The ten months that Luther spent at the Wartburg were highly auspicious for both the reformer and his work. Unburdened of his usual daily routine, Luther was able to compose the fundamental theological texts that would anchor his teachings and prove essential for the reform of worship and church order that followed. His time at the Wartburg was characterized by a productive tension between otherworldliness and an almost universal presence in this world. With marked similarities to other vital eras of transition—think, for example, of Nelson Mandela, imprisoned yet fully part of events in South Africa—Luther lived alone and removed but was at the same time a presence in the midst of the Reformation. On his letters he noted the address of the sender as 'on the mountain', 'in the land of the birds', or even 'from the Isle of Patmos'.[29] He had taken on the role of apocalyptic visionary and prophet previously adopted by John, who 'was on the island called Patmos because of the word of God and the testimony of Jesus' (Revelation 1:9).

In fact Junker Jörg was far from isolated. He remained the centre of the Wittenberg reforming circle even if he was not physically present—just as almost ten years later he had to stay at Coburg while Melanchthon represented the Protestant cause at the Imperial diet in Augsburg. He followed events back home in Wittenberg closely. When, under the pressure of such great responsibility, Melanchthon rued that without Luther those who remained in Wittenberg were 'going astray without a shepherd', Luther wrote by return contradicting his friend, 'So long as you, Amsdorf, and the others are there, you are not without a shepherd. Don't talk that way, lest God be angered, and we be found guilty of ingratitude. Would that all the churches, at least the collegiate churches, had one-fourth of your share of the Word and its ministers'; confidence and joy should grow from the knowledge one was acting as was pleasing to God and harmful to Satan.[30]

For all Luther's ties to his other colleagues in Wittenberg, the reformer placed particular hope and trust in Melanchthon, who was just twenty-four years old, giving expression to that relationship through a Scriptural parallel: 'You surpass me now and succeed me as Elisha followed Elijah with a double portion of Spirit—which may the Lord Jesus graciously bestow upon you. Amen.'[31] For just a moment it seemed that Melanchthon might cut himself loose from Luther as Karlstadt had done and adopt radical means of renewal, but his deviation was only momentary; he returned to Luther's side, metaphorically, and would stay there for the remainder of his friend's life.

Several times a week letters or packages with manuscripts or books would go back and forth between Wittenberg and the Wartburg, and Luther was therefore informed about developments in Wittenberg and the Empire and about ongoing scholarly debate. Deliveries from the Wartburg brought Luther's friends the manuscripts of new texts in quick succession. Spalatin and Melanchthon acted as Luther's publishing agents, receiving instructions from the author about the order in which his works were to appear and the desired quality of the printed text. While they were permitted to make editorial changes, no iota of theological content was to be touched.[32] Misunderstandings and tensions were unavoidable in the circumstances. While seeking to fulfil Luther's wishes, Spalatin also had to bear in mind the political situation and the possible implications for the Electoral Saxon government. When he advised moderation or even proposed delaying publication for tactical reasons, as was the case for a politically embarrassing attack on Albrecht of Brandenburg, archbishop of Mainz, the man of God ensconced on his mountainous Patmos flew into a rage and rained down abuse.[33]

Looking beyond such friction, surely unavoidable in the highly charged atmosphere of those years, we see Luther continuing to find support in the community of Wittenberg scholars that had proved so constructive during earlier discussion of reform of the university curriculum and during the debate over the indulgence. He compared notes with Spalatin on political and tactical matters and with Melanchthon on problems of translation and interpretation. For Luther's temperament and his zest for action everything moved too slowly, however, and seemed too impersonal. He wrote of his delight in receiving hot off the press in Wittenberg the first passages of Melanchthon's *Loci communes*—described on the title page as the 'most noble articles of the Christian teaching'—but added:

> I wish I could be with you to settle the question of the vows. It is not good to debate in a letter. While one writes quite verbosely about something the other person already knows only too well, one omits what the other person is most interested in, as for instance happened with regard to the question of confession.[34]

For Luther the months spent in silence and seclusion high in the mountains of the Thuringian Forest were the most productive of his literary life. While historians of theology are surely right to date the inspired breakthrough earlier, during Luther's stay at the Wartburg the issues preyed on the reformer's mind to such an extent that he worked on several texts at the

same time. In November 1521, for example, he published in short succession
a theological statement on the Mass, a polemical work against the relic
collection at Halle, and the Wartburg Postil, a sermon collection.

He started with the work he had had to leave lying on his desk in
Wittenberg as he set off for the Imperial diet. He wrapped up his scholarly
commentary on the Psalms, begun years earlier, with an extensive elucida-
tion of Psalm 22. Although he intended to return to this project, his huge
workload meant that this version became definitive. He then completed his
interpretation of the Magnificat, from Luke 1:46–55, the song of praise by
the Mother of God that lay very close to his heart. While his epigones would
no longer hold Mary in such high regard, the reformer saw in Mary the
epitome of the human freely chosen through the grace of God, not in
response to what she had done but as a 'lowly maid'. For Luther, Mary
was the original biblical model of Protestant election through grace.[35] At the
same time he turned his attention to fundamental lessons for politics and
history: on one hand, he stressed the insignificance of human authority in
the eyes of God: 'He has brought down the powerful from their thrones,
and lifted up the lowly' (Luke 1:52); on the other hand, he emphasized the
need for power and authority in the world: 'For while the world stands,
authority, rule, power, and seats must remain',[36] with 'seats' understood as
the authority of kings and magistrates.

He also resumed the regular battles that he had been required to fight ever
since the publication of the Ninety-Five Theses. His opponents had been
reinvigorated by the events of the Imperial diet and were not as incompetent
when it came to employing the media as their usual portrayal by historians of
the Reformation would suggest. The theological faculties at the universities
of Cologne and Louvain set the tone of the academic defence, while Paris
remained reticent. The leading figures were Jakob van Hoogstraten, a
Dominican from Cologne, who had been demoted after his abortive attack
on Reuchlin but now found his way back into the position of inquisitor, and
Jacobus Latomus, a Dutch theologian recently called to Louvain who shared
von Hoogstraten's inquisitorial passion, a calling he would direct at Erasmus
a few years later. In early summer Luther heard news of a polemical text
published by Latomus in May 1521 in which he had again justified Luther's
condemnation as a heretic following his disputation with Eck at Leipzig in
1519. He responded immediately, adopting the uncompromising, combative style of debate that was in keeping with his unconditional responsibility
to the truth but gave his opponents good reason for complaint and for

adopting a similar tone in turn. In the substance of his reply Luther stressed the innate sinfulness of humankind, which was not erased by baptism, a teaching that undermined conventional works righteousness. No less effective than the argumentation was the biting irony contained in the pamphlet sent out from the Wartburg into the wider world, which exposed the Louvain professor and his like-minded colleagues in Cologne and elsewhere to public ridicule.[37]

Luther's treatment of his German arch-enemy Cardinal Albrecht of Brandenburg (Figure 25) was very similar. Thunderbolts rained down from the Wartburg on Albrecht's plan to exhibit in Halle his large collection of relics for veneration. Luther's text 'Against the Idol at Halle' (*Wider den Abgott von Halle*) was a polemical work so biting and so lacking in any of the political prudence that was all the more advisable in light of the Imperial bann that even advance notification of its appearance was cause for

Figure 25. Cardinal Albrecht of Brandenburg, archbishop of Mainz, by Albrecht Dürer, engraving, 1519; the Small Cardinal.

consternation at the Saxon court. Spalatin had warned Luther immediately that 'the Sovereign will not allow anything to be written against Mainz', but Luther countered unapologetically, 'For the sake of the sheep of Christ, we must resist that most atrocious wolf!' The 'public peace' that was Spalatin's concern was nothing in comparison to the 'eternal peace of God'.[38]

All the same, before his pamphlet was printed, Luther approached the archbishop directly, in a personal letter of 1 December 1521. In order that the letter would reach its recipient quickly, Luther had it sent by Melanchthon to Wolfgang Capito, who since spending time in the humanist atmosphere of Basel had had some sympathy for Luther and the Reformation and as cathedral preacher at the court in Mainz and Albrecht's personal adviser now exercised significant influence.[39] Luther could not have thought he would win over the archbishop with his letter, which was lacking in political acumen, even haughty and imperious. Twice, he wrote, he had already turned to Albrecht, but without receiving a satisfactory response. As the sinful indulgence campaign took place in Albrecht's name and with his knowledge, he could have turned the storm against the archbishop personally, but, Luther wrote, to date he had spared Albrecht personally and 'the ruling family of Brandenburg', in other words, the Hohenzollern dynasty.[40] But he could not allow himself to continue to do so, because the cardinal 'has now again erected at Halle that idol [his collection of relics] which robs poor simple Christians of their money and their souls'. Therefore he must make clear to Albrecht that 'if the idol is not taken down, my duty toward divine doctrine and Christian salvation is a necessary, urgent and unavoidable reason to attack publicly Your Electoral Grace . . . and to show all the world the difference between a bishop and a wolf'. He gave Albrecht fourteen days to respond with a 'definite and speedy reply', with a clear change of course; otherwise he, Luther, would make public his declaration of war on the veneration of relics at Halle. As if making fun of all those who thought the Imperial and ecclesiastical banns at all effectual, he threatened, 'Your Electoral Grace should not at all think that Luther is dead. He will so gladly and joyfully rely on that God who has humbled the pope and will start a game with the Cardinal of Mainz such as few people expect.'

Albrecht responded promptly, writing from Halle on 21 December with evident diplomatic skill and, influenced by Capito, even with reference to the core of Luther's theology: 'I recognize that I need the grace of God for I am a poor sinful human being . . . and without the grace of God there is nothing good in me.'[41] His words could no longer have the desired effect on the warrior of God on his Thuringian Patmos. Luther wanted action and he wanted to see real change in church practice, but the archbishop was evidently not prepared to act. Luther sent his polemical text into the world, and in so doing launched an attack on the Hohenzollern prince himself, the primate of the church in the Empire.

Initial Plans for Evangelical Renewal of the Church

Despite Luther's pleasure in polemic and in confronting his opponents, the focus of his scholarly work was not on creating definitive doctrinal statements but on the evangelical renewal of the church. He deemed three fundamental innovations most urgent: (1) an evangelical order of worship, which would eliminate the sacrifice of the Mass and in which the sermon would be central; (2) radical pruning of the personnel of the church—their number had grown dramatically during the late Middle Ages, with priests, monks, nuns, lay brothers, and semi-clerical, or semi-lay, religious groupings—in light of the doctrine of the priesthood of all believers; (3) communication of the word of God in the vernacular by means of appropriate sample sermons and a German-language Bible.

The elimination of the unique, sacrally defined priesthood ran in parallel with the establishment of a communal, sermon-focused worship service, without the Mass and celebrated by a trained evangelical preacher. The theological rationale behind this rupture in the nature of Christian worship demolished the fundaments of the Roman Church. Luther set the explosives in two extensive scholarly treatments. The first of these texts, completed by the end of May 1521, addressed confession and was dedicated to Franz von Sickingen, who had been one of the first to introduce evangelical communal worship; the second text, on the Mass, was complete by the beginning of November 1521.[42] In neither text did Luther deviate from his essential position, but while his theological stance was unconditional, when it came to the practical consequences he was more patient, counting on growing conviction and the non-violent victory of the word of God. Aural confession was retained but was now voluntary, and the pastor, who heard confession, was no longer an intermediary between the confessing sinner and God, for that elevated status of the priest was incompatible with Luther's rethinking of the priesthood's theological foundations. Even the rumour of

a text by Luther on confession was so alarming to the Franciscans of
Wittenberg that they asked the elector to forbid its publication.[43]

Luther completed two texts on the theology and practice of the Mass in
autumn 1521: 'On the Abolition of the Private Mass' (*De abroganda missa
privata*) and 'On the Misuse of the Mass' (*Vom Mißbrauch der Messe*).[44] Both
works took aim at radically minded reformers in Wittenberg and elsewhere
who were rushing into summary abolition of the Mass without providing
sufficient theological grounds for their actions. The immediate impetus for
Luther's texts was provided by a vehement and largely undigested list of
theses by Karlstadt, and in particular by Karlstadt's claim that any Christian
sinned when he or she received communion during the Mass in one form
only, in the bread alone. To Luther's mind, Karlstadt had reversed victim
and offender, and his pastoral responsibilities required Luther to spring to the
aid of the former. In an extensive treatment of the words of institution,
Luther drew up the foundations of the evangelical communion service and
countered the unevangelical exclusivity of the priesthood of the papal
church with the itinerant priesthood of Christ, the sole model of priesthood
provided by the New Testament.[45] When he departed this world, Luther
insisted, Christ had given the priestly office to all Christians without any
need for consecration by the church. The practical consequences were
entirely those adopted by the radicals in Wittenberg. Luther, however,
legitimized his interpretation not as primarily revolutionary, but as a
'democratization of the path to salvation'.[46]

Celibacy and the vows taken by monks and nuns were closely tied in with
the priesthood and the theology of the Mass. Here, too, the hermit in his
Thuringian mountain retreat found that he needed to respond to circumstances in the wider world, and specifically to events in Wittenberg—
changes had been rapidly introduced to the Mass, the first marriages of
priests had taken place, and individual monks had left the Augustinian
monastery—that were taking place without his say and threatened to leave
him in their wake. Both celibacy and monastic vows were existential issues
for Luther: outwardly he appeared as Junker Jörg, but inwardly he remained,
and intended to remain, an Augustinian monk. It had long been clear to him
that theologically both concepts were inventions of the papal church with
no Scriptural foundation, a view that when aired publicly in his treatise 'To
the Christian Nobility of the German Nation' had found great resonance
throughout the Empire. Luther was well aware that his position would
rattle both church and state, and he was therefore scrupulous when it

came to its realization. He was as opposed to the immediate closing of all monasteries, with their nuns and monks hounded out into the world, as to the storming of the bastion of celibacy on the stead of passion. To Luther, the danger that the impetus would come not from inner religious conviction but from worldly desire seemed very great. On these issues, as in all other issues concerning ecclesiastical order, he intended to look to persuasion and discernment and to theological argumentation found in published works and sermons.

During the first weeks of his exile he had been unsettled by the steps Karlstadt had taken against celibacy and in favour of the marriage of priests, for he believed their theological justification superficial and feared 'that he will attract malicious defamation of himself and of us'. He was also concerned about the pressure that might be placed on Christians unprepared for the far-reaching consequences, asking, 'Dear God, do our Wittenbergers want to give women to the monks as well?' and noting, 'They will certainly not force a wife on me.'[47] When he heard of the first official marriage of a priest—Bartholomäus Bernhardi, priest in Kemberg, which lay about fifteen kilometres south of Wittenberg, married in May 1521—he congratulated his former student and recognized his courage. When, however, as if a dam had broken, in the weeks that followed dozens of priests throughout Germany established the first Protestant pastors' families, Luther kept his distance from their abandonment of their vow of celibacy. In putting his unconditional theological views into practice, Luther was led by a realism that he had learned in his entrepreneurial parental home. He found it hard to look beyond the practical implications for those who had broken their vow, for ecclesiastical law dictated that a priest who married immediately lost his office. If a priest was expelled, then, Luther prophesized with a certain gallows humour and an ability to paint a picture that was all his own, 'two stomachs would suffer want, and all who may come from them'.[48]

Luther was clear that he intended to 'remain a monk and to live accordingly';[49] to him it seemed inconsequential 'whether I retain or lay aside the cowl and the tonsure'.[50] Unsettled by seeing many of his supporters in Wittenberg and beyond leave their monasteries in rapidly growing numbers, alongside his other scholarly tasks Luther turned to examining the theological foundations of monasticism and celibacy. To regain control of the innovations being introduced against his will in Wittenberg and to provide Scriptural justification, in September 1521 he drew up his 'Theses on Vows' (*Themata de votis*),[51] 139, or 141, theses that addressed the religious declarations before God that were the pillar of the priesthood and monastic life in the Roman Church. Luther addressed the text to the 'bishops and deans of the Wittenberg church, who are disputing over the vows taken by those who are members of religious orders'. The letter to Melanchthon that accompanied the text made evident that while the theses were directed against the teaching of the papal church, they were also designed to counter that teaching's overly simplistic revocation by his colleagues in Wittenberg. If it was indeed the case, as Luther suggested Melanchthon believed, that 'a vow should be nullified if one is not able to keep it, so that the vow is not maintained in sin', then all vows, including 'the divine commandments' were to be nullified. Therefore, Luther continued, a distinction must be made between evangelical vows desired by God and therefore valid, and those, like the vows taken by monks and priests, that were human inventions.[52] 'The Judgement of Martin Luther on Monastic Vows' (*De votis monasticis iudicium Martini Lutheri sententia*), a treatise on the same theme, followed on 21 November, furnished with the dedication to his father that we noted earlier, when we discussed Luder's entering the monastery.[53]

Both works were made widely available and garnered considerable attention from supporters and opponents. The vows taken by priests and monks had been the subject of much discussion in reform-minded circles during Luther's absence, but Luther now repositioned the debate. For Luther the theological heart of the problem lay not in whether a vow had to be kept, but in whether that vow, given 'in a free and evangelical attitude', was lawful and pleasing to God, in which case, he wrote, 'then it is right that you keep your vow and fulfil it'.[54] Here again guidance was found in the freedom of the Christian and election by the grace of God postulated by Paul. Vows taken specifically in order to earn salvation, such as those given by monks and priests within the papal church, ran counter to the commandments of God and were obstacles on the path to salvation; they must be abandoned, for, as the first of his theses stated, 'everything that is not of faith is sin'.[55] Only the vow of baptism is valid, by which God binds God to every Christian. The freedom granted to every human must not be constrained by unscriptural coercion, Luther insisted, as had been the case with the vows of celibacy taken by priests, monks, and nuns.

Just like the Wittenberg radicals Karlstadt and Zwilling, Luther believed monasticism and celibacy were not part of an evangelically reformed church. Luther's reasoning, however, was not anthropologic and negative, based on human weakness and the resultant shortcomings of monasteries and priestly households, but rather theological and positive, rooted in evangelical God-given freedom. The plausibility and legitimacy that Luther's position gave not only to departure from the monastery and the marriage of monks or priests but also more generally to Reformation innovations were immediately evident: 'That will turn public life on its head,' prophesized Johannes Bugenhagen when, in early September and as a guest in Melanchthon's home, he was the first to read the manuscript with Luther's theses, newly arrived in Wittenberg. His host immediately agreed: 'That is truly the beginning of the liberation of the monks and nuns'.[56]

Equally aware of the implications, Luther's opponents were greatly alarmed when Luther's rejection of monastic vows was published at the end of February 1522 and, having been immediately translated into German, was reprinted throughout the Empire. Monks loyal to the papal church would have been particularly eager to see Luther's arguments refuted, and several Latin treatises by the Roman party appeared in quick succession, filled with so much scholarly substance that Erasmus could confirm with satisfaction the 'careful response' to Luther's 'highly garrulous' book. But neither the rebuttals nor their praise by the prince of humanists could stop the condemnation of monasticism in its tracks, at least not in Germany. Johannes Cochläus, one of Luther's sharpest critics, blamed the reformer's perfidious tactics—Luther, he opined, had not responded to the solid counterarguments that had been made in Latin in order to keep the refutation of his own position from the people.[57]

Alongside his reckoning with the unscriptural practices of the papal church, Luther addressed the practical consequence of that criticism by throwing himself into the creation of a new evangelical worship service focused on the community and the sermon. In May 1521 he recommended work on his Postil, a collection of model sermons for each Sunday through the church year. He demonstrated how the lectionary text might be interpreted in an evangelical sense, offering guidance for the many pastors who were not fully familiar with the new teachings. The impetus behind this collection of sermons had come in late 1519 from the Saxon elector himself, whose main concern had been to ensure uniformity within the Saxon-Thuringian territorial church as it underwent such significant transition. It is certainly possible, however, that lurking in the background was a concern to divert his professor of Bible, who was proving ready for a fight, from his literary brawl with his opponents. As the Postil was intended as a hand-book for pastors, the first edition, which appeared in March 1521, even before Luther left for the diet at Worms, had appeared in Latin. Now ensconced at the Wartburg, Luther reworked the entire original concept: the pastors of the nascent evangelical church were to be given not just guidance on evangelical theology but also instruction on how to engage their congregation from the pulpit as did Luther—how to 'look them in the mouth'. Luther ended his German-language sermon collection on this note, and it was published in parts in Wittenberg from summer 1521.[58]

The defeat of the old and the establishment of the new: for Luther, sitting at his desk in his study high in the Thuringian Forest, these two tasks were superimposed, as this collection of German-language sermons, later known as the 'Wartburg Postile', makes evident. Just one example: the complaints from the Franciscans of Wittenberg about Luther's text on confession, which we noted above, were immediately passed on to the reformer by Duke John, who requested his response. To counter Luther's teaching on the sacraments by proving that there *were* biblical foundations for confession, the monks had invoked the account in Luke's gospel (17:11–19) of Jesus' healing of ten men with leprosy. Luther took up their challenge and provided his own interpretation of the same passage in a sermon that he included in his Postil.

'I Was Born for My Germans'

Along with the Luther Bible, the sermons of the Wartburg Postil gave definitive shape to the culture of German Protestantism for generations to come, leaving their mark not only on the exegetical tradition and preaching style of the pastors, but also on the spiritual thinking of those who heard the word of God in church and at home alongside family and household members. With his usual sober grasp on reality, Luther was well aware of the limitations of some pastors. In order that it might not happen that 'everyone will preach his own ideas, and instead of the Gospel and its exposition, we again shall have sermons on castles in Spain',[59] he recommended that if on occasion a pastor lacked either the inspiration or the words for his own sermon, he could simply read out one of the sermons by Luther that appeared in the Postil, advice that might still usefully be heeded today. The remarkable pedagogic impact of the model sermons on aural and oral culture even beyond Protestant Germany must not be overlooked. In preaching, as in so many other fields, including schooling and catechizing, Catholics learned from Luther. The great Bavarian and Austrian preachers of the baroque era, figures such as the renowned Augustinian Abraham a Sancta Clara in Vienna, had no reason to fear comparison with their Lutheran rivals.

The decision to change the language of the Postil sermons from Latin to German had a bearing that reached far beyond the collection's function as an aid for Protestant pastors. The switch was in part a response to Luther's enthusiastic reception by the many thousands of individuals encountered on the Rhine and during his travels through Hesse and Thuringia who hung so closely on the words of his sermons. This experience remained with Luther when, at the Wartburg, he made the definitive break that took him irreversibly down the path evident in his treatises 'To the Christian Nobility of the German Nation' and 'The Freedom of a Christian' of the previous year. In a letter of November 1521 the reformer had written, 'I am born for my Germans, whom I want to serve.'

National Socialists and the German Christians of the National Socialist era reinterpreted—and thereby deeply discredited—this statement to their own ends, as they did also with Luther's self-stylization as 'prophet of the Germans',[60] which explains why today these words are often ignored by Lutheran church historians or mentioned only somewhat shamefacedly.[61] But Luther's pronouncement deserves our attention both for what it can tell us about the reformer's sense of self and for the light it throws on where Luther stood within the complex events of his age; it must not be allowed to exist only as misinterpreted by nationalist perceptions of a later age. It is an expression of the Old European humanist cult of nation, of the humanist concern to find the origins of the French in the Gauls, of the Dutch in the Batavians, of the Swedes in the Goths, and of the Germans in the Germani. In this same context belongs Luther's significantly later statement about Arminius, the victor over the Roman general Varus, whom, he said, he 'loved from the heart', continuing, 'if I were a poet, I would want to celebrate him'.[62] Such focus on poetry and language serves to demonstrate once again that Luther's interest in Germanness was primarily cultural and not political.

The theological core was formed by the role in God's plan for salvation assigned in Scripture to the people. For Luther those 'people' were not Germans in a nationalist sense, but the people of God, and more specifically in his case those to whom he had been called to bring the unadulterated word of God. For this German people to understand the message sent to them by God, it would have to be communicated to them in a language they could understand. Here, then, is the real context for the statement 'I am born for my Germans'. Luther made this pronouncement to Nikolaus Gerbel in Strasburg, a lawyer, humanist, and pioneer of the new artistic and religious spirit and it followed on from a listing of the texts on which Luther was working at the Wartburg. Luther reported that these works—remarkably, the translation of the Bible is not included in his list—would be composed, and here is the decisive phrase, *omnia vernacula*, 'all in German'. All these works would be in the language of the people, not in Latin.

The profession of allegiance to 'my Germans' is everything but nationalist and the related reorientation to the German language was neither new nor surprising. At the end of the fourteenth century and in the fifteenth century in particular, a new lay piety based on the written word had emerged, accompanied by the increased production of texts in the vernacular. This development, which had begun in the Low Countries but then spread through the north and middle of Central Europe, can be laid largely at the door of the *devotio moderna*, the devotional movement that proved particularly popular amongst the urban laity of north-west Europe and also influenced the young Martin Luder. Existing plans for reform of the church had already recognized a role for the vernacular, too, as can be seen, for example, in the *Libellus ad Leonem X* of 1513, a broadly conceived reform project drawn up by Paolo Giustiniani and Vincenzo Quirini, members of the Camaldolese order, a reform branch of the Benedictines, on the occasion of the Medici pope's accession to the papal throne. While theologically their plan had nothing in common with Luther's anti-papal turn—although both concepts criticized the luxury of the papal court and the un-Christian power politics of the papacy—just like Luther Giustiniani and Quirini were clear that the Bible must be translated and the vernacular used during worship services:

> For of what use is it [they asked] that every day the holy Gospel and parts of the Letters of the Apostles are read out in the church in Latin [which was itself not one of the original languages of Scripture] and also Psalms sung, when neither those who read them out [i.e. the priests] nor those who listen understand.[63]

Here history takes something of an ironic turn. In that moment their call for the vernacular and other similar requests made by Roman reformers were discredited and fell entirely on deaf ears, yet only a little later when raised by Luther, such demands spread like wildfire throughout Christendom north of the Alps.

When he talked of serving the Germans, Luther spoke in precisely the same spirit as the two Italians almost ten years earlier, when they had called for the use of Italian, and more generally for the vernacular, in worship by the universal church. Luther emphasized the linguistic element in his reforms for at its theological core his call for the re-establishment of the pure Gospel was also focused on language. He understood his avowal of loyalty to the Germans and to the German language very functionally, with his eye on the task to which he believed himself called—he was to spread the original word of God amongst humankind, which he understood in terms of universal Christendom and not as a national German Christendom. This approach distinguished him from the Bohemian Hussites, even if he saw himself as their theological successor. Nothing was further from his mind than a German-language imperialism, whatever in practice his contribution to the German language and its spread beyond the boundaries of the Empire would be. The language of scholarship throughout Europe, and for Luther too, was Latin, which explains why he translated many of his works into Latin after they had first appeared in German. The translating culture of his age was highly developed and translation went both ways. When the Gospel was to be proclaimed outside German-speaking lands, then it should be read and heard in the relevant language of the people, even when politically inopportune, as in the case of its subsequent translation into Croatian and Slovenian by Primus Truber, a Lutheran.

The best-known fruit of Luther's concern for 'his Germans' was the translation of the New Testament that the reformer began towards the end of his stay at the Wartburg. It was only logical that the emphatic reorientation towards the German language would embrace the Bible. Luther's translating of the Bible had its roots in his renewed evangelical theology, but it was fed by late medieval reading-based lay piety and its vernacular culture. Printing had brought a new dynamic to this movement such that by the beginning of the Reformation a good dozen Bibles or part-Bibles had already appeared in High German with a handful also in Low German. Luther's translation work, which he mentioned for the first time in two letters of 18 December 1521,[64] was therefore not as much a product of a lack of Bibles in German as of the excess and confusion of existing translations. Tellingly, according to a later Table Talk, the impetus for his translation came from Melanchthon, for whom this hotchpotch of texts was a horror. According to Luther's account, in the first week of December 1521 he had returned to Wittenberg incognito and while staying with Melanchthon he was called on by his friend to translate the New Testament because the versions currently available were

not made from a single mould: 'One person had translated the gospel of
Matthew and another that of Luke. So he also wanted to bring into the light
and into a right order the letters of St Paul, which he believed had become
rather dark or obscured.'[65]

The circle of reformers in Wittenberg urgently wanted to see a German
New Testament with a distinctly Protestant character, which explains the
emphasis placed on the letters of Paul. Luther's achievement with his Bible
translation went far beyond his original theological and church-political
goals, for the translation that he began immediately on returning into exile
not only provided the desired uniformity and Protestant flavour but also
proved a remarkable literary achievement. The 'Luther Bible', a complete
translation of both Old Testament and New Testament first published in its
entirety in 1534, left its imprint on German cultural life, both linguistic and
literary, for centuries to come. The impact may have been greatest in
Protestant areas, but it was not restricted to them. The Luther Bible did
much to give the German language an advantage and an attractiveness in
northern Europe and central Eastern Europe that ended in Scandinavia only
with the barbarism of Nazism and in the east even more recently, as English
became the lingua franca of globalization.

Luther was well prepared for his translation work. He had begun to study
Greek and Hebrew in Wittenberg and had continued his linguistic work with
new enthusiasm at the Wartburg. Above all, however, he was aided by what
appears to have been a natural talent when it came to the German language
that he had honed in the great treatises of 1520 and polished in the sermons in
his Postil. His secret, he later revealed, was 'to look the people in the mouth'
(dem Volk aufs Maul schauen). His linguistic skills were combined with a
remarkable familiarity with Scripture that was much admired by his contemporaries. As a final piece, biblical scholarship had reached a whole new level of
critical philology with the appearance in Basel in 1516 of Erasmus' Greek
New Testament, with its critical apparatus and accompanied by a Latin
translation. It is very likely that Luther drew on this revolutionary edition of
the Bible at a very early date, even as he was preparing his Wittenberg lectures
on the Letter to the Romans. We do not know, however, whether he also had
a copy to hand at the Wartburg, although he was certainly able to draw on the
Greek edition of the Bible by Nikolaus Gerbel, humanist in Strasburg, a copy
of which had been sent to him the previous May.

He began his translation of the New Testament in mid-December and
completed the work in a creative flurry within only a few weeks. When the

commotion at Wittenberg caused him to return there definitively in early March 1522, he carried the completed manuscript with him in his luggage. After the first turbulent days, which were entirely dedicated to the altercations with the radicals, he went through the manuscript line by line with Melanchthon. Printed by Melchior Lotther over the course of the summer, the text was sent out into the world on 21 September under the title 'New Testament German' (*Newes Testament Deutzsch*) and quickly became renowned as the 'September Testament'. Within only a year Luther's translation had been reprinted some dozen times, in locations ranging from nearby Grimma to distant Basel. In the years before Luther's death another twenty printings appeared, with the texts that appeared after 1530 following the revised version on which Melanchthon and Luther had worked between June and December 1529.

Having restored peace in Wittenberg, in summer 1522 Luther turned to the translation of the Old Testament. This time he worked not alone but as a member of a team, the 'Bible commission'. Luther usually composed the first draft of the translation, which was then revised by the larger grouping, drawing on the philological expertise of Melanchthon for the Greek and Matthäus Aurogallus for the Hebrew and with contributions from Bugenhagen and on occasion from Spalatin, sent by letter. In view of the high cost to the purchaser and also in the interests of the publisher, the Old Testament appeared in stages—in July 1523 the five books of Moses were published in Wittenberg by Melchior Lotther; the following year saw the publication of the historical books the Psalms in January and September, both printed by Luther's friend Cranach, who in addition to his artists' workshop and apothecary now owned, with Christian Döring, a print shop.

The woodcuts, both large and small, which illustrated the Luther Bible and contributed significantly to its success were created in Cranach's artists' workshop. Although Melanchthon was the principal consultant, Luther also advised the artists on the theological context of the images they were creating, and not infrequently the reformers would provide detailed instructions about how the Bible illustrations should look. Unlike the Swiss reformers and the radicals in their own camp, the Wittenberg theologians were not opposed to images, which they valued for providing a window onto the Bible and its Reformation interpretation.

By October 1524, when Cranach printed the third instalment of the Old Testament, which comprised the Song of Solomon and the Book of Job, the translation of the Bible was three-quarters complete. More immediate tasks and logistical difficulties meant that the appearance of the remainder took another ten years, printed in small sections. At last, in September 1534, the first Wittenberg edition of the complete Bible appeared on the market, accompanied by an indefinite permission to print granted by the elector to its three publishers, Moritz Goltze, Bartholomäus Vogel, and Christoph Schramm.

But the work was not yet done. The New Testament underwent constant revision—in 1531 the Bible commission established for that task was already meeting several times a week. In additional to the Hebrew and Greek scholars, Justus Jonas, Caspar Cruciger, and on occasion other theologians too joined in on the project. The minutes were kept by Georg Rörer, who had been Luther's secretary since the late 1520s and whose skills had already been tried and tested when he recorded Luther's sermons and lectures. The German translation that soon became widely known as the 'Luther Bible' was therefore a joint work that better merited the name 'The Wittenberg Reformers' Bible'.

Every German-speaker who even glances through the Luther Bible will find examples of its outstanding language and sentence construction that over the centuries have never lost their force. Until very recently any articulate German-speaker might have drawn from his or her store of vocabulary expressions such as 'he whose heart is full, his mouth overflows' (*Wes das Herz voll ist, des geht der Mund über*) or 'to throw pearls before swine' (*Perlen vor die Säue werfen*) or 'to shake the dust from one's feet' (*den Staub von den Füßen schütteln*) without any need to acknowledge citing the Luther Bible. The version produced by the Bible commission, which polished Luther's earlier translation, was the Bible of generations of German-speaking Lutherans until it was recently replaced by modern versions whose emphasis on 'unbiased language' often results in a text with far less flavour.[66]

The Wittenberg Bible proved an immediate best-seller and remained so for centuries. It also became a model for translations into other languages, not just Dutch, French, and English, but also Scandinavian and Slavic languages. Despite the multifaceted involvement of Luther's colleagues, only Luther appeared on the title page, as 'D. Mart. Luth.' Some justification for that decision can be found in Luther's way with words, which turned the frequently meticulous scholarly philological considerations of the various experts into a unified and fluent language. Above all, however, crediting only Luther was a commercial decision by the publisher. Luther's name could guarantee the sale of an expensive publication. The unbound edition of the complete Bible of 1534 cost two gulden and eight groschen, the equivalent of almost one month's salary for a journeyman bricklayer in central Germany.[67] The complete Bible was therefore most likely to be purchased by princely courts, scholars, and more prosperous merchants. When acquired within a less elite social context, it tended to become a family Bible, passed down through the generations. While Luther was naturally delighted by the commercial success, more important to him was that the translation provided every Christian with access to the word of God, whether by reading the text or by hearing the text read, and that it reflected as far as was possible the original language of the Bible.

The translation and cleansing of the Bible contributed fundamentally to Luther's self-identification as proclaimer of the word and prophet of God. He had informed his readers as early as the preface to the partial translation of 1523:

> Though I cannot boast of having achieved perfection, nevertheless, I venture to say that this German Bible is clearer and more accurate at many points than the Latin. So it is true that if the printers do not, as usual, spoil it with their carelessness, the German language certainly has here a better Bible than the Latin language—and the readers will bear me out in this.[68]

V

Contesting Interpretation within the Evangelical Camp

The Struggle with the 'False Brothers'

Reformation by Means of 'Insurrection and Rebellion'?

Luther had triumphed, but in almost the same moment, he discovered that there were limits to what he could achieve. Two painful realizations grew: he did not have a monopoly when it came to interpreting the rediscovered evangelical truth, and his grip on the reins was not firm enough to allow him to preside over the transformation of church and society. Construing the Reformation in his own way, Andreas Bodenstein, known as Karlstadt, dean of the theological faculty, hastily introduced changes at the town church in Wittenberg. Unlike Melanchthon, who listened attentively for the signals reaching Wittenberg from the Thuringian Patmos, Karlstadt was little bothered by whether his actions would be approved by Luther. He had no intention of taking Luther's sensitivities into account when it came to giving practical shape to the new Wittenberg theology. Accounts of the dramatic innovations undertaken by Karlstadt and his like-minded ally Gabriel Zwilling, one of Luther's fellow Augustinians, always reached Junker Jörg at the Wartburg only after the fact. Luther believed that the business of Reformation was reserved for him alone, but now he sensed matters escaping his grasp. As all of history was part of the salvation narrative, the devil must be personally responsible for the redirection of his plans, and the devil would surely do his utmost to obfuscate the truth of Scripture at the very place it had been rediscovered, by whispering in the ears of Luther's weak, misguided colleagues.

Initiated by Karlstadt and his supporters, the 'Wittenberg unrest' held the town in thrall for several months. Viewed retrospectively, these events can be located as one of the numerous urban movements that flared up in late medieval cities in an attempt to align secular and ecclesiastical affairs with the interests of their citizens. The anticlerical riots that caused such fear amongst the Catholic clergy were part of that tradition: students and journeymen chased priests from their altars, ripped the missals from their hands, and mocked and derided all men of the church, above all Franciscans and Antonite monks. Such goings-on were hardly unheard of, but Luther's theologically innovative and deeply felt attacks on the failings of the church had brought a new dynamic and plausibility to the traditional protests of the citizenry and a well-established urban anticlericalism. In Wittenberg, unlike in earlier urban protests elsewhere, demands for innovations in the ecclesiastical life of the town did not prove highly contentious, and the Saxon court and the elector's local administration initially allowed events to develop unchecked. For the Saxony authorities all that was important was that university and foundation chapter were of one mind on the Mass and that town council and citizenry were ready to follow their lead.

In October 1521 Augustinian Gabriel Zwilling preached against the veneration of the sacraments and the sacrifice of the Mass and advocated that the Lord's Supper be distributed in both kinds. The subsequent introduction of a new order of service, without the Mass, at the town church ran smoothly. Shortly afterwards, following another sermon by Zwilling, thirteen Augustinian monks left the Wittenberg monastery, and the citizenry again put up no protest. Zwilling now ministered as a member of the laity, and his appearance in the pulpit dressed in regular clothing was simply accepted. The campaigns against the saints and their depictions in the church, formerly deemed sacred, were more spectacular. The attacks were at first only verbal, made in sermons, theological disputations held at the university, and in Karlstadt's treatise 'On the Removal of Images' (*Von der Abthuung der Bilder*), but eventually, at the beginning of 1522, the assailants turned to iconoclasm. On 10 January, the former monks dragged pictures, statues, and altars out of the monastery and onto the courtyard and set them alight. Similar events appear to have taken place at the town church, or at least so ran an accusation that spread rapidly, in part the work of Luther, and has always provided the lens through which the unrest in Wittenberg has been viewed; whether that accusation is justified cannot be verified, for our only source material is a related resolution by the magistrates, issued on 20 January.

The Wittenbergers had sought to use the corporative authority of the community to implement the new teachings, an approach that was consistent with contemporary interpretations of the legal rights of the urban community. Such rights were increasingly likely, however, to collide with the new claims of the early modern territorial state, and as a result the Electoral Saxon government and the Imperial government in Nuremberg inevitably deemed the events in Wittenberg rebellious. Following his unexpected return to Wittenberg in March 1522, Luther spoke out volubly against the innovations, turning what had occurred into a theological, inner-Protestant rebellion. The overhasty reconfiguring of church and society would place too great demands on the theologically unprepared populace, he feared, and would give opponents a political boost. His criticism was aimed at the writings and actions of Karlstadt in particular; he judged Melanchthon's similar thinking more leniently. Only a few months earlier Luther had seen no reason to intervene and had played down not-insignificant anticlerical outbursts as student hijinks. Visiting Wittenberg incognito at the beginning of December, he had even given the innovations his blessing, writing to Spalatin, 'Everything else that I hear and see pleases me very much.'[1]

Back in the solitude of his retreat in the woods, Luther began to worry as matters quickly intensified in the early New Year. Following the 'iconoclasm', the Electoral Saxon government—the elector, we should recall, was a pious collector of saintly relics—demanded an investigation. Additionally, the implications for the university were particularly ominous. As a result of the turmoil, numerous students had already left Wittenberg, and Melanchthon even considered joining the exodus. Both these threats were highly charged. If the university at Wittenberg were no more, the institutional basis necessary for the development of an evangelical theology based on philology would be lost. If the Electoral Saxon regime decided that chaos reigned in Wittenberg, then its political support might be withdrawn, to say nothing of those amongst the princes of the Empire and the Imperial government who would be eager to use civic rebellion as grounds for a root and branch destruction of the teachings emanating from Wittenberg.

Throughout his life when his achievement seemed threatened Luther responded with the assurance of a sleepwalker, and this instance was no different. Within his own camp he staked his claim to definitive and unassailable interpretative authority. The wind was to be taken from the sails of his opponents, especially Imperially influential Duke George of

Saxony, all too close by, who was very ready to use the opportunity presented by rebellion in Wittenberg. 'A Sincere Admonition by Martin Luther to all Christians to Guard against Insurrection and Rebellion' (*Eine treue Vermahnung an alle Christen, sich zu hüten vor Aufruhr und Empörung*), written in December 1521, was widely distributed the following month in pamphlet form. In laying out the principles that would guide the reformation of church and world, this repeatedly reprinted and highly influential text stated unconditionally that whether its concerns be religious or political, a Lutheran reformation could never be founded on either violence or rebellion. At that moment, as throughout his life, Luther's maxim was that the word of God alone, and therefore instruction by pastors and doctrine, would bring victory for the rediscovered evangelical truth. By implication right order and peace would follow, but Luther was not motivated by inherent pacifist convictions; here, as always, his purpose was transcendent and tied to salvation: the fall of 'the pope and his anti-Christian regime' would not come from the use of human force but 'from the word of Christ, which is the breath, the rod and the sword of his mouth', according to the apocalyptic prophecy of the prophet Isaiah, 'He shall smite the earth with the rod of his mouth and with the breath of his lips he shall slay the wicked.'[2]

Later, after the Peasants' War of 1525 had taught Luther that the self-will of the individual who heard the call of Christian freedom was not so easily tamed, the reformer recognized a need to modify his original position. Evidently the word would not be able to prevail of its own accord through orderly channels. Non-violence needed to be protected and promoted by the legitimate actions of prince and magistrate, called by God to that task.

To Wittenberg, 'Under a Far Higher Protection'

In spring 1522 Luther's actions were again determined by an uncompromising referentiality to Christ. He wrote to the elector that he had 'received the gospel not from men but from heaven only, through our Lord Jesus Christ', and therefore he could henceforth 'boast and call myself a minister and evangelist'.[3] Those who believed themselves bound by the rediscovered Christian truth, he wrote, should 'make no reference to my name; let them call themselves Christians, not Lutherans. What is Luther? After all, the teaching is not mine. Neither was I crucified for anyone.' Party designations and particularity were not his thing: 'The papists deservedly have a party name, because they are not content with the teaching and name of Christ, but want to be papist as well.' His approach was emphatically universal: 'I neither am not want to be anyone's master. I hold, together with the universal church, the one universal teaching of Christ, who is our only master.'[4] His words were also a defence against the derogatory characterization of the evangelical movement as 'Lutheran', a term that had been employed by Eck in 1520 in much the same manner as the related earlier movement in Bohemia had been denigrated as 'Hussite'. Those who represented the evangelical churches followed the reformer's example and consistently refused to term themselves 'Lutheran'—or at least they did so up until the second half of the sixteenth century, when, as confessionalization advanced, the orthodoxy of the Formula of Concord of 1577 was proudly designated 'Lutheran' to make evident that it contained, and safeguarded, the pure teachings of the reformer.

As Luther faced the dual threat to both his life and his work, his universalist subordination to his 'master Christ' gave him the strength to keep to the path that he believed he must follow, refusing to be led astray by his personal situation or the interests of others. Under pressure from the radicalization of the Wittenberg movement, in January Luther announced that he would leave the Wartburg and return home.[5] Alarm bells sounded at the Saxon court, then in residence at the hunting castle of Lochau, today Annaburg, where a sharp exhortation prompted by the unrest in Wittenberg had recently been received from the Nuremberg Imperial administration, which governed Germany during the Emperor's absence. At the same time, the bishop of Meissen had announced plans for a visitation that would provide a clearer picture of the unsettling events on the ground. If Luther, still under Imperial bann, should be found in the very city where the unrest was taking place, then political reprisals from the Empire would seem unavoidable. The elector called on Johann Osswald, his representative in Eisenach, to visit the 'prisoner' at the Wartburg and firmly forbid him from returning to Wittenberg, for 'it would not be to the good were he to allow himself to be seen publically in the present circumstances'.[6]

Luther was fully aware of the danger, and also of the difficult situation in which he would put the Electoral Saxon regime. But he did not hesitate. He did not even pause to reply to his ruler, waiting to respond only once the die was cast and he was already on his return journey to Wittenberg. The letter he wrote 'in haste' on 5 March, the final night of his journey, spent at Borna by Leipzig, can take its place as one of the greatest historical statements of the freedom of the individual, which for Luther was founded in a faith in God that nothing on earth could shake. The author was concerned not with justifying his actions but rather that the Elector 'not be disturbed' in hearing of his disobedience, 'for if I would be a true Christian I must be everyone's consoler [even for the great and the good] and do no harm to anyone'. He wrote that he had 'a thoroughly unaffected love and affection for Your Electoral Grace above all other sovereigns and rulers' and that his own life was of no matter here, a life that he would willingly sacrifice for the sake of the pure Gospel, which was his only concern; he continued, 'Your Electoral Grace knows (or, if you do not, I now inform you of the fact) that I have received the gospel not from men but from heaven only, through our Lord Jesus Christ.' Without ingratiation or presumption, but with a candour that could hardly have been surpassed, he underscored his independence of, even superiority to, any secular ruler. In this specific instance that secular ruler was his territorial ruler, whose authority Luther consistently acknowledged, and with whom, he professed, he had a personal bond. Luther thanked the elector for shielding him from the execution of the Imperial verdict and for his concerns for Luther's life, as expressed in his most recent instruction. Such earthly benevolence, however, while so important, must not be allowed to cloud the sacred perspective, which alone guaranteed protection from, and the courage and freedom to face, all earthly dangers. The elector, Luther wrote, 'has already done far too much and should do nothing at all', for God wished the matter to be left in God's hands. 'If Your Electoral Grace believes, then Your Electoral Grace will be safe and have peace. If Your Electoral Grace does not believe, I at least do believe and must leave Your Electoral Grace's unbelief to its own torturing anxiety, such as all unbelievers have to suffer.' Luther was 'going to Wittenberg under a far higher protection than the Elector's'.

In language that was both witty and clear, Luther made his resolve part of an image designed to extinguish any remaining aggravation at the electoral Saxon court: 'If the condition that exists in Wittenberg existed in Leipzig, I would go to Leipzig even if (Your Electoral Grace will excuse my foolish words) it rained Duke Georges for nine days and every duke were nine times as furious as this one.' When it came to the attitude the Electoral Saxon government should adopt, Luther continued, in secular matters the government should confidently abide by the 'Imperial constitution' and 'by no means offer any resistance or request such resistance or any obstruction on the part of others', so, in other words, the ruler should not act counter to Imperial law in order to defend Luther against possible violence to his person. Responding like an Old Testament prophet, Luther turned secular authority on its head, or relativized its significance in light of sacred history, which is, in the end, all that matters: 'I have no intention of asking Your Electoral Grace for protection. Indeed I think I shall protect Your Electoral Grace...he who believes the most can protect the most.' Finally, undaunted, Luther discharged his pastoral responsibilities for the elector: 'Since I have the impression that Your Electoral Grace is still quite weak in faith, I can by no means regard Your Electoral Grace as the man to protect and save me.'[7]

These are not the words of a prince's lackey, a vilification that the rebels of 1525 would soon use against him, but they are also not the words of a revolutionary set on subverting the affairs of the world, a characterization of Luther readily invoked in our secularized world. When Luther spoke against violence, he was speaking of the non-violent progress of the word of God. For many of his contemporaries the complexities of his stance and his personality were already too great—they were neither able nor willing to understand him. Thomas Müntzer, for example, who during Luther's absence had briefly joined Karlstadt in Wittenberg and would soon become Luther's principal opponent in the Protestant camp, picked up only on Luther's opposition to radical change in church and society and taunted the reformer as the 'soft-living flesh at Wittenberg'.[8]

But Luther was talking a language that Elector Frederick understood. Frederick accepted Luther's prophetic claim and its legitimization of the intransigence of 'Doctor Martinus'—the name the elector always respectfully used for his Wittenberg professor of Bible—and directed Saxon politics accordingly. The submission that charismatic religious leaders often demand of their followers did not characterize their relationship. Prince and reformer each followed his own path, without questioning the freedom of the other to make decisions and take action in his own sphere. This experience, also largely typical of Luther's subsequent relationships with Frederick's successors, first his brother John and then John's son John Frederick, reinforced how the reformer viewed the political. The secular and spiritual domains were separate, but they were complementary, not antithetical. Luther's positive experience with his territorial ruler meant that both the context and nature of his teachings on law and authority were very different from the context and nature of the political thought of western European Calvinism. In place of collaboration with the secular authorities, Calvinism, a product of the later Reformation of the second half of the century, faced active opposition.

The elector allowed the obstinate Augustinian monk to have his way. As a precaution he instructed Hieronymus Schurf, who was professor of law in Wittenberg but held a secondary position as an electoral councillor, to ensure that Luther's presence was not the cause of further disturbance. On no account was Luther to preach 'at the foundation at the castle', in other words at the chapel associated with the elector's court. Anything said or done at the castle would have official character, and the Saxon government might then be held responsible. Schurf was also instructed to ensure that Luther agreed to compose a letter suitable for publication in which he formally notified the elector of his reasons for returning to Wittenberg and recorded that he had done so without the approval of the electoral regime. The reformer could agree to these conditions without difficulty for he believed it his God-given responsibility to dampen the waves of unrest.

Back at the Helm, Preaching

With his sudden reappearance in Wittenberg at the beginning of March, Luther must have seemed to the Wittenberg community much like the angry Moses who descended from Mount Sinai to put an end to the dancing around the Golden Calf. Like Moses, Luther was soon back in charge. He secured for himself the authority to determine what the Reformation was and what shape that Reformation would take, in Wittenberg and Electoral Saxony at least. In keeping with his prophetic role, preaching and the proclamation of the word were his means to that end. Every day for a week, Sunday to Sunday, he entered the pulpit in the town church of Saint Mary to explain from Scripture how church and world must be ordered. He spoke directly to the residents of Wittenberg, whom he described in the letters he wrote during this period as 'my community', or as 'my stall' that the devil had invaded. He wore the habit of an Augustinian monk to preach and moved back into the monastery to live, demonstrating visibly that he did not agree with those who had rushed to leave the monastery and had introduced innovations to the worship service.

Cranach, both artist and friend, recorded Luther in this role in an image that was quickly distributed to the world. Luther appeared as a youthful monk. He is no longer the professor of Bible sporting a doctor's cap, or the saint-like saviour of Worms; now he is the preacher and herald of the new

Figure 26. Martin Luther, by Lucas Cranach the Elder, painted between 1522 and 1524, when Luther no longer had his monk's tonsure but still wore his monk's habit.

order. Externally he wears the traditional clothing of the monk, but the real substance lies in his proclamation of a new theology—as is subtly suggested by his full head of hair, which represents the distancing of his message from the monastic life of the Roman Church. During his journey from the Wartburg back to Wittenberg, Luther had not resumed the tonsure of Dr Martinus Luther that Junker Jörg had abandoned.

A preacher dressed as a monk but without the tonsure (see Figure 26)—this image illuminates how Luther believed the rediscovered evangelical truth could be enacted in a world in which the minds of most Christians were still ruled by centuries of false exposition by the Roman Church. He declared his position powerfully in his Wittenberg 'Invocavit sermons', named after the Sunday in the church year that fell on 9 March 1522, the date he began his sermon cycle. Only Christ and the grace of God can save humanity. The order imposed by the radicals was therefore nothing more than a new enslavement that destroyed the freedom so recently won. Turning to each disputed theme in turn, he sought to demonstrate that freedom and love of the weak, and not the strict letter of the law, could bring about the evangelical renewal of church and society. He recorded, 'I condemn the idea that Masses are considered sacrifices or good works; but I do not want to lay hands on the unwilling or the unbelieving, or curb them by force.'[9] He adopted this position repeatedly as he addressed all the issues that Karlstadt and his followers amongst the magistrates and church community had wished to regulate through radical action, from the presence of images in the church to the fate of monks, nuns, and priests.

Eyewitnesses reported the powerful impact of Luther's week-long preaching series, as the sincerity, enthusiasm, and persuasive powers of the reformer won over the Wittenberg community and leading members of the town council. Even Hieronymus Schurf, austere lawyer and electoral official, was impressed. Deeply moved, he reported to the Electoral Saxon court:

> that great joy and rejoicing has started and grows for both the learned and friends among us from Doctor Martin's arrival and preaching, by means of which each day with irrefutable evidence of our errors he shows us, who are poor, misguided, and vexed, how by means of divine aid we can find again the path of truth . . . such that evidently and clearly the spirit of God is in him and works through him.[10]

The new church order with its sweeping changes was quietly dropped, along with the radical innovations that it had introduced. To appease Luther, he was honoured with plentiful quantities of beer and wine and cloth for a new habit. Although Gabriel Zwilling had so recently stood at Karlstadt's side calling for radical cleansing and transformation, he now rejoined Luther; his commitment was so great that soon after Luther arranged for him to become pastor at Altenburg and Torgau, two particularly prominent locations.

'Here all things have been well restored by Doctor Martinus,' Melanchthon could report with relief to Spalatin on 20 March. The elector believed his faith in Luther vindicated. The rest was up to Saxon diplomacy as, with an eye to the political context, Luther was asked to revise the statement that had been required from him about his unilateral decision to return to Wittenberg. That declaration then made its way to the Imperial government via Hans von der Planitz, the Electoral Saxon representative.[11] The result was as desired: the Imperial government was reassured, and Duke George of Saxony expressly absolved his cousin from any involvement in Luther's actions. That the man who had preached against the unrest in Wittenberg was an outlaw of the Empire and had been excommunicated by the church was left off the table—in legal terms an absurdity, but politically certainly feasible when we consider the tacit agreement that meant that the Imperial bann did not apply in Electoral Saxony. The Augustinian monk was now free to appear in public in the elector's residence town of Wittenberg and throughout Ernestine Saxony, regardless of his continuing status as an outlaw in the rest of the Empire, and he was free to take into his own hands the Reformation of the territorial church in Electoral Saxony. Anyone who worked with Luther or even simply entered his house no longer needed to fear the penalties that might be imposed by the laws of the Empire and the church on those who had contact with an individual under Imperial or ecclesiastical bann.

Reformation by Persuasion Only

Two complementary principles characterized Luther's early evangelical reform of the church: (1) consideration of the weak and reconciliation with the repentant amongst those who had gone astray; and (2) the radical battle with Satan, who 'here amongst my herd is trying to do much damage'. If the eternal enemy of the truth was to be stopped in his tracks, each person who served as a tool of the devil must be condemned and isolated, and it made no difference to Luther whether that individual was part of the papal church or came from within his own ranks. In spring 1522 Karlstadt, Luther's colleague on the theological faculty at Wittenberg who had debated with him against Johannes Eck at the Leipzig disputation, was forbidden to preach or publish in Wittenberg. Karlstadt had not been silenced, however, for he continued to publish outside Wittenberg, in Nuremberg, for example, and found other pulpits from which he could broadcast his divergent and increasingly mystical and spiritualistic theology for the renewal of church and world. The alienation of the two men, both personal and professional, was now irredeemable.

In 1523 Karlstadt became pastor in the Thuringian town of Orlamünde, on the upper reaches of the Saale, far from Wittenberg. There he established his counter-model of a radical evangelical church, without infant baptism, which garnered support in surrounding areas, reaching as far as Jena. In August 1524 the two adversaries met again in person, in Jena and Orlamünde, but the only result was a hardening of the fronts. Luther was resentful that in the district where Karlstadt was being well received, for the first time his own preaching failed to bring communities over to his way of thinking. Instead, he encountered the stubborn resolve of the common man that less than a year later, in the course of the Thuringian Peasants' War, would cause him such problems. In Kahla, in the shadow of the command-ing electoral Saxon castle of Leuchtenburg, his path to the pulpit was partially blocked by a demonstrative sign of the rejection of images, for he had to clamber with difficulty over a broken crucifix. He subsequently declined to preach in Karlstadt's home parish of Orlamünde, probably because he feared that he would find himself facing an uncontrollable challenge from the congregation. All the more embittered, then, was the clash of views at a communal gathering, when Luther found himself facing not Karlstadt, whom he had brusquely expelled from the church, but the community itself, which was principally composed of self-confident peasants who insisted on their right to elect the pastor, on the removal of images, and on the validity of inner mystical knowledge of the truth of God. By the time Luther departed, Karlstadt and the 'fanatics' of Orlamünde were his irre-concilable enemies. His opponents saw in Luther a man who had betrayed the very Gospel that he himself had rediscovered. Shortly after cutting themselves off from Luther, the peasants joined the uprising.

By this time Karlstadt had already left Saxony. Banished by the Electoral Saxon government, he travelled through southern Germany, was active in Rothenburg ob der Tauber, and ended up in Strasburg. Over subsequent centuries, all the mystical and spiritualist strands of Protestantism would invoke his views on images and the Lord's Supper and his rejection of infant baptism, the antithesis of the theology of Wittenberg. While Luther sought to counter Karlstadt's appeal wherever he could, he performed his Christian duties nevertheless. He took part in the baptism of Karlstadt's son Andreas, with the agreement of the child's mother, in the absence of his father, choosing to leave it to God to decide whether it was honest and heartfelt; Luther's wife even stood as godparent to Karlstadt's son.[12]

Having wandered through southern Germany, in 1525 Karlstadt was declared an outlaw, for while in Rothenburg ob der Tauber he had estab-lished links to the rebellious peasants. Luther secretly offered him refuge in Wittenberg, although only on condition that in future he neither voice nor publish his views. His stay was short, and Karlstadt soon was seeking to realize his Anabaptist-spiritualist counter-model to Luther's Reformation in East Frisian Oldersum, under the protection of a local humanist-educated nobleman. Yet even in this notoriously independent region Luther's influ-ence caught up with him. Karlstadt would find peace only in the 1530s, when he moved to Zurich and Basel. Within the Reformed areas of the Swiss Confederation Luther was esteemed as the courageous champion of the indulgence theses directed against Rome, but the steely authority over the doctrine and order of the church that he had secured during the Wittenberg unrest of 1522 was not recognized.

Victory over the Prophets of Zwickau

In spring 1522 as Luther energetically grasped the helm again in Wittenberg, the attack on the old order elsewhere in the Empire was well under way. The exhortations he had sent from the Wartburg had neither prevented monks from abandoning their monasteries in great disorder,[13] nor held in check the waves of attacks on clerics and their economic and legal privileges in the towns. Against the will of its author, the Reformation message fuelled the anticlericalism already well entrenched in medieval towns. In many places, including neighbouring Erfurt, the citizens took part in an all-out attack on the local clergy. Particularly unrestrained was the response in the weaving and trading town of Zwickau, at the foot of the western Erzgebirge, which lay within Electoral Saxony and was an important hub for long-distance traffic running north–south and east–west. In Zwickau Luther's priesthood of all believers was understood literally—weavers and blacksmiths, and even women, preached and expounded the word, in the process challenging the authority of every established office of the church. Alarm bells sounded for the professor of Bible, for whom exegesis was about educated interpretation not inner mystical illumination. Additionally he understood his prophet-hood as exclusive, as the grace of God revealed through study of Scripture to him and to his supporters. Events in Zwickau were principally the work of three lay preachers who would soon be known as the 'Prophets of Zwickau'—Nicolaus Storch, a weaver, Thomas Drechsel, a blacksmith, and Markus Thomae, called Stübner, who had studied in Wittenberg— but behind them all was none other than Thomas Müntzer, the very theologian who soon would unite mystical theology with social revolution to produce an opposing model of reform. Müntzer emerged during the Peasants' War as Luther's most influential adversary. From August 1520 to April 1521 he had preached at the parish church of Saint Katharine in Zwickau, broadcasting his mystical ideas and in effect encouraging the creation of separatist conventicles distinct from the church community.

In late 1521 Nikolaus Hausmann, pastor of Zwickau and a friend of Luther's, persuaded the town council to respond. The three 'prophets' fled to Wittenberg at the end of December and put their largely incoherent views to Melanchthon. The spiritualism, pronounced prophetic character, and eschatological visions of the men from Zwickau, and not least Stübner's rejection of infant baptism, were a cause of great concern for Melanchthon, already alarmed by events in Wittenberg as he stood guardian for Luther while the latter remained at the Wartburg. His report to Luther received in return an admonition to level-headedness and confident examination of the spirit of the Prophets of Zwickau.[14] Melanchthon was to proceed without fear and without inappropriate lenience; he should examine the men in light of a catalogue of Scriptural criteria, testing whether their views were indeed in keeping with God's word. Their supposed 'conversations with God' were nothing but devilish deception. Luther also decisively rejected the incipient Anabaptism that he encountered here for the first time. He could find no mandate for adult baptism anywhere in the Bible, he wrote, where 'according to apostolic custom, and in the time of the apostles, small children were baptised'.[15]

The disputes with Karlstadt and with the Prophets of Zwickau were Luther's first experience of the 'false brothers',[16] who for him were nothing other than creatures of the devil: 'I have always expected Satan to touch this sore, but he did not want to do it through the papists. It is among us and among our followers that he is stirring up this grievous schism, but Christ will quickly trample him under our feet.'[17] In his dealings with the Prophets of Zwickau and with other 'false brothers', the reformer would consistently retain this pronounced distinction. He was always prepared, however, to enter into discussion. His Invocavit sermons having calmed Wittenberg, he was willing to receive Markus Stübner on two successive evenings at the beginning of April, followed by meetings with Drechsel and Storch in late summer. Their conversations produced intense dispute over who represented the voice of God, over what 'my God would deny your God'.[18] For Luther there was no question: he alone had been commissioned by God to speak as God's prophet. In his discussions with the men from Zwickau and other false brothers, he wrote, he must therefore have 'been talking to the Devil incarnate'.[19] Accordingly, he was aggressive in their encounters, treating them not as fellow interlocutors, but as individuals who had gone astray and were in error and must be forced back onto the right path with scoldings and reprimands. In his guests' inability to appreciate his 'friendly and fraternal admonitions'—they preferred instead to up and leave in anger—he saw Satan at work again.[20]

Only a few years later Kaspar von Schwenckfeld, a member of the Silesian nobility and an early supporter of Luther, had a similar experience. As councillor to the ruling duke, Schwenckfeld had introduced the Reformation to the small territory of Liegnitz as early as 1522. When it came to the doctrine of the Lord's Supper, however, he followed his own path, which led close to the Swiss, and he fostered a spiritualism that was indifferent to any form of church organization. Luther met Schwenckfeld's request for recognition of his theology with complete incomprehension; all that Schwenckfeld received in return was excommunication that forced him underground with his supporters and into an itinerant life far from home. The Wittenberger had to hand a term that he used to isolate the Prophets of Zwickau, Schwenckfeld, or others like them, shutting them off from his Reformation: he designated them 'fanatics' (*Schwärmer*), for they refused to be satisfied with the rationality of the word of God and its exposition by office holders called to that task, insisting instead on spiritual inspiration and a mystical experience of God.

At various locations, principally in rural areas, the three Prophets of Zwickau continued to make known their vision of evangelical doctrine, but they remained highly individualistic, with little interest in establishing a comprehensive church order that could rival that of the Reformation church in Wittenberg. Schwenckfeld similarly attracted followers, but the spiritualistic nature of his teachings meant a clandestine existence. Thomas Müntzer was a different case, however. In the years between 1522 and 1525 he grew to be the most influential and most dangerous of Luther's challengers within the evangelical camp.

'He Who Has Not Seen Luther in Wittenberg Has Seen Nothing'

For the moment Luther had defeated the false brothers, and he was able to tighten his authority over all aspects of the renewal of the church, both theoretical and practical. The rebel celebrated at Worms for his stand against false, in other words unscriptural, authority was now, in Luther's own eyes too, the bringer of order and bearer of evangelical authority. All the strategic elements of evangelical church renewal came together in Wittenberg, or rather, we might envisage a network reaching out from Wittenberg across Germany and Europe bearing a methodical church reform from which the evangelical urban, territorial, and state churches of the modern age emerged. Wittenberg had become Luther's own cathedral see, a German Rome. 'Anyone who has not seen the pope in Rome and Luther in Wittenberg is thought to have seen absolutely nothing'—evidently agreeing with this widespread maxim, in 1523 Johannes Dantiscus, Polish ambassador to the court of Charles V and a member of the Roman Church who would rise to be bishop of Ermland, stopped off for three days in Wittenberg as he journeyed home from Spain. He did not rest until Philip Melanchthon had arranged for him to meet the celebrity residing at the Augustinian monastery. After they had dined together, Dantiscus was one of the first to experience Luther's 'Table Talk', later so renowned, at a time when Luther was still living in the midst of his fellow Augustinians.

Like so many pilgrims to Wittenberg, students from all over the world but also princes and statesmen, the Polish ambassador experienced for himself the reformer's self-confidence, which had grown with his victory over his opponents within the Reformation camp. 'Luther's face', he recorded:

> is like his books; his eyes are piercing and sparkle almost uncannily, as one sometimes sees in those who are possessed . . . One perceives his pride and great arrogance very readily: he is completely uninhibited in his scolding, disagreeing, ridiculing, and taunting of the pope, the emperor, and several other princes . . . At home he dresses such that he could be taken for a courtier; when he leaves the house, he wears the habit of his order.

Despite Luther's outbursts against his opponents, with which the Pole could not agree, even at this early date the overall impression was of benevolence and hospitality, for which later, too, when he was married and had his own household, Luther would be praised: 'We drank wine and beer in great humor. In that respect he seems to be a "good chap" [ein guter Geselle], as one says in German.' In his letter to the bishop of Poznán from which this character sketch is taken, Dantiscus stated, 'In the holiness of his lifestyle, which we often extol in him, he is no different from us others [i.e. other priests]',[21] evidence that the Catholic party did not possess only the warped image of the reformer created by anti-Reformation propaganda.

The report that Dantiscus composed during his travels in the early days of the Reformation suggests that Luther demonstrated both foresight and a good grasp of reality when he insisted that the 'weak' must be convinced before new church practices were introduced. As Dantiscus travelled through the Elbe plain, where storms and floods had destroyed the crops, he heard harsh words and even curses directed against Luther by the despairing peasants. He was told that Luther had led the people astray by having them eat meat during times of fasting and that God's anger had therefore devastated the land. Luther, who had grown up only a stone's throw from the rural experience and had recently visited relatives in the villages around Eisenach, was the last person to fail to take the fears of the 'common man' seriously. Such anxieties only confirmed for him that the way forward must be paved with preaching and writing that patiently explained his new theology.

Against Müntzer and the 'Murderous Gang of Peasants'

Is the Freedom of the Christian Also the Freedom of the Peasant?

Two years later the reformer found himself facing a decision that would have tragic implications for the peasants and also, in a certain respect, for him. Along with the Imperial knights who three years earlier had tied the interests of their estate to the struggle for evangelical freedom, the peasants, too, were amongst those who were losing out with the profound changes that accompanied the transition from the late Middle Ages to the early modern period. They lost out through the construction of the territorial state, which imposed further dues on the peasants in the form of what were in effect state taxes and required them to accept legal and institutional innovations. And they lost out with the demographic upswing and the Europe-wide agrarian boom it produced: the growth in population in Europe caused the demand for foodstuffs to soar, but only those who had the right to market such products were in a position to profit from the surge in demand, being able to offer grain, milk, cheese, and meat for sale at markets local or more distant. Peasants rarely had much sway, other than in exceptional instances, as was the case for the free peasants of Friesland and Prussia and in individual Alpine regions who achieved a prosperity to which rich silver artefacts that can be found today in local museums still testify. The greater the potential receipts from agrarian production, the harder the feudal lords squeezed their peasants, making constantly higher demands, either directly, in the form of products of the land, or indirectly, in the form of ever-increasing monetary levies. Peasants of greater means, who could produce more from their lands, were able to bear this increased burden better than those who worked only mid-sized or small landholdings, which caused antagonism and tension in the villages themselves. The odds were in favour of those who had that material advantage, but they became longer for all others. The situation was particularly oppressive in areas where the law required that lands be divided up following a death, which meant that peasant landholdings were constantly partitioned. Regions in which this practice was common, in south-west Germany, in Franconia, and in Hesse up to Thuringia, formed the heartland of the rebellion.

The pressure on the peasants came not only from the noble and urban owners of the land they worked, but also from the many ecclesiastical foundations, which had been badly shaken by Luther's teachings. Some nobles provoked the peasants through their particular cruelty or, simply, their thoughtlessness: the countess of Stühlingen, at the Upper Rhine, decided to force her peasants at harvest time to collect snail shells on which yarn could then be wound. The great abbeys, monasteries, and prelatries of southern Germany were much detested and would be the first to feel the wrath of the peasants. As for the knights, for the peasants, too, the anticlericalism that had become so widespread in the late medieval period played an important role, but equally decisive for the peasants was that productive moment of fusion with Luther's new evangelical theology, specifically with the concept of the law of God and with the communal principle. Like the reformer, the peasants desired that the life of both the individual and society be based on an unconditional dependence on the law of God, on the 'Evangelium', which the peasants saw as both instruction and way of life.

> It is our conclusion and final opinion that if one or more of the articles set forth here is not in agreement with the word of God (though we think this is not the case), and this disagreement is shown to us on the basis of Scripture, we shall withdraw such an article—after the matter is explained to us on the basis of Scripture.[22]

This text comes from the final article of the Memmingen manifesto, drawn up by the rebellious peasants in March 1525, which borrowed unmistakably from the words used by Luther in 1521 at the Diet at Worms as he refused to recant. The manifesto was published in pamphlet form and distributed throughout the Empire, promoting the peasant cause very successfully. Many of the local letters of grievance on which the peasants of Memmingen drew to construct the Twelve Articles—with the assistance of Christoph Schappeler, evangelically minded town pastor, and Sebastian

Lotzer, a furrier and lay theologian—had also cited the law of God. The articles gave the peasants' protest, which had been fragmented both geographically and temporally, a programmatic and universal framework. The 'old law' to which the peasants had previously turned to defend themselves against the unifying innovations of ruler or local landowner was applicable only regionally, or even locally, which had meant it could not be used as the foundation of a broader, overarching communal campaign. That deficiency had now been overcome, for with the introduction of the Reformation, God's law alone could be used to legitimize concrete peasant demands, and the peasant protest could exist as a national movement. Additionally, the galvanizing appeal to God's law meant that the battle was being fought not simply for earthly ends, but for the sake of God's kingdom.

The second link between the Reformation and the demands of the peasants lay in the communal principle, whose social and political volatility we have already encountered in the context of the Knights' Revolt. Protestant communal Christianity fitted well with the attempts of the peasants to remove village self-governance from the grip of the ruler and, when possible, extend their self-determination. In the peasants' demands this affinity with the Reformation was articulated in light of the church community, with the first of the Memmingen articles demanding the community be able to elect the pastor. This claim was a decisive step in a simplification of the complicated medieval process of appointment to a parish, where various institutions recognized in canon law, including incorporation, patronage, and curacy, had increasingly left the parish priest alienated from the simple religious needs of his flock.

An elected priest would be far more likely to reside in the village, where he could bring to all Christians, whatever their social standing, the church's sources of grace, and, in the words of the peasants, 'preach the holy gospel to us clearly and purely'. The article continued, 'he is to add no teaching or commandment of men to the gospel, but rather is always to proclaim the true faith and encourage us to ask God for his grace.' The pastor was to receive the tithe on grain, which previously the peasants had been required to hand over to the church without any ability to influence how it might then be used. Donations to the church were to be administered by the community and used to meet that community's ecclesiastical ends, which encompassed not only direct support for the pastor but also, for example, care of the poor. The small tithe, on fruit and household animals, was to be abolished as one 'which men have invented'.

Reformation ideas aligned with the peasants' concerns about the nature of the church in their midst but, even more importantly, they aligned with a communal understanding of society. The Articles of Memmingen also addressed communal lands: in many places the collective use of meadows and fields that belonged to the community had been usurped by the local lord, and local landowners had unilaterally reserved for themselves the peasants' stake in fishing, the hunting of small game, and the use of the forests, declaring it part of the local lordship. The articles demanded that such rights 'should revert to the entire community', and that 'the community should be free, in an orderly way, to allow anyone to take home what he needs' from the forests, 'with the approval of a supervisor appointed by the community'.

The peasants, even more than Sickingen and the Imperial knights, emphasized the sacral and Christian character of both the ecclesiastical and secular communities: the village, as the peasant *communitas*, was framed in terms of Christian fraternity, and the relationship with the local lordship, which the great majority of peasants had no thought of abolishing, was to be guided by 'fraternal love in Christ'. So, for example, if common land claimed by the peasants had been rightly purchased by the local lord years or decades earlier, then compensation would be paid. Such 'fraternal love' was also to underpin the assessment of all levies and services, which should never be set so high that survival was made impossible. Additional services should be appropriately remunerated.

The peasants identified a particularly blatant violation of Christian fraternal equitability in the death duty (*Todfall*), the payment due to the noble, urban, or ecclesiastical *Leibherr*, or personal lord, on the death of the head of a family. The *Leibherr*, who was not necessarily also the *Grundherr*, or leaser of the land, used this opportunity to increase his stake in the burgeoning agricultural profits. In the eyes of the peasants, 'widows and orphans' were being 'shamefully robbed' by precisely those who should 'guard and protect' them, turning on its head the core idea of the medieval world order that dictated that the lord should provide his subjects with defence and protection, which meant also attending to their social welfare, in return for the services they provided. For the peasants enthused by Luther's teachings, the re-establishment of evangelical fraternity would be the means to restore the health of that relationship.

The 'Christian Association' created in Memmingen at the beginning of March 1525 by the three Upper Swabian peasant groupings gave concrete form to the rebellious peasants' notion of how society should look. Open to members of any estate, the union was to cause no harm to 'anyone, be he spiritual or secular'; its intent was to increase fraternal love amongst the people. Arbitration, its members believed, would bring an end to the crisis in the relationship of peasant and lord. They called for the creation of a council of judges comprising statesmen and Reformation-minded theologians and led by Archduke Ferdinand of Austria, the Emperor's representative, and Martin Luther; the council would rule on the demands of the peasants and seek to ensure the restoration of Christian love amongst the estates.[23] Whether their ideas were utopic wishful thinking or whether the rediscovery of the Gospel had brought a real possibility that the peasants' political and social concerns might be understood in light of Christian fraternity would become clear over the months that followed. The course of events depended in large measure on how the Wittenberg reformer, so highly esteemed in Germany and by the common people in particular, would respond to the peasants' cause.

Luther had long idealized the peasant, whom he saw as a pure and true Christian in a world blighted by depravity and profit-seeking. He was confronted with demands of the southern German peasants for the first time in mid-April 1525: in the course of an inspection that ran from 13 April to 6 May, as he travelled through the Harz forelands and into Thuringia near Weimar, he was presented with copies of the Twelve Articles (see Figure 27) and the Christian Association drawn up by the peasant assembly at Memmingen. The peasants had called upon him to adjudicate their demands, and he immediately took up that task. His verdict was published in a pamphlet entitled 'Admonition to Peace, a Reply to the Twelve Articles of the Peasants in Swabia' (*Ermahnung zum Frieden auf die zwölf Artikel der Bauernschrift in Schwaben*). This first text addressed to the peasantry was composed in Eisleben on 20 April, at some distance therefore from the events of the uprising and at a time when news of peasant violence and plundering in Upper Swabia had yet to arrive. Luther still had reason to believe that the conflict could be stilled by a Christian exhortation to all parties. His 'Admonition to Peace' appealed to the conscience of each side: he called on 'you princes and lords, and especially you blind bishops and mad priests and monks' to recognize that they alone were responsible 'on earth ... for this disastrous rebellion' and that 'the peasants have just published twelve articles, some of which are so fair and just as to take away your reputation in the eyes of God and the world'. He praised the peasants for their willingness to embrace the directives they found in the Bible but

Die Grundtlichen vnd rechtē
haußt Artickell / aller Bawrschafft vnnd Hynderseßenn der Geistlichen vnnd Weltlichen Oberkeyten / von welchen sie sich beschwert vermeynen.

Bawrschafft

Figure 27. The Twelve Articles, adopted in March 1525 by the peasants' assembly at Memmingen, published in 1525 in Erfurt by Hans Stürmer.

warned them that the 'heinous wrongs' of the authorities did not entitle them to use force: 'Christians do not fight for themselves with sword and musket, but with the cross and with suffering, just as Christ, our leader, does not bear a sword, but hangs on the cross.'[24]

Luther or Müntzer

Luther's concluding prayer that God 'either reconcile you both and bring about an agreement between you, or else graciously prevent things from turning out as you intend [through the use of force]' went unheard.[25] Editions of Luther's call for peace were available throughout Germany by the beginning of May, but blood had already been spilled by both parties some time earlier, and a peaceful settlement was no longer on the cards. A spectacular act of revenge at the beginning of April fuelled anti-peasant propaganda for decades: following the capitulation of the town and castle of Weinsberg, Count Ludwig von Helfenstein, the Habsburg commander of the castle, and fifteen knights were forced to run the gauntlet through the pikes of the peasants until they collapsed and died. The countess was taken in triumph to Heilbronn; her transportation in a dung cart was all the more appalling to the nobility as she was an illegitimate daughter of Emperor Maximilian and therefore aunt of the current Emperor. Soon after, the monasteries and castles of Bamberg were stormed; their inhabitants were killed and furniture, paintings, and sculptures destroyed. When events are viewed more broadly, then it is evident that such destructive violence was not the rule. These episodes brought the peasants no advantage, and they only strengthened the resolve of opponents who were determined to seize the moment to break the intractable peasants, as they saw them, once and for all. By the time Luther issued his call for peace, reflection, and mutual understanding, the ruling authorities had already responded with brute force. At the end of May, Jäcklin Rohrbach, instigator of the bloody scene at Weinberg, had fallen into the hands of the Swabian League, and its noble members had piled up the wood for his pyre with their own hands. Georg Truchsess von Waldburg ensured Rohrbach's death in the flames was long and painful, a warning for anyone who might in future dare to challenge the power of the princes. The peasants he had previously led had already broken with Rohrbach, but this canny decision could not help them—the princely army paid back every peasant act of violence many times over.

The peasant rebellion that had broken out in southern Germany soon spread to the north, and to Thuringia, where it erupted at the end of April in the storming of monasteries and castles. The threat of chaos was all the greater as now the peasants were no longer on their own: joined by mineworkers and discontented townspeople their uprising had grown into a broad popular movement. Suddenly Luther found himself in the midst of the events and felt called to respond on two fronts—to ensure Thomas Müntzer, his most dangerous opponent within the Protestant camp, was stopped in his tracks; and to call on the authorities, in his case the Saxon ruler, to take action against the chaos and anarchy, standing alongside them in their struggle against disorder.

Since his dismissal from the parish at Zwickau in spring 1521 Müntzer had led a restless itinerant life. Relating his eschatology, which was increasingly combined with ideas of social revolution, he travelled to Bohemia and to Prague and then returned to Saxon and Thuringian lands. He stayed briefly in Wittenberg, in his home town of Stolberg in the Harz, and at the monastery of Cistercian nuns at Glaucha. He consistently found small groups of enthusiastic supporters, but he also consistently raised the suspicions of the authorities. From spring 1523 until summer 1524 he held the office of pastor in the small electoral Saxon municipality of Allstedt, south of Eisleben, where Luther had been born, without having been called to the post, as was legally required, by the elector. He managed to remain for a longer time only in Allstedt, even as Duke George of Saxony and the counts of Mansfeld, which lay close by, issued harsh mandates against him and his followers, for the Electoral Saxon government, within whose jurisdiction Allstedt lay, did not become involved, and Luther, too, initially left Müntzer to his own devices.

On 13 July 1524 Müntzer had the opportunity to preach before Duke John and his son John Frederick at the castle high above the town. The potential to influence Electoral Saxon ecclesiastical politics was all the greater because the ruling elector, Frederick, had been seriously unwell for some time, and the influence of his brother and nephew was growing. Along with his Prague Manifesto of 1521, which had announced the arrival of the church of the End Times, Müntzer's 'Sermon to the Princes' (*Fürstenpredigt*) on the prophet Daniel, which was quickly published in 1524, is a key text for Müntzer's mystical visions. Luther immediately recognized a shocking challenge in the sermon, for Müntzer had portrayed himself as the new Daniel and therefore as a councillor sent from God, the very role that Luther claimed for himself. There was no real danger, however, that the princes would fall under the sway of Müntzer's visions and apocalyptic dream interpretations, and Müntzer's call for force to be employed to make the authorities accept the Gospel was unrealistic. Müntzer drew his followers in Allstedt into a formal union in order that they might immediately create God's kingdom on earth, but he was ordered to appear at the court at Weimar and forbidden to preach or publish. His arrest now imminent, at the beginning of August 1524 he fled in the night over the walls of Allstedt. By mid-August he was leader of a popular Reformation movement in the Imperial city of Mühlhausen, a short day's journey to the west.

Luther had already gone onto the offensive in June 1524—and therefore immediately before Müntzer preached his 'Sermon to the Princes'—when he published a pamphlet entitled 'An Open Letter to the Princes of Saxony concerning the Rebellious Spirit' (*Eyn brieff an die fürsten zu Sachsen von dem auffrurischen geyst*). He had called on the princes to banish the 'spirit at Allstedt' and to reject sharply his teachings, according to which 'we Christians are to destroy and storm churches'.[26] A letter he sent that autumn to the mayor, council, and community of Mühlhausen had similar intent. Although he had been forbidden to publish, Müntzer responded with two pamphlets, printed in Nuremberg, in which he blasted his Wittenberg adversary. Even their titles derided Luther: 'A Highly Provoked Vindication and a Refutation of the Unspiritual Soft-Living Flesh in Wittenberg' (*Hoch-verursachte Schutzrede und Antwort wider das sanftlebende Fleisch zu Wittenberg*) and 'A Manifest Exposé of False Faith, Presented to the Faithless World' (*Ausgedrückte Entblößung des falschen Glaubens der ungetreuen Welt*). In their wordcraft and acerbity Müntzer and Luther were worthy rivals. Distinguishing himself from the soft-living Luther, Müntzer laid out the principles that would guide him in future: the days when he, like Luther, had been solicitous of the 'great Hanses' of this world were past; now was the time for furious force to be employed to ensure authority be transferred to the people and the world ordered unconditionally according to the will of God. Like Luther, Müntzer spoke and thought like an Old Testament prophet, but while Luther, with his equally fiery temperament, was ready to take long, slow breaths when it came to the implementation of his theology, Müntzer's prophethood propelled him into action and to the immediate realization of the Kingdom of God.

The antagonism between these two fundamentally different theologians took a new turn in April 1525, when their war of words became an armed struggle. On his return from a fact-finding mission through the areas of south Germany where the peasants had risen up, in March 1525 Müntzer set his torch to a popular revolt in Mühlhausen. The council made up of the urban elite was toppled and replaced with an 'eternal council', its members recruited from the supporters of the social-revolutionary reformer. Unlike Luther when he faced unrest in Wittenberg, Müntzer saw rebellion and the use of force not as a threat, but as an opportunity for the Gospel. Less than a week after Luther had called for calm in his 'Admonition to Peace', written in Eisleben, Müntzer assumed the mantle of leader of the anti-Wittenberg Radical Reformation, when, on 26 April, he arrived at Eichsfeld with a body of men from Mühlhausen and directly intervened in the peasants' struggles against local landowners and the territorial regime. Travelling in the Harz forelands and eastern Thuringia, near Weimar, Luther was only a few hours distant from the events that ensued.

Rebellious peasants and princely armies were lined up against each other. Also at stake now, at the high point of the Thuringian Peasants' War, were two irreconcilable models of reformation and evangelical renewal. In his celebrated teaching on the two kingdoms, to which we will return in detail, Luther carefully distinguished between theology and politics, between the religious-spiritual and the material-earthly. Müntzer positioned himself in the social-revolutionary tradition of the medieval reform movements that equated the internal and the external in order that the world as a whole might be sanctified. With the enthusiasm that had once propelled Joachim of Fiore or Girolamo Savonarola in Italy and the Taborites of Bohemia, Müntzer preached of the onset of the thousand-year kingdom of Christ as foretold in Revelation. When the 'great Hanses', the princes, close their ears out of self-interest, the people must reach for their swords in order to separate the human wheat from the chaff and thus prepare the world for the final kingdom. In this radical theology the extrovert activism of the Old Testament vengeful prophets was united with a deep interior piety of the cross. God's revolutionary signed the letters he addressed to his former comrades and to peasants, citizens, and princes, 'Thomas Muntzer with the sword of Gideon' or 'Thomas Muntzer, a servant of God against the godless'.[27] He believed the apocalyptic moment had arrived, in which God would punish the powerful of the world and place the sword in the hands of the elect that they might fight for the authority of the apostolic community, which would be drawn together to become the church of the End Times.

Taking Refuge with the Authorities

Having composed his 'Admonition to Peace', Luther found that the flames of rebellion were raging in Thuringia and that he was at the seat of the fire. Again he saw his authority under threat, and this time that threat was Empire-wide. He could no longer be sure that the devil, whom he saw behind all that was happening, would not strike a successful blow against the Gospel after all. Only peace and order, he believed, and not war and violence, could bring the Gospel victory.[28] Additionally, in February the Emperor had triumphed against his French foes outside Pavia, and now nothing seemed to lie in the way of his intervention in Germany. It is hardly surprising that Luther's mood became doom-laden.

Yet such fears did nothing to shake his certainty that he was on the right path or to reverse his resolve to speak out against breaches of the peace with proclamations of God's word and calls to the authorities appointed by God to keep the peace. The inspection he had begun in mid-April was continued, and he preached at almost every location he visited (see Map 1)—in the Harz and the Harz forelands in Wallhausen, Stolberg, and Nordhausen, and in eastern Thuringia in Weimar, Orlamünde, Kahla, and Jena. At the castle of Wallhausen, which lay to the west of Sangerhausen, he preached before the local lord, Freiherr von Asseburg, on Matthew 7:15: 'Beware of false prophets, who come to you in sheep's clothing but inwardly are ravenous wolves.'

Luther's sermons were not received by everyone with equal enthusiasm and acquiescence. They also provoked open dissent, even anger—some of his audiences protested by ringing bells or creating a racket in other ways, and he was also threatened physically. Where previously he had been carried on a wave of enthusiasm and agreement, now, in the midst of social unrest, he had to make the bitter discovery that in the eyes of the people he was the emissary of hated princes and lords. These addressees had no desire to know anything of the crucified Christ as the model of patient suffering before injustice, as demanded by the 'Admonition to Peace' and as preached to them by Luther. Their theology of the cross was that of Thomas Müntzer, who understood the suffering of Christ as a call for the establishment of God's kingdom on earth by force.

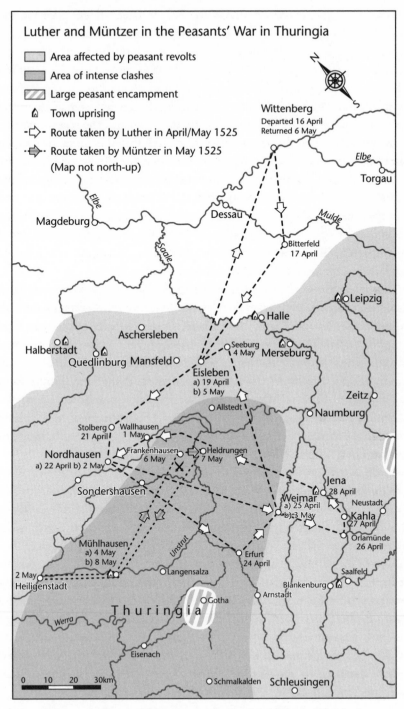

Map 1. Luther and Müntzer in the Peasants' War in Thuringia

In light of this experience, the Wittenberger placed all his hopes in the princes and the magistrates. When the divine order was in danger, Christian authorities were entitled, even required, to use legitimate force. Twice, on 25 April and 3 May, he attended the court at Weimar and was disconcerted to find that the Electoral Saxon regime was reluctant to launch any military action against the peasants. Despite the extensive rioting nearby, Duke John continued to insist that negotiation was the way forward. He appears even to have considered renouncing his own office and his right of succession in the electorate. The elector was dying at the Saxon hunting castle of Lochau; he was freed from all earthly cares on 5 May 1525. At the height of his struggle with the infernal powers, not only was Luther robbed of his proven protector, but he also discovered that Frederick the Wise, like his brother John, was not prepared to use force against the peasants and from his deathbed had urged that all milder possibilities be sought.[29]

All that news could only have increased the reformer's apprehension, perhaps even thrown him into something of a panic. Even the counts of Mansfeld, with whom he felt a particularly close bond, seemed hesitant. In a surprise attack at the beginning of May, Count Albrecht had taken the village of Osterhausen, which had been occupied by the peasants, and had killed or banished those who had rebelled, but his councillors were working hard to dissuade him from any further use of force. Passing through Seeburg on his journey back to Wittenberg, Luther quickly composed a letter to Mansfeld councillor Johannes Rühel, to whom he was related by marriage, in which he earnestly warned Rühel, 'I urge you not to influence my gracious Lord, Count Albrecht, to be soft in this affair.'[30]

Heavenly omens only seemed to confirm his worries: 'A child has been born here in Wittenberg without a head and another with twisted feet,' he reported, and, even more alarming, 'Philip [Melanchthon] and I, we saw a rainbow in the night last winter, above the Lochau', so above the hunting castle at which half a year later Frederick the Wise would die.[31] For Müntzer the rainbow was guarantee of divine approval and support, but for Luther it was a symbol of the anger of God and presaged menacing events on earth. He reassured his friend Myconius in Gotha that despite the chaos he still believed in Christ's victory over the powers of darkness,[32] but that victory required that the princes do their duty as Christian authorities and not hesitate to re-establish order and peace, cost what it will, at this decisive moment in the history of the world and salvation when Satan threatened to crush the rediscovered Gospel. As the prophet of God,

Luther believed himself duty-bound constantly to remind the authorities of their responsibility.

In this apocalyptic mood, immediately following his return to Wittenberg late on the evening of 6 May, Luther composed his summons 'Against the Robbing and Murdering Hordes of Peasants' (*Wider die räuberischen und mörderischen Rotten der Bauern*),[33] undoing the mild tone of his 'Admonition to Peace', composed two weeks earlier. His condemnation of the peasants animated Luther's contemporaries and posterity like no other text and earned him harsh criticism. This five-page work which, unlike the 'Admonition to Peace', a good thirty pages long, was not written for the peasants but intended for the princes alone, contained statements that were simply monstrous:

> Therefore, dear lords, here is a place where you can release, rescue, help. Have mercy on these poor people! Let whoever can stab, smite, slay. If you die in doing it, good for you! A more blessed death can never be yours, for you die while obeying the divine word and commandment in Romans 13, and in loving service of your neighbor, whom you are rescuing from the bonds of hell and of the devil. And so I beg everyone who can to flee from the peasants as from the devil himself; those who do not flee, I pray that God will enlighten and convert. As for those who are not to be converted, God grant that they may have neither fortune nor success. To this let every pious Christian say, 'Amen!' For this prayer is right and good, and pleases God; this I know. If anyone thinks this too harsh, let him remember that rebellion is intolerable and that the destruction of the world is to be expected every hour.[34]

These words are shocking even to the well-disposed reader and even when we bear in mind that long before and independently of Luther the princes of southern Germany had already adopted a bloody solution to the rebellion and that the text would not yet have reached the hands of the princes' mercenaries who ten days after its composition massacred the peasants at Frankenhausen. The unrestrained outburst of anger and sanction of bloody warfare were entirely Luther's, and their presence within his way of thinking and spiritual existence must be acknowledged not to give them historical relativity, but rather to make them comprehensible.

Luther saw the devil at work—to the injury of the Gospel but also to the eternal ruin of everyone who fell for the devil's blandishments and did his bidding. This reading of the situation explains his apparently cynical call on the lords to take pity on the peasants and save them through stabbing and smiting. Anyone, be he mercenary or prince, who should fall in the struggle against the peasants led by Satan, Luther wrote, could be comforted by the knowledge that he had participated in a work pleasing to God and therefore had received God's blessing. His first text, the 'Admonition to Peace', had justified the hesitation of the princes and their councillors to take action against the 'poor people', but the outbreak of violence and chaos had changed the situation fundamentally. Therefore, Luther continued, he was bound to withdraw his call for leniency and shake the princes into action against those who had broken the peace and now caused disorder: 'This is not a time to sleep. And there is no place for patience or mercy. This is the time of the sword, not the day of grace.'[35] His words were those of an Old Testament prophetic 'princely sermon', or even a 'princely scolding', but they also record Luther's anxieties, and even his doubts. The hesitation of the Saxon and Mansfeld territorial rulers had led him to fear that he had lost the vital political involvement that could guarantee the peace and earthly order of central Germany that were surely essential if the Gospel was to thrive.

Luther's Triumph and Its Cost

Quickly it became evident that the German princes had no need of a prophetic wake-up call. Landgrave Philip of Hesse, just twenty-two years old, had already proved himself in his victory over Sickingen and the rebellious Imperial knights. Independently of Luther's admonition, Philip had resolved to come to the rescue of territorial rule in central Germany by again employing an iron fist, this time against the peasants. At the beginning of May he had made short shrift of the rebels in the lands of the abbeys of Hersfeld and Fulda, 'pacifying' in the process his own territory. Now he moved into Thuringia and joined with dukes George of Saxony and Henry of Brunswick, both of whom had remained loyal to the Roman Church—in the face of a common enemy, princely solidarity won out over religious difference. On 14 and 15 May 1525 the well-equipped and well-led princely army faced the united but ill-disciplined Thuringian peasant force at Frankenhausen, which lay between Mühlhausen and Allstedt, the two principal centres of Thomas Müntzer's activities. Goliath faced David, for the peasants had no cohesive leadership, little experience of pitched battle, and hopelessly inferior weaponry. Military calculation meant nothing to the rebels, however, as they gathered on a hill to the west of the town, for Müntzer, Luther's counterpart and a similarly rousing preacher, stood at their head and declared that victory would be theirs and the kingdom of God would dawn in the here and now—not, as the Wittenberger had told the princes' soldiers, following their death in combat—with its realization on earth immediately after the battle.

Müntzer's 'Sermon to the Princes' had proved futile, but while the authorities failed to respond to his appeals, the people had rallied to this inspired preacher in their thousands, with the rebellious peasants joined by miners from around Mansfeld, by urban artisans and manual workers, and also by a scattering of the civic ecclesiastical and political elite. Corralled in a wagon fort near Frankenhausen, they confidently awaited the princes' army, flying a silk banner sporting a rainbow and carrying the commanding words of their leader in their hearts:

> Go to it, go to it, while the fire is hot! Don't let your sword grow cold, don't let it hang down limply! Hammer away ding-dong on the anvils of Nimrod, cast down their tower to the ground! As long as they live it is impossible for you to rid yourselves of the fear of men. One cannot say anything to you about God as long as they rule over you. Go to it, go to it, while it is day! God goes before you; follow, follow![36]

Müntzer's exhortation was no less bloodthirsty than Luther's. Ultimately, however, Müntzer's men would be not the perpetrators but the victims. The military engagement over, some 5,000 of Müntzer's followers lay dead on the battlefield and on the streets of the town, to which they had fled as a last resort. Six hundred were taken prisoner, including Müntzer himself, the prophet of the Last Judgement, which had now caught up with him. The princes' army, with its well-armed horsemen and foot soldiers, had had the advantage from the beginning and lost only six men. The figures tell the story—of the bloodlust of the princely forces and of Müntzer's self-delusion.

From prison two days after the battle, Müntzer wrote to his followers in Mühlhausen. He had been misunderstood by the people, 'for they sought only their own interests and the divine truth was defeated as a result'. The 'disaster' at Frankenhausen had a clear reason: 'Everyone was more concerned with his own self-interest than in bringing justice to Christian people.' Here was no cynicism, but rather an expression of the fact that Müntzer, too, had not seen the revolutionary reconfiguration of the world as the means to create a better life on earth for the poor. Just as for his Wittenberg counterpart, his ultimate intent was couched in light of the salvation narrative, in 'bringing justice to Christian people' in the struggle with Antichrist. Now he saw that he had taken the wrong path to reach that goal. He therefore called on the community in Mühlhausen to 'seek the mercy of the princes', and he trusted, he wrote, 'that you will find the princes disposed to show you mercy', and even more clearly, 'I wanted to declare this at my departure, to relieve my soul of the weighty burden of conniving at further insurrection, so that innocent blood can cease to flow.' His words were surprising, even though the princes' torturers may well have helped him reach the conclusion that it was time to reject violence. After torture that also led to his retracting his teachings, on 27 May 1525 Müntzer was beheaded in Mühlhausen, along with fifty-three of his supporters. He never lost his trust in his God. 'My salvation and blessedness in the face of fear, death and hell be with you, dear brothers,' he had written to the community in Mühlhausen ten days before his execution, relating that he was content 'since it is God's good pleasure that I should depart hence with an authentic knowledge of the divine name'.[37]

The Swabian League pacified first Württemberg and Swabia and then, by early June, Franconia, while in the Rhineland and Alsace at much the same time as the victory in Thuringia the elector of the Palatinate allied with the Duke of Lorraine to crush the rebels in two battles that were particularly bloody. The peasants' resistance was broken. Only in distant Samland, north and west of Königsberg, between the Vistula and Curonian Lagoons, and in the Alps, the Habsburg lands, and the archbishopric of Salzburg could echoes of the southern and central German uprising still be heard up until summer 1526. Under the leadership of Michael Gaismair the peasants of Tyrol and Salzburg fought through to several further victories. The continuing revolt did not radiate out, however, into other parts of the Empire.

These events had far-reaching implications for the social and constitutional history of Germany, although the much-touted thesis that the peasants were henceforth excluded from political life is false. Equally profound were the consequences for the Reformation. Luther's call for stabbing and smiting had become a gruesome reality at Frankenhausen. As few people were aware of the true sequence of events, for many his 'harsh book', as Luther himself would soon describe his pamphlet, had caused the fury of the princes' army. His opponents in Leipzig accused him of hypocrisy, suggesting that because his electoral Saxon protector had died, he had thrown himself and his declarations of loyalty at Duke George of Saxony. And indeed, in speaking out against the rebellious peasants, Luther had turned the tables on rulers loyal to Rome who claimed that the Reformation was nothing more than sedition. Even Luther's supporters and friends were consternated: the community at Zwickau had seen the compassion and fraternal love in Christ that Luther had constantly preached trampled underfoot. The authorities also treated his radical attitude with suspicion: Mansfeld councillors Rühel and Kaspar Müller called on Luther to make a public statement; his companions in Wittenberg feared for his reputation, and for their own.

Initially such concerns had little impact on Luther. That confidence stemmed from his conviction that in addressing the worldly questions of rebellion and obedience, of rights and duties, he had simply stated what the Gospel taught. On 23 May, when he learned from his brother-in-law in Mansfeld of Müntzer's end and of the great numbers who had died in the battle at Frankenhausen, he expressed his regret, but then, unmoved, cited Matthew 26:52: 'All who draw the sword will die by the sword.' On 30 May he lectured Amsdorff defiantly: 'In my opinion it is better that all of the peasants should be killed rather than that the sovereigns and magistrates should be destroyed, because the peasants take up the sword without God's authorization'[38]—a harsh statement, even a terrible declaration, not least because the conscience behind it appeared entirely at peace. Luther may have been judging in light of the salvation narrative, which for him was the only perspective possible, but his judgement holds hints of an almost fundamentalist fanaticism.

Luther's first public statement came some three weeks later, on 4 June, and was made from the pulpit. His thoughts were tied up with his approaching marriage, which followed ten days later and provided his opponents with additional ammunition. Judiciousness was still lacking: 'Some useless yammerers construe what I wrote against the peasants almost maliciously,' he ranted right at the beginning of his sermon, which found a wider audience when published as a pamphlet with the title 'Dr Martin Luther's. Defence of the Book against the Robbing and Murdering Peasants'. (*Verantwortung D. Martin Luthers auf das büchlein wider die Reuberischen und mörderischen Bawern*). For Luther his responsibility lay in his duty, which he had identified, to see subjects returned to obedience to their embattled superiors. He had fulfilled that duty, he insisted, according to his own means, in promulgating the will of God. With evident pride in his success as an author he put in their place 'those clever clogs... who wanted to tell me how I should write'.[39] At the beginning of July he felt forced to provide a more extensive vindication, 'because the little book that I published against the peasants has given rise to so many complaints and questions, as though it were un-Christian and too hard'.[40]

His 'Open Letter on the Harsh Book against the Peasants' (*Sendbrief von dem harten Büchlein wider die Bauern*), one of the first works he wrote after his marriage and the 'kissing week' that followed (which will be addressed in the next chapter), tackled the problem in the form of a response to the concerns of Mansfeld chancellor Kaspar Müller. Yet, he wrote, he certainly did not understand his friend's worries about his hard words, and he would most like to stop his ears against 'those blind, ungrateful creatures who seek nothing in me but causes of offense'. In his appeal to the princes he had merely done his duty as a preacher, he insisted, in calling on all people, authorities, and subjects, to act in accord with the word of God. He provided, however, an extensive theological basis for his position in the temporal implications of the Gospel, which distinguishes between two kingdoms: the spiritual kingdom of God, in which compassion and mercy reign, and the kingdom of earth, in which the anger of God and the relentless struggle against evil are sovereign. The tool to be employed in the kingdom on earth by the authorities responsible for order and law is he continued, 'not a wreath of roses or a flower of love, but a naked sword'. God has therefore given the authorities 'not a featherduster [literally, a foxtail], but a sword', in order that they might take action against evil in the kingdom of earth with all severity. Christian authorities, but not tyrants, are a prerequisite for the implementation of mercifulness and a policy of peace.

This passage is remarkable in giving expression to the doctrine of the two kingdoms, first formulated by Luther in 1523; we shall return to this teaching when we consider Luther's political thought. In relation to the peasants, he was simply repeating what he had already said in his 'harsh book', now refined in light of more recent events. His Christian instruction was not intended, he wrote, for 'these furious, raving, senseless tyrants, who even after the battle cannot get their fill of blood . . . It makes no difference to these bloody dogs whether they slay the guilty or the innocent, whether they please God or the devil.' Such 'scoundrels and hogs' amongst the princes are unteachable, but their subjects must 'put up with them, when God plagues us with them'.[41] Those amongst Luther's supporters who, like the reformer himself, were convinced that the authorities had an essential part to play in the restoration of the pure Gospel were by and large content with this explanation. Luther succeeded in keeping the evangelically minded princes on board with the Reformation, while although he sought to taint Luther with association with rebellion, Duke George of Saxony faced an uphill struggle in convincing even his Catholic peers that Luther should be mentioned in the same breath as Müntzer.[42] Yet the reformer's remarkable popularity and authority had been badly damaged, above all, naturally, amongst the peasants.

The theological tragedy of the Peasants' War lay not so much in the failure of Müntzer's revolutionary concept—contemporary historical constellations had ensured it never really had a chance—as in its impact on the two rival modes of church renewal. Both forms had become more opaque and had forfeited something of their reputation—the mystical-eschatological strand as a result of Müntzer's irresponsible leadership, and the strand associated with the Wittenberg Reformation and its authority figure, Luther. Years later, however, it would be evident that the reformer had learned something from the reaction to his ruthless pamphlets after all, for, he recorded, he had sworn never again to pick up his pen in times of war.[43]

'His Death is a Weight around My Neck'

Statements made by Luther in letters and to his friends and family make evident that he was not unaffected by the suffering of the peasants and that on occasion he sought to mitigate the results. In late June, as he still presented an impassive face to the public, in a letter to Amsdorff he calculated the suffering with appreciable dismay: 'in Franconia eleven thousand peasants were killed...In the Duchy of Württemberg six thousand peasants were killed; elsewhere in Swabia ten thousand...Rumor has it that the Duke of Lorraine has killed twenty thousand in Alsace. Thus the poor peasants are being killed everywhere.'[44] Seeking relief for a citizen of his home town of Eisleben who had landed in prison in Mainz, Luther even turned to his arch-enemy Albrecht of Brandenburg. Although he intervened specifically on behalf of this single individual, at the same time he called more broadly for judiciousness and moderation on the part of the princes. They must realize that 'this rebellion was not calmed by human hand or council, but by the grace of God, who took pity on all of us, and especially the authorities'. Instead of giving thanks as was right and fulfilling their duty of compassion 'to the poor people', Luther recorded, 'too many...treat the people so cruelly and are so ungrateful to God, as if they wantonly want that the anger of displeasure of God and the people be awoken again and directed against them.' Justifying his call for the use of force made at the high point of the rebellion, Luther continued by noting that it had been good that the response had been serious and heated:

> for the people ... had been seen to be rebellious and obdurate. Now that they have been struck down, they have become other people and are worthy of receiving not just punishment but also grace. Too many are tearing the sack on both sides [behaving without restraint]; moderation is good in all things, and mercy triumphs over judgement (James 2:13).[45]

Luther found no similarly conciliatory words for Müntzer. His arch-rival was for Luther the instigator of rebellion and a creature of the devil: 'Anyone who has seen Müntzer can say that he has seen the devil incarnate in all his wrath.' Even in death Müntzer remained a danger, for he was now seen as a martyr. To be able to counter that characterization, Luther wanted to be familiar with all the details, 'for it is useful to know how that proud spirit behaved'.[46] Later, however, in a Table Talk of 1533, despite his conviction that he had done nothing wrong with his response in 1525, the reformer permitted himself to admit his part in the fate of his 'false brother': 'And so I killed Müntzer; his death is a weight around my neck. But I did so because he wanted to kill my Christ.'[47]

VI

Arrived in the World—
Marriage, Family, and a Large
Household

A Wedding as a Sign of the End Times

'Far from yielding to the lascivious impulses of his blood, like fat Luther marrying a nun on leaving the cloister...' The reformer's marriage has frequently been described in just such terms, here in the words of Belgian-French author Marguerite Yourcenar (1903–1987), the first female member of the Académie Française.[1] The persistent cliché is based on a malicious invention of Luther's opponents that some of his contemporaries were all too willing to parrot. The reality was very different. Averse to overhasty innovation, Luther remained celibate for a good many years after he had launched his assault on monastic life. After leaving the Wartburg in spring 1522, he returned to live in the Augustinian monastery in Wittenberg and resumed his monk's habit, wearing normal clothing only on occasion and within the monastery walls. He appeared in public without his monk's habit only from October 1524, almost three years after the appearance of his text 'On Monastic Vows', which contained his theological delegitimization of monasticism.

As criticism of the monastic life had welled up, material support for the monastery had dwindled. As a result, the condition of the large building at the eastern city wall deteriorated, and funds for the maintenance of those who remained at the monastery ran short. With only Luther and prior Eberhard Brisger still living at the monastery and the latter preparing to marry, the reformer decided he was no longer prepared to hold the fort and asked the elector to provide him with a small house somewhere nearby.

Marriage was not part of the plan. His supporters repeatedly urged Luther to align his own lifestyle with his teachings, but for Luther individual Christian freedom applied in this instance just as it applied to other issues associated with the new Christian order. He would make his own decision. 'If you are married,' he wrote, 'whether to a Christian or non-Christian, a virtuous or an evil mate, you are not on that account either saved or condemned. If you are unmarried, you are also on that account neither saved nor condemned. All this is free, free.'[2] In autumn 1524 he informed his trusted friend Spalatin that he was not at all minded to marry. Yes, he wrote, he felt 'my flesh or sex', for he was not made of wood or stone, but marriage was out of the question, 'since I daily expect death and the punishment due to a heretic'.[3]

The uncertainties facing a declared outlaw appear to have given Luther cause to shrink back from finding a wife, but he may also have been happy to avoid the malicious comments of his opponents that would surely follow his marriage. Although he could readily shake off accusations about the purity of his teaching, he had no desire to provide his opponents with a moral target. Some of his friends, specifically Melanchthon and Schurf, were fully in agreement. It is understandable that a man in his early forties who knew women only as members of his family or from the lives of saints and who as a priest had been exhorted to 'speak only a little and briefly'[4] with women in the confessional would be somewhat shy and reserved. All would change, however, in spring 1525, on the spirited initiative of a young nun who had embraced his teachings and left her monastery.

Katharina von Bora

On the night before Easter Sunday 1523 Katharina von Bora fled from the Cistercian convent of Marienthron in Nimbschen by Grimma together with eleven other nuns similarly animated by Luther's words. Hidden in a covered wagon belonging to Leonhard Koppe of Torgau, a carter who delivered supplies to the convent, they returned 'to the world'. That they had to conceal themselves in herring barrels, as the legend would soon run, seems unlikely and is at any rate not proven by the sources. Where was the carter, who knew Luther personally, to take his human load if not to Wittenberg? Only there would the former nuns be safe from the severe punishment that both canon and Imperial law laid down for those who fled the monastery and for those who assisted their flight. Additionally there the nuns, now freed from their captivity, could find the advice and support that would help determine what they might do next.

Like so many others the length and breadth of the land, the former nuns of Marienthron looked first to Luther. The reformer 'was burdened by so many matters and so many cases, especially regarding marriage and the priesthood', he complained in these days, that he hardly knew where to turn next.[5] Nevertheless he immediately took up the cause of the escaped nuns, whose arrival in Wittenberg had caused something of a sensation. On 10 April he wrote was what in effect an open letter to their co-conspirator, whom he deliberately addressed as 'his particular friend, cautious and wise', reassuring him 'that maidens are divinely permitted to leave monasteries'. As usual Luther saw his best defence in the offensive: he himself had prompted the trader's involvement in the flight of the nuns; there was nothing furtive about Koppe's actions and he need not have the bad conscience of a thief, for he was a 'holy robber', who 'had freed these poor souls from the imprisonment of human tyranny'. To liberate their flight of any trace of unseemliness, Luther named each of the twelve nuns individually, 'in order that everything be an open book'. For its public audience, his letter portrayed their departure from the monastery as an exemplary act of Christian freedom. As the events had taken place on the night before Easter Sunday, a redemptive interpretation lay readily at hand. Their liberation had taken place 'at the right time before Easter', for Christ had also taken prisoner the imprisonment of the people, or, in other words, had defeated death.[6] That same month, April 1523, the letter was printed as a pamphlet and when in response more nuns left their monasteries, Luther saw the opportunity for a further publishing offensive. An account of the experience of one nun who had fled the monastery of Neu Helfta by Eisleben, was published under the title 'A Story of How God Helped a Nun. With an Open Letter by Martin Luther to the Counts of Mansfeld' (*Eine Geschicht, wie Gott einer Klosterjungfrau ausgeholfen hat. Mit einem Sendbrief Martin Luthers an die Grafen von Mansfeld*).[7]

In the close-knit social world of Wittenberg, Luther was unavoidably drawn into the practical problems facing the 'liberated' nuns, particularly as several, including Katharina von Bora, lived at the home of Lucas Cranach, where Luther was frequently a guest. His concern to justify their flight theologically combined with a personal interest in their future fate. That fate was uncertain, for in the society of his day, a respectable and secure existence for a woman was possible only within her original family, as a member of an ecclesiastical community, or in marriage. For those former nuns who either did not want to return to their families or were unable to return to their families, suitable new circumstances had to be found. For the majority that challenge was quickly met, as a whole slew of former priests, as well as pastors and professors, were looking for wives.

But Katharina von Bora's case proved problematic. Katharina was as lacking in means as she was determined to use her newly won Christian freedom to determine her life for herself. She came from a poor rural noble family with a small estate in Lippendorf, south of Leipzig, that was only just able to support the family of the heir. Katharina had probably been born right at the end of the fifteenth century, and aged four or five she had been given to the Benedictine convent at Brehna by Bitterfeld. When ten years old, she had moved to the Cistercian convent at Nimbschen, where, in 1515, aged around seventeen, she had taken her vows. She would have had no memories of a family life when, in her early twenties, she resolved to use that new Christian freedom to try her hand at life in the world. Although she had had no say over her admission to the monastery, she had not lived there unwillingly. Her education had been decent, including the basics of Latin, and she had matured into a determined individual of strong character. In Katharina, Luther encountered evidence of the achievements of monastic life, not its corruption.

Courting

By the end of 1524 all of the nuns who had fled the convent at Nimbschen had either returned to their families or married; all, that is, except Katharina von Bora. It looked as if an engagement was in the offing with Hieronymus Baumgärtner, a student in Wittenberg and son of a patrician family in Nuremberg, but her prospective husband's parents baulked at a daughter-in-law of no means. In October 1524 Luther admonished Baumgärtner, who had returned to Nuremberg, 'If you want to hold on to your Käthe von Bora, then hurry up, before she is given to another, who is actually here.'[8] His reference was to his younger colleague Caspar Glatz, whom the Wittenberg theologians envisaged as a husband for the last of the former nuns. But they had reckoned without the bride herself. Katharina succinctly declared that she had 'neither desire nor love' for Glatz. Her pronouncement irritated the marriage broker, who found the young noblewoman 'proud and arrogant',[9] and he responded, 'What devil will have her? If she doesn't want this one, she may find she has to wait a while for another.' The young woman did not want to wait any longer; she wanted to choose for herself. She bluntly informed Nikolaus von Amsdorff, who discussed the marriage issue with her on 23 or 24 March, that she planned, 'if it is possible and is the will of God, to take Doctor Martinus or Mr. Amsdorff in marriage'.[10]

Evidently Luther was no longer so adamantly opposed to his own marrying. He wrote jokingly to Spalatin that he had had the possibility of 'three women all at the same time' but had behaved so unskilfully that two of them decided to take other available husbands and the third was being held onto by a thread.[11] One of the two candidates who backed off was, as Luther later recounted in a Table Talk, Eva von Schönfeld, a former fellow nun of Katharina's who had also lived in Cranach's home and whom he had preferred over Katharina.[12] When, finally, only the third possibility, Katharina von Bora, remained, Luther moved quickly to ensure that that thin thread became a secure knot.

We cannot term theirs a love match, even if the groom would soon congratulate himself on his choice and although the couple quickly developed a deep conjugal love. Luther the monk was not impelled into marriage by sexual desire; with a clear head, he gradually made the decision to marry a woman who was partial to him and needed support. Here was the 'rational' in its Lutheran manifestation, with even this most private of decisions formed by the immediate historical context and part of sacred history. We should recall that the worst of all weeks of the peasant uprising in central Germany fell in March and April 1525. As agents of the devil the peasant armies had taken up arms against the rediscovered Gospel, and therefore, Luther was convinced, he must necessarily set an example himself: 'To vex and spite the devil and all his opponents I will still marry my Käthe,' he informed Amsdorff, his confidante. Writing from the heart of the rebellious lands in Mansfeld he declared at the beginning of May, 'Well, if I get home, I shall prepare for death with God's help, and await my new lords, the murderers and robbers.' Again he believed himself caught up in the eschatological struggles of the Last Days, in which he was prepared to lose his life. His marriage project had become a final existential and redemptive statement, a second 'here I stand, I cannot do otherwise', and he again declared, 'If I can manage it, before I die I will still marry my Katie to spite the devil.'[13] The invitation to their small wedding celebration struck the same note: as lords, priests, and peasants were arousing such a clamour about his 'small book against the peasants' and were threatening him with death, he wrote, he would ensure with his marriage, 'that for my end I will be found in the state created by God and will have retained about myself nothing of my previous papal life'.[14]

Luther's defiant resistance of the courses of the world, so typical of the reformer, determined that his wedding took place precisely as the violence and excesses reached their height. The decision to marry, made some time earlier, had been taken for a number of reasons. There was his father's expectation that following the early death of several of his siblings, Martin would ensure the continuation of the family.[15] Hans Luder would hardly appreciate his oldest son's shrinking from marrying when he had recommended everyone else take that very step, and his son may well have felt that it was time to act on the offer of reconciliation that he had made to his father in the preface to 'On Monastic Vows' and broadcast for all to read. For it even to be possible for him to do so depended on a change of attitude without which, whatever his strength of will, the decision to marry would have been unthinkable, and therefore also the happiness that he so quickly discovered in that union. For years as both author and counsellor he had addressed the issue of marriage, a connection with women that supplemented interactions in daily life, but now, finally, his reserves about living together with a woman had to disappear. With a degree of self-irony, in April 1525 he noted his surprise: 'It is rather strange that I, who so often write about matrimony and get mixed up with women, have not yet turned into a woman, to say nothing of not having married one.'[16]

The Wedding—Maligned on Earth, Hailed in Heaven

Having identified the way forward that seemed right for both him and the internal credibility of his teachings, Luther acted as he always acted—decisively, without hesitation, and shrewdly. Those who might have sought to dissuade him from marrying or discouraged him from a relationship with Katharina von Bora[17] were left in the dark—even his closest colleague, Melanchthon, who complained just as bitterly about his lack of knowledge as about the reformer's expected loss of reputation:

> On June 13, Luther unexpectedly and without informing in advance any of his friends of what he was doing, married Bora; but in the evening, after having invited to supper none but Pommeranus and Lucus the painter, and Apel, observed the customary marriage rites. You might be amazed that at this unfortunate time, when good and excellent men are everywhere in distress, he not

only does not sympathize with them, but, as it seems, rather waxes wanton and diminishes his reputation, just when Germany has especial need of his judgment and authority. These things have occurred, I think, somewhat in this way: The man is certainly pliable; and the nuns have used their arts against him most successfully; thus probably society with the nuns has softened or even inflamed this noble and high-spirited man. In this way he seems to have fallen into this untimely change of life.[18]

Only a small group were invited to attend the event itself, their presence necessary so that they could testify to the legality of the marriage and bear public witness that it had taken place. In addition to those mentioned by Melanchthon, Cranach's wife was also in attendance—and therefore the family for whom Luther had stood godfather and who for some time now had been hosts of the bride—as well as Justus Jonas, dean of the theological faculty and close comrade-in-arms of the reformer ever since he had accompanied Luther to Worms. Jurist Johannes Apel was not a close friend of Luther's, but he was likely included because he too had recently married a former nun. The marriage received its church blessing from Bugenhagen, as pastor at the town church. As was usual, the ceremony took place in private in the living quarters of the groom, and therefore in this case in the former Augustinian monastery, which soon would be regarded only as the home of Luther and his wife. At 5 p.m. on 15 June 1525, Luther and Katharina were married. Regulation of the property brought by each party into a marriage could often be a drawn-out process that followed the ceremony but was in this instance unnecessary, as neither party owned anything. The freshly married couple were therefore accompanied immediately to their bedroom, where, in the presence of the witnesses, they lay down together in the marriage bed. The next day the witnesses participated in a small celebration.

It was customary for the newly married couple to attend church ceremonially the day after their marriage, but in this instance that event and the celebration of the wedding were put off until 27 June, as the plans had been kept secret and the guests therefore still had to be invited. Even when they did occur, the festivities were more modest than was usual for a respectable wedding, which would usually be marked with plentiful gifts, a lavish meal, and much public innuendo. A small crowd of family members and friends attended as guests—Luther's parents, relatives, and friends from Mansfeld, his close colleagues, including Melanchthon, and also Leonhard Koppe, the carter from Torgau whose courageous act had brought the bride and groom together. These men were naturally accompanied by their wives, another sign that the all-male world of the monastery and Luther's bachelor years was now behind him. In addition to the presents from the guests, the celebration, which took place in the living quarters of the new couple in the Black Monastery, was made possible by the twenty gold gulden with which the town council honoured them. Elector John, who had very recently succeeded his brother as elector, provided 100 gulden for the fitting out of the new household. That gift marked a new turn of affairs for both Luther and Katharina, who as a result became owners of personal property for the first time in their lives.

Neither humbleness nor lack of means lay behind the absence of the large and impressive celebration that Luther's status and exemplary role might well have invited. The restraint stemmed from a concern that his marriage at such an incongruous time might cause him to be 'disdained and disparaged' by the people. Even confidence that in heaven 'the angels will laugh and the devils will cry' did not help.[19] He did not dare to invite his friends in Mansfeld formally, 'because of how the times are now in the lands', and he did not even inform the counts 'my gracious lords' of his wedding.[20] He tied events closely together in his letter of invitation to Nikolaus von Amsdorff, who had been called as pastor to Magdeburg. Responding to the worried questioning of his friend, he confirmed, 'that I was suddenly married to Catherine', not in a moment of 'passionate love nor burning for my spouse', but 'to confirm what I have taught by practicing it'.[21] His request for support at the celebration of the wedding was immediately followed by his statement on the peasants who had been killed that we encountered at the end of the previous chapter. That was, however, no triumphant reckoning, but rather, much like the request he sent to his arch-enemy in Mainz that mercy might be shown to the defeated, an attempt to rein in the spirits that he had summoned.

When we consider the relative leniency shown by Luther in the weeks following his marriage, we may be tempted to see something positive in the coincidence of the joys of marriage and the suffering of the peasants, a concurrence that was disparaged by many contemporaries and has continued to be viewed critically by historians. Marriage and a routine existence in the company of his wife (Figures 28 and 29), and soon also his children, evidently brought a certain easing to the emotional life of the reformer and a clearer sense of the mundane human experience. That mellowness was only evident, however, when God's order was not under any threat, as was the case following the defeat of the peasants. His obsession with his work and the

Figures 28 and 29. Martin Luther and Katharina von Bora shortly after their marriage, by Lucas Cranach the Elder, 1526.

stridency of his scholarly debate were unaffected; indeed, the new support that he found in his marriage and family lent him wings. 'I was hoping', sighed Erasmus in spring 1526, 'that Luther's wife would calm her husband down'[22]—a reference to the treatise on the bondage of the will, written at the end of 1525, with which Luther had sharply countered the humanist avowal of free will.

The inopportune marriage in the midst of the Peasants' War would long prove troubling, and not only for Luther's opponents. In Wittenberg, the magistracy had to step in against an upstanding citizen who abused Luther and his wife publicly because she believed that the marriage of a monk and a nun dishonoured the married state. Even friends and colleagues took a while to come to terms with the new situation, although Melanchthon got there first, having made clear in his letter of complaint to Joachim Camerarius that in principle, so when the timing was put to one side, Luther 'has done nothing that seems to me worthy of censure or incapable of defense'. He also answered the 'rumor . . . that he had previously dishonored her', condemning the allegation as 'manifestly a lie'.[23] Such gossip was naturally welcomed with open arms in the Catholic camp. Even the otherwise graciously reserved Erasmus, who in September 1524 had broken for good with Luther with his treatise 'On Free Will' (*De libero arbitrio*), poured ridicule on the Wittenberger. 'Delightful news', he wrote on 10 October 1525:

> Luther has put aside the philosopher's cloak and taken a wife (may heaven bless and prosper the event!). She is an attractive young lady from the distinguished family of the von Boras, twenty-six years old, but dowerless, who abandoned the life of a vestal some time ago. And in case you should have any doubts that the marriage was blessed by heaven, a few days after the singing of the wedding hymn the new bride gave birth to a child![24]

A few months later he had to concede, 'There is no doubt about Luther's marriage, but the rumour about his wife's early confinement is false; she is said, however, to be pregnant now.'[25]

Amongst Luther's opponents hardly anyone was willing to summon the generosity of spirit shown by Erasmus and confess to error or malicious gossip. As a result, the stigma of uncontrolled sexuality as the reason behind the surprising marriage was long retained, unquestioned, in the Catholic image of Luther. Worse still were the accusations against Katharina von Bora who was vilified in nearby Dresden and Leipzig as a 'faithless nun' and disreputable 'dancing maid', who had thrown herself at the Wittenberg monk, while in Spain she was allotted a career in a brothel before her marriage.[26] Hieronymus Emser, court theologian in Dresden, who had been carrying on an intense quarrel with Luther for years, turned the reformer's eschatological judgement that the pope was Antichrist against him, prophesying that the sacrilegious marriage would inevitably produce the Antichrist. Non-partisan when it came to matters of logic, Erasmus recognized a double-edged judgement, for as he commented with a refined irony, 'If there is truth in the popular legend, that Antichrist will be born from a monk and a nun ... how many thousands of Antichrists the world must have already!'[27]

A New Normality—Sexuality and Conjugal Love

The reformer would have expected nothing else of his opponents and held that their attacks only confirmed his belief that in marrying he had continued to fulfil God's commission. Now a new life began for Luther, a life that he quickly learned to value. The newly married couple appear to have enjoyed something of a honeymoon, during which Luther put his lecturing and preaching on hold and only completed the most necessary correspondence, which included writing to his friends to inform them of his new, married, status. Years later he spoke in his Table Talk of 'kissing weeks'[28] and still marvelled at the sudden change to his everyday experience:

> Man has strange thoughts the first year of marriage. When sitting at table he thinks, 'Before I was alone; now there are two.' Or in bed, when he wakes up, he sees a pair of pigtails lying beside him which he hadn't seen there before. On the other hand, wives bring to their husbands, no matter how busy they may be, a multitude of trivial matters. So my Katy used to sit next to me at first while I was studying hard and would spin and ask, 'Doctor, is the grandmaster the margrave's brother?'[29]

If we remain with the contemporary sources and leave to one side both the polemic of Luther's opponents and modern psychological interpretations that are very much products of the nineteenth and twentieth centuries, then we can recognize that sexual desire did not propel Luther into marriage. The reformer discovered and accepted his sexuality within marriage. Called to account, his opponents, both contemporary and subsequent, can provide no concrete evidence to sustain their interpretation, which leaves us with all the less reason to doubt Luther's own statements, from an early comment made while still a monk that the torments of his soul were not the product of unfulfilled longing for 'women' (*mulieribus*) to the confession made privately to his friend Amsdorff only a few days after his marriage, that he sensed 'God has willed and brought about this step. For I feel neither passionate love nor burning for my spouse, but I cherish her.'[30]

But soon, as sexual desire became a vital part of his personal experience, he discovered and sanctioned that drive as God-given fulfilment of humankind even in this world. Not long before his marriage he had assured monks and nuns that the renunciation of desire required super-human effort of which only very few amongst many thousands, with the help of God, were capable.[31] In his later works and in his practical pastoral care he insisted that every individual can live out his or her sexuality, indeed *must* live out his or her sexuality in a certain form, namely, in a timely and appropriate marriage. Sex outwith marriage was for Luther an offence against the order of creation:

> Just as it is a supreme necessity and strict commandment when God says, 'You shall not kill. You shall not commit adultery', even so it is an equally supreme necessity and strict commandment—indeed, a much higher necessity and

stricter commandment—that 'You shall be married. You shall have a wife. You shall have a husband.' (Genesis 1:27, 2:24)[32]

Marriage was part of both heavenly and earthly order, and adultery was therefore 'a sin against the Holy Spirit, and civil authority, against domestic life'.[33]

The reformer was remarkably prolific in his comments on sexual matters, yet not from obsession or frivolity but because he was asked for his opinion on cases brought before the marriage court and as he sat around the table with his friends. His Table Talk demonstrates that the absolute association of sexuality and marriage was radically new and far from convincing for everyone.[34] But Luther was not to be moved: brothels were to be closed, as he had already achieved in Wittenberg in 1521, and attempts to have them reopened, as in Freiberg at the end of 1540, would be staunchly opposed.[35] Luther acknowledged the challenge for young men, and in particular for students in Wittenberg for whom he provided pastoral care, who were not in a position to marry. But sex before marriage was whoredom and must be punished by both state and church. He advised the young men 'to pray and to ask God for a pious girl for marriage'.[36] However naïve that statement may sound today, it was consistent with the reformer's view of the world and of people. Sexuality and marriage were for Luther not just part of the divine order but also part of the eschatological struggles of God's plan. In paradise men and women are united without lustfulness. On earth, however, the Fall had poisoned sexual desire, so that even those called by God to marriage suffer on its account. Only in marriage is that suffering mitigated. Those who are unmarried, by contrast, are imperilled, quite literally, by the temptations of the devil: to permit sex outside marriage or even to permit brothels, especially in a university town, was 'to allow the devil to rise up against God and to promote the kingdom of the devil. Here someone stands against God and wishes to destroy the kingdom of God— the devil itself.' Fully in the grip of the devil were, the reformer believed, all 'sodomites', a term used for both homosexuals and those involved in bestiality, and also all those whose desire for women 'is corrupted, as with Italians and Turks'[37]—thereby Luther combined existing national stereotypes with new religious stereotypes directed against Catholics and Muslims.

Luther sharply distinguished the deep fulfilment of sexual desire within marriage from such experiences of the devil. Found in the giving and experiencing of pleasure, that fulfilment was immanent and of the world and was the responsibility of the husband: it is one of the worst of sins, he informed the audience of a lecture on Genesis, to be like the Old Testament Onan, 'to produce semen and excite the woman, and to frustrate her at that very moment'.[38] His words were an admonition against coitus interruptus, the standard form of contraception of his time, but they also told of a sexual interaction that took the female partner seriously. Yet the high esteem in which Luther held marriage and sexual relations within marriage was about more than just the existential concerns of this world. Here he found what was in effect secular fulfilment of the religious knowledge of grace and secular manifestation of the freedom of the Christian. Both were rooted in God's eternal faithfulness to humanity.

This reality explains why a man who only shortly before had defended his celibate life so vigorously, and had distanced himself from any idea that he might marry, spoke immediately after his marriage of the 'hell of celibacy', which would destroy the Christian. His criticism of celibacy grew in proportion to his burgeoning appreciation of marriage and family life. Entirely in keeping with his categorical personality, every time his life took a new direction, he turned his back decisively on what he had cast off. 'To forbid marriage and to damn marriage', as did the strictures of Rome on celibacy, was to forbid a natural right, 'just as if one wanted to forbid eating, drinking, sleeping etc.'.[39] Above all, this reversal was a product of his eschatological understanding of good and evil: if marriage and sex within marriage were an imperative of God, then celibacy could only be the work of the devil, as the opposing force in an eternal struggle with God. Strictly speaking this position was directed only at unscriptural compulsory celibacy, which was an invention of the papal church, but in practice it produced a general denigration of the state of being unmarried. The marriage and household of the reformer took on a model character, presenting a norm both for evangelical pastors and professors and for Protestants more generally. The consequences of the reformer's new theology of marriage were hardly any less far-reaching than those of the theology of grace that formed the core of his Reformation. The monopolization of legitimate sexuality within marriage and the resulting persecution of violations by both church and state left a permanent mark on both private and public life in Protestant Germany and Europe even into the last century.

The somewhat distant regard in which Luther initially held his wife soon became marital affection, even real love. He looked back on a time when he lay seriously ill far from home, and remembered, 'Oh, how I longed in my heart for my family as I lay deathly ill in Schmaldkalden! I believed that I would never again see my wife and my little children. What aching that being apart and separation caused me.' And he affirmed this 'natural love' full-heartedly, precisely as a man who dedicated his life first and foremost to the true knowledge of God: 'No one is so spiritual who does not feel that inborn natural inclination and love; for it is a great matter for the union and fellowship between man and wife.' Marriage was therefore 'indeed a holy estate'.[40] In the letters that he wrote regularly to his wife when he was away from home, this marital love was evident in his bantering forms of address: 'to the hands and feet of my dear housewife'; 'my holy and diligent wife'; 'my sweetheart housewife'; 'most holy Frau Doctor'. Even the very last of his letters, sent by an aging Luther during a journey to Mansfeld, recount this almost youthful joy in their togetherness and a longing to return home soon, while Katharina's letters in return record her constant worry about the health of her husband as he travelled away from home.

Death was familiar in Luther's home, as generally in the pre-modern world of Old Europe. For Katharina it was almost part of everyday routine, for she had constant and real concerns about her husband's well-being. In spring 1537, when on his way to the diet at Schmalkalden, Luther became seriously unwell. His death seemed to everyone so imminent that he dictated his will, and a carriage was organized to bring Katharina to his deathbed.[41] Although in the end he did make it back to Wittenberg, where he recovered after a long recuperation, the shock of the experience was not easily eradicated. From then on, whenever Luther travelled, Katharina would become extremely fearful, and she begged her husband to look after his health. Luther, for his part, tended to play down the danger, writing to her playfully on what would prove to be his last journey, and only a few days before his death, of a loose stone hanging over his head in his 'secret chamber' that fell down when lightly touched by workers summoned to attend to it. He called on Katharina at home in Wittenberg to trust in God: 'I have a caretaker who is better than you and all the angels; he lies in the cradle and rests on a virgin's bosom, and yet, nevertheless, he sits at the right hand of God, the almighty Father. Therefore be at peace. Amen.'[42]

For his part, Luther repeatedly envisaged the death of his wife, especially at the beginning of 1540 when already entering menopause she lay somewhere between life and death after an especially difficult miscarriage. With nothing more to be expected from any medical intervention, Luther wrote beseechingly to the elector to ask that he be excused from an official journey, again to Schmalkalden, which was already in the works. He wanted to stay by the side of his wife in Wittenberg, praying for her recovery. By the end of March Katharina was able to take over the reins of the household again, as Luther immediately informed Justus Jonas with delight, 'My Käthe respectfully greets you. She has me tell you that, sitting on the throne of her majesty in her household, she is learning again to be angry and to scold and almost to curse the careless, burdensome, and disobedient maid.' Looking back in his Table Talk he acknowledged, 'I asked God to let my Käthe live for me . . . and he also gives her the property at Zöllsdorf and bestows upon us additionally a rich and fruitful year.'[43]

His fear for the life of his wife influenced his theological reading of God's purpose for women. In 1522, while still a monk, Luther had written in his work 'On Married Life' (*Vom ehelichen Leben*)—which we might be tempted to think was like asking someone blind to describe colour—of the death of a woman in childbirth as being in accord with the laws of nature: 'Whether she is tired and finally bears death, that does not matter, let her bear death, she is there for that reason', continuing, 'It is better to be healthy for a short time than to live for a long time unwell.' Fifteen years later, when he had a wife and children himself, he bemoaned the death of an acquaintance in childbirth:

> It must be the greatest sorrow and heartbreak when two pious married people who have got on well with each other, and love and value each other, must physically separate themselves from each other. Our lord God is the greatest breaker of marriages, he brings together and then again separates from each other . . . For how slippery and volatile is our life! Ah, it must cause such pain when a married couple who love one another are thus separated.

And now, after his own wife had so nearly died as a result of her pregnancy, deeply moved, he wrote a letter of consolation published as 'Comfort by Dr Martin Luther for Women for Whom It Has Gone Wrong in Childbirth' (*Ein Trost D.Martini Luthers für die Weibern / welchen es ungerat gegangen ist mit Kinder geberen*), which was published in 1542 in Wittenberg along with Bugenhagen's exposition of Psalm 29, 'which also is on the baptism of children. And also on unborn children and on children who cannot be baptised.'[44]

'Mr Käthe'

'In Order That the Doctor Acts as I Want'

Luther's love for his wife was accompanied by admiration for her great capabilities. Katharina proved to be extraordinarily adept when it came to running his household—she was as able to ensure the daily provision of her family and their guests at mealtimes as she was skilled at running a student hostel and acquiring property or the lease on land. Luther's letters to his wife are full of praise, and it was by no means only in jest that he addressed her as 'My Lord Käthe', 'sow haggler', or 'lady of Zöllsdorf'. His words endorsed her various undertakings that meant that their family income grew and was secure, in particular the purchase of property, first a large market garden near Wittenberg and then the small noble manor of Zölls-dorf, south of Leipzig near the village of Kieritzsch, which she purchased in 1540 from her brother at a favourable price and with a subvention from the ruler.[45]

The dominant role of a woman in the household and in financial matters was likely to arouse ill-spirited gossip in the small world of Wittenberg. 'I must get the doctor used to something different in that he should do as I will,' Katharina was reported to have said within only a few days of their marriage, words attributed to her even by her close friend Nikolaus von Amsdorff, in a statement he made two decades later during arguments about the provision for Katharina following her husband's death. The funds that she had used to acquire the small manor belonging to her family were said to have been 'taken from the doctor through his body and mouth'. The accusations continued: against the will of her husband she had made herself mistress of the former Black Monastery 'in order that many rooms and chambers could be added from which each year much more could be earned'. These spiteful accusations came not from Catholic opponents but from men and certainly also women in Luther's own camp who begrudged the former nun, who had arrived in the town with nothing, the carte blanche she had received from the reformer and the successes that had resulted. The nineteenth century had its own problems with Luther's headstrong and confident wife. The editor of the relevant source material sought to blur the very evident discrepancy between his own bourgeois-paternalistic era and the age of the Reformation when he wrote in response to the allegations, 'The master and focus of all the large household was no other than Luther himself, a lifelong role he also played for his Käthe.'[46]

Yet the reformer never was master in his own home in the way that these words suggest. The two decades he had spent as a member of monastic communities had inculcated restraint and modesty, and, additionally, work stretched him to his limits from morning to evening, and he was in no position to be actively involved in the affairs of his household or family. He knew nothing of financial matters for he had never even learned to deal with money. There was little ready cash available in the early days of their marriage, nor indeed later. The chair that Luther had held as an Augustinian monk had been unsalaried; the elector now provided it with an income of 200 gulden per year, raised after 1536 to 300 gulden, a high salary comparable only to that received by Melanchthon. Yet for a large household even these sums were nothing like enough. Luther did little to change the situation in any fundamental way; he absolutely refused, for example, to take an honorarium for his books or to charge his students for their attendance at his lectures.

The Extended Household at the Black Monastery

Considering his financial situation, the reformer could only look gratefully on his wife's ability to tackle their financial constraints as an act of providence that relieved him of the responsibility of meeting the material needs of his family. The enterprise that the '*Lutherin*' (the female form of 'Luther' in German, and the name she was called, respectfully, by contemporaries) led was rather complicated. Sometimes regularly, but sometimes only on occasion, her husband's salary was supplemented by deliveries of produce. The Danish court sent one ton of butter and one ton of herring each year. Town councillors, publishers, and more prosperous supporters of the Reformation paid their respects with silver beakers, rings, medallions, or similar objects. If there was spare cash to hand, Katharina would invest it profitably, largely, in light of her flair for the practical, in property, which then also provided her family and others who lived in the house with produce of the land. Luther had his study in the house, probably still in the first floor of the southern addition,[47] and each day at mealtimes experienced for himself just how many fellow residents in his home had to be fed. He was therefore well aware of the challenges. He responded as was his way, adding to his 'Wondrous Accounts of Doctor Martin and Käthe', the rhyming lines, 'For I, poor

man, keep the household accounts, where I am supposed to spend my money
/ and I am to do so in seven places / but it always flies hither and thither.'[48]
Words of praise found in his Table Talk make unmistakable reference to
Katharina and to Proverbs 31:10–31:

> A pious, God-fearing wife is an extraordinary treasure, more noble and more
> precious than a pearl, for the husband depends on her, trusts her in all matters.
> There will be no shortage of nourishment. She is joyful and makes her husband
> joyful and gives him no sorrow, and throughout his life gives him love and no
> pain, can handle flax and wool, and likes to work and be creative with her
> hands, is productive in the house and is like a merchant ship that brings many
> wares and goods from distant lands. She gets up early, feeds the servants, and
> gives the maids their just part. Considers a field and buys it and lives from the
> fruit of her hands, plants vines and tends them well, attends and cares with
> joy which is deserving... likes to work and works hard. She reaches out to
> the poor and gives her hand to those in need, gives to poor people and lives to
> help them. She oversees what is happening in her home and is not lazy in
> eating her bread.[49]

Despite the witty light-heartedness Luther employed to distance himself
from Katharina's housewife's worries, he was evidently aware that the need
to run a profitable enterprise might cast his wife in a bad light. In his will
drawn up in 1542 he called on all his good friends, 'to be witnesses for my
dear Katie and to help defend her, when some idle gossips want to trouble or
defame her, as though she perhaps had a sum of ready cash on the side,
which she would purloin or embezzle from the poor children'. As the law of
his day gave the husband complete testamentary authority over the possessions and estate of a married couple, no matter who had been responsible for
their acquisition or oversight, Luther left to his wife:

> the little holding at Zülsdorf, the same that I have purchased [!] and made
> useful, absolutely as I have had it up to now; secondly, as a dwelling the house
> of Bruno which I have bought under the name of my man Wolf; thirdly,
> beakers and valuables, such as rings, necklaces, gratuities, gold, and silver,
> which should be worth about a thousand gulden.[50]

Thanks to his wife's domestic skills and financial ability, Luther's household
eventually became one of the wealthiest in Wittenberg. The value of the land,
animals, and precious objects he possessed in 1542, the year of the Turkish
tax, was calculated at 7,079 gulden and was rivalled only by the wealth
of the Cranach family with their art-producing business. In the former

Augustinian monastery Luther and his wife were able to run what the middle class of the nineteenth century would have called a 'large house' (*großes Haus*), but their home was not the grand town palace of a modern bourgeoisie, and it had little to do with the portrayal of status, power, or culture. Luther resided in the Old European 'complete house' (*ganzes Haus*) of the early modern professor, which was under the direction of his wife. Judged by today's criteria it was both private and public—private in that it provided for family members and house guests, and public in that it served the scholarly and student communities. It was primarily a business concern, an enterprise designed to make a profit. To this extent the critics of Katharina Luther the 'business woman' were absolutely right.

Their commercial enterprise was not a radical innovation. It was usual for a professor to run a small private student hostel, known as a *Burse*, for which the layout of the Black Monastery was already particularly suitable. The top floor had always been intended for student rooms, and Katharina needed only to restore those quarters, which had become dilapidated. More unusual, and a cause of envy, were the scale and success of her hostel, where between ten and twenty students could lodge, with some of them receiving full board. Archaeologists made a very rare discovery when they uncovered ceramic water holders that would have hung in each room to supply the student-lodger; the reliefs on these vessels displayed the fundamentals of Lutheran theology—'Law and Grace', 'Faith Alone', and other such themes—as depicted by the Cranach workshop in Wittenberg. The students' eagerness to live in the former Augustinian monastery, which had not been a popular residence in its previous incarnation, can be readily explained by the status of the reformer. To live under the same roof as Luther was not just an honour but also beneficial for their studies and, above all, for their subsequent careers in the evangelical church currently under construction. When his time allowed, Luther turned his attention to the students and to other members of the household, especially during his soon-to-be-famous discussions around the table. All material concerns fell, however, to his wife, who oversaw up to ten employees; when the Luther family was at its largest, the household included boys, maids, a cook (female), a coachman, a swineherd, and other support.

From the start the young and newly married Katharina had to do much herself. First she needed to establish a more or less functional household, and she began with the bed. Luther the monk had never aired the straw, and the straw sacks were not up to the task of providing a mattress for the married couple. New household supplies also needed to be acquired, for as each monk had left the monastery, he had taken with him furniture as well as equipment from the kitchen. As the monastery buildings were far too large for the young couple and also in a very poor state of repair, a smaller more liveable space had to be established within their walls. With his usual directness and flair, Luther wrote to the elector in 1532, 'If I had wanted to build a house, then I would probably not have wanted to build it in this pigsty.'[51] In light of their lack of funds, the couple's living quarters were initially somewhat makeshift. Only at the beginning of 1530 were the necessary renovations and additions begun, creating a suitable space for the Luther family, which now included children, and for those who resided with them. For the store of provisions, two regular cellars and a special wine cellar were constructed, and in the western part of the living space a brew house was added, where Katharina brewed the beer required by her household and the hostel. With the construction of an extended kitchen on the garden side of the building and with stabling available for the horses along with stalls for the smaller livestock, all the forms of space required by a large household were to hand. After the mid-1530s a comfortable apartment for the immediate family was constructed in the first upper storey, with a living room—which today forms the 'Luther parlour' (*Lutherstube*) in the museum—five further rooms with fireplaces, and two chambers that were likely used as bedrooms. Eventually sufficient funds were available to have the old impractical public bath used by the monks turned into a new bathroom suitable for the needs of the family.

The crowning conclusion to the renovation was the doorway leading from the northern main courtyard into the house, created by stonemasons as a magnificent late Gothic portal with niches that functioned as seats (Figure 30). The design was the work of the mistress of the house herself. Above the two stone seats to the right and left of the door was the Luther rose—a white rose with a red heart and the black cross of Christ, which as a monk Luder had selected for his seal and now had long functioned as a symbol of his courage and his Christ-centred theology. Ever practical, Katharina was careful to ensure that the new door would be wide enough to permit the passage of the various goods that were to be transported into the storerooms and kitchens. She gave the elaborate and expensive doorway to her husband for his birthday in 1540. Aged fifty-seven, the 'doctor'—the usual form of address for Luther, often also used by his wife, as the title 'professor' was not customary—received a distinguished entrance to the rooms in which he worked and lived, and in other ways, too, he was now granted a certain ease in his daily life. Yet the work on the convent building as a whole was still not complete. In his final years Luther would complain that he had always been hard-pressed 'to maintain the roof, glass, and iron', even though, as he noted, 'the third part [the eastern] is not fully constructed'.[52]

When it came to the food and drink required to meet the daily needs of the family and the other members of this large academic household, extensive arrangements had to be in place for purchases to be made at market, for the maintenance of livestock, and for the leasing, development, and cultivation of gardens, fields, and orchards. All these arrangements, too, were the work of the mistress of the house, and Katharina dealt with them so expertly that the provisioning of the household generated a profit that could then be invested in property.

Figure 30. Katharina Doorway, Lutherhaus, Wittenberg, a gift to Luther from his wife, Katharina, for his fifty-seventh birthday.

Over the course of the years, Katharina formed a reliable prop for the work of the Reformation and was even in a certain respect Luther's collaborator. She was involved in overseeing the printing of his texts, and when Count Günther von Schwarzburg requested that Luther find him a suitable pastor, Luther noted that Katharina 'as a wise woman and doctor... might also give counsel'.[53] Luther urged his wife to read the Bible for herself and told her much about the theological and ecclesiastical problems he was facing, as can be seen, for example, in a detailed letter to his wife in which he described the negotiations with Zwingli undertaken at Marburg in 1529.[54] Conversely, Katharina's opinions and mindset influenced Luther, as we will see again when we consider his attitude towards Jews. Reporting to his wife on the cold he had acquired as he walked alongside his coach, underdressed, through a Jewish village, he added, 'Had you been here, however, you would have said that it was the fault of the Jews or their god.'[55]

Table Talk

In the evening, as family and guests sat around the dining table, the mood was determined by the master of the house, and his words were recorded by eager note-takers and preserved for posterity as his 'Table Talk'. We have no comparable record for the contributions of the mistress of the house, who made all of this possible. Our knowledge of her labours was gleaned only much later from account books and, most recently, from archaeological excavations at the Luther House. Full appreciation of Katharina has come only with the more recent work of social historians and historians of gender.

The discussions took place in either Latin or German, partly during the meal itself and partly afterwards, when a smaller group gathered in the sitting room. Meals took place in the former refectory on the ground floor, which was large enough to accommodate around one long table all the members of the household—which when students were included could number on occasion between 35 and 50 people—as well as colleagues and friends from the town. The master and mistress of the house sat at either end of the long table. Katharina was the only female member of the group that subsequently assembled in the sitting room, and she was fully involved in the discussion, even when it was in Latin.[56] She was not enthusiastic, however, about having note-takers record what was said at her table.

The surviving texts of those discussions fill six volumes of the Weimar Edition (*Weimarer Ausgabe*), the modern critical edition of Luther's works. They give us Luther's own words, but filtered and honed by the minute-takers, who worked from notes they had written at the time and created the final version of the text from their memories of what had been said. Modification or even deliberate falsification is extremely unlikely, partly because in the sixteenth century people generally had very good memories and partly because several records of each conversation were usually made, giving historians the opportunity to compare one against the other. From its very first edition, published by Johannes Aurifaber, the reformer's last secretary, in German in 1566, the 'Table Talk' was an immediate success. We do well to remember, however, that the authoritative and edifying character acquired by many of the reformer's words and statements that have thus survived should not be applied retrospectively to the original conversations in the refectory or sitting room of the Luther House.

These social gatherings were a continuation of the evening conviviality that Luder had enjoyed while still living as a monk, as we heard reported by Dantiscus, the Polish ambassador. They would often take place several times a week and were attended by Luther's Wittenberg colleagues and friends, in particular Melanchthon, Bugenhagen, Justus Jonas, and Caspar Cruciger, sometimes with the addition of members of the elector's court or visitors from elsewhere. Those who gathered were not there simply to ask the Great Man questions and sit back to hear his answers; they were equal partners in the discussion and their opinions were valued by the master of the house. Johannes Mathesius who lived with Luther in the 1540s and later wrote the first biography of the reformer, reported that it was not uncommon for Luther to come to the table straight from his work and, still deep in thought, to speak little during the meal. On occasion, in keeping with former monastic practice, the meal would be eaten in silence. Only when the meal was over would the master of the house launch the conversation, with a question along the lines of, 'So, what's new?' Colleagues or external guests would speak first, with the younger members of the gathering following on. Directed by Luther or one of the older guests, the conversation concentrated on individual issues and problems drawn from theology, on the politics of church, Empire, or electorate, or on economic, educational, or marriage-related concerns. As a rule, the master of the house concluded the discussion, summing up with his final words, a practice that while in keeping with the customs and culture of such discussion can also be attributed to Luther's reputation and prophetic sense of self.

The conversation was not limited to weighty themes. Topics might be drawn from the everyday, or from news from Saxony or farther afield, reports of spirits, witches, monstrous births, or natural phenomena, even on occasion from idle tales or gossip. That the discussion repeatedly returned to the experiences of the head of the household and the narrative of his Reformation activities was in part a product of his self-consciousness, but it also followed from the natural curiosity of the younger participants and visitors. In the last years Luther's natural dominance not infrequently became almost larger than life as he addressed posterity in an act of self-memorialization.

'Children Are the Most Loving Pledge of Marriage'

The successful business enterprise and the illustrious company gathered around his table were not the most radical additions to the household of the theologian and professor. Truly revolutionary was that the household was headed by a married couple and had at its heart a family with children. In this respect, too, the Luther House was exemplary, as a model for the home of an evangelical pastor. It was singular, however, in the size of its household and the number and breadth of the roles and functions it performed, both public and private. Also without parallel was the scale of the work that the reformer managed to achieve, often surrounded by the noise of children and the business of the household. Conditions were so turbulent that Prince George of Anhalt was urgently advised to abandon his plan to lodge at the Luther House during a stay in Wittenberg.[57] Luther did not seal himself off, unlike those mandarins of the nineteenth and early twentieth centuries who decreed their studies should be treated as inner sanctums that would only be entered under exceptional circumstances and with prior approval. The reformer took his responsibilities as a father very seriously, but he did not neglect his official duties as professor, preacher, pastor, and regent of his new church as a result.

Although Luther's immediate family were part of the greater household, its members formed a distinct unit and were the reformer's primary concern when it came to caring and providing for those around him. That inner circle was formed by the married couple and their children, but also by several children of relatives—first, from 1529, the four children of Luther's deceased sister Margarete, and, subsequently, two further nephews from Luther's side of the family and a nephew and great nephew from Katharina's. This inner circle, too, was not a typical pastor's family, let alone comparable with the small families of the modern age.

Paternal Love

Much that we know of the relationship between parents, and especially fathers, and their children in the pre-modern world seems alien today, even repellent. Yet the love and intimacy that characterized these relationships are still impressive. Parents and children lived in close proximity and interacted very naturally. Children were a constant presence in the Luther House, even in Luther's study. He reported of his five-year-old son, 'When I'm writing or doing something else, my Hans sings a little tune for me. If he becomes too noisy and I rebuke him for it, he continues to sing but does it more privately and with a certain awe and uneasiness.'[58] Luther always held his children in his mind's eye as he travelled—he might search out gifts, for example, at a yearly fair[59]—and sometimes he travelled with an actual image. As the Imperial diet met at Augsburg in 1530, Luther's favourite daughter, Magdalene (Figure 31), kept him company in a painted portrait hung on the wall of his sitting room, brightening for him those anguished

Figure 31. A posthumous portrait of Luther's favourite daughter, Magdalene (1529–42), by Lucas Cranach the Elder.

weeks in Coburg, which was a relief for his companion Veit Dietrich, who, visibly gladdened, informed Katharina, 'You did a very good thing when you sent the doctor the likeness, for through the picture he obliviates beyond measure many of his thoughts. He has attached it to the wall opposite the table where we eat.'[60]

From Coburg Luther sent his 'beloved son little Hans Luther at Wittenberg', just four years old, a letter in which as a reward for his son's being such a good boy in his studies and at his prayers, he told the story of:

> a pretty, gay, and beautiful garden where there are many children wearing golden robes. They pick up fine apples, pears, cherries, and plums under the trees, and they sing, jump, and are happy all the time. They also have nice ponies with golden reins and silver saddles. I asked the owner of the garden who the children were. He replied: 'These are the children who love to pray, learn their lessons, and be good.' Then I said: 'Dear sir, I also have a son. His name is Hans Luther. May he too enter the garden, eat of the fine apples and pears, ride on these pretty ponies, and play with the other children?' The man answered: 'If he likes to pray and study and is good, he may enter the garden.'[61]

The story has a clear religious didactical purpose and was recounted for good reason, but it is also a witness uncommon for its time of the sympathetic understanding of an adult for a small child.

For Luther marriage and sex had a value beyond simply their associations with children. He was clear, however, 'Intercourse can easily come to pass... but children are the most loving pledge of marriage, they bind and preserve the bond of love. This is the best wool from the sheep.'[62] Long before his own marriage he had declared in his text 'On Married Life' that the education and care of children were bound up with faith, and had commented on fathers:

> When a father goes ahead and washes diapers or performs some other mean task for his child, and someone ridicules him as an effeminate fool—though that father is acting in the spirit just described and in Christian faith—my dear fellow you tell me, which of the two is more keenly ridiculing the other? God, with all his angels and creatures, is smiling—not because that father is washing diapers, but because he is doing so in Christian faith. Those who sneer at him and see only the task but not the faith are ridiculing God with all his creatures, as the biggest fool on earth. Indeed, they are only ridiculing themselves; with all their cleverness they are nothing but devil's fools.[63]

Before he became a father—his first child, a son, was born on 7 June 1526 and baptized 'Hans' after his godfather Johannes Bugenhagen—Luther would have had no opportunity to make the elegant story of this sermon his own. But now, aged forty-two, he was fully engaged with the most practical problems of child-rearing. He reported joyfully of Johannes, aged one and a half, 'He has learned today how to bend his knees and crap in every corner, and indeed he did a fine job for me of crapping in every corner.' The Table Talk note-takers recorded how the reformer held a child on his lap who 'shitted and pissed'.[64] In 1530, even as he sat in Coburg tormented by fears about whether his teachings were being conveyed correctly at the Imperial diet at Augsburg, he weighed in on Katharina's attempts to wean one-year-old Magdalene, about which his wife had written to him, advising:

> I think it would be good if you want [to stop nursing her], [but] gradually, so that at first you omit one feeding per day, then two feedings per day, until [the child] clearly stops [nursing by herself]. So George von Grumbach's mother, Lady Argula, has advised me; she has been with us here, and had dinner with us.[65]

The Luthers had six children in all, over the course of eight years— Johannes was followed at the end of 1527 by Elisabeth, and in May 1529 by Magdalene, called Lene, who was her father's favourite, in November 1531 by Martin, and at the beginning of 1533 by Paul. The youngest of his children was Margarete, born in December 1534 when he was already fifty-one years old, and Luther recognized that with his many health concerns, it was highly unlikely he would see her grow into adulthood. When Margarete was only four years old, her father wrote to her godfather requesting that one day, when he himself was dead, he find her a suitable husband.[66] As was so common for families in this age, for the Luthers death was not just a premonition but also a very real experience. Two of their daughters died as children. Elisabeth's death, aged nine months, was a cause of deep sorrow for her parents, but they were comforted by a new pregnancy that followed soon after. 'I have another daughter in the womb,' rejoiced the expectant father,[67] a remarkable statement on two accounts: he identified himself with his wife, which was very unusual for the time, and he was right—his next child was indeed a daughter. It is hardly surprising that when Magdalene was born, six months after the death of her sister, she found a particular place in Luther's heart. But the Luthers also lost Magdalene when she was still a child. At the beginning of September 1542 Luther ordered his oldest son, Hans, now aged seventeen, to return home from Torgau, where he was at school. 'I ask you,' he wrote to an acquaintance in that town, 'to be quiet to my son about what I am writing to you: my daughter Magdalene is ill and almost in her last hour; in a short while she might depart to the true Father in heaven, unless God has decreed otherwise. She herself longs so much to see her brother.'[68] Magdalene died on 20 September, surrounded by her family and just thirteen years old. Her father held her in his arms and comforted her in her last moments: '"Dear Magdalene, my little daughter, you would be glad to stay here with me, your father. Are you also glad to go to your Father in heaven?" The sick girl replied, "Yes, dear Father, as God wills." The father said, "You dear little girl!"'[69] Trust in God provided assurance that Magdalene had gone to a new and happier life and that her father on earth must defer to her heavenly father. But the loss still caused deep pain. Three years later Luther the father continued to experience the anguish that her death had caused him and, still grieving, commented that he would never be able to forget her.

Paternal Authority

While Luther evidently loved his children, the principles that guided how they were to be raised show little sign of paternal sympathy for the emotions, thoughts, and actions of children. While that absence was in keeping with contemporary attitudes towards children, surely his own upbringing also played its part, first in a parental home where the rod was not spared and then in a monastery where unconditional obedience was required. In one Table Talk Luther pronounced with a touch of humour that a regime as strict as that of the Turks was required if one was to become the master of one's children, an attitude that likely stemmed from his experience of the bevy of children growing up in the Luther House and from his belief that boys should be raised more strictly than girls. He had great things planned for his oldest son—as had his own father when Luther was a boy—and therefore tended to joke with Hans less than with his daughters and kept a close eye to ensure he was not indulged.[70] His other sons, too, had to become used to close monitoring of their studies from an early age—they were supervised by a preceptor or tutor and at age eight began to learn languages and theology from Melanchthon and rhetoric from their father. 'Your physical and spiritual father', Luther might sign a letter to one of his sons. Having been enrolled at the university when only seven years old, aged thirteen Hans was the opponent at a promotion and received his bachelor's degree. Even when studying in Torgau and therefore absent from Wittenberg, he remained under the strict oversight of his father, who bluntly reminded him that his mother, sisters, brothers, and aunt Magdalene 'are looking forward to a successful progress and conclusion of your studies'.[71]

While monitoring for success had its rationale, the severity, even brutality, with which Luther punished disobedience can seem incomprehensible today. 'He thinks he has escaped the whip, but the whip shall be his reception committee,' he let it be known of his nephew Florian von Bora after Florian, having left the Lutheran household while still an adolescent, had behaved improperly away from home.[72] The threat he directed at Hans—'I would rather have a dead son than an unruly son'[73]—is likely repulsive even to the reader eager to avoid evaluating the child-raising principles of the sixteenth century in light of today's anachronistic standards. Particularly disturbing is Luther's employment for his sons of the very methods employed by his own father that had caused him suffering and left disobedience his only recourse. Even his great liberating experience of God was forgotten: the undeserved grace of God was not in evidence here—when it came to the raising of children, the rules were set not by the merciful God of the Reformation but by the censorious and demanding God of an earlier age.

Children of Luther's time had their own way of dealing with such outbursts. 'If you should become a lawyer, I'd hang you on the gallows,'[74] Luther is said to have threatened his son Hans as an adolescent—with the result that Hans studied law and became councillor at a princely court, precisely the highly regarded, aspirational position that Hans' grandfather Hans Luder had wanted for his son Martin. Only Luther's second son, Martin, fulfilled the heartfelt wish of his father and studied theology, although without great success—he died aged thirty-four without having completed his studies and likely of alcoholism. The youngest son, Paul, had a notable career, though not as a theologian but as a medical doctor and personal physician at a number of prominent courts, first for Saxony-Gotha, then for Brandenburg, and finally at the electoral Saxon court in Dresden.

Margarete, Luther's youngest child and only surviving daughter, born late in his life, followed the path that we saw her father setting down for her in his letter to her godfather. She married Prussian councillor Erhard von Kunheim and was mother to nine children. Although Luther argued that girls should also be educated and although the knowledge that his own wife acquired in the convent was impressive, Luther had no thought of an independent career outwith marriage and family for either his own daughters or any other well-raised evangelical woman. When we think of the manifold possibilities for an independent life available to women in the medieval and early modern Catholic Church, it is again evident that Luther and his Reformation did not directly launch the modern.

All this—the severity, paternalism, and authoritarianism Luther demonstrated in raising his own children and the children invited into his household—was entirely in keeping with the usual relationship of parents, and especially fathers, and their children. In Luther's home this relationship was more deliberate, and it was underpinned theologically by the relationship between God and humankind. When one of his children was being insubordinate, Luther offered a rough rebuke: 'How have you earned or why should I love you so much that I should make you an heir of all that I have. Shitting, peeing, crying, you fill the whole house with screaming—yet I must have so much concern for you?' That exclamation was the deep groan of an overly taxed father, but it is impossible to fail to hear within it the Reformation doctrine of grace, carried over here onto the relationship between father and child.[75]

PART THREE

Prophetic Confidence,
but Temporal Failure,
1525–1546

I

Evangelical Renewal of Church and Society

Wittenberg as Luther's Cathedral Town

Particular Reformation, not Universal Reform

The year 1525 was for Germany, as with the defeat of the peasants the early modern territorial and princely state was decisively established. The year also marked a turning point for Luther. With his marriage to Katharina von Bora, the monk became a family man and was located once and for all in the midst of the everyday world. His relationship with the broader public also changed, a shift that should not be read as evidence that the popular Reformation had now become, irreversibly, a Reformation dictated from above, by ruler or magistrate, as has been detected by those who theorize about an 'early bourgeois revolution'. While the disillusioned peasants had to resign themselves to the established ecclesiastical situation or participate in what were in effect 'private' underground mystical or Anabaptist practices, the urban popular reformation remained conspicuously vibrant. There the communal church comprising the citizens of the town continued to gain ground into the second half of the century and was still championed at the beginning of the seventeenth century.

The fundamental changes directly affected Luther, in his attitude towards life, his 'national' status, and the potential reach of his social and ecclesiastical activities. Although peace and order had been re-established, only at first glance was he a victor. Certainly the battle between the two irreconcilable models of evangelical reform of church and society had been decided in his favour. His realistic model had won through, with the kingdoms on earth and in heaven kept distinct, while the unified model in which heaven and earth were made one, as advocated by Thomas Müntzer, had been discredited. In truth, however, both forms of church renewal could now seem suspect, the mystical-eschatological as a result of Müntzer's irresponsible leadership at Frankenhausen, and that of the Wittenberg Reformation. Luther had in effect lost twice—he had lost his popular reputation and he had lost room to manoeuvre with the princes.

His status amongst the common people had suffered because he had appeared as the agent of the princes, not the advocate of the weak and oppressed, and because he had celebrated his marriage in the very moment that the rural communities were overwhelmed by suffering and sorrow. The political constraints came because the pressure created by Müntzer and the peasants had revealed just how dependent his Reformation was on the support of the authorities. During the Peasants' War the reformer never betrayed his inner independence and absolute personal and God-given purpose, as we saw in the text justifying his return from the Wartburg; nor would he ever do so in future. But this was a subjective freedom that found its limits in the political reality when it ran counter to the interests of the princes, whose power and self-confidence had grown significantly with the defeat of the peasants, such that now they were the deciding force in Germany.

The early and unwavering alliance that Luther formed with the princes and with their territorial state was not unpolitical, as claimed, unhistorically, by those who projected the behaviour of Lutherans in the nineteenth and twentieth centuries back onto the reformer himself. Much the opposite was the case: the decision in favour of an alliance with the authorities was evidence of a political sensibility that the 'false brothers' in the Protestant camp lacked.

In 1525 the weight in the political alliance between Reformation and early modern state had shifted distinctively in favour of the temporal ruler. Unavoidably, these new circumstances had an impact on the scale of Luther's field of action. In taking sides so decisively against the rebels, Luther had ensured that a symbiosis of Reformation and territorial ruler or of Reformation and town magistrate was the sole possibility. The age of rebellion transitioned into an era of consolidation. Where Luther's writ ran, the new order adopted a model that placed the evangelical territorial or urban church under the protection of the authorities, even though at its core his theology was still conceived in light of the independent communal church.

Consolidation in individual territories and towns saw hopes for the universal success of the Reformation compromised and contracted. Optimism was replaced by more sober prospects. The politics of Electoral Saxony had not changed in any fundamental way, and the new elector had not distanced himself from the Reformation. The decisive shift was in Luther's subjective evaluation of the moment in which he was living, his chapter in the narrative of salvation. He did not question his theology or doubt the path laid out for him by God, but his temporal perspective was now longer—his certainty that the course of the Gospel would soon be fulfilled in this world had faded. At the end of April 1525, in the throes of the Thuringian Peasants' War, he had taken a strong personal stand against that chaos, and for the first time he had seen his preaching derided and mocked. In that moment he had believed that were the peasants to succeed, the world would become the spoils of his devilish opponents and the opportunity for its evangelical renewal would have been squandered.

The Older Luther—Pessimistic but Unremitting

The princes' ruthless measures against the rebels had banished Luther's eschatological nightmare, but the experience left its mark. In the second half of the 1520s, the rallying of his opponents and the narrowing of the possibilities did not go unnoticed by a figure of Luther's spirit, always alert to the shifting constellations of his age. The result was the transition from the optimistic Eleutherius-Luther of the earlier years of his adulthood, ready to take on the world, to the realistic and pessimistic older Luther. In July 1525, in his 'Open Letter on the Harsh Book against the Peasants', he had already given expression to the pessimistic image of the world and humankind that would increasingly shape his attitude, describing how, 'If the peasants became lords, the devil would become abbot; but if these tyrants became lords, the devil's mother would become abbess.' He explained:

> Therefore I wanted to do two things: quiet the peasants, and instruct the pious lords. The peasants were unwilling to listen, and now they have their reward; the lords, too, will not hear, and they shall have their reward also. However, it would have been a shame if they had been killed by the peasants; that would have been too easy a punishment for them. Hell-fire, trembling, and gnashing of teeth in hell will be their reward eternally, unless they repent.[1]

Luther had envisioned the discovery of the pure Gospel resulting in a universal reform of the church that embraced not only Christianity but also, as a logical consequence, all other peoples too, and not least Jews, from whom the true Christ had remained hidden only because of the scheming of the papacy. But that vision had been compromised. In Rome and amongst the rebellious peasants Satan had rallied forces for an attack on the redis-covered Gospel, and as a result the universal reform of Christianity could no longer be expected in the foreseeable future. Luther placed all his hopes instead in the particularism of the territorial reformations, from which would emerge the territorial evangelical churches that have remained characteristic of German Protestantism up to the present day.

The changes that distinguished the young Luther from his older incarna-tion also left their mark on his personal bearing. In his late forties Luther became in both behaviour and appearance his own monument—Frederick William I, the second king of Prussia, wrote of acting 'steadily as a rock of bronze' (*stabilisiest wie ein Rocher de bronze*), words that can equally be used in describing the considerable subject of the Luther portraits of these years (Figure 32). Inevitably, his increasingly pessimistic world view came through in his theology, forced from him by the unsympathetic treatises of his opponents, and of Erasmus in particular. Clear explanation of the human will's lack of freedom was needed, the darker side of the coin whose other,

Figure 32. Martin Luther, by Lucas Cranach the Elder, 1532. This depiction of Luther, by which he is readily recognized today, was reproduced in the Cranach workshop more than 1,000 times.

resplendent, face assured the sinner of the grace of God. The pessimistic realism in Luther's theology and anthropology was coupled with recognition, initially somewhat indistinct but by the end of his life irrefutable, that his universal concept had been abortive.

That turnaround was clear to Luther, but sober realization was for him no reason to doubt his cause or cease his work. The opposite was very much the case, for he was certain that unceasing activity was essential if God's prophet on earth was to succeed in replanting and securing the Gospel in both church and society, at least in locations that remained receptive after 1525. Right up until the end of his life, Luther never stopped. He expanded his evangelical theology and defended it successfully against attack from both the Roman Church, by then fully launched on its counteroffensive, and dissenters within his own camp, in particular those who championed an anti-sacramental teaching on the Lord's Supper. In theoretical discussions and with practical suggestions, he pushed ahead with the reordering of church and world in accord with the Gospel—he drew up ordinances for Urban and territorial churches, for the care of the poor and of the elderly and sick, and for schools and universities, with an eye to a basic education for both boys and girls, and he wrote legal opinions and turned his attention to visitations and church discipline; the list could go on. He was in no doubt that he should also continue his regular duties as professor and preacher, and on occasion as pastor, in Wittenberg. He was also always on call for his large circle of friends and supporters outside Wittenberg, ready to provide specific advice and words of comfort in moments of existential crisis.

Alongside the activities we can consider his routine business, Luther functioned as what today might be termed a political consultant or spiritual advisor. His Saxon territorial ruler and also other evangelical princes within the Empire and farther afield looked to him for theological opinions or pastoral support in delicate political matters and issues of conscience. That responsibility proved especially burdensome, and even painful, in 1530, when the evangelical estates planned to respond to the renewed condemnation of their religion at the Imperial diet at Augsburg by forming a defensive military alliance and sought Luther's views on the theological legitimacy of resistance against the Emperor.

The centre of Luther's world remained Wittenberg, where he inhabited a space bounded by writing desk, lectern, and pulpit. For all that he repeatedly vented divine wrath at the insufficient faith and poor morals of the citizens and students of Wittenberg, 'the small and poor town that now had a great name' remained for him the new Jerusalem. In Wittenberg the evangelical truth had been rediscovered and in Wittenberg the renewed church had taken concrete form.[2]

Christian Civic Virtue and Moral Discipline

Luther the reformer and prophet of God believed that his responsibilities reached beyond doctrinal purity into behavioural mores. Irrespective of his separation of the spiritual and temporal worlds, he kept a close eye on the ecclesiastical and civic community. Unlike the clergy of the Roman Church, who claimed a standing distinct from that of regular citizens, Luther viewed himself as a full member of his community and as responsible, like all citizens, for the public good, and therefore for moral order and social peace.

Both Luther's commitment to the redemption of the Christian and his concern for the civic community are evident in his conflict with Hans von Metzsch. As bailiff and town captain, Metzsch was one of the most capable and most influential state officials within Electoral Saxony, but he was also intemperate, proud, and haughty. Metzsch and Luther had initially worked well together, as during the visitation of 1528, when the former had proved himself a loyal supporter of the Reformation. By the end of the decade, however, the rift between the two men was so great that in a Table Talk Luther openly acknowledged, 'Hans Metzsch is my enemy and I am his enemy'; that enmity, Luther recorded, was not a product of any direct harm to Luther but stemmed rather from Metzsch's un-Christian lifestyle, which was particularly problematic because he was a public official.[3] Luther reported, 'Our captain, Hans Metzsch, has time and again been admonished by me, kindly but seriously, to stay away from harlotry and dealings with prostitutes', but the only answer Metzsch could give was that he could not be without women.[4] As a result the reformer excommunicated Metzsch—aged over forty and the highest local official—'on account of his fornicating' and eschewed any further personal contact.[5]

The town captain respected both elements of Luther's response, not least, it seems likely, as he was eager to avoid the public scandal that would result from his rebuffing at the communion table or ostracism within society, but he did not change his behaviour and indicated that he was not prepared to marry. Luther therefore brought the case to his ruler, acknowledging, 'It is not for me to be concerned with the affairs of secular government, or to disparage Your Electoral Grace's officials'; his concern was rather that he give the elector warning that he believed himself bound to speak out 'by means of public preaching and judgment' against the elector's own official.[6]

Luther was clear that Metzsch's actions threatened the salvation of the Christian community and also the security of both town and electorate: 'Metzsch may be a good soldier, but I would not want him to defend me in an emergency, since he does not have before his eyes God who has thus far miraculously protected us without striking a blow, and daily still preserves us.'[7] His concerns were not solely about Metzsch's un-Christian behaviour, for he also accused the electoral official of having acted high-handedly when the medieval city wall was being reconstructed as a modern fortification. Metzsch had moved the project forward without the agreement of the town council, which in spring 1531 had been greatly perturbed when Metzsch had had almost 100 metres of the old town wall torn down, making it possible to enter the town unobserved and unchecked for several months.[8] Luther believed his responsibility extended into circumstances that were entirely a matter for the civic community and emphasized for the elector just how alarming Metzsch's actions had been for the inhabitants of Wittenberg, writing, 'For I know very well how concerned one has been until now with the gates of the city, so that the city would be properly locked.' That fear had also gripped the parents of students at Wittenberg, who had expected their sons would be safe. Wittenberg, he wrote, was a 'good, peaceful, and law-abiding town', but the trouble caused by the headstrong town captain was threatening to turn all the citizens, who 'might get tired of Metzsch's stubbornness, cursing, and tyranny', against the territorial ruler.[9]

We do not know of any direct consequences of Luther's intervention. The modernization of the town fortifications continued, and for the time being Metzsch evidently continued to claim that he could not live without women. Evangelical moral discipline eventually won the day, however, for in 1533 the town captain finally married and had to ask the reformer for his sins to be forgiven: 'I am a lost sheep. I acknowledge my sins and long for absolution.' Luther granted him his request and offered a prayer of gratitude that God had called the town captain 'out of whoredom and into holy matrimony'.[10] Their reconciliation did not last. Evidently Metzsch and his family fell into line with the ecclesiastical and civic mores of Wittenberg for only a few years. By the end of the 1530s the official's relationship with the church, the citizens, and the university was again so fraught that Luther re-excommunicated him. Along with general accusations of un-Christian and arrogant behaviour that suggested disdain for God's word and God's servants and antagonism towards the authorities, this time the specific complaint focused on misconduct during the supply crisis faced by Wittenberg, and experienced throughout Germany and Europe in those decades as harvests proved unable to meet the needs of the rapidly growing population. The elector's residence claimed precedence when it came to the provision of fish and grain, and supplies for the inhabitants of Wittenberg were insufficient. We do not known whether Metzsch's fault lay in profiteering, a failure to take remedial action, or simply an inability to respond effectively to the crisis. In this instance the ruler intervened, and Metzsch was transferred to Colditz. He did not fall out of princely favour, however, and when he died in 1549, the elector expressly honoured him as his 'true subject, councillor, and servant'.[11]

Luther's disciplinary measures against the prominent electoral official, one instance amongst other similar actions, document his special position within Wittenberg and Electoral Saxony. They illuminate the principles that guided his actions both in the church and in the world more broadly. They also illustrate, however, how he adopted and influenced a broader trait of his age, the 'social discipline' that was characteristic of European societies in the transition from the medieval to the early modern and encountered in both the ecclesiastical and the political. Social discipline began as an urban phenomenon, found amongst the citizenry and in certain ecclesiastical circles, above all the mendicant orders. With the Reformation, ecclesiastical discipline and social discipline became fundamental features of Latin Christendom. While a component of all the Christian confessions and present in all the confessional territories, such discipline was particularly characteristic of Calvinism, where it was both intense and institutionalized, and of the Roman Church, where it could be found in confessional practices and in the spiritual exercises of the new orders, especially the Jesuits.

Luther followed less formalized disciplinary paths, but he, too, had the Christianization of society by means of control and correction as his goal. His response to the unruly town captain demonstrates that he condemned wilful and egotistical behaviour as both un-Christian and anti-Christian and that he was ready to employ ecclesiastical sanctions against such conduct. The social and political prominence of the 'sinner' was no deterrent for Luther; to the contrary, he believed such standing demanded the adoption of a model Christian lifestyle. Calvin did not rest until the sinful and unregenerate members of the old political elite were forced from Geneva and a new council receptive to his Christian order took its place. Luther forwent a similar demonstration of power in Wittenberg, limiting himself to advising and admonishing, although his words were forthright and blunt. For Luther the duties of the theologian and the prophet came with political responsibility. As he informed the elector, 'Should something later go wrong, I would not want to be blamed for having been silent to the disadvantage of Your Electoral Grace.'[12]

Luther did not feel called to enforce his evangelical moral norms as perfectly and as relentlessly as did Calvin and the Reformed presbyterians, with their institutionalized and formalized church discipline. He saw no need for the evangelical order to be constructed and secured by legal means; reference to Scripture was inherently sufficient. In 1521 as he stood before the Imperial diet at Worms he had declared himself the prisoner of the Bible he held in his hands,[13] and similarly, in disciplining Hans von Metzsch he referred to his duty of obedience to the biblical text. Asked by a dining companion, 'Is fornication also a sin if I don't take another man's wife but an unattached wench, as long as I am myself free too?', so without adultery being committed, Luther pointed out to his interlocutor that Paul had made no distinction between prostitution and adultery. He insisted that he neither was able to lay down the law nor wished to do so and called on the questioner to look to the biblical text: 'I can't make a law for you. I simply point you to the Scriptures.'[14]

In additional to the biblicism that was so typical of Luther, when it came to ethical and moral issues, he drew also on the traditional tried and tested communal norms of civic society, norms typical of the feudal world of Old Europe. That approach can be seen particularly clearly in his second excommunication of Metzsch, where in addition to chastising the town captain for his infringement of the Christian love due one's neighbour, the reformer also punished the noble-seigneurial violation of the solidarity of the civic community, demonstrating a communal philosophy that was in keeping with his origins and with his communally focused theology. All the more remarkable, then, were his actions in another prominent case involving discipline. In the early 1530s stormy altercations broke out in Zwickau over how the town pastor was carrying out his office. The reformer refused to acknowledge either the church community's claims to co-determination or the town council's rights of patronage. Instead, in contradiction of all collective and communal norms, he excommunicated Stephan Roth, town

clerk and representative of the magistracy, and for over a year prevented
the vacant pastor's post from being filled. In practice he had placed Zwickau
under 'interdict', the prohibition of all religious activities practised by the
Catholic Church that he had so vehemently criticized. He did not even baulk
at naming his response in these terms.[15] As the territorial church adopted the
Reformation, the communal ecclesiastical approach of the early Reformation
was lost. Luther's concern was now that the rights of the early modern state be
secured within his territorial church, as had been evident in the instructions
drawn up for the Electoral Saxon visitation of 1527.

The conflicts in Zwickau reveal something more, and something that
would trouble the reformer for years. At the height of his influence, the
outbreaks of anger and tactlessness so characteristic of Luther could make it
hard, and on occasion even impossible, for the reformer to form a balanced
judgement. He relied entirely on the account given by the party that shared
his own political-ecclesiastical position and simply ignored the explanations
of those with whom he was not in sympathy. Roth, who retained his links to
Luther despite his excommunication, had a point when he accused Luther of
harming the Gospel with his credulity, rash judgement, and humiliating
insults.[16] Luther's prejudiced and high-handed intervention in the conflicts
in Zwickau does not show him in a good light. His quick temper and
vehemence meant that he was susceptible to such derailments, especially
when, as in precisely these years, he was tightly wound and overburdened
with work.

Pastor and Preacher

Spiritual reassurance, not discipline, formed the core of Luther's pastoral role
as he advised and aided individuals and the community as a whole.
He continued to hear confessions, although he castigated the Roman
Church for its confessional practices. The most personal expression of his
pastoral care is provided by his letters of consolation, sent to sustain individuals far from Wittenberg in times of need. We have already encountered
such letters in discussing the spiritual torments of Georg Spalatin, Luther's
early friend and colleague.[17] This form of pastoral care had been practised in
the late Middle Ages, in particular in the context of mysticism, but Luther
used the pastoral letter in a somewhat different, and distinctly Reformation-
related, way, in which personal and psychological empathy were bound
together with theological exposition of Scripture. Luther wrote more than

one hundred such letters.[18] In addressing suffering communities, several were almost Pauline in character and were part of the public conflict with opponents of the Reformation. The majority, however, were intended for specific individuals and were entirely private in nature, designed to console or fortify the recipient in the face of death, when distressed in body or spirit, when experiencing religious persecution, or when suffering spiritual fears. Correspondence was sent to members of all the estates: to princes such as Frederick the Wise and Joachim of Anhalt, to members of evangelical communities, and also, naturally, to Luther's close friends and colleagues. In the midst of other urgent business, Luther would still work with great care on such letters, giving much attention not only to their theology and psychology, but also to their literary style; those intended for the better educated were written in Latin and the remainder in his compelling German. Some recipients passed on Luther's letters for friends and acquaintances to read, and they in turn made copies that were circulated. This process contributed significantly to Luther's popularity and renown as a pastor, bolstered by the publication and wide distribution of collections of letters of consolation that soon followed.

Personal concerns were always tied in with evangelical theology and active encouragement of the Reformation. We see that unity of purpose particularly clearly in the letter of consolation Luther sent to Melanchthon in summer 1540. While in Weimar on his way to the religious colloquy at Hagenau, Luther's sensitive and emotionally fragile friend became ill, evidently as a result of his worry that he would be unable to hold his own before opponents of the Reformation. Melanchthon feared that the Catholics would exploit the two reformers' entanglement, which had recently become public knowledge, in the bigamy of the landgrave of Hesse (to which we will return very shortly) and that he would be unable to respond. Luther countered by insisting, in true Pauline manner, that his friend place his trust in God, knowing that in the midst of uncertainty assurance was guaranteed. With God Melanchthon could hold his head high and venture on: 'Fear not, we will win, although we are sinners.' There was no point, Luther insisted, in fretting oneself to death, and mournfulness would only distract from the one who had been victorious over death.[19]

Luther comforted and fortified those who despaired or mourned principally through an evangelical piety focused on Christ. 'He who defeated the devil and directed the princes of this world, will not he also right your present shame?' His recommended remedy always was to embrace the *gaudium* or the *delectatio*, the joy of God's creation. Behind suffering and tribulation Luther saw lurking none other than Satan himself—how could it be otherwise in the struggle against those possessed by the devil? But one should not torment one's self by launching into a wrestling match with Satan, but rather 'righteously scorn him, just as when one scorns and ignores a dog that barks aggressively, such that it doesn't only not bite but also ceases to bark'.[20]

However earnestly Luther addressed his pastoral tasks, he always held his highest and most important call to be preaching. He liked to call himself 'preacher' or 'evangelist' at Wittenberg.[21] He usually preached without a written text, recording:

> I cannot preach or compose a sermon as an art. I do not tend to look at all pieces individually, but rather only at the main piece, on which the gist of the whole sermon is based. And while I am talking, something might occur to me that I had not given great thought to previously. For if I was to address all the words and talk of all parts specifically, then I would not get through very quickly.

Many of Luther's sermons could therefore only be published from transcripts made by listeners. Not infrequently that record was the cause of some surprise to Luther, who commented on the printed version of his exposition of the Letter to the Galatians, 'for now it seems even to me to be remarkable and I find it hard to believe that I have expounded and treated this letter of Saint Paul so extensively and with so many words'.[22] In these years he also wrote sermons that were specifically intended for publication, adding to the collection of model sermons for the less articulate pastor that he had begun at the Wartburg. The new contributions were in part assembled and prepared for publication by a man we have recently encountered, Stephan Roth, rector and later town clerk in Zwickau. By 1527 Luther's postils covered virtually all of the annual cycle of lessons.

Luther the preacher was heard far beyond Wittenberg, and his published sermons were undoubtedly the most spectacular form of Reformation publicity. For centuries Protestant pastors and preachers would be guided and taught by those printed texts. If anything justifies the equation, already made by contemporaries, of Wittenberg with Rome, then it is Luther's presence and impact as the preacher of Wittenberg. But marked differences between the pope's role in Rome and Luther's role in Wittenberg must also be acknowledged. However often Luther entered the pulpit, he never spoke from that space *ex cathedra*, in order to pronounce decrees of faith. And no Roman pope ever preached as frequently or as emphatically as the reformer, who at times gave sermons daily, and on occasion, when he preached both in the church and to his companions at home in the Black Monastery, sometimes even more than once each day. From March 1528 to June 1529, while Johannes Bugenhagen, the Wittenberg town pastor, was in Brunswick and Hamburg overseeing the introduction of Reformation ordinances, Luther in effect acted as Wittenberg pastor in his place, preaching regularly during the week, on Wednesdays on Matthew's gospel and on Saturdays on John's gospel. A similar pattern occurred from October 1530 to March 1532, while Bugenhagen continued his ordinance-related mission in Lubeck. When he travelled, Luther might preach even more often than when at home in Wittenberg, partly because of the high demand from those who wished to hear the famous man in action, but also because Luther felt such a strong call to proclaim God's word. Even age and illness could not bring him to stop preaching. The sermon that he gave at Wittenberg on Sunday, 17 January 1546, before leaving to attend negotiations at Eisleben, would soon prove to be the final occasion on which he could be heard preaching in his 'cathedral town'. In the course of the travels that followed, however, he entered the pulpit a further five times, both in Halle during the journey and in Eisleben, where he preached for a last time on Monday, 15 February, three days before his death.

While the Luther House in the former Augustinian monastery provided a private setting for Luther's theological and authorial activities and for convivial mealtimes, the pulpit offered a public stage, where he proclaimed the word 'for the town and for the world'. Luther's preaching in Wittenberg was the evangelical counterpart to the pope's *urbi et orbi* blessing in Rome. In his treatise 'The Misuse of the Mass', written at the Wartburg, Luther had declared the proclamation of the word to be the cornerstone of the new evangelical worship service. In emphasizing that Scripture recorded that Christ had conferred his priesthood on all the faithful, Luther delegitimized the Roman priestly caste and the sacrifice of the Mass that they administered.[23] From now on, he insisted, the heart of the service should be formed only by the preaching of the word, 'For a priest ought to preach, as is written in Zechariah in the second chapter: "The lips of a priest should utter nothing but the law and wisdom of the Lord."' And, he noted, in addition to the priesthood of all Christians, the Bible states unequivocally that 'there is not more than one office of preaching God's Word, and that this office is common to all Christians; so that each person may speak, preach, and judge, and all the rest are obliged to listen'.[24]

When it came to giving concrete form to the faithful's responsibility to preach, Luther set narrow boundaries. In so doing, he distinguished himself from the 'false brothers', who believed that all who felt illuminated by the Spirit were called to expound the word. Luther, by contrast, insisted on a particular qualification for the preaching office that involved proper study, a formal call, and, above all, individual aptitude. In order that 'the proper respect, discipline, and order may be maintained', only those who have 'a good voice, good eloquence, a good memory, and other natural gifts' should preach. In keeping with the thinking of his age, he considered only men to be candidates for the office of preacher, but he also distanced himself from the male monopoly of the Catholic priesthood. From Paul's words that 'the women should keep silence in the church', Luther noted, the papal church drew the argument that 'preaching cannot be common to all Christians because women are excluded'. He continued:

> My answer to this is that one also does not permit the dumb to preach, or those who are otherwise handicapped or incompetent. Although everyone has the right to preach, one should not use any person for this task, nor should anyone undertake it, unless he is better fitted than the others.[25]

His argument against the call of women to the preaching office was thus tactical and time-specific, and it no longer held when, as was the case from the end of the nineteenth century, women could acquire the same qualifications as men.

Throughout his life, Luther preached with all seriousness and real passion. He was the professor of Bible who in 1517 had taken up the struggle with Rome, but he was also the original preaching pastor, as symbolically depicted in the famous portrait on the Wittenberg Reformation altar, a product of the workshop of Lucas Cranach, where Luther was shown in the pulpit with one hand on the Bible while gesticulating with the other like a prophet, pointing to the image of Christ and his redemptive act (Figure 33). After giving up the monk's habit entirely in October 1524, when in the pulpit Luther wore the full cloak of the late medieval professor from which would later develop the standard clerical robes of the Protestant pastor. Zwingli and the other Swiss reformers immediately divested themselves of all the vestments and regalia worn by the medieval priest when he celebrated the Mass. Luther's concern for continuity and

Figure 33. Martin Luther preaching, depicted by Lucas Cranach the Elder on the Reformation Altar in Wittenberg Town Church, 1547.

stability extended, by contrast, also to clerical garb, for he held that especially when it came to worship, it was important not to unsettle the people by introducing unnecessary changes or by making alterations too quickly. For the celebration of the Lord's Supper he therefore continued to wear a chasuble, although somewhat simplified, without the pomp of the maniple and other signs of rank. For Luther what a pastor wore was not a matter of principle but rather part of the 'adiaphora', those things that were neither mandated nor prohibited for salvation. The freedom of the Christian left it to the individual pastor in his Lutheran community to decide exactly what he would wear—with the result, which did not bother the reformer, that from parish to parish and subsequently from territorial church to territorial church Lutheran worship looked different.

When it came to worship, the niceties of dress and appearance were the last things on the reformer's mind. To preach was for him the most noble of duties and a service to the Wittenberg community, which he saw as the model for universal reformation, for it provided an example of how the pure word might be preached and how an order of worship might be constructed around that proclamation of the word. All eyes were indeed on the town on the Elbe, those of his supporters and his opponents alike. The wish to hear Luther preach was great. He appeared principally in the pulpit of the town church of Saint Mary, but he also preached repeatedly at the castle church, usually when word had been received that one of the princes of the Empire and his retinue were in residence. On his return from the Wartburg in 1522, we will recall, Luther had been forbidden by Frederick the Wise from preaching in the castle church, which in light of its ties to the ruling dynasty was in effect the official church of the state, but the reformer's Invocavit sermons of that same year gave the elector cause to reverse his position. Luther was now brought in to preach at the Wittenberg castle church, and later also at the castle church at Torgau, during what were in effect state visits, when Electoral Saxony used the opportunity to display publicly its identification with the reformer and his work. The sermons Luther gave before ruling princes such as the dukes of Pomerania and Mecklenburg, the grand master of the Teutonic Order Albrecht, duke of Prussia, and the duchess and crown prince of Brunswick–Lüneburg played a very significant part in ensuring the spread of Lutheran teachings and the introduction of Lutheran church ordinances outside Wittenberg and Saxony—in Brunswick Lüneburg, Pomerania, and Mecklenburg, and in the lands of the Teutonic Order in Prussia, which lay to the north-east, beyond the borders of the Empire. Philip, the young landgrave of Hesse, did not visit Wittenberg for himself, but he entrusted the reformation of his lands to Franciscus Lambert, a pupil of Luther's, and he swung fully over to the Saxon model when it became clear that in a number of essential matters Lambert had departed from Wittenberg.

Luther soon developed a style of preaching that was very much his own and largely disregarded the scholastic tradition and the rules of the *ars praedicandi*. While he employed the humanist model of philological interpretation of the Scriptural text, he did not allow himself to be led by the humanists' fascination with classical rhetoric. His style was lively, and he spoke without a script, using only notes or his memory, and often improvised, as if in lively dialogue with the literal sense of the text. Contemporaries characterized his preaching as powerful and 'heroic', a sign of the divine inspiration of this learned doctor who had no need of the tricks of dialectics and rhetoric.

Luther delighted in expounding the word of God in series of sermons. Sermon and lecture thus sat side by side, such that the exposition Luther provided for the worshipping community from the pulpit and the interpretation he provided for students in the lecture hall were different in degree but not in kind. The sermon series that were published were very similar to his printed lectures,[26] and the latter, too, were as a rule produced from transcripts made by members of his audience. Even the two audiences were also not so very different. Luther addressed his sermons to all those resident in Wittenberg, irrespective of their social status or level of education, but that audience naturally included his students and colleagues at the university. He began, from 1519 to 1521, with two series of sermons running in parallel, one on the Old Testament and one on the New Testament. He followed with his exposition of the letters of the Apostles—beginning with the First Letter of Peter, from May to December 1522—which in light of his radical emphasis on the meaning of Scripture he placed above even the gospels, recording:

> Thus one apostle has recorded the same things that are found in the writings of the other. But those who stress most frequently and above all how nothing but faith in Christ justifies are the best evangelists. Therefore St. Paul's epistles are gospel to a greater degree than the writings of Matthew, Mark, and Luke. For the latter do little more than relate the history of the deeds and miracles of Christ. But no one stresses the grace we have through Christ so valiantly as Saint Paul does, especially in his Epistle to the Romans. Now since greater value attaches to the words of Christ than to his works and deeds—and if we had to dispense with one or the other, it would be better for us to do without the deeds and the history than to be without the words and the doctrine— these books that treat mainly of Christ's teaching and words should in all conscience be esteemed most highly. For even if Christ's miracles were non-existent, and if we knew nothing about them, His words would be enough for us. Without them we could not have life.[27]

As we would expect, he also gave sermon series on the gospels and the
Psalms, and he preached no fewer than three series on Genesis—from 1519
to 1521, in 1523/24, and from May 1535, with numerous interruptions,
until shortly before his death. In Genesis, almost more than anywhere else,
he found models and stimuli for his narrative imagination, insisting,
'All examples and accounts, indeed the whole text, lead through and
through to knowledge of Christ.'[28] This Christ-focus provided him with
grounds for a creationism—somewhat naïve from today's perspective—that,
in responding to a query from Spalatin, led him to insist that 'one cannot
force the meaning of the words of Moses without reason'. For Luther, God
really had created the world in six days and the snake was an actual snake,
used by the devil as a tool against God and humankind. Where he identified
room for a rational reading that did no damage to the meaning of the words,
he would use it, believing, for example, that the words spoken to Cain came
not directly from the mouth of God, but rather from a priest, as intermediary. For all the very high value he put on the divine word, he did not
replicate the absolute adherence to Scripture of many of his radical critics.
He employed a historical-critical approach in his exposition of the Ten
Commandments in particular. His theology defined his methodology, in
particular the Reformation division of Law and Gospel, which enabled a
Christological interpretation of the laws of the Old Testament. He described
the Mosaic laws as 'the Jewish Saxon Mirror' [Sachsenspiegel], suggesting that
they were a form of popular law geared to specific needs. He did not
relativize the laws as a result, but he did permit them a historical dimension,
and also a philosophical character, in as much as he understood them as
natural law, intelligible to all of humankind. He also expected those who
heard his sermons to be able to grasp philological criticism when necessary:
when he preached on the First Letter of Peter, for example, he made
extensive reference to possibly corrupt places in the text.

Not all Wittenbergers detected the fire of the Gospel burning in
Luther's sermons, let alone proved willing to adopt a lifestyle that was in
keeping with Scriptural norms. Town captain Metzsch was only one
example amongst many. His by-faith-alone theology meant that the
reformer would have held that only God could decide whether and how
his preaching of the word bore fruit amongst his audience, and yet he was
still profoundly disappointed when the Wittenbergers misunderstood the
message of Christian freedom that he brought them by feeling free not to
attend worship. The response to his catechism sermon, given four times a

year, was similar—neither nobility, nor townspeople, nor peasants displayed any enthusiasm for being taught again and again the same matters of
faith and on top of all that teaching, for allowing themselves to be
examined. Exasperated, by 1527 Luther had to admit that 'no one responds
to it, rather the people become so rough, cold, and lazy, that it is a disgrace,
and many do even less than before'. But, he insisted, the sermon should not
just 'resound richly in one's ears', but instead must 'go into one's heart and
have an effect within'. Where only outward behaviour was affected, he
saw 'pure hypocrisy'.[29]

In 1529 the crisis erupted publicly, and Luther thundered from the pulpit
with all the holy anger of an Old Testament prophet: 'I do not wish to be
the herdsman of such sows who want nothing other than fleshly licentious-
ness. I offer you pearls, and [as you spurn them] you will have mash instead.'
In light of their lack of gratitude for their Scripturally learned doctor, he was
ready to hand them back over to the 'tyrannies of the pope' and the
judgement of his unscrupulous officials.[30] Their sins would not go unpun-
ished, he warned the Wittenbergers, and that punishment was already lying
in wait everywhere—epidemics and starvation; the murderous Turks; the
Emperor, who was resolved to go to war against pure teaching. But nothing
could be laid at his door; the obdurate had only themselves to thank for what
lay before them. At the beginning of 1530 the reformer finally went on
strike, refusing to preach, and broke his silence only in order to take
Bugenhagen's place as town pastor while Bugenhagen was away from
Wittenberg carrying out a short visitation. Even the ruler was alarmed, but
he was unable to placate the angry evangelist, neither through his offer to
discipline the Wittenbergers nor through reference to the schadenfreude of
Luther's opponents, an argument that in almost all other instances would
have convinced Luther.[31]

With his departure for Coburg the reformer became absorbed in very
different problems. Luther would not have been Luther if by the time he
returned in mid-October he had not forgotten his anger and thrown himself
full force back into preaching to the Wittenbergers. Yet his relationship with
the Wittenberg community never remained harmonious for long. The
following year he was already complaining about the 'thick ears' of his
audience and their disdain for both word and sacraments, and about loose
morals when it came to contact between men and women. Within only a
short time, the relationship was so dysfunctional that he turned his back on
his cathedral town and swore he would never return.

When he preached beyond the walls of Wittenberg, Luther was spared such frustration. The people streamed to see and hear the celebrity. When he was in Zwickau in 1522, Luther preached in all the town churches, one after the other, and then also preached from a window at the town hall to the masses who had gathered in the marketplace having travelled in haste from the surrounding district and even from the distant mining towns of Annaberg and Schneeberg. For precisely such occasions the reformer developed a specific form of travel sermon, in which he concentrated on the major and fundamental questions of his Reformation theology such as the two regiments or divine and human justification. He gave one such sermon in 1529 in Marburg, shortly before his return from his abortive discussions with Zwingli about the Lord's Supper.

In Protestantism's Headquarters

With Wittenberg Luther's cathedral town, the reformer's study functioned as the administrative heart of German and European Protestantism. This modestly furnished room located in the first floor of the southern extension, near the family's living quarters,[32] served the reformer for two decades as a locus of intellectual endeavour. Here theological tenets were formulated, here the strands of a Europe-wide communication net intersected, and here advice was disseminated as Luther crafted his responses both to private concerns and needs and to great political matters. No longer was this space occupied by a tormented soul and the scene of theological searching; here instead plans were drawn up for the transformation of Reformation ideas into a new evangelical ordering of church, politics, and society.

Unlike Cranach, friend of Luther and business entrepreneur, in his large artists' workshop nearby, Luther had no army of assistants to call upon. The production of Luther's treatises, sermons, reports, and letters—on occasion a remarkable forty in one day—was almost entirely the author's own work. He might have the assistance of an amanuensis or secretary. That help did not always live up to expectations, as was the case with Wolfgang Seberger, Luther's first secretary, whose fussiness and doziness were the focus of Luther's mockery; others, however, like Georg Rörer and Veit Dietrich proved highly capable when it came to creating order, following discussions, or even stimulating theological thought.

Rörer, just nine years younger than Luther, was also personally close to the reformer. After the death of his first wife, a sister of Bugenhagen's, he lived in the Luther House with his newborn son, Paul, until he remarried. As he could write a form of shorthand, he was able to produce accurate transcriptions of lectures and sermons given by the reformer, which in part he published himself. Later he oversaw and directed the complete Wittenberg edition of Luther's writings. In 1529 he acted as Luther's secretary at the Marburg colloquy, an office he took up again at the request of the elector, who also paid his salary, in 1537, this time in order to provide Luther with assistance for his Bible revisions and to take the minutes at the meetings of the Bible commission. In Jena after Luther's death and the Schmalkaldic War, catastrophic for the Ernestine line, Rörer dedicated himself to the reformer's written legacy and produced another four volumes as part of the Jena Luther edition.

Veit Dietrich acted as Luther's secretary from 1528 until 1534, when he fell out with Katharina over the students' boarding costs. Dietrich was repeatedly called on to provide assistance when the aging reformer was poorly or unwell. He took down letters dictated to him, kept records of important conversations, and organized the storing and archiving of letters and drafts. His transcripts of sermons given by Luther on varying occasions in the circle of his family and friends produced the 'house postile' (*Hauspostille*), which he published in 1544.[33] Luther's final secretary was Johannes Aurifaber, who began work at the Luther House in 1545, accompanied Luther on his last journey, and made a name for himself by being present at Luther's death and as collector and editor of his posthumous publications.

We have a description of Luther's study provided by the reformer himself, in a letter sent to a former fellow Augustinian, Wenzeslaus Linck, in Nuremberg:

> Every day I am so overwhelmed with letters that my table, benches, footstools, desks, windows, chests, boards and everything lie full of letters with questions, causes, complaints, requests etc. The whole weight of the church and the community falls on me for the spiritual and secular office holders perform their duties so badly.[34]

As age and illness began to limit his creative energies, even this indefatigable worker in the vineyard of the Lord had to step back. In summer 1544 he refused a request from Anton Lauterbach, who had long resided with him at the Luther House and was now superintendent at Pirna, for a text on the principles of church discipline. Where was he, 'an exhausted and poor old man', to find the strength and time to undertake such a project, he asked, continuing that he had to write endless letters and that all the world pestered him for treatises and reports—the electoral princes were waiting to receive his written advice on how to tackle drunkenness, particularly widespread at evangelical courts at the time, others wanted him to write for them on clandestine engagements or against the sacramentarians, yet he was also meant to produce a glossary for the whole Bible.[35] When at just this moment the Electoral Saxon chancellor asked Luther to provide a report on Martin Bucer and Philipp Melanchthon's text with plans for the Reformation in the archbishopric of Cologne, Luther brusquely informed him that he was 'fed up with the great prattling I sense here from that blabbermouth Bucer... and have no desire beyond all measure for it. If I am now to read it all, then my gracious lord must give me space until my lack of desire abates.'[36] Old and sick, the reformer only wished to be left in peace to live and fall asleep one final time.[37]

But precisely in these months, as the political outlook for the German Protestants darkened so dramatically, there could be no talk of a peaceful existence. Fearful and apprehensive, Luther had to look on as Emperor Charles V signed the Peace of Crépy with his arch-rival Francis I of France and agreed to a ceasefire with the Turks; with his back now covered, Charles could turn to military action in the Empire against the Protestants, an event to which we will return.

Travelling for Work

The reformer's advice and help were also sought beyond the walls of the town on the Elbe. The daily routines of Wittenberg were therefore repeatedly interrupted by travel, principally within Electoral Saxony but on occasion also to friendly neighbouring territories, to Anhalt, Mansfeld, and, most distant of all, Marburg in 1529. His journeying did not take him beyond Protestant central Germany. In part the Imperial bann, still in place, was responsible for his restricted movement and accounts both for his failure to attend the Imperial diet held in 1530, the 'Confession Diet', when his route to Augsburg was blocked by the Catholic bishoprics in Franconia, and for his decision not to participate at the religious colloquies held in 1540/41 in Hagenau, Regensburg, and Worms. Additionally, however, we can recognize in Luther's itinerary a deliberate concentration on the Electoral Saxon, and soon also Ducal Saxon, heart of German Protestantism, a region that was in effect regarded as the model for evangelical renewal.

The majority of his journeys were short and Luther remained close by Wittenberg while he preached in villages and towns or visited co-workers with whom he was friendly—so, for example, in April 1536 he travelled to Eilenburg to visit Caspar Cruciger, his colleague on the Wittenberg faculty and assistant in the Bible translation, whose second marriage he performed, before giving the wedding sermon the following day; in the 1540s he visited Nikolaus von Amsdorff in Zeitz several times. Most of the time Luther spent away from Wittenberg, however, was given to developing and organizing churches throughout the territory. Initially individual communities approached him with requests for advice and assistance as they drew up evangelical church ordinances. At the end of April and beginning of May 1522 he travelled to a number of locations in Electoral Saxony—Borna, Altenburg, Zwickau, and Torgau—and hardly back in Wittenberg, he left again, on 10 May, to return to Borna and visit Eilenburg. He supplemented, in both breadth and depth, his discussions with the magistrates with programmatic preaching on fundamental Reformation issues such as the appointment of the pastor, marriage, baptism, and good works.

Later, when the principal concern was the creation of a uniform territorial church, the reformer participated in the first great visitation of Electoral Saxony, which required him to travel throughout the electorate. He was accompanied, we should note, by Hans von Metzsch, town captain in Wittenberg, who had no problem with the organizational principles of the Reformation church. From the end of 1528 to the beginning of 1530 the commission visited communities from Grimma and Colditz in the south to Belzig and Brück in the north. The work undertaken away from home was very important, but problems came to the fore in Wittenberg that were the inevitable result of the reformer's prolonged absence. Students turned their backs on the Leucorea in droves because without Luther the provincial university 'at the limits of civilization' held little attraction, especially when Melanchthon was also travelling. The government responded immediately and on 12 March 1529 recalled the reformer from the commission, incidentally along with their official Metzsch, who was urgently needed on account of the construction of the Wittenberg fortifications.[38] As the visitation provided invaluable insight into the realities of parish life, Luther pressed to be allowed to resume his involvement. The Electoral Saxon government agreed, but Luther was to be included only on occasion and only for a few days at a time, as in the case of the visitation of the northern district of the electorate begun on 14 January 1530, when he was permitted to attend only in Belzig and Brück, in order that he could be back in Wittenberg to preach on 22 January.[39]

Requests that reached Luther from outside Electoral Saxony were usually dealt with by letter or via a suitable pastor, often one of Luther's students. If the matter concerned somewhere in central Germany, however, he would frequently travel in person—for example in 1521 he travelled to Wörlitz to advise the three princes of Anhalt on the reformation of their churches and to preach before them. In 1539, Duke George, Luther's opponent in Ducal Saxony, was succeeded by his brother Henry, who immediately called for a change of course that would lead into evangelical waters. Luther oversaw in person the introduction of the Reformation in Leipzig that Whitsun. At the site of his bitter defeat by Johannes Eck two decades earlier, Luther now gained the upper hand at last. Similarly, in Naumburg in January 1542, in the presence of the elector, Luther consecrated his long-standing Wittenberg colleague Nikolaus von Amsdorff as the first evangelical bishop of the bishopric of Naumburg-Zeitz, at the same time using his authority to open up the territory belonging to the bishopric to intervention from Electoral Saxony.

Again and again Luther had to travel to the Electoral Saxon court—some forty times to Torgau and on occasion also to Weimar. There he acted for the princely family as both pastor and spiritual adviser, at weddings, for the baptisms of children, in times of sickness or death. He preached to the court, and to its guests and political allies—in Torgau, for example, in 1528 to Christian II of Denmark, in 1531 to Duke Henry of Saxony, the great hope of the Protestants in the neighbouring Albertine territories, and in 1536 even to an embassy from Ferdinand, Catholic King of the Romans and brother of the Emperor.

As we will see in greater detail, Luther was also employed as a counsellor in political affairs at the court, for in these years such matters usually had a religious dimension. While it has been proposed that after 1525 and as a result of his stance during the Peasants' War and the death of his patron Frederick the Wise Luther lost influence or standing with the Saxon government, his itinerary certainly suggests otherwise. In spring 1526 he was drawn into the negotiations for the alliance with Philip of Hesse. When the Protestation at Speyer in 1529 and the Augsburg Confession of the following year established definitively that two hostile confessions now existed within the Empire, Luther's advice for the government of Electoral Saxony became indispensable, for no one could represent the evangelical faith and the organization of church and world that stemmed from that faith more authentically than the reformer himself. He was, and he remained, the greatest human and cultural capital that Saxony could invest in its ecclesiastical and Imperial politics. As a worthy space was required at court for the representation of the new, renewed ecclesiastical order, Elector John Frederick had a new church built, intended specifically for evangelical preaching, at the castle of Hartenfels, his Torgau residence, which he arranged for Luther himself to consecrate, in October 1544. When the estates had decisions to make on religious matters, Luther was just as indispensable to the diet as he was to the court. In March 1528, along with his colleagues Bugenhagen and Jonas, he undertook an arduous winter journey to the territorial diet at Altenburg, where possible imminent Catholic military action was discussed. The reports on which the threat was based soon proved groundless, a deception cunningly constructed by the Ducal Saxon councillor Otto von Pack, who hoped his financial problems would be solved by betraying—or better yet, selling—word of an offensive Catholic alliance in Breslau to easily excited Landgrave Philip of Hesse. At the end of the 1520s the Empire seemed to be on the brink of religious war. Fortunately, Luther had kept a level head when he appeared at the diet and had succeeded in discouraging the prince and the estates from a pre-emptive first strike, arguing that the Bible only allowed the use of force in self-defence, as a response to an actual attack. Later he was called on to attend such political deliberations all the more frequently, both in Weimar and repeatedly in Schmalkalden in Hesse, where he was present at meetings of the leadership of the Schmalkaldic League, formed in 1530 to defend Protestantism.

But the reformer's longest journeys, in terms of both distance covered and time away from Wittenberg, were undertaken for the confessional cause. In autumn 1529 he travelled to Marburg in the landgraviate of Hesse for the religious colloquy with Zwingli, and the following spring he went to Coburg, on the south-western edge of the electoral state, bordering Catholic Franconia, where he stayed until October to observe the Imperial diet at Augsburg from the last safe vantage point for a man still under Imperial bann. We should not forget that conditions for travel at the time meant these trips were strenuous and time-consuming. Travel to Marburg, for example, took all of the second half of September and involved stops in Torgau, Grimma, Altenburg, Jena, Weimar, Erfurt, Gotha, Eisenach, and from Creuzburg on the Werra on into Hesse. After four days of discussion, from 1 to 4 October, the return journey was immediately launched. On the evening of 18 October, so after a journey lasting over a month, the reformer and his travelling companions were home again.

Luther also repeatedly brought words of consolation to ailing colleagues who were also his friends and to poorly princes. In summer 1534, for example, he journeyed to Prince Joachim of Anhalt-Dessau, and in 1540 to Melanchthon, when his friend became extremely unwell on that journey to the religious colloquy at Hagenau.

Travel for travel's sake or for relaxation was as uncommon for the Wittenberger as it was for the majority of his contemporaries. At the beginning of 1540 he had purchased for his wife the estate of Zöllsdorf south of Leipzig, where Katharina and the children would then often stay. Luther rarely found the time to make the journey, which took around a day and a half from Wittenberg. At the end of 1531, so overworked that it was evident to everyone, he accepted an invitation from Hans von Löser, the Saxon marshal, to recuperate and 'to drive away the buzzing and weariness of my head through physical exercise'[40] at Löser's castle at Pretzsch, half a day's travel up the Elbe from Wittenberg. The nobleman had in mind the pleasures of the hunt, yet the reformer preferred not to join the company of the hunters but instead to contemplate the goodness of God and to relax to the magnificent words of Psalm 147:

> Praise the Lord, O Jerusalem! Praise your God, O Zion!
> For He strengthens the bars of your gates; He blesses your sons within you.
> He makes peace in your borders; He fills you with the finest of the wheat.
> He send forth His command to the earth; His Word runs swiftly.
> He gives snow like wool; He scatters hoarfrost like ashes.
> He casts forth His ice like morsels; who can stand before His cold?
> He sends forth His Word, and melts them; He makes His wind blow, and the
>   waters flow.[41]

Recording his thoughts in writing evidently also contributed to Luther's recuperation. His exposition of the Psalms, written in the midst of nature, was published by mid-January 1532, with a dedication to his host that was in effect a thank-you for his short holiday in the beauty of God's nature.[42] In years to come, Luther would repeatedly stay with the marshal, but he never saw such a break as an opportunity to forget his duties as a theologian; to the contrary, it was a time to meet the responsibilities of his office by expounding the word or administering the sacraments.

In light of Luther's ties to Wittenberg as his *stabilitas loci*, one journey stands out markedly. At the end of July 1545 the reformer left his 'cathedral city' on a search for a suitable place to which to move. He informed his wife from Zeitz, the first stop on his flight from Wittenberg, 'I shall be on the move, and will rather eat the bread of a beggar than torture and upset my poor old [age] and final days with the filth at Wittenberg which destroys my hard and faithful work.'[43] His reference was evidently to his differences, already noted, with influential circles in Wittenberg over the concrete form evangelical faith and life should take. Magistrates and university leadership tended to take a stance on such issues that was more pragmatic than the reformer liked, for Luther was adamant about the moral radicalism of the Gospel. As he fled, he painted a dark prophetic vision for his wife:

> As things are run in Wittenberg, perhaps the people there will acquire not only the dance of St. Vitus or St. John, but the dance of the beggars or the dance of Beelzebub, since they have started to bare women and maidens in front and back, and there is no one who punishes or objects. In addition the Word of God is being mocked. Away from this Sodom!

He gave his wife instructions to sell up all they owned and move to the family estate at Zöllsdorf in order that during his lifetime he could be sure she would have a secure existence as a widow, for he believed that after his death 'the four elements at Wittenberg certainly will not tolerate you'.

In the weeks that followed his departure from Wittenberg, Luther made his way through central Germany, to friends such as the von Schönfelds at the castle of Löbnitz by Düben, who were indebted to Luther because he had taken in Margarete von Schönfeld in Wittenberg when she fled the monastery along with his future wife, Katharina; to merchant Scherl in Leipzig; to colleagues such as Amsdorff in Zeitz, Jonas in Halle, and Joachim Camerarius, professor in Leipzig, who provided him with accommodation on his second visit to the university town. Yet even as he fled, he remained true to himself and retained his active commitment to building up the evangelical church. He preached regularly; in Zeitz he took part in the interrogation of Naumburg cathedral preacher Georg Mohr, who had been accused of being too close to the hostile Catholic canons of the cathedral chapter; he inducted the new evangelical bishop George of Anhalt to the bishopric of Merseburg; and he also took the opportunity to end the scandal caused by a member of the cathedral chapter's living with a woman to whom he was not married—by presiding at the marriage of the couple himself.

The background to and specific reasons for Luther's flight were not as obvious as his letter to his wife suggests. All we do know for certain is that the reformer was unhappy with circumstances in Wittenberg. He sent that message with its typical unbridled anger and flood of abuse evidently counting on his wife to make his feelings known in Wittenberg and at the court. His closest colleagues doubted that the letter, which Katharina passed on to them, contained the real reasons for his peculiar behaviour. Highly principled man that he was, poor Melanchthon immediately sought in himself a cause for his mighty friend's anger. To keep the court fully informed, Melanchthon travelled to chancellor Gregor Brück in Torgau, and Brück then raised the alarm at court. The chancellor could not resist the opportunity to scoff a little: somewhat smugly he informed the elector that the sale of home and property would not be easily achieved, for even Wittenbergers 'who do not have such valuable houses and property to sell as he does' had not been finding buyers.[44]

But in light of his intense temperament and readiness to display the anger of a divine prophet, with Luther anything was possible. Everyone at court knew that his departure from Wittenberg would rock the electorate, and what was more, Melanchthon had also threatened to leave. Elector John Frederick may well have groaned inwardly at the escapades of his star professors, but he still did all he could to calm the stormy waters. He immediately set Matthias Ratzenberger, his personal physician, to Zeitz with a letter for Luther that not only expressed his concern but was also kindly framed, and he also had Ratzenberger present evidence of agreement with Melanchthon, showing concrete arrangements were in place should Luther come around. On one hand, the letter noted the elector's concern about the potential risk if Luther, still under Imperial bann, were to travel in the vicinity of Catholic territories without an electoral escort. On the other hand, the letter put to Luther that it had been impossible to tackle his complaints about the Wittenbergers because he had not laid them out sufficiently clearly. Both letter and ambassador left Luther in no doubt that the elector would do all he could to fulfil Luther's wishes and that he would do his prince and his territory a 'particular favour' if he would 'return to us and again to Wittenberg'.[45]

We do not know the details of the negotiations and their outcome. Ratzenberger's accounts suggest that he met Luther in Merseburg and brought him back to the court at Torgau with a protective escort. From there the reformer then finally returned to his cathedral town and to his family, arriving home in the late evening of 17 August or in the night on 18 August. His return brought to an end an episode that, viewed objectively, seems to have had its origins not so much in the failures of the people of

Wittenberg as in the burdens of old age and in distress caused by a contrary world, specifically the detested Council of Trent, whose opening loomed. The electoral regime's robust assurances of future support in times of trouble would have made Luther's return easier. Even more important, however, was the entreaty that Luther recognize that at this delicate moment—the estates in Worms were in the midst of discussing evangelical participation at the papal council, against which Luther had fought so hard—nothing would incite so much 'jubilation . . . amongst those opposed to the word of God' as a permanent rift between Luther and the town so associated with his Reformation.[46]

Wittenberg's Theology, between Rome and Zurich

Between 1515 and 1520 the young Luther had achieved all that was necessary in terms of theological innovation or any other form of theoretic breakthrough; now that new evangelical theology was to be nurtured and brought on. On one hand such cultivation involved the assertion and legitimization of Luther's theology against the theology of Rome, in a challenge to both medieval tradition, which the Wittenbergers rejected as unscriptural, and the new anti-Protestant theology employed by the Roman Church as a weapon in the battle against Luther's teachings. On the other hand, this fostering required the erection of a barrier that would protect Luther's theology from aberrant teachings within the Reformation camp. The conflict with the 'false brothers' largely took a backseat, other than in the case of the Anabaptists and their creation of a New Jerusalem in the Westphalian cathedral town of Münster in the early 1530s. Since the late 1520s the principal quarrels had been with the evangelicals of southern Germany and the Swiss Confederation who developed and aggressively promoted a variant of Protestant theology that was clearly distinct from that of Luther. Huldrych Zwingli in Zurich and Martin Bucer in Strasburg had been at the forefront of that movement, but from the late 1530s that role fell increasingly to French exile John Calvin. Calvin was first active in Strasburg and Basel as a member of relatively small exile communities, but after his return to Geneva in the 1540s he established a Reformed model of the church, soon termed 'Calvinist', that in western Europe and eastern Central Europe rivalled, and was in part more successful than, the Wittenberg model.

Disputing Theology

Having been nourished by debate as he grew into a reformer, Luther was ready to take on all these challenges, and he responded with energy and passion. In the process he and his opponents laid the foundations of early modern 'controversial theology'—focused on, and thus intensifying, the differences between the various churches—which in Germany in particular would deeply influence the culture of the word, both written and spoken, until well into the next century. The mediation attempted by humanists with their *'via media'* theology, which had in mind a compromise between Protestant and Catholic renewal, had only limited impact and in the end was crushed between confessional fronts. Given the atmosphere, the religious colloquies that the politicians repeatedly urged the theologians to hold could only fail. Luther participated in person at only one such gathering, the Marburg colloquy held in 1529, where the Lord's Supper was discussed with the Reformed theologians of the Swiss Confederation and southern Germany. His recognition while in Marburg that even members of the evangelical camp remained obdurate in the face of his truth only strengthened Luther's iron resolve to defend and enforce the exclusivity of that truth. He laid no stock in religious colloquies involving Roman theologians and therefore could confidently leave them to Melanchthon, who represented Wittenberg theology at these and similar gatherings.

Whenever theologians from the Roman camp threw down the gauntlet, Luther was ready to pick it up. We have already heard of his debates of the early 1520s with Eck, Cochläus, and members of the theological faculty at Louvain, and later, too, he gave significant time to defining his position against that of his opponents. As products of the Enlightenment and secularization, and with the devastating ideological conflicts of the twentieth century still all too vivid to us, we are historically divorced from this controversial theology, born in the disputes between the reformer and his opponents, which repeatedly broke out in new exchanges until into the seventeenth century. As we recognize its contribution to the suffering and chaos of the religious and political wars of that earlier age, our aversion and incomprehension will likely grow, but for Luther such disagreement offered a welcome vehicle for bringing his truth to the public with uncompromising clarity and for purifying his message of any ambiguity or possible misinterpretation. In terms of ecclesiastical politics such contestation was not productive. Every emphasis on or intensification of disparity only complicated attempts to bridge differences or to ensure, at least, that they did not become poisonous. The reformer was willing to run that risk, even heighten the danger, for he believed that in matters of faith and belief any compromise could be noxious. He feared the opportunity for salvation for both himself and the world, rediscovered after such long agonies of the soul, might be squandered, and therefore grasped unhesitatingly every opportunity for debate that would signpost the path that must be taken, no matter how devastating the results for the transitory earthly world might be.

Luther's opponents shared his opinion entirely and acted just as he did. These debates therefore honed not just Lutheran theology but also papal theology, and as a result they laid the spiritual foundations of the early modern Roman Catholic confessional church, which took shape in parallel to the Protestant churches. The works produced by Luther's opponents had real substance. Alongside a rethinking of priestly life and devotion, the Roman Church also took theology in new directions. Innovation was especially evident in Spain, where church reform had already begun in the fifteenth century. At the university at Salamanca a theologically renewed scholasticism flourished. Dominicans Francisco de Vitoria and Bartolomé de Las Casas, born in 1483 and 1484 respectively and thus of an age with Luther, explored new theological questions not as part of an existential search for individual salvation, as Luther had done, but under the impact of the revolutionary discovery of unknown cultures and non-Christian peoples in south America. The debates generated by Luther's new theological paradigm brought a new dynamic and greater potency to medieval scholastic theology. After the initial breakthrough of the years 1517 to 1520, Luther sharpened his reformed theology in the heated disputes of the 1520s, 1530s, and 1540s, but at the same time his opponents, too, honed their teachings and the definition of their Rome-loyal theology.

Luther's confrontations with Johannes Eck, Cardinal Cajetan, Johannes Cochläus, and the faculties of theology at Cologne and Louvain—and these are just the adversaries we have already encountered—led to clarification of central theological issues by both sides as they tackled topics such as penance, purgatory, the value of the history of the church, and above all the basis for and nature of papal authority. Melanchthon's *Loci communes* of 1521, a comprehensive account of Reformation teachings, was followed in 1525 by the corresponding handbook for the medieval tradition, Johannes Eck's *Enchiridion locorum communium*, on Roman theology. Cajetan refined his existing work on scriptural interpretation the mediatory role of the church in the salvation of the faithful and faced criticism from the orthodox within his own camp as a result. The theological faculty at the university in Louvain was not in as bad shape as the biased comments of the reformer suggested, a verdict that later generations accepted unquestioningly. In their debates with Luther and the theology of Wittenberg, the theologians of Louvain crafted the pillars of the early modern Roman confessional church. While in 1521 it had been easy for Luther to make Jacobus Latomus, who betrayed a lack of skill,[47] seem ridiculous; in Latomus' colleague Johannes Driedo, several times dean and rector at Louvain, Luther faced an opponent of a different cut. Beyond the dispute with Luther, Driedo's anti-Protestant controversial theology brought a redefinition of the theological and organizational underpinnings of his own church that would be taken up at the Council of Trent and declared canonical. This innovation can be seen in Driedo's account of the sinner's ability to receive faith and grace through inborn reason and free will and in his work on the relationship between Scripture, tradition, and doctrinal authority and on the redemptive work of Christ.

When it came to debating the sacraments, no less a figure than Henry VIII, king of England, entered the fray against Luther. As we have seen, in 'On the Babylonian Captivity of the Church', Luther had attacked Roman sacramental teachings, accepting only the three core sacraments of baptism, the Lord's Supper, and confession/penance as legitimate. In so doing he had sharply rejected the traditional *ex opere operato* doctrine, the thesis that the holy sacraments required no human effort to be efficacious, and had declared instead that the sacramental blessing was dependent on the faith of the recipient. In his 'Defence of the Seven Sacraments against Martin Luther' (*Assertio septem sacramentorum adversus Martinum Lutherum*), published in London in 1521, the English king rejected Luther's position and thereby prepared the ground for the permanent canonical status of all seven sacraments within the Roman confessional church; the sacramental teaching of the medieval church had only established that number incidentally. The pope expressed his gratitude by presenting Henry VIII with the Golden Rose and title of *defensor fidei*, defender of the faith, the greatest honour Rome could give to a layperson.

The flood of controversial theological writings launched by Luther and the Reformation did not result in only confrontation and conflict. As each side propelled the other on, Protestant and Catholic teachings were fortified in a process that elucidated in turn the spiritual and cultural foundations of the modern age.[48]

Against Erasmus and Humanist Free Will

The most significant debate, with ramifications still felt today, was sparked by questions about the extent and nature of human will, an issue that went to the anthropological heart of both Roman and Reformation theology. Luther's opponent was no less a towering figure than Erasmus of Rotterdam (Figure 34) to whose humanist and optimistic declaration on the freedom of the will, he had responded with his treatise on the bondage of the human will, the logical consequence of his Reformation by-faith-alone theology, which was constructed on a pessimistic image of humanity—humans, Luther insisted, can achieve nothing by their own efforts. With this issue fundamental to both Reformation and Roman theology, Luther was bound to be drawn into debate, and he participated with not only philosophical and theological clarity but also biting irony.

In the course of his dispute with Erasmus, with unwavering radicalism Luther intensified objections to works righteousness that he had raised in his early Reformation writings and to the humanists' associated optimistic image of humanity. He had drawn an ineradicable line in the sand. Again, as the parties debated each defined its position, on this occasion determining with great clarity two fundamentally different positions on the role of humanity in this world, particularly politically and socially, and on human capability.

Luther's dispute with Erasmus in 1525/26 over the freedom, or lack of freedom, of the human will documents his command of the central theological and philosophical issues, but it also demonstrates that the reformer had his finger on the pulse of his times, knowing just when to make their differences public. The stridency of the language can be alienating for today's reader. Contemporaries were horrified even by the announcement of Luther's forthcoming work. Heinrich Stromer, personal physician to the archbishop of Mainz, who actively sought reconciliation, prophesized 'a great future tragedy'.[49] Yet for Luther the polemic was advantageous, even necessary, for it undermined other approaches, including well-intentioned obfuscation.

The first move was made by Luther's opponents, who felt challenged to refute the theological essence of the Reformation positions developed in Luther's great treatises of 1520. They sought an unimpeachable authority the

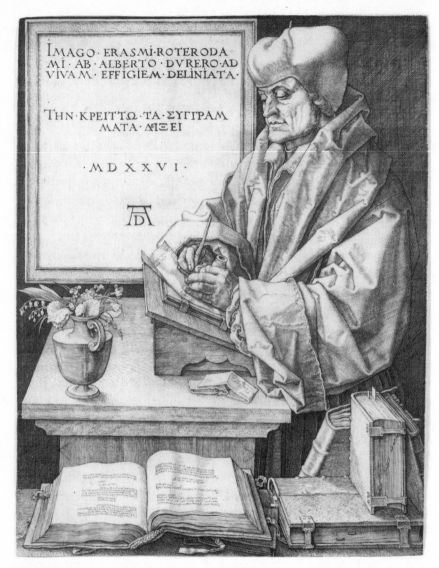

Figure 34. Erasmus of Rotterdam, by Albrecht Dürer, engraving, Nuremberg, 1526.

equal of, even superior to, the Wittenberger, and who better then than Erasmus, the leading light of the humanists who had preceded Luther as a media star, as we might say today, a role he had in some respects invented. Erasmus long baulked at the task, but his early sympathies for the reformer, which he had continued to express to Pope Leo X even after Luther had been declared a heretic,[50] cooled significantly. Additionally, he was increasingly alarmed by what he saw as the attention-grabbing popularist behaviour of the former Augustinian monk. Above all, Erasmus was irritated that Luther's intrepid public performance had forced him to quit his Basel bolt-hole, where, behind closed doors, he had been able to pour elegant scorn on Rome without further consequences.[51] When it came time to show his colours, step-by-step he distanced himself from Luther. He even broke off his correspondence with Melanchthon, with whom he was close on many issues, for over four years.

Before 1525 their differences had not yet been made public in printed texts or programmatic debate; both parties had limited themselves to pointed barbs in letters or private conversation. It was the kind of half-public quarrel within humanist circles that was typical of the times, at least until Luther's appearance created a new and broader public. Luther continued for several years to position himself indirectly in the debate with Erasmus, knowing that comments made to friends or students either orally or in writing would be passed on and would eventually reach his opponent.

As a young humanist, Joachim Camerarius, Luther's colleague at the philosophical faculty in Wittenberg, felt equally drawn to both the reformer and Erasmus. When, in spring 1524, Camerarius travelled to Basel, Luther used the opportunity to re-establish direct contact with Erasmus. He began the letter that Camerarius carried with him by noting that although he had expected Erasmus, 'as the greater and older man', to end the silence, he, out of charity, would make a beginning. What followed in his letter, however, was no offer to enter into discussion of the facts, let alone an attempt at reconciliation. Erasmus was again accused of timidity and moral cowardice in the face of Rome. Above all the Wittenberger's claims to possess a superior truth could not be missed. Admittedly, he wrote, 'the affair has progressed to such a stage that there is little danger to be feared for our cause, even if Erasmus should fight us with all his might', but he advised Erasmus to keep silent, noting, 'There is quite a difference between being stung once by Erasmus and being attacked simultaneously by all the papists.' Luther required from Erasmus nothing other than capitulation and intellectual self-abandonment. 'If the Lord defers giving this [disposition] to you', he continued to Erasmus, 'then I ask you, if you can do nothing else, in the meantime to be only a spectator of our tragedy', refraining from further interference.[52]

As even Lutheran church historians must admit,[53] the letter was hard and almost too much. Luther could not have believed that an approach of this ilk would foster the neutrality of the highly respected but notoriously sensitive and vain Erasmus. Was the letter, then, a product of the naivety of a new celebrity obsessed with his own version of the truth—surely how Luther appeared to the long-established leader of European intellectuals? We have reason to doubt that interpretation and to identify behind the apparent impetuosity a deliberateness that always determined Luther's actions—the new Reformation truth was to be taken to the public, cost what it might, and any attempt to dilute that message must be frustrated.

Luther again got what he wanted. Erasmus did not address the personal attack and very deliberately insisted that for him, too, the Gospel was at the heart of the matter. However, when he received Luther's outrageous letter, he was already working on a refutation of the audacious Augustinian monk, encouraged not least by crowned heads of Europe who included Emperor Charles, Henry VIII of England, and Duke George of Saxony. His highly praised 'On Free Will' (*De libero arbitrio*), which with humanist erudition championed the freedom of the will, could therefore be published very quickly to clarify his position; it was already available in summer 1524. Luther then responded with 'On the Bondage of the Will' (*De servo arbitrio*). A public debate, ultimately unavoidable, was launched, and Luther had the undivided attention of the leading minds of Europe as he laid out for them the essence of his rediscovered evangelical theology.

In the end, Erasmus had no real choice if he wanted to avoid appearing to sympathize with the heretic, or, worse still, to support him actively. During a stay in Louvain he had already heard his philological-historical critical methods vilified in public lectures as the soil from which the rebellion had sprung. In a complaint to the rector he had asserted that he was neither prosecutor, nor patron, nor judge of Luther, but the conservatives' growing suspicions were not to be quelled by his avowals. In Cologne the Dominicans had already banished Erasmus' works from their library. It was impossible not to recognize that every day that passed without the required reckoning with Luther was another day of suspicions stoked.

Once 'On Free Will' had appeared, the politically minded members of the Roman Church could breathe more freely, especially as the work was immediately praised highly in philosophical and intellectual circles. Erasmus had charged full on at Lutheran theology, with an attack on the Reformation teaching of justification by faith alone and its essential assumption that anything deliberately done by a human for the sake of his or her salvation was essentially sinful. Where Luther, joined by Melanchthon in his *Loci communes* of 1521, condemned the concept of the freedom of the human will as a defilement of the Gospel by heathen philosophy, Erasmus emphasized the ties between theology and philosophy, between faith and reason. Where the reformers saw free will as the antithesis of divine predestination and as a belittlement of Christ's redemptive act, the humanists justified free will and cemented its significance. Erasmus had written, 'By free choice . . . we mean a power of the human will by which a man can apply himself to the things which lead to eternal salvation, or turn away from them.'[54] Certainly his interpretation no longer took the somewhat naïve form that had appeared in his paraphrase of the Letter to the Romans of 1517—which had been mocked in Wittenberg as theological dilettantism—because in that work, as its author would eventually concede, free will had been inserted into his paraphrase. He now formulated a middle position, which agreed with Luther as far as it identified the precedence of grace but also left room for human effort, which Luther denied absolutely. Just as the reformer believed the provision of grace to be inalienable for it was solely and absolutely the work of God, the humanist insisted on personal responsibility as the basis of his positive anthropology, which defined humans in light of reason. He could not conceive of human responsibility either philosophically or theologically without freedom of the will and freedom of choice.

Erasmus had set out his treatment in his 'diatribe or discourse on the freedom of the will' and elegantly drew his reader into his chain of thought. Erasmus himself ensured that his real addressees knew of his text, for he sent the work, along with a friendly cover letter, to Wittenberg, although not to Luther, but to Melanchthon. In a letter dated 30 September, the latter responded by expressing his joy in seeing their common rejection of the radical position adopted in Zurich and held out the prospect of a sympathetic reception by Luther and a tempered response.[55]

In similar cases, Luther's response could be expected by return of post, but in this instance both supporters and opponents had to wait over a year to learn of the reformer's reaction. The delay can undoubtedly be attributed to the rush of events surrounding the Peasants' War and Luther's marriage, but trepidation about the finality of the imminent break also played its part. That trepidation did not run counter to the outspoken tone of the letter sent to Erasmus the previous year, for there only the theological competence of the Rotterdamer was at issue, while his philological and editorial achievements were for Luther beyond doubt. Luther would have doubtlessly read Erasmus' explication of free will immediately, but he only

dipped his own pen into the inkwell to reply after Joachim Camerarius
wrote to Katharina asking that she urge her husband to compose a reply, or
so Luther recalled in a Table Talk from 1540.[56] When he did set to, Luther
wrote with no hesitation or trace of reticence. There was no longer any
thought of sparing his highly respected opponent, or of any moderation in
either argument or language. All that counted now was the truth and on that
point he neither would nor could admit 'that Erasmus has suggested anything that is correct'.[57]

Luther's treatise 'On the Bondage of the Will', the first substantial text he
wrote after the Peasants' War and his marriage, appeared in December 1525,
initially in Latin, but followed only a few weeks later by a German version
prepared, evidently in parallel to the Latin text, by Justus Jonas.[58] The title
alone was a powerful blow against Erasmus and those amongst the humanists
who sympathized with Rome. Luther's introductory explanation of his
surprising long silence—he had seemed 'not only willing to accept, but
eager to seek out, opportunities of this kind for writing'—led immediately
into a general attack. That he had said nothing did not stem from fear of
Erasmus, whom he awarded without hesitation 'a palm such as I have never
yielded to anyone before ... you are far superior to me in powers of
eloquence and native genius'. He explained, 'it was, then, neither pressure
of work, nor the difficulty of the task, nor your great eloquence, for any fear
of you, but sheer disgust, anger, and contempt, or—to put it plainly—my
considered judgment on your Diatribe that damped my eagerness to answer
you.' In Luther's view, Erasmus had used 'rich ornaments of eloquence' to
convey trash, 'like refuse or ordure being carried in gold and silver vases'.[59]
The principal section followed step-by-step Erasmus' argument, producing
a comprehensive but rather uneven text. But the treatment of the subject
matter itself was then all the more rigorous and securely anchored, following
a tried and tested strategy that avoided any whiff of concession and gave no
space to terminology or argument that might suggest to an opponent that
contrary positions could be reconciled.

'On the Bondage of the Will' was the fanfare that announced the full-out
Reformation assault on the optimistic illusion which, empowered by innate
reason and their ability to do good, humans could achieve salvation unaided.
In future there could be no thought of explaining away the differences
between the 'old' Roman theology and the 'new' evangelical theology as
inconsequential. Where humanists and supporters of Rome found comfort
in the possibility that humans could achieve perfection, Luther found peace

for his soul precisely in despair, for in that existential abyss, indeed only in that existential abyss, could he experience the unfathomable grace of God:

> Admittedly, it gives the greatest possible offense to common sense or natural reason that God by his own sheer will should abandon, harden, and damn men as if he enjoyed the sins and the vast, eternal torments of his wretched creatures, when he is preached as a God of such great mercy and goodness, etc.... I myself was offended more than once, and brought to the very depth and abyss of despair, so that I wished I had never been created a man, before I realized how salutary that despair was, and how near to grace.... Nothing has been achieved by them [attempts to defend the goodness of God] except that the ignorant have been imposed upon by empty talk and 'contradictions of what is falsely called knowledge'. Nevertheless, there has always remained deeply implanted in the hearts of ignorant and learned alike...the painful awareness that we are under necessity if the foreknowledge and omnipotence of God are accepted.... They [all men] are quickly compelled by inescapable logic to admit that just as we do not come into being by our own will, but by necessity, so we do not do anything by right of free choice, but as God has foreknown and as he leads us to act by his infallible and immutable counsel and power.... There is no such thing as free choice, though this fact is obscured by the many arguments to the contrary and the great authority of all the men who for so many centuries have taught differently.[60]

As the Reformation message penetrated the philosopher's obfuscation of the truth, humankind's absolute dependency on God was again revealed. And thus the dispute with Erasmus had, in Luther's eyes, fulfilled its purpose. He did not respond to the two further pamphlets composed by Erasmus in defence of the freedom of the will. In 1537, when a complete edition of his works was being planned in Strasburg, Luther wrote that he considered 'really a book of mine' only 'On the Bondage of the Will' and his catechism.[61] The Lutheran doctrine of the unfree will appeared in both the 'Instructions for the Visitors of Parish Pastors in Electoral Saxony' of 1528 and the Augsburg Confession of 1530, although in the somewhat attenuated form deployed by Melanchthon, the humanist, to call off the dispute between Erasmus and Luther without abandoning Reformation theology.

Today, to those of us who take the capacity for human reason as a given, Erasmus' position may well appear more plausible, and certainly more sympathetic. With an eye to how Luther can be put to work today, church leaders may be tempted to temper the uncompromising character of the reformer's thought precisely on this issue, or to pass it off as historically contingent. To do so, however, is to fail to recognize that the anthropology

of the modern era followed only from the destruction of traditional, theologically legitimized self-confidence and the unconditional rejection of all
human claims to self-sanctification, and that this new dynamic altered the
very foundations of church, state, and society. Awareness that humankind
lives in circumstances over which it has no control, a recognition often
voiced in the disorientating crises of the modern world, can be placed more
readily at Luther's door than at Erasmus'. For all that, however, we must also
recognize that for Luther evil was never an abstract; evil was the concrete
work of the devil. On that point Luther was anything but modern.

The Real Presence of Christ on Earth—The Lord's Supper and Baptism

Luther's life with the devil as the absolute enemy of God was for him utterly
real, but just as real for him was Christ as the reconciling power of God not
just in sacred history but also in events of this world. From that reality emerged
his understanding of Christ's presence in the sacraments, an issue on which it
would prove impossible to build consensus within the Protestant camp.
Differences were particularly marked when it came to the Lord's Supper,
but baptism was also contested. All the reformers shared Luther's criticism of
the complex sacramental doctrine of the papal church, which he had already
expressed in 1520 in his reform treatise 'On the Babylonian Captivity of the
Church', and the majority embraced his view that of the seven traditional
sacraments of the church only baptism, the Lord's Supper, and penance were
legitimate.[62] At the same time, however, his theological explanation of the
new evangelical teaching on the sacraments immediately met with objections.
The fundamental dependence of the sacramental agency of baptism and the
Lord's Supper on the theology of justification was not in question, nor was
there any doubt amongst reformers about the doctrine that emerged from the
link to justification that meant that the sacraments could only affect salvation if
they were received with faith in the grace of God. The critics' concern was
that Luther had not gone far enough. They insisted that the implications for
how the Protestant sacraments should be both defined and practised were far
more radical than Luther was willing to allow.

The first objections were directed at the immediate baptism of newborn
infants, a practice retained in Wittenberg as completely self-evident.
Disagreement was voiced by the 'false brothers' in Saxony and Thuringia
and also, particularly strongly, by the Anabaptist movement that emerged

in Zurich and in certain locations within the Empire. Luther's opponents
could invoke the infants' lack of faith, which they had not yet acquired, for
Luther himself had made faith a condition of the salvific effect of the
sacraments. They were equally opposed to the demonological elements,
in particular exorcism, which were preserved in the first version of the
Wittenberg baptismal rites, published in 1523. Luther had retained the
banishment of the devil from the soul of the newborn child as an element
of the ritual only out of consideration for those whose evangelical convictions were weaker, and he was therefore able to strike it without any
difficulty when he reworked the 'Small Book on Baptism' (*Taufbüchlein*) in
1526. But infant baptism was an altogether different matter. On this issue
he was ready to go to battle. Theological treatments of the issue intended
for a popular audience, such as the pamphlet 'On Rebaptism, to Two
Pastors' (*Von der Wiedertaufe an zwei Pfarrherrn*) of 1528, provided him with
one weapon, but he also armed himself with his Small Catechism, published in 1529. Its fourth section, 'The Sacrament of Holy Baptism', had
the subheading, 'In a simple way in which the head of a house is to present
it to the household'; this simple way took the form of questions and
answers, as in:

> What gifts or benefits does baptism grant?
>
> Answer: It brings about forgiveness of sins, redeems from death and the devil,
> and gives eternal salvation to all who believe it, as the words and promise of
> God declare.[63]

Through his catechism, the guiding principle used by Luther to counter all
rationalizing criticism of child baptism was thus passed down from generation to generation, through instruction in the church and at home. The rest
was the work of the grandiose visualizations of Jesus' concern for children
produced in Cranach's workshop, seen by a broad public and therefore able
to leave a deep imprint in the Lutheran consciousness. Even in the secularized present, almost nothing brings people into church like the wish to have
their children baptized before family and friends.

Most of the reformers, including Zwingli, shared Luther's theological
explanation of child baptism. Protestant authorities insisted child baptism be
continued, not least because it provided the simplest means of monitoring
how the population was growing or shrinking and of controlling the sexual
behaviour of their subjects. Anabaptism, whose followers believed only adult

baptism legitimate, remained on the margins, although the movement did survive, largely underground, throughout the Empire and Europe. No baptism meant no entry in the register of baptisms, the only demographically useful record produced in the early modern, pre-statistical world; when Anabaptists then also refused to bear arms, their isolation was complete. To their contemporaries Anabaptists had become enemies of the state.

Disagreement over the Lord's Supper played out differently. The nature of communion was the principal point of contention amongst Reformation theologians, and that disparity was evident in the varied forms of Reformation worship and community life. For decades internal Protestant disputes over the Lord's Supper were repeatedly rekindled and stoked with great learning, but also with a brutal ruthlessness that could result in the expulsion of those who dissented. The argument over the Lord's Supper overlapped at points with the dispute with the humanists over the free, or unfree, will. Luther's antithesis was Huldrych Zwingli, the Zurich reformer and humanist, who left no room for a sacral meaning and wanted the Lord's Supper to be understood in rational inner-worldly terms.

Luther's redefinition of the Lord's Supper had two central elements: first, the administration of the 'lay chalice', which meant that the wine, and therefore the blood of Christ, was no longer reserved for the priest but was available to the whole community as they participated in the Lord's Supper, another logical consequence of the priesthood of all believers; secondly, the radical rejection of transubstantiation, the essential transformation of the earthly bread and wine into the heavenly body and heavenly blood of Christ, which remains constitutive of the Mass as celebrated in the Catholic Church today. The decisive distinction from the Catholic Church was, and remains, transubstantiation; the lay chalice, by contrast, could, and still can, be permitted by Rome, as it was in the fifteenth century for the descendants of the Hussites, in the sixteenth century at times in German lands in order to keep the Reformation at bay, and also today on special occasions or in special circumstances. Both the lay chalice and the rejection of transubstantiation were common to all Protestants, but for a group of reformers that was not enough, not for spiritualists such as Müntzer, Karlstadt, or Schwenckfeld and not for those strongly influenced by humanism such as Johannes Oecolampadius in Basel or Zwingli in Zurich. They demanded the elimination of all magical and sacral elements in the sacraments, which were, they believed, incompatible with the spiritual nature of God's action. The Schwenckfeldians eventually abandoned celebration of the Lord's Supper entirely. For Zwingli and like-minded reformers it seemed implausible that the body of Christ could be present in any real sense in the bread and wine used in the celebration of the Lord's Supper on earth.

By contrast, Luther insisted that the celebration of the Lord's Supper had a sacred core, which he defined in terms of the 'real presence' of the Lord even without transubstantiation, which meant for him that Christ was actually and truly present amongst those who ate the bread and drank the wine in his name and with the promise of his words of institution. For decades Protestants would be embroiled in fierce conflict over this doctrine of the real presence, with even fellow Protestants damned or banished. Those conflicts eventually also raged within the Lutheran camp itself, for after Luther's death the distinction between his understanding of the Lord's Supper and that of Melanchthon, which had been swallowed for the sake of their friendship, became a matter of public debate. The result was a poisonous confrontation over the theological problem of ubiquity, which raised the question, not easily answered logically, of how the presence of Christ was to be defined, for that teaching put Christ in the position to be in heaven at the same time as he was on earth, amongst the guests at his Table.

In the mid-1520s the challenge to the Wittenberg teaching on the Lord's Supper came from theologians in southern Germany and the Swiss Confederation, led by Zwingli, 'people's priest' in Zurich, where he had particular responsibilities for preaching. Their alternative to the doctrine of the real presence of Christ in the Lord's Supper was an earthly immanent interpretation, which understood the event as simply a meal of remembrance. The performance of the rite that they adopted was accordingly prosaic: the elevation of the host was abandoned (it ended in Wittenberg only in 1542); where Luther continued to use communion wafers, Zwingli and his colleagues now introduced plain bread; the participants no longer knelt to receive but instead sat around a table as if at a usual meal. The innovations were all the more blatant to the community because they were played out not just in print, in the to and fro of the pamphlet debates, but also before their very eyes, as the faithful celebrated the Lord's Supper. This was, however, only a visible sign of theological difference that ran deep and of disparate Reformation cultures determined in part by the varying extent of humanist influence on the Wittenberg and Swiss Reformations. We must not identify anything nationalistic here, for the German-speaking Swiss lands were essentially part of 'Germany', and the Zwinglian form of Reformation theology was definitive for a generation in neighbouring southern German lands and in the more distant Low Countries and the county of East Friesland. The first wave of the Danish Reformation was also strongly informed by southern German, and in effect Swiss, theology.

In central Germany the south German and Swiss teachings gained their strongest foothold in the landgraviate of Hesse. Luther had aroused much interest in Hesse in 1521, when he travelled through the territory on his way to and from Worms. Additionally, traditionally close ties existed between the landgraviate and Electoral Saxon Thuringia. Soon after his first meeting with Luther at Worms, the landgrave of Hesse had decided in favour of the Reformation, but for internal unrest and external political repercussions to be avoided, doctrinal clarity and a single coherent church presence were vital. Dogmatic differences threatened to scupper plans for the political alliance of Protestant Imperial estates that lay close to the heart of Philip of Hesse, without doubt the greatest political talent in the Protestant camp. With good reason, then, on 22/24 April 1529 as the decree stigmatizing Protestants in the law of the Empire was issued at the Imperial diet at Speyer, the young landgrave invited the adversaries to a religious colloquy in order that they might find a way to eliminate their religious differences and establish the basis for a Protestant-wide defensive alliance.

This meeting, attended with some reservation by the Saxon theologians, took place in the first days of October in the Hessian landgrave's castle high above Marburg and was dedicated almost entirely to the issue of the Lord's Supper. At the outset the atmosphere was friendly. Luther joked, if somewhat sarcastically, when he greeted Bucer as 'You rascal', evidently a reference to Bucer's recent entry into Wittenberg publishing. Zwingli initially kept in the background, and with his Swiss tunic and dagger appeared somewhat out of place alongside the other theologians in their clerical or academic garb. The gathering was by no means a theologians' retreat. Those who had travelled to Marburg lived with the court at the castle, and the discussions, which took place in a resplendent room designed to impress, were presided over by the landgrave in person and by his cousin Ulrich, Duke of Württemberg. The presence of the Duke of Württemberg, who was under Imperial bann and at the urging of the Habsburgs had been ousted by the Swabian League from his lands, gave the gathering distinctly political overtones. The event was launched with a humanist-inspired welcome and eulogy given by Euricius Cordus, who had just been called as professor of medicine to Marburg, the first university founded as a

Protestant institution. The crowds who heard his speech were large, drawn from the town and university and from farther afield. In addition to his colleagues Melanchthon and Jonas, who would be directly involved in the discussions, Luther's cohort alone consisted of his assistants Rörer and Dietrich, Caspar Cruciger, who was the Wittenberg castle preacher, and Friedrich Myconius, pastor in Eisenach, and Justus Menius, pastor in Gotha, who had both joined the Wittenberg party as it travelled to Marburg. Among those who had accompanied the opposing faction was Jacob Sturm, mayor of Strasburg, who carefully assessed the possible political consequences of the theological positions adopted. Others had come to Marburg of their own accord, attracted by the appearance of such theological heavyweights and aware that landmark decisions were in the offing. They included Gerhard Westerburg, a member of the radical spiritualistic camp, who travelled to Marburg after Karlstadt had been refused the escort he had requested. Johannes Campanus from the Low Countries brought his own compromise proposal, with which, however, he made no headway.

Only the active participants subsequently, on 5 October, put their names to the fifteen Marburg articles (Figure 35). Their signatures formed distinct blocks (Figure 36): the Saxon theologians Luther, Melanchthon, and Jonas appeared higher on the page, while the Swiss and south Germans—Zwingli, Oecolampadius from Basel, and Martin Bucer and Caspar Hedio from Strasburg—added their names at the base; dividing these two groupings were Andreas Osiander from Nuremberg, Stephan Agricola from Augsburg, and Johannes Brenz from Schwäbisch Hall, as representatives of the south German towns that sided not with Zwingli but with Luther. The signatories had not formed a homogeneous group with all members on an equal footing. In accord with the practice of ranking speakers at Imperial diets or diets of the estates according to their social standing, the opinion leaders for each party—Luther and Melanchthon; Zwingli and Oecolampadius—sat at two tables placed directly in front of the presiding landgrave.

On the Saxon side, Luther himself was the principal speaker, indeed almost the sole speaker. He was allocated the first contribution, which followed the formal opening of the gathering by the Hessian chancellor. Well aware of the explosive potential of the issue of the Lord's Supper, again, as also years earlier at Worms, he cited Scripture as his only criteria. Now, however, he spoke not as an intimidated monk but as a self-assured reformer and faction leader.

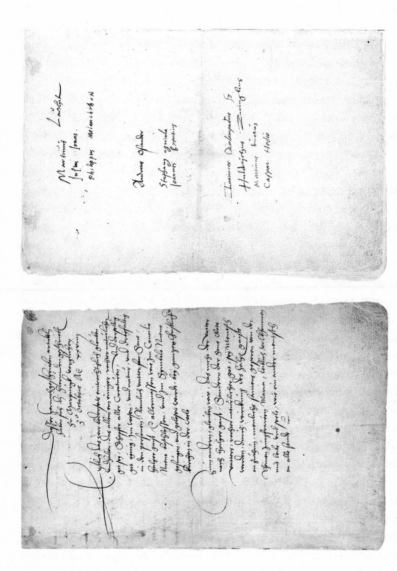

Figures 35 and 36. First page and final page with distinct groupings of signatures of the Marburg Articles, drawn up at the Colloquy of Marburg in 1529.

In both his oratory and his tactics, Luther showed himself highly skilled. He immediately staked out his ground, and throughout the discussions that followed he did not concede an inch. Yes, he had accepted the landgrave's invitation, but only to attest to his beliefs where others erred, not to open his opinions to negotiation. He immediately listed a complete catalogue of such errors, which his interlocutors would need to abandon before they would even be in a position to discuss the Lord's Supper. Freefall was halted only by agreement with Luther's demand that all points of difference would be recorded in the protocol of the meeting, and thus, as it were, certified. With this step the nature of the discussions was also decided: there would be no attempt to find a middle way; each party would attempt to refute the other and force it to renounce its errors. The key issue remained the problem of how Christ was present in the Lord's Supper. Here the divide between the parties ran very deep and would not be bridged at Marburg, or even for centuries to come. For Luther there was simply no question—in the Gospel Christ stated 'this *is* my body' and therefore the bread and wine *are* the body and blood of the Saviour. Neither his opponents' proposal that here, as so often, Christ had been talking figuratively nor a rational approach that excluded the possibility of ubiquity could achieve anything. Evidently at Marburg, too, the ever-present temptation of Satan was to be resisted: on the tabletop in front of him Luther wrote in chalk *hoc est corpus meum* ('this is my body') and then covered up the words with a cloth that lay over the table.

By the third day of discussion, a Sunday, all that was left to do was to confirm that the talks had failed. In an upsurge of personal obligation that was entirely characteristic, Luther approached his opponents, expressed his gratitude for the friendly and collegial atmosphere, and requested their indulgence for his sharper moments, for, he noted, he was only flesh and blood. But when, evidently moved, Zwingli asked in response for Luther's friendship and it seemed the existential differences over the Lord's Supper might be masked, Luther's gruffness returned. 'May God have you come to your senses,' he responded, which his opponents naturally immediately countered with the selfsame request. The reformer remained unmoved when Jacob Sturm, one of the cleverest and more influential men of his age, spoke of his concern that grave political consequences might follow for the southern Germans if Luther did not recognize their position as legitimate, for they would be left vulnerable to being seen as like Anabaptists and sectarians, who had been condemned in Imperial law. Of just as little avail was Martin Bucer's plea that Luther at least acknowledge a shared

Reformation spirit. For Luther, the Lord's Supper had salvific significance; anyone who thought differently was in no way at one with him.

Luther was at least prepared to participate in the formulation of the concluding articles, which the landgrave believed necessary if plans for the pressing political alliance were to be realized. Of the fifteen articles, which were largely drawn from an earlier text devised by Luther and Melanchthon solely on the basis of Wittenberg teachings, fourteen testified to consensus amongst the participants. Even the last article, on the Lord's Supper, recorded agreement—on the importance of the sacrament, its distribution in both forms, and the rejection of the Mass and of transubstantiation. But the article then acknowledged differences over the nature of the presence of the body of Christ, and all the world, with Luther leading the way, knew this additional sentence contained the decisive statement. The published articles, of which there were soon over twenty editions including translations into Low German and Dutch, were read as evidence of the division in the Protestant camp. This evidence was compounded by the catchy terms 'sacramentarians' (*Sakramentierern*) and 'fanatics' (*Schwärmern*) that Luther attached to his opponents, entirely unjustified in as far as they seemed to imply contempt for the sacrament. The devastating political impact was soon felt, for at the Imperial diet held at Augsburg in 1530, the southern German and Swiss theology, soon to be distinguished from that of Luther through the designation 'Reformed', was condemned and its proponents excluded, just like Anabaptists, from the protection of Imperial law. This decision helped pave a path that would lead Germany generations later into the great thirty-year-long territorial and religious war.

Untiring in his efforts to find a compromise, Strasburg reformer Martin Bucer did finally present a complicated theological formula that was accepted, and included in 1536 in the Wittenberg Concord, by Luther and his colleagues, much to the relief of those who thought in political terms.[64] However, the wording sidestepped the central problem of how Christ was present when the sacrament was received, and as a result the concord was accepted only by the south German Reformed and not by the Swiss. In the course of the sixteenth century additional attempts were made to find a common basis, on the Lutheran side above all by Philip Melanchthon, and amongst the Swiss not least by Genevan reformer John Calvin. None of the proposed formulae with their many theological subtleties proved viable. The internal Protestant divide sealed at Marburg was overcome only in 1973, in a concord agreed at Leuenberg by Basel, when Lutheran and Reformed committed to a fellowship of the Lord's Supper.

For Luther compromise on the Lord's Supper was psychologically impossible. He framed the problem solely in existential terms, which for him meant it was a matter of salvation. Any variation from his position could only be the soft whisperings of the devil sent into the world to divert humankind from the correct path. All those who disagreed with him, Schwenckfeld and Zwingli alike, however different from each other they might be in their teachings, were nothing other than despisers of the sacrament, and with the salvation of humankind at stake, all possible means must be used to force them to submit. A year before the meeting at Marburg he had informed the Protestant public in his 'Confession concerning Christ's Supper' (*Bekenntnis der Artikel des Glaubens*), a text as artless as it was brilliant, 'I am not drunk or irresponsible. I know what I am saying, and I well realize what this will mean for me before the Last Judgment at the coming of the Lord Jesus Christ.' It was his intention, he continued, to remain by his position on the Lord's Supper until his death and beyond. 'If in the assault of temptation or the pangs of death', he concluded, 'I should say something different—which God forbid—let it be disregarded; herewith I declare publicly that it would be incorrect, spoken under the devil's influence.'[65] This highly personal confession was made public, but again Luther had no intention of asserting his position by force. He also accepted Melanchthon's repeated attempts to find a compromise formula, efforts that made evident that Melanchthon was not at one with him over the real presence, even though at times their difference of opinion created a tension between the two leading figures of the Wittenberg Reformation that was almost unbearable, at least for Melanchthon.

The existential, salvific dimension, present from the start, meant that Luther never gave any ground on the real presence of Christ in the Lord's Supper, neither in response to theological argumentation nor in light of ecclesiastical or political realities. In 1544 Emperor Charles V made peace with his arch-enemy Francis I of France in the treaty of Crépy. Within the Empire and more broadly in the context of European politics, the Protestant estates of the Empire found themselves in a precarious position. Unity within the Protestant camp was essential. Yet just when the political situation looked promising, Luther rubbed salt into the wound of continuing antagonism over interpretation of the Lord's Supper. In 1542 Hermann von Wied, archbishop of Cologne, had become Protestant. It now seemed possible that the reformation and secularization of this ecclesiastical electorate would give Protestants the majority of the votes in a future Imperial election; additionally, the lower Rhenish lands of the archbishopric, which bordered the Habsburg Low Countries, were very strategically located. But political calculation was not Luther's thing: when Amsdorff sent him a copy of the Reformation articles drawn up for Cologne by Melanchthon and Bucer, along with a warning that 'there is concern that they do not follow the pure teaching in all things',[66] Luther was immediately ready for a fight. Having read the text, he bluntly informed Gregor Brück, the Saxon chancellor, who hoped for a conciliatory response in the midst of the political crisis:

> it goes on at some length about the use, fruit, and honourableness of the sacrament, but it mumbles on the subject of the substance [whether it is the body of Christ or whether it only stands for the body of Christ], such that one cannot tell what it thinks in this matter. Nowhere does it emerge whether the real body and blood are received orally ... For that reason I have had enough of it and have unendingly little taste at all for it.[67]

Neither this lack of appetite nor consideration for Melanchthon, one of the authors of the text for Cologne, prevented Luther from providing a flaming rejoinder. Indeed, he 'preached such pointed sermons on the matter in Wittenberg and referred so coarsely to Philipp [Melanchthon] that Philipp said to Dr Brück that if Luther were to continue in such a manner then he was minded to leave'.[68] The 'hideous work' expected by Melanchthon appeared on 30 September 1544, its confessional character evident even in its title: 'Short Confession on the Holy Sacrament' (*Kurzes Bekenntnis vom heiligen Sakrament*).[69] The Protestant world could at least permit itself a sigh of relief that the text was directed not against Melanchthon and Bucer, but entirely at Zurich and Heinrich Bullinger, who now oversaw Zwingli's legacy. With the appearance of the Zurichers' response only a few months later, in the form of a rebuttal entitled 'True Confession of the Servants of the Churches in Zurich' (*Warhaffte Bekanntnuß der dieneren der kirchen zu Zürich*), the wounds formed at Marburg were being reopened in high acrimony. Each side listed in detail the other's every violation of the fraternal Christian forbearance promised fifteen years earlier, and Luther even demanded that all Wittenberg theologians put their names to his list and thereby expressly join in his condemnation of the Zurich position on the Lord's Supper. The intention was deliberately inward-looking, designed to ensure that any dissenters in his own camp were bound to the radical Lutheran explanation of the Lord's Supper. The plan failed because—as a moment of calm reflection would surely have made evident— Melanchthon could not reconcile such a sharp condemnation of the south German and Swiss teaching on the Lord's Supper with his own conscience. The anathema of the 'Short Confession', with its denunciation of the Zurich position on the Lord's Supper, was the reformer's final word on this matter, and when Luther died over a year later, the orthodox amongst his pupils saw this position as an inheritance they were bound to defend. With Melanchthon remaining true to his conciliatory position, the stage was set for another War of the Diadochi, both inescapable and destructive, as those left behind after Luther's death fought over his inheritance.

These circumstances again illuminated clearly the reformer's unconditional and unwavering belief in his faith and his truth. This conviction shaped his actions in the final years of his life just as much as it had determined his behaviour at Worms in 1521. A 'prisoner' of the word of God, he was unable to make any concessions, not for friendship's sake, as Bucer had hoped, let alone as a political tactic. He was not prepared to legitimize, or even tolerate, a political alliance whose dogmatic basis remained unresolved. Whether that meant snubbing the political leadership of the Protestant Imperial estates, as was the case with Philip of Hesse in 1529, or heightening an existing political crisis, as happened in the mid-1540s, was of no consequence. His attitude was a huge burden for political Protestantism, even long after his death. As the confessional age dawned, foreign policy also became increasingly confessionalized, yet dogmatic agreement on the central articles of faith was now essential for enduring political alliances. As a result the Protestants, divided over the issue of the Lord's Supper, were dangerously weakened as they faced the dogmatically unified Catholic camp. The Calvinist and Reformed political leadership were well aware of the problem, but they proved rarely able to convince their Lutheran partners to shake hands across the confessional divide.

Academic Commitments

In ensuring that Reformation theology took root and thrived, Luther's regular activities in Wittenberg were no less important than the rehearsal of theological differences, which occupied Luther far beyond the examples discussed here. His Wittenberg routine comprised academic teaching and examination, in which, after a break from 1521 to 1524, Luther again became fully involved, and also the work of the Wittenberg Bible

commission undertaking the revisions to his translation, a task discussed
earlier. This work on the Bible reveals that for all the reformer's theological
originality and individuality, intellectual exchange amongst colleagues was
so significant that we can speak of a 'collective Wittenberg authority' that
oversaw the development and establishment of Lutheran theology, composed of Luther, his constant theological interlocutor Melanchthon, the
town pastor Bugenhagen, Justus Jonas, replaced by Georg Major after
Jonas transferred to Halle, and Caspar Cruciger, who although a student of
Melanchthon's was highly respected by Luther.

Something similar can be seen in Luther's academic instruction, and in
particular in the disputations, whose import for a systematic theology has
only recently been made evident.[70] Particularly revealing are the later
disputations of the 1530s and 1540s, for they provide evidence of Luther's
uninterrupted theological creativity even as he aged. As was standard practice in German universities, in Wittenberg disputations were a regular
component of academic training and examination. Anyone who wished to
receive an academic degree, and a doctorate in particular, had to participate
in a public disputation in which he defended theses supplied by a member
of the teaching body, usually the chair of the committee. To force the
candidate to take a clear stance, the theses were usually highly didactic,
which makes this type of source especially interesting for historians of
theology. Additionally, as the theses had to be published—usually as a
single sheet exhibited in advance—we have better access today to Luther's
disputations than to his lectures, very few of which are available as recorded
by Luther.

In the early 1520s Luther was already using this academic responsibility as
an opportunity to present, in the form of theses, the central theological issues
currently preoccupying him and to have these questions aired by the degree
candidates and members of the examining board in a public disputation. The
contentious issue of the extent and limits of the human will was discussed in
this context precisely at the time that Luther was himself debating the issue
with the humanists. In 1522, with the overhaul of academic study at
Wittenberg that accompanied the Reformation, the disputation process
was dropped, but it was resumed after 1533, and Luther used his participation in a good dozen such academic occasions to give account both for
himself and to the academic public of the central issues of faith in Reformation theology—on the doctrine of justification in five disputation theses on
Romans 3:28, on the necessity of faith for salvation, on evangelical

ecclesiology and Christology, and finally on the Trinity, in his last disputations of late 1544 and mid-1545. Emerging from the question of God, his
whole theology embraced European thought since the classical age, as is
particularly impressively demonstrated in a run of theses from early 1536
entitled 'On humankind' (De homine / Über den Menschen), with its focus on
the relationship of faith and reason in the history of the European church
and the history of ideas, a question posed again at the beginning of the
twenty-first century by Pope Benedict XVI. While he valued the achievements of philosophy highly, for Luther again there could be no doubt:

> Philosophy or reason . . . know almost nothing of humankind, not the effective
> cause and correspondingly not the final cause of humankind. There is no
> possibility that humans . . . in and of themselves can recognize themselves until
> they have recognized themselves in their source, which is God. [For that
> reason] from the fullness of its knowledge theology defines the whole and
> perfect human.
> [In this world] until the likeness of God is restored and will be completed . . .
> humans find themselves in sin and day by day are increasingly justified or
> disfigured. For that reason Paul did not hold these kingdoms of reason even
> worthy of being called 'world' but preferred to call them instead 'the
> fashion of the world' (1 Cor. 7:31).[71]

The 'antinomian' dispute emerged from such academic disputation and
proved to be one of those inner-Wittenberg theological conflicts that after
the death of the reformer would plunge German Lutheranism into severe
crisis. In this instance the debate was over the relationship between law and
grace, which in Luther's doctrine of justification belonged together as
polarities that were indispensable for the justification of humankind before
God. But Johannes Agricola, pupil of Luther and rector of the school in
Eisleben, disagreed with Luther and demanded the strict separation of the
two: he believed the Gospel alone to be the authority in matters of faith and
justification before God; the law and the commandments served only to
establish proper behaviour on earth and therefore belonged not in the
church but in the town hall. Bugenhagen and Melanchthon objected
energetically to Agricola's position, while initially Luther was primarily
concerned to bring his opponent back into the Wittenberg consensus.
Luther eventually became convinced that Agricola was more concerned
with raising his profile than with the issue itself, and he welcomed Agricola's
call to Berlin, even if, as he added sarcastically, he believed Agricola's vanity
made him more suited to be court fool than court preacher. This assessment

makes it all the less surprising that immediately after Luther's death, antagonism again broke through, with the radical guardians of Luther's
legacy mocking Agricola for his involvement in Charles V's Augsburg
Interim as *Scheissleb* (shitty liver), a play on the name of Agricola's home
town of Eisleben.

The Luther Rose and Marian Piety

Our picture of the reformer's theology would be incomplete and one-sided
if we did not consider, even briefly, manifestations of his faith that in spite of
their inherent Protestant character did not become the subject of polemical
debate and altercation. Perhaps the most beautiful example lies in the
theological meaning of his signet ring (Figure 37), which bore the famous
Luther rose with the cross at its heart, which he sketched as 'a symbol of my
theology' on 8 July 1530, in the midst of the highly testing time spent at
Coburg, for Nuremberg's town clerk and reformer, Lazarus Spengler:[72]

> There is first to be a cross, black [and placed] in a heart, which should be of its
> natural color, so that I myself would be reminded that faith in the Crucified
> saves us. For if one believes from the heart he will be justified. Even though it is
> a black cross, [which] mortifies and [which] also should hurt us, yet it leaves the
> heart in its [natural] color [and] does not ruin nature; that is, [the cross] does
> not kill but keeps [man] alive. For the just man lives by faith, but by faith in the
> Crucified One. Such a heart is to be in the midst of a white rose, to symbolize

Figure 37. Martin Luther's gold signet ring, given to the reformer by Electoral
Prince John Frederick at Coburg in 1530. Staatliche Kunstsammlungen Dresden
Grünes Gewölbe.

Figure 38. The Luther Rose, woodcut, 1530. A white rose set against a sky-blue background holds a red heart containing a black cross; a gold-coloured ring surrounds the image.

> that faith gives joy, comfort, and peace; in a word it places the believer into a white joyful rose; for [this faith] does not give peace and joy as the world gives and, therefore, the rose is to be white and not red, for white is the color of the spirits and of all the angels. Such a rose is to be in a sky-blue field, [symbolizing] that such joy in the Spirit and in faith is a beginning of the future heavenly joy; it is already a part [of faith], and is grasped through hope, even though not yet manifest. And around this field is a golden ring, [symbolizing] that in heaven such blessedness lasts forever and has no end, and in addition is precious beyond all joy and goods, just as gold is the most valuable and precious metal.[73]

The Luther rose (Figure 38) and its theological import deeply shaped Lutheran spirituality and the Lutheran mentality. Today, when Luther's controversial theological writings often have only historical relevance, the white rose with the red heart bearing the black cross at its centre is possibly the strongest visual representation of the reformer and his theology of Christ and theology of grace.

A very personal theology and religiosity is evident also in the reformer's distinctive Marian piety. Orthodox Lutherans and enlightened liberal Protestantism were very ready not to dwell on what they saw as a rather awkward remnant of Catholicism; more recent ecumenism has emphatically made use of Luther's Marian piety in its own interests. The significance of the mother of God in Luther's lifetime has only emerged more clearly through recent research into the history of theology. The key text is Luther's 'Magnificat Translated into German and Expounded' (*Das magnificat verdeutschet und ausgelegt*), on Mary's song of praise in Luke 1:46–55. Spoken by

Mary, pregnant with the Redeemer, in response to her relative Elisabeth's declaration of her blessedness, in the Vulgate this prayer begins with the word 'magnficat' and was one of the most read and most recited Scriptural texts of the age, receiving much attention from theologians. Their esteem was explicitly shared and defended by the reformer, who recorded, 'It is a fine custom, too, that this canticle is sung in all the churches daily at vespers, and in a special and appropriate setting that sets it apart from the other chants.'[74]

Luther turned to the Magnificat while he was at the Wartburg. In a moment of uncertainty and intense deliberation as he debated his theological anthropology with Jacobus Latomus, theologian at Louvain, Luther immersed himself in the song of the 'Blessed Virgin Mary', a mystical and spiritual text utterly unsuited for polemic or debate. Again he functioned as both pastor and reformer, translating the text into German and explaining the hymn of the mother of God for the laity, seeking to fulfil his responsibility to bring them solace and recount their blessedness. He dedicated the work to the electoral prince John Frederick, who was just eighteen years old, partly in gratitude for the protection afforded by his family but above all in order that the text might serve to fortify spiritually and help educate the future ruler, as an example of the genre known as 'mirrors for princes' (Fürstenspiegel). He wrote in the dedication of wishing that:

> the tender mother of God herself procure for me the spirit of wisdom profitably and thoroughly to expound this song of hers, so that your Grace as well as we all may draw from it wholesome knowledge and a praiseworthy life, and thus come to chant and sing this Magnificat eternally in heaven.[75]

The reformer maintained his positive image of Mary throughout his life. He decisively rejected attempts to find a rational explanation of the virgin birth, which proposed for example a dual construct for Mary, as virgin and as mother. No, he declared succinctly and decisively on 2 July 1533, the Feast of the Visitation of the Blessed Virgin Mary, 'Virgin and mother are one person'. For him Mary was 'eternal . . . and remained an eternal, holy and blessed mother'.[76]

Luther's explication of the Magnificat, like his Marian piety more generally, displayed a new, Reformation image of Mary in which the mother of God was extolled not for her ability to broker salvation but for her humility and acceptance of the will of God and held up as a model of a life pleasing to

God. Accomplished historians of theology may well find, as one has written, that as one reads Luther on the Magnificat, one will unavoidably be left with the sense that Kant's ethics must have been formed within the new historical departure for Western Christendom that is found in Luther's words.[77] But this discussion moves us beyond the boundaries of biography. Luther's Marian piety was not a product of polemic or debate intended to differentiate. Only after Luther's death did the mother of God become a figure of confessional difference, and even enmity, when Catholic Marian devotion located her at the pinnacle of the baroque heaven of the saints and, in response, Protestant orthodoxy identified this Blessed Mary as a favourite bogeyman.

To Craft an Evangelical Church Order and Ensure the Christian Education of Children

Luther's criticism of the institutions of the Roman papacy was just as central to his Reformation theology as were his teachings on grace and justification. Even today, as Protestants and Catholics find common ground on justification, institutional differences still run deep and continue to present practical barriers, with little room for compromise. For Luther, only grace can justify and only through Christ, an inalienable truth that made equally clear that a church founded on the Gospel did not require, and should not have, priests who functioned as intermediaries between God and humankind or a pope on the Roman model. Christ stands at the head of his church, both its visible institutions and the invisible community of the faithful. The pope and the hierarchies of priests and prelates, Luther insisted, were not just unevangelical but even anti-evangelical and had to be abolished. In usurping the headship of the church that is Christ's alone they had proved themselves creatures of the devil, who seeks to infiltrate the church and thereby wreck God's plan for salvation. In 1520 Luther had declared that the Wittenbergers were convinced 'that the papacy is the seat of the true and incarnate Antichrist'. If the pope was not prepared to undertake fundamental reform, he continued, which meant nothing less than the abolition of his own position, then 'for the salvation of souls all things are permitted' to be used against him.[78] If the papacy was not willing to accept its days were over, as the reformer very soon recognized was the case, then the evangelical and pope-free church was to be erected at least in those towns and territories where the authority of Rome and Rome's supporters did not run.

No less clear was the line Luther drew on the other side, to separate off the radical elements in his own camp. The church of Christ required ordained servants, educated and formally installed, who would expound and preach the word of God. As early as 1520, in his text 'The Freedom of the Christian', he had already qualified his priesthood of all believers, recording, 'although we are all equally priests, we cannot all publicly minister and teach'.[79]

On one hand, the rigour of Luther's evangelical theology and of the principles he applied to church and society helped secure the Reformation church, not only the territorial and urban churches of Germany and the national churches of northern Europe, but also the churches of Lutheran minorities within Catholic areas of the Empire and in eastern Central Europe. On the other hand, however, the construction of those churches could not advance him towards his real goal, the universal reform of the Christian church to which he believed he had been called by God. He was not ready to acknowledge that with every change to the nature of the church, even if that innovation was rooted in the Gospel, he distanced himself further from such total reform of Christendom, leaving behind both the Roman Church and the 'false brothers', in which category he placed all those within the Reformation camp who did not think as he did. The reformer's aim was to create a united Christendom that looked again to the Gospel, but, as many contemporaries reproached him, instead he divided religion. The resulting complexities of Latin Christianity, in both attitude and organization, helped drive the emergence of the modern 'Europa'—initially multiconfessional, but soon ideologically pluralistic—with which from the seventeenth century Latin Christianity increasingly identified, another secularizing consequence of Luther's Reformation. In the moment of victory and at the height of his influence, Luther already bore a hint of tragic failure.

Luther would not remain unaware of the dichotomy between the success that was the construction of separate Reformation churches and the complementary failure that was the division of Christendom. A realist, however, he was not to be diverted from what seemed to him necessary. The declaration 'If I knew the world was to end tomorrow, I would still plant an apple tree today' is a twentieth-century invention falsely attributed to Luther, but it holds a certain truth. The realization that his every success only fuelled his opponents strengthened Luther's conviction that he was advancing down the path assigned to him by God. His confrontational understanding of sacred history taught him that there was no reason to expect that the reconstruction of the evangelical church could run smoothly, and he was in no doubt that Satan, consumed by destructive desire, would seek to halt its renewal. Working through his creature the Antichrist who occupied the papal throne in Rome, Satan would not only defend his anti-church, but also lead its counter-charge. Luther therefore did his utmost to ensure the success of the individual reformations, initially in Electoral Saxony and subsequently in other parts of Germany and Europe, which held his doctrine to be pure, but he never surrendered his hope that one day, even if not during his lifetime, from these regional models of an evangelical ordering of church and society would spring a universal reformation of Christendom, even of humankind.

Medieval Models for Reform and New Reformation Creations

The construction of the evangelical church was manifestly animated by Lutheran Reformation theology, but the influence of late medieval reform, both legal and organizational, is equally patent. Much that Protestant-dominated Reformation research of the nineteenth century deemed innovative had origins that reached back generations. Often secured by concordat, the ruler's authority over the church in the late medieval period—a royal authority in areas outside the Empire, but exercised by the local territorial ruler within the Empire—anticipated the early modern church. For Protestant ecclesiastical historiography the late medieval Mass-priest, appointed to say the Mass at one of the numerous altars within so many churches, was the epitome of the flawed and futile development of the pre-Reformation clergy. A modern perspective, by contrast, sees in such individuals not pointless and often ill-disciplined clerics but men whose position was not so unlike that of the town clergy who were subsequently responsible to a Protestant town council. Such continuity is all the more revealing in the case of those who held endowed preaching positions, which had been established in towns throughout Germany in the fifteenth century in order that the quality of the church service might be raised in line with the improved education of the urban population. Territorial rulers and urban magistrates took on functions in the church that had previously been the preserve of the bishops. Melanchthon could draw on medieval developments when he justified the Reformation ruler's intervention in ecclesiastical matters with reference to the secular prince's responsibilities as an 'emergency bishop', duty-bound to take action when the bishops of the Roman hierarchy refused to introduce essential improvements. And the moral discipline, work ethic, and worldly asceticism that ever since Max Weber have been attributed to Protestantism were also not so very new.

When they came to design an evangelical church and society, Luther and his allies could therefore look to medieval tradition, but they understood their reforms as new and quantitatively different, for their concerns were not primarily political or administrative but rather evangelical. The existing desire for a renewal of the church had begun to be realized in many places, but fuelled by Reformation theology it now gained a new momentum. For generations the inhabitants of the larger Imperial towns had sought to reform the churches in their own setting in light of their religious needs and to reflect the legal and organizational realities of their communities. In giving the urban and princely appropriation of the church a new plausibility, Luther eliminated barriers that had frequently stood in the way of the realization of such late medieval reforms. Above all, Lutheran theology of grace and communal theology offered a coherent dogmatic basis that allowed earlier selective or isolated reforms of worship and church order to join together to form an integrated ecclesiastical presence within town and territory.

While significantly independent reformations were carried out in, for example, Imperial cities such as Strasburg and in Zurich and territories such as the landgraviate of Hesse, eyes remained fixed on Electoral Saxony and Wittenberg, where, under Luther's energetic leadership, a counter-Rome took shape, in terms of its legal and ecclesiastical order. The practical path to evangelical renewal of the church was anything but revolutionary, for Luther had no desire to alter or overturn the existing order. Rather, his concern was for the elimination of all those non-Scriptural additions— religious communities, legal statutes, institutions, ceremonies, and the like—that had adhered to the body of the church over the centuries since the early church. For Luther such embellishments were not just unhelpful but also harmful. Their removal would result from instruction and encouragement to recognize the truth; it must not be overhasty or in any way violent. Even those weak in faith and slow to understand were to appreciate the need to return to the evangelical condition desired by God.

The social and political order was to be disturbed only when it openly contravened divine command and stood in the way of the Gospel message of salvation. Luther abhorred violent incursions into the ecclesiastical or secular order such as broke out for the first time immediately after his appearance at Worms, which had been followed by iconoclasm; occupation of churches; disruption or mocking of church services, processions, and the veneration of the saints; refusal to pay the church tithe; persecution of clergy; and storming of monasteries. He equally detested the separatist movements that turned away from the universal church and towards private gatherings, as in the case of the Prophets of Zwickau, the spiritualists who looked to Karlstadt and Müntzer, and the Anabaptists. For the reformer such activities were the work of Satan, who sought to defile the rediscovered pure doctrine and to plunge humankind into ruin.

Luther's evangelical church ordinances, which emerged from his theology of grace, were, however, no less radical, as was evident for all to see in monks and nuns who left their monasteries; priests who married; the cessation of Masses said without a congregation present; preaching in German; abandonment of relics, of the veneration of the saints, and of the promises of the indulgence; redirection of pious endowments; secularization of church property for the care of the poor, sick, and orphans; evangelical education within the family and in schools and universities; and, not least, regular salaries for those who served the church.

Such extensive reform could only be accomplished through communal effort. Individuals and institutions with very varied jurisdictions and interests worked together to provide theoretical explanation and to ensure its practical realization—ruler and territorial government; Wittenberg professors and pastors, led by Luther; local officials and urban magistrates; and individual communities that grasped the initiative and developed their own model solutions—as in Leisnig on the Freiberger Mulde, just a short day's journey south-east of Wittenberg.

Beginnings in the Communal Church—The Leisnig Common Chest Ordinance

Luther possessed no blueprint for a new order. Occupied with the elaboration of his theology and entangled in disputes carried out in print, initially he tended to respond to questions brought to him, rather than follow a preset plan. He justified the abandoning of monastic life, the marriage of priests, and the abolition of the Mass only retrospectively, in letters, treatises, and scholarly treatments. When it came to the outward organization and financial regulation of the church, the situation was similar. The delegitimization of the priesthood and of the church's financial underpinnings had severed a vital nerve in the medieval community, and a solution had to be found with all haste. On one hand at issue were the appointment and payment of the evangelical pastorate to which the colourful late medieval society of priests and religious orders, who had lived from the endowment of altars and other similar benefices, had been reduced; on the other hand at issue were arrangements for care of the poor, elderly, and sick, which had been financed by the pious gifts that were now so criticized.

Embracing the Reformation idea of Christian freedom, local communities took reform in hand, in Wittenberg—even during Luther's absence at the Wartburg, as we have seen—in Augsburg, where influential humanist and town clerk Konrad Peutinger long banked on compromise, and then in Nuremberg, Regensburg, Strasburg, Magdeburg, Kitzingen in Franconia, and so forth. In Electoral Saxony local communities also led the way, in the elector's secondary residence Altenburg, and in Borna, Zwickau, and Leisnig. In spring 1522, these communities looked to Wittenberg for advice and assistance, providing Luther with an opportunity to set down his essential position on ecclesiastical law. In April and May 1522 he participated in local discussions with magistrates and congregations, and in his writings justified communal self-determination and self-government. In his customary programmatic sermons, he answered from Scripture the burning questions of the day about the constitution and organization of the church. In Altenburg he preached on Christ's appointment of his disciples as his representatives and as leaders of the church (John 20:19f. in the morning, John 20:21f. in the afternoon); in Zwickau he preached on consecutive days in the church of Saint Mary and the church of Saint Katharine on the relationship between faith and good works, on marriage, and on infant baptism, which the Zwickau radicals had rejected; in Borna he preached on Misericordia Sunday on the responsibilities of good pastors and bishops according to John 10:11–12: 'I am the good shepherd. The good shepherd lays down his life for the sheep. The hired hand, who is not the shepherd and does not own the sheep, sees the wolf coming and leaves the sheep and runs away— and the wolf snatches them and scatters them.'

The difficult conditions, both legal and political, faced by the church in Leisnig drew Luther back in autumn 1522 and spring 1523. The three programmatic texts that resulted established a model for evangelical churches far beyond their practical application for the church in a single town in Electoral Saxony. One of these texts concerned the appointment of the parish pastor and established, according to its title, 'That a Christian Assembly or Congregation Has the Right and Power to Judge All Teaching and to Call, Appoint, and Dismiss Teachers, Established and Proven by Scripture'. The second, 'Ordinance of a Common Chest', which began with a preface by Luther entitled 'Suggestions on how to deal with ecclesiastical property', provided a model for evangelical care for the poor and social welfare that became known as the 'Leisnig Common Chest Ordinance' (*Leisniger Kastenordnung*), named after the chest, usually a large wooden trunk secured with metal fastenings, in which money for the needy was kept. Finally, the third text, 'On the Order of Worship in the Community' (*Von Ordnung Gottesdiensts in der Gemeinde*), concerned the character of the Reformation preaching service.

These plans for an evangelical church presence in the town of Leisnig provide impressive evidence of the communal roots of the Reformation. At the outset Luther had no thought of a Reformation constructed from above. Anchored in Christian freedom and the priesthood of all believers, the right 'to judge all teaching and to call, appoint, and dismiss teachers' gave to the rural communities and the citizens of the towns the original task of reforming the church in their village or town according to their own lights. Conflicting secular privileges, such as rights of patronage, were to yield to the God-given privileges of the community. The right to elect the pastor that was derived from the priesthood of all believers came with a communal responsibility to follow an orderly process in making that appointment. As a Christian community cannot exist without 'teachers and preachers who administer the word', a selection process in accord with Scripture must be employed to ensure the appointment as pastor or preacher of those 'who are found to be qualified and whom God has enlightened with reason and endowed with gifts to do so'.[80]

Luther's recommendations on the future use of church income also reinforced the church community and the communal ownership of ecclesiastical property. While the reformer greatly criticized what he believed to be parasitical profiteering by the papal church from the misguided willingness of pious Christians to endow the church, he was determined to see such gifts of money and possessions, mainly land, appropriately repurposed. Even if pious bequests could no longer be used for their original purpose, he insisted that on no account were 'greedy bellies [to] grab these ecclesiastical possessions', perhaps while invoking the reformer himself. The possessions and income of the monasteries had been given 'for the glory and service of God', a purpose that was now redefined in Reformation terms. The best way of meeting that original intent in an orderly manner was surely 'to devote all the remaining property to the common fund of a common chest, out of which gifts and loans could be made in Christian love to the needy in the land'.[81] Luther also insisted, however, that whenever the property of a church or other endowed institution was redirected to new ends, consideration must also be given to those who were currently living from that income: provision must be made for monks or nuns who did not wish to join the Reformation, in the form of either assistance during the remainder of their lives or capital that they could use to support themselves in the world. Current leases on land or property belonging to the church should not be revoked; only when the contract expired or the current holder died were these possessions to be added to the common chest. Again we find evidence of Luther's anti-revolutionary principles—even as necessary changes were realized, those affected were to be spared uncertainty and suffering.

Both poor relief and the choice of pastor had already been issues of the moment, independent of the Reformation. As the population grew rapidly, food and work had come to be in short supply. Unable to earn a sufficient living, more people turned to begging or occasional thievery, and the authorities issued ordinances for the poor with strict measures designed to control and discipline the army of beggars and vagrants. In the works-based piety of the papal church the beggar had a function, for those who had the means could become almsgivers or benefactors for the sake of their salvation; grace-based piety allowed for no such possibility. In Protestant areas beggars were above all a social problem, 'as a result of which', according to Luther, 'much harm is done to the land and the people', if it was not resolved by a 'rich common chest'. At the end of the century Queen Elizabeth of England would seek to clear beggars from the highways by making care of the poor the responsibility of their home communities.

Equally topical was the community's ability to select its pastor, a practice that had been far from unknown in the high Middle Ages and was still being exercised in certain parts of Europe. In most German towns and villages, however, that right had long since been lost, having passed into the hands of the local nobility or ecclesiastical institutions. For the inhabitants of the towns and amongst the more substantial peasantry of the fertile Baltic marches and the Tyrol, greater education and a self-conscious lay piety had increased sensitivity about any form of tutelage. And where was communal self-determination any more pressing than in the provision of town or village with a suitable pastor to serve as a good shepherd?

It is therefore no surprise that the community's selection of its pastor and the Leisnig common chest ordinance, which the reformer praised as 'a common example', were emulated everywhere. When the rebellious peasants took the evangelical transformation of their village churches into their own hands, they could invoke Luther: 'First', so began their Twelve Articles, well known throughout Germany, 'we humbly ask and request—in accordance with our unanimous will and desire—that in future the entire community have the power and authority to choose and appoint a pastor.'[82]

By 1525, however, the limitations of the communal church in Leisnig were already evident. The community had been able to select its pastor, overturning the claims of the hitherto powerful Cistercian monastery close by the town, which held the right of patronage, but it had been successful only with the support of the ruler, who fended off the protests of the abbot. The common chest was to be administered by the community, but Luther had assigned the authorities a key role in the secularizing of the monasteries.[83] Intense conflict broke out in Leisnig, for hardly had the ordinance for the common chest appeared, with a foreword by Luther, before the Leisnig town council realized that if the administration of church funds and poor relief fell to the church community, it would lose significant social and political sway. Apparently anxious to have control of these funds, the council suspended the common chest ordinance, which had already been passed and had Luther's approval, and took the administration of the common chest into its own hands. Luther protested to the territorial ruler about this reinterpretation of his recommendations for the communal church in favour of the town council's political authority, but he received no response—an effective dampener on his hope that the communal constitution could be recast without great difficulty in light of the apostolic model. In his sermon of 23 December 1523 the reformer again made the case for a Christian and communal-based constitution and for the care of the poor and sick to be in the hands of the community, but added 'but we don't have the people for it, therefore I do not trust beginning it until God makes more Christians'.[84]

In the meantime feasible options and active allies for the cause of ecclesiastical renewal had to be sought, especially as it was not just in Leisnig that

Luther's vision of the word emerging spontaneously from below, out of the communities, proved idealistic. When the first reports from the inspection of individual communities lay before him, Luther had to acknowledge the poor conditions in the parishes: 'No one contributes anything, no one pays for anything, Mass fees have been abolished, and there are either no rents or they are too small. The common man pays so little attention and respect to preachers and pastors.'[85] Theologically the switch from the communal Reformation to Reformation from above was unproblematic, for according to Luther's ecclesiology—unlike for the later English congregationalists, for example—an individual community was not in and of itself the church. The longer the process of renewal took, the more Luther became concerned that the nature and organization of the Christian community within each town, territory, or kingdom be as uniform as possible. Following the revolt of the peasants he was convinced that only the authorities could guarantee the social peace that he held essential for the construction of the evangelical church. For Luther and the majority of his contemporaries it was self-evident that the responsibility to ensure peace and security also encompassed religion and the church.

The politics of the Empire pointed in the same direction. A resolution passed by the Imperial diet at Speyer in August 1526 permitted the estates— in other words the territorial rulers and the magistrates of the Imperial towns—'in matters concerning the edict [the 1521 Edict of Worms against Luther] to live, rule, and act as each hopes and believes it can answer before God and his Imperial Majesty'. The Imperial estates alone, so only the political authorities, were to determine the nature of the church within the territories and Imperial towns.

Instructions for the Saxon Visitation

In light of this context, Luther's ascription after the mid-1520s of responsibility for the new ordering of ecclesiastical affairs to his Saxon ruler is perhaps evidence of his political acumen. It is not easy, however, to determine precisely his role in the process, begun in 1525, that created the Protestant early modern territorial church, with the ruler sovereign over the church. We should not immediately assume that all instances of cooperation with ruler or town magistracy were part of a deliberate agenda designed to bring about the establishment of a church regime under their political authority. Evidently Luther saw no contradiction in principle between the rights of the church community and the rights of the authorities. The Leisnig ordinances had been designed around a communal church, but he had never doubted that the ruler was also part of the equation.

Throughout his life, the reformer identified the church with the community, not with a hierarchy of office holders or with an ecclesiastical bureaucracy. Indeed, he would have been happy to erase the term 'church' altogether. In 1539 he was still bemoaning the 'misery connected with this meaningless and obscure word'. Rather than talking of the 'church', one should speak of 'Christian holy people',[86] ordered through the community. The collaboration of the ecclesiastical community with secular authorities, more specifically with the early modern state, was necessary, Luther insisted. Each had its own remit and responsibilities. The 'state' has the right, indeed the God-given duty, to call on its subjects to support the church financially, and if necessary to force them to cooperate 'just as when one uses force to ensure that they give to and serve in the making of bridges, pathways, and roads, and in other incidental needs of the territory'.[87] The communities, which could take the form of church-related institutions such as universities, and individuals such as the theologians who held office as professors or pastors, were free to regulate internal matters such as worship, pastoral care, sacraments, and confession.

Luther laid out how he conceived the Saxon territorial government's regulation of external matters in three programmatic letters written in autumn 1525 and in 1526 and addressed to Elector John, who had now taken up the reins of government in Electoral Saxony and had publicly stated his support for the Reformation. The first of these texts, dated 31 October 1525, made evident the breadth of the reorganization that Luther envisaged, for he was not thinking in terms of a narrowly defined reform of the church, understood as a social subsystem. University reform was a precondition for a functioning evangelical church, and the ruler, Luther insisted, must now, at last, ensure that the necessary improvements in higher education were undertaken. Payment of parish clergy and the maintenance of church buildings, parish houses, and schools required the ruler's 'attention and action... as the secular authority'. As 'God's faithful instrument' the ruler was responsible, according to Luther, for preventing 'that in a short time there will not be a parsonage, a school, or a pulpit functioning and [that] thus God's Word and worship will perish'.[88] For Luther reformation meant a general reform of church and society; the church was to be renewed, but so too was education, so closely associated with the church, from elementary schools in town and countryside to Latin schools and the territory's university.

The German princes are often portrayed as having used the Reformation to their own ends, as a means to increase their authority within their own territories, and yet the Electoral Saxon government declared its misgivings about such comprehensive engagement. It was especially concerned about the unmanageable financial burden. It would be almost two years and take further missives from the reformer before the government gave in to his urgings.[89] While the resolution of the Imperial diet at Speyer of 1526 that gave the Imperial estates the right to reform the church within their own territories played its part in that decision, so too did Luther's success in allaying the concerns of the elector, as head of the Saxon household. The reforms, Luther had reassuringly declared, could be supported by the ample funds available from monastic possessions and endowments, 'given in the service of God', which were sufficient to finance the evangelical church along with all its related responsibilities, such as education and care of the poor. Only in places where the parish income was insufficient would it be necessary to insist to the community that 'they reward those who toil, as the Gospel states', and if that encouragement was of no avail, then the costs would be borne 'by the town hall or otherwise'.[90]

Luther's proposal for 'a visitation of all the parishes in all the princedom' was also accepted. To this end the electorate was divided into four or five districts, each of which was to be visited by two nobles or princely officials. Luther's alternative suggestion makes evident that at this point he was certainly not thinking that the territorial ruler would have exclusive sovereignty over the church: if the ruler eschewed the effort, then the towns or nobility could undertake the visitation—in other words the estates could take the place of the ruler.[91] A year later, when Luther fleshed out the form of the visitation in consultation with Gregor Brück, the Saxon chancellor, there was still no talk of a purely princely body. The visitation commission was to have four members, 'two responsible for the income and possessions, and two for the teachings and personnel',[92] so administrative officials were to the state as well as experts in theology and pastoral care representing the church, who ultimately would be appointed by the university and not the elector.

Luther's proposals were elaborated at a gathering of theologians and government officials and then approved by the elector on 16 June 1527 as instructions for a visitation. This process launched the territory-wide visitation carried out between 1529 and 1531, which laid the foundations of the evangelical territorial church in Electoral Saxony and became a model for the Reformation in other territories. The princely regime was now very clearly in charge, able to appoint or dismiss at will the members of the commission named by the university, as was the case, as we have seen, for Luther himself. The reformer would have liked to continue his participation, but in the end his workload allowed him to be only marginally involved in the realization of the visitation for which he had advocated so strongly. The theological leadership of the visitation commission was taken by Melanchthon, who composed his renowned 'Instructions for the Visitors of Parish Pastors in Electoral Saxony' (*Unterricht der Visitatoren an die Pfarr-herrn im Kurfürstentum zu Sachsen*), an extensive statement of Reformation theology intended equally for the instruction of pastors and for the improvement of the material, spiritual, and moral well-being of the community and of the behaviour of its members. An explanatory and broadly framed preface by Luther was added to the text, in which the reformer allocated this first great ecclesiastical-political undertaking by a Protestant territorial state a place in a history of Christianity that reached from the early church up to the contemporary papal church.[93] Luther's approbation gave Melanchthon's text and the visitation proceedings more broadly a decisive theological and political legitimacy.

Luther both desired and helped bring about the shift towards a territorial church. Why, however, did he choose to invest so completely in the secular authorities, and specifically in the Saxon elector? Why did he not favour an episcopal constitution, which would have given the Saxon church far greater independence, perhaps even under Luther himself as Saxon primate? Even if for some reason—perhaps because of his Imperial bann and his excommunication—he shrank from assuming that role himself, surely other excellent candidates for the office—Bugenhagen, Jonas, or even Melanchthon—could have been found without difficulty. Luther had no fundamental problem with the idea of the office of bishop, and indeed he installed his Wittenberg colleague Nikolaus von Amsdorff as bishop of Naumburg-Zeitz. His preface to Melanchthon's 'Instructions for the Visitors of Parish Pastors in Electoral Saxony' is full of praise for the holy bishops of the ancient church. He stated openly that with the medieval episcopacy's having abandoned its ministering responsibilities 'we would like to have seen the true episcopal office and practice of visitation re-established', but no one had felt called to that role, for no one had been certain that such was the will of God. It therefore had been necessary to turn to the elector, who as a temporal authority constituted by God was able to act, indeed was required to act, in light of the Christian love that he held in common with all Christians. His involvement, Luther wrote, was pleasing to God and 'a happy example which all other German princes may fruitfully imitate'.[94]

Aside from any personal reserves, behind Luther's forgoing of an episcopal constitution for Electoral Saxony undoubtedly lay a judicious grasp of the realities of power. From the beginning the ruler had held a key role in the organizational transition from the old church to the new evangelical church, for often political clout alone—as we have seen in Leisnig—decided whether the community's desire to call a Reformation preacher would prevail against the opposition of the individual or institution that had traditionally held the legal right of appointment. In May 1522, when the right of patronage held by a provost in Halle stood in the way of the community of Eilenburg's ability to appoint to the parish, Luther called for the intervention of the elector, who as a 'Christian brother' must confront the wolves and tend to the salvation of the people.[95] As we have seen, in the late Middle Ages the local temporal authorities had become increasingly involved in the regulation of church affairs, making all the more plausible Luther and his fellow reformers' call on those authorities to act now.

Evangelical ecclesiastical law—very much the work of Philip Melanchthon—legitimized the involvement of the princes or magistrates within their evangelical territorial or urban churches in light of the authority exercised by 'emergency bishops'. With the bishops of the papal church refusing to enact the necessary reforms, the temporal authorities, 'pre-eminent members of the church' responsible for its external order, became emergency bishops in their place. They had been entrusted with maintaining both tablets of the law brought down by Moses from Mount Sinai: both the temporal, as holders of worldly authority, and the spiritual, as leading members of the church. Ruler and magistrate were able to take on such roles within the church not because they held political power, but by virtue of their personal piety. They had no authority to make decisions concerning the internal affairs of the church, over doctrine or the cure of souls, for example, for according to God's law the regulation of such issues fell to the church alone and was exercised by ministers of the word (*ministerium verbi*) or duly called theologians and pastors.

That the territorial and urban churches of German Lutheranism would be controlled from above and by temporal authorities was now set in stone. From the middle of the century the independence of those who ministered spiritually was reduced step by step, with the pastors demoted to quasi-servants of the state. The consistories were the most important organs of church government, and although their membership was intended to include equal numbers of theologians and legal councillors, the secular authorities soon dominated. Rulers and magistrates also claimed the right to intervene in internal church affairs, even though ecclesiastical law clearly differentiated between competencies in external and internal matters and placed the latter in the hands of the clergy alone. Both before and after the Reformation the authority of Catholic princes over the church was always limited to external matters, and this claim to jurisdiction over the internal affairs of the church therefore marked a qualitative shift.

This expansion of the authority of the temporal powers had never been Luther's purpose. Even more alien to his intentions was the distortion of the Reformation balance of the rights of the state and the rights of the church found in ecclesiastical jurisprudence of the nineteenth century. Yes, the construction of territorial and urban churches was for Luther a logical consequence of his visitation model, but he would refute any attempt by the temporal authorities to assume competence *in sacra*, over the spiritual core of the church. He could not do otherwise, for such claims stood in stark opposition to his teaching on the two regiments or kingdoms. Here we can usefully recall those disputes in Zwickau in the early 1530s, when Luther even employed excommunication and interdict in defending the church from incursions into its internal affairs. He responded to those who criticized the Lutheran rulers' involvement in the regulation of the church by pointing out 'our princes do not force [their subjects] to faith and to the Gospel, but only remedy the external abuses [of the papal church]'.[96] Luther was no forerunner of the established church. Some Lutheran pastors believed themselves fully entitled to criticize prince and magistracy when they contravened the fundamental principles of the Lutheran church; only in the nineteenth century did the pastors themselves become pillars of the state.

Luther was not unaware of the tension between his early ideals of a communal reformation and the subsequent princely character of his reformation, an incongruity that increasingly tormented him in old age. Admittedly the Saxon electors took their role as protectors of the church very seriously and did all they could to ensure the success of the Reformation—John Frederick even staked his possessions and his life on this cause. Yet, almost inevitably, their church politics repeatedly became bound up in secular concerns, and above all in the consolidation of princely power, internally in relation to their subjects and the estates, and externally in relation to Emperor and Empire. Eventually Luther could no longer hide his alarm: the evangelical church, he insisted, should not be making every-thing worse than it had been in the papal church. In the papal church the bishops were princes; in the evangelical church the princes were threatening to become bishops, which, he opined, was much worse.[97] His worries about whether the Reformation church in Saxony and elsewhere was in accord with Scripture helped produce the increasingly pessimistic view of the world that came to dominate his last years.

Evangelical Reform of School and Family

Luther always sought to keep a certain distance from ecclesiastical law and issues of church order. His suspicions about lawyers and wheeler-dealers typified by Wittenberg town captain Hans von Metzsch ran deep. He was all too happy to leave the necessary exposition of ecclesiastical law and the legal relationship of church and state to Philip Melanchthon, while the practical work of designing constitutions for Lutheran territorial and urban churches was shouldered by Johannes Bugenhagen, the Wittenberg town pastor. Bugenhagen provided half of central and northern Germany and also Denmark with church ordinances, demonstrating a particular concern for alms and the common chest. Luther had laid the theological groundwork, but in giving Luther's ideas practical form Bugenhagen was the founder of Reformation welfare systems for the elderly, poor, and sick. Luther concen-trated instead on the broadly staged reform of education for both youth and adults and on the improvement of morals and conduct in accord with Gospel norms, above all in marriage and within the family.

Luther had recognized early on that his Gospel-based teachings would only win through if the people were able to understand the word of God. Ignorance and lack of education in rural areas, and also sometimes in towns and amongst the nobility and even the clergy, made two things clear to him: all the population should be much better educated, and universities must produce in sufficient number qualified theologians able to expound the word intelligibly and correctly and to provide pastoral case for communities. His wish for university reform was therefore accompanied by a heartfelt desire to see a comprehensive network of urban and village schools established. Again he looked to the authorities, both princes and magistrates, to discharge their duties, in this instance as 'the highest guardian of young people'.[98]

In spring 1524 Luther published his renowned treatise 'To the Councilmen of All Cities in Germany that They Establish and Maintain Christian Schools' (*An die Ratsherren aller Städte deutsches Lands, dass sie christliche Schulen aufrichten und halten sollen*), a work still lauded today.[99] The text was occasioned by a profound concern that the widespread rapid changes would lead not to an improvement in education but to its collapse. While the humanists, and in particular Ulrich von Hutten with his call 'Oh the times, oh the customs' (*O tempora, O mores*), had celebrated the upsurge in learning and education, Karlstadt and other radicals had declared academic studies unnecessary, for in the new age now dawning, the divine spirit would communicate directly with humankind, with no need for learned interpretation. According to Luther, such ideas were music to the ears of the avaricious, especially amongst the nobility, providing them with cover for their seizing of income given to support schools and universities; it was also grist for the mill of a pragmatism, found throughout society, that was sceptical of education and held that children needed to be taught only how to provide for themselves.[100]

With all the prophetic self-assurance that so animated Luther in these early years, he threw himself into the breach opened up by his false brothers. Behind their hostility towards education lurked none other than the devil himself, who sought to sow ignorance in order that the divine truth again be hidden. 'For the sake of God and our poor young people,' he implored the magistrates, 'such insidious, subtle, and crafty attacks of the devil must be met with Christian determination.' Even if the salvation context were put to one side, the authorities still had non-spiritual grounds for launching an educational offensive:

> My dear sirs, if we have to spend such large sums every year on guns, roads, bridges, dams, and countless similar items to insure the temporal peace and prosperity of a city, why should not much more be devoted to the poor neglected youth—at least enough to engage one or two competent men to teach school?[101]

The reformer was not just concerned for the education of the people more generally; he also wanted to see elite education safeguarded. Luther believed that humanist learning had seen a golden age dawn in Germany, bringing forth the best and most knowledgeable men, ornaments of philology and all forms of learning, with skills that could be used to communicate the Gospel. However resolutely he challenged the theological competence of Erasmus and other humanists, he was equally firm in valuing humanist education, in particular knowledge of ancient languages. To be able to understand and propagate the divine truth, it was not enough to read the Bible in German, as Luther's critics in the radical Protestant camp preached. For—and remember, these are the words of the acclaimed translator of the Bible into German—'in proportion then as we value the gospel, let us zealously hold to the languages'. Learning and languages do us no harm but rather 'are actually a greater ornament, profit, glory, and benefit, both for the understanding of Holy Scripture and the conduct of temporal government'.[102] With an invigorating polemic he added that anyone who believes languages and learning to be an unnecessary luxury should also demand that Germans give up silk, wine, spices, and other expensive goods. Luther was certainly aware of the challenges of financing education, but he had a simple solution. The teaching of children and promotion of learning are pleasing to God, he noted; indeed God requires such work. Therefore nothing was more obvious than that schools and higher-education institutions should be supported from all the endowed income and possessions that the papal church had demanded for indulgences, requiem Masses, fraternities, and 'more similar such swindles'.

The school issue accompanied the reformer throughout his life. Its continued presence is a sign that his admonitions did not bear great fruit and that improvements came only slowly, but it is also evidence of the almost unmatched gravity and urgency with which he promoted schooling and education. In 1530, even as he waited at Coburg consumed by worry about the reception of his teachings at the Imperial diet at Augsburg, Luther composed a fervent exhortation, which he published not in the form of a pedagogical treatise but under the title 'A Sermon on Keeping Children in School' (*Eine Predigt, dass man Kinder zur Schule halten solle*). When the work was republished in 1541 Luther added a commanding preface and headed the text with Jesus' words 'Let the small children come to me'. The prophetic purpose and essential links to salvation were even more evident in this first national 'educational initiative' than in his earlier text addressed to the magistrates, but so too was a secularizing dynamic that meant that subsequent generations valued education highly but viewed it as independent of any religious purpose:

> Therefore let everyone be on his guard who can. Let the government see to it that when it discovers a promising boy he is kept in school. If the father is poor, the resources of the church should be used to assist. Let the rich make their wills with this work in view, as some have done who have established scholarship funds. . . . this way you do not release departed souls from purgatory [as was promised benefactors in the Roman Church], but, by maintaining God's offices, you do help the living and those to come who are yet unborn . . . so that they are redeemed from hell and go to heaven; and you help the living to enjoy peace and happiness.

At the conclusion Luther reinforced the argument as a whole with words that possess strong Old Testament overtones: 'Well, then, my beloved Germans, I have told you enough. You have heard your prophet.'[103]

In keeping with his belief in an indissoluble connection between evangelical Christendom and education, Luther always wished to see schools and the education of children included in any visitation. When it came to financing education, the towns and territories essentially acted as he had proposed. Ecclesiastical possessions and the libraries of monasteries and other foundations, and not infrequently also church and monastic buildings, were given over to the support of schools and universities, as for example in Göttingen and Zurich and later for the university at Helmstedt. Church property was thus reallocated according to a Reformation interpretation of the benefactors' original intent, but it was not secularized in a modern sense. The reformer was very conscious, however, that the activities of the territorial states or the towns in the cause of education would come to nothing if they did not have the support of parents, a view reinforced by visitations. In his pamphlet sermons of 1530 and 1541 and in many additional sermons, Luther strongly cautioned parents again and again that it was one of the foolish things of this world when 'the common people appear to be quite indifferent to the matter of maintaining schools [and are seen] withdrawing their children from instruction and turning them to the making of a living and to caring for their bellies'. Additionally it is a 'horrible and un-Christian business', everywhere doing 'great and murderous harm . . . in so serving the devil'.[104]

More important for Luther even than school and university was the Christianization of the social unit formed by the family and the household, where not only children but also members of the wider household could be educated in the evangelical faith and a Christian way of life. In an age in which family could be conceived of only in relation to marriage, marriage itself played a central role in the reformer's pedagogical and social thinking. Such had been the case even during the initial phase of the Reformation, when Luther had challenged the sacramental character of marriage and advocated for priests and nuns to be able to marry; subsequently his own experiences as husband and father influenced the new evangelical theology of marriage, sexual relations, and family.

Although he did not hold marriage to be a sacrament, Luther was absolutely clear that it had been ordained by God and underpinned Christian fellowship. Marriage therefore required not only the nurture of church and state but also their supervision and control. As early as 1522, in his work 'On Married Life' he had already pronounced on the obstacles to marriage laid out in detail in the canon law of the medieval church, in particular permitted degrees of kinship between a husband and wife. Only on the issue of celibacy did Luther deviate significantly from the traditional tenets of matrimonial law, which he followed closely, for example, when it came to the very varied grounds that allowed the dissolution of the otherwise unshakeable bond of marriage. Theology, not law, determined Luther's thinking, and in his 1522 text he addressed the question of 'how to live a Christian and godly life', in order 'that we may say something about the estate of marriage which will be conducive toward the soul's salvation'. His response reflected justification by faith alone and his scepticism about the human will: 'I say that flesh and blood, corrupted through Adam, is conceived and born in sin . . . but God excuses it [the sinful married couple] by his grace . . . and he preserves in and through the sin all that good which he has implanted and blessed in marriage.'[105] Marriage was no longer a sacrament, but the church retained its responsibility because in married life humankind was close to both sin and grace.

To Luther marriage was, on one hand, 'God's good will and work' and, on the other hand, 'an outward, bodily thing, like any other worldly undertaking'.[106] Scholars of evangelical ecclesiastical law therefore defined marriage as a 'res mixta', a combination of the spiritual and the temporal, and it was therefore to be regulated by both church and state. Where exactly the boundary between their competencies lay was unclear. As a result, when the Electoral Saxon visitation articles were being drawn up in the late 1520s, a dispute broke out between theologians and state officials over which aspects of marriage the church would examine and which fell a priori entirely under the jurisdiction of the state and whether pastors should be given instructions on how to deal with marriage-related issues. The state officials, and Spalatin in particular, were particularly concerned about the possible political and legal implications and advised against detailed new regulations.[107] Luther agreed, and as a result the wording that appeared in the visitation ordinances under the heading 'On Marriage' (Von Ehesachen) was both brief and non-specific. The pastors were instructed simply to 'teach and act sympathetically and reasonably',[108] and to ensure that Christian liberty not be misunderstood as freedom of the flesh. Challenging cases were to be brought to the local official or to the prince's chancellery and thus handed over to the matrimonial jurisdiction of the state.

Luther's Catechism

The most effective tool in establishing and securing the evangelical church in the long term was Luther's 'Small Catechism' (Der kleine Katechismus), in effect a manual for Christian faith and life. First published in 1529, this compendium of evangelical belief and conduct had gone through more than sixty editions by Luther's death. It had been immediately translated into Latin and numerous other European languages and remained in use for centuries. 'The deplorable, wretched deprivation that I recently encountered while I was a visitor has constrained and compelled me to prepare this catechism, or Christian instruction, in such a brief, plain, and simple version,' Luther recorded in the preface.[109] The plan had its roots in Luther's declaration of 1526 of the need for an account of 'everything that a Christian needs to know' in the form of a catalogue of questions and answers—'child's play', as he termed it—for, he wrote, 'enough has been written in books, yes, but it has not been driven home to the hearts'.[110]

The four pillars of Christian belief and conduct were to be embedded in the hearts of children by means of the catechism: the Ten Commandments, the Confession of Faith, the Lord's Prayer, and the sacraments of baptism, confession, and the Lord's Supper. Each theme was addressed in a play of questions and prescribed answers. Scripture was cited prominently, introduced by the question, 'Where is that written?' The intention was that both children and the adults responsible for their Christian education could learn clearly and easily what it meant to be baptized, to receive communion, to confess one's faith, and to say the Lord's Prayer; no longer then would they 'live like simple cattle or irrational pigs'.[111] Children would reach that goal only if pastors and catechists always used the same formulation for each article of faith and never employed any of the various versions of the Ten Commandments or the Confession of Faith readily found after 1,500 years of Christianity.

The wording of the catechism immediately produced a novel standardization of the fundamental Christian texts. Learning through repetition and questioning was to be followed by comprehension, which would be fostered by the pastor, who was to explain, as simply as possible, each article of the catechism in turn. Laws of the kind established by the papacy were declared poisonous; only instruction on the benefits of a Christian life or the harm caused by an un-Christian life would enable individuals to grasp the truth. Anyone who stubbornly resisted learning the tenets of faith was not to be allowed to participate in the sacraments and should be excluded from family meals by their parents or the head of the household. If those penalties proved ineffective, then the individual was to be banished by the authorities.[112]

Responsibility for instruction in the catechism fell to both pastor and community. Above all, however, Luther insisted, 'Let all their lesson learn with care, so that the household well may fare', drawing in the Christian household, and the married couple who headed that household in particular.[113] Luther saw the head of the household as pastor and bishop of his own community (*episcopus et dominus pastor illorum constitutus*).[114] Essentially, Luther's ideal of an evangelical church was thus not just a communal church but also a family church. Very likely, his experiences with his own family and in his own home, as a father and as head of the large household in the former Black Monastery, enabled Luther to compose a small catechism that was equally remarkable both pedagogically and theologically.

Sin and Confession

Church discipline, distinctive of Calvin and institutionalized in the Reformed church, was not part of Luther's church order. Disciplining and excommunication were ad hoc individual matters, as we have seen in the cases of Hans von Metzsch, the Wittenberg town captain, and the magistrates of Zwickau and their town clerk Stephan Roth. Calvin believed Scripture made church discipline part of the true church and insisted, therefore, that church elders, as regents within each community, were required to consider disciplinary cases regularly, usually weekly; Luther, by contrast, rejected any such formalized process. This striking difference between the two reformers' models for the organization and constitution of the church was a product of their divergent ecclesiologies, but character and personal experience also played a role—on one hand, Calvin, the stern lawyer and exile, thought in systematic and formalized terms and as the leader of stranger churches existing in alien surroundings had learned to prize the community's moral and doctrinal purity; on the other hand, Luther, the theologian and pastor, thought in terms of the individual Christian and how she or he could be turned away from the path to ruin.

For all Luther's great concern for the orthodoxy of the doctrine and organization of the church, the individual was always his focus, and when it came to doctrinal and moral issues each person was to be persuaded, not disciplined, onto the correct path. His primary concern was the salvation of the individual, not the relentless cleansing of the church and civic community of sin and error. Confession, to which Luther dedicated a chapter in the small catechism, stood as surety for a life that would lead to salvation. In his eyes, more important, than a list of transgressions were repentance and faith that the forgiveness pronounced by the confessor was absolution granted by God directly. Formalized, ritualized, and without inquisition by the confessor, the process of confession that he laid down was based on the faithful's self-determined self-scrutiny and free acknowledgement of having sinned. That faith was Luther's essential concern is very evident in the query 'Do you also believe that my forgiveness is God's forgiveness?', to be posed by the confessor before he was permitted to absolve the sinner, who had answered in the affirmative, with the formulation, '"Let it be done for you according to your faith" [Matt. 8:13]. And I by the command of our Lord Jesus Christ forgive you your sin in the name of the Father and of the Son and of the Holy Spirit. Amen. Go in peace.'[115]

Outcomes: The Confessional Churches and Confessional Cultures of the Modern Age

Today both educational and religious sociologists laud Luther's pedagogical texts as the first impulses behind the great success story of education and learning in the modern age, a story that they see as a lasting achievement of Protestant confessional culture. Luther's contemporaries, however, were divided over whether with his impassioned appeals to chancelleries, town halls, and families the reformer was ultimately seeking to stem an educational and moral catastrophe that he, and his Reformation teachings, had caused— like the magician's apprentice who could not be rid of the spirits that he himself had called up. In one corner were Catholic controversial theologians such as Johannes Cochläus, whose polemic ran much along these lines, but they were joined by some humanists, above all Erasmus of Rotterdam. In the other corner were the Protestants, confident that Luther alone had provided the momentum for the first educational revolution of the modern age.

When this debate broke out again in the nineteenth century against the backdrop of the *Kulturkampf*, in the face of Catholic critics such as Johannes Janssen and Ignaz von Döllinger, the dominant Protestant scholarly world insisted on 'the enormous indirect impact of Reformation ideas on the history of education and scholarship, the salutary deliverance and cultivation of the intellect through the purification of moral attitudes', to cite the introduction to Luther's educational treatise of 1524 in the Weimar edition of 1899.[116] The thesis that the origins of modern scholarship lay in Protestantism, and its complement, that Catholicism was divorced from learning, were thought irrefutable. Today, with the liberal arts, and history in particular, no longer confessionally branded, we can assess the confessional contribution in a more sober and more nuanced manner. There are parallels with Luther himself, who praised humanist scholarship and its linguistic tools as prerequisites for the consolidation of the Reformation and the evangelical transformation of society.

Luther can be given credit for reining in the spiritualistic and popularist currents in his own camp that declared religion and education incompatible. A particular success lay in his rousing calls that enlisted the political authorities and parents for his educational cause and thereby anchored educational culture far more broadly within society than had been the case for earlier humanism. A similar example is provided by the training of pastors in both theology and languages. As the reformers themselves evince, highly educated theologians and pastors could also be found before the Reformation, but that such scholarly training became a qualification acquired by the whole corpus of pastors and theologians, eventually including those within the Roman Church, was the work of none other than Luther himself.

In 1546, as the reformer was carried to his grave, he left behind in Electoral Saxony an evangelical church organization that could function, and was already functioning, as a model for a whole run of territorial and urban churches in other parts of the Empire and within Europe more broadly. By the same token he had deeply influenced the Saxon territorial state and its politics and the social and cultural life in both town and countryside for both community and family. The endurance of that achievement when only a few months later the Emperor triumphed over the alliance of Protestant princes and drove Luther's ruler from his electorate was the work of the city republics of central and north Germany that asserted their Lutheran confessional identity in unconditional opposition to the Emperor.

When Lutheranism faced its greatest threat since the beginning of the Reformation, it was saved not by the princely territorial church, but by its anchoring in a civil religion. The driving force within the towns came not from the magistrates but from a coalition of citizens and Lutheran pastors. In the intermingling of the traditional civic spirit of Old Europe and a Lutheran communal Christianity, towns such as Magdeburg, Brunswick Hamburg, Lüneburg, Rostock, and many others found legitimacy and a will to resist demands for political and ecclesiastical obedience made by the supreme head of the Empire.

In the middle years of the century the communal character of the early phase of the Reformation again triumphed. For a moment it had seemed that in Germany a tradition of civil and civic Lutheranism would be consolidated as a counterpart to the civil and civic Calvinism that was taking root in western Europe at precisely this time, but soon the towns, too, veered towards, or were forced to become part of, the urban and territorial ecclesiastical regime directed from above. We should not lose sight, however, of the possibilities for a communal church and civic republic inherent in Luther's ecclesiology and church order, rooted above all in the Lutheran Christian household. The territorial churches that became characteristic of German Protestantism in the following centuries were not in accord with Luther's vision of Christian freedom and self-determination and of the Christian ecclesiastical community.

When the fight for survival in the mid-sixteenth century was won, the evangelical form of church and society forged by Luther and his Wittenberg colleagues was quickly consolidated in the Lutheran confessional culture that profoundly shaped political, social, and private life in Germany, Scandinavia, and parts of eastern Central Europe over the following centuries. In parallel, and entirely complementary to this Lutheran success story, a very similar development took place in those territories and towns that had kept their distance from Luther's teachings, either willingly or at the insistence of the authorities. The post-Reformation Catholic confessional church took shape, with its corresponding confessional culture, as a reaction to the processes described here for the Protestant territories. This Catholic confessional church was just as much a new church for a modern age as were the confessional churches of the Reformation.

Each of these modern confessional churches and confessional cultures claimed to possess the truth. By the end of the sixteenth century more than a few representatives of a rigid confessionalism were ready to assert that claim in well-nigh fundamentalist style, whatever the cost. The resulting chaos of the great religious and political wars made clear that only the permanent separation of claims to religious truth and claims to political power could produce a sustainable ordering of relations within and between states. With this realization the confessionalism that had erupted out of the Reformation was staunched. Only then was the way free for the ideological pluralism of modernity, which encompassed the major confessions as well as those forms of faith whose proponents the reformer had opposed as 'false brothers', and also, eventually, non-Christian religions and non-religious world views.

II

'But We Christians Are Part of a Different Struggle'—Facing the Demands of the World

W ith the reformer's appearance before Emperor and Empire at Worms in 1521, grand politics gained a grip on Luther that it would never relinquish. His new understanding of God was highly charged, for he had redefined not only the life of the individual lived in faith, but also church, state, and society. The challenge for rulers was unprecedented. The 'Luther Affair' was present in some form in almost every significant development or decision of the age, just as, conversely, the great political events of the Empire and Europe always concerned Luther in some way. As Luther refined evangelical theology through disputes with his opponents and as the evangelical territorial church in Electoral Saxony took shape, momentous decisions were also being made within the Empire and in Europe. Often neither context nor problem was new, having emerged earlier and independently of the Reformation, but now they were unavoidably drawn into an association with the Luther Affair. Such was the case above all for the power politics of the Habsburgs in the Empire and in Europe more broadly, but there was even a global dimension, generated by the contest with the Ottoman Empire in the east and by Iberian overseas interests in the west.

Charles V left Germany immediately after the conclusion of the diet at Worms. He did not return to the Empire for nine long years, and when he did so, to preside over his second Imperial diet in person, at Augsburg in 1530, he faced a Protestantism that in the meantime had become organizationally, confessionally, and politically established. Initially Charles V had been diverted from Luther and the circumstances in Germany by the dangerous revolt of the Comuneros, urban and rural Castilian rebels who, outraged at new taxes introduced on the Iberian Peninsula, threatened to topple Habsburg rule and were subdued only after a lengthy struggle. The conflict with Francis I, king of France, over pre-eminence in Europe erupted at the same time, and with it the series of wars against the French Valois dynasty that, interrupted by only temporary truces, accompanied Charles V for the rest of his reign. This struggle played out initially in the Italian peninsula, where at stake were control of the kingdom of Naples, where the French challenged Habsburg rule, and hegemony in the north, above all in the duchy of Milan.

In these circumstances the popes could not avoid taking a stand, both diplomatically and militarily. The Papal States was one of the five powers that thus far had guaranteed the political balance in Italy, and it was not going to take the involvement of a foreign power as simply a matter of course. Power politics thus made confrontation with Charles V unavoidable, with the very man so recently courted as Emperor-Elect because of the Luther Affair. The high point of that confrontation was the notorious Sack of Rome of 1527, when for weeks German mercenaries in Habsburg employ plundered the Holy City, a traumatic experience that long burdened the relationship of Rome and the papacy, the Imperial dynasty, and the Germans. Luther and his Reformation were similarly long discredited in Italy, especially as the soldiers' dealings with the artistic achievements of Rome could hardly have been more boorish. Marauding mercenaries incised anti-papal and pro-Lutheran graffiti into the newly painted and still-radiant frescoes at the Villa Farnesina. By inscribing the word 'Babylon' on the church tower in a cityscape, they declared the Wittenberger's message in the midst of the glory of the Renaissance papacy—the whore of Babylon sat in Rome and the pope was Antichrist. The Romans saw only a combination of German heresy and Teutonic barbarism.

To the clashes within Europe were added the conflicts with the Islamic Ottoman Empire, which, repeatedly supported by Francis I, challenged Habsburg authority in the Mediterranean, from North Africa, and in the east, from the Balkans. On land, in south-eastern Germany, the brunt of the defence against the Turks was borne by Charles' brother Ferdinand, as archduke of Austria and from 1526/27 also king of Bohemia and Hungary. At sea, the battle was fought by Charles and Spain, partly in alliance with other Christian Mediterranean powers. Highly spectacular and closely followed in the Christian world were Charles' attempted invasions on the coast of North Africa where the Turks ruled, of Tunis in 1535 and Algeria in 1541.

While all these events kept Charles V in suspense, the Reformation in Saxony and Germany could unfold largely undisturbed, even, from 1526, safeguarded by an Imperial recess issued at the diet at Speyer. The contrary decree of the second diet of Speyer in 1529, which restored the edict of Worms in all its severity, was also associated with the external challenges facing the Habsburg representatives at the head of the Empire. This time the onus fell not on Charles V but on Archduke Ferdinand, his brother and representative in the Empire. The proposition sent to the German king from Spain establishing the issues that were to be discussed at the diet and providing pre-prepared resolutions did not arrive in Speyer in time, and Ferdinand was therefore able to set the goals for the meeting himself and redirect the diet sharply away from Luther and his supporters and towards the interests of the Catholic majority. Ferdinand had his eye firmly on the urgent need to ensure that the majority of the estates rallied behind granting financial assistance for the Imperial defence against the Turks, for news had just been received of a new offensive. (Within six months the Ottoman cavalry would have advanced into the Habsburg hereditary lands, right up to the gates of Vienna.) Today we know that Ferdinand acted against the wishes of his brother: against the backdrop of continuing war with Frances I, Charles had intended leaving the Luther Affair unresolved, with the assurances of 1526 still in place.

Even without Charles' instructions, the Imperial diet of 1529 failed to put an end to the Reformation, which emerged legally more secure and bolstered by stronger political alliances. With Electoral Saxony at their head, six princes and a good handful of Imperial cities presented a 'protestation', an appeal against the resolution of the diet that was a standard legal tool in such instances. In the protestation they declared their obedience to Emperor and Empire in all things other than religion, in which they claimed the right to act according to their consciences and for which, they declared, they were not bound by majority decisions. 'Protestantism' was thus formulated in a context that was doubly, if contradictorily, determined by power politics—by Charles' responsibilities in Spain and conflict with France, and by Ferdinand's interests in the defence against the Turks in south-eastern Germany.

The differences between the Habsburg brothers, illuminated at Speyer by the issue of how to deal with the religious question, were not fundamental but rather tactical. When Charles was again secure in his Spanish saddle and as the conflict over supremacy in Europe moved in his favour, he left for Italy, where, through personal dealings with Clement VII, whom he had recently attacked so mercilessly, he sought to prepare the ground for the intervention in the Empire and in the religious issue that had been repeatedly postponed. Clement VII, who had long manoeuvred between Habsburg and Valois and always had one eye on the interests of his own Medici dynasty, recently forced out of Florence, now put his eggs in the Habsburg basket, hoping to ensure the re-establishment of Medici rule in Tuscany. With the renowned admiral Andrea Doria also siding with the Habsburgs, bringing with him his Genoan fleet, Imperial interests had gained the upper hand in Italy. The French forces had been forced to abandon their siege of Naples and had been practically wiped out during their retreat. A run of peace treaties resulted, agreed by Charles V with the pope at the end of June 1529 at Barcelona, with Francis I in early August at Cambrai, and finally, one day before Christmas, in Bologna with the mid-sized and smaller states of Italy.

And, finally, in October 1529 the Austrian capital city of Vienna, which had been besieged by the Ottomans, was relieved, bringing relative peace on the Turkish front. Now the Emperor's hands were no longer tied. After some ten years he could again turn in person to the Empire and to the religious issue. He could do so now with increased majesty and greater legitimacy, for political rapprochement with the papacy had cleared the path for his Imperial coronation, previously blocked by the estrangement that had set in soon after Worms, leaving Charles forced to settle for the title 'Emperor-Elect'. The holy event took place in February 1530, and although it was held not in Rome but in Bologna, the most northerly of the towns of the Papal States the coronation was performed with all the accumulated ceremony of centuries and splendour of the Renaissance. Side by side under the baldachin, a ceremonial canopy, Emperor and pope rode together to the church, in the midst of a long procession. Here was a demonstration of unity and resolve registered and comprehended by all of Europe, and above all by the German Protestants.

Strident Onlooker of the Imperial Diet at Augsburg

A Conciliatory Appeal by the Emperor

On 21 January 1530, before his coronation, Charles had called an Imperial diet at Augsburg, employing a tone that gave real hope to Luther's supporters amongst the Imperial estates, who had so recently been snubbed at the Imperial diet at Speyer. The talk was of overcoming 'past errors', and of the need, in the name of 'he who is our saviour . . . to hear the evaluation, opinion, and mind of each in love and good will, and to compare with our own Christian truth', in order that 'we all live under a single Christ, in a common church and in unity'.[1] Irrespective of this moderate tone, however, the second visit to Germany by the Emperor, so recently crowned and anointed by the pope, was characterized by a consciousness of majesty greater than on his first visit, to Worms. Above all, the Emperor was imbued with a sense of his responsibility, as one anointed by Christ, for the purity of doctrine and the unity of Christendom. Additionally, following the sudden death at the beginning of June of Mercurino Gattinara, his long-standing grand chancellor, in Innsbruck, before the gathering at Augsburg, Charles had taken the reins of government into his own hands.

The creation of an independent Imperial policy on religion and the church was no easy matter. It required the plotting of a challenging course between various opposing fronts: between Pope Clement VII, who continued to reject calls for a general council that came from the Protestants and from Charles himself; the Protestant Imperial estates who, like Luther, distinguished between the 'Roman bloodhounds' and the Emperor and set their hopes on the latter; and, finally, the radical anti-Lutheran ultramontane element among the Catholic Imperial estates who were spoiling for the opportunity to make short shrift of the 'heretics' and who even before the diet assembled were already irritated by the moderate tone of its announcement.

The Protestants—a term in use by this date to describe the evangelically minded Imperial estates in light of their 'protest' of April 1529 against the Imperial resolution of Speyer—recognized that they needed to justify their actions before the Emperor. In an appeal to Charles V they explained why they believed they were not required to submit to a majority in matters of religion or their conscience; the document was delivered to the Emperor in September, while he was in Piacenza. In Germany the chancelleries of the Protestant princes and town magistrates became a hive of activity, with Philip of Hesse even drawing up plans for a military offensive. However, a precondition for any common political action, be it diplomatic or military, was that the inner-Protestant differences on doctrine be overcome, a disagreement that with the failure of the Marburg colloquy on the Lord's Supper at the beginning of October had seemed to have become all the greater, even irreconcilable. The theologians held a key role, for doctrinal and confessional questions were central not only to internal Protestant debates but also to the estates' justification before the Emperor. In Electoral Saxony their advice was initially found primarily in collective reports produced by the Wittenberg theologians as a group, with Luther a participant but not the principal member. When the announcement of the upcoming diet reached Electoral Saxony at the beginning of March 1530, the chancellery's diplomatic and confessional-political efforts only increased.

At the diet of Augsburg of 1530 the interweaving of politics and religion that was so typical of the centuries before the Enlightenment proved particularly intense. Where in 1521 Luther had acknowledged his faith and his teachings as an individual, now the collective confession of the evangelical church, much developed in the meantime, was at stake, represented by princely rulers and civic magistrates. Again Luther had a central role. After adopting his unfortunate stance on the peasants' revolt, for some years he had remained in the background of Imperial politics. Now he stepped forward into the limelight again, for as the Emperor's announcement of the diet made clear, Imperial politics were tied up more than ever with the religious questions that he had posed. If, as some historians have suggested,[2] in the mid-1520s Luther really did lose some of his influence at the Electoral Saxon court, then his activities in 1529 as theological advisor and political expert must be deemed his comeback. Certainly, unlike some of his theologian successors, he never thrust himself forward into that role. Political consulting, as we might call it today, was abhorrent to him, for it exposed him to the demands of politicians and lawyers, which he deeply detested. Nonetheless he could not withdraw from that task, for the evangelical authorities, principal among them his own ruler, were not ready to forgo his advice. And he believed himself called to take a stand when the word of God that he had rediscovered was under threat.

Luther prepared himself thoroughly for the approaching diet. In March he had called on his Wittenberg community to pray for success, for the tyranny of the Turks and the false sects would be debated and therefore 'the diet is a matter for us all'. He would have liked to have stood before the Emperor again, but from the outset it was clear that Luther could not be present in person, in part because of the danger he would face as a condemned 'heretic' but also out of respect for the Emperor, who could not be expected to meet an outlawed rebel. Luther was involved, however, in all the preparatory consultations and was in effect 'virtually' present at the diet itself, in the form of letters, reports, warnings, and admonitions, and also in the words of pastoral reassurance that he sent to Augsburg from the Electoral Saxon castle at Coburg.

In the Kingdom of the Jackdaws

On 3 April 1530 Luther and his Wittenberg theologian colleagues left for Torgau, from where they would travel together with the elector and his court towards Augsburg. Evidently the Saxon officials wanted to ensure they had time before the beginning of the diet to work with the other Protestant Imperial estates *in situ* and formulate the defence of their position that they would send to the Emperor. The Electoral Saxon delegation arrived in Coburg on Good Friday, 15 April. Luther preached several times in the town, and when the court continued its journey he moved late on the evening of 23 April into quarters at the castle high above the town, from where he would follow the events of the succeeding months in the Imperial city of Augsburg, over 200 kilometres to the south. No longer did he have to make do with cramped quarters in an auxiliary building, as had Junker Jörg at the Wartburg almost ten years earlier. The reformer took up residence in two spacious rooms in the princely wing itself that he fitted out with a small working library. On the wall he wrote the words from two Psalms, as if to relieve the distress of the moment: 'I shall not die, but I shall live, and recount the deeds of the Lord' (118:17), and 'For the Lord watches over the way of the righteous, but the way of the wicked will perish' (1:6). Opposite his writing desk he hung the portrait by Cranach of his one-year-old daughter, Magdalene, which his wife had sent on to him. With him was his secretary Veit Dietrich, who assisted him in his scholarly work and with his endless correspondence but was also his conversation partner and his companion in a loneliness that could often be oppressive.

As when at the Wartburg, in the north-western Thuringian Forest, now ensconced high in the southern Thuringian Forest, the hermit was aware of the magnificence of the natural world around him, in which he readily saw a metaphor for the existential situation that he and his work currently faced. Aesop, the Greek writer of fables, whom he would soon engage more intensely, may have served as his model. Immediately after his arrival at the castle, Luther informed Spalatin that while in Augsburg there was still uncertainty about when the Imperial gathering would begin, he had come 'here right into the midst of a diet', namely the diet of the jackdaws, 'magnanimous kings, dukes and other noblemen of the kingdom, who seriously care for their belongings and offspring, and who with untiring voice proclaim their decisions and dogmas through the air'. They disdained 'such holes and caves as you people call—with but little reason—palaces', and lived in God's free heavens:

> They also show contempt for the foolish luxury of gold and silk...All are equally black, all have dark blue eyes, all make the same music in unison, yet with a pleasant difference between the voices of the elders and the youngsters...As far as I could tell from the interpreter of their resolutions, they have unanimously decided to make war throughout this whole year [first] on the barley...and then on the summer and winter wheat, and whatever else are the best fruits...Yet our [noblemen] are better off in one point—they have a less expensive and more tolerable market than your [noblemen] at Augsburg.

He continued, 'We sit here with great pleasure in [this] diet...the unanimity of all their voices, which are so saturated with beautiful melodies, also delights us beyond measure...these fathers of the fatherland and preservers of the commonwealth [are made] extremely agreeable and pleasant to us.' Finally, he asked Spalatin to excuse such a long letter dedicated entirely to jackdaws; it was, he wrote, written as a joke, but as a 'serious and necessary joke which should chase away the thoughts seizing me'.[3]

The almost five months that Luther spent 'in the kingdom of the jackdaws', from mid-April to early September, were not only a time of tension, anguish, and unrest on account of the confessional negotiations at Augsburg. We have already heard of his continued involvement in family affairs in Wittenberg, and of his caring letter to Hans, his four-year-old son, with its paternal account of a magnificent garden with amusing children's games. Above all, however, and replicating his experience at the Wartburg in 1521/22, he used the solitude of the Electoral Saxon castle to turn to work that he had repeatedly put off. 'This place is certainly extremely pleasant and most suited for studying,' he wrote on the very first day to Augsburg, and held out the prospect of work on 'the Psalter...the prophets, and... Aesop'.[4] Within the year he had published extensively on the Psalms and the Prophets, partly in the form of translations and partly in commentaries. At the end of May 1530 Luther received word of his father's death. He subsequently put to one side his translation of Aesop's fables, which he hoped would be used both in schools and for the instruction of children at home; as with his Bible translations, his goal with the fables was to cleanse the text of later objectionable additions. Increasingly taken up with the events at the diet, he found himself unable to return to his work on

Aesop, and the completed thirteen fables were only published posthumously, in Jena in 1557.[5]

Luther would not allow himself to be diverted from preaching. His sermons always took their bearings from personal and current circumstances, and therefore in works such as his 'Sermon on the Cross and Suffering' (*Sermon vom Creutz und leiden*) and in his notes on justification he turned again to the fundamentals of evangelical belief. His Coburg sermons were immediately printed both in Wittenberg and elsewhere, and they later appeared together in a collection entitled 'Nine Sermons that Luther Gave at Coburg in the Year 1530' (*Neun Predigten, welche Luther zu Coburg in dem Jahr 1530 gehalten*).[6] Additional work from this period included a treatment of translation and the veneration of the saints entitled 'An Open Letter on Translating and the Intercession of the Saints' (*Ein sendbrieff von Dolmetzschen und Fürbitte der heilligen*); a pamphlet we have already encountered on schooling, 'A Sermon on Keeping Children in School'; and a text in which he spoke out against neglect of the Lord's Supper, his 'Admonition to the Sacrament of the Body and Blood of Christ' (*Vermahnung zum Sakrament des Leibes und Blutes Christi*).

Above all the prophet of Sinai and the herald of the new Zion[7] was held riveted by the events at Augsburg, which he sought to influence through letters and 'admonitions'. He was in constant contact with the Electoral Saxon delegation, but he also addressed himself to the Imperial diet as a whole and to individual members, with Catholic participants certainly among them. Hardly had he arrived at Coburg when he sent his 'Exhortation to All Clergy Assembled at Augsburg' (*Vermahnung an die Geistlichen, versammelt auf dem Reichstag zu Augsburg*),[8] which attracted considerable attention. His appeal was not framed as an offer to negotiate; it was a repeat of his call to the bishops to do their duty at long last and eliminate abuses within the church. Were they to do so, Luther wrote, he would happily acknowledge their authority; by failing to do so, they were playing into the hands of the sectarians and raising the prospect of turmoil in the Empire. Luther would hardly have expected this much-repeated call to bear fruit on this occasion. His 'Exhortation' was propagandistic groundwork, and there was little real expectation that it would influence the content of the discussions that were to follow.

The situation was different in the case of a later letter addressed to Cardinal Albrecht of Brandenburg. In June, immediately after the reading of the Protestant confession of faith by Jonas and Melanchthon, Luther heard that the archbishop of Mainz was adopting a conciliatory course in the discussions. Without hesitation he turned again to address his adversary directly. In his open letter, published in Nuremberg, we find, most unusually, Luther in the role of supplicant. He did not rail or threaten or seek to convince this prince of the church of the truth of his message; instead he promoted the cause of peace. Albrecht, he wrote, had heard the confession of faith and could neither condemn nor refute it. The Protestants therefore 'do not deserve to be so harmfully condemned, so dreadfully persecuted'. And as it can be assumed that 'our opponents will not accept that teaching', there can be 'no hope that we . . . will become of one mind on teachings'. He therefore asked the elector:

> to work with others to ensure that that part will keep the peace and believe what they will and allow us to believe this truth that has now been confessed before their very eyes. It is well known that no one should or can be forced to believe, that is not in the power of the emperor or of the pope.

He no longer had any hope, Luther wrote, that the archbishop of Mainz and his fellow believers would allow themselves to be convinced by the truth. His plea was for external, political peace, which he emphatically described as a concern for 'Germany, poor, miserable, abandoned, despised, betrayed, and sold, my beloved fatherland, for which, as is my due, I want nothing bad but grant rather everything that is good'.[9]

To see in these conciliatory words merely empty tactics or to accuse Luther of fickleness would be not only to misrepresent Luther's character and attitude but also to miss the mark entirely when it came to understanding his political theology or Christian politics, which distinguished between the worldly and divine kingdoms, between action taken for the sake of one kingdom or the other. In the cause of coexistence in this world, Luther could offer Cardinal Albrecht, and with him all adherents of the Roman Church, peace and mutual toleration. To do so had no implications for the unconditional obligation to God to bear witness to the evangelical truth, and even if necessary bear the burdens and sufferings of war, although—a point to which we shall return— only as a defensive measure, not in order to spread the religious truth.

Contesting the Confession of Augsburg

The direct conflict with opponents who remained loyal to the Roman Church was only, however, a side stage. Luther's focus was on the leadership of the Protestant party in the deliberations, and on Electoral Saxony in particular. Theological responsibility fell on Melanchthon, with whom over the next weeks and months Luther would be in close contact by letter, in order that Melanchthon might not be diverted from Luther's own line. Luther's very first letter situated the discussions at Augsburg firmly in sacred history: Christendom, Luther wrote, was in the grip of two 'last woes'—on one hand the Turks and the Mohammedans, against whom he would inveigh with cries and entreaties to heaven, and on the other hand the 'domestic monsters' who raged in Augsburg. Melanchthon and he had been granted the ability to recognize and bear those burdens, he recorded 'but precisely this violence', he added with an assurance drawn from Scripture, 'is a witness and prophet of the end [of Satan] and our redemption'.[10] The immediacy of those links between contemporary events and the salvation narrative precisely in the Coburg months is evident in Luther's translation of the Book of Ezekiel, which related the apocalyptic threat to Israel from the army of the satanic prince Gog to the current threat from the Turks as an expression of God's 'anger and rod because of Christian sins'.[11]

For Luther visions of the End Times were not grounds for lethargy or resignation; they invigorated his vigilance and zest for action. Nor was he to be halted by his troublesome health, not even by a fainting attack that left him unable to work for several days in May. As was usual, he saw in all forms of adversity the work of the devil, and the devil was to be defied. 'Now then, if the devil eats me, then, if God wishes, he will devour a purgative which will constrict his stomach and his arse. And why not? Anyone who wants to have Christ must suffer.'[12] When, at the beginning of June, he learned of the death of his father, the certainty that he had brought 'the light of the truth' to the world and his gratitude 'that he [his father] has lived to now and has been able to see this light'[13] helped him overcome his great sorrow. In long and intensive daily prayers he was able to strengthen his conviction that God would not allow his cause to fail in Augsburg, but would instead lead on to an eternal victory. 'A Christian must be as sure of the fulfillment of his prayer as he is of the truthfulness of God';[14] this maxim, declared several years later in his exposition of the gospel of John, helped him through the painful days of isolation at Coburg, as the negotiations at Augsburg repeatedly threatened to plunge him into despair.

In Augsburg itself the theological leadership of the Protestant cause lay in the hands of Philip Melanchthon. Although in his apprehension he constantly sought to coordinate his decisions with Luther, in light of the distance their letters had to travel, often he was forced to rely on his own decision-making. He could also consult the theologians who were to hand in Augsburg, and turned particularly to Johannes Brenz, the staunchest representative of Lutheranism in southern Germany. Exchanges with Luther could be slow and faltering; at one particularly critical moment their correspondence was interrupted for more than two weeks. Melanchthon was constantly aware that the reformer was watching him warily from Coburg, and the need to be able to justify his actions proved a heavy burden on Luther's 'surrogate', the role that Melanchthon, for all his theological independence, believed he was playing. In long prayers he threw himself and his worries before God, but he still read every new letter that arrived from Luther tensely and fearfully. When Luther doubted the resolution of his representative, his letters could be adamantly direct, even inflammatory and offensive. Much concerned about their impact on the sensitive soul of his friend, Luther would follow such dispatches with missives full of words of comfort, counselling Melanchthon that he should keep the work that he found so demanding 'within the limits that will conserve your body, so that you don't kill yourself and then claim that this has happened as a result of obedience to God. For one serves God through no means more than through not doing anything.'[15]

At this point, Melanchthon was working flat out on the Saxon defence, in order that it would be ready before the arrival of the Emperor. He looked in particular to two previous texts—the Articles of Schwabach of summer 1529, probably composed by Luther himself, which had been presented to Margrave George of Brandenburg-Ansbach in Franconian Schwabach to serve as the basis for the Reformation in his territory; and the Articles of Torgau, one of the reports drawn up in March 1530 by the Wittenberg theologians collectively at the request of the elector, so with a view to the approaching defence before the Emperor. The draft of the defence was sent immediately to Coburg for approval, and Luther notified the elector by return, 'I have read through Master Philip's Apologia, which pleases me very much; I know nothing to improve or change in it, nor would this be appropriate, since I cannot step so softly and quietly [leise tretten].'[16]

As would become evident, this postscript was highly unfortunate. After Luther's death Melanchthon's opponents would read Luther's words as fundamental criticism of his colleague's confessional politics and chided him as 'one who steps quietly' (Leisetreter). Such was certainly not Luther's intention in 1530. He used the term with a light irony, in some respects even with a certain self-irony, suggesting that with his careful and cautious ways, Melanchthon had accomplished something that Luther would neither have attempted nor have achieved. His words were to be understood as a tribute to Melanchthon as diplomat, in serving, in effect, as foreign minister when representing the theology of Wittenberg at the diet of Augsburg and subsequently at the various religious colloquies.

Luther's approval was all the more important as in the meantime it had become clear to Melanchthon and to the Electoral Saxon court that the text with which they defended themselves must essentially take the form of a *Confessio*, a pan-evangelical confession of faith that as many of the Protestant estates as possible would support. Before the start of the diet this collective policy had a considerable success, when Landgrave Philip of Hesse, who tended to side politically with the Reformed Swiss and southern Germans, affiliated himself with the confession of faith. Melanchthon and the political leaders of Electoral Saxony were mightily relieved when, after the confession of faith had been read before the diet at the beginning of July, Luther at last abandoned his doubts and without reservation praised, 'Yesterday I carefully reread your whole Apologia, and I am tremendously pleased with it.'[17]

Keeping the Protestant front as united as possible proved essential. Even before the negotiations began, the Protestants faced a change of mood at the Imperial court. Immediately after his entry into the predominantly Protestant Imperial city on 15 June, Charles issued a strict prohibition of evangelical preaching and, additionally, he ordered the Protestant Imperial estates to participate in the Corpus Christi procession to be held the following day. Where once the Protestants had hoped that at Augsburg, as at previous Imperial diets, they would be able to profess their teachings in public sermons, now they found themselves forced to participate in one of the great, and to their minds objectionable, moments of image cultivation by the papal church. The darkening of the atmosphere was very likely the product of pressure from Rome, but it was also a result of the death of Mercurino Gattinara, Charles' humanistically inclined grand chancellor, who had consistently rejected the radical demands of the curia and had seen the diet at Augsburg as an opportunity for mediation. He had even proposed that Erasmus of Rotterdam be included in the diet's discussions, in order that the disputed religious issues could be discussed, without external pressure, at the highest intellectual level, with the hope that a joint resolution would then be possible. Instead, however, even the Imperial proposition read out at the opening of the diet, on 20 June, proved sharper than expected, for it made unambiguously clear that the Protestants should expect to face Imperial disfavour if the religious issue was not 'changed around and returned to what is best'.

Irrespective of such signals, the parties still agreed that discussion of the religious question took precedence over all worldly matters, even the financial aid for the war against the Turks that was so important to the Habsburgs. In the very first week of proceedings, an event occurred before Emperor and Empire that was almost as significant as Luther's appearance at Worms: on 25 June the Protestant estates presented the Emperor with their 'Confessio' in both Latin and German, which, in accord with standard procedure at Imperial diets, was then read aloud, a responsibility that fell to Christian Beyer, Electoral Saxon chancellor, who recited the German version. Originally designed to explain the changes undertaken in Saxony as the abolition of abuses, now the Electoral Saxon defence had become a comprehensive confession of faith.

The first part of the text, which would soon gain renown as the Confessio Augustana, the Confession of Augsburg, laid out, largely unpolemically, issues of faith and doctrine according to Wittenberg theology. The Protestants' position was rooted in the apostolic confession of faith and therefore represented the true tradition of the early church, distinct from, on one hand, the papal church, as represented at Augsburg by Johannes Eck in particular, and, on the other hand, the dissenters within their own camp, the 'false brothers', Anabaptists, and 'sacramentarians'; the last was a pejorative term used for the Reformed, who thus were excluded from the evangelical church. Only in the second part did the text seek to justify the individual changes that had been made to existing practices within the church—the introduction of communion in both kinds, with both bread and wine, the marriage of clergy, the abolition of the sacrifice of the Mass, the evangelical understanding of the office of bishop, and the associated reordering of the church.

In Electoral Saxony, Hesse, Brunswick-Lüneburg, Anhalt, and the Imperial cities of Reutlingen and Nuremberg, which were soon joined by German Imperial cities lying further south, the confession had the backing of not just most of the Protestant estates, but also the most important of the Protestant estates. As a result the Confession of Augsburg immediately became the most significant dogmatic pillar of German Protestantism. Only Strasburg, Constance, Memmingen, and Lindau kept their distance, providing a little later their own confession, the Confessio Tetrapolitana, or

Confession of the Four Cities, which included a Zwinglian interpretation of the Lord's Supper.

Electoral Saxon policy had sought, and had achieved, two goals: first, Saxon church politics had been justified before the Emperor and the Catholic majority amongst the Imperial estates and, secondly, a majority of the Imperial estates that had opted for Protestantism were united in their support of the Wittenberg version of the Reformation and had been distinguished sharply from Anabaptists, Spiritualists, and Reformed Swiss and southern Germans. The confessional politics of Electoral Saxony and its allies, with their theology the work of Melanchthon, were largely in line with the position Luther had established shortly before at Marburg. For Luther, all politicking, with an eye to advantages in this world, had been infiltrated by evil, indeed by the devil himself, even if those advantages were very tempting, as was the case with the alliance of Lutherans and Reformed sought by the landgrave of Hesse. The only defensible politics were those founded on a common confession of pure doctrine. As was usually the case, the Wittenberg theologians fell into line with Luther, where they were joined by the elector and his councillors. All agreed without question that their actions should be guided by Scripture and that there was no one more knowledgeable of Scripture or more capable when it came to the interpretation of Scripture than their own Wittenberg professor of Bible.

Expectations for the diet and views on the tactics to be employed did vary, however. Luther rejected further discussion, for any attempt at mediation would necessarily open up the pure word to negotiation. The Saxon officials and Melanchthon the optimistic humanist thought compromise possible and did not wish to see that eventuality excluded at the outset. Here—and not in the anxieties of Melanchthon or the impetuosity of Electoral Saxon politics—lay the reason for the tension, which tormented both parties, between the Saxon delegation in Augsburg, who had to enter into negotiation and wanted to do so, and its spiritual leader at Coburg, who saw everywhere the betrayal of God and of God's commission.

This struggle over the direction taken by confessional politics at the Augsburg Imperial diet, at times almost acrimonious, could have led to a personal falling out of Luther and Melanchthon and to a rift that would have been catastrophic for the Reformation. This outcome was avoided by the two men's deep and ultimately unshakable mutual trust, built up during long years of working side by side on reform of the university and of religious faith. The two men wrestled with each other and with themselves in the common cause of the Gospel, each according to his own temperament: at the castle at Coburg was Luther, the prophet of Sinai, resolute, convinced of his mission, and always ready to meet the devil head-on as the devil sought to extinguish in the world the truth so recently rediscovered; in Augsburg was Melanchthon, with the discriminating mind of the humanist and scholar, always ready to listen to opposing opinions and to explore all possible options for mediation.

Misgivings and a Reality Check

The presentation of the Confession of Augsburg did not mark the end of the religious proceedings at the diet. Commissioned by papal cardinal legate Campeggio, Johannes Eck, Luther's old sparring partner, drew up the '*Confutatio*', the Roman Church's refutation of the Confession of Augsburg. The response was so intransigent that even the Emperor had his doubts. After revision, it was read before the diet on 3 August. Likely influenced by this apparent hesitation, Melanchthon continued to hold out hope of conciliation and entered into new negotiations with Imperial representatives and with the papal theologians, with many qualms about whether his approach would pass muster with Luther. He was certainly not driven by any vain desire to take up a place before the prelates of Rome or the great men of the Empire; the point of reference for all his actions was, and remained, shared Wittenberg theology.

But Luther doubted Melanchthon, and there is good reason to accuse him of lacking faith in his colleague and friend. Cut off from reliable news for days, and sometimes even for weeks, Luther feared the worst, namely that Melanchthon would fail to stand by his confession of faith and for the sake of rapprochement and peace would be tempted to water down the text. Luther's mind may have run to his own experiences with unctuous temptations that could be resisted only with all the abruptness and incivility that he, but not Melanchthon, possessed. Over the following weeks, he showered Melanchthon with suspicions, insinuations, reproaches, and insults: 'I hate completely beyond measure your miserable concerns', 'Your philosophy, and not theology, causes you anguish... [because] in your rhetoric you have no *locus communis*: it is called faith', 'You struggle against yourself, your greatest enemy, who gives the Devil so much to use against you', 'I certainly pray diligently for you and I regret that you, you incorrigible leech, make my prayers so futile', and so on.[18] Via Spalatin he informed the Saxon government, 'I am not pleased to hear of your astounding endeavour to create agreement between the pope and Luther. But the pope will not want it and Luther refuses to tolerate it.' And, finally, on 20 September to Jonas, short and clear: 'I am nearly bursting with anger and indignation. I want you to break off the negotiations and return. If war breaks out as a result, then war breaks out. We have prayed and acted enough.'[19]

Understandably, Heinz Scheible, Melanchthon's most expert biographer, reproached Luther for his behaviour, suggesting that the Luther who resided at Coburg was no longer the guide and friend of the Wartburg but rather an aging figure who fell victim to his own moods as he saw events slide out of his control.[20] Certainly, Luther's outbursts were hardly helpful. Melanchthon, who undaunted continued to ask for advice, frequently ended his reading of these letters no better informed than when he began: at the end of June, for example, to his query about where there might be room to manoeuvre on the issues of the lay chalice and the marriage of clergy and in particular in the matter of the private Mass, on which the opposing side placed particular weight, he received the brusque response that more than enough had already been conceded, but found in the hastily added postscript, 'As I have always written, I am ready to concede all things [to the opponents] if only the gospel alone is permitted to remain free with us.'[21] Luther also suffered vicariously with Melanchthon and sent him letters of comfort in which he sought to fortify him through his faith. In part this support was necessary—who but Melanchthon could have accomplished at Augsburg what was needed?—but it was also an expression of Luther's fraternal Christian sympathy. While Luther was still in command, in one respect, underlined by the events in Augsburg, his earlier optimism had now faded: he could no longer believe that he would succeed in bringing all of Christendom over to evangelical thinking. At Marburg he had been pained to see the incorrigibility of Zwingli and the south Germans; now the Imperial diet had again demonstrated the incorrigibility, which he believed wilful, of his Roman opponents. Further evidence of the battle of the Last Days was to be found in the unremitting onslaught of the Islamic Turks and in the 'hardening' of the Jews. We should hardly be surprised to see the courage of his convictions and his zest for action increasingly covered by a veneer of disdain for the world.

Luther would be proved right. In the subsequent deliberations of a large caucus of princes from the Imperial diet, the differences remained unbridgeable, and the discussions that Melanchthon held with theologians from the opposing party also changed nothing. A final act provided categorical evidence of the failure of all the attempts at mediation. In response to the Roman *Confutatio* and at the request of the Electoral Saxon regime, Melanchthon had produced an *Apologie*, in defence of the Lutheran *Confessio*, which the Protestant estates attempted to present to the Imperial ruler on 22 September. The Emperor refused to accept the text, thereby demonstratively giving his support to the *Confutatio* more decisively than Rome could hardly have hoped. His action also signalled that in his opinion the Protestant confession of faith had no foundation in either the church of the Empire or the law of the Empire. The door had closed on the possibility of an Imperial reform policy that might have united earlier Spanish reforms with the new Lutheran demands for reform in Germany. Not only had no agreement been reached, despite all the hopes, but now the disagreement between Rome and Wittenberg over both doctrine and ecclesiastical law had been elucidated and cemented in formal statements of faith. The fundamental ideological and political enmities of the confessional age had appeared on the horizon. Even within the Protestant party the confessional politics of Electoral Saxony had not been entirely successful, for the Reformed Confessio Tetrapolitana only made the doctrinal distinctions more evident and more profound.

Melanchthon's Augsburg confession had long been accepted by Luther himself. In the letter to the archbishop of Mainz discussed above, Luther referred to the Confession of Augsburg quite naturally as 'our confession', and when Nuremberg reformer Lazarus Spengler inquired apprehensively at Coburg whether too much had been conceded in Augsburg, Luther reassured him, 'for even if Christ plays as if a little weak, he has not as a result been forced from his seat'.[22] In one way the failure of the negotiations in Augsburg reinforced the theological unity of the Wittenberg theologians. As the Emperor had refused to accept the first, hastily composed version of the *Apologie*, Melanchthon had the opportunity to revise and clarify the text, beginning the task with such enthusiasm during his journey back to Wittenberg, undertaken together with Luther, that the latter is said to have snatched the quill from Melanchthon's hand, reminding him, 'One cannot serve God only with work, but also with celebrations and resting.'[23] In its final version, published in September 1531, Melanchthon's *Apologie* was thoroughly Lutheran in character, with the doctrine of justification, the heart of Lutheran theology, used to define the other articles of faith.

In the long term, beyond Luther's lifetime, the Confession of Augsburg proved a viable theological platform and became in effect the Magna Carta of Lutheranism, both in Germany and farther afield. Additionally, with the diet of Augsburg of 1530 the Lutheran form of the Reformation became a stable presence in the political realities of the Empire, increasingly even in geographical areas originally influenced by Zwingli. In the political and legal proceedings of subsequent diets the only Protestant doctrinal statement recognized was the Confession of Augsburg—at Nuremberg in 1532 for the first time—and with the Religious Peace of Augsburg of 1555 the confession became part of the Imperial constitution.

Against Ecumenism, Religious Colloquies, and a Council

The presence of three confessional statements at the diet of Augsburg proved to be a first step in the direction of the confessional age, that period during the late sixteenth and early seventeenth centuries in which religion, formulated around *confessio*/confessions, determined the essential character of both politics and society. In Imperial legal thinking, the status of the confessions was summed up by the formula *religio vinculum societatis*, religion binds society together, which made religion necessary for social peace. For those active in 1530, however, the lasting division or differentiation of Christendom into opposing and irreconcilable confessional groupings or political power blocs was not a given. Certainly, no one wanted to accept that might be the case—not the Emperor and his brother Ferdinand, made king of the Germans in 1531, not the Imperial estates and the political leadership of the opposing religious parties, and also not the theologians, the majority of whom continued to yearn for agreement. Above all such was not the case for the people themselves, those 'simple' Christians and subjects in town and countryside still very far from having been 'confessionalized' in one direction or another. Even as they emphatically advocated for the Reformation or— rarely in this period—for the papal church, most people still envisioned a single, unified church.

Having proved unfruitful at Augsburg, the search for agreement on the divergent theological positions was continued at several religious colloquies, for which the political authorities, especially the Emperor with his profound concern for a religious peace, repeatedly pushed. At the end of the 1530s and in the early 1540s such theological conventions took place at frequent intervals: 1539 in Leipzig, on a more local level; in spring 1540 in Hagenau, presided over by King Ferdinand; again in 1540, in November and December, in Worms led by Imperial chancellor Nicolas de Granvelle; and finally, soon after again, in spring 1541 at Regensburg, in parallel to the Imperial diet called to that city. Specific propositions were even made with the so-called 'Worms Book' of late 1540 and the Regensburg proposals for union, but neither party was ready to put its weight behind those texts: the Protestants had concerns about the teachings on the Lord's Supper, confession, and the church; the papal contingent felt that the statements on double justification were ambiguous. The Augsburg Religious Peace of 1555, which gave Lutheranism the protection of Imperial law, called for further discussions, 'for the Christian, amicable, and final settlement of the matter of religion and faith'.[24] The religious colloquy subsequently held in Worms in 1557, continuing the attempts to find peace, produced no agreement.

Luther was not present in person at any of the colloquies. His experiences at Marburg in 1529, where he had found the intransigence of Zwingli and his fellow Reformed incomprehensible, and the analogous course of events with the Catholic party a year later at the diet of Augsburg, had left Luther with the unshakable sense that both Zurich and Rome were impervious to his holy truth.

Luther therefore laid no stock in ecumenical endeavours, however theologically or philosophically sophisticated they might be. Such was especially the case when, as with the ecumenical efforts of Georg Witzel, Roman designs were glaring. Luther's scorn and ridicule were all the sharper in this instance because Witzel had originally supported the reformer and had married. After his conversion, he had been called by one of the counts of Mansfeld, who had remained Catholic, to, of all places, Eisleben, the town of Luther's birth. At the heart of Lutheranism, but from a Catholic enclave formed by the church of Saint Andrew, the newly Catholic priest advocated for an ecumenical return of the Protestants to a conservatively reformed papal church. His case was complicated by his marriage while still a Protestant pastor, and certainly his married status caused him embarrassment. He took advice from Johannes Cochläus, Luther's arch-enemy, who was experienced in dealing with heretics; Cochläus instructed him that his wife could remain at his side within their household, but that he should say nothing about her being his wife and even deny they were married if necessary. The Catholic ecumenical project was wounded when Cochläus' advice became public: a gust of wind blew the compromising letter into the neighbouring garden of the evangelical pastor, feeding the Lutherans with easy material for satire and moral indignation.

Theologically Witzel's Roman ecumenism had left Luther largely unmoved, but such was not the case for Erasmus' work 'On Restoring the Unity of the Church', published in autumn 1533. Luther believed himself challenged once again, and Melanchthon feared that 'passions of old' would poison the atmosphere between the two enemy camps once and for all. Although he had already broken with Erasmus, Luther had continued to follow the literary output of the man he deemed his real antithesis, and in this instance he responded to Erasmus' ecumenical proposals with an extensive refutation. He chose not to enter into dialogue with Erasmus, but to turn instead to public media, with an open letter addressed to Amsdorff.[25] Unlike Melanchthon, Luther preferred that the differences between the two men be laid out clearly, rather than allowing their peaceable disregard for each other to continue, which explains his letter, in effect a manifesto, which was immediately published. No one else would likely have been sharper in tone and less compunctious in addressing the prince amongst humanists, so highly respected by Protestants too. The consternation was all the greater because Erasmus and his admirers saw in his text on the unity of the church something of a legacy of the great humanist and a last attempt to escape the current polarization. Luther was not able, or willing, to show forbearance let alone deference, for he believed the whole business to be evidence of pernicious vanity and of a craving for the admiration of the prelates of the devil's church. Again, as also when they had exchanged blows earlier, he chiefly denounced Erasmus' philosophical and rhetorical elegance, in which he believed lurked a frivolity that he deemed ill-suited to, and even contemptuous of, the word of God. The 'tyranny of ambiguity', he wrote, only sows tares amongst the wheat. It creates an inducement and a temptation to accept in church and world a clouding of the re-established purity of the Gospel for the sake of peace and unity. And therefore, Luther wrote, Erasmus' work should be banished from schools. Additionally, Luther believed that the establishment of clear dividing lines would be in Erasmus' own interest, for it would protect him from the enemies within his own camp who accused him 'of being a Lutheran'.

This polemic no longer found any great resonances. The scholarly world saw only the long-superseded skirmishes of two worthy old men. The silence even in Wittenberg was both eloquent and awkward. After Erasmus' death, in 1536, Luther spoke of the humanist only occasionally, in lectures or in his Table Talk. He appreciated Erasmus' *Adagia*, a collection of proverbs, which he was happy to use, although he criticized Erasmus' heroization of ancient morals. The dirty work of a Christian peasant or a Christian maid, so he taught his students, counted before God for far more than the heroic actions of classical heroes—Luther was essentially taking his leave from the Renaissance and from humanism and announcing the arrival of the confessional cultures of the late sixteenth century.

Holding no stock in texts on the re-establishment of the unity of the church, Luther could only think conversation and negotiation pointless, and even damaging to the pure word of God. They might lead to compromise, which was the work of the devil and would result in the betrayal of the Gospel truth. Luther usually recommended against participation by the Electoral Saxon theologians at the religious colloquies, although that advice tended to fall on deaf ears. Electoral Saxony neither was able nor wanted to stand up against the pressure coming from the Emperor. Again representation of Wittenberg theology fell to Melanchthon. As we have already heard, as he travelled to Hagenau in 1540, the responsibilities associated with that role almost killed him. The Wittenbergers remained concerned for his well-being, although in the end he proved more robust than Luther. When it came to deciding who should attend the colloquy at Regensburg, Luther emphatically cautioned the elector not 'to send Philip, who is so dangerously unwell, to such a pointless religious colloquy in which they only deride us and we lose time and money'.[26] Notwithstanding his fear that Melanchthon might allow himself to be drawn into dangerous compromise, Luther stood by and consoled his friend as he carried out his weighty task: 'The Lord', he wrote to Melanchthon in Worms in November 1540, 'who has called you to profess the things of his church in his name, will give you the mouth to speak and wisdom, and he will stop up the mouths of those who say godless things, in his honor and for the salvation of the elect.'[27]

Melanchthon withstood the pressure and at the colloquies did all he could to fulfil Luther's expectations and his own wish for unity and peace amongst Christians. To that end, he was prepared to make more concessions than was Luther—to the Roman Church when it came to the formulations employed, even for the doctrine of justification, and within the Protestant camp in order to build bridges for the doctrine of the Lord's Supper. In late April 1541 the religious colloquy that had been transferred from Worms to Regensburg at the beginning of that year was relaunched. Those participating—Eck, Julius Pflug and Johannes Gropper on the Catholic side; Melanchthon, Bucer, and the Hesse theologian Johannes Pistorius on the Protestant side—were presented with an Imperial plan for union that was to be used as the basis for their discussions, and the elector demanded that Luther also declare his opinion. The reformer believed he had been vindicated in his belief that such discussions could only bring dilution of the religious truth and should therefore be rejected. This 'circuitous, cobbled-together document,' Luther and Bugenhagen succinctly reported, proposed that 'they are right and we are also right'. Yet despite their own uncompromising stance on the matter, the two authors did not forget the difficult position faced by their colleagues on the ground in Regensburg, and at the end they requested that the elector 'not write too harshly to Philip and the others of our party, in order that he should not grieve himself to death'.[28] At the instigation of the elector of Brandenburg, in June 1541 a delegation arrived in Wittenberg seeking to go over Melanchthon's head and deal directly with Luther in order to find a solution to the debated issues, but Luther stood fully behind his friend.

Luther would eventually see the pope convene the general council that he had demanded immediately after the publication of his Ninety-Five Theses and for which the Imperial estates and the Emperor had repeatedly called. Successive popes had either failed to pursue the plans for a council or had deliberately thwarted those plans, as was the case with the Medici pope, Clement VII, who had feared that his illegitimate birth might be debated, producing demands for his resignation. Paul III (1534–1549) was the first to pursue an active pro-council policy—in 1536 he called for the church gathering to meet in Mantua or Vicenza—but in spring 1538 he was forced to delay the opening of the council indefinitely.

Commissioned by the Saxon elector, at the end of 1536 Luther worked on a confessional statement that the Protestants could use to counter the papal position at the council, should the opportunity arise. That text was presented to the meeting of the Schmalkaldic League held in Schmalkalden in February 1537 and would subsequently—as we will explore later—be deemed a confession of faith in its own right, known as the 'Schmalkaldic Articles'. In 1538/39 the reformer fleshed out his position in an extensive text entitled 'On the Councils and the Churches' (*Von den Konziliis und Kirchen*),[29] an account that would prove to be his final word on the matter. Some twenty years after his first ardent call for a council, his attitude towards that assembly of the church had become far more sober. That the popes held themselves to be superior to the council was not his only problem; a painstaking study of the history of the general council, drawing on all the most modern resources available to him, established for Luther that God's people should trust not the inerrancy and immutability of the decrees of the council, but the word of God, through Scripture alone, *sola scriptura*. If that were acknowledged, then participation at the deliberations would be possible, for Protestants valued the church so highly that, Luther wrote, 'we are prepared to perish leaving neither hide nor hair behind, rather than to see the church suffer harm or loss'.[30]

Here was an offer to work together with the Roman Church on reform, although admittedly only on condition that that church was prepared to abolish itself. That possibility was certainly not part of Paul III's plans for the council. The reformer rejected these plans vehemently, for he believed that the unfettered control of the council by the pope and the curia destroyed the very foundations of Christian freedom.

According to Roman reckoning, the council that did meet, convening for the first time in Trent in December 1545, following a renewed summons, was the nineteenth general council. However, this council did not represent all of Latin Christendom: it came some two decades too late, and it granted the Protestants, who in the meantime had established their own confession and their own church constitution, neither equal status as participants nor unrestricted discussion of the contentious religious issues. Additionally, when it came to the status of the pope within the church, very evidently the only possibility available to the council was that it confirm his existing position, with no prospect of altering, or even abolishing, his function, a non-negotiable for the Protestants. With the required parameters therefore lacking, Luther believed that Protestant participation would be pointless, even counterproductive. He had already written in July 1545 to Amsdorff that for the Imperial diet currently in session at Worms to order the Protestant estates to participate in the council under the threat of possible political repercussions would be a 'monstrosity' and 'the wisdom of Satan':

> The Pope shouts that we are heretics and that we must not have a place in the council; the Emperor [in fact this position had been adopted by King Ferdinand] wants us to consent to the council and its decrees. Perhaps God is making fools out of them . . . that they condemn us and at the same time ask for our consent. But this seems to be their raging wisdom . . . [that] they could be in a position of publicly decrying us as incorrigible people who are willing to listen neither to the pope, nor the church, not the Emperor, nor the empire, and now not even to the council, which we ourselves have so often requested. . . . But it is the Lord who will ridicule the mockers. . . . Let the pope first acknowledge that the council is superior to him, and let him listen

to the council [even] if it speaks against him—just as his conscience testifies against him—[and] then we shall discuss the whole matter. They are insane and stupid.[31]

The Protestant princes and magistrates were of the same mind. No Protestant theologians participated in the council, which as a result became the first council particular to the confessional Roman Church in the modern age. The council produced the Tridentine decrees issued in 1563 and the first modern self-contained confession of the Roman Church, the *Professio fidei Tridentina*, the equivalent of the Lutheran Confession of Augsburg of 1530.

Alliance and Resistance—Drawing Political Teachings from Scripture

Back in Wittenberg

By late summer 1530 the religious negotiations at Augsburg were getting nowhere and gradually the Protestant estates began to depart from the Imperial diet. The first of the Electoral Saxon delegation to leave was electoral prince John Frederick. On 14 September he visited Luther at Coburg, failing at first to recognize the reformer, who had acquired a full beard. John Frederick acknowledged Luther's service with the gift of a valuable signet ring, with the Luther rose as the coat of arms, which had been made by one of Augsburg's renowned goldsmiths. Luther was delighted, even if the princely ring, intended to be worn on top of a glove, was far too large for his bare scholar's hand.[32] He did not accept the prince's invitation to join his company for the trip home, however eager he was to return to his family. The worry was too great that unwarranted concessions might be made in Augsburg at the last moment. His sermon before the electoral prince was directed at preventing just such an outcome. In Augsburg, he warned, the devil was trying 'to tear us from our faith', but anyone who resisted could be sure that God would bring his own through all danger. Luther had recognized, however, that the battle would soon be over for the moment, and therefore he sent word to his wife, in a letter that he gave to his 'Most Gracious Lord' to take with him, that he would return home in early October.[33]

He arrived back in Wittenberg on Thursday, 13 October, at seven in the evening, following a journey of around eight days, during which he had preached repeatedly, at Schleiz, Altenburg, and finally also at the electoral residence town of Torgau. His life resumed its usual pattern, but having been absent for six months, Luther found he had little time to give to his wife and children. In response to a request from the landgrave of Hesse, the very week he arrived home he had to begin work on a record of the events at Augsburg that would fortify the faithful. Problems within the territorial church in Electoral Saxony also required his immediate attention, above all the falling out in Zwickau of pastor Konrad Cordatus, whom Luther had recommended, and Stephan Roth, the senior town clerk.[34] Naturally Luther also preached in the Wittenberg town church on the Sunday after his arrival home, and he threw himself back into his teaching. From autumn 1530 to spring 1532 Johannes Bugenhagen was in Lübeck, where he was involved in the construction of the evangelical church and for a year and a half Luther also served as Wittenberg town pastor, leading worship and providing pastoral care.

Political Counsel at Times of Crisis

Despite this demanding double burden, Luther continued to write. The calendar records that in the week of his return alone, four texts were made ready for publication: his 'Admonition concerning the Sacrament' (*Vermahnung zum Sakrament*), his treatise 'The Keys' (*Schlüsselgewalt*), and two psalm expositions, for Psalms 111 and 117. The following week 'Dr Martin Luther's Warning to His Dear German People' (*Warnung D. Martini Luther an seine lieben Deutschen*) was very nearly complete. Luther also began to forge plans for a new publication, specifically a text on the Jews. As he complained to his companions around the dining table, he was preaching four times each week, giving two lectures, providing his legal opinion, as a theological expert on specific marriage-related issues, trying to stay on top of his mounting correspondence, and at the same time writing books; all this work, he was in no doubt, was a task set for him by God.[35]

Repeatedly Luther had to put his usual daily responsibilities on hold while he provided the territorial government with advice. The week after his return from Coburg he was called to Torgau, from 26 to 28 October, to discuss the implications of the Emperor's decision to steer back into open opposition to Protestantism. With a Catholic majority present at the diet,

Charles had been able to obtain an Imperial resolution that restored all the severity of the Edict of Worms of 1521. With the heretic safe in Coburg or in Electoral Saxony and Luther's Reformation a reality in half of Germany, the suggestion that the resolution might be executed throughout the Empire was even more unrealistic than it had been nine years earlier. For the present the idea of a war on heresy, which certainly had its supporters in the Imperial camp, was unrealizable. The Catholic estates were not prepared to take military action against fellow members of the diet, and in the curia suspicions were again being aroused that Charles might become overly powerful and threaten the Papal States. In any case, with the Turkish armies again surging forward into Hungary and the Habsburg hereditary lands, the Emperor and his brother Ferdinand were dependent on the financial assistance of the Protestant estates. The Imperial government was repeatedly forced to grant temporary toleration. Thus in August 1532 at the Imperial diet held at Nuremberg, an Imperial mandate established that no cases involving religion were to be heard before the Imperial Chamber Court, the Imperial supreme court, hence granting the Protestants a free hand in regulating the nature of the church within their own lands.

The political realists in the Protestant camp were clear that any gains were likely only temporary, a product of current constellations, and that the fundamental threat from Imperial politics and from the power politics in play had not been lifted. Trusting in permanent protection by the French king, the enemy of the Habsburgs, would be equally futile. The Protestant camp therefore felt called to create, through political and military alliances, a shield that would protect it from the sword of Damocles that hung over it. Both political unions and military resistance were from the start interwoven with religious confession, and therefore no decisions were to be made without involving theologians—neither on resistance, where the interpretation of law and authority required Scriptural guidance, nor on alliances, where whether common political cause could be made with the Reformed, who did not recognize the Confession of Augsburg, was to be clarified.

As noted, Luther had already taken a stand on alliances and resistance: in 1528 at the territorial diet held at Altenburg a response had been needed to the report, later proved false, from Otto von Pack, councillor in Ducal Saxony, that the league of Catholic princes formed at Breslau was about to attack. In the heightened Imperial tensions of autumn 1530 the political plans of the evangelical authorities went much further, and were legally and ethically therefore more complex, for at stake was not just the relationship between individual estates, but the relationship to the Emperor, the head of the Empire.

The positions adopted by the Wittenberg theologians are recorded in material produced collectively, and we therefore often cannot trace their origins with any certainty to a single individual. As a rule, the drafting of the testimony fell to Melanchthon, but even if Luther did not hold the pen in his own hand, the results follow lines he had established. This framework was evangelical in a radical or, more precisely, biblical sense, for the reformer often drew on examples from the Old Testament. The stances taken on apparently entirely secular matters such as the relationship between authorities and their subjects, the right to form alliances and to resist, or economic or financial questions make very clear how unconditionally and extensively Luther lived and judged on the basis of Scripture. According to his reading, the Bible permitted only a single response to the threat of danger, namely, the renunciation of force and a strict limitation to self-defence. He remained by those principles throughout his life, although as the confrontation in the Empire reached a crisis point, he did finally have to accept some modification.

On Two Kingdoms and Two Regiments

Luther's political thought was rooted in Scripture; it was a political theology whose core remained consistent—from his early Reformation pamphlets, via his response to the rebellious peasants in 1525 and the peace offer made to Cardinal Albrecht of Brandenburg from Coburg in 1530, to the statements of the 1530s and 1540s on the right to form alliances and to resist. When he discussed the activities of the Christian, be that a Christian prince or a simple individual, Luther distinguished on the model of the church father Augustine, if not always entirely clearly, between the two kingdoms and the two regiments associated with them—the kingdom of God, in which God reigns through his word and his Gospel and fights sin with his law, and the kingdom of the world, which is threatened by evil in the form of the eternal enemy and therefore must be ruled by the authorities with sword and force in the name of God. Only in the early twentieth century did the term 'the doctrine of the two kingdoms' become established as a designation for the fundamental character of Luther's political theology, introduced by Karl Barth.

Luther did not take a theoretical model as his starting point; he began from the concrete problems of Christian activity in the world. The fundamental problem lay in the apparent contradiction, often challenging for Christians to grasp, between, on one hand, the commandments of Christ to love and to renounce violence and, on the other hand, the experiences of Christendom in this world. At the heart of this issue were rulers, who, like his contemporaries, Luther understood as authorities. He had the actors of his own day very much in mind: the Saxon electors, his territorial rulers, and their territorial state, but also the Emperor and the Holy Roman Empire, with which Electoral Saxony and the other Imperial estates were linked according to both divine and human law.

Luther's first great political text, written in 1523, carried the title 'Temporal Authority: To What Extent It Should Be Obeyed' (*Von welltlicher Uberkeytt, wie weyt man yhr gehorsam schuldig sey*). The work was dedicated to his territorial ruler, Duke John of Saxony, brother and co-regent of Frederick the Wise. In a series of sermons given in Wittenberg and at the court in Weimar, he had already treated the tension between the renunciation of violence demanded by Christ and the right to exercise force claimed by the authorities.[36] At that moment for Luther personally the question of the extent to which a Christian was bound to obey the authorities in matters of religion was particularly acute. Several princes, with neighbouring Duke George of Saxony amongst them, had recently forbidden their subjects from owning or reading works he had written. His text on the secular authorities therefore had a double task. On one hand, it considered 'temporal authority and the sword it bears, how to use it in a Christian manner', placing itself within the tradition of the late medieval 'mirror for princes', which sought to restrain and bring moral principles to the heightened sense of power of the Renaissance prince, as found most recently in the highly praised mirror for princes dedicated by Erasmus of Rotterdam to Charles V. On the other hand, the text sought to explain 'to what extent men are obligated to obey it [temporal authority]',[37] that is, to show Christian subjects facing increasingly oppressive demands from princes and magistrates the extent and limits of their right to self-determination and their ability to take political action of their own accord.

Authorities who prohibited their subjects from accessing Luther's writings and thereby withheld from them the rediscovered word of God were, for Luther, just as much in error as were the sectarians, who believed themselves perfected in Christ and therefore sequestered themselves from the imperfect world. Two fundamental truths of Scripture determined how the Christian must act. First, the temporal laws and the sword, understood as the penal power of the authorities, were established by God for the ordering of the world. As 'the authority which everywhere exists has been ordained by God', all those not called by God to rule have a duty of obedience, for 'he then who resists the governing authority resists the ordinance of God'. Secondly, since the Fall two kingdoms have existed, namely 'the kingdom of God' and the 'kingdom of the world', in each of which a different regiment obtains: in the temporal regiment of the kingdom of the world the human acts through temporal means and the authorities must use the sword and force to keep evil in check; in the spiritual regiment of the kingdom of God, God rules over God's people and fights against sin and does so only with God's word and the love of Christ.

Luther's awareness of realities and his pessimistic view of humankind paved the way towards a viable teaching on Christian action in the world that allowed him to retain Christ's commandments about love and the renunciation of violence. Since the Fall, Luther insisted, it must be recognized that, 'the whole world is evil and ... among thousands there is scarcely a single true Christian'. In the instance that 'anyone attempted to rule that world by the gospel and to abolish all temporal law and sword ... he would be loosing the ropes and chains of the savage wild beasts and letting them bite and mangle everyone', such that, he added with such a wonderfully immediate image, 'I would have the proof in my wounds'. For Luther the actions of the Christian on earth included the use of the sword—on which point he was at odds with the Anabaptists and the spiritualists—military service, oath-taking, and other concerns of a citizen of this world. But he did not see such earthly responsibilities—and here he distinguished himself from all those who promoted theocracy—as a commandment to establish the Gospel or the kingdom of God on earth. The task took the form of service to one's neighbour, what today we might call 'civic duty', 'since a true Christian lives and labors on earth not for himself alone but for his neighbor'.[38] This position formed the theological basis of a tract written in 1526, still under the shadow of the Peasants' War, entitled 'Whether Soldiers, Too, Can Be Saved' (*Ob Kriegsleute auch in seligem Stande sein können*)[39] and also of his texts on war with the Turks written in 1529 and 1530, however questionable all his exhortations to the use of force may seem today.

Luther's explanation of the extent and limits of secular authority has a dual character, as practical instruction for rulers on Christian conduct by those who hold political power in this world and as pastoral guidance in the cause of the salvation of those who exercise such authority: princes and statesmen, Luther wrote, are a 'rare prize in heaven'—a maxim later generations enjoyed citing—for it is not entirely impossible for them to achieve heavenly bliss, as long as they accept 'that God's word will neither turn nor bend for princes, but princes must bend themselves to God's word'.[40] Their political actions must not 'extend too far and encroach upon God's kingdom and government'. The lordship of the princes concerns only 'life and property and external affairs on earth, for God cannot and will not permit anyone but himself to rule over the soul'. Even though princes are 'consummate fools'—Luther was clearly taking aim at the authorities who forbade their subjects to read his works—'they must confess that they have no power over souls. For no human being can kill a soul or give it life, or conduct it to heaven or hell.'[41] Thus temporal authority with its claims to the obedience of its subjects concerned only the kingdom on earth. The responsibility of that temporal authority, according to Luther, was to punish peremptorily and without hesitation those who are evil and to nurture paternalistically those who are peaceable.

The guiding principles that Luther laid out for the Christian ruler were clear-cut: the ruler must be more clever than lawyers and must understand more than can be found in all the books of law. The ruler's actions must be of service to his subjects. His lands and his peoples are not there for his use; rather he is there for their use. He must therefore keep a strict eye on the 'high and mighty and . . . his counsellors', so on statesmen and officials, and while not treating them with contempt, he must also not trust any of them. Above all he must not allow himself to be hustled into war, and he must never repay a wrong with an even greater wrong but must abide by the proverb 'he cannot govern who cannot wink at faults'.[42]

At this time Luther rejected on principle the taking up of arms against a superior authority such as the Emperor or the German king, for to do so would contravene the ordering of the Empire established by God. War against lordships, or 'states', which were legally equal or inferior was lawful only when the protection and security of one's lands and people were at stake and attempts at reconciliation had failed.

Seen as a whole, then, Luther's political theology was concerned with the rights of the people, in effect the rights of subjects, to religious self-determination and the inviolability of their consciences, and also with astute and lawful action by rulers that was rooted in the contemporary Imperial and territorial constitution. The doctrine of the two kingdoms contained no double moral standard that combined the religious ethics of one kingdom and the Machiavellian apparatus of the other. By means of a specific distribution of power, Luther's doctrine established what modern terminology would designate a 'balance of power': externally the claims and rights of the authorities to the bodies of their subjects were set against the right of God to the souls and the consciences of God's people, over which the temporal authorities had absolutely no sway; internally, within the temporal regiment, the balance was between the ruler's power to punish and the ruler's duty to nurture.

The acknowledgement that the kingdom on earth has its own regiment with its own ethics and its own instruments designated the political realm an autonomous space, free of theology, a space that Luther no longer entered with religious directives in hand. Another principle, concerning the individual's personal responsibility for his or her soul, was also formulated here. Although to talk of freedom of the conscience at this date would be anachronistic, the conscience of the individual had been declared off-limits to political manipulation. In 1520 Luther had rejected the claims of the pope and his Roman Church when he wrote of the freedom of the Christian; in 1523 in his text on temporal authority, he set clear limits to secular power and established, again in the terminology of today, fundamental rights for every individual: 'How dare the mad temporal authority judge and control such a secret, spiritual, hidden matter as faith?'[43]

Right of Resistance and the Schmalkaldic League

In the late 1520s, when the issues of obedience and resistance re-emerged with a new urgency, Luther remained by his constraints. With the announcement of the Emperor's return to the Empire and the possibility of political and military coercion, at the beginning of 1530 the Saxon government resolved to forearm, hoping for a positive response to a question put to the reformer for his expert opinion: 'Should his Imperial Majesty...dare to overrun us and use force against us for the sake of the word of God, whether we are bound to suffer such or whether we in turn may halt such use of force'. But Luther was not to be moved from his position that 'he who strikes back is in the wrong', even princes, who at that time—and not in accord with the Imperial constitution—he believed subjects of the Emperor without office and therefore bound to obey. Naturally, obedience that was counter to God's truth could not be required of them, but passive disobedience was the only form of resistance permitted, even to the point of forced exile. Unlike Philip of Hesse, who believed that as a 'full Christian' he did not in 'all good conscience' have to suffer in silence, Elector John accepted Luther's moral counsel and passed the text on to his confessor with the charge that he always remind the elector of what Luther had written.[44]

Where previously the theological and ethical problems of political action had been treated theoretically and with an eye to the future, in autumn 1530 with the Augsburg Imperial recess they gained an additional dimension. Unlike in the case of the Speyer resolution of the previous year, now the Emperor himself stood behind the renewed threat of Imperial action against the Protestant estates. It was clear that the estates were only safe from the power of the Emperor as long as in the wider political arena Charles' hands were tied. The constellations of the international power system could change at any time as the result of a battle or diplomatic agreement. The issue of the right to resist was more pertinent than ever and was tied in a distinctive manner to the problems of authority and obedience. Was the Christian commandment to obedience unconditionally binding even in the case of this Emperor, who was hostile to the Protestants, or did the resolutions of Augsburg make military precautions legitimate, and if so, what form might these take?

In light of the duty of obedience, reiterated by Luther in the spring, everything now depended on whether the Emperor, the authority set over the princes by God, had acted lawfully. That question was tackled in a whole run of theological expert opinions produced in autumn/spring 1530/31, and by no means did all share Luther's assessment.[45] Amongst the Wittenberg theologians, Bugenhagen and Amsdorff had favoured resistance from the start. Above all Philip of Hesse and his jurists advocated, in letters and expert opinions, for the right to resist. Evidence of Luther's readiness to test all the matters of this world against their compatibility with Scripture is found in his willingness to hear such arguments and his agreement that he would be included in the reports issued collectively by the Wittenbergers when, finally, they deemed active resistance theologically justified. That cooperation is all the more remarkable because the Protestants of Franconia, in particular in Brandenburg-Ansbach and the Imperial city of Nuremberg, led by orthodox Lutheran reformer Johannes Brenz, remained unswervingly by the original stance and rejected all active resistance.

The relaxation of Luther's position on resistance had already begun at that consultation at Torgau that he and his Wittenberg colleagues had been ordered to attend immediately after his return from Coburg. There they were 'communicated a note' with a quintessential version of a legal opinion drafted by the 'doctors of law' under the leadership of former chancellor Gregor Brück. Luther's theological objections from March had not been taken into account. Instead, drawing on canon law and Roman civil law and in part also on natural law, the document summarily established that the Emperor had violated the responsibilities of his office and that therefore resistance was permitted. This view was in accord with the concerns of the landgrave of Hesse, recently expressed in a letter, about the application of the biblical commandment to obedience to the Imperial constitution. The electoral princes, Philip of Hesse had written, are partners in the Empire while the head of the Imperial institution is only an elected Emperor and therefore 'it is evidently the case that no emperor has ever had the power in German lands to demand forcibly a single gulden from a prince'. Additionally, as the recent history of the resistance of the Bohemians and the Swiss demonstrated, he continued, active resistance was by no means novel.[46]

Luther was loath to follow these arguments and did so reluctantly. Again the distinction between the two kingdoms and between the two regiments was decisive. Legal scholars had proved that here was a situation in which the constitution of the Empire permitted resistance, he opined, continuing, 'We have always taught that one may allow the temporal laws to exist, to be valid, and to be upheld as they are because the gospel does not teach against the temporal law.'[47] Here was no theological justification of the use of force, with the divine order established by a holy war, but rather simply recognition that jurists and statesmen could employ the tools of their earthly regiment in their own kingdom. In practice the jurists aligned themselves with the Lutheran teaching on the two kingdoms, as for example when Chancellor Feige of Hesse found a right to resist in natural law, but insisted that he had no competence to judge whether that 'might happen with God and good conscience'.[48]

However small the concession granted by the Wittenberg professors may seem, agreement from the theologians had cleared the way for unreserved negotiations over united action, which were held in late 1530 and early 1531 in Schmalkalden, in Hesse, and quickly proved fruitful. The official Protestant defensive alliance, named the Schmalkaldic League after the location where it had been formulated, was formally created on 27 February 1531 in Saxon Torgau. The long-debated Protestant military alliance had become a reality, and it was soon to be joined by the large majority of the Imperial estates that accepted the Confession of Augsburg. Brandenburg-Ansbach and Nuremberg did not become members but instead held firm to their orthodox Lutheran position and continued to reject any active resistance. Nonetheless, the Schmalkaldic League stretched across all the Empire, from Strasburg in the south-west to Pomerania in the north-east, and from Constance in the south to Oldenburg in the north (see Map 2). Negotiations over possible alliances with England and France were launched, although without any concrete result. In the mid-1530s the league's army comprised 2,000 cavalry and 10,000 foot soldiers, who were under the command of the league's two leading players, Electoral Saxony and Hesse.

If Charles should issue a call to arms against the Protestant Imperial estates, 'the emperor would not only act in contravention of God and divine law but also in violation of his own imperial law, vow, duty, seal, and edicts'[49]—Luther quickly published this insight, won from the legal opinion provided by the Saxon jurists, for a wider audience in 'Luther's Warning to His Dear German People'. Where previously he had preached obedience to the Emperor as the highest authority appointed by God, now he wrote of not only the right but even the duty—as the Gospel was under threat—of disobedience as the guiding principle for political action. For the simple Christian this meant continued passive, suffering disobedience. The princes and their governments, however, were now allotted distinctly enlarged and evangelically legitimized scope for action in their earthly kingdom. In addition to the power of the sword that Luther had always granted them in internal matters, now they also had theological validation for political alliances and military resistance to the Emperor.

Nevertheless Luther continued to be careful to maintain a certain distance from the affairs of the world. If war should occur as a result of the resistance that had been permitted, then he would have to accede to the others in his party and await God's council and judgement. 'It is not fitting for me, a preacher, vested with the spiritual office, to wage war or to counsel war or incite it, but rather to dissuade from war and to direct to peace,' he recorded. If, however, it should come to war, he continued, 'I will surely hold my pen in check and keep silent and not intervene as I did in the last uprising', a reference to the Peasants' War.[50] He had learned his lesson, and the political discussion of the right to resist and the right to form an alliance had shown him that precisely as a divine prophet he must not confuse which kingdom and regiment were his domain.

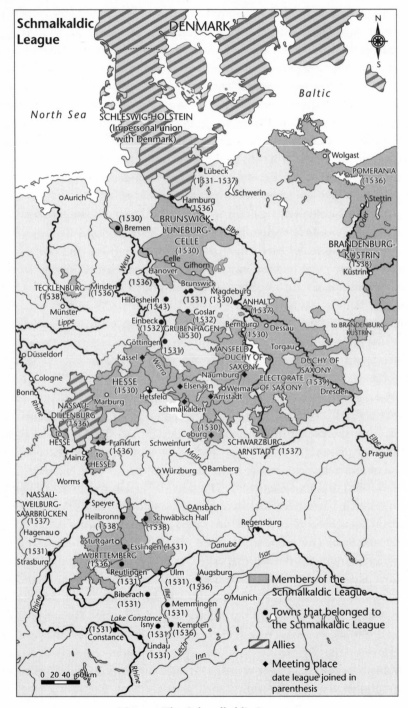

Map 2. The Schmalkaldic League.

With his new approach to resistance Luther edged closer to political reality. His high estimation of Emperor and Empire was in ultimate effect a romanticized and backwards-looking delusion and no longer corresponded with the realities of political power in Germany or with the full constitutional reality. Even as the princes acquired sovereign rights, they retained their feudal responsibilities to the Emperor, but they were not the Emperor's subjects; they carried the weight of the Empire alongside the Emperor, of an Empire that could not be ruled without them. In particular when it came to the practicalities of power politics, of the economic system, and—as nothing could make clearer than had the Luther Affair—of ecclesiastical and cultural politics, they were the equals of the Emperor, not least because the latter had little access to instruments of power within the Empire, and, just like the princes, was reliant on his own lands for resources and as a power base.

Earlier, in the fifteenth century, the Imperial head and the estates had become embroiled in a tenacious struggle over the modernizing or reform of the Imperial constitution. Preliminary steps had been taken under Emperor Maximilian but where they would lead was not yet clear. As a result every shift in the power relations of Emperor and estates also—and indeed especially in the religious question—was a move towards resolution of the reform of the Empire to the advantage of either the Imperial crown or the estates. Luther's acknowledgement of the practical realities of this political rivalry gave the Protestant politicians legal space to manoeuvre, but it also meant that Luther himself viewed the political situation with new eyes.

On this basis, Saxony and its allies now had a clear framework for their political action over the coming years, and as a result Luther the political consultant returned to the wings. He still continued to call for moderation, however, and to warn against an overly hasty willingness to use force, which meant that he repeatedly clashed with the position adopted by Landgrave Philip and his Hesse theologians. In the early 1530s his life again became dominated by his daily endeavours in the Wittenberg offices of German and European Protestantism—the translation of the Bible, theological disputations, personnel matters, and advice for evangelical communities.

Countering Political Catholicism and the Anabaptists of Münster

With many princes rejecting the Reformation, Luther found himself increasingly concerned with political Catholicism. Particularly demanding was the dispute with Duke George of Saxony, who indefatigably sought to keep Luther's teachings at bay from his lands, which not only neighboured but in some cases even intermingled with the lands of Electoral Saxony. At the beginning of the 1540s Luther bitingly mocked Duke Henry of Brunswick, who was equally adamant in his Counter-Reformation stance, with his polemical text 'Against Hanswurst' (*Wider Hans Worst*),[51] which while certainly uncouth and vituperative, was also virtuosic. He thereby opened a strategically important door for the spread of his teachings within central Germany. For Luther the dispute was something of an elixir that seems to have lightened days darkened by pain, illness, and age.

A similar impression is provided by the dispute that Luther had entered into several years earlier with Cardinal Albrecht of Brandenburg, his adversary from the early days of the Reformation. At the beginning the conflict focused on Albrecht's anti-evangelical ecclesiastical policy and on his suspected influence on the dukes of Saxony and Brunswick, whom we have just encountered. Luther was particularly alarmed when at Whitsun 1534 Albrecht cleansed the council of his residence town of Halle of all supporters of the Reformation, thereby overthrowing the constitution of the town. A highly suspect legal case followed, in which the cardinal employed, as was not uncommon at the time, his powers of high justice as territorial lord to bail himself out of a political fix. He used his chamberlain, wealthy merchant Hans Schönitz, as a sacrificial pawn—condemned on the basis of a confession extorted under torture, Schönitz was executed in order to cover up irregularities in the territorial finances. The rage of Luther the prophet at the machinations of the ecclesiastical prince was so great that even the evangelicals amongst Albrecht's fellow members of the estates were left aghast. The Hohenzollerns protested sharply at Luther's unrestrained accusations, and even Duke Albrecht of Prussia, who revered Luther, expressed his indignation. Luther had to justify himself before former chancellor of Electoral Saxony Brück and ultimately his publications were closely censored.

The reformer was especially outraged that the cardinal had had the execution carried out before the case brought before the Imperial Chamber Court by the Schönitz family had been heard. For Luther, whatever one's place in society, one was strictly bound to follow the processes laid down by the law. He was giving expression to a development that moved apace during the sixteenth century and that today historians term 'juridification' or, better, 'judicialization', whereby the unregulated use of force was replaced by the regulated implementation of the law.

Luther gave similar advice in the case of a feud that gained literary prominence in the nineteenth century when it was used as the basis of Heinrich von
Kleist's novella *Michael Kohlhaas*. Having sought revenge through violent
means, Hans Kohlhase turned to Luther for advice and assistance. In a letter
of 8 December 1534 Luther insistently warned Kohlhase not to dwell on
retribution. While Kohlhase undoubtedly had a right to protect his reputation, Luther acknowledged, he must not do so by committing a sin or acting
unlawfully. His feud would lead only to sinfulness and roguery and would
burden his conscience 'for you knowingly should destroy so many people, for
which you have no right'. Luther proposed that instead he should act peaceably
and pursue his interests through legal means. If, however, 'he should not obtain
justice, then there can be no advice other than to suffer injustice'.[52]

Finally, during this phase Luther also had to grapple with the Anabaptist
Kingdom of God created at Münster. From 1534 until June 1535 the New
Jerusalem ruled by Jan of Leiden as 'King of Münster' held all of Germany in
suspense, theologians and men of the church no less than princes and
statesmen on both sides. Fearing not least that practices at Münster might
catch on in many circles where the Reformation was not yet secure, Luther
intensified his theological dispute with the Anabaptists, with, for example,
his great sermon series on the biblical foundations and correct understanding
of baptism.[53] With their constitutional revolution and their introduction of
the community of goods and polygamy, the Anabaptists of Münster challenged the fundamental order of the age and gradually became a political
problem that the reformer also had to address. The need to respond was
all the greater because Luther's opponents in the Catholic camp, such as
Johannes Cochläus, held Luther and his teachings responsible for the perversion of all the established norms. Additionally, the Saxon government
commissioned Luther with using his ecclesiastical connections in Westphalia
as a source of more detailed information about what was happening. Better
informed about the specific circumstances after the arrival of a report from
Soest in autumn 1534, Saxony responded. Luther believed another great
theological debate with the Anabaptists unnecessary and therefore instead
limited himself to the prefaces of works by others.[54] He held that polygamy,
the community of goods, and the eschatological kingdom were so evidently
anti-Christian that there was no need for theologians and the church to give
these revolutionary innovations their attention. The responsibility to restore
order, he opined, fell solely on the temporal authorities. In his eyes the

Anabaptists were the cause of disorder, and according to Luther's political theology disorder could never be condoned and was to be put down with the sword.

In June 1535 Münster was seized by the combined military forces of the German princes, united in extraconfessional solidarity, and the Anabaptists were punished mercilessly. The Wittenbergers subsequently publicized their position in an account entitled 'That Secular Authority Is Obligated to Defend against the Anabaptists with Physical Punishment' (*Dass weltliche Oberkeit den Wiedertäufern mit leiblicher Strafe zu wehren schuldig sei. Ettliche Bedenken zu Wittenberg*), composed according to the now-standard pattern whereby the text was written by Melanchthon and Luther added his name as one of the signatories.[55] The Wittenberg theologians were responding to a request for advice from the landgrave of Hesse, who to date had punished Anabaptists only with banishment.[56] From the start they emphasized this matter was not one for the 'preaching office', for it was not given the use of the sword. The responsibility to act fell entirely to the temporal authority, although it should punish only the obstinate who closed their ears to admonition. For those who accepted admonition and renounced their error, 'it is Christian to show them mercy'. Religious errors were not to be punished, only offenses against the 'physical regiment', a reference to the fundamental opposition of the Anabaptists to temporal authority. Such infringements, they recorded, were a product of their teachings that Christians must not acknowledge any authority, must not swear—Anabaptists therefore refused to take the oath, which was fundamental in constructing the obligations of the civic community and of the feudal system and the early modern state— must not own any possessions, and were entitled 'to leave the women they have married' for religious reasons.

As religion did not provide a fundamental right to punish, or even an obligation to punish, medieval heresy law was not relevant. With the designation of Anabaptism as rebellion, however—a verdict that was not limited to the extreme form found at Münster—the Wittenberg report made a decisive contribution to the radicalization of the authorities' policy on the Anabaptists. It made no difference that Luther added to the document in his own hand the words, 'This is the general rule, but may our gracious lord always show mercy along with punishment according to the circumstances.'

In light of the events at Münster and strengthened by theological statements made by both sides, in Germany—unlike in the Dutch Republic of the seventeenth century—the authorities continued to persecute Anabaptists for generations, deeming them rebels and fundamental enemies of the early modern state. The tragedy was compounded by the authorities' complete inability to see the entirely peaceable foundations of Anabaptism, which were abandoned by and large only by the Anabaptist grouping that gained power in Münster. Anabaptist leader Menno Simons, who was also from the Low Countries, reacted by immediately re-establishing non-violence as a fundamental tenet, which then became characteristic not just of his own followers, the Mennonites, but also of Anabaptism as a whole.

Papal Council and Luther's 'Testament Regarding Religion'

In autumn 1536 grand politics entered the stage again. In a bull issued on 2 June 1536 Pope Paul III had called a council of the church, which was to meet the following May in Mantua. The princes should also attend for the sake of countering heresy, improving Christian morals, and restoring a peaceful unity. A demand made repeatedly for the last decade and a half had now been met. Many had given up hope, and in light of the measures against Luther's teachings put in place in the meantime by Rome and the Emperor, they were uncertain how they should react. The Saxon elector was inclined to ignore the invitation, and the theologians were suspicious that what awaited them was an auto-da-fé on the model of Hus' experience at Constance in 1415. As we have heard, Luther took absolutely no stock in this council, which had been called on the sole authority of the pope and could certainly not be deemed a free gathering. He even doubted that it would take place. 'If the pope summoned me I wouldn't go,' he informed those sitting around the table, 'I'd scoff at his summons because he's our adversary.' Commenting with self-irony on the impact of his excommunication he continued:

> But if the council publicly asked me I'd comply, for I'd be welcome and I'd be received in a friendly fashion. . . . If you, my dear Katy, went with me and acknowledged that you were Luther's wife, you'd be burned to death even if in other respects you honored the whole papacy. The Lord keep me in his Word! For I have very bitter enemies.[57]

His refusal to attend was not the end of the matter for Luther. The elector heard from his jurists just how politically and, especially, legally complicated and dangerous the matter was. As the custodian (*Vogt*) of the church, the

Emperor was legally entitled, in light of his temporal authority, to execute any decisions that might be passed at the council, and the law provided no grounds for opposition. The question of resistance thus emerged again, this time in a highly complex context for both Imperial and ecclesiastical law. John Frederick, who had become elector of Saxony in 1532, had been raised by Spalatin and had been drawn to Luther's theology since his youth. He was not going to make a decision on this issue without taking theological advice. On 24 July he requested that his Wittenberg theologians provide him with their expert opinion on the council. In September 1536, Luther was called no fewer than three times to the court at Torgau, where he provided counsel but also, and above all, preached to the political decision makers and tended to their spiritual needs in order to fortify them at this particularly difficult moment. Dated 6 December 1536 and the work of Melanchthon, the collective report of the Wittenberg theologians was based entirely on the doctrine of the two kingdoms and gave the politicians a free hand in temporal matters, for, it recorded, 'the Gospel permits all natural and warranted protection and defence as established in natural law or otherwise by the temporal regiment.' This position was in keeping with the advice given in 1530, with the only change Melanchthon's citation of natural law in the rationale, in addition to the temporal regiment. Luther was the first to sign the document, and added his affirmation: 'I will also act with prayer, even where it is to be with the fist.'[58]

But Elector John Frederick was not yet satisfied. In addition to the legitimization of his temporal decision, he wanted assurance that he was on firm ground in religious and confessional terms. On that front, only Luther's opinion counted. In light of the reformer's advancing years and his troubled health, for some time the Saxon court had harboured a desire for Luther to compose a comprehensive account of his teachings that could then serve as his testament. The plan was partially conceived as a means of forestalling the unholy quarrels that it was feared would break out amongst the evangelical theologians after the reformer's death. Now, at the end of 1536, the moment had come for Luther to compose his 'testament regarding religion', having received the commission from former chancellor Brück in late August. The text would then be ready in time to be presented at the gathering of the members of the Schmalkaldic League that was planned for the beginning of February 1537 and could be approved by those present. Luther threw himself into the task with his usual energy, but on 18/19 December he suffered a heart attack, and he had to dictate the final paragraphs to two colleagues.

Luther's 'Schmalkaldic Articles', as the confession soon became known, would long preoccupy the Lutherans of Electoral Saxony and of Germany as a whole and was the cause of much debate—first at the end of December in Wittenberg, at a gathering of Electoral Saxon theologians; then in February 1537 at the diet held at Schmalkalden; and eventually, in summer 1538, by a broad public, after Luther arranged for its publication—previously the text had only been circulated internally.[59]

The diet that opened at the great council chamber in the town hall of Schmalkalden on 10 February 1537 was the most splendid and most significant in the history of the military league. Eighteen princes and twenty-eight envoys from the towns attended, accompanied and counselled by no fewer than forty-two theologians, as well as ambassadors from Denmark and France and observers sent by the Emperor and the Holy See. Luther presented his articles, which were to function as the basis for decisions made in confessional politics. The article on the Lord's Supper was the cause of renewed intense debate, as the southern German members of the league believed themselves excluded. Strasburg, in particular, an essential member of the league in light of its fiscal, diplomatic, and military contributions, felt snubbed. Melanchthon had his own concerns about the tactical implications of the unambiguous and radical rejection of the papacy, which he believed removed all room for negotiation, and he looked for an alternative approach. With many of the political leaders, led by Philip of Hesse, expressing concern about the text, the Saxon elector forwent official discussion of the articles by the diet. In any case there was no political need for the diet to address the text, as all the members of the alliance unanimously opposed any involvement with the papal council.

At the last moment Bugenhagen and Amsdorff arranged for the theologians present at the diet to meet together. Bugenhagen stood firmly behind Luther's article on the Lord's Supper, having even intensified the wording of Luther's original version. At the conclusion of their discussions the participants were presented with the text to sign. Only the southern German theologians refused. From amongst the Wittenberg theologians, however, Melanchthon recorded his reservations:

> I, Philip Melanthon [sic] also regard the above articles as true and Christian. However, concerning the pope I maintain that if he would allow the gospel, we, too, may (for the sake of peace and general unity among those Christians who are now under him and might be in future) grant to him his superiority over the bishops which he has 'by human right' [iure humano].[60]

Serious illness prevented Luther from attending either the political negotiations or the meeting of the theologians. Despite suffering that serious heart
attack before Christmas, he had still undertaken the demanding eight-day
journey to Schmalkalden, in the middle of winter, travelling through
Thuringia and the Thuringian Forest and, as usual, preaching repeatedly
along the way. Hardly had he arrived in Schmalkalden when he was stricken
with bladder and kidney problems. Initially he continued to preach in the
town church, and when he became too weak, he still attended several of the
daily worship services held in that church, although he avoided the cold
nave in favour of a small robing room above the sacristy. He was living in
two rooms on the first floor of a large three-storey half-timbered building,
the house of the *Rentmeister*, a Hesse official. On 11 February he held a short
service there, but he was too weak to be able to leave his quarters. Fearful for
the life of his reformer, the elector arranged for a doctor and his medications
to travel from Erfurt, and then also a barber surgeon from Waltershausen,
who was to remove the kidney stones. Luther's health still did not improve,
and he did not want to die in foreign Hesse. On 26 February the sick man
began the journey back to Wittenberg, accompanied by the doctor from
Erfurt and several colleagues. The journey in an unsprung, or hardly sprung,
travelling coach via the bumpy roads of the Thuringian Forest was agonizing, but it brought its own blessings—shortly before reaching Gotha he
passed the stones and, on this occasion, he survived. He still needed to take it
easy, however, and the patient and his caregivers therefore arrived back in
Wittenberg only on 14 March, after a two-week-long journey.

The Schmalkaldic Articles contained Luther's final word on all confessional
and doctrinal issues. He used the opportunity to establish for eternity, as it
were, his position on all those theological issues that he believed had not
been spelled out clearly in the discussions held at Augsburg in 1530 and
subsequently. He was less prepared than ever to mince his words, and he
showed no consideration for other theological opinions within the Protestant
camp, let alone for political interests or political calculation. As he had done in
those decisive moments twenty years earlier, he again made central the
evangelical doctrine of the justification of the individual through faith alone.
He was preparing the ground for after his death, and he therefore saw less
reason than ever to give way or compromise on this truth, or on any other
doctrinal truth. He would not be deterred by the unwillingness of the
Schmalkaldic League to address his 'testament' or by the hesitation of a

number of theologians in his own camp to identify with all the points in his confession. He even took Melanchthon's tactical manoeuvring in his stride. All the greater, then, was his delight in the unwavering faith of Elector John Frederick in both his reformer and his reformer's confession, for it guaranteed that even after his death the newly discovered Gospel would have a powerful champion on earth. That conviction was reinforced when, in 1544, John Frederick presented the articles as officially published to the Imperial diet at Speyer in order that the German public and all of Christendom might see that Electoral Saxony's religious and ecclesiastical politics were built on theological foundations that the reformer himself had formulated.

In 1538 Luther had already arranged for the articles to be published privately. Paul III had first changed the location of the council from Mantua to Vicenza and then, in April 1538, had postponed the council indefinitely, and Luther no longer entirely discounted the possibility that a pope might be willing 'to convene a truly free council in a serious and genuine spirit, without deception and treachery, as would be his duty'. Should that happen, then 'this confession' would be ready—to which, Luther also recorded in the preface, 'I have held fast . . . and by God's grace, I will continue to hold'—as a precautionary measure, to defend against the attacks of not only opponents but also 'the poisonous people . . . among our . . . unfaithful associates'.[61] He intended his text to act as a compass for his ruler, Elector John Frederick, and indeed the elector set his bearings by the articles when he was plunged into political and personal crisis only a few months after Luther's death, when the Emperor launched his long-feared attack.

However, the reformer's confession could not guarantee harmony amongst the theologians. Melanchthon's delicate distancing from the text, however nuanced and, in the end, loyal to Luther, would play its part in ensuring that immediately after the Emperor's victory, Luther's legacy was contested by his heirs. The tensions that Luther and Melanchthon, bound by a Christian fraternal understanding of their common task, could absorb, now produced deep enmities and bitter public polemical battles between, on one hand, the Gnesiolutherans, who claimed to be the only 'genuine' Lutherans, with Matthias Flacius Illyricus, a pupil of Luther's, at their head, and, on the other hand, the Philippists, led by Melanchthon, who were deemed crypto-Calvinists and accused of wholesale betrayal of Luther's inheritance, for they appeared to incline towards Calvin's teaching on the Lord's Supper, and when it came to church politics, they were ready to accept the Imperial Interim and thereby make concessions to the Roman Church.

Revealingly, recourse to Luther's Schmalkaldic Articles initiated an end
to this fraternal warring in the mid-1570s. His text was subsequently
absorbed into the Book of Concord in 1580, where it formed a central
pillar of Lutheranism within the Empire, a Lutheranism largely freed of
anything Philippist.

The Dilemma of the Landgrave of Hesse's Bigamy

'Unbounded Sexuality' or 'An End to Double Standards'?

The turbulence over the appropriate response by German Protestantism to
the Roman plans for a council was hardly over—or rather had been placed
on the back burner by the postponement of the council—when the reformers and the Saxon leadership of the Schmalkaldic League faced a problem
that was hardly any less explosive. At first glance this problem seemed a
private matter, and the reformers, called on to provide their opinion,
attempted to treat it entirely as such. But just as the confessional problem
was per se a political issue, so too the pastoral care required in this case had
political import, for the matter concerned one of the most powerful of the
princes of the Empire and a leading figure of political Protestantism, on a par
with the Saxon elector. Additionally the issue at stake had profound implications for both Imperial and ecclesiastical law. Philip, landgrave of Hesse
(Figure 39), was not inclined to comply with the Emperor and the law of
the Empire when it was not in his interests to do so, and he was also not
willing to have his sexual desires reined in by established norms. Philip had
been married since 1523 to a daughter of Luther's opponent Duke George
of Saxony (George the Bearded), but he permitted himself a profligate
extramarital love life, which evidently neither his wife nor the pastors of
Hesse dared challenge. In light of the Wettin family inheritance arrangements, the Saxon sister-dynasty was politically interested in what happened
at the Hesse court; like the majority of their contemporaries, at least amongst
the nobility, they were largely unconcerned, however, about extramarital
relationships.

In summer 1539 the fine veil of religious and personal disingenuousness
was abruptly torn. The landgrave, whose wife had just given birth to their
seventh child, encountered Margarete von der Sale, a seventeen-year-old
lady-in-waiting at the court, and immediately desired her, just as he had

Figure 39. Philip I, landgrave of Hesse (1504–1567), as a young man, by Hans Krell, painted between 1560 and 1570.

desired dozens of women in the past. Von der Sale's mother, however, who held a high position at the court of Philip's sister Elisabeth von Rochlitz, was not ready to tolerate the purely sexual relationship that Philip demanded. As it was not equivalent to marriage and in particular did not give any children inheritance rights, she was also not willing to accept her daughter's living in 'concubinage', a form of relationship widespread in ruling houses of the age that ensured the partner a certain social status. She demanded a legally binding church wedding that would create a legitimate second marriage.

Philip was in a bind, for the moral demands of the leading theologians of the Reformation, which he defended with such passion, were very high, a response to the turpitudes of the Roman Church, and those demands focused in particular on issues concerning marriage and sexual relations. Philip's quandary came with serious risks, for bigamy was not tolerated in Imperial law. According to the Carolina—this strict legal code setting out procedure in capital crimes had been established by Charles V just a few years earlier and had only been adopted for Hesse by Philip with great hesitation—bigamy was punishable by death. Additionally, any suggestion of polygamy was theological dynamite. Ever since the New Zion had been established in Münster in 1534/35, polygamy had been seen as a sign of heresy and had been tackled by both Catholic and Protestant princes, including the landgrave of Hesse in particular, with recourse to the sword. But Philip, a crafty tactician, saw a way out from this messy situation: Luther himself, with all his authority in theological and moral matters, would provide him with a declaration that could function as a legal certificate of no objection.

Philip had in mind nothing less than a theological statement that the bigamous second marriage he was planning was legitimate in the eyes of God and humankind, with certification, if possible, that nothing stood in the way of the eternal salvation of the landgrave. For all his temerity, Philip was not prepared to convey his wishes directly to Luther, for personally they were hardly on the best of terms. He could well imagine the storm of anger he might face.[62] Here, too, however, a way forward was quickly found. Philip confided in his personal physician, who was treating him for a serious illness at the time, likely syphilis, which was so widespread. His physician recalled that since the Marburg colloquy on the Lord's Supper, Martin Bucer had been in the debt of the landgrave, and he asked the Strasburg reformer to make the landgrave's case before Luther and Melanchthon. Initiated into the circumstances by a long discussion with Philip in person, Bucer not only delivered a letter from the landgrave but also participated in the Wittenberg reformers' deliberations.

Fair judgement of Philip and his desire for pastoral counsel is not easy. Historians have often used the spirit of their own age as their point of reference and therefore have seen in Philip's bigamy an expression of 'unbounded sexuality' and 'the great stain on the history of the Reformation and in the life of Luther' (the scandalized judgement of the moralistic nineteenth century) or have defended him as a 'honest bigamist' who forced 'an end to double moral standards' (a present-day judgement made in the context of an omnipresent sexuality).[63] Let us free ourselves from such anachronistic conclusions and try instead to understand this matter, too, on its own sixteenth-century terms.

What stands out in the landgrave's behaviour is that deep religious longing and secular deviousness could coexist. On one hand the landgrave was undoubtedly a committed, Bible-led Christian who suffered deeply at the sinfulness of his actions. For over a decade he had taken communion only rarely and exceptionally, evidently fearing that he would suffer eternal damnation if he approached the Table of the Lord impenitently and not willing to change his ways. During his long illness in 1539, when he believed he was on the cusp of death, one fear tormented Philip until it became almost unbearable: had he squandered his chance at eternal salvation through his sexual escapades, which he seemed unable to halt? God appeared to have punished him by giving him syphilis. His moving descriptions for the reformers of the anguish of his soul and his conscience and his requests for pastoral counsel that were in effect pleas that he might be rescued from eternal damnation were hardly feigned. It is certainly possible that a religiously and legally legitimized second marriage with Margarete von Sale, whom he desired so passionately, could have appeared to him a suitable way of freeing himself from the extramarital sexual desires that were deemed sinful.

On the other hand, Philip tackled the concerns of his conscience with all the usual slipperiness and unscrupulousness of a politician, skills that had long been second nature to him and that Luther found abhorrent. Philip did not even stop short of blackmail.[64] He ended his request with an undisguised threat: if the reformers were not prepared to give his second marriage their theological blessing, then to the great detriment of the Reformation he would be forced to change sides and turn to the Emperor, or even to the Roman curia, who ever since their arbitrary annulment of the first marriage of Henry VIII of England had had the reputation of being able to find a solution for even the most delicate of sexual circumstances.

Similar Circumstances in the Catholic Camp

It would be anachronistic to believe the religious in Philip's demands cancelled out his shrewdness. If we use the circumstances of his own age as our yardstick, then his behaviour can appear even courageous and consistent. Certainly he did not take refuge in an irregular cover-up of the kind adopted by the decisively Catholic Duke Henry of Brunswick, the antihero of a text by Luther we have already encountered, his pamphlet entitled 'Against Hanswurst'. Henry of Brunswick would never have dreamed of using a second marriage to sidestep public condemnation of his relationship with Eva von Trott, just seventeen years old and a lady-in-waiting to his wife. When their relationship, which had produced three children, could no longer be kept secret, he staged a farcical fake funeral for his lover in Gandersheim; in the meantime the young woman had fled to a remote castle where the extramarital relationship could continue, far from the court and out of the public eye, and over the following years it produced further children.

The deception-based model used in Brunswick produced just as unhappy an outcome as the bigamy-based model employed in Hesse. Von Trott's parents did not believe that their daughter had really died, and in 1541 they lodged a complaint against Duke Henry at the Imperial diet held at Regensburg. The scandal, now made public, fell into the lap of the Protestants, for they were wrapped up in a bitter feud with the Duke of Brunswick, who had very recently badly snubbed the elector of Saxony by refusing to allow him to pass through his territory. Luther himself took the matter to heart and in his polemical pamphlet 'Against Hanswurst' he revealed and thundered against the hypocrisy of the duke and his moralizing outrage at the drunkenness and gluttony of the Protestant princes. Henry himself, Luther wrote, was guilty of 'shameful whoredom and adultery' and, worse still, of blasphemy and of insulting God. With his fake funeral, Mass, and office for the dead, 'he makes a jester's cap out of both God and the Christian faith, as if death, resurrection and eternal life were nothing but a joke or a piece of tomfoolery.'[65]

Here was a theme that could divert attention away from Luther's own problems with Philip of Hesse's bigamy. Luther called Albrecht of Brandenburg, archbishop of Mainz, into the dock too. The cardinal, Luther wrote, had mixed together fleshly desires and sacred deeds when he undertook 'whoring and adultery while feigning holiness'.[66] His reference was to the relationship of the archbishop with the daughter of a baker in Mainz, which, rumour had it, Albrecht had taken as far as adding his lover's remains to the relic collection he kept in his residence town of Halle.

Pastoral Care and Politics

Despite its evident dishonesty, the Brunswick affair encumbered the Catholic camp far less than the landgrave of Hesse's bigamy burdened the Protestants. Philip's request to the theological leadership of Protestantism was an imposition that made them directly and personally responsible, along with the Saxon elector, to whom Bucer presented the landgrave's demand as he travelled through Weimar on his return journey. The whole affair must have sat uneasily with Luther from the start, for he had mistrusted the landgrave of Hesse ever since their first encounter at Worms in 1521, when Philip had provoked him with his brazen questions about marriage and sexuality.[67] On the other hand Luther did value Philip as a 'remarkable man ... [who] has his [propitious] star', continuing, 'He has a Hessian head. He can't rest, nor does he give in. If one thing is finished he'll undertake something else shortly after' and acknowledging the political contribution Philip was willing to make to the Reformation from his territories at the heart of Germany.[68] Above all, as a pastor Luther could not refuse the pastoral support for which he had been asked, even if it might have weighty consequences. Months later the reformer would lament, 'It lay heavily about our hearts, but because we could not refuse to accept it, we thought we might at least rescue our consciences.'[69]

On 10 December 1539, at the conclusion of their discussions, a vote was taken by the theologians that would weigh heavily on Melanchthon and on Luther in particular for many years, and that proved harmful to the Reformation itself. The text of their message to Philip had been drafted by Melanchthon, but only after hours of discussion with Luther, who also voted in its favour. The reformers confronted the landgrave unsparingly with the sinfulness of his life to date, although they also commended that he 'earnestly bewailed it, and showed pain and remorse for such sins', and encouraged him to continue to do so. At the same time they decisively rejected Philip's argument that he was allowed to have several wives because God had permitted the same of the patriarchs of the Old Testament. According to the reformers, Christians were to be guided by the New Testament, where Christ had established that a man could be one flesh only with a single woman. However, in this specific instance, conscience and salvation were on the line, and therefore an exception was possible, but only in the form of a personal dispensation, which was relayed to the landgrave in the form of confessional counsel.

Luther and Melanchthon saw clearly the cost of this pastoral advice. Almost imploringly, they pointed out to the landgrave that this permission was not to be understood as a general rule to be publicly proclaimed, or as a new law. Their words were pastoral counsel designed specifically for the landgrave and were intended only to satisfy the exceptional situation in which he now found himself. Philip was in effect forbidden from making their advice public; instead he should treat the woman who might be his second wife as his mistress, which would cause little stir as many princes lived in concubinage and therefore the people were well used to it. The reformers also warned the landgrave of the immense political consequences that might result from his second marriage and their counsel's becoming common knowledge. The enemies of the Gospel would deem the Protestants to be just like the Anabaptists of Münster, 'who took several wives at once', and even like the anti-Christian Turks. In his own territories, disclosure would provoke a revolt by the 'furious' estates directed against the Reformation. If he should decide to change sides and ally with Emperor and pope— unmoved, the Wittenberg theologians turned Philip's threat back on him—he would gain nothing, for he would only be discredited as a 'disloyal, false man who has forgotten how to be a good German'.[70]

However one views the matter, one thing is clear, which was also clear to those involved: for the first time since the beginning of the Reformation, and perhaps for the first time in his life, Luther was not free to make his own decision. Undoubtedly he abhorred the circumstances in Hesse, and in this instance, too, his temperament would have led him in a certain direction, urging him to inform the landgrave in no uncertain terms of the sinfulness of his love life and to demand Philip's unconditional repentance and adoption of the morals of Christian marriage. He had not caved in to the excesses of Hans von Metzsch, the wayward Wittenberg town captain; he had pilloried him publicly and forced him to marry. However much the two Wittenberg reformers tried to convince themselves, and the wider world, that their scandalous confessional counsel to the landgrave of Hesse was a pastoral matter, their politically rooted caution is unmistakable, as they sought to protect German Protestantism from the loss, or even just the aggravation, of one of its most important and most capable leaders.

The reformers had to run the risk that one foul deed would beget another. The logics of the affair meant that their pastoral advice could not remain secret, simply an arcane detail of the Reformation. The landgrave wanted an official and legally binding second, bigamous, marriage precisely in order that his relationship could have a public presence, particularly for the sake of his wife's social status and the inheritance rights of any children they might have. From the beginning the landgrave had had a broader public in mind. Rumours of the wedding began to circulate and when they were confirmed by Elisabeth von Rochlitz, all that remained for the landgrave to do was to insist the Wittenbergers make their recommendation public.

Melanchthon, who had consistently cooperated more closely with the landgrave, was more deeply entangled in the whole business. Unwittingly he had accepted an invitation from the landgrave to travel from the diet that was under way at Schmalkalden to the nearby castle of Rotenburg on the Fulda. On 4 March 1540 he had unexpectedly found himself attending the dubious wedding itself, which was held in the castle chapel. But the disastrous results—disastrous for Imperial politics and ecclesiastical politics alike—landed most heavily on Luther, not least because the landgrave had sent him a large barrel of Rhineland wine, which his adversaries all too easily interpreted as a bribe. Over the months and years that followed, Luther found himself facing what today we would call a significant image problem: he had lost the trust of his public. He faced this problem with the same consistency he had always shown. Even as his enemies gloated and his supporters cringed, he was not prepared to depart from a position that had been deemed faithful to Scripture.

For Luther this evangelical truth had been conveyed as private confessional counsel, from which one could not generalize and which therefore should not be made public. Luther consistently refused to address the issue directly and instead took refuge in obfuscation and subterfuge. He first deployed this tactic within his own camp. In May 1540 Anton Lauterbach, superintendent in Pirna, asked for a reaction to rumours that the Wittenbergers had permitted Philip to enter into a second marriage; Luther had to contrive a way of not betraying the truth but at the same time not misleading his friend.[71] Even after Philip's sister had let the cat out of the bag and there was no longer any doubt that the bigamous marriage had taken place, he continued with his former strategy, proposing, 'In a quarter of a year this tune will be played out too . . . I expect worse things than this', and 'Just be calm! It will blow over. Perhaps she will soon die.'[72] A little later he provided the Saxon elector with a detailed account of the events, reluctantly certainly, but aware, as he argued, that as the landgrave had made the matter public, he was entitled to follow suit. As he also acknowledged, the elector needed to be fully informed if he was to be able to defend himself against the serious accusations being made against him at the court in Dresden. Yes, he admitted, in order to avoid public upset he would rather have kept the confessional advice secret, but he insisted that he had nothing to keep from the elector, 'nor am I ashamed of that advice'.[73]

Luther continued to demand strict secrecy from Philip, but Philip had now been in contact with the Imperial party in hope of dissuading Charles V from prosecuting him in accord with Imperial law; the Emperor allowed himself to be paid off with concessions made by the landgrave in the Treaty of Regensburg of June 1541, which severely limited Hesse's room to manoeuvre, in particular in relation to France and in the west of the Empire. Luther was untroubled by these developments, secure in his belief that he had made his decision on the basis of Scripture and that he was at peace with God: 'I don't know why I should worry about these things,' he recounted, 'I'll commit them to our Lord God...He has undoubtedly helped us out of greater troubles.' The harsher the attacks and the stormier the public commotion, the more certain he was of his case. Where initially he had bemoaned, 'Oh, dear God, how we must suffer tumult and scandal', only a little later he was defiantly stating, 'We neither should yield nor want to yield. We must bear the devil and his muck as long as we are alive. I had thought I would lead a peaceful old age, but it was not to be. Well, we must dare to take him on.'[74]

For Martin Brecht, the great church historian and biographer of Luther, his subject's behaviour was 'neither immoral nor a matter of double standards, but it was rather exercising Christian freedom, which a pastoral counsellor, unlike a judge, could do'.[75] While we may well agree with that interpretation, we should not forget the personal tragedy that in this instance was bound in with the exercise of Christian freedom. Following on from this unloved but unavoidable confessional counsel, Luther could not proceed with the directness and sincerity that he had consistently demanded of the papal church. This was certainly not the first time, he admitted to those gathered with him at his home, that he had provided counsel that mediated between the human weaknesses of the flesh and the sinner's longing for salvation. Now for the first time, however, he was sharing an experience well known to the confessors of the Catholic Church, both in the Middle Ages and up to today, when public suspicions fall upon a confessor who cannot defend himself because of the secrecy of the confessional. Additionally, he who had always passionately pointed to the mote in the eye of his Roman opponents, now for the sake of the Gospel carried a beam in his own eye.

Economics, Society, and a Lived Reality

'Lend, Expecting Nothing in Return' Is Not Feasible in the World

In the late 1530s economic and social problems again intensified in Germany and in Europe more broadly. The extended demographic upturn that had begun in the mid-fifteenth century had led to such a widespread increase in population that even a small-scale local harvest failure could mean price rises and starvation. Additionally, the inflow of South American silver had reached a level where it fuelled inflation and currency devaluation. Wittenberg and the surrounding regions of central Germany were less directly affected than the great trading cities of western and southern Germany, yet here, too, many people had reason to complain of price rises and food shortages. Luther was well aware of the problems, and he had been required to respond to such hardship as both pastor and spiritual councillor. As for every other aspect of life, he also drew his economic and social advice and admonitions directly from Scripture. Where greed and profiteering trampled underfoot the commandment to love one's neighbour, Luther turned to ecclesiastical penalties, even excommunication.

Again and again the reformer spoke of fundamental problems in contemporary economic and social systems—in treatises and letters, but above all as he sat around the table with friends and colleagues in the evening. Scholars of later centuries have sought to draw from these various texts something that might be deemed an economic theory, or at least a monetary theory. For Max Weber and Ernst Troeltsch Luther's scattered comments on usury are evidence of the backwardness or double standards of his financial ethic. Subsequently, for anti-capitalist ideologists of the twentieth century Luther became a key witness in defending an anti-modern economic theory and economic policy, with his 'struggles against the excesses of interest charging' seen as anchored 'in a healthy sense of justice for his people' or with a place reserved for him in 'the history of political economics'.[76] Such assertions are problematic in two regards: first, Luther had absolutely no interest in establishing an economic theory, and, secondly, his comments on the charging of interest and on other economic issues are given an import that they were never intended to carry. Luther's comments always addressed specific contemporary circumstances, which he viewed not in the context of any systematic economic or monetary theory, but in the context of the Christian life, with his pronouncements based on Scripture, and remarkably frequently on the Old Testament. His knowledge was limited almost entirely to his narrow central German circumstances, and he hardly even registered links to a broader geographical framework, let alone addressed global demographic and climatic developments or the accelerated money supply, of which he and his contemporaries were generally unaware.

Early in the Reformation Luther published three treatises that addressed the charging of interest. His 'Short Sermon on Usury' and 'Long Sermon on

Usury' were published in 1519 and 1520 respectively and his treatise 'On Trade and Usury' (*Von Kaufshandlung und Wucher*) in 1524, with the latter an extended version of the 'Long Sermon' that included extensive treatment of the mercantile family businesses of southern Germany.[77] The texts were part of Luther's Reformation project and closely associated with the elaboration of his evangelical theology. Since the high Middle Ages theologians and church leaders had participated in a debate over whether and under what conditions canon law's prohibition of the charging of interest could be circumvented. That debate had become all the more topical and all the more intense with the rise of early capitalism and mercantile capitalism in northern Italy, and now also preoccupied secular bodies. Years before the controversy over Luther's theses on the indulgence, an interest rate of five per cent had been defended in a disputation by none other than Johannes Eck. He had come under fierce criticism as a result, with suspicions that the position he adopted was the product of a bribe from the Fuggers, the Augsburg bankers.

As in the great Reformation treatises of 1520, in his texts on usury and monopolies Luther's concern was to ensure that the church and the world would be cleansed in accord with the Gospel. No church that was the successor of Christ could enter into dealings with usurers or monopolists; that church should abstain from all financial dealings. Secular activities, be they economic or political, must observe the Gospel's commandment to love, and this commandment obliges the Christian to provide selfless assistance, which includes the loan of money and possessions without the charging of interest.

Yet when he addressed the economic and social questions of his age, Luther did not fall back on the biblical radicality of the spiritualists and Anabaptists. He acknowledged that the historical framework had changed and that the more sophisticated reality of the mercantile financial world could not be regulated by simply adopting the norms of early Christianity. Luther believed, however, that all activities of the world, including the economic, must still conform to the fairness and impartiality of Christian love, a stance he maintained when challenged by the radical positions adopted within his own camp, above all by Jakob Strauss, pastor of Eisenach. Strauss declared the charging of interest to be a sin no matter the circumstances, an approach that threatened to unsettle the Saxon government's Reformation politics.

In 1525 Luther used a query from the town council in Danzig as an opportunity to provide an extensive explanation of the foundations of

Christian monetary and economic thinking. The Gospel is ambivalent, Luther explained: Christ had said, 'lend, expecting nothing in return' and therefore interest charging is completely unevangelical. This was, however, 'a spiritual law, according to which one cannot rule'. For the activities of the temporal world, interest charging is possible, even necessary, but must be 'arranged as is fair. For all laws and practices must be subject to fairness as their rule and their master.' Anyone who lends money must not expect advantages in return, and while that person is due compensation, the return must not be arbitrarily high, determined, as we might say today, by market forces, but must be fair and equitable for both parties. Under these conditions, Luther allowed the Danzig council to charge interest, and proposed a limit of five per cent, a figure that was much in line with the expectations of his day, as evident from Eck's contribution to the disputation mentioned above and from German Imperial diets. Luther laid particular worth, however, on flexibility in the payment of the interest, in accord with the circumstances and standing or wealth of those involved: a 'person of substantial wealth who has already long received', so someone who had already achieved high profits by lending out the capital both could and should set an appropriate part of the interest against the 'principal', the capital that was to be repaid. A different tack was to be taken if creditors and recipients of the interest were 'old and without means', in which case one must not 'take the mule from its trough and turn them into beggars, but give them the interest for their lifetimes, as love and natural fairness teach'.[78]

The distinction between, on the one hand, the commandment that Christians should love one another—'lend, without receiving'—and, on the other hand, the receipt of interest set at an appropriate level from activities in the world does not add up to a moral double standard. Here, rather, we see how the doctrine of the two regiments and the two kingdoms played out in financial matters. As the temporal authorities are responsible for the regulation of the kingdom of the world, Luther saw it as the duty of the government to regulate monetary affairs and economic activities equitably for all: 'Emperor, kings, princes, and lords ought to watch over this matter, look after their lands and people, and help and rescue them from the gaping jaws of usury.' Economic reform was for him inalienably part of the evangelical renewal of church and society. The anger of an Old Testament prophet thundered again: if those who ruled did not undertake the required reordering of the monetary system and instead continued to 'serve the papal tyranny, burdening lands and people more and more heavily as time goes on', then the time would come, 'when the land can no longer endure them but has to spew them out'.[79]

Luther was particularly hard on the southern German family businesses and their early capitalist or mercantile practices. In the prodigious profits typical above all of the Fuggers, with their involvement in long-distance trade, mining, and banking, Luther saw an exploitation of the people by monopolists that was inimical to God, for they were destroying the corporative ordering of society. 'How could it ever be right and according to God's will', Luther asked, 'that a man in such a short time should grow so rich that he could buy out kings and emperors?' Monopolists had made it such that all the world had to comply with the economic rules that they dictated, with the result that gains made one day were already lost by the following year. The monopolists themselves, however, 'are always dealing with permanent and sure gulden for our temporary and uncertain pfennigs. Is it any wonder that they become kings and we beggars?' Luther deemed the profits of early modern mercantile practices to be the product of 'great injustice and un-Christian thievery and robbery'. Assuming the mantle of a Robin Hood, he praised the contemporary challenge to Imperial law by the robber knights as the warranted backlash of those who had been cheated, not to 'excuse the highwaymen and bushwhackers' but as a sign of divine justice: with the government failing to prevent the wrongs committed by the monopolists, 'God uses the knights and robbers to punish the wrong-doing of the merchants'.[80]

Against Usurers and Speculators

Some fifteen years later, the inflation and supply problems that accompanied the population explosion produced a crisis that again drew Luther's attention to the economic context, not least because he was directly affected by the galloping deterioration. To date, Luther recorded, he had been able to live well on a salary of 200 gulden; now, however, he needed 300 gulden, for everything that a household required was dearer, and was continuing to become even more expensive.[81] Even when provisions were normal, there was good reason to complain that Wittenberg did not have adequate 'bread or other supplies for then it was all so expensive'.[82] In subsequent years ever more frequent acute supply crises had threatened catastrophe. In autumn 1538 a plague of mice intensified the problem to the extent that no more flour was available. When a drought set in the following spring, famine

Figure 40. Lucas Cranach the Elder self-portrait, aged seventy-seven, 1550.

brought many people to the brink of death. On 7 April 1539 Luther admonished the town council, but in the evening, as he sat with his friends, he was advised by his friend Lucas Cranach (Figure 40), mayor of Wittenberg at the time, that the magistrates were powerless: the remaining grain was being held back by landowners in order that they might charge higher prices as the need became all the greater. As a result, on 9 April Luther addressed a letter of protest directly to the elector and called on him to take action immediately against the nobility, who were using the grain 'to profiteer so shamelessly, to the destruction of the land and its people'.[83]

For Luther, as for most of his contemporaries, the source of the economic crisis and the suffering of the people was not population pressure and the broader economic climate it created but rather the un-Christian behaviour of the people. In their greed, noble landowners and even peasants were holding back grain in order to achieve a higher price; profit-seekers were thus speculating with the daily bread. Most pernicious was the pre-emptive, low-cost purchase of whole fields of grain as they were sown or as their crops ripened. In the craving for great profits, Luther wrote, the commandment to Christian love was not just ignored but knowingly transgressed. The temporal authorities were duty-bound to punish such malfeasance. In times of need, they must 'force the peasants, citizens, nobility and all who have it to sell their grain'.[84] But the roots of this evil could only be tackled through a change in attitude and a return to the mandates of the Gospel, which meant that responsibility lay not just with politicians and economists but also with theologians, and with pastors in particular.

Luther therefore did not limit himself to appeals to the authorities. He attended personally to the acquisition of grain for the suffering community of Wittenberg. Where, as in neighbouring electoral Brandenburg to the north, the export of grain was forbidden, he sought an exemption from the relevant authorities.[85] Above all, however, he spoke and published in the cause of a fundamental improvement of the moral premises behind economic activities. On the first Sunday after he had written to the Saxon elector urging him to take action, Luther entered the pulpit at the town church and held what his Table Talk recorded as 'a hard and pointed sermon against the greed of the profiteers'. According to Luther they fully deserved the curses they were receiving and were the greatest enemy of the land, for they were strangling the people with their profiteering and greed. He continued his sermon by treating Proverbs 19:17: 'Whoever is kind to the poor lends to the Lord, and will be repaid in full.'[86] Several months later he turned not to Emperor, princes, or magistrates but to the pastors, with a tract entitled 'To Pastors, That They Should Preach against Usury' (*An die Pfarrherrn, wider den Wucher zu predigen*). Luther recorded that he was placing all his hopes in the pastors' ability, through their sermons and admonitions, to bring about change, for since he had first written on the subject fifteen years earlier profiteering had not decreased; indeed in the meantime, usury no longer appeared to be viewed as sinful but was seen instead as 'a virtue and something honourable, as if one is showing the people great love and doing them a Christian service'.[87]

On one hand the text is characterized by Luther's sense of the imperfection of humankind—'they say that the world cannot be without usury. That we know to be true. For no regiment is so rigid and stately that it can defend against all sins.' It recognized the complexity of financial affairs and acknowledged that those who loan money need to be protected from delinquent debtors. If payment of interest or repayment of capital did not happen, the creditor might in turn be forced into debt, or even into ruin, if, for example, left unable to complete an outstanding business transaction such as the purchase of a field. The responsibility for establishing the details of the damage done and deciding what compensation was due fell to secular law and to the lawyer, whom in this context, and exceptionally, Luther judged positively. On the other hand, precisely in matters concerning money, Luther again insisted on the evangelical commandment to love. Only the

Christianization of the individual and of society could counter the fundamental evil that was the unscrupulous pursuit of profit. Almost imploringly, Luther warned the pastors to resist attempts to cause them to doubt their own part in the struggle against usury—whether by those who extolled financial dealings as a service to neighbour and society or by the radicals in their own camp who condemned such dealings wholesale. Undeterred by such extreme opinions, the pastors were to 'preach the dreadful and terrible examples of how God and even the devil dealt with usurers and the parsimonious, killed them in body and soul without honour and exterminated their line'. Every individual, whether his office was temporal or spiritual, was duty-bound, wrote Luther, to punish this vice and protect the pious. In financial matters, too, every Christian was to 'hold to his conscience as a measure of his estate and his office'.

In this matter, as always, Luther's pessimistic view of the world was offset by his optimistic trust in the Gospel and in the conscience that it held prisoner. Economic offences such as usury or grain speculation were to his mind just as ineradicable as sin generally, but that was not the end of the matter. Rather than capitulate, one was to counter evil tenaciously with word and Gospel. 'Secular and civic trade and provisioning that are just and meet and without greed and deception' were necessary and were not reprehensible. Luther held a 'purchasable interest' (*käuflicher zins*), which was secured by a lien (*Unterpfand*), to be neither usury nor sinful as long as 'all can see for themselves that it is a fair and honest purchase', in other words that the interest rate was not set too high.[88] The reformer thus expressly legitimized the *Rentenkauf*, the most important and most widespread form of credit of his time, which saw the creditor purchase for a set sum an annual rent that was then charged against a house or field that he had mortgaged but could continue to use. Common in Latin Christendom since the thirteenth century, this form of financial transaction had been declared a 'purchase' by the legal minds of the church and therefore did not contravene the prohibition on usury.

In insisting on the traditional idea that the *Rentenkauf* was a material object, Luther could still oppose the loaning of money in a modern sense. This interpretation is confirmed from a Table Talk of around the same date. Luther had been asked whether a poor man who lacked any collateral should be permitted to take an unsecured loan in order that he might acquire a business that would enable him to escape poverty. Luther answered with a decisive 'no', and added, 'He shall live within his poverty and feed himself with God and honour, not sin or do wrong, for the money is round and digestible, and will soon be gone ... One should make the people abide by their manual labour and exhort the rich to the work of compassion.' It was of prime importance for the stabilization of the current situation that, despite such fundamental conservatism, Luther approved the *Rentenkauf*. This financial instrument was used not just by individuals or church institutions but also by kings, princes, and city magistrates, who were not yet able to draw from their regular income the enormous sums needed for the construction of the early modern state. In harmony with canon law and the Imperial diets, Luther helped surmount the inflexible and long-outdated medieval position on interest. The five per cent interest rate that he thought appropriate would not, however, prove tenable in the century of the first 'price revolution'. At the beginning of the 1540s he learned from his companions around the table that the Emperor was permitting interest rates of twelve per cent to be charged in the Low Countries; Luther responded with a scandalized early modern 'No way!'[89]

Calling and Estate

Luther also had a dual perspective on the society of his time—normative, which for him always meant biblical, and pragmatic, in light of the sinfulness of the earthly world. We must bear in mind, however, that the very idea of 'society' as a philosophical or descriptive category was as alien to him as it was to his contemporaries. When he spoke or wrote of what we might call 'society' today, he was thinking in terms of the 'church' or 'community of God' and its proper order. As his model for this organization, Luther, like the reformers of the papal church, adopted the traditional concept of the three estates (*Drei-Stände-Lehre*), developed by the church father Augustine and worked out in detail in the medieval period. Society was divided functionally into three estates: the ecclesiastical, the political, and the economic. This division was based on a cosmic 'harmony through inequality' drawn both from the order of creation and from natural law. This divinely ordained harmony was achieved through each individual's carrying out, and being content with, his or her responsibilities for the community as a whole according to the role allotted by God, usually by birth.

Luther made no changes to the essential features of the traditional three-estates doctrine, and for him everything came down to the maintenance of stability and order, although the theological turn that he had introduced did bring new emphases to this model, which again makes very clear that he was no social revolutionary in the guise of a theologian. It is hardly surprising that Luther's core understanding of society is present in the great theological debates over the correct meaning of the Lord's Supper. Living according to the order, or institutions, established by God—'the office of priest, the estate of marriage, the civil government'—humankind received salvation not from monasteries or other religious institutions but through Jesus Christ alone. Those who engaged in such works 'are altogether holy in God's sight'—as servants of the word, financial administrators, or sacristans for the church community; as princes, judges, administrators, chancellors, clerks, or state servants; and as 'fathers and mothers who regulate their household wisely and bring up their children to the service of God'.[90]

With the evangelical delegitimization of the priestly estate, all the related social forms of late medieval society in both the church and the world were also dissolved—gone were the religious orders, the religious foundations, the collegiate institutions, the confraternities for men and for women, and the many in-between forms of religious or semi-religious membership of the clerical estate. Ecclesiastical society and society more broadly were thereby radically simplified. Above all, the status of marriage and family was greatly enhanced, becoming the sole possible form of life for a Christian. This simplification was in accord with a radical secularization of society— not in the sense of a de-Christianization, but rather in the sense, typical of early modern Europe, that the religious was no longer contained but instead taken out into society and throughout the world more broadly. Everything done by the three estates within their individual contexts of church, econ- omy, or politics is 'pure holiness and leading a holy life before God. For these three religious institutions or orders are found in God's Word and commandment; and whatever is contained in God's Word must be holy.'[91]

This new appreciation of what it meant to be active in the world also, and especially, had an impact on the individual's 'calling', which with Luther was given both conceptual and practical significance that left a deep impression on the European modern age. Although here, too, in principle the trad- itional teaching of the medieval period was retained, it underwent a shift that saw the collapse of the long-undisputed superiority of the clerical *vocatio* in the face of Reformation theology. Now in Protestant societies only the individual's 'call' to action in the world was deemed valid. Over succeeding centuries Luther's Bible translation would provide a vital impetus for the spread of the modern ethos of this calling, found for example in his translation of 1 Corinthians 7:20–22: 'Each person shall remain in the call to which he was called. If you are called as a servant, do not worry ... For he who is called as a servant in the lord is the Lord's freed man.'[92] For Luther, unlike Calvin later, achievement was not of the essence for this calling, and neither was achievement a means of social advancement. Key for Luther was that all forms of service, carried out honestly and faithfully, be pleasing in the sight of God:

> Therefore, it happens that a pious maid does what she is ordered and according to her office sweeps the yard or carries out the manure, or a servant in the same way plows and drives a team—they are walking straight toward heaven on the right road; while another goes to St. James [shrine of Santiago de Compostela in Spain] or to church, and ignores his office and work, is walking straight toward hell.[93]

Work became the heart of an inner-worldly holiness. Luther's translation of Psalm 90:10 became famous but was distorted by business entrepreneurs and politicians in the nineteenth and twentieth centuries and is often avoided with some embarrassment by Protestantism today: 'Our life ... if it has been delightful, then it has been one of effort and work.'[94]

Luther's teaching on calling and work was not designed to increase productivity or, as Max Weber correctly identified in Calvinism, to free the capitalist spirit.[95] Only in Reformed thinking, and within Calvinism in particular, did the Wittenberg reformer's sense of the presence of religion in the world intensify into a modern work ethic. For signs of election to the hereafter to be found in inner-worldly asceticism and economic success—which classical sociology of religion identified as the cultural motor that propelled society towards modern rationalism and capitalism—was more characteristic of Reformed western Europe than of Lutheran Central or northern Europe. A similar model could be found in the rise of the natural sciences. The decisive impulses for the disenchantment of a world ruled by witches, demons, comets, and other magic forces and for their rational scientific explanation were found not in areas where Lutheranism was dominant, but rather in the Reformed culture of western Europe, in for example the famous anti-witch text 'The World Bewitched' (De betoverde weereld), the work of Balthasar Bekker, a Reformed preacher.[96]

Luther's ethic put significant hurdles in the way of the economic and social progress of the individual. Social stasis was the order of the day. Yet even within these traditional boundaries, Luther's teachings on estate and calling provided a thrust towards secularization that would have profound implications.

For Luther, his teachings on the three estates and on calling did not form models for the social realities of his own time or of a later age. They provided instead a yardstick that he could use to determine how far communal life had departed from the biblical ideal as a result of human sinfulness. His words were not intended as a social-political programme that was to be turned into reality; they formed an admonition never to relinquish the struggle to bring an evangelical ordering to the world, even if on earth the devil repeatedly gained the upper hand and although only Christ himself, in the struggles of the End Times, will defeat evil once and for all and erect the perfect heavenly church.

As the reformer aged, his conviction grew that the behaviour of society was determined not so much by biblical norms as by the temptations of the devil. On this point also, the year 1525 was a turning point. Where before 1525 he had seen himself as the son of a peasant, acknowledging thereby not so much the social realities of his parental home as his sympathies for the natural state of the order of creation, from 1525 he saw in the rebellious peasants only the agents of the devil. Even when the peasants had been defeated and had returned to tilling the land in peace, he still principally saw in them the negative: their money-grubbing and miserliness, their indifference to the word of God, their unwillingness to provide for pastor and village church. Similar can be said of his reading of the other estates. He was on good terms with individual citizens, nobles, and even rulers, as we can see in the examples of the captains of the Wartburg and Coburg castles, Hans von Berlepsch and Hans von Sternberg respectively, and he was friendly with the Saxon von Löser family, even spending his holidays at their castles. With all the greater suspicion, then, he watched what he identified as a lack of morals amongst the upper circles grow apace. Everywhere, amongst merchants and nobility, and even amongst the peasants, he saw at work 'the great Hansen with their chains of yellow gold and riding their stallions', with an eye solely on money and profit, lacking any Christian modesty in their showy furs, and seeking only their own advantage without any love for their neighbour in mind. Town captain Hans von Metzsch, against whose arbitrary actions he repeatedly protested, was for Luther the epitome of the haughty official, proud beyond his status. Unlike in the text addressed to the Christian nobility of 1520, later Luther rarely had a good word to say of the local nobility, whom he deemed morally degenerate and presumptuous.

When it seemed that the Saxon nobility were thwarting the elector's plan to send the electoral prince for a university education, he raged to those sitting with him around the table that the nobility were tyrannical, obstreperous, overbearing, arrogant, and scornful of study and education, adding, 'they are doubly possessed with all seven deadly sins'.[97] Princes, even those who supported the Reformation, were, we can helpfully repeat, 'rare game in heaven',[98] for they did not keep a close eye on their officials, were immoderate in their eating and drinking, and tormented their subjects, yet they did not even know how to govern themselves.

On Witches and Gypsies

The conventionality of Luther's image of society can be seen particularly clearly in his statements about marginal groups. The poor were to remain honourably poor in the sight of God, or at any rate not raise capital that they might use to support their activities and thus improve their economic situation. Like his contemporaries Luther used the term 'gypsy' as code for 'thieves who have flocked together from all over the world and wander the countryside looking for the opportunity to do harm and unnerve Christians with their tall stories and stealing'. And for Luther, as for his contemporaries, witches were a social reality. He shared the views of his age on magic and witchcraft and was prepared to believe the rumours of 'witches and sorceresses' in the vicinity of Wittenberg who 'were stealing eggs from the nests of hens, milk, and butter', responding, 'one must show them no compassion. I myself wish to see them burned.'[99] He was not, however, a veritable witch finder of the type that several generations later would provoke a witch craze in Germany, and in certain instances he favoured clemency over the full force of the law.

Luther's statements on gypsies and witches were also made within a theological context. Like the Turks and the Jews, with whom they were usually cited in a single breath, gypsies were Satan's helpers in his final struggle against Christ; witchcraft was a falling away from God; in their magical activities witches and magicians were committing a 'crimen laesae Maiestatis divinae', high treason against the sole legitimate sovereignty of God. At the same time witches were very much part of Luther's conception of society, with clear consequences for the social well-being of the community. The witch craze of the late sixteenth century and first half of the seventeenth century was particularly virulent in Lutheran areas of the

Empire. Even subsequently, Luther's certainty that the devil was active in the world and constantly threatened to extinguish the new light of evangelical truth led Lutheran theologians and the authorities that they influenced to see in every magical manifestation, a rural and urban commonplace, a pact between the individual practitioner, usually a woman, and the devil, against which the sword was to be deployed.

Christian Conduct in the World

Luther cannot be listed amongst the economic theorists of the modern age. Economic and social politics were of secondary importance to him, relevant solely as they emerged from his theology, which was rooted decisively in the Gospel. Indirectly, however, the Lutheran Reformation was part of the economic history of its age, as a result of, for example, the abolition of the numerous saints' days. Along with the Bible, the agrarian world of central Germany in which Luther lived provided the context for his understanding of economy and society. As a monk and university professor he had no contact with money on a daily basis, let alone any relationship with savings or investments. When, eventually, he was head of his own household, his capable wife oversaw their accounts and investments, although Luther was legally responsible for their administration. Overall he had no real under-standing of the early or mercantile capitalism that developed during his lifetime in southern Germany; in particular, from where it spread through-out the Empire, and especially to the brisk economy of central Germany. He stood aghast at its growth, with no appreciation of the possibilities it presented, for example, for the poor.

Money matters were for him 'crude idolatry, for one venerates and prays to the great god Mammon, which is money and possessions and such like'. He saw such 'crude idolatry' all around him, 'filling the world'.[100] His works on usury and other comments on economy and society found little reson-ance and were not adopted into theoretical observations on economy and society. Only in the late nineteenth and twentieth centuries did histo-rians grant Luther a place in political economy, building on Karl Marx, who had seized upon Luther's fulminations against the burgeoning monetary economy of the sixteenth century to declare him a forerunner of his own capitalist theory; Luther was now an actor in the age of the 'early bourgeois revolution'. Today Luther's positions on economy and society are certainly still discussed, but only in a dehistoricized form and in terms of a financial ethic, as guidance used for managerial training or by an aspiring economic power that, like China, does not want simply to copy the capitalistic ways of 'the West'. This approach is very much a product of our own world and is entirely distinct from Luther's world, which provided the terms of reference for his thought and actions.

The immediate social impact of Luther's Reformation theology lay elsewhere, in what today we might term the experiential realm or the mentality of the age. The new theology of grace and salvation launched an evangelical Christianization that brought salvation to the world in new ways, conferred through one's estate, and above all through marriage or a 'call' to action in the world. A powerful thrust towards secularization ensued, not because religion was forced out of the world but precisely the reverse: religion was brought into, and acted in, the world. The implications for daily life were profound, for peasant and townspeople as much as for noble, prince, and, not least, the administrative and political elite whose ascent Luther observed with keen interest. For many generations to come, in Lutheran areas thoughts, actions, and attitudes, along with a cultural identity—defined as distinct from Catholics or the Reformed or the 'sects'—would be deeply influenced by this new, of-the-world Wittenberg theology and spirituality, even when the individual was not religious. Either way, each individual was part of the community, and thereby also a member of an evangelical 'confessional society' and 'confessional culture' that for centuries would be moulded by Luther's culture of the word and by his interpretation of heavenly and earthly realities, by his Bible, by his hymns, which entered the memories and hearts of almost everyone, and not least by his catechism, with its easily recalled instructions for how to behave drawn from the Ten Commandments.

Very deliberately Luther had eschewed collective coercion as exercised by the Calvinist presbyterial church. He looked instead to the individual conscience, but unlike the Roman Church he abandoned obligatory confession in favour of allowing the individual to decide whether to confess personally to his or her pastor. On the whole, evangelical thinking and behaviour were more deeply anchored in daily life, not increasingly detached, for in numerous ways the individual was brought into close contact with the proclamation and exposition of the word.

Culturally, Lutheran societies tended to be sober and not highly sensual. Where Catholicism emphasized the visual, the religion displayed to Lutherans was restrained, if we ignore the later baroquization of many church spaces, whose message was more about the splendour of the prince than the splendour of religion.[101] Pithily put by Thomas Kaufmann, Lutheran confessional culture took the form of a 'piety and churchiness based on hearing, the least concrete, least spectacular, and least visible of the senses'.[102] Socially, and in a certain way politically also, for centuries to come Luther was present in towns and villages in the persons of the pastor, the pastor's wife, the sexton, and the schoolteacher. That Lutheran presence entered deep into the social and cultural realities of these communities, even if the local noble looked down disdainfully on the pastor and his family, the peasants only very unwillingly provided financial support for the church, and urban intellectuals made fun of excessive Lutheran piety and pastoral self-importance.

Here is not the place to explore the similar 'Christianization'—similar although built on different theological foundations—that was eventually also experienced by the Roman Church, renewed by Tridentine reform, but in that process we can identify another impulse that was a product of Luther's life and of his impact on the society and culture of modern Europe.

III

Conflicted Emotions—God-Given
Joy and Apocalyptic Fear

'The years of our life are three score and ten; at the highest they are
fourscore. What is best in them is trouble and toil, for they pass by
rapidly and we fly away'—so ran Luther's translation, made many years earlier,
of Moses' prayer in Psalm 90. Undoubtedly as he wrote he had his own life in
mind. Even though he always consoled himself that 'toil and trouble . . . are
mitigated in the regenerate, who believe and hope in God's mercy',[1] it must
have become harder for him to cope with his daily labours, particularly as they
tended to grow, not contract. The worsening political situation in the Empire
and for the church heightened tensions and thus increased the pressures of his
work, while at the same time the rapid spread of the Reformation throughout
Germany and Europe spawned new questions that ranged across theology,
church order, and moral discipline and also concerned mundane personnel
matters. Some of this work was distributed amongst the theologians in
Wittenberg—town pastor Johannes Bugenhagen was responsible for issues
concerning church ordinances, and Melanchthon operated in effect as foreign
minister, responsible for Imperial politics and religious colloquies—but Luther
felt that the final responsibility was his, and his workload had grown greater
than would be usual for someone of his age today.

In his final years the reformer's daily tasks were performed under the
shadow of conflicting feelings and emotions. He had known illness and pain
since a young man. For all his appreciation of the joys of the senses, his body
was ultimately a 'maggot sack that daily rushes closer to the grave',[2] the
decaying vessel for the immoral soul that longed for eternity. As his health
concerns grew and his labours threatened to overwhelm him, death
appeared to him all the more frequently. In 1545, for example, he recorded
in the preface to the new edition of the Wittenberg Bible, 'I do not believe

I will live long enough to go through [revise again] the Bible', and that he was 'now too weak for such work'.[3] His consciousness of eternity could induce a longing for death. On what would prove to be his final journey, he informed his travelling companions that when the negotiations in Eisleben were over, 'I want to go home, lie myself down in a coffin, and give the good stout doctor to the worms to devour',[4] and it was not the first time he had expressed such sentiments.

The courses of this world left Luther deeply dejected: in spring 1545 in the preface to the complete edition of his Latin works, he warned the reader that Satan was 'strong and evil, now also very furious and savage'.[5] He could see clear evidence of this satanic anger in the politics of the Emperor and of his Catholic opponents, but the devil's work could also be identified in the actions of some Protestant princes: 'Interest rates and greed have burst in like a flood and are defended under the law. Also, disrespect, lust, extravagance in dress, gluttony, gambling, pomp, and all kinds of bad habits and evil. Subjects, servants and workers in every trade are insubordinate,' he had complained in the later 1530s.[6] At the end of his life he was tormented above all by the council of the church that had just met for the first time, in 1545 in Trent, which, as we have noted, he believed to be the spawn of the devil and the Roman Antichrist. Divisions in his own camp also caused him concern. The rediscovered Gospel appeared to him—surely with good reason— weakly anchored in the hearts and minds of the people, and therefore that the Reformation would thrive was by no means guaranteed. Even where he 'had preached the Gospel with great trouble and effort for some thirty years', he felt that in the end he was in Sodom and Gomorrah. Almost beseechingly he urged the Wittenbergers 'to respect this grey head' in order that they might learn how to resist the devil, the flesh, and the world.[7]

Luther never lost his faith in God, the courage of his convictions, or his confidence that he was God's prophet. His much-admired determination and his youthful fighting spirit were unabated. But his usual animation was now joined by the impatience of age, and his words became all the more unbridled and all the more aggressive. Yet in the midst of tumultuous debate and even as he despaired about the vale of tears on earth, he was able to find moments of relaxation, whether in artistic pursuits or in the elemental refuge provided by family and friends. He was buoyed in particular by his wife, as we can read from the touching letters that he wrote to Katharina during that last journey into Mansfeld territory, correspondence filled with new endearments, continued teasing, and respect for her intelligence and practical skills:

'To my kind and dear Katie Luther, a brewer and a judge at the pig-market';
'To my dearly beloved mistress of the house, Catherine Luther, a doctor, the
lady of Zölsdorf [and] of the pig market, and whatever else she is capable of
being'; 'To the highly-learned woman Catherine Lüther, my gracious
mistress at the house at Wittenberg'.[8]

Earthly Pleasures—Painting, Poetry, and Music

'I Have No Sympathy with the Iconoclasts'

It would be wrong to portray Luther as an aging curmudgeon. Even as his
body failed him and he was overburdened with work, he looked for, and
found, joy in God's nature and in the arts. This point in our account of his
life seems the right moment to turn our attention to Luther's love of art,
poetry, and music, and in particular to his own artistic endeavours in word
and music. We enter a private world but, as was typical of his age, not one
that formed its own bubble, sealed off from public life. For Luther and his
contemporaries a close relationship existed between, on the one hand,
leisure-time artistic pursuits and, on the other, the arts as a vehicle for
conveying the ideas of the Reformation. Luther's personal artistic involvement was focused on language and music, most consummately as merged in
the evangelical hymns he composed, the reformer's most original creation.
Yet he also valued the visual arts and was well aware that images could be
employed to help spread his message, an appreciation that can be seen most
clearly in his friendship with Lucas Cranach and his manifold cooperation
with Cranach's workshop.

When, in the early 1520s, iconoclasts insisted the interior of churches be
cleansed of all pictorial representations, Luther opposed them firmly. In his
soon-renowned Lenten Invocavit sermons, given in March 1522, Luther
taught the Wittenbergers:

> I must admit that images are neither here nor there, neither evil nor good, we
> may have them or not, as we please. This trouble has been caused by you; the
> devil would not have accomplished it with me, for I cannot deny that it is
> possible to find someone to whom images are useful.[9]

Only a little later he maintained, 'my image breakers must also let me keep,
wear, and look at a crucifix or a Madonna, yes, even an idol's image, in full

accord with the strictest Mosaic law, as long as I do not worship them, but only have them as memorials'.[10] Once freed of the delusion that the worship of images could bring redemption, wrote Luther, each person can and should find delight in artistic depictions: 'Images or pictures taken from the Scriptures and from good histories... I consider very useful, yet indifferent and optional. I have no sympathy with the iconoclasts.'[11]

The fruitful cooperation of the Wittenberg reformers and the Cranach workshop was built on precisely these foundations, whether in the images printed for the Wittenberg Bible or in remarkable painted altar depictions of evangelical theology as found in the Church of Saint Wolfgang in Schneeberg (Figure 41), but with the prime example in the Wittenberg town church itself. Although the great Wittenberg Reformation altar (Figure 42) was dedicated only in April 1547, a year after Luther's death, its theological iconography, in which baptism, Lord's Supper, preaching, and penance formed the four pillars of the Protestant church, had been worked out by Melanchthon and Luther much earlier, in the 1530s.

The Reformation print was an artistic achievement of a somewhat different nature and the forerunner of the political caricature. Luther was directly involved with many of these satirical images, ensuring that the many people

Figure 41. Front view of an altarpiece in the Church of Saint Wolfgang, Schneeberg, by Lucas Cranach the Elder, 1539, the first altarpiece he painted for a Protestant church.

Figure 42. Front view of the Reformation Altar, by Lucas Cranach the Elder, Town Church of Saint Mary's, Wittenberg, oil on panel, 1547. On panels around the central depiction of the Last Supper, Philip Melanchthon baptizes (left), Johannes Bugenhagen hears confession (right), and Martin Luther preaches (below).

who were unable to read had access in pictorial form to the words with which he raged. He took a real, even mischievous, pleasure in the dry humour and intellectual perspicuity of such depictions, which exposed his opponents mercilessly. A series of biting Cranach caricatures illustrated his pamphlet 'Against the Papacy at Rome, Created by the Devil' (*Wider das Papsttum zu Rom, vom Teufel gestiftet*), to each of which Luther added an earthy quatrain; the result has been deemed the most audacious product of the long and bitter struggle between Rome and the Reformation.[12]

Luther's attitude towards images was by no means simply utilitarian. Pictures gave him genuine pleasure and were an integral part of his life, as in the case of the portrait of his young daughter Magdalene that was with him at Coburg in 1530. He also valued and cherished the double portraits of his father and mother and of himself and his wife. These portraits, too, are evidence of how the private and the public overlapped. He and his family were certainly fortified by and delighted in such pictures, but for Luther these images were also testimonies and tools of his cause, with no sense that their private enjoyment and public propagandistic application were incompatible.

Thus the double portrait of Luther and Katharina was intended to condemn priestly celibacy and promote the Protestant notion that pastors should marry. When news reached Luther that the church council was to meet, the reformer responded that he would have liked to send a copy of the image of the married couple to Mantua to 'inquire whether they prefer marriage [to celibacy]'.[13] He was in no doubt that having seen that depiction, the fathers of the council would inevitably resolve in favour of the marriage of priests. As he set out to depict the couple, and with Luther's advice surely ringing in his ears, Cranach bore the public impact of the portrait in mind: he chose to depict not the intimate love of bride and groom but the honour associated with the new estate of two people legitimately bound together in marriage. He was picking up on the tradition of the late medieval double portrait used by the nobility and members of the civic elite to symbolize and proclaim the alliance that came with their new married status. The double portrait of Luther and his wife was immediately put into production, with one contemporary surmising that a thousand copies had been made. Reproductions were included in the art collections of Protestant princes, but they could also be found in the homes of Protestant pastors and of the most humble members of their parishes. The Luthers' double portrait was even popular in Catholic Venice, where it stood for religious freedom. In 1540 Venetian painter Lorenzo Lotto noted in his diary that he had given his nephew, in whose house he was currently living, a gift of two small pictures with portraits of Luther and his wife.[14]

'When I Write, the Words Flow to Me'

Luther and the Wittenbergers were not averse to images, and certainly not supportive of iconoclasts. Luther's personal artistic endeavours focused, however, on poetry and music, and his most creative artistic achievement united both forms in producing the hymn in its Protestant, or more specifically Lutheran, incarnation. When it came to writing, he had a natural talent. 'I have a quick hand and a swift memory. When I write, the words flow to me. I don't need to push or press'—thus he explained his tremendous productivity, which has hardly been rivalled by a German-language author since. Statisticians have calculated that his average annual output was 1,800 printed pages, so five pages a day. Often the ink was not yet dry on manuscripts carried to Hans Lufft's print shop. In 1517 Luther published two works in German; in 1523 he published no fewer than 345, which meant that around two-fifths of all works published in German that year were penned by the reformer.[15] His output in 1523 was certainly exceptional, but in the course of 1528 he still produced sixty works in German.

Two idiosyncrasies meant that Luther was read and absorbed, seared into the memories of generations to an extent hardly replicated by any other author. The first of these quirks concerned the geographical centrality, literally, of his birth and upbringing and thus also of his language. In his age so many dialects were spoken in Germany that 'people who live only thirty miles apart cannot easily understand each other'. Luther's central location was a stroke of luck that proved of remarkable significance. Luther situated himself thus:

> I do not have a specific, special, or personal speech in German, but instead use the common language that means I am understood by those from both the north and the south. I use the language of the Saxon chancellery, which is copied by all princes and kings in Germany; all imperial towns and princely courts write as does the Saxon...chancellery, and therefore it is the most common German language.[16]

Modern philology only reinforces that position, suggesting that a Luther from the far north or southern fringes of the Empire would in all likelihood have failed to catch on linguistically.

The second quirk concerned Luther's apparently inborn sensitivity to language and to how it was heard, which was united with a remarkable creativity when it came to new words and figures of speech. In his Bible translations, Luther 'looked the people in the mouth' and wrote himself into their cultural memory with radical formulations and images. The same can also be said of his letters, pamphlets, sermons, and postils, and above all of his catechism, from which generations of German Lutherans drew not just their faith but also their language, including newly created terms that are now part of every German's vocabulary.[17]

Luther thought, wrote, and spoke vibrantly and vividly, especially when it came to the memorable natural imagery that he used to describe and praise God and God's creation. Where the limits of the human imagination made it hard to grasp that whole, he listed instead specific elements that brought to life complete worlds for his audience or reader: 'God daily and abundantly provides shoes and clothing, food and drink, house and farm, spouse and children, fields, livestock, and all property.'[18] He used assonance and alliteration to emphasize what he believed important.[19] When his words were intended to ridicule an opponent, Luther did not stop at satire and irony, but also employed sarcasm and cynicism, often combined with a very coarse and foul choice of language. The most holy and the most profane appeared alongside each other. In one Table Talk he spoke of his opponents' reaction to the Duke of Hesse's bigamy: because they were not willing to heed the arguments of the Wittenberg theologians, 'God will harass the people. As far as I'm concerned, I'll use the foulest words and tell them, if they're unwilling to look Morolf [the reference is to Philip of Hesse] in the face, to look at his behind.'[20]

Intriguingly, Luther's strong language marked a shift in oral culture. Into the eighteenth century, in a magic-laden ceremony held at Easter, the Catholic Church still cursed stubborn sinners and heretics, including the Wittenbergers by name. In light of the new evangelical interpretation of the relationship between God and humankind, Luther was neither able nor wanted to resort to the language of cursing. He tackled his opponents instead with an earthly punishment dealt out in insults and vituperation. He thus brought a new accent to the oral culture of an age that for generations to come would still believe in the magical power of cursing formulas, as evinced by the witch craze that took hold in Germany, including Lutheran areas, not many years after Luther's death.

The hearts of the people would be reached not by means of sterile writing but through vivid expression, so ran Luther's maxim as an author, for, he insisted, 'it is the nature of the word to be heard'.[21] In his 'Treatise on the Last Words of David' (*Von den letzten Worten Davids*), he noted that 'anyone learns German or any other language much better from oral conversation at home, in the marketplace, or from a sermon than he does from books. Written characters form dead words; oral speech forms living words.'[22] What was needed for everyday communication in the world was needed all the more to communicate the word of God: 'Eloquence is joined to wisdom,' Luther lectured. 'God, who gives wisdom, also gives the word, so that we can speak ... Christ says, "I will give you a mouth and wisdom." '[23]

While his linguistic talents had their part to play, undoubtedly the Bible taught Luther how to communicate, for in Scripture he found clarity and imagery and learned of the power of the word. The proclamation of the

Gospel was always Luther's primary and greatest concern, but his associated joy at a well-turned phrase is also unmistakable. 'To say much with only a few fine brief words, that is an art and a great virtue,' he wrote, a rule he followed even when theology was not his subject.[24] We see this principle in action in the reworking of Aesop's fables that he undertook at Coburg. In this instance his concern was moral improvement, as he sought to help individuals to learn to live a life pleasing to God and beneficial to their neighbours. As an introduction into 'the external life of the world', Luther maintained, he knew of few books apart from the Holy Bible that could outdo Aesop in being useful, elegant, erudite, and well considered.[25]

Alongside these pedagogical and moralistic concerns, Luther had another goal. The most frequently read version of Aesop's tales, found in a collection by Heinrich Steinhöwel, had done no favours to the language of the Greek fables and failed to replicate their literary merits. Luther's aim was to enhance this existing collection in order that it become 'a more lively and more delightful Aesop, but also edifying, virtuous, and useful'.[26] Luther wrote of the fables as a source of art and wisdom, insisting they should not function as idle, showy gossip. Aesop, he insisted, had written not frivolous entertainment for the uneducated but in order that 'one can sit happily together and discuss such fables of an evening at the table with children and the members of the household in a way that is useful and enjoyable'. Luther therefore selected fables that he believed would entertain his readers but at the same time teach them about imprudent human behaviour such as foolishness, hatred, jealousy, and pride. Among his translations were tales about the rooster and the pearl, the wolf and the lamb, the lion and the donkey, the frog and the mouse, the sheep and the dog, and other constellations drawn from the animal kingdom. One recounted the story of the dog that was carrying a piece of meat in its mouth when it spied its reflection in the water; thinking he saw another dog and another piece of meat, the animal snapped at his reflection and the piece of meat he already had fell into the water and was lost. Luther recounted the moral of this tale: 'One must be content with what one has been given by God. Anyone who despises what is lesser will never become greater. Anyone who wants to have too much will in the end receive nothing. Some lose certainty for the sake of uncertainty.'[27] As we know from the letter that Luther sent from Coburg with his account of the diet of the jackdaws, when he was in cheerful mood and had the time, the reformer enjoyed composing his own fables, employing lively verbal imagery.

During the last decade of his life, Luther became fascinated by popular proverbs, which he proposed be collected and published. He began to compile the sayings of which he himself was aware and contacted his friends to request that they look out for further examples: Wenzeslaus Linck, for example, was to have all descriptions, rhymes, and songs in use in Nuremberg and Franconia tracked down and recorded.[28] Unlike his contemporaries Erasmus, Johannes Agricola, and Sebastian Franck, who also published collections of popular proverbs,[29] Luther's interest in proverbial wisdom had theological intent, but he was also motivated by authorial ambitions and linguistic-political objectives. He wished to see Latin texts succeeded by German versions that deployed sayings 'made so good that they will appeal to everyone'.[30] Unlike the Greek and Latin collections of proverbs assembled by Erasmus, Luther's project was designed not to serve humanist scholarly interests but to ensure the people would be instructed in their own tongue, ahead of the language of the educated elite.

The proverbs that Luther gathered—by his death he had collected almost 500[31]—unerringly gave voice to a popular wisdom still found in sayings used today: 'what would muck be if it did not stink'; 'stand like oxen on a mountain'; 'dogs bark much but do not bite', 'many hands make light work'. Others serve to portray individuals and types: 'lard in his neck', 'fire in his arse', 'walks on roses', 'does not cover his mouth', 'acquires horns', 'the more men know, the worse they grow'. Others still encapsulate moral or social maxims: 'a clear lie is not worth an answer', 'what is not yours, leave it lying', 'it tastes of the barrel [suggesting the origins of a person or object are evident]', 'he who has something of his own, treats it as if grasping into a salt container [so carefully and in moderation]'. And an expression that portrayed the work ethos of the Reformation in popular terms: 'faithful labourers pray twice'.[32]

'I Love Music'

The power of Luther's language was accompanied by a great love of music. In a letter written from Coburg in 1530 he noted, 'except for theology there is no art that could be put on the same level with music, since except for theology [music] alone produces what otherwise only theology can do, namely, a calm and joyful disposition.' Evidently, comradeship amongst music lovers meant that Luther was even willing to overlook confessional and cultural differences, on which he was otherwise so inflexible, for this letter was sent to Ludwig Senfl, court musician to the Catholic dukes of Bavaria to whom, as the reformer admitted at the start of the letter, his name was mud. He could hope that no harm would come to Senfl from receiving this letter, 'for who, even among the Turks, would censure him who loves art and praises the artist?'[33] Luther may well have been planning to produce a major theoretical text on music or a lecture on its nature, achievement, and significance, but only an outline of such an undertaking exists. Under the title 'Concerning Music', Luther formulated five succinct points:

I love music.

Its censure by fanatics does not please me

For

1. [Music] is a gift of God and not of man.
2. For it creates joyful hearts.
3. For it drives away the devil.
4. For it creates innocent delight, destroying wrath, unchastity, and other excesses.

I place music next to theology.

   This is well known from the example of

   David and all the prophets, who all

   Produced poetry and songs

5. For [music] reigns in times of peace.

It will be difficult to keep this delightful skill after us.

The Dukes of Bavaria are to be praised in this, that they honor music.

Among our Saxon [Dukes] weapons and cannons are esteemed.[34]

For Luther, when it came to music, the practical, not the theoretical, was paramount. He was introduced to music while a school pupil, principally, as was usual, through singing in a boys' choir. In Erfurt music was part of the curriculum of an arts degree. By that stage Luther was already an enthusiastic music lover, or so we are told by Crotus Rubeanus, who remembered him as 'knowledgeable in music and philosophy', a description that seems confirmed by Luther's repeated references to the extensive repertoire of songs and church music he had acquired during his youth.[35]

Luther played both flute and lute, using the latter, his principal instrument, to accompany singing. The status of the lute in Luther's day was much like the status of the piano today: the lute could be played solo, in an orchestra, or to provide accompaniment, and it could be heard both in civic and court circles and in church. In addition to music intended specifically for the lute, lutenists performed pieces written for several instruments and both secular and spiritual music for voice. Anyone who played the lute had access to all the multi-voiced music of the time, provided that lutenist, like Luther, had mastered the art of 'intabulation', the ability to transcribe pieces that had been composed for voice or other instruments.[36] The instrument was to be played regularly, for according to a dogma of music pedagogy of the day, 'sounding the lute is an art / do not use it frequently and your learning has been for nothing'.[37] Even his greatest opponents could not deny the reformer's lute-playing skills. In 1521 Johannes Cochläus noted that as Luther travelled to Worms, the Wittenburg monk's lute-playing attracted the attention of the people like once the ancient singer Orpheus; Cochläus' disdain could not entirely disguise a degree of admiration.[38]

Music making and singing were part of everyday life in the Luther House. Visitors noted that 'there was often and much singing'. According to a report by Matthäus Ratzenberger, the family doctor and a frequent guest at the house, after dinner the reformer would fetch his part book from his study in order to sing polyphonically with his sons and the students who were present.[39] The music making left the head of the household 'so merry and happy in spirit, that he simply could not tire of or become satiated by the singing, and he was able to speak so marvellously about music'. Again private activities undertaken while unwinding with family and friends were closely bound in with Reformation activities intended for the broader public. This report on singing in the Luther House comes to us from no less a figure than Torgau cantor Johann Walter, Luther's principal partner in the musical reworking of evangelical worship.[40] For the reformer, music was both a song of praise for God and a token of God that brought him joy and confidence in even the worst of circumstances. In December 1538, after an evening of singing motets, Luther pronounced with that inimitable combination of artistic sensibility and coarse imagery, 'in this life in the shithouse there have been such noble bounties; what then will happen in that eternal life where all is perfect and delightful?'[41] He was convinced that music already accomplished much that was good in the world, a view he incorporated for both readers and singers into the rhyming preface to the Wittenberg songbook:

> Here where company sings so well there can be no angry spirit. Here no wrath, strife, hatred and jealousy remain; all heartache must yield. Covetousness, anxiety and all else that begins with severity will depart accompanied by all sadness.

'So that the Word of God May Be among the People Also in the Form of Music'

That unusual alliance of love for music and skill with words made possible the Wittenberger's possibly greatest and certainly most original artistic achievement—the creation of the German Protestant hymn. On entering the monastery the student at Erfurt had sold, along with the remainder of his possessions, the lute he had previously played at many a happy gathering. With the advent of the Reformation, however, he saw such self-denial as a false devotional rigorism, as even a pernicious attempt at self-sanctification. His emphatic recognition that he was a new and free man—as expressed in the change of his name to Eleutherius/Luther—was followed by his joyous resumption of music making and singing, which for him now formed an original expression of evangelical theology:

> For God has cheered our hearts and minds through his dear Son, whom he gave for us to redeem us from sin, death, and the devil. He who believes this earnestly cannot be quiet about it. But he must gladly and willingly sing and speak about it so that others also may come and hear it. And whoever does not want to sing and speak of it shows that he does not believe and that he does not belong under the new and joyful testament, but under the old, lazy, and tedious testament.[42]

Luther's songwriting began as early as 1523, in connection with the liturgical work undertaken as part of the creation of a new evangelical order of worship. At the end of that year, he informed Georg Spalatin, still one of his closest collaborators, '[Our] plan is to follow the example of the prophets and the ancient fathers of the church, and to compose psalms for the people in the vernacular, that is, spiritual songs, so that the Word of God may be among the people also in the form of music.' He needed to bring on board suitable poets for this project, such as Spalatin himself, who was more talented, Luther wrote, than he. In transferring the Psalms into song, however, one should avoid 'any new words or the language used at court'. He continued, 'In order to be understood by the people, only the simplest and most common words should be used for singing; at the same time, however, they should be pure and apt; and further the sense should be clear and as close as possible to the psalms.'[43] This was an audacious and entirely new undertaking that would soon be replicated elsewhere, in particular in the context of Reformed–Calvinist culture. The first Witten-berg communal songbooks, published in 1524 and 1529, were a novelty that had tremendous impact. Before Luther's time, singing, even on occasion in German, had been part of the worship service, but the particular innovation here lay in the production of a whole body of songs to be performed in church that were deliberately in German.

Alarmed at the dismal state of the piety and Scriptural knowledge displayed by congregations in Saxony, on his return from the Wartburg the reformer threw himself into the systematic construction of an evangelical Scriptural culture and devotional experience. He placed particular hope in the communal songbook, a project launched long before 1529, the year his great pedagogical works for the community—his two catechisms and the expanded new edition of his prayer book—appeared. Music can bring inspiration and joy, he recognized, but, additionally, communal singing would not only enhance the liturgy of the evangelical worship service but also embed knowledge of Scripture and Christian moral commandments.[44] Luther's appeal for help had largely fallen on deaf ears, generating no response from Spalatin or any others. The reformer therefore set to himself. He is known to have authored thirty-four songs with verses, four liturgical songs, four biblical rhymes for use on gravestones, and a rhyming preface for a hymnbook, and he also reworked two existing songs. Of the thirty-four hymns by Luther, no fewer than twenty-four were written in just one year, in 1524. His example soon found enthusiastic emulators, and edition by edition, the evangelical communal songbook became more extensive. Its appearance signalled the birth of the Protestant hymn and of the poetry-composing pastors and children of the manse who would leave such a marked impression on German literature.

Scholars of literature and music may well be right. Luther did not fulfil any literary ambitions with his hymns; his texts are not of consistent lyrical value, and some of his rhymes and meters are reminiscent of the Meistersinger and to the more perceptive ear lack purity. His hymns have been seen as the product of a talented and on occasion inspired amateur poet. He seems to have counted out the syllables, perhaps tapping on the table as he gave each the same weight.[45] Whatever the virtuosity of his melodies and ability to set new words to an old tune, his musical possibilities were limited. As he frankly admitted, he lacked the skill to produce a motet of the kind composed by Senfl, the Bavarian court composer whom he so admired, 'just as he cannot preach a Psalm as I can'.[46] His hymns were not art for art's sake; they served to proclaim the Gospel, to strengthen the community spiritually through praise of God, and above all to provide the individual through communal singing with the joyous assurance of his or her inclusion in the Christian community.

The general populace, for whom these songs were designed, took up the reformer's hymns enthusiastically, with a fervour that was not limited to Lutheran churchgoers. A century later, Luther's compositions were joined by the hymns of Paul Gerhardt, the finest of his hymn-writing successors. For generations their songs quickened Christian faith through word and music, whether during worship, with the family, or anywhere people came together to sing. Luther composed songs to mark almost all the central elements of the Christian message—for baptism and the Lord's Supper and for the Lord's Prayer and the Ten Commandments. For the ninth commandment, he devised the lyrics: 'You must not lust after your neighbour's wife or house or anything else; you must wish him well, as your heart wishes you well.'[47] For Whitsun Luther provided a medieval hymn rendered with three additional verses, on faith, love, and hope, and the words 'Now we ask the Holy Spirit above all for the sake of the true faith, that the Holy Spirit will protect us at our end when we return home out of this misery'.[48] Then there were translations of the Psalms or new versions in German. In Psalm 130, for example, the second verse strongly recalls the Reformation move away from works-based piety to a piety of grace:

> Out of deep need I cry to you, oh God, hear my call. Turn your gracious ears to me and open them to my plea . . . For only your grace and favour can forgive sins. Our efforts are otherwise for nothing even if our lives are of the best. No one can boast before you, all must fear and live in your grace.[49]

Similar were the reworkings from the existing Latin treasury of songs, such as that undertaken at the time of the menacing Turkish offensive of 1529, adapted from a sixth-century Latin antiphon: 'Graciously grant us peace Lord God in our time, for there is no other who can contend for us but you alone, our God.'[50]

A not-insignificant number of Luther's hymns became spiritual folksongs. 'From Heaven on High I Come to You' (*Vom Himmel hoch, da komm ich her*) is still regularly sung at Christmas. In Luther's time and long after, the song, whose fifteen verses recount in great detail the events in the stable at Bethlehem, was performed as a type of nativity play. Subsequently its melody even served as a dance tune, to which those gathered to celebrate Christmas, especially in Scandinavia today, dance around the Christmas tree. Here is an expression of the emotional joy of Lutheran confessional culture, which unlike Reformed or Calvinist culture found nothing pernicious in dance. With reference to children, Luther warded off cheerless criticism that held dancing to be essentially sinful: 'Young children dance without sin; do the same and become a child, then dancing will not harm you. Otherwise, if dancing were a sin in itself, then we must not permit children to dance.'[51] Performed in intimate family groupings and at large festive gatherings and sung and staged within the church, 'From Heaven on High I Come to You' records particularly effectively how the songs of the reformer could serve as a bridge between the private sphere of family and home life and the public world of the church and civic community.

Other chorales by Luther also moved beyond the church community or the circle of educated burghers. Exceptional folklorist Johann Gottfried Herder was sure that the people, 'who have more sense and imagination than studying savants', not only liked to sing songs such as 'A Mighty Fortress is Our God' (*Ein feste Burg ist unser Gott*), 'All Praise to You, Jesus Christ' (*Gelobet seyst du Jesu Christ*), and 'Christ Lay in Death's Bonds' (*Christ lag in Todesbanden!*), but also, having been formed by the songs they had learned as children, took them to heart.[52] Even those who like Friedrich Nietzsche drew a sharp dividing line that separated off Luther and the world of Lutheranism were knowingly or unknowingly caught in their spell; although Nietzsche felt nauseated by 'Luther's hideous, arrogant, peevishly envious abusiveness' and declared that Luther 'felt out of sorts unless he was wrathfully spitting on someone', when confronted by a premonition of sudden death, in almost the same breath Nietzsche took refuge in the evidently inimitable hymn writing of the reformer, recording, 'In the midst of life we are surrounded by death.'[53]

Turks and Jews: An Eschatological Threat

In the last two decades of Luther's life, moments of relaxed confidence experienced in good company or when creatively engaged alternated abruptly with moments of unrestrained aggression, even destructive fantasizing, that encompassed everyone and everything Luther believed inimical to faith and his way of life, or that he found simply alien. He directed this anger against opponents within the Christian camp, but he also increasingly took aim at members of non-Christian faiths, so against Jews and Muslims, with the latter largely subsumed under the expression 'the Turks'.

In Luther's still popular chorale 'Preserve Us, Lord, by Thy Dear Word' (*Erhalt uns Herr bei deinem Wort*) we find evidence of how an artistic expression of faith in God could be combined with an unflinching destructive impulse. While the hymn demonstrates Luther's powerful way with words and music, it also reveals a fearfulness and a readiness to employ force. In mid-1542 a rumour circulated that pope and Turks had agreed to unite against the Protestants. In response Luther composed this work, which appeared under the heading 'A Children's Hymn, to Be Sung against the Two Arch-enemies of Christ and His Holy Church, the Pope and the Turk', in which the singer implored God for assistance in 'the slaying of the pope and the Turks'.[54] Neither lyricist nor singer was in any doubt that help would come and that the evangelical Christians' cause would win the day if they remained true to the Reformation message. As so often in verses and texts written by the reformer, the immediate concern was to provide words of comfort for those in great distress. At the same time, however, Luther constructed a concrete picture of the enemy that Lutherans retained for many generations, even those who lived in parts of Germany or the United States where they were unlikely to encounter a Catholic, let alone a Turk or other Muslim. Only in the second half of the twentieth century, as Germany became more culturally and religiously diverse, was the expression 'the slaying of the pope and the Turks' replaced by the more neutral 'the slaying of your enemies'.

In the 1520s Luther had already spoken and written of 'the Turks', who stood for all of Islam, and of the Jews. The public and unambiguous position he adopted was founded on the truth claims of Christianity, thought self-evident in his time. The language and argumentation of his early texts were considered, and on occasion even contained a degree of understanding for members of other religions, with a tone that was more concerned than condemnatory. A radical change occurred in the 1530s. Now the aging Luther wrote with merciless viciousness against both Jews and Turks, with evidence of an uninhibited destructive craving. Again the explanation can be found in his apocalyptic vision of the End Times. 'I am beginning to get fired up against the Turk and Muhammad, since I am aware of Satan's fury, which is unbearable and which rages so powerfully against bodies and souls. Therefore I shall pray and weep aloud and will not be silent until I see that my shouting has been heard in heaven,' he wrote at the end of April 1530 in his first letter from Coburg to Philip Melanchthon. He saw a similar struggle taking place at Augsburg, against the 'domestic monsters of our Empire'.

The ire of both Turks and papacy he interpreted as 'these last two woes, which come down upon us and range among us with the violence of the last day'. But, he concluded with absolute certainty, 'precisely this violence is a witness and prophet of the end [of Satan], and of our redemption'.[55]

Luther on the Turks—Contemporary and Sacred Interpretation

Luther's texts on the Turks and on Islam were composed against the backdrop of the political and cultural conflict with the Ottoman Empire in which Latin Christendom had been embroiled since the fall of Constantinople to the Turks in 1453. The challenge was twofold. First, the Islamic-Turkish empire was lined up against the Christian-Habsburg empire, with Germany's principal focus on events in the south-east, where the Ottoman cavalry were pushing forward towards Vienna and the Holy Roman Empire. Secondly, and closely related, the Christian monopoly of religion on the European continent and of culture and lived experience appeared under threat. It is therefore hardly surprising that despite Luther's distinct lack of interest in power politics, he returned repeatedly to the Turkish issue— usually critically and negatively, but on occasion positively. The Turks were most likely to appear in his letters and in his Table Talk at moments of acute threat or when the Imperial diet was set to discuss defence. In his theological writings the Turks and Islam were deployed by Luther as a warning to Christians and as an admonition that they not neglect their Christian faith. The Turks' principal role, however, came from the part they were given in Luther's portrayal of the earthly events of sacred history. He took up this theme in three substantial treatises and two text editions. 'On War against the Turks' (*Vom Kriege wider die Türken*) was written at the end of 1528 and published in 1529, 'Army Sermon against the Turks' (*Heerpredigt wider den Türken*) appeared in 1530, and, finally, 'Appeal for Prayer against the Turks' (*Vermahnung zum Gebet wider die Türken*) was published in 1541. His 'Tract on the Religion and Customs of the Turks' (*Büchlein von der Religion und den Sitten der Türken*) of 1530 was a translation with commentary of a report that had appeared in Latin of an imprisonment by the Turks in the fifteenth century and 'Brother Richard, Refutation of the Koran' (*Verlegung des Alcoran Bruder Richardi Prediger Ordens*) was the 1542 translation into German of an Islamic handbook from the late thirteenth century, to which Luther added a preface and his own response, entitled 'Refutation by Martin Luther' (*Verlegung Martini Lutheri*).

Each text was very much a product of its immediate political context, which explains the more intense output around 1529/30, when Vienna was besieged and leading political and ecclesiastical figures doggedly pursued military and moral defences against the Turks. Luther had contemporary realities very much in mind, which meant both the distress and fear felt by the people generally as well as the political and military threats to those areas in the path of the Ottoman offensive in the Balkans and on the Mediterranean. He not only gave defensive military measures his blessing but also called for a war against 'the Turks', whom, in keeping with the fashion of his age, he accused of all conceivable forms of brutality. In his 'Army Sermon against the Turks' he encouraged Christian mercenaries 'to make use of their fists and confidently lay into, kill, rob and do as much damage as they want'.

In line with his doctrine of the two kingdoms, Luther assigned the right to wage war against the Turks to the secular authorities alone, and to the Emperor in particular. This war would be fought to defend their subjects from harm to their person or damage to their property; it was not a holy war, fought for the sake of religion. Luther was clear that neither papacy nor any other ecclesiastical authority had jurisdiction when it came to resistance to the Turkish threat. He was very aware of the effect of the Turkish threat on the politics of the Empire and, by extension, on his Reformation's prospects. Not only were the Emperor and the Habsburgs distracted politically by the Ottomans and by the French king, who repeatedly cooperated with the Ottomans, but the Protestant Imperial estates used the opportunity provided by the Emperor's need for financial support for the war against the Turks to extract religious and political concessions.

Luther's assessment of the religious and cultural implications of the sudden confrontation between Christendom and the Islamic Turks was thoroughly realistic. He undertook the translation of the Latin repudiation of the Koran by Richard, a Dominican monk, because he suspected that Islam might prove attractive to some Christians. First the Arabian Saracens had been successful and now they were followed by the Turkish Ottomans, wrote Luther, and 'the common man, according to flesh and blood, is easily attracted to where no cross is visible, but only property and honor in this life, which is also the orientation of Mohammed's Koran'. It was therefore essential that the Koran be refuted and Christians fortified in their faith. They were to be shown, Luther continued in his preface to the translation, that 'while Mohammed obtains victory, success, power, and honor in the world by the wrath or permission of God, we Christians carry the cross of our Lord and shall be blessed not here upon earth but in the life to come'.[56]

Although they were entrenched in contemporary realities, Luther's writings on the Turks and on Islam were essentially theological and religious texts, concerned only superficially with the constellations of the international political system. This character is evident even in his very early pronouncements, from the time of the indulgence controversy in 1518. In his explanation of the fifth of his ninety-five theses, he argued that the pope was unable 'to remit any penalties except those imposed by his own authority or that of the canons'. His thesis countered papal claims with the concept of 'God's correction and scourging', imposed by God for the sinfulness of humankind even upon the innocent, as proved in many places in the Bible. 'Who would doubt that this punishment is beyond the power of popes?' Luther asked. 'No pope or priest is able to override the rod of God', he continued, yet such is the claim of the pope and the Christian secular authorities when they appeal for a war on the Turks:

> Many . . . even the 'big wheels' in the church, now dream of nothing else than war against the Turk. They want to fight, not against iniquities, but against the lash of iniquity and thus they would oppose God who says that through that lash he himself punishes us for our iniquities because we do not punish ourselves for them.[57]

Not unexpectedly, this thesis immediately produced virulent criticism from his opponents and incomprehension in his own camp. The curia did not see a theological argument; it saw only a pro-Turkish, and therefore anti-Christian, plea. *Exsurge Domine*, the papal bull of 1520 that threatened Luther with excommunication, cited this element of Luther's text as evidence of the heretical in his teachings. However shocking to his contemporaries, this approach to the Turkish threat belonged to the existential core of Luther's criticism of the church. Luther's concern—unrecognized or deliberately overlooked by his opponents—was not for the pragmatic issue of whether, how, and under whose leadership Christendom might or must take military action against the Ottoman Empire. For the reformer the Turks and Islam were part of his theological concern with how the individual is justified before God and the role played by penance. Luther's position on the Turks was therefore wrapped up with his penitential theology and formed part of the transition that was the Reformation.[58]

Luther's later statements on the Turks and on Islam were also framed theologically, and specifically by the narrative of salvation. For Luther, the Ottomans were the enemies of the German people and of Christians in general; like 'a pirate or highwayman' they robbed the land and caused the people to perish. He held, therefore, that the European powers were permitted to, indeed required to, resist. Even more significantly the Turk had a redemptive role, for 'he is God's rod and the devil's servant; there is no doubt about that', who roused Christians and caused them to repent.[59] For the reformer the real threat came not from the death and destruction wrought by the Turks but from the false complacency fostered by the curia's suggestion that military defence against the Turks was all that was needed. Just as Rome touted a fraudulent sense of security through the sale of the indulgence, the endorsement of military action as the only necessary response to the challenge to Christendom posed by 'the Turks' would also lead to ruin, for it too stood in the way of true repentance.

Like the Antichrist in Rome, the Turks also were 'enemies of our salvation', and agents of the devil. But the Turkish threat was also a God-sent opportunity, for it would open the eyes of Christians to their sinfulness and at the last moment, as it were, bring them to repentance and true atonement. Protestant pastors were to seize the opportunity: 'Every pastor and preacher ought diligently to exhort his people to repentance and to prayer . . . God makes known how well pleased he is with true repentance or amendment made in faith and reliance on his Word.' The answer to the Turkish threat to the redemption of the individual Christian and of all Christendom did not lie with the armies of this world, for Luther wrote, 'The emperor is not the head of Christendom or defender of the Gospel or the faith. The church and the faith must have a defender other than emperor and kings'—Christ alone safeguards salvation. He continued:

> This man [the Christian] is not to fight physically with the Turk, as the pope and his followers teach; nor is he to resist the Turk with the fist, but he is to recognize the Turk as God's rod and wrath which Christians must either suffer, if God visits their sins upon them, or fight against and drive away with repentance, tears, and prayers.[60]

The Jews—From Personal Experience

As we turn to Luther's attitude towards Jews, we must bear in mind, even more than when we consider his attitude towards 'the Turks', that this study is not concerned with the reception of the reformer; its purpose is to locate Luther's thought and action in the historical context of a world in spiritual and material transition. Such historicizing requires much effort and faces significant challenges, but it is essential if we are to avoid viewing an individual who was a product of the sixteenth century only through the lens of the crimes of the twentieth century. Luther has been identified as foreshadowing the National Socialist attempt at annihilation of the Jews, an interpretation that some Protestant pastors have felt compelled to adopt in atonement for the guilt they bear for the actions of Lutheran bishops under National Socialism. During the Second World War, Allied propaganda drew a line that ran 'from Luther to Hitler', implying a continuity that even today can still provide a chapter heading in an academic text.[61]

All too understandably, even scholars who approach the sources critically have overlooked the historical distinction between the religiously determined anti-Jewishness of Old Europe and the racial anti-Semitism of the modern age. In place of 'goodness and meekness', they argue, Luther preached 'hatred and the destruction of human worth'[62]—a summation that is both right and wrong. It is right because Luther's preaching against Jews was merciless, as he adamantly called on the authorities to drive them out; it is wrong if 'the destruction of human worth' suggests physical eradication on racial grounds. Above all, however, this formulation is misleading in attributing to Luther a historical causality that had meaning only for later generations. The dreadful words of hatred against the Jews for which Luther was responsible did not lead directly and inevitably to the Holocaust carried out under National Socialism. Anyone who declares Luther to have been Hitler's forefather has failed to pay sufficient attention to decisive cultural, political, and social developments that lay between the Reformation and National Socialism and for which Luther was not responsible.

Luther's approaches to the Muslim Turks, on one hand, and to the Jews, on the other, stemmed from their shared context within his End-Time-orientated Reformation theology. The Turks threatened the people of God from without; the Jews threatened the people of God from within, from the midst of Christian societies. Lived experience generated a fundamental difference: from the outset Jews had been participants in the German social world, which even as a persecuted minority they had helped shape through their economic, political, and, not least, religiously determined cultural activities; by contrast, the Turkish and Islamic threats were external to the Empire.

For Luther direct contact with Jews was anything but routine. Significantly, he lived far from the Jewish centres of his age, which since the late medieval pogroms survived only in towns in the south and west of Germany. Jews had been forced out of central Germany, where both town magistrates and territorial rulers, with the Saxon Wettin family to the fore, had banished Jews from their lands and in the process destroyed centres of Jewish culture—in Magdeburg and Erfurt, for example—that were amongst the oldest in Germany. Before setting off on a pilgrimage to the Holy Land, in 1494 Elector Frederick the Wise specifically confirmed the mandate expelling the Jews from Saxony that had been issued in 1432, citing the enmity of the Jews towards Christ and Christ's mother, Mary.

Since a child, Luther had only known towns and districts populated solely by Christians, with no Jewish residents, let alone a Jewish community. Places where a permanent Jewish presence was tolerated, as in the villages of Daberstedt and Hochheim by Erfurt for which privileges had been granted by the archbishop of Mainz, must have seemed exceptional. He would have seen Jews on occasion in the large city of Erfurt, with its extensive trade and fairs, and perhaps also in Mansfeld territory, where for economic reasons they were on occasion permitted to travel and trade. In Wittenberg, by contrast, where Luther spent most of his life, Jews were encountered only as they had been memorialized—in the name of the 'Street of the Jews' (*Jüdenstraße*) directly behind the town church, where Jews had lived before their expulsion, and in the so-called 'Jewish sow' depicted on the southeastern gable of the town church (Figure 43), one of the most repugnant of the mockeries that dragged the religious sensibilities of the Jews through the dirt, here by means of an obscene association with an animal that Judaism held to be unclean.

Luther experienced an exclusively Christian urban and rural society as his everyday norm. This experience explains his sudden alarm on unexpectedly encountering a Jewish settlement outside Saxony. He then did all he could to induce the authorities to expel these Jews—an event to which we will return—and to restore what was for him normality.

As a reformer, too, Luther never established closer contact with Jews. Yet his relationship with Jews was still different from that with Turks, for Jews were present in the Empire and therefore part of his lived environment. What was more, the reformer and the Jews, or more specifically their

Figure 43. Stone carving of the so-called Jewish sow (*Judensau*) on Wittenberg Town Church, *c.*1440, cited by Luther.

theological and political leadership, lived and worked within comparable constellations that addressed similar problems. The major transitions within European society since the end of the fifteenth century also brought radical change for Jews that was accompanied by profound fears as well as some optimism. The construction of territorial states in Germany held out the possibility of increased legal and institutional security in the form of princely or civic Jewish ordinances. At the same time, however, it presented Jews with new problems. The traditional protections afforded by the universal powers, the Emperor and the pope, had faded even to the point of meaninglessness. As judicial authority passed from Emperor to princes or to the magistrates of the Imperial towns, the territorialization of the regulation of the Jews led to the fragmentation of Jewish legal rights and Jewish life, endangering the unity of the German Jewish community. No less serious were the economic and social transitions. In the face of global businesses such as that of the Fuggers in Augsburg, the monetary and financial services offered by Jews became increasingly marginalized, and they lacked the opportunity to compensate for this loss with a reorientation towards trade, manufacturing, or the acquisition of property. At the same time, amongst urban artisans and merchants, who also felt threatened by the changes under way, resentment against Jews grew. The negative Jewish stereotype of the early modern period was established, initially independently of the anti-Jewish teachings of the theologians.

In religious-cultural terms, too, the Jewish diaspora in the Empire and throughout Europe found itself imperilled by the radical changes. The forced baptisms on the Iberian Peninsula and the end of Sephardic Judaism in south-western Europe that they heralded gave the theological leaders of the Ashkenazi Jews of Central and eastern Europe reason to fear that the Christian Inquisition might also seek to destroy their religious and doctrinal traditions. At the same time Jewish and Christian cultures were not entirely isolated from each other, as was long and incorrectly thought the case, for each party was aware of, and responded to, the debates in the cultural milieu of the other.

It is not surprising, then, in light of the existence of such commonalities even alongside so very many differences, that the younger Luther reached out to Jews and, conversely, that Jews responded to the Reformation and to the reformer's texts on Jews. Initially it seemed rapprochement might be in the offing, with Luther telling Jews of an end to medieval oppression, and with some Jews speaking in celebratory terms of the reformer as liberator and anticipating that he would bring about lasting improvement in the relationship between Jews and Christians. The messianic and apocalyptic streams that emerged in German Judaism precisely in these years, feeding novel and high expectations for the future, were also a direct reaction to Luther and the Reformation. Soon, however, it became apparent that the expectations of both parties rested on misunderstandings and in the long term would burden, rather than ease, their relationship. Theological and spiritual revitalization gave Jews a new self-confidence that spurred them on to resist the demands of their Christian environment, not least when it came to Luther's anticipation of their conversion. Conversely, this reinvigorated determination helped dash the reformer's expectations that Jews would convert and from the 1530s gave him cause to decry their obduracy. Now he even invoked the possibility that this newly attractive Judaism might lead Christians to convert in great number and as a result descend to eternal damnation.

Luther's limited personal contact with Jews strengthened this web of expectations and fears. His first closer connection with Judaism came through a convert, whom he got to know in the early 1520s when it was proving so hard to fill the newly created chair of Hebrew at Wittenberg. As established Hebrew scholars were difficult to find, the Wittenbergers found themselves turning to and entering into negotiations with baptized Jews, as was the case with Werner Einhorn of Bacharach, Matthaeus Adrianus from Spain, and Bernhardus Hebraeus, who from summer 1519 to Easter 1520 was interim professor at Wittenberg and in 1521 was again in the town, as a private instructor. Bernhardus Hebraeus, formerly Rabbi Jacob Gipher, had been baptized in his home town of Göppingen in 1519, much influenced by Luther's writings and by his sermons in particular. He subsequently studied theology in Wittenberg, and then in Erfurt and Leipzig. All the world, including Luther, usually called him 'the baptized Jew Bernhard'; apparently he did not merit a surname, unlike all who were born Christian, a sign of a social divide that could not be overcome even by conversion. After his marriage to a maid of Karlstadt's, Bernhard lived in the small Electoral Saxon town of Schweinitz, an easy day's travel east of Wittenberg on the Black Elster. Luther stood godfather at the baptism of his first child. Subsequent encounters are also likely to have taken place, as on occasion Luther visited the elector's castle at Schweinitz. In 1534 Bernhard was sexton at a Saxon village church. For unknown reasons, he became poverty-stricken and, suspecting his wife had committed adultery, left his family.

For Luther, Bernhard was initially the image of the ideal 'good Jew'. He saw Bernhard as the herald of a wave of conversions, even the conversion of all Jews, which would be unleashed by the rediscovery of the Gospel. When Justus Jonas translated into Latin Luther's text 'That Jesus Christ Was Born a Jew' (*Daß Jesus Christus ein geborener Jude sei*) in order that it would be available to educated Jews, Luther provided a programmatic dedicatory letter addressed 'To the baptised Jew Bernhard'. The text, he wrote, was intended 'to strengthen and assure your faith in Christ, whom you have lately learned to know in the Gospel, and now that you are baptized in the Spirit you are born of God'. He continued to Bernhard, 'I hope that by your labor and example Christ may be made known to other Jews, so that they who are predestined may be called and may come to their King David, who feeds and protects them.'[63] When Bernhard's family fell apart, Luther and Melanchthon each took one of his children into their families. Bernhard himself received support from Luther and other reformers in the form of occasional alms or small paid jobs. More than this, Luther informed Justus Jonas in 1535, he could not do, 'as I have been called on by God to support so many in my home', but he would very much like to help the good man, he wrote, 'as he is a guest in the church of the gentiles and at home in the church of the Jews'.[64]

The example provided by Bernhard makes evident the limits of Luther's reception of baptized Jews, even in the early breakthrough years of the Reformation, when he still expected many conversions. In the Catholic world baptized Jews such as Paul of Burgos in Spain could rise to hold high office in the church, but it seems never to have crossed Luther's mind to appoint Bernhard, one of his own theology students, as an evangelical pastor. He failed to mention Bernhard on any of the many occasions during these years when he received requests from rulers or communities for recommendations of suitable clergy. Even during the early years the reformer was evidently possessed by a latent fear that baptized Jews might subvert the Reformation and lure Christians to Judaism; subsequently that fear would become almost pathological.

Luther's good relationship with Bernhard was an exception, for the reformer was highly suspicious of converts and constantly sensed trouble. When after only a few months in Wittenberg Johann Böschenstein, the first professor of Hebrew at the university, proved unwilling to limit himself to working on behalf of the theologians and instead also taught rabbinic writings, Luther berated him—without warrant, it seems—for being a convert and Christian in name alone who was judaizing, seeking to seduce Christians to convert to his original Jewish faith. The stay of Matthaeus Adrianus, a Spanish convert, in Wittenberg proved similarly short. Adrianus found himself clashing with the reformer, who considered that Adrianus, a Hebraist highly respected amongst humanists, was using his linguistic talents to teach Luther, now a world-renowned theologian, about the New Testament and to criticize his doctrine of justification. Initially Luther also placed much hope in Werner Einhorn a convert from Bacharach, but after moving to Ingolstadt, Einhorn took up with Luther's opponents and was denouncer and witness in several heresy trials. Initially these specific conflicts had little impact on Luther's broader thinking about Jews for they registered as personal relationships gone wrong, but they gained increased significance when, in the 1530s, for reasons of theology and church politics, his image of the Jews became increasingly negative.

Through the Ninety-Five Theses and his appearance at Worms, Luther had become well known to Jews in the Empire. For a good number of their theological and political leaders Luther even became an authority in whom they placed hope and with whom they sought closer contact. Amongst Christians an unfounded rumour would eventually circulate that while Luther was still in Worms two Jewish theologians had challenged the new hero of Christendom to a theological disputation, from which Luther had emerged with a splendid victory. Luther himself provides us with evidence of a visit to Wittenberg in the 1530s by three Jewish scholars who wished him to participate in a Jewish–Christian religious colloquy. No such discussion appears to have taken place, and Luther later spoke of the encounter with detachment, even derision: recalling the event in the 1540s, in an account that was not without a certain prejudice, he reported that the Jews had intended to find in him 'a new Jew', a hope strengthened 'since we Christians were starting to read their books'. When he 'forced them back to the text', however, 'they soon fled from it', in other words, they did not want to accept its strict Lutheran interpretation. They invoked their rabbis, whom, they insisted, they were obliged to believe just as Christians relied on 'the pope and the doctors', an effective card to play against Luther, who, while speaking emphatically of the freedom of the individual Christian, insisted that doctors of theology knew best. Despite this discord, Luther continued, he had ensured that the Saxon authorities guaranteed the Jewish visitors free passage, only soon to discover that 'they called Christ a "tola"', a rightfully hanged highwayman.[65]

Josel of Rosheim

Far more important than any such encounters was Luther's contact at the end of the 1530s with Rabbi Joselmann ben Gerschon, generally known as Josel of Rosheim. Born in 1476, Josel was a few years older than Luther. A merchant resident in the small Imperial city of Rosheim in Alsace, since the 1520s he had been the elected *parnas u-manhig* for the Jews of the Holy Roman Empire. As 'forerunner and leader' (the modern translation of his office, contemporaries spoke of him as 'commander'), Josel was unceasingly active on behalf of his fellow believers. He had access to the princes of the Empire and to Charles V personally, who as king in Germany was patron of the Jews. He had discussed the position of German Jewry with Charles on the periphery of Charles' coronation at Aachen, and again soon after at the Imperial diet at Worms in 1521, and then again in 1530 at the Imperial diet at Augsburg. An experienced political figure and close observer of events, Josel was in no doubt that as territorialization advanced in Germany, he could not limit his activities to the renewal of royal and Imperial privileges. If the Jewish presence was to become legally entrenched, the princes and magistrates of the Imperial cities would need to be won over, for only then would the position of German Jews be brought into line with the altered Imperial framework and new power structures.

Not surprisingly, Josel immediately launched into action when, at the beginning of August 1536, Elector John Frederick issued a mandate that compounded the prohibition on Jews' settling within Electoral Saxony, in place since 1432, by revoking their right to stay temporarily or to travel through Saxony. We cannot be sure what led to the issuing of this mandate, including the extent of Luther's involvement. We do know that shortly before, Luther had met with the elector and endorsed his policy towards Jews, but we also know that the leadership of the German Jews included Luther in their political calculations and hoped to win him over as an ally for their repositioning within the Empire and within Christian society. The absence of any fundamental enmity between Protestants and Jews in these years is evident in the good, even friendly, relations between Josel of Rosheim and numerous Christian political leaders and south German reformers, in particular Wolfgang Capito in Strasburg.

Furnished with their letters of recommendation addressed to the Saxon elector John Frederick and to Luther, the 'commander of the Jews' travelled to central Germany hoping for constructive negotiations of the sort he had participated in at other princely courts and at the Imperial court. In Electoral Saxony, however, neither John Frederick nor Luther was prepared to talk to him, and Josel could advance no further than the outer circles of the Saxon court. Without doubt, the internal political organization of the Jews had unsettled the reformer and caused him to shrink back from a meeting with their leader. Josel's successes on behalf of some individual Jewish communities and of German Jewry as a whole suggested that the image of the Jews Luther had created in the 1520s did not reflect reality. His prognosis of 1523, which had appeared in his text 'That Jesus Christ was Born a Jew', had proved incorrect, for Jews eluded evangelical indoctrination and saw no need for either religious and spiritual rescue through conversion or social liberation through integration into the majority Christian society. To the contrary, at the same time as Christendom was being shaken awake by the Reformation, Jews were experiencing a religious-spiritual renewal and retrenchment that empowered them to seek to secure their political and social situation and consolidate their Jewish identity, as Josel of Rosheim had recently impressively confirmed at a theological disputation with Protestant scholars held on the periphery of a princely gathering at Frankfurt.

This news was unwelcome and incomprehensible to Luther, who wanted no part in any Jewish intervention with Elector John Frederick. Unlike reformers such as Capito, Luther had never allowed Jews and their Hebrew culture any independent worth, let alone considered the possibility of a partnership—at the time of the reform of the university at Wittenberg, he had deemed Hebrew the servant of theology. He experienced the spiritual renewal of the Jews and their political and social self-confidence, evident in the activities of Josel of Rosheim, as a threat to his Reformation and therefore, like all other opposition, as machinations of his devilish opponent that were to be frustrated by all possible means.

Luther became all the more convinced of that assessment when news reached him from Moravia that a group of Christians were celebrating the weekly Sabbath not on Sunday, as had been the practice throughout Christendom for more than a thousand years, but on Saturday; additionally, their newborn male children were being circumcised. Today it is evident that the origins of this community, immediately condemned as Sabbatarians and Saturday believers, were Christian and Anabaptist. Its innovations were not based on the Jewish model but had emerged from study of the Old Testament. Horrified, however, both Catholics and Protestants believed they had identified an example of 'judaization', of the destructive influences of the Jewish cult on Christians. Luther's reaction was particularly harsh, and in his sharply worded pamphlet of March 1538 entitled 'Against the Sabbatarians' (*Wider die Sabbather*) he railed against both Jews and misguided Christians.

As Luther always assumed that God would ensure events turned out as he believed fit, he did not plan to leave the commander to stew in ignorance, and instead addressed an extensive letter 'To the cautious Josel, Jew of Rosheim, my good friend'. He showed no sign of any sympathy for Josel's goals within the Empire and no interest in the spiritual-religious renewal amongst Jews, for they were simply evidence of Jewish obduracy and evil intentions towards Christians, and in particular towards Luther's newly discovered evangelical truth. 'My heart has been, and still is, that one should treat the Jews kindly,' he wrote, but the Jews had responded to this benevolence such that 'you curse and blaspheme your own flesh and blood, Jesus of Nazareth, who has done you no harm, and . . . if you could you would rob his followers of everything they are and have'. Jewish exposition of Scripture that contradicts the Christian interpretation is, Luther insisted, nothing other than a curious and unsustainable twisting and fudging of the evident truth of Christ the Messiah. He informed Josel, 'because your people so shamefully misuse my service and undertake such things, which we Christians cannot accept from them, they themselves have thereby taken from me any influence that I otherwise might have had with dukes and lords'; Josel should therefore seek to have his matter brought before the Saxon elector by someone else.[66]

Luther's stance was absolute and irreversible. The situation had changed, for now Jews could no longer place any hope in the reformer. In essence, however, Luther's own position had not changed, for—as the letter makes absolutely clear—his early plea for cordial relations with Jews never implied a possible exchange between Christians and Jews or any form of convivial interaction; Luther's sole purpose had always been to make his evangelical insights available to Jews in order that at last religion and society in Germany and Europe might be uniformly Christian. In Luther's eyes, Jewish failure to cooperate had made that milder approach pointless; now he urged the authorities to expel the Jews in order to safeguard Christian society.

In general the secular authorities took up Luther's call, with the Saxon elector first to act. In 1539, likely as a result of the furore throughout the Empire, he had moderated his Jewish mandate of 1536 by allowing Jews passage through his lands on certain conditions, but in 1543 he returned to the absolute prohibition of 1536. At that time he had referred, almost verbatim, to the words of 'the honourable and most erudite, our dear devout Martin Luther, doctor of scripture' that only a short while earlier had warned against the lies of the 'obdurate Jews about the right and true Messiah, Christ our saviour' and about their destructive implications for the Christian people.[67]

Luther's final encounter with anyone Jewish came at the beginning of 1546, just fourteen days before his death. The reformer was on his way to participate in negotiations needed by the quarrelling counts of Mansfeld when, near Eisleben, the town of his birth, he passed through, he wrote to his wife, 'a village in which many Jews are living'. His response will form part of our account of the final days of his life.

Early and Later Texts on the Jews

Personal experience played no part in determining Luther's image of Jews, which was formed instead from Scripture and its exposition according to

Reformation theology. At their core his views remained impervious to any actual contact with anyone Jewish. The texts in which he made reference to Jews were not the product of social, economic, or even racial concerns; their perspective was theological, bound in with the evangelical renewal of the church, a church that for Luther was universal in character and therefore included Jews. What he wrote about Jews should therefore be read against the background of the various stages of his career and the work he undertook for his Reformation cause during each phase. His stance varied according to his assessment of the progress of, or threat to, his evangelical message.

With his final years characterized by a pessimism about the world, visions of the End Times, and fears for his life's work, the reformer's language when he spoke or wrote of Jews became increasingly hateful, full of abusive obscenities and bloodthirsty fantasies about their destruction. The later Jewish texts document the dark underbelly of the reformer's remarkable way with words. His 'revelling in vulgar and sordid expressions'[68] was extreme even for an author who never held back with his choice of words, and all the more remarkable as in the early years when he had harassed popes and rebellious peasants with his aggressive polemic he had spared the Jews. At that earlier date he had courted Jews and had sought to protect them from their non-Reformation opponents. Before the Reformation when lecturing on the Psalms and the Letter to the Romans, Luther had looked critically at how the Scriptural role played by Jews fed the current relationship between Jews and Christians. With the Reformation the Jewish question took on new meaning for Eleutherius-Luther. In the early years of the Reformation, as the whole of the Christian world seemed to open up to his teachings, he looked to Jews with pastoral optimism, earning reproach from his opponents, who claimed he was judaizing and abandoning Christian positions in favour of rapprochement with Jews.

The title of Luther's first text on the Jews was certainly remarkable: 'That Jesus Christ Was Born a Jew'. The work was written in 1523, at a time of euphoria as the rediscovered evangelical truth spread rapidly and a movement from below, emerging from the communities themselves, optimistically sought to give Christian life evangelical form. Luther embraced the Leisnig Common Chest Ordinance as a fundamental communal act of renewal, and he was similarly convinced that the new theology would also take root amongst Jews, who would become part of this Christian revival. Now at last the age when the papacy had obscured the evangelical truth was over, an age in which Jews had not received the pure word of God but instead had been persecuted and marginalized; 'they have dealt with the Jews as if they were dogs rather than human beings,' Luther had written.[69] According to the lewd imagery of the dedicatory letter 'To the baptised Jew Bernhard', the popes had acted towards the Jews like 'a bawd [who] may teach a girl to be a harlot and afterwards charge her with not living in virginity'.[70]

This papal response was to be replaced by evangelical tenets that would henceforth govern the relationship between Jews and Christians. As 'blood relatives, cousins, and brothers of our Lord', Jews were to be treated as friends and instructed in that rediscovered evangelical truth harmoniously, in order that they would become 'right good Christians'. In these years Luther called for patience when it came to the 'weak', a reference to Christians who had not opened themselves to the Reformation, and similarly he warned against too intense instruction of the Jews, 'for they have been led astray so long and so far that one must deal gently with them'. He insisted that the traditional approach be abandoned immediately and completely. Above all, invented tales of Jewish guilt for the death of Christ and 'of having Christian blood if they don't stink, and I know not what other foolishness' must cease. Luther asked, 'So long as we thus treat them like dogs, how can we expect to work any good among them? Again, when we forbid them to labor and do business and have any human fellowship with us, thus forcing them into usury, how is that supposed to do them any good?' Jews should be permitted to leave their ghettoes, and prohibitions on guild membership and other economic restrictions should be lifted.[71]

A radical shift in the relationship between Christians and Jews seemed to be taking shape. Yet even if we did not know that within only a few years this Jewish-friendly position would be abandoned, we would likely still be able to recognize that Luther's early stance was based on an idealistic misconstruing of the religious and social dynamics of the evangelical renewal of Christendom and to observe that he was mistaken in his judgement of what Christians would be prepared to do. His hopes for those Jews who turned to Christianity were far greater than those of the pre-Reformation church, which had been content with baptism. The pressure created by his alien expectations, so divorced from reality, eventually meant that Luther veered into a much more radical and confrontational attitude.

Even this first solicitous text was not the product of a willingness to engage with contemporary Judaism, let alone to launch a dialogue with Jewish theologians and philosophers. The young Luther was already mistrustful of the humanist exchanges of Christians and Jews, which now had a significant history, in which reformers such as Andreas Osiander in Nuremberg, Wolfgang Capito in Mainz and later Strasburg, Konrad Pellikan in Basel or Zurich, or Sebastian Münster, cosmographer in Basel, participated. To Luther's prophetic self, his rediscovered evangelical truth was so self-evident and could be so easily grasped by everyone, including Jews, that it was logical, indeed necessary, that they become part of the renewed Christianity of the Reformation. Any philological or theological engagement with contemporary Jews and their texts would only be counterproductive and even potentially dangerous, for it would provide the devil with a lair from which to thwart the evangelical renewal of Christendom or even lure Christians to Judaism.

Luther never seriously attempted to convince Jews that in its essence Christian teaching conformed with 'their own true faith'.[72] In a letter to Josel of Rosheim he did mention a booklet with which he hoped to win over Jews and bring them 'to your promised Messiah',[73] but the project was never realized. His reference cannot have been to the pamphlet 'Against the Sabbatarians', discussed above, which he published soon afterwards, for that text was utterly unsuitable for recruiting Jews. None of Luther's subsequent sermons or publications talked to Jews as a body or to their representatives; they talked only of them. His audience comprised his evangelical fellow Christians and his intention was to warn them of the dangerous machinations of the Jewish spawn of the devil.

Luther's knowledge of Judaism and Jewish culture came not from Jews or their writings but from the words of Antonius Margaritha, a convert from Judaism, who, like many an apostate, was highly derogatory about his former co-religionists and their faith and practices. Although in a public disputation with Josel of Rosheim held at the Imperial diet at Augsburg in 1530 Margaritha had been exposed as a slanderer and had been banished from the diet, Luther based his later works principally on the Old Testament and on Margaritha's anti-Jewish handbook, entitled 'The Whole Jewish Faith, Together with a Thorough and Truthful Account of all the Regulations, Ceremonies, and Prayers both for Family and Public Worship, as Observed by the Jews throughout the Year'.[74]

Through Luther, Margaritha's hate-filled clichés and stereotypes found a broad audience, especially via Luther's text 'On the Jews and their Lies' (*Von den Juden und ihren Lügen*). The aggressive and contemptuous tone of this polemical work, which was published in 1543 and covers almost 150 pages of the Weimar edition of Luther's collected works, makes understandable the response of one contemporary evangelical theologian who 'has regretted' that Luther had died three years too late. Luther's attacks in this work and in his subsequent Jewish texts demonstrated the marked shift in his attitude and expectations. The open-minded optimism of the early years had become the depressing realization that opposition, even within his own camp, was growing and that universal reform of church and society would not be realized in his lifetime. He now listed the Jews amongst the forces that opposed him, alongside the pope, the 'fanatics', and the Turks, for the Jews not only obstinately resisted the evangelical truth that was readily evident to every honest individual, but also did all they could to tempt Christians from the true evangelical path.

Luther elucidated his position in the introduction to his work. A text that he had been sent had informed him, he wrote, that 'these miserable and accursed people do not cease to lure to themselves even us, that is, the Christians', and that they were being successful, even though he had never thought possible 'that a Christian could be duped by the Jews into taking their exile and wretchedness upon [themselves]'. He had to counter-attack, 'so that I might be found among those who opposed such poisonous activities of the Jews and who warned the Christians to be on their guard against them'.[75] The converted Christians he mentioned were evidently the 'Sabbatarians' we encountered earlier, the grouping in Moravia with Anabaptist origins, which had introduced circumcision; as noted, Luther had already launched a campaign against this movement in his 1538 pamphlet 'Against the Sabbatarians'.

The later Jewish writings were not the work of the optimistic liberator from tradition or the visionary who had foretold how Christian and Jew would come together. Jews were no longer errant brothers who could be won over for evangelical Christianity by instruction; they were now Satan's agents who must be forced onto their knees without mercy in order that their evil-intentioned perversion of Scripture would not lead faithful Christians into error. And therefore, Luther wrote, 'I do not wish to have anything more to do with any Jew. As St. Paul says, they are consigned to wrath; the more one tries to help them the baser and more stubborn they become. Leave them to their own devices.'[76]

Such premises make unsurprising that all Luther's theological and Scriptural explanation of, for example, the claimed inheritance of Abraham, circumcision, the promised land in Palestine, and the teaching of the coming of the Messiah, led only to abuse and imprecation: the Jews are pernicious distorters of Scripture, 'a useless, evil, pernicious people, such blasphemous enemies of God'; some among them 'believe what a cow or a goose believes'; and 'they were and still are obliged to obey him [God]; but they were hardened and ever resisted, blasphemed, and cursed'. To preach to them would be like 'preaching the gospel to a sow'. The fabricated tales that two decades earlier he had condemned as inventions of the medieval church were now set out as actual events; there was every reason to believe the accusations of 'contaminating wells, of kidnaping and piecing children'. Even the presence of the sow sculpture in the parish church in Wittenberg was used as an opportunity to spread in all their degrading detail the established stereotypes of the everyday life of Jews.[77]

The plans for the integration of the Jews into Christian society as equals were replaced by a popular image of parasitical worthlessness that served and intensified any and all resentments: 'They live amongst us, enjoy our shield and protection, they use our country and our highways, our markets and streets', and in so doing they deceived the authorities such that 'our princes and rulers sit there and snore with mouths hanging open and permit the Jews to take, steal, and rob from their open moneybags and treasures whatever they want'. If a thief steals ten gulden, Luther wrote, he is hanged; 'but when a Jew steals and robs ten tons of gold through his usury, he is more highly esteemed than God himself'. Jews mock the Christian of whom they take advantage and say to one another, Luther wrote, putting words into their mouths: 'We do not labor, and yet we enjoy prosperity and leisure. The accursed Goyim have to work for us, but we get their money. This makes us their masters and them our servants.'[78]

Now Luther taught that because of their asocial behaviour, and above all because they reviled Christ, Christ's mother, and Christ's teachings, Jews could not be accepted within the evangelical community and were even a threat to that communal existence. They jeopardize the salvation of society and of each individual, he claimed, for when the rightful anger of God is turned upon them, it will also strike Christians who have tolerated these accursed creatures. For this punishment to be avoided, princes and lords, with the support of pastors and preachers, must put in place concrete counter-measures. 'I shall give you my sincere advice', Luther wrote:

> first, to set fire to their synagogues or schools and to bury and cover with dirt whatever will not burn, so that no man will ever see a stone or cinder of

them . . . Second, I advise that their houses also be razed and destroyed . . .
Third, I advise that all their prayer books and Talmudic writings, in which
such idolatry, lies, cursing, and blasphemy are taught, be taken from them.
Fourth, I advise that their rabbis be forbidden to teach henceforth on pain of
loss of life and limb . . . Fifth, I advise that safe-conduct on the highways be
abolished completely for the Jews . . . Sixth, I advise that usury be prohibited to
them, and that all cash and treasure of silver and gold be taken from them and
put aside for safekeeping . . . Seventh, I recommend putting a flail, an ax, a hoe,
a spade, a distaff, or a spindle into the hands of young, strong Jews and Jewesses
and letting them earn their bread in the sweat of their brow, as was imposed on
the children of Adam   (Gen. 3).

Indeed, it would be best, Luther proposed, if the Germans 'emulate the
common sense of other nations such as France, Spain, and Bohemia, etc.,
compute with them how much their usury has extorted from us, divide this
amicably, but then eject them forever from the country'.[79]

'Diluted Jewish Blood'

Luther maintained his hate-filled polemic against Jews, Muslims, and in his
view errant Christians to the end of his life. The essential characteristics of his
thought and actions in response to those of other faiths can therefore be
found here. The later Jewish texts are shocking even before they are read
against the background of the modern anti-Semitism of Lutheran bishops
during the Third Reich. The reformer recognized that those of other faiths
were equally human, an essential difference from the racial anti-Semitism of
the National Socialists and Hitler. Moments of compassion do emerge. But
Luther had no thought of dialogue. His concern was entirely with safeguarding his position and to this end he believed any measure against Jews
justified, even their banishment and the destruction of their communities.
He was aware of the human suffering that would result, but he was ready to
accept that outcome, just as he had been willing to accept the implications of
the treatment of Müntzer and the 'false brothers'.

Despite those destructive fantasies—'set fire to their synagogues or
schools . . . so that no man will ever see a stone or cinder of them'—Luther
allotted the Jews a special place amongst his opponents. For the professor of
Bible, they had been and remained the people of God of the Old Testament,
but the anger of God had fallen on 'contemporary Jews',[80] who had, he
held, entered into a pact with the devil. They remained, however, the blood

relatives of his heavenly Lord for 'the Messiah . . . is after all their kinsman, born of their flesh and blood, and the true seed of Abraham, of whom they boast'.[81] Four days before his death, in this 'Admonition against the Jews' (*Vermanung wider die Juden*), Luther insisted that 'Jewish blood has now become more diluted and impure',[82] a statement that brings to mind the racial anti-Semitism of the National Socialists. His words should be understood, however, in terms of the narrative of salvation and not as racially framed in speaking of biologically impure blood. The reformer arrived at his formulation not from a racially founded fear that German or Christian blood would be contaminated but from his fear that the Jews of his own time were moving further from recognizing Christ as their promised Messiah, their blood relative.

Hostility towards Jews, undoubtedly fostered by Luther's words, turned into racial anti-Semitism in the twentieth century. In that era Lutheran bishops amongst the German Christians adopted the anti-Semitic racial theories of the National Socialists and ceased to regard baptism as a sign of fraternal unity that knew no racial boundaries. In so doing they decisively departed from the reformer's own teachings, for even as Luther called for the destruction of Jewish communities, he always insisted that Jews who converted should be treated as 'brothers'.

Even the elderly Luther's perspective on the End Times held salvation to be universal and available to all, including Jews. He retained his vision of a Christian church that included Jews and the heathen as a New Jerusalem. Jews could not be brought into this church by force; only the mercy of God would lead them there and in the End Times open their eyes. Luther's salvation-based perspective had as little room for conversion by force, on the Spanish *converso* model, as it had for *limpieza de sangre* biological purity of the blood, a concept that had emerged in the Iberian Peninsula in the late fifteenth century. 'May Christ, our dear Lord, convert them mercifully'[83]—so ran the prayer that ended his shocking anti-Jewish tract of 1543. His final adamant exhortation to the counts of Mansfeld to banish all Jews also contained a proviso: 'If, however, they convert, give up usury, and receive Christ, then we will gladly regard them as our brothers.'[84]

End Times and Defending against False Believers

Here the alien in Luther and his era is so jolting that we need to adopt an ethnological approach that will allow us to recognize both his lack of mercy and sympathy for the very human fate of dissenters in this world and his fraternal concern when eternal salvation was at stake. For Luther, as for most of his contemporaries, each human stood in the tension between the realities of this world and the next. The eternal fate of the individual in the hereafter was far more significant than that individual's limited lifespan on earth. Each individual and each individual's actions are part of sacred history. This individual does not have power over his or her fate or over the fate of the world; he or she is part of an impenetrable cosmic event in which God and the devil, the power of light and the power of darkness, fight for supremacy. The individual is not without self-will and has room to manoeuvre, but sinfulness and lack of willpower mean that he or she can easily be tempted by the devil's machinations from the path to salvation established by God in Jesus Christ. Under the popes the Roman Church had become an agent of evil, the incarnation of Antichrist. God had called him, Doctor Martin Luther, to take up the fight and to cleanse the church. As the prophet of God he was to return the people to the path to salvation, including Jews, Christ's blood relatives. Their failure to respond to his prophetic words could be evidence only of obduracy.

The final version of 'Preserve Us, Lord, by Thy Dear Word', a song we have already encountered, illuminates how Luther framed his quarrels with those who did not share his beliefs. The first verses, in which the singer called on God for protection from 'the slaying of the pope and the Turks', were followed by the words:

> Give thy people one mind on earth,
> Stand with us in our final strife
> And lead us out of death to life.[85]

'One mind': a uniform and dogmatically pure faith should rule on earth, in every land, in every town, and in every village. Only then, the reformer believed, would the salvation of the individual and of society as a whole be safeguarded. He conceived and lived his relationship with non-Christians entirely through the Bible. His concern was not for the confrontations of this world but for the struggle for salvation that overarched all earthly constellations and events. From the start, his conception of the End Times had shaped Luther's theology, and ever since the horrors of the Peasants' War his emotions, too, had been caught up in apocalyptic fears and visions of the ultimate battle. Right up to the moment of his death Luther never doubted his evangelical cause, but he was equally certain that the powers of evil never rested. His 'final battles'[86] were against his devilish opponent and all his earthly creatures who wished to divert humankind from the single path that led to eternal salvation. He needed to ensure that his supporters were well armed for the struggle they would face after his approaching death.

Luther's inability to enter into dialogue with those who did not agree with him and his determination, despite personal anguish, to oppose them mercilessly as opponents of God were the dark flipside of Luther's prophetic conviction. The final battle of sacred history could end only with validation and victory or with defeat. Certainly, that the battle of the End Times would be fought according to rules that were not the rules of wars on earth must not be overlooked. Throughout his life, as during the Peasants' War or in the Turkish pamphlets, the reformer called without moralistic qualms for the use of force. He made a promise of salvation to Christian soldiers that is reminiscent of the fundamentalist vision of paradise held by Islamic holy warriors: 'If you die, you will never find for yourself a more blessed death. For you die in obedience to the word of God and God's command (Romans 13:4ff) and in the service of love that saves your neighbour from hell and from the shackles of the devil.' Here too, however, he distinguished between the earthly and heavenly kingdoms. Force can be used only in the conflicts of this world and must be directed against the pope or the Turks, so not against their religion but only against their claims to authority in this world; the soldiers who thus fight do so 'not as Christians, but as servants and subjects of the emperor'. This battle is a good and Christian work that can secure the soldiers' salvation, yet not because they are fighting for the kingdom of God, but because as Christians they must be 'upright, obedient, and loyal subjects' who 'owe to their secular ruler ... obedience and such service'.[87]

In the battle of the End Times true Christians will fight Turks, Jews, and the pope, as all are forces set against God, but they will not fight with earthly powers. Luther legitimized the use of military force against the pope or the Turks not in religious terms, as an instrument of a holy war, but as an inner-worldly matter, as an instrument of the secular authorities and not the church, of Emperor Charles and not the Christian, according to the personalization in his first Turkish text. If necessary, arms can and must be taken up against the pope, but only against the pope as a secular power, as Emperor Charles had done at Pavia and in the conquest of Rome: 'I do not advise men to wage war against the Turk or the pope because of false belief or evil life, but because of the murder and destruction which he does,' Luther had written. Entirely distinct from this power struggle is war waged for religious and spiritual reasons: 'The first man, Sir Christian, has been aroused against the papacy because of its errors and wicked ways' and his weapons are not soldiers and might; he fights only 'with prayer and the word of God'.[88]

However wildly and belligerently Luther declaimed against Turks and Jews and however distorted his image of the enemy, he had no thought of recruiting holy warriors to take up arms against them. If he did pronounce anything like a holy war, then he did so only in a spiritual sense and not as the destructive military campaign so often encountered in the history of Christianity. Individuals who participated in religious war were to be armed spiritually, above all with prayer and the proclamation of the word; force and terror were not their weapons. Where today Islamic suicide bombers are glorified in religious terms, Luther's blessing of soldiers who fell in war had no ties to a religiously motivated act of violence and was concerned only with the use of force in an earthly context, in a war intended to defend or re-establish order and peace against external enemies such as the Turks or internal threats such as the rebellious peasants.

Luther did not call for a holy war. He did not send into battle holy warriors who understood the world in fundamentalist terms and fought in order that God's kingdom might be realized on earth or to avenge offences against God's holy order. Force in that sense was preserved for God alone, who is an absolute God and has no need for human assistance in God's kingdom.

We may be tempted to see this distinction as naïve or pedantic and perhaps even as cynical, not least because so soon after Luther's death Germany and Europe were overwhelmed by the chaos of the religious wars. The holy warriors of the confessional age could not invoke the reformer, however, neither in the bloody civil wars between Beggars and Catholics in the Low Countries and between Huguenots and the Catholic League in France, nor in the great confessional and political wars of the early seventeenth century. In the middle of the seventeenth century a Christian fundamentalism that cannot be laid at Luther's door was overcome by a separation of religion and politics that was in part possible because of Luther's distinction between the secular and spiritual kingdoms and the recognition that each operated within its distinct sphere.

IV

Dying in Christ—'We Are All Beggars, That Is True'

I n his last year of life, Luther was, he reported to Jakob Probst in Bremen, a former fellow monk in Wittenberg, 'an old man, decrepit, poor, tired, numb, and in the meantime as good as one-eyed'.[1] His decline was evident to those around him, including his friend Lucas Cranach, who in 1543 preserved Luther's advancing years and afflictions in an unembellished portrait (Figure 44).[2] Luther's physical decline naturally had an impact on his productivity: where between 1516 and 1530 he had published some 360 original works, in the following fifteen years his output roughly halved, to only 184 works. When he saw the need, however, he was still ready to invest all possible energies in what he believed a just cause, whatever the personal cost. He commented on Cranach's portrait of 1543, which depicted him as an infirm man, with a distinctive if weak script but fortified by his faith in God:

> Cast your burden on the Lord, and he will sustain you; he will never permit the righteous be moved (Ps 55:22). We should work, but we are to leave God to worry. For our worry is nothing. In the meantime we could have done much that is good, but has been prevented by our worrying.[3]

When concerns for his health threatened to overwhelm his wife, he repeated that message: 'Pray and let God worry. You have certainly not been commanded to worry about me or about yourself. "Cast your burden on the Lord, and he will sustain you," as is written in Psalm 55 and many more passages.'[4]

His trust in God's care meant that Luther paid little heed to the waning of his own powers. Throughout his life he had willingly risked his health, and by his final years he was constantly on the edge of collapse. Yet the demands he faced remained just as great, for by now he was deemed an authority on all matters, those of the world as much as those of salvation.

Figure 44. The elderly and ailing Martin Luther, by Lucas Cranach the Elder, 1543.

To Mansfeld, to Save Mining and the Evangelical Church

In winter 1545 everyone's fears seemed about to be realized. Now sixty-two years old, Luther continued to observe his responsibilities rigorously, and three times in close succession he travelled to Mansfeld in a wagon that provided him with little protection from the harsh winter weather, from 3 to 11 October 1545; from 22 December 1545 to 7 January 1546, so over Christmas; and finally from 23 January to 18 February 1546. He was accompanied on the first two journeys by his colleague Melanchthon, whose presence was a product of their close bond but still somewhat reluctant in light of Melanchthon's own delicate health; the necessary assistance on the third and final journey was to come from his sons. By this date his health was extremely precarious. To his ongoing agonizing digestive troubles and kidney and bladder problems were now added obesity, a heart weakness, and the significant damage to his left eye already noted. Increasingly often he was too weak to leave his bed, and he repeatedly became cognitively impaired or even fainted. Repeatedly death seemed near. To tackle these problems and to try to keep his constant headaches at bay, he had been advised by his doctors to use a caustic treatment to keep a wound on his thigh from healing, probably to prevent blockages in the blood flow. With his mind completely given over to the tasks that awaited him in Mansfeld territory, Luther forgot to take the caustic agent with him on his last journey. Just two days before his death he recalled 'how dangerous it is' to neglect this therapy, and he wrote to Melanchthon to ask him to fetch the substance from Katharina and send it to him via a messenger.[5] It is not at all surprising that his wife and his friends did not want to let him travel. The Saxon elector, too, as he informed his Mansfeld cousins on receiving news of Luther's death, would 'have preferred to see Martin of blessed memory spared this matter when an old and worn-out man'.[6]

But there was no point trying to stop Luther. Right to the end the reformer set his own rules, which in this instance allowed him to tackle a task that had been close to his heart for years. At issue were the encroachments of the counts of Mansfeld on the mining industry, through which they hoped to improve their notoriously bad finances, a product of the repeated division of their lands. They terminated the leases on the *Herrenfeuer*, the smelting works in Mansfeld that, unlike the *Erbfeuer*, were owned not by the master smelter himself but by the territorial ruler, intending that they would be 'state-run' in future. In economic and financial–political terms the decision made a great deal of sense, especially as precisely in these years German mining was facing competition from the more profitable silver production of South America, but the plans alarmed those who would be affected, rousing their protests.

Luther's willingness to become involved stemmed from two factors. First, he acted out of familial solidarity, for his brother Jakob and brother-in-law Paul Mackenrot saw their economic well-being threatened and called on their influential Wittenberg relative for support, and Luther responded all the more energetically when he recognized the broader economic implications: 'where mining should decline, this damage would not be good for the whole of Germany'.[7] Secondly, the actions of the counts of Mansfeld ran counter to his notion of a Christian economic and social ethic. At the beginning of 1536, as the administrative changes to the smelting enterprises

were being planned, he had written to the Mansfeld chancellor Kaspar
Müller, to whom he was related by marriage, that he had 'no hope at all,
for my theology tells me that man's planning [a reference to the worldly
interests of the counts] and God's blessings are against one another'.[8]

The counts of Mansfeld also became hopelessly enmeshed in family
altercations, which were hardly unusual in smaller territories where the
modern principle of primogeniture had not yet been established but were
potentially life-threatening for lands such as Mansfeld, where the original
dynastic castle had already been divided amongst several lines and the lands
themselves were fragmented. The church in Mansfeld territory was also
affected, specifically its right to appoint to the principal church in Eisleben,
the church of Saint Andrew. Luther believed the spiritual and social order of
his 'beloved fatherland' to be under threat and repeatedly called on the
counts to find a peaceful solution; additionally, he prompted Michael
Coelius, the Mansfeld castle preacher, to appeal to the consciences of the
counts of Mansfeld.[9]

Finally, Luther addressed an extensive letter to Count Albrecht, a strong
supporter of the Reformation and also the driving force behind the economic
changes. He was unsparing in his harsh criticism and urgent admonitions, but
he also provided pastoral advice. The count, Luther wrote, must surely already
sense that he was in the grip of the devil, and that he 'was already cold and had
come to Mammon', where he thought only 'of becoming rich'. God would
not allow him to continue to oppress his subjects, and if he did allow it, he
would 'let the county go to ruin in poverty, for it is his (God's) gift, which he
can easily take back again'.[10] When Albrecht responded with indignation to
these threats, Luther turned to the powerful neighbours and feudal superiors
of the Mansfeld counts, to Duke Maurice and Elector John Frederick of
Saxony and to Elector Philip of Hesse, to encourage their intervention on
behalf of the master smelters. At the beginning of October 1545 he proposed
to the counts that as 'the child of their lands' he act as mediator, although he
also strongly warned them again against behaving in a manner that was
'unchristian and unhuman'. His specific concern was the justified demand of
the smelters and affected merchants that the counts either take on the business
debts along with the operations or allow them to continue to run their
smelting works on the existing terms for two more years, to give them time
to pay off those debts themselves.[11]

The first discussions took place between 22 December and 7 January but
proved inconclusive. As a result, after only a few days of rest, on Saturday,

23 January, Luther set off again, this time in the company of a larger group. Along with his servant Ambrosius Rudtfeldt, his assistant Johannes Aurifaber, and his colleague and friend Justus Jonas, who joined the party in Halle, he was accompanied by his three sons, Johannes, aged nineteen, Martin, aged fifteen, and Paul, aged thirteen, who were to use the opportunity to visit relatives in Mansfeld territory. The travellers had to break their journey in Halle because, as Luther, evidently in good humour, wrote home, 'a huge female Anabaptist met us with waves of water and great floating pieces of ice; she threatened to baptize us again, and has covered the countryside', and the ferryman deemed a crossing of the swollen River Saale too dangerous. As the River Mulde, which flowed further east through Dessau, was also impassable, a return to Wittenberg was also not possible. For three days they were 'captive . . . at Halle between the waters'.[12]

Luther did not lose his stride, and on the Tuesday, the Feast of the Conversion of Saint Paul, he entered the pulpit in the town church. There, in addition to marking Paul's experience on the road to Damascus, he again called to account the papacy and their 'antics' directed at the saints and good works. The people of Halle, drawn in droves to hear him preach, experienced the Luther that Germany had now known for a quarter-century—daggers drawn and keenly alert to how he might most effectively publicly counter his opponents and their errors. He was not to be deterred from again directing his ire against the 'damned cardinal', a reference to Albrecht of Brandenburg, who had been his principal opponent, and his collection of relics held at Halle, even though Albrecht had died the previous September and the relics had long before been transferred from Halle to the archbishop of Mainz's residence at Aschaffenburg.

Luther the preacher had lost nothing of his way with words and images. How the people, duped by the cardinal, had run to be shown 'the milk of our dear Lady', he recounted, yet what they had really seen was 'rather the milk of some goat or ram'. The residents of Halle also experienced Luther as chastiser, as he passionately sought to preserve his work. In order that the town of Halle remain steadfast by the Gospel, the town council, he announced, must at last 'find courage to drive the foolish, mangy monks out of town'. Imploringly he urged, 'hold the Word in love and esteem', for ultimately only the grace of God can safeguard the Reformation; otherwise, 'it readily and quickly comes to pass that the masks and monkeyshines, the dead bones or relics (such as the cardinal of Mainz had) replace the pure and salutary Word of God'.[13] Since Luther was a young man, his theology and his approach to living had been shaped by his belief that all things on earth were dependent on the grace of God alone. Now, convinced that his work was under attack from the forces of darkness as never before, this conviction became all the more radical and existential.

After a mounted Mansfeld troop sent to escort the party helped them cross the still-dangerous River Saale, late on Thursday, 28 January, the travellers arrived at Eisleben. Luther took up residence at the home of Johann Albrecht, the town clerk, on the marketplace, not far from the counts' castle.[14] The fainting attack that he had experienced shortly before arriving in Eisleben was forgotten in the joy that here, in his home town, he would be able to help 'my dear lords', as he always termed the counts of Mansfeld, to find a solution to the conflicts between them. The final fourteen days of his life were anything but oppressive or even filled with pain. Much to the contrary, Luther energetically launched himself into the negotiations and was able to record some early success. The warm and respectful hospitality he received gave him great pleasure, as did the good wine, the beer that sat well in his stomach, helping ease his bowel problems, the game, and the fine fish, all sent to him by the counts. He preached regularly, worked each day on his correspondence, entertained Protestant princes such as Johann Heinrich of Schwarzburg, Albrecht of Mansfeld, and Wolfgang of Anhalt, and conferred with Levin von Emden, syndic in Magdeburg, about civic issues. As in Wittenberg, time around the table was spent not only in reflection but also in bantering. Luther could not refrain from one more opportunity to chastise lawyers for being bad Christians, to which Levin sharp-wittedly responded, 'Now that laypeople have power from the Christian teachings to judge, they also want to arbitrate on the business of the world.'[15]

The Mansfeld issues could not be resolved simply by Christian admonition, preaching, and prayer. Even though the counts greatly respected their theological mediator, the very real opposing concerns, full of intricate detail, could not be banished by good intentions and persuasion. Discussions took place at the castle every second or third day, with Luther, in light of his physical weakness, only in attendance for one to one-and-a-half hours. His patience was tried as negotiations dragged on. It took ten days for the counts' interests in the 'new town' at Eisleben to be defined, a process that seemed to Luther even more complex than the founding of the new town itself, some half-century earlier. 'We have enough to eat and drink, and could have a good time,' he complained to his wife, 'were it not for this disgusting business.'[16] Only his sympathy for his homeland had prevented him from simply abandoning the whole business 'in my anger'. The pride and obstinacy of the counts had made him 'become a jurist, but this will not be to their advantage. It would have been better had they let me remain a theologian.'[17] Finally he, too, turned to the ruses of the lawyer. To put pressure on the counts and hasten the proceedings, he arranged for Melanchthon to acquire a letter from Gregor Brück, the Electoral Saxon chancellor, that would require him to return home to Wittenberg immediately to attend to urgent matters. It seems hardly likely that Luther felt such lawyer's subterfuge meant he was a 'bad Christian', for he attributed the political and legal difficulties he faced to 'Satan [who] harasses us with his wickedness', and such wickedness could legitimately be thwarted by all means possible.[18]

His feint proved unnecessary, for the counts' councillors were able to untangle the knots without any external pressure. The settlement was laid out in two agreements: the first, signed by Luther and Jonas on 16 February, regulated with the agreement of all the counts the ecclesiastical and school ordinances for the county, and in particular the disputed rights of patronage, the responsibilities of the Eisleben superintendent, and the stipends of pastors and teachers. The second agreement covered secular affairs and was signed the following day, Wednesday, 17 February, explicitly in Luther's name, although because of his infirmity the reformer had had to leave the final editing of the text to the other mediators, Wolfgang of Anhalt, Johann Heinrich of Schwarzburg, and Justus Jonas.[19] Partly with an eye to the urgent need to let the ailing reformer begin his journey home, in the end a number of problems thought more minor had been put to one side, to be tackled the following May—with the result that even the memory of the reformer could not prevent the counts from entering into a new, long-unresolved conflict. Luther's involvement was therefore only successful in the long term when it came to the regulation of church and schools.

Luther's Final Sermons—Preaching against Turks, Jews, and the Devil

However weak he felt and however often he was distressed by the progress of the negotiations, Luther was not to be diverted from expounding the word of God to the populace of his homeland, to the residents of Eisleben and the many people who travelled to Eisleben from surrounding areas to hear the famous reformer preach. During his stay in Eisleben of just over two weeks he preached in the church of Saint Andrew, which lay opposite the house where he was living, no fewer than four times: on Sunday, 31 January, immediately after his arrival, on the following Tuesday and Sunday, and finally on Monday, 15 February. He spoke of Christology and ecclesiology as he preached on the nature and meaning of the Saviour and his church. His first sermon tackled the account of the storm on the Sea of Galilee and the two natures of Christ that that narrative made evident: the truly human Christ required sleep, while the truly divine Christ had command over the forces of nature. He interpreted the ship that carried the Saviour and his frightened apostles through danger as a metaphor for the evangelical church and its safeguarding of the salvation of its members.

On the Tuesday, the Feast of the Presentation of Christ in the Temple, his sermon was more restrained but full of empathy for the fate of Mary and of mothers in general. He attributed the 'impurity' of women who had recently given birth—found in Scripture and lifted by a rite performed in church six weeks after the birth of the child—solely to the will and law of God, stripping it of the dark magic in which it had been wrapped by popular belief and popular religion. He used the example of this purification ritual to reiterate the core evangelical truth that, while monks may believe themselves holy because they follow a rule, being law-abiding is not inherently beneficial, for humans profit only from their knowledge of the love of Christ and the grace of God, which leads them to act for the well-being of their neighbours.

On Sunday, 7 February, Luther turned to the sinfulness of humankind that is a product of the weaknesses of the flesh, issuing a moral and ethical warning but with a dose of sober realism: 'Even if the human body is ugly, repulsive, leprous, and impure, nevertheless we need the filthy sack and cannot do without it.' Hope, he impressed upon the community, therefore is found in grace alone, *sola gratia*. As the devil always lurks, this gift requires vigilance from the sinner: 'You should know that your sins have not been forgiven so that you should be secure and snore away, as if you had no more sins.'[20]

And his last sermon, given on Monday, 15 February. With apparent premonition, Luther struck a final chord sounded in the name of Christ, but unmistakably also his own work, drawing together admonition and consolation:

> Only come to me; and if you are facing oppression, death, or torture, because the pope, the Turks, and emperor are attacking you, do not be afraid; it will

not be heavy for you, but light and easy to bear, for I give you the Spirit, so that the burden, which for the world would be unbearable, becomes for you a light burden. For when you suffer for my sake, it is my yoke and my burden, which I lay upon you in grace, that you may know that this your suffering is well pleasing to God and to me and that I myself am helping you to carry it and giving you power and strength to do so. So also say Ps. 31 and Ps. 27: 'Let your heart take courage, all you who wait for the Lord,' i.e. all you who suffer for his sake. Let misfortune, sin, death, and whatever the devil and the world loads upon you assail and assault you, if only you remain confident and undismayed, waiting upon the Lord in faith, you have already won, you have already escaped death and far surpassed the devil and the world.

Luther's final words spoken from the pulpit implored the community with a message that he, too, was to take to heart: 'Cling only to Christ's Word and come to him.' Then he broke off—much more about this Gospel remained to be related, he sighed, 'but I am too weak and we shall let it go at that'.[21]

The Eisleben sermons bear the unmistakable signs of a last testament. With the end of his life, perhaps even his imminent death, before he eyes, he wanted to convey one last time to the inhabitants of his Mansfeld homeland the essential points of the evangelical truth and beseech them to remain true to the pure word of God. Awareness that he would not be able to serve the people and admonish them as God's prophet for much longer heightened the resolution and force of his words, a character also typical of the final urgings of others who seek to ensure that their ideas will survive or their teachings will be supported even after they are gone. For the elderly Luther, however, the campaign to ensure his legacy was something more, for the legacy was understood as part of sacred history. His whole life long, Luther was convinced, he had been participating in the battles of the End Times, and his responsibility was to bring Satan, the cosmic opponent of God, to his knees, along with his creatures of the earth. In the early years, as the Reformation erupted and Luther was celebrated throughout Germany, he had engaged that battle joyfully, knowing that victory would soon be his. By the end of his life, however, events had taught him a different lesson. The papal church was consolidating, in Hungary the Turks were assailing the Christians, and even the Jews were advancing, or such he believed was the message of the Sabbatarianism that was emerging amongst Christians in Bohemia. All these events were for Luther signs of the apocalyptic battle of the End Times of which his life, and his approaching death, was part—a consciousness, indeed an experience, that gave his own 'final battle' an almost obsessive character.

Turks, heathens, Jews, even the devil himself were omnipresent in the sermons Luther gave in Eisleben, above all on the first Sunday when his text told of the storm on the Sea of Galilee and Christ's rescue of the fishing boat. Luther interpreted these events as a model for the evangelical communities in the present, which just like that small ship, were threatened by hostile forces under the command of the devil. More than three dozen times he hurled the name 'devil' or 'Satan' at his listeners, on occasion several times in one sentence and in staccato in the final passages. His intention is clear— he wanted to shake the supporters of the Reformation awake in order that after his death they would be ready, and armed, to face the onslaught of his satanic adversary and his allies on earth—Turks, heathen, Jews, sects, and, naturally, the Roman Antichrist.

Luther treated Jews specifically one more time. His comments were stimulated by the current situation in the county of Mansfeld and by a related personal experience during his journey. Just outside Eisleben, as he had immediately reported to his wife, he had been travelling in his open wagon 'through a village in which many Jews are living', when he had become dizzy with the cold. It was his own fault, he stressed, although, he noted, 'It is true that when I passed by the village such a cold wind blew from behind into the carriage and on my head through the beret, as if it intended to turn my brain to ice.' He distanced himself from direct blame, reporting to his wife, 'you would have said it was the fault of the Jews or their god'.[22]

Read closely, this letter does not bear evidence that Luther maintained an occult-fed anti-Semitism. The association of black magic with Jews was not his, but his wife's, for Katharina appears to have developed her husband's radical negative picture of Jews by ascribing to Jews a role as a destructive force inimical to God not only within the narrative of salvation but also tangibly within the world. The reformer did not claim his wife's view as his own. The episode had evidently left its mark upon him, however, contributing to his immediately putting all his efforts into ensuring that the Jewish community was expelled from the vicinity of the town where he had been born.

Luther's short, seven-page memorandum entitled 'An Admonition against the Jews' (*Vermanung wider die Juden*) was a product of the sermons given in Eisleben. It was addressed to the territorial rulers, but was intended also indirectly for the people of Mansfeld, to whom he would have propounded the essential passages from the pulpit.[23] Again he was impelled by a sense that soon he would 'never preach to you again' and by his concerns about the survival of the Reformation. He was convinced that if the evangelical communities were to remain after his death 'diligent in the Word of God's grace', all the internal enemies of the Gospel would need to have been expelled from their midst. In Halle those enemies had been identified as the monks loyal to Rome; now, in Mansfeld, they were the Jews, and specifically those who lived in Rissdorf, near Eisleben, under the protection of one of the countesses of Mansfeld. To continue to tolerate these people who constantly mocked the Christian Lord was to 'be a participant in the sins of another', Luther wrote.[24] He therefore called on the territorial rulers in what he himself termed 'a sufficiently blunt way if anyone wishes to pay attention to it'[25] to banish Jews from their lands immediately.

It was in this last 'blunt' admonition that the reformer went as far as to include a sentence we have already encountered: 'Jewish blood has now become more diluted and impure.'[26] Centuries later racial anti-Semites within Lutheranism were able to take hold of these vile words and give them their own interpretation.

This unbounded attack on Jews and other opponents during Luther's final years should not be written off as simply evidence of a final fury. Luther was motivated by a concern for the survival of the evangelical church that was united with a profound fear that after his death Satan would find it easy to extinguish the light of the newly rediscovered divine truth. Other reformers also suffered existential fears, especially Calvin, who repeatedly saw himself poised on the edge of a hellish abyss. The Genevan reformer tamed his fears through an iron self-discipline found also in his words. Luther, by contrast, gave his verbal fantasies free rein in his great sermons of admonition in order to win in the struggle against Satan and, above all, in order to ensure that after his death the efforts of the evangelical church in that same struggle might never diminish.

Only recently Luther had demanded of the counts of Mansfeld that when it came to the restructuring of the smelting industry, they showed Christian concern for the needs of the people, yet now he had no scruples in advocating that for the sake of his imperilled Reformation, uncompromising action be taken against Jews and against all others who in his eyes were wrong-thinking. The absolute evangelical purity of the territorial or urban church and of its associated society more broadly was tantamount for Luther. Here he had no doubts—only dogmatic purity and religious unity could guarantee the survival of the true Gospel, and only then would the devil and his human creatures be denied all opportunity to lead true-thinking Christians astray. At the end of his life Luther thus assembled an ominous legacy that contained a powerful call for internal religious and ideological unity and integration, and for external radical disassociation, with a clear demarcation that separated off both Jews and non-evangelical churches and beliefs within Christendom.

The Final Message—Dying in Christ

In the middle of February, as it seemed agreement was at last looming in the Mansfeld disputes, Luther informed his wife that he would soon be return-ing home. He wanted to celebrate before his departure what had been achieved and ensure that personal ties between the two brothers Count Gebhard and Count Albrecht were re-established. He informed his wife, 'I shall ask them to be my guests so that they may talk with each other. For until now they have been silent, and in writings have shown much bitterness toward each other.'[27] His death, surprising despite all the omens, prevented him from experiencing that joy.

On Wednesday, 17 February, two days after he had had to break off when preaching in the church of Saint Andrew, Luther again felt so faint that he had to cancel his plans to participate in the final negotiations and remained instead in his quarters. In an extensive account composed the night that Luther died, his colleague and friend Justus Jonas recorded that during that morning Luther had moved restlessly through the room, sensing that he was near death: 'I was born and baptized here in Eisleben, perhaps I am also to die here?' In the course of the day he experienced chest pain and difficulty breathing, which convinced him all the more that death was near. But he was not to be kept from his usual mealtime experiences: he spent the evening in good-humoured company and appears to have eaten and drunk undaunted. Around eight o'clock he went to bed, prayed, and fell asleep. A good two hours later he awoke, evidently because the pain in his chest and his breathlessness had increased. As he was very cold—also it was wintertime—the bedroom was heated.

Those staying at the same house gathered in the sickroom—his two younger sons (Johannes, the oldest of his sons, was staying with his uncle Jakob in neighbouring Mansfeld), Justus Jonas, Aurifaber, his servant Rudtfeldt, castle preacher Michael Coelius, and his hosts. Around one in the morning, Luther started up again out of sleep. Feeling cold, he moved restlessly back and forth in the room as the pain in his chest continued to grow. The two town doctors were called. In the meantime Count Albrecht and the countess had rushed to the house from the town castle, which lay only a few steps away, and tried to bring some relief to their esteemed Luther, with the countess rubbing him with Aquavit.

Jonas and Coelius, the theologians present, were eager to ensure that Luther experienced a Christian death. Extreme unction and other deathbed rituals practised by the Roman Church were out of the question. All the more important, then, were pious prayers that focused Luther repeatedly on his 'heavenly Father, eternally merciful God', and a final confession of faith. In one of the increasingly shorter moments when he was fully conscious, the dying man was asked by his two colleagues: 'Dearest father, do you confess Christ the son of God, our saviour and redeemer?' All those standing around the bed later bore witness that he had answered with a clear 'yes'. Very soon after he fell unconscious for the last time. Attempts to revive him failed. Death came between two and three o'clock in the morning, the result, according to Melanchthon and the doctors, of a *'cardiogmum'* or *'periculosas angustias pectoris'*, a narrowing in the heart, which today we would term a heart attack.[28]

For all their commitment to truthfulness, those present at the deathbed wanted to provide supporters and opponents alike with a particular image of the death of the reformer. More authentic than their reports is therefore a final memorandum found on Luther's writing desk. His notes, written on 16 February, the day before he found himself on his deathbed, were intended solely as a personal aide-memoire:

> No one should think he has tasted the Holy Scriptures sufficiently unless he has ruled over the churches with the prophets for a hundred years. Therefore the miracle is so inordinate 1. of John the Baptist, 2. of Christ, 3. of the apostles. Do not try to delve into this divine Aeneid, but bow your head and worship its traces. We are beggars, that is true.[29]

'We are beggars'—those words from his final sentence, the sole German sentence in a text that is otherwise entirely in Latin, can be understood as a summation of his realist anthropology. A theological meaning is, however, also unmistakable, which leads us to suspect that his words formed notes for his next sermon, in which, continuing the series, he planned to present another core element of Reformation theology. 'We are beggars' gives expression to the Reformation theology of humility (*humilitas*) in one of the malleable images so loved by the reformer. Humankind appears before God not with the capital acquired through Catholic works-based piety but as a beggar with nothing to his or her name other than faith in Christ and in the grace of the heavenly Father.

The significance of the deathbed scene reached far beyond the events themselves. On one hand, a Protestant death rite was not so much created as given unsurpassable symbolic meaning. As presented to the public by its eyewitnesses, Luther's death became just as much part of the Reformation as was the promulgation of the Ninety-Five Theses almost thirty years earlier. The dying man and the theologians at his side would certainly have had the great medieval tradition of the *ars moriendi*, the art of Christian dying, in mind, as evident in the prayers and above all in a Latin formulation spoken three times: 'Into your hands I commit my spirit, deliver me, God of truth' (*In manus tuas commendo spiritum meum, redemisti me deus veritatis*). Essentially, however, as Protestant theologian Heinrich Bornkamm recognized, the reformer 'died an unmedieval death', without receiving the last rites, without any appeal to the saints, without any consecrated object, such as a rosary, and without having allowed himself to be dressed in a monk's habit in order that the merits of his order might offer him protection when he stood before the throne of God to be judged. Luther, Bornkamm reminded us, had long since deemed all human and ecclesiastical inventions meaningless when it came to the moment of death, when the true nature of the individual appeared before God.[30]

On the other hand, the death scene, or more precisely, the reports of the death scene, had a role to play in the Protestant church's self-affirmation at a moment of great danger. Those reports, and the 'official' report composed by Justus Jonas in particular, had been written with their public and propagandist effect in mind. And so it had to be. They recounted the death of the person who had rediscovered the evangelical truth and had founded the Reformation church; now it was necessary to prove that his work could survive without him and—in accord with contemporary perception—that God truly had stood behind him and would now continue to protect his orphaned followers.

That Luther's opponents would use his death to try to bury his work along with the heretic himself had already been evident during the reformer's lifetime. In 1545 he had published a translation of and caustic commentary on a pamphlet recently published in Italy. The text told of his disreputable death and of a final instruction to his supporters to place his body on an altar to be venerated; in the morning, when the people had opened the grave, they had found that it was empty of a body but 'full of such a sulfurous smell that it made all sick who stood round about'.[31] Anyone who read those words would have known what they meant. Medieval tradition said that heretics doubted or even recanted their teachings at the end of their lives. In a sulphuric haze the devil would rob the heretic of his or her soul, and that heretic would die an agonizing death, documented by the body's distorted facial features and twisted limbs. The Wittenbergers themselves were not free of such notions: in 1542 Luther had commented on the death of Karlstadt, 'a friend writes from Basel that Karlstadt has died and adds a fantastic story: he insists that some ghost comes to Karlstadt's grave and moves around in his house, making all kinds of noise by throwing stones and gravel.'[32] Something similar had been said by Veit Dietrich of Johannes Eck, the opponent of Luther's early days, when he commented that Eck had died 'such a hideous death', insane and refusing the sacraments, that it could not have been 'something simply natural'.[33]

For the Protestant theologians who inherited Luther's legacy it was therefore very important that the world—both friend and foe—be shown that the prophet had died a Christian death in his evangelical faith, full of serene confidence in his God. Like all other eyewitness reports, the official record of the death, commissioned by the Electoral Saxon government and quickly published by Jonas, Coelius, and Aurifaber in March 1545,[34] established in great detail all the particulars and phases of the death, in order that Luther's end was documented as a confident, peaceful, and Christian passing in faith, right up until he drew his last breath, a moment that all those present registered as quiet and with no sign of fear. To provide objective corroboration of the reports of those who had been present, an artist living nearby was called in the night to record Luther's peaceful features very shortly after his death (for a copy by Cranach of the original, now-lost, sketch, see Figure 45). The next day Lucas Furtnagel, a painter resident in Halle, hurried to Eisleben to draw the deceased, now laid out, and to create a death mask in wax, from which he subsequently created a plaster cast in his workshop in Halle.

D.M.L. Nat° 1483, 10 No: Obiit 1546. 18 Feb:

Figure 45. Martin Luther on his deathbed, by Lucas Cranach the Elder, following a lost sketch made by an artist in Eisleben immediately after the reformer's death, 1546.

In the ideologically highly charged atmosphere, however, it could hardly be expected that even all these efforts could prevent the defamation of Luther's death by his opponents. And so was born the tale that a despairing Luther had committed suicide. Even at the end of the nineteenth century this rumour could still make for a publishing success, until voices raised even in the Catholic camp put an end to such nonsense.[35] For Luther's supporters, however, the record of his death and his death mask anchored their self-assurance, holding firm their Protestant identity in the face of attack during the period of transition that followed the death of the founder of their faith. In Halle, second only to Eisleben in its ability to boast of particular ties to Luther's death, a life-size Luther doll was created in the seventeenth century with the help of the death mask, providing what was in effect a waxwork display designed to edify and be venerated by Luther pilgrims.

Decisions about what would happen with Luther's corpse and how the reformer would be memorialized fell in the first place not to the theologians but to Elector John Frederick and his counsellors. They were in no doubt that now, more than even during the lifetime of the reformer, it was essential to consolidate the evangelical faith of the people and close ranks against external attacks. The tactical considerations noted here are of more interest to historians than they were to contemporaries; completely independently of such concerns, news of Luther's death was met with deep grief and despondency as it spread initially through the territory of Mansfeld and in Electoral Saxony, then through central Germany and the Empire as a whole, and finally even farther afield, throughout the Protestant world. Captured in ceremonial, this distress could be used to root evangelical teachings more deeply within the communities and within each individual Protestant Christian. The Emperor and the Catholic estates had long been preparing for a military attack and must be shown that even after the death of the founder of their church, the Protestants of Germany lacked neither theological nor political leadership.

What had been impossible while Luther lived now became possible with his death—he became as it were the property of the state, collateral, both ecclesiastical-religious and political-social, for Saxon and German Protestantism. The plea of the counts of Mansfeld, doubtless uttered at a time of deep distress but naïve nevertheless, that they be allowed to bury the dead reformer in the county of Mansfeld, his home territory, was rejected by the elector without extensive explanation. The funeral and interment were a matter for Electoral Saxony and its theologians.

Mourning, Burial, and Memorialization

The great ceremony of mourning began in Eisleben and was initially the work of the theologians. Justus Jonas took control. At 4 o'clock in the night, so very shortly after Luther had died, Jonas dictated a letter to the Saxon elector and had it taken by mounted messenger to Torgau. During the morning he also informed the theologians in Wittenberg and requested that they call on Katharina to break the news to her gently. He arranged for the death mask to be made and gave the first eulogy. In the course of the day the body, dressed in a collarless shroud, was laid out in a tin casket in the house where Luther had died; on the following day it was carried in a procession, accompanied by bell-ringing and singing, to the town church of Saint Andrew. The counts and their families, along with the princes who had travelled to participate in the negotiations, had paid their respects to Luther in the house where he had died; their subjects, both urban and rural, took their departure from the reformer in the town church the next day, on Friday, 19 February.

That afternoon Justus Jonas gave the funeral sermon—before counts, lords, and some 4,000 additional mourners. This evangelical public heard from the pastor the details of the reformer's Christian death, a process soon repeated in innumerable communities in territory after territory. Jonas had already adopted the combative tone that would be deployed by Protestantism in the coming days and weeks to show that Luther's followers not only were far from defeated but also remained true to the teachings of the deceased reformer and ready to defend them against all comers. Published and therefore immediately widely received, Jonas' sermon employed an image of the goose and the swan that would become very popular in the age of confessional Lutheranism (Figure 46): at the stake the Czech reformer Jan Hus had prophesized to the papal church that he, the goose, a translation of the name 'Hus', would soon be followed by a swan, who would sing better and more successfully. Finally Jonas cited Luther himself, with the reformer's message to the Roman Church: 'When living I was the plague to you, pope; in death I will be your death.'[36]

Following the sermon, the coffin was sealed. Ten citizens kept vigil by the body through the night. That evening a letter arrived informing the counts of Mansfeld and Jonas that the Saxon elector had resolved 'to have the body buried at our castle church' and requesting that the counts provide an escort for the remains as far as Bitterfeld, the first town on electoral Saxon soil; Jonas was to accompany the coffin all the way to Wittenberg.[37]

The next morning a second sermon followed, given this time by Michael Coelius, the Mansfeld castle preacher, who already had to counter the first rumours of a sudden death. These rumours came either from the branch of the house of the counts of Mansfeld who had remained members of the Roman Church or from the small circle of Catholics who lived under their protection in Eisleben. Whichever the case, Johannes Landau, the Catholic apothecary, had composed an account of events that differed from that of the evangelicals and had sent it to Regensburg, to counter-reformer Georg Witzel, who had formerly been active in Eisleben. That same year, his report was published by Luther's arch-opponent Johannes Cochläus, translated into Latin in order that the Catholic version of how Luther had died might be read throughout the educated world.[38] After Coelius had given his sermon, the body of the reformer was transported to Wittenberg, accompanied by relatives, theologians, and a guard of honour composed of forty-five men on horseback, including several counts and other rulers. Thousands of people who mourned or were simply curious lined the way; in the villages and towns bells rang out.[39]

Figure 46. Luther and the Swan, painting on a choir stall in the Brüdernkirche, Brunswick, 1597.

After a stop in Halle, where Jonas again preached and citizens again held vigil, the following day at Bitterfeld an electoral Saxon mounted troop with two counts at its head took over the escort, travelling first to Kemberg and arriving the following day, Monday, 22 February, at Wittenberg.

There Gregor Brück, as representative of the territorial government, had received the news of Luther's death on the morning of the day he died from a mounted messenger sent from Torgau. As Jonas had wanted, Luther's wife had been informed by her husband's theologian colleagues. Despite her constant worries about her husband's health, she was unprepared for the news, for only a few days earlier she had received a letter from Luther in which he had announced that he would soon be returning home, had talked at length of the good food he was enjoying, and had scoffed boisterously at the rumour that 'Doctor Martin has been led away', in other words, that he had died.[40]

Although Luther had tirelessly encouraged her to resign herself to the will of God, Katharina was not to be consoled at her loss. Just how deep her grief

was at the death of her much-loved and much-admired husband is evident
from a letter to her sister-in-law Christina von Bora that her candour makes
all the more moving:

> The mercy and peace from God the Father of our beloved lord Jesus Christ,
> kind beloved sister. I readily believe that you have a heartfelt sympathy with
> me and with my poor children, for who would not readily be saddened and
> troubled on account of such a dear man as my beloved husband was, who
> served so well not just a town or a single country, but the whole world.
> For that reason I am so sad that I cannot tell of my heartfelt suffering to a
> single person and do not know where I will find my senses and my courage.
> I can neither eat nor drink, and also not sleep. And if I had had a principality or
> empire, I would not have suffered so much if I had lost it, as when our dear
> Lord took this beloved and worthy man from me and not just from me, but
> from the whole world. When I think of it, I can neither speak nor write for
> pain and crying (as God well knows).[41]

Katharina's grief was joined by material concerns. No formal support existed
for the widows and orphans of even the highest servants of the state; royalties
were generally meagre, and in any case Luther had largely forgone payment
for his publications. The wife of such a famous husband feared the worst,
that she would be unable to pay the debts she had accrued, as was evidently
usual, in making purchases to cover her household's daily needs from the
tradespeople of Wittenberg—another small but startling encounter with the
alien world in the age of the Reformation. The family were freed from their
acute plight only by a gift of twenty gulden given, at the urging of some of
Luther's friends, by the elector as a sign of his gratitude.

That Monday in February 1546 when the deceased reformer arrived back in
his cathedral town, the pressing concern was not the grief and worries of his
family but the image of Protestantism, how the new church that was a
product of that first act in 1517 would portray itself both religiously and
politically. The stars seemed as ill-aligned for this evangelical church within
the great world of Imperial and power politics as they were for the material
security of the Luther family in the small world of Wittenberg. Luther had
seen the storm clouds gathering: he had ended his final letter to Katharina,
'Some say the Emperor is thirty miles away from here, near Soest in
Westphalia; some say that the Frenchman [Francis I] is hiring mercenaries
and that the Landgrave [Philip of Hesse] is doing the same. But let them say
and sing; we shall wait for what God will do.'[42] The electoral Saxon

government was well aware of the demands of the situation. The ceremonial surrounding the burial of the reformer was to display again the triumph of Luther and Electoral Saxony over the old forces and in so doing make manifest the bereaved's intention to hold fast to Luther's word and his teachings.

Under instruction from Torgau, the elector's officials in Wittenberg had done everything possible to prepare for precisely such a display of confidence and self-assertion. The founder of Electoral Saxony's territorial church and of European Protestantism would be buried not in the town church, the first evangelical parish church, but in the Castle Church, a state church in effect, and thus at the burial site of the ruling dynasty. Yes, that interment was a high honour, but it was also an appropriation by the Ernestine dynasty and the electoral Saxon state. The burial itself was similarly designed as a ceremony of state, with widow and family, university, town residents, and church community each given a role to play.

All was already decided by the time Luther's body was carried, early on the morning of Monday, 22 February, through the Elster Gate, the place where a quarter-century earlier the reformer had burned the papal bull. Here the family had gathered along with the court and town, their members marshalled by their estate. A great funeral procession formed and processed through the town, accompanied by the ringing of bells, from the Elster Gate to the castle, passing crucial sites of the Reformation: the Black Monastery, which was now known as the Luther House, Melanchthon's home and the buildings of the university, the town church of Saint Mary, the marketplace with the home and workshop of Lucas Cranach, and then on to the Castle Church.

At the head of the funeral procession were the school-pupils and the clergy, followed by sixty-five men on horseback under the command of the electoral commissioners as representatives of the ruler and of the counts of Mansfeld. The hearse followed, pulled by four horses, much in contrast with the rather miserable covered wagon in which Luther had left Wittenberg not quite three weeks earlier. Immediately behind the hearse came the family, with Luther's widow and daughter along with other 'matrons' on a low horse-drawn cart, and Luther's three sons, brother Jakob, and three nephews from Mansfeld along with other relatives and close friends on foot. Carefully grouped by estate followed the university community—first rector, princely and noble students, and the older and more renowned professors led by Gregor Brück, Melanchthon, Jonas, and Bugenhagen, and then the younger professors and masters and the members of the town council. Last in the procession were 'the splendid number of students' and the citizens of Wittenberg. Those who had not been allocated a place in the procession—residents of the town as well as those who had travelled from nearby villages—gathered at the side of the street or in the marketplace to participate in the mourning.

Attended by as many as a thousand mourners, the funeral held at the Castle Church combined an evangelical worship service with an academic memorial service. Hymns of mourning and a funeral sermon given by Johannes Bugenhagen (see Figure 47), who was town pastor in Wittenberg and Luther's own pastor, were followed by an academic memorial address given by Philip Melanchthon in Latin and immediately printed in several editions in both Latin and German. The publication of Melanchthon's address had a twofold purpose—in the world of the educated elite, his observations on the life and death of the reformer were to serve as a defence against polemical attacks by Luther's opponents; in the everyday world they were to absorb the shock felt across the board, by Lutheran parishioners and their pastors, at princely courts, and amongst the urban magistracy.

Given at the open grave, Melanchthon's oration formed the first high point of the Protestant memorialization of Luther that had begun in Eisleben as the reformer drew his final breath. The reformer's closest colleague and friend, to whom the leadership of Saxon and German Lutheranism had now fallen, set the tone for how the Protestant world would remember their prophet and church father. Near the start of the oration he spoke of 'the reverend doctor Martin Luther, our most dear Father and Preceptor, whom many wicked men have most bitterly hated; but whom we, who know that he was a minister of the gospel raised up by God, love and applaud', continuing, 'We also have the evidence to show that his doctrine did not consist of seditious opinions scattered by blind impulse, as men of epicurean tastes suppose; but that it is an exhibition of the will of God and of true worship, an exposition of the Holy Scriptures, a preaching of the Word of God, that is, of the gospel of Jesus Christ.' Melanchthon, who so often had suffered under Luther's lack of restraint, did not deny his friend's human weaknesses. 'Some by no means evil-minded persons,' he noted, 'have complained that Luther displayed too much severity', but he located Luther's temperament within the salvation narrative, with which Luther had framed his actions and which must now be continued by his successors: 'I will not deny this [Luther's severity]. But I answer in the language of

vnd Martyrern/der iiij. Theyl.   cccxxiij

Nach dem die Oratio geendet/haben die Leich hin-
getragen/etliche gelehrte Magistri darzů verordnet/wel
che die Leich in dz grab gelassen/vnd also zur růge gelegt/
Vnd ist also das theür Organum vnd werckzeüg des hey
ligen Geystes / der Leib des Ehrwürdigen D. Martini/
allda im Schloß zů Wittemberg / nicht fern vom Predig
stůl (da er am leben manche gewaltige Christliche Predi-
gen/für den Chur vnd Fürsten zů Sachsen/ vnd der gan-
tzen Kirchen gethon) in die erden gelegt/Vnnd wie Pau
lus j. Corinth.xv. spricht/Gesäyet in schwachheyt/das er
auffghe an jhenem tage/in ewiger Herrligkeyt.

Zů einem solchen Christlichen abscheydt auß disem
ellenden leben/vnnd zů der selben ewigen seeligkeyt/helffe
vns allen/ð ewige himlische vatter/ so gemelte D. Mar-
          Eg   tinum/

Figure 47. Luther is buried in the Castle Church at Wittenberg as
Johannes Bugenhagen preaches the funeral sermon, from Ludwig Rabus'
martyrology, *History of God's Chosen Witnesses, Confessors, and Martyrs*
(in German), vol. 4, Strasburg, 1556.

Erasmus, "Because of the magnitude of the disorders God gave this age a violent physician."' To provide transconfessional corroboration of his evangelical reading of contemporary events and of Luther's role, Melanchthon had called as his witness no less a figure than Erasmus of Rotterdam. After death, their differences and conflicts were drowned out by their common clear thinking and good intentions at a time of transition. Melanchthon sought to take the wind from the sails of those who following Luther's death, 'falsely affirm, that intricate disputes have arisen, that the apple of discord has been thrown into the Church'.

To define and safeguard Luther's status for the present and in sacred history, Melanchthon called up a great sweep of forerunners that included the prophets of the Old Testament, the apostles, and the church fathers, including Augustine in particular, on one hand, and the classical heroes Solon, Themistocles, and Scipio, on the other; in this truly impressive gallery of witnesses to and ancestors of a European Christian presence, he specifically highlighted 'our leaders, Isaiah, John the Baptist, Paul, Augustine, and Luther'. Dig deeper and it is evident that this trailblazing unity of humanism and Protestantism had stronger ties to the orator than to his subject. Nevertheless, over the following centuries this lineage formed a vital continuity in the memorialization of Luther and for Protestantism's self-identification. Returning to the present, Melanchthon ended his speech with an appeal to those who mourned that they should 'reflect on the perils that now threaten the whole world'. To prevent the truth of Luther's teachings from being corrupted, he warned, 'Let us be more diligent in regulating our lives and in directing our studies, always holding fast this sentiment: that so long as we retain, hear, learn, and love the pure teaching of the gospel, we shall be the House and Church of God.'[43]

At the end of the ceremony a group of masters from the university lowered the coffin into the open grave. Rapidly and widely distributed, the official report concluded:

> and so that worthy instrument and tool of the Holy Spirit, the body of the venerable Doctor Martin was laid in the ground there in the castle at Wittenberg not far from the pulpit from which during his lifetime he gave many powerful Christian sermons . . . that he will be raised on that day in glory (Paul, 1 Corinthians 15:43).

First, however, that heavenly glory was to be given expression here on earth, in the Castle Church at Wittenberg, in a monument of truly princely quality. For the grave the territorial government commissioned a panel in

Figure 48. Luther's epitaph in the Castle Church at Wittenberg, copy from 1892 of the original bronze in Jena by Heinrich Ziegler the Younger, which was based on a design by Lucas Cranach the Elder, 1548.

bronze (Figure 48), a material associated with power, with an image of the man laid to rest beneath it that had all the qualities of princely portraiture of the age, an honour that was unprecedented for someone of lowly origins. The political catastrophe that overtook the Ernestine line the following spring meant that these plans were not realized as had been intended. By the time the bronze grave covering was ready, Wittenberg was in the hands of the victorious Dresden branch of the Wettin family, and there was naturally no desire to leave the epigraph in their grasp also. The monument was eventually displayed in the parish church at Jena, the town to which the Ernestine branch had transferred their university.

Despite all the political fluctuations Wittenberg was not to be denied, however, and soon 'pilgrims' were arriving from throughout the Protestant world. A generation earlier Frederick the Wise had assembled his treasury of relics in Wittenberg as an expression of medieval works righteousness and as a means of increasing the sacral significance of his dynasty. Now this same town became the central memorial of Protestantism, which was here to stay. In the Castle Church a carefully conceived plan unfolded. The graves of the electors Frederick the Wise and his brother John the Consistent would sit alongside Luther's grave, joined later by that of Philip Melanchthon, to form a highly coherent dual display of state and church. The earlier relic project, at which the Reformation had taken aim, had supported the territorial and status claims of the Wettin dynasty; this new display expressed deep Protestant piety, but it also reinforced the early modern electoral Saxon state through similar sacral legitimization.

The memorialization of Luther soon spread from Wittenberg throughout the Protestant world and could be found largely in churches but also on occasion in town halls or castles. Memorials of Luther were most frequently artistic, with larger-than-life full-length images of the reformer common. Luther often appeared in a double portrait alongside Melanchthon, and in churches in northern Germany in particular, he was depicted according to the revealing 'Luther and the swan' motif discussed above, which brought to the fore links to Czech martyr Jus Hus, now raised to the status of 'pre-reformer'. Luther was also a presence in the homes of citizens and richer peasants, depicted on decorative glazed stove tiles that portrayed the reformer, the Reformation, or confessional themes and reminded their viewers, whether host or guest, who they were and where they belonged.[44]

Elsewhere, too, the early modern princely state and its confessionalized society created their own sacral-cultural display, a programme also embraced by post-Tridentine Catholic confessional states, above all Bavaria. This model undoubtedly had its greatest success in Protestant territories, continuing even through to Prussia-Germany with its various entwined expressions of dynasty and Reformation—the Memorial Church (*Gedächtniskirche*) and Imperial

Cathedral (*Kaiserdom*) in Berlin; the Wittenberg Castle Church, renovated by Prussia, with its bronze Theses Doors (*Thesentür*) and highly visible Confession Tower (*Bekenntnisturm*); and the mock-up of the house in which Luther had died in Eisleben, where the hero's death scene was recreated Prussian-style (almost two centuries earlier a dispassionate enlightened spirit had ensured the real deathbed was burned in order to inhibit a cult of Luther relics. The highly charged Prussian Luther memorialization of the nineteenth century responded to the modern age and modernity's demands on Protestantism. That the Wittenberg of 1546, and of Luther's lifetime, belonged to another, completely alien world was quietly forgotten.

Reformer and Emperor, Again

The storm clouds gathering over the funeral soon burst. Determined to use military means against the Protestants, the Emperor had reached the necessary agreements with the pope and with individual princes of the Empire. His brother Ferdinand was on board, and he also won as allies the Duke of Bavaria, who since the death of Duke George of Saxony had been the most important exponent of the Counter-Reformation amongst the German princes, and Protestant Duke Maurice of Saxony, who was eager to acquire the electoral status held by his Wittenberg cousins. In July 1546 the Emperor placed Philip of Hesse and John Frederick of Saxony under Imperial bann— officially not on account of their religion but because they had taken up arms against their fellow prince of the Empire Duke Henry of Brunswick and had held him prisoner—an act that marked the start of the war. The Protestant defensive union, after which the 'Schmalkaldic War' was named, proved able to field a powerful military force in response, but the military leadership was so inept that after some initial success the forces of the Schmalkaldic League were destroyed in a single battle. On 24 April 1547 elite Spanish units within the Imperial army crossed the River Elbe at Mühlberg, a half-day's journey from the electoral Saxon seat of government at Torgau, and put to flight the Saxon army, caught unaware while worshipping. They soon captured elector John Frederick in the Lochau Heath and took him prisoner. With the speedy capitulation of the landgrave of Hesse, the Protestant union was at an end and nothing stood in the way of the Emperor.

Following the defeat at Mühlberg, Lutheranism's cathedral town was now protected only by its walls, the very fortifications whose construction two decades earlier Luther had commented on with loathing and ridicule. But even its city walls could not save Wittenberg. The town capitulated in mid-May, and a few days later the Emperor triumphantly entered the heretics' lair. At the grave in the Castle Church, Charles and Luther met for a second time—or perhaps a third, if we include their long-distance duel at Coburg/Augsburg in 1530[45]—and for a moment it seemed that Rome's anathema and the Imperial bann had caught up with the reformer. The verdict that condemned Luther as a heretic could now be executed posthumously. The Emperor needed only to give the sign, and the fate that had befallen the English reformer John Wycliffe would be shared by Luther: in 1428, forty years after Wycliffe's death, his remains had been exhumed and burned.

The radical anti-Protestant party, led by Spaniards and representatives of Rome, appear to have encouraged the Emperor to have Luther's body disinterred and burned. Dresden painter Adolf Friedrich Teichs (1812–1860) drew the viewer into his powerful historical depiction entitled 'Emperor Charles at the Grave of the Reformer' (Figure 49), where he depicted the moment of decision, when, to the consternation of the hardliners, the Emperor made clear that he would not follow their advice and would leave the grave undisturbed.

Whether played out to a dramatic climax in the Castle Church or a carefully considered decision, Charles' pronouncement was both a political calculation and an expression of his personal religiosity. Just like the Augustinian monk, after their first encounter in 1521 the Emperor had resolutely followed his decision to its logical end. The confession that Charles had composed in 1521 was not the work of a medieval heretic-hunter, but, again like Luther, Charles was no early modern confessionalist. The fate that overtook Martin Bucer only a few years after that last encounter between Emperor and reformer in Wittenberg reveals how, with the emergence of a new generation of rulers, the world changed in the middle of the century. In the late 1540s the Strasburg reformer had moved to England where, based in Cambridge, he supported the reformation of the Anglican Church introduced under Edward VI; he died in February 1551 and was buried in Great Saint Mary's in a ceremony similar to that held for Luther. In 1554 Mary I became queen of England and established an inflexible confessional Catholicism—she had Bucer condemned as a heretic, and his corpse was disinterred and burned along with copies of his books.

Charles' restraint at Luther's grave was politically astute. The Emperor's principal concern was to ensure that his victory brought lasting peace to

Figure 49. *Charles V at Luther's Tomb*, by Adolf Friedrich Teichs (1812–1860), 1845.

Germany. He had no doubts that the only route to pacification required that Protestants be returned to the lap of the universal Christian church. Charles therefore imprisoned the Protestant leadership and even threatened them with death. He used the Imperial diet immediately called to Augsburg— termed the 'armoured' diet in light of the presence of Spanish troops—as an opportunity to issue an interim religious and ecclesiastical order, which made a number of concessions to Luther's supporters in the short term, but was intended in the long term to return them to the authority of Rome. A good year after the death of the reformer, it seemed that the Reformation and the evangelical church that had grown from the Reformation were similarly about to be consigned to the grave.

In the end the Emperor's military triumph did not bring a fundamental return to Catholicism; much to the contrary, Protestantism emerged strengthened from this existential crisis. In part this result can be laid at the door of the political inconsistencies within the Imperial pacification plans, but three other factors were also decisive: first, the fortitude and faithfulness of John Frederick and Philip, Protestantism's imprisoned and humiliated leaders, which brought both men the honorary title 'the Magnanimous'. With his refusal to abandon the teachings of the Wittenberg reformer, John Frederick, the Saxon elector, was willing to risk his electoral status, his land, and his life. His loyalty to his beliefs became a model for a wider self-confidence amongst Lutherans, for his family and dynasty just as for theologians and parishioners.

The second factor that helped rescue Lutheranism was none other than the 'Judas of Meissen', the name given by Ernestine pamphlets to Duke Maurice of Saxony on account of his alliance with the Emperor and the Counter-Reformation Imperial princes. Yet Maurice had never intended to betray his faith. He did welcome his blood money, received in spring 1548 at the Imperial diet at Augsburg in the form of the Saxon electoral title, which had been taken from his imprisoned cousin, deemed to have committed high treason, and he also besieged the Lutheran city of Magdeburg. He was far more concerned, however, with his own political interests than with the implementation of the Imperial Interim. Soon after, he changed sides and organized the anti-Imperial princely rebellion of 1552, which had dual political intent: to defend the rights of the estates against the threatened dominance of the Emperor and to save Lutheranism. Maurice was also the first of the German Imperial princes to look to an alliance with an external power as a means of securing internal interests. At the castle of Chambord on the Loire he entered into a military union with Henry II of France, the arch-enemy of the Habsburgs, which was directed against Charles V. This combination of Lutheran confessional politics and Machiavellian power politics would not have pleased Luther at all, but it was essential for the defence of his worldly achievement, and not only in the crisis of the mid-sixteenth century.

The reassertion of Lutheranism after its defeat in the Schmalkaldic War was not by any means the work of the princes alone. It was also the achievement of urban Lutheranism—the third factor that made possible Lutheran survival. As we saw in the context of Luther's reworking of the constitution of the church, for just less than a generation during the crisis caused by the Interim, Lutheranism held the upper hand in the city republics of central and north Germany,[46] anchoring Lutheran confessional culture for the long term in an assertive civic society. In alliance with their resistance-preaching Lutheran pastors, the Lutheran citizenry formed an opposition to Imperial religious politics that sprang from their communal and civic religion and had wide social reach. 'The Interim, the Interim, the devil lies behind it'[47]—this satirical verse, heard throughout Lutheran Germany, pointed out to everyone, and to the strategically alert authorities in particular, what really stood behind the placatory Imperial compromise formulations on religion, namely, a systematic re-Catholicization of the kind already successfully implemented by the Habsburgs in other parts of their global empire, above all in the Low Countries.

The insurmountable resistance of the Lutheran city republics and the princes' revolt of 1552 forced Charles to allow John Frederick, the former Saxon elector, to return as duke to his remaining possessions in Thuringia, at Weimar, Gotha, and Eisenach. The Emperor himself experienced an ignominious retreat in the cold of winter to Villach, protected from the rebels' armies by the natural barrier created by the Alps. It was the beginning of the end for Imperial hegemony. Charles left his brother Ferdinand fully empowered to agree a temporary truce with the rebels, established in 1552 in the Peace of Passau, and to build on that achievement with a permanent peace. With the religious peace agreed at the Imperial diet held at Augsburg in 1555, German Protestantism was formally recognized in Imperial law indefinitely and, as soon would become apparent, permanently. After his defeat at Metz by the French king and his Protestant German allies, Charles abdicated—the only abdication in the history of the Holy Roman Empire— divided his lands between his brother Ferdinand and his son Philip, and withdrew to Spain, spending the remainder of his life in an unassuming villa at the Hieronymite monastery of Yuste, in Extremadura.

The Emperor could see that all the plans he had brought to his first Imperial diet, at Worms in 1521, had come to naught. Politically, his conception of a modern, universal empire had collapsed in the face of the emergence of the early modern state, above all in France but also in the German lands, where the territorial princes would soon be sovereign in practice. His failure was also religious and ecclesiastical. The traditionalist unity to which he had professed his allegiance with a highly conscious sense of sacred majesty had been countered first at Worms by a single Augustinian monk and then by half of Germany. Yet neither the defeat of his political model nor the failure of his vision of the church could rattle Charles' religious convictions. In his faithfulness, he was entirely the equal of his opponent at Worms.

In terms of their religious devotion Emperor and rebel were not, in the end, as very different as they and their contemporaries thought. Each day when he was at Yuste, Charles would gaze upon Titian's 'La Gloria'. The painting, which he had commissioned and then brought with him from Brussels to Spain, depicted the Final Judgement, with the Emperor, dressed in a penitent's shirt or shroud, kneeling before the throne of the triumphant Trinity, with his wife, who had predeceased him, and his aunt, who had raised him, by his side. In Titian's heaven, somewhere between the medieval and baroque heavens, the three figures receive a highly personal final judgement, without the support of martyrs, saints, popes, or founders of religious orders. On 21 September 1558, as Charles lay on his deathbed and was to prepare himself for the transition to the next world, he armed himself with a simple crucifix, handed to him by Bartolomé Carranza, Dominican monk and archbishop of Toledo. The Emperor died with a faith in Christ that was very similar to the 'faith in Christ alone' teaching of his Wittenberg opponent. The guardians of doctrinal and moral confessional purity spied a possible infringement. Archbishop Carranza was called before a tribunal to justify the Christocentric character of his pastoral care, and even the Emperor posthumously fell under suspicion of heresy.

Freed from polarizing confessional impulses, we can see that the Christocentric devotion of the Reformation and of Imperial, pre-Tridentine Catholicism sprang from a common root. The deathbed scene in Yuste should be understood in light of the pre-confessional, Christ-focused piety of the *devotio moderna*, which so greatly influenced both the devotional instruction received by Charles as a young prince of Burgundy at the Habsburg court at Mechelen and the spirituality of Martin Luder, student and monk.

Epilogue

Failure and Success: Luther and the Modern World

A Changed World and Luther's Part in Changing It

Viewed in light of the Christian attitudes of their age, Luther does not prove to be so very different from his Imperial opponent. In 1521, as he spoke out before Emperor and Imperial diet in favour of an evangelical renewal of the church, Luther, too, thought of Christendom only in universal terms. By the time of his death, however, early modern particularist forces were as evident in the reform of the church as they were elsewhere. The universal evangelical renewal of Christendom had become the discrete reformations of the Lutheran or Reformed territorial and urban churches. In place of the unity and peace that Erasmus, for one, had sought for Christendom, estrangement and hostility now dominated. Soon the German territories, and Europe more broadly, would be trapped in an unremitting struggle over political and confessional-cultural supremacy, conflict that even contained signs of a fundamentalist desire to see the enemy eradicated. Luther's self-assertion had meant that, just like the Protestant churches, the post-Tridentine renewed Roman Church had inevitably become a particularist church and its head, the pope, a particularist prince, no matter how much he might continue, even up to the present, to insist upon the universality of his church. Just like the papacy, Luther and all the confessional churches that emerged from the Reformation abided by their universalist-couched assertion that they alone represented the truth, signalling clearly the discrepancy between claim and reality.

At the midpoint of the Reformation century Imperial rule had also become particular. The Reformation had eroded the sacrality of the Holy Roman Empire, and the foundations of Imperial political power had been weakened by the dividing up of the Habsburg possessions: European and global interests were assigned to the king of Spain; the Holy Roman Empire passed to Charles' brother Ferdinand and his successors, their political power limited to Germany and the border zones of eastern Central Europe.

The world in which Luther and Charles V died was not the world of their encounter in Worms. That broad shift is now customarily seen as marking Europe's transition into the modern age. There can be no doubt that both men, Charles V just as much as Luther, contributed fundamentally to that transformation. Their contributions were, however, dissimilar, and each echoed quite differently for posterity. Where later generations celebrated the Wittenberger as the motor of the modern age, and even modernity, they saw the Habsburger as its dampener. In order to understand Luther's contribution to and position within the history of Christendom and history more generally, we have to consider the roots of this clichéd view popular in Germany.

Luther hoped that the restoration of the evangelical truth would inaugurate a new era of belief, but the idea that he was authoring revolution was as alien to him as it was to those who celebrated and joined with him in bringing about that transformation and those who rejected and feared the innovations he advocated. The model that divided up history into epochs was a later creation. Historians and philosophers of the nineteenth century, and Georg Wilhelm Friedrich Hegel (1770–1831) and Leopold von Ranke (1795–1886) in particular, turned Luther into the hero of a new age, providing the Protestant bourgeoisie of Germany with a philosophical and historical rationale for deploying the reformer in their response to the rapid advance of modernization in their own age. The interpretation of the Wittenberger's actions as revolutionary served to legitimize their world-altering activities and to place Germany at the head of progress. That Protestant historical model proved so powerful that on the eve of the descent into National Socialist barbarism, Adolf von Harnack (1851–1930), the most significant Protestant theologian and director of scholarship of the early twentieth century, could pronounce without any qualms, 'The modern age began along with Luther's Reformation on 31 October 1517; it was inaugurated by the blows of the hammer on the door of the castle church at Wittenberg.'[1]

Since then both the confessional and the nationalist values that underpinned this interpretation have been called into question. The inevitable progress of history towards the modern, however, that 'modern' is defined, is also contested. The famous depiction of the Augustinian monk in Wittenberg as the cudgel-wielding Hercules Germanicus who humbled the authorities of his age is now no longer read as evidence of Luther's intent to clear a path for the modern age but deemed instead testimony to the ingenious media strategy adopted by the reformer and his supporters. Having been repeatedly cited as an expression of the revolutionary consciousness of the age of Luther, the famous Copernican woodcut 'The Breaching of the Old Image of the World' (*Durchbrechung des alten Weltbildes*) was exposed some time ago as a historicizing interpretation produced in the nineteenth century.

From the French, Spanish, and Italian perspectives, the Reformation has always been a German, and therefore limited, event. The broader European context provides support for French historians who speak not of *the* Reformation but of an 'age of reforms' (*temps des Réformes*), referring to ecclesiastical and religious reformations that stretched from the fourteenth century to the mid-seventeenth century. Luther was at the heart of this transition. He was its product, and his contribution in driving it forward was unsurpassed.

The End of Universalism

Just like all the other actors of his age, Luther understood 'religion' in universal terms—for the reformer it was the sole truth for an evangelically renewed Christendom. As God's prophet he was responsible for bringing that truth, which alone could save, to all peoples and for ensuring its implementation everywhere. Charles V's political universal project failed, but so too did Luther's theological and ecclesiastical universal project. The outcome was momentous. Cultural and political differentiation within Europe, the modern concept of liberty, and in the long term even the ideological pluralism without which modern society would be unthinkable were all only possible when universalism no longer held sway. Such ideas would have been utterly alien to both Emperor and reformer.

The Habsburgs could not prevail against the militant particularism of separatist territories and nations. Kings, princes, and their subjects were no longer prepared to form a single universal *populus Christianus*, with the Emperor as *sacerdos Christi*, Christ's anointed one, their representative and ruler. The future belonged to 'sovereignty', the aspiration of all rulers and republican magistrates, with its theoretical foundations supplied by French royal jurist Jean Bodin.[2] In the Empire the official end of the religious unity of the 'holy empire' in 1555 meant also the end of the dream of a German Imperial state. The right to construct the early modern state had passed from the crowned head of the Empire to the princes of the Empire. Charles V had sought to create a modern monarchy in Germany with a strong king or Emperor at its head, but the princes appropriated ultimate legal and political power for themselves. As a result Germany would henceforth be character-ized by its multiplicity of territorial states.

A similar situation prevailed in Europe more broadly, where Charles V's idea of a graduated political order that climaxed in the office of the Roman Emperor had proved abortive. Nevertheless the Emperor was able to safe-guard the authority of the Habsburg family, although he did so not through a universal monarchy but by means of a dual hegemony established at the time of his abdication, when his authority was divided between the Spanish Habsburg line, which retained its supremacy for another century, and the Austrian Habsburg line, which exercised Habsburg interests in central and eastern Europe. Charles V thus became one of the founding fathers of the modern state and the modern world order, but this role was involuntary and a product of failure.

The real loser in the creation of this political and cultural new order in Europe was the pope. Luther had sought, and was largely responsible for, the pope's disempowerment, but at the same time, the political enfeeblement of Rome was not the reform of the church for which he had hoped. The lasting internal stability given to the papacy in both ecclesiastical and political terms by the Council of Trent had its roots in the early form of absolute elective monarchy, with the pontiff at its head, established in the fifteenth century. The mixing of the spiritual and the secular that Luther had criticized so vehemently remained an essential characteristic of the papal church for centuries. The Roman Church also retained its claims to universality, even though with the self-assertion of the Reformation this universality had become a fiction; the papal church was now a modern particularist confes-sional church just like its Reformation rivals. The early modern papacy never managed to resolve that mismatch, no matter how splendid its portrayal of its claims to universality. At the end of the Reformation century, Sixtus V (1585–1590) launched a reconstruction of Rome that tackled the layout of the urban space. In a pugnacious response to the German

Reformation, the design staged the narrative of salvation throughout the Eternal City, and in giving salvation space, as it were, within Rome, claimed it for the renewed Catholic Church. In the mid-seventeenth century in his design of Saint Peter's Square for Alexander II, Gian Lorenzo Bernini (1598–1680) portrayed the universal authority of the Roman Church in global terms. Yet in these same years the particularity and political insignificance of the papacy in practice were very evident. At the peace conference held at Münster at the end of the Thirty Years War, fought over religion and territorial power, the curia struggled tooth and nail against the secular political order of the Peace of Westphalia, but the international community of states, Catholic and Protestant alike, simply brushed aside its protests.

Luther's Success and Its Preconditions

It is harder to draw up a balance sheet of successes and failures for Luther than for the Emperor and the popes. Hardly any other figure had anything like the same influence on the transition that had begun in Europe in the late medieval period. Even when viewed in the context of a longer 'age of reformations', Luther still stands out as *the* reformer—he consolidated existing reforming impetuses and provided them with a new energy and a new dynamic. His opponents also profited from his response, above all Ignatius of Loyola, the reformer of the papal church, who seems inconceivable without the provocation provided by Luther. Because of Luther, the Reformation era and the period of confessionalization that followed marked the apogee of a secular turn that neither grew from nor focused on church and religion alone.

The medical 'syndrome' provides useful illustrative parallels. A complex syndrome will be the product of numerous independent factors, but some of those factors will be particularly decisive. The innovations and transitions in Europe during the late medieval period and the first century and a half of the early modern period were similarly determined by a number of independent factors, but in the end with Luther religion became *the* decisive factor, in providing not only meaning and explanation but also a driving force that brought about cultural and social change.

We must recognize that this dynamic was generated by an understanding of religion that is not replicated today, even within Protestant churches. Luther was just as immersed in that different religious mentality as were Charles V, the popes, and all his other contemporaries. Luther thought and acted in a premodern world that is entirely alien to us, a world in which demons and angels were a constant presence and everything on earth was part of a higher transcendental reality.

For Luther the present was always part of the narrative of salvation, especially when it came to the renewal of church and world according to Gospel criteria. Luther understood religion eschatologically, in that he always thought in terms of the end of the world and its transformation into eternal heavenly life. Religion thereby acquired a dynamism and efficacy that were invigorated in early modern Europe by the Reformation. That revitalization might prove constructive and positive but could also be evil and destructive.

Luther had originally envisioned a universal reformation of Christendom by means of a restoration of the Gospel that would bring about the peaceful reconciliation of the fragmenting powers of his time. This vision was not to be realized. He had sought a renewal of Christendom that flowed outward from the church community and ushered in a Christianization of the world; instead he generated the particularism of territorial and national churches. For Luther, however, such setbacks were simply defensive positions, adopted in light of the realities of the situation, from which, he was sure, the pure word and the evangelical church would one day advance to become universal.

In 1521 Luther had stood before the leading figures of church and world to defend his teachings as a lone monk without influence, power, or symbolic capital. With that picture as our starting point, whatever the limits of his achievement, we have good reason to think Luther victorious. He helped establish the terms of the debate over a new order for Latin Christendom, or Europe as it would soon be called, a change in terminology that recounts a secular reframing of the continent and its culture to which his courageous rebellion contributed. As history reached a crossroads,[3] the Wittenberg reformer played a decisive role in determining which path it would take, although that path did not always lead where he had intended, and on occasion even went in an opposite direction.

The ability of this Augustinian monk from the 'edge of civilization' to hold his ground before the most powerful men of his age can be attributed to courage, heroic self-assurance, and prophetic confidence, which stemmed from his sense that he was God's messenger. Those characteristics had also produced earlier martyrs who had opposed the authorities in the name of their faith, above all Jan Hus. Luther's particular strength was his ability to stick to his task undeterred, allowing neither coercion nor temptation to divert him from his cause. He surrendered nothing to those within his own camp who impatiently sought to hasten change, and he resisted the elegant admonitions of Erasmus, the prince of humanists held in such high esteem by all parties, who called on Luther to silence his views and content himself with peaceful compromise. Such responses required a steely character that would make it possible for him to 'dig out the roots and stumps, chop out the thorns and underbrush, and fill in the potholes', for, as we recall, at the high point of the conflict over his teachings, the reformer characterized himself as a 'rough woodsman'.[4] A little-known sketch of the reformer by Lucas Cranach the Elder masterfully catches Luther's will to act, even something almost brutish in the reformer's character. Luther's ruthlessness can come across as obstinacy or even pig-headedness, but it was a condition of his success.

Where Luther resisted his enemies, his friends and allies had to tolerate Luther: Philip Melanchthon, who patiently suffered his friend's diatribes and generously recognized his intellectual greatness; the Saxon electors, who tolerated Luther's every dissent and aligned their politics with his vision, even to the extent of staking their lands and their lives; Georg Spalatin, an intelligent companion in the early years of the Reformation who later, as pastor in Altenburg, was brought to the point of collapse by a reproach from Luther. Their loyalty was to the common cause that Luther represented so compellingly, but it was also a result of engaging character traits that made Luther's volcanic temperament bearable—his pleasure in art and literature; his enjoyment of conversation and good company, which meant that even when the pressure of work was very great or an external threat loomed, he was cheerful and confident as he gathered with his family or a wider circle of guests; his openness and frankness, which allowed both opponents and supporters to know exactly where they stood with him. His interest in others, his ability to respond with tender words and gentle gestures, enabled his severity and crassness, especially in his speech, to be almost forgotten. The letters of consolation he wrote to those who were sick, mourning, searching, or doubting show that he was both serious and gifted when it came to pastoral care, with his advice trusted and his admonitions followed.

Luther's strength of character was joined with two talents without which his rapid success throughout Germany would have been impossible: his outstanding ability when it came to crafting his public profile and his feel for the politically decisive forces of his age. The potency of his language and the creativity of his images and argumentation along with the effort he invested and his command of the pulpit made Luther more suitable than any other to become a star of the first media age. Those skills allowed him to spread his teachings throughout Germany and beyond, supported by a whole army of printers, painters, and graphic artists. His words echoed not just amongst the educated elite but also amongst the people more broadly. As the defeat of the popular rising of the peasants demonstrated, however, the Reformation would not have been secure in the long term if Luther's political sensibilities had not led him to allies who were right for his cause and uniquely dependable.

If revolution really was possible in 1525 and if the peasants had a genuine opportunity to transform politics, society, and the economy at the last moment, there would be reason to deny Luther's political intuition. But we would need also to deny that power had already shifted in favour of the princes and their territorial states and that in the mid-1520s, whatever their broad appeal, Luther and his Reformation still faced a precarious situation. In 1547 the dangers of any association with rebellion were made evident even to rulers as powerful as John Frederick of Saxony and Philip of Hesse when the Emperor declared them guilty of high treason and brought them militarily to their knees. In deciding that the princes and the magistrates of the Imperial towns would be the bearers of his Reformation, Luther demonstrated a keen ability to recognize the only political authorities of his time that were both able to act and dependable. At the same time, however, he had to run the risk that his achievement would become part of, or even subordinate to, the calculations of these authorities' secular interests in the form of evangelical territorial or urban churches.

Luther's original concept of a universal reformation of church and world failed, but its very failure launched fundamental cultural and social-political change that was more profound and more consequential than anything set in motion by Charles V. Luther rebelled against the papacy and against papal claims to absolute sovereignty within Christendom, revealed by the Renaissance popes not only in previously undreamed-of expressions of power but also in a worldliness that was repugnant to so many of the devout. Abandoned by the universal authorities of church and Empire, Luther entered instead into an alliance with the princes and the early modern state and in the process became the reformer, and finally even the church father, of a new evangelical faith and of a modern particularist confessional church. Without calling into question the universality of faith and of the invisible church, he demolished medieval universalism and repudiated the legitimacy of its Imperial–papal dual headship. Ecclesiastical and confessional differentiation gave additional impetus to the political and social differentiation of Christendom that had begun in the late medieval period, driving it onwards to the birth, in the firestorm of the European confessional wars, of an international system comprising legally equal particular states.

No less than universality, this cultural, political, and ideological differentiation within Europe had its roots in the Middle Ages, but it was the Reformation that gave it its religious legitimacy and modern dynamic. In the long term this process would foster the shift to the secularism, pluralism, and freedom of conscience of the modern age. This too, had not been Luther's goal, but it was another unintended consequence of his thinking and his actions.

The Confessional Church and Confessional Culture of the Modern Age

As the Wittenberg Reformation stood its ground against all that Rome and the Emperor could throw at it and with the creation of additional Protestant churches elsewhere—Reformed and Calvinist in the Swiss Confederation and western Europe, Anglican in England—Europe experienced a powerful shift towards ideological and institutional diversity. The early modern confessional churches and their confessional cultures left a deep impression on the continent, intellectual and cultural as well as political and social. This impact was a product of mutual antagonism, even enmity, but it also resulted from fruitful competition in response to provocation, and not infrequently was generated through osmosis and exchange.

Luther was successful even, and specifically, in Rome. Medieval traditions fostered the papal church's early modern revival, but in the face of opposition from a more powerful curia, the reforming enthusiasm of the late medieval period had largely tailed off by the beginning of the sixteenth century. Rome needed to hear the wake-up call that emanated from Wittenberg if it was to launch the rapid renewal necessary to ensure it was not left at a profound disadvantage. In the end the Roman reforms also enabled a transition into the modern age, even if that process was built on spiritual and institutional foundations that were not those of the societies and churches of the Reformation.[5]

The papal church that emerged from the reforming Council of Trent was not the medieval universal church against which Luther had rebelled. Just like the confessional churches of the Reformation, the Tridentine Catholic confessional church was also a new church of a modern age. After Luther the popes were even more reliant on the assistance of the secular rulers than they had been when under threat from late medieval conciliarism. As a result, even in Catholic areas of Germany and Europe, religious and ecclesiastical authority that had been exercised by the church now passed into the hands of the state. Much as in Protestant areas, this process was tied in with the territorialization and regionalization of organization and administration, in Catholic lands above all when it came to the appointment of bishops and authority over the clergy in general. The Gallicanism of the modern age in France is only the best-known example, for in the Spanish church and in the territories of the Empire that remained Catholic, above all the dukedom of Bavaria, the stronghold of the old faith in southern Germany, secular rulers dedicated much energy to ensuring that they also had a decisive say in the appointment of bishops, the administration and use of church property, the disciplinary supervision of the clergy, educational and training institutions, universities and colleges alike, ecclesiastical institutions that catered for social welfare or cared for the sick, and so on.

Catholic renewal had Luther and his competing Protestant Reformation to thank above all for new impetuses in education. No less a figure than the Jesuit Peter Canisius, so influential in southern Germany, soberly registered that the Catholic Church had fallen behind when it came to schools and universities, and he immediately launched into a race to catch up; in the Catholic areas of Germany his Counter-Reformation catechism performed a role very similar to that of the Lutheran catechism in Protestant territories.

Emulation of Luther's work on the catechism was only one element of Rome's extensive response. As in Protestant lands, new modes of thinking and behaving reached many layers of society, but in the early modern Tridentine church, those innovations were the work of the reform orders, above all the extensive Jesuit network, and were adopted in particular by princes and nobility, by the new political and educational elites, and by the burgher class. The rural areas were initially little affected, but the situation for Protestantism was hardly much different. In response to Luther, Catholic agents of confessionalization also sought to effect the Christianization of society as a whole, to encourage self-searching and self-direction, and to create a programmatic bond between religious interiority and a moral and responsible life within the family, the church, and the town or village community. As a result of Luther's evangelical renewal, a 'modern Christianity' also emerged within renewed Catholicism, fostering a 'bourgeois spirit' (*esprit bourgeois*) throughout Europe. The efforts of the reform orders 'contained enough novelty with regard to the family and society, as well as in the manner of living one's religion, to disquiet the champions of tradition', Louis Châtellier has noted.[6] Where married and family life in the Luther House in Wittenberg served as the model for the Protestant burgher family, the cult of the holy family, promoted above all by the Jesuits, became exemplary in Catholic societies.

Without the pressure and challenge from Luther, the Renaissance papacy characterized by Alexander VI Borgia, Julius II della Rovere, or even Leo X Medici would have hardly been in a position to undertake such a radical revitalization of religion. With the reforms of the Council of Trent, wrung from the popes only by Luther's Europe-wide success, religion re-emerged as the focus of the papal church, enabling it to make its own contribution to the history of the modern age in Europe. The successful staging of religion celebrated by today's popes, among young people in particular, is also Luther's success, for the reformer remedied religion's developing anaemia and returned its existential power. The Catholic Church may not want to celebrate the five-hundredth anniversary in 2017, but it should feel invited to join Lutherans in honouring the Reformation.

State and Politics

In the secular world, the impetus Luther brought to the processes of differentiation benefitted the early modern state above all, first in the Protestant parts of Europe and then, in modified form, in Catholic lands. Soon after Luther's death, the authorities in the evangelical territories of Germany seized the opportunity to bring the recently created territorial churches directly under their jurisdiction. They claimed decision-making power not only for the external affairs of their territorial churches but also, on occasion, for internal matters such as ritual and confession, an authority that Luther had unwaveringly reserved for theologians. Additionally they claimed broad competences over matters previously solely or largely in the hands of the church and in so doing gained access to core activities of the modern state, such as care for the sick, old, and needy, the regulation and control of marriage and the family, and schooling and university education. The issues in which the state could intervene were now far more numerous. At the same time the political continued to become more autonomous or secularized, such that step by step politicians felt released from the religiously founded responsibilities that in his teaching on the two kingdoms Luther had imposed on Christian authorities in the world.

This territorial church governance of later Lutheranism not infrequently saw religion as a tool that could be employed to political or social ends, a development that was not in accord with Luther's fundamental principle of the freedom and right to self-determination of the church, both as a community and for individual Christians. The Saxon reformer would have had no time for the ideology of 'Throne and Altar' dominant in nineteenth-century Prussia and, incidentally, a product in many ways of traditional Hohenzollern 'court Calvinism'. The alliance with the National Socialists entered into by individual Lutheran bishops and 'German Christians' could not be reconciled in any way with his teachings. Yet these developments, the grim result of Luther's decision to commission the princes as emergency bishops for the cause of the Gospel, are also part of the history of Luther's influence.

The outcome was similar when it came to political activity and political consciousness more generally. Luther did not believe himself to be at the beck and call of the secular authorities. For the sake of peace and good order he demanded obedience to lawful authorities; a servile spirit and obedience for obedience's sake were, however, entirely alien to him. If pure teaching and the evangelical ordering of state and society were in danger, then dissent and Christian self-assertion, and any concomitant suffering, were required. He acknowledged an active right of resistance for individuals and authorities who were thus constitutionally empowered. Despite the acceptance of an extensive role for the state in ecclesiastical affairs from the mid-sixteenth century, the memory of Luther's successful rebellion against traditional authority remained alive in Lutheran churches and could be deployed to justify both individual and collective action. The lay Christian participated in the life of the church in concrete form each Sunday not simply passively, in hearing the word of God, but also actively, in confessing the evangelical faith and, above all, in singing hymns. The independence of the pastors was not completely eradicated with their submission to the supervisory authority of the temporal authorities; on the whole the Lutheran pastorate behaved like loyal employees of the state, but some pastors and theologians were prepared to drag princes and magistrates over the coals as Luther himself had always done. Greater engagement with authorities brought with it a more deeply rooted willingness, even responsibility, to censure those same authorities. Even though the right of active resistance was limited to specific office holders, on occasion Lutheran Christians were both ready and able to resist actively in response to injustice.

And yet, the early modern urban, territorial, or—as in Sweden—national churches eclipsed the freedom of the self-determining Christian and the early communal church. While civic Calvinism remained firmly anchored in the political culture of western Europe, the tradition of a civic Lutheranism in central and northern Europe, which in the mid-sixteenth century had still been capable of collective political action, even active resistance, faded away. The two branches of the Reformation therefore contributed in different ways to the creation of an open, participatory political culture, partly as a result of their singular origins. Calvinism drew on a tradition of underground, exile, or independent churches free of secular authority and on the maritime and libertarian character of western Europe, in particular in the Dutch mercantile republic. Other than in a few solitary communities, neither feature shaped German Lutheranism.

The broader historical context sent the church in a specific direction, but so too did Luther. He never disavowed the rudiments of the communal church found in his early theology, but he subsequently embedded them within the structures of the territorial church. While, as we have seen, that tactic was based on an accurate assessment of prevailing power constellations, it decisively weakened the communal principle. The sense of political responsibility that was both deep-rooted and pervasive in Calvinist societies did not develop under Lutheran auspices. Democratic tendencies associated with the self-government of church and community have correctly been linked to the presbyterial and synodial constitution of Calvinism, but any such democratic leanings were blocked in Lutheranism. The transition to the modern form of the participatory evangelical lay church took place for Lutheranism only in the nineteenth century and even then faced resistance. Luther and his reception played their part in ensuring that in the nineteenth century Germany, a 'delayed nation', had to begin its 'long road West'.[7]

Toleration and Pluralism

Pluralism and tolerance were not the children of the Reformation, only, at best, its grandchildren. Certainly Luther's appearance turned 'tolerance' into a pressing problem addressed by humanists in particular, above all Erasmus amongst Catholics and Melanchthon in the Lutheran camp. In an age of differentiation and exclusion, their ideas were unlikely to thrive, and the prospects for more extreme notions of toleration were even bleaker. By the mid-sixteenth century Europe's spiritual and cultural core had been divided into a number of confessional churches and confessional cultures, each of which continued to insist on its own universal truth claim, which excluded any other truth. Christians left no room for mutual toleration, let alone for the toleration of adherents of any other religion.

Toleration in its modern sense was alien to Luther. He was unable to imagine a plurality of religious truths.[8] Yet his ideas and actions provided toeholds for the subsequent development of freedom of conscience and toleration. First there was a thesis he had defended at the Leipzig disputation, 'the burning of heretics is against the will of the Holy Spirit', and his appearance before Emperor and Empire at Worms, where he had refused to recant on the grounds that faith is an internal spiritual concern in which the authorities of this world cannot intervene. Throughout his life he continued to insist that faith cannot be forced and that no one wields authority over the soul. In the early years, when he still assumed that the evangelical word of God would quickly prevail, he supported freedom of expression: 'Let the spirits collide and fight it out,' he had written,[9] even if the words the spirits spoke were heretical.

The experiences of the Peasants' War and the increasing opposition to the Wittenberg model of reform caused Luther to back away step by step from this 'liberal' position. In the final days of his life, he was practically obsessed with the requirement, dictated by the narrative of salvation history, for absolute ecclesiastical and dogmatic unity and Protestant social purity. He charged the authorities with ensuring this need was met, if necessary through force, although force meant expulsion, not fire or sword, which Luther, unlike many other religious leaders of his time, did not wish to see employed against dissenters.

This unconditional demand for dogmatic purity formed the dark side of the religious renaissance that Luther introduced, and not just in determining the character of the church but also in helping shape the society and politics of the nascent modern age. One generation later, as religious differences escalated into the fundamental enmities of the modern confessional system, the maxim 'religion is the bond of society' (*religio vinculum societatis*), under-stood in terms of both sociology and political theory, grew pervasive, with its suggestion that only the cord of a single religion could bind society together and guarantee internal peace.

In a long-term perspective, both the rescinding of this principle of unity and purity and the emergence of tolerance and freedom of opinion were fostered by the Reformation. Here, then, is yet another outcome that Luther had not intended. For generations the idea of tolerance, articulated above all by those rejected as 'false brothers', would remain an undercurrent in Germany with little real impact. Toleration largely prevailed against the dominant ideology of uniformity not as a concept or a programme but as a reality—*via facti*, by means of fact, in a contemporary formulation; in other words toleration happened because none of the competing confessions was able to win out absolutely. Against the will of the theological leadership of all the confessions, in Germany as also across and in some cases within the other European states, multiconfessionality by region became established. As mobility was an economic necessity in Europe, contact between confessions, and even their intermingling, was unavoidable, and in more and more locations people belonging to different confessions lived alongside one another, creating cracks in the edifice of uniformity.

The multipolar Europe of the various confessions was still far from pluralistic in a modern ideological sense. The process of religious-ideological differentiation begun by Luther would have to pass through further major battles before it could arrive at modern pluralism. In the first half of the seventeenth century, irreconcilable confessional enmities joined with no-less fundamental competition amongst the early modern states over political power, a product of the egotistical idea of sovereignty, to force Europe into an age of religious and territorial war, at the high point of which both friend and foe, along with the faith of all parties, seemed poised to descend into chaos. The situation was saved only by the separation of religion and politics that was recognized in the great peace treaties of the mid-seventeenth century by Protestant and Catholic—except the Papal States—alike, which harked back to Luther's teaching on the two kingdoms. Politics became autonomous, and the states and their leadership were freed from the responsibility of defending the universal truth claims of the individual confessions. As a result, religion was unburdened of its comprehensive responsibility for all aspects of private and public life, and therefore also of the compulsion to integrate and stabilize church and society. Politics and religion are kept apart in the modern world in a way that would have been unthinkable for Luther but is nevertheless a consequence of his Reformation.

From the mid-seventeenth century the confessions relaxed and eventually abandoned their universal truth claims, allowing the extra-confessional Anabaptists and other forms of 'false brothers' who had been forced underground to re-emerge gradually without risk. Ultimately this path could also be taken by non-Christian religions, above all by Jews but also by deists or atheists. Only then did modern pluralism and individualism come into being, for a modern toleration was now in place that permitted freedom of conscience not only for one's own confession but also and especially for dissenters and strangers. For Luther this would have been nothing less than proof of the victory of Satan, evidence of the triumph of evil. His rebellion against the exclusive and authoritarian truth claims of the ecclesiastical hierarchy had had very different motives, yet it paved the way for the tolerance of the modern age and for contemporary pluralism.

Christians and Jews

Evaluating Luther's long-term impact on the relationship between Christians and Jews is particularly challenging. Luther's religiously and eschatologically founded anti-Judaism is not the same as modern racial anti-Semitism. His call on the German authorities to expel the Jews as in Spain and England was not designed to lead to their extermination and was not a precursor of the Holocaust carried out under National Socialism. No direct path led from Luther to Hitler. But the Reformation cannot be cleared of the charge that its unbounded attacks—although not on those who were ethnically other, on religious outsiders and those who 'denied the truth'—helped poison attitudes towards Jews in the nineteenth and twentieth centuries. Luther's later Jewish writings would not have been read in every Protestant household, not even in the homes of all pastors, but his attitude towards Jews was well known and would have had an impact simply because Luther was Luther and in the nineteenth century Luther was reimagined by his supporters as a superhuman hero of the German people.

Individual Lutheran Christians, like individual Catholics, Calvinists, and Anglicans, took a courageous stand against the racial fanaticism of the National Socialists and gave aid to threatened Jews, but Lutheran confessional culture failed to erect a firewall against the National Socialist destructive mania. In countries of western Europe where Reformed Protestantism was very influential, intellectual exchange between Jews and Christians had begun in the seventeenth century, and for residents of towns such as Amsterdam the coexistence of Christian and Jew was taken for granted. That reality was to some extent a product of the distinct social and economic situation in western Europe, but it stemmed also from ecclesiastical and theological tradition, and then again from the experience of diaspora and otherness that generations of Calvinists shared with Jews, not infrequently even at one and the same location, as, for example, in Hamburg.

A number of Luther communities also endured flight, expulsion, and minority status, and in the Catholic Rhineland were even persecuted, living 'under the cross', as members of underground churches. But theirs was not the widely disseminated, collective experience that might have moulded Lutheran confessional culture and sown seeds of sympathy for the other or for minorities. From the start Luther had been incapable of dialogue with those who did not think as he did, the downside of the prophetic self-confidence that was essential to his success. Additionally, he never had anything like the personal experience of exile of Reformed theologians such as John Calvin or John à Lasco—the latter left Poland for Emden and London, from where he was expelled; then, in the harshness of winter, with his stranger community he was denied refuge in port cities of Denmark and northern Germany. In his final years, as we have seen, believing the eschatological final battle was at hand, Luther developed what was well-nigh a phobia about all that was alien. His norm was and remained the single-faith 'pure' society in which ecclesiastical and civic communities were indistinguishable.

Freedom and Conscience

Understandably, the reformer left a lasting and distinct impression on his own confessional church and confessional culture. His rejection of the papal and priestly church was revolutionary and has continued up to the present to define the institutional and cultural profile of Protestantism. This transition was radical because it was rooted in salvation—'We here are convinced that the papacy is the seat of the true and incarnate Antichrist',[10] he had written in 1520. Alongside the doctrine of justification, salvation was at the heart of Lutheran theology. Characterization of Wittenberg reform as reform of a religious order that lost its way overlooks this theological component. The elimination of the papal and priestly offices brought revolutionary change to

Protestant Germany and Europe that reached well beyond the church and into culture, society, and politics—the clerical estate was no longer included at diets of the estates, for example—and the economy. For the politics of the church today, the Reformation paradigm shift in how the pope was viewed has left the divide between the Protestant and Roman Churches unbridgeable, despite good-willed ecumenical intentions.

With the abolition of the priestly estate, whose sanctified members were able to intervene before God, now every Protestant Christian had a direct relationship with God. They no longer had to be prepared to defend their thoughts and actions before the hierarchy of the church, for now they were responsible only to their consciences. Although revolutionary in the context of the age of the Reformation, this new understanding did not usher in individualism and subjectivism in their modern sense. To find their early signs, we must look instead to the aesthetical and philosophical thinking of the Renaissance, to Dürer's individualistic artistic approach, for example, or to Ulrich von Hutten's authorial subjectivity. For Luther, Christian identity, characterized by a direct, personal connection to God, was realized in community, as were Christian freedom and the priesthood of all believers; the upshot was the development of new spheres of action, but not as a precursor of liberalism or a plurality of opinion. For Luther, freedom came with 'bondage' (*Knechtschaft*) in the form of ties to Christian norms, in particular in a commitment to the well-being of one's neighbour.

For Luther, freedom of conscience, for which he had advocated so impressively in Worms, meant in concrete terms 'imprisonment' in the word of God, being bound by religion. He understood 'conscience' as a theological quality that was associated not with behaviour but with the person, with the being and salvation of the individual. A good conscience is not a sign of conformity with norms and moral codes; a good conscience is, simply, faith.

The Lutheran idea of the priesthood of all believers posited that all people are fundamentally equal before God, in particular in light of God's assurance of salvation. When it came to the ecclesiastical reality, however, Luther juxtaposed the priesthood of all believers with the office of pastor. In Lutheranism the priesthood of the faithful was supplemented—or, we might say, mitigated—by the preacher and pastor, who alone were permitted to proclaim the word and administer the sacraments, having been expressly approved for these roles by their training, call, and ordination. This pastoral preaching was performed within a church, set apart as a consecrated building. On this point Luther had retreated, for in 1520 in his 'Treatise on Good Works', which admonished the pope for the ostentation of his church buildings, Luther had explained that prayer 'under a straw roof or in a pigsty' was far more threatening to the papacy than magnificent churches that lacked such 'unconquerable prayer'.[11] He backed down from that position soon after, alarmed by the protests of the 'false brothers' against all external order, holding that preaching should be held in 'an orderly, public, reverent assembly ... and one should not seek out secret concerns to hide away, as the Anabaptists do'.[12] Within Lutheranism the church building became and remained a sacred site for worship of God and the proclamation of God's word.

Politically and socially, too, no room was left for freedom of conscience in its modern sense. For Luther Europe and Christendom were identical. At best, Jews or even Muslims could live here only with special permission and this authorization could be revoked. It was the duty of the authorities to ensure that every individual was baptized immediately after birth and thereby admitted into the Christian community and church. Rejection of infant baptism or the Trinity was a punishable act no different from atheism.

A Faith That Is of the World

Against his will, Luther assisted at the birth of the pluralistic and liberal modern; indirectly and involuntarily he contributed to the emergence of modern tolerance, pluralism, and liberalism, and to the economics of modern society. His deliberate personal legacy to the modern age lies elsewhere, in the rediscovery of religion and faith as elemental forces for the individual and for society. Just when the lustre of religion threatened to be outdone by the aesthetic and political brilliance of the secularized Renaissance papacy, the Wittenberg monk defined humankind's relationship with God anew and gave back to religion its existential plausibility. His bold reasoning and courageous presence provided religion with the position it then held for centuries to come within both private and public life in the modern age. As a result of the Protestant Reformation and the reformation of the papal church, for which Luther had provided the impetus, religion influenced the culture, society, and, not least, politics of the modern age and was therefore able to play a decisive part in the radical transition that produced European modernity.

The rebellion of the Wittenberg Augustinian monk, motivated by his concerns about salvation, turned the sixteenth century into an era that would be eulogized by Goethe as an epoch 'in which faith ruled'. Renaissance, humanism, and, above all, the Roman curia, with its worldly involvement in power politics and artistic statements, had been treating religion as splendid ornamentation for culture and philosophy; an apprehensive people had either to be content with empty sacred routine or to take flight to the irrational practices of popular religion. But Luther gave religion a new legitimacy and a new reality by means of a radical new understanding of a personal God through whose grace all people are drawn into relationship with God without any need for intermediaries or ritual. God again became real—in the souls of the people and in their daily activities in the world. For many people, both educated and uneducated, both lord and subject, both rich and poor, religion had been given back its existential significance and became the guiding principle for all thoughts and actions. The search for a single defining quality acquired by history from Luther and the Reformation, for what was singular and exceptional, brings us to this qualitative renewal of religion. This innovation had its roots in the theology and devotional practices of the late Middle Ages, but it flowered only with Luther.

More important still is that Luther redirected the secularization that had taken hold of religion into a new 'worldliness' (*Welthaftigkeit*). Previously monasteries, abbeys, religious foundations, and other consecrated locations had provided the principal, and prominent, setting for faith and for the activities that sprang from faith; now the Christian individual and Christendom as a whole were to live out their faith and prove themselves in their faith in their everyday experiences in the world.

Luther's teaching on justification, which formed the theological core of his rebellion against the papal church, reached out beyond the narrowly religious to have momentous impact on mentalities and behaviour. The transition from medieval works-based piety to evangelical grace-based devotion founded on the 'by faith alone' principle set a course towards a modern vocational ethic that determined the Christian's correct action in the world. The 'holiness' previously reserved to the priestly life and especially to the life of the monk was now brought into the world. In serving the community (*ecclesia*), the family (*oeconomia*), and the state (*politia*), this holiness provided a new dynamic that the special status of the clerical calling (*vocatio*) had previously held back from the world.

With Luther's eschatological theology uniting faith and world and identifying the world as the place where salvation unfolded, that which was of the world became part of salvation. Marriage, sexuality, work, and politics were all re-evaluated and given a new legitimacy. A dynamic that had been absent when medieval performance-based devotion had held sway was now present in both private and public life. To believe without acting in the world was now just as sinful and far from God as was acting in the world without believing. On this basis religion would help shape the modern world for centuries, culturally, socially, and politically.

Our image of the emergence of the modern age in Europe is distorted if on one hand we stamp Luther a revolutionary because he took on the authorities of his own time and yet on the other hand deem his focus on religion and the resultant confessional era a step backwards, a form of demodernization, leading away from the rationalism and freedom of the Renaissance. Instead, we need to recognize that in assigning religion an original authority, subservient to neither philosophy nor art, and in identifying the world as the setting in which religion functioned and proved itself, Luther unleashed a dynamic that contributed fundamentally to the secular reshaping of early modern Europe and, in the longer term, to the emergence of the modern.

At a time of profound suffering for humanity, Dietrich Bonhoeffer found in Luther a guide and an anchor. Bonhoeffer's reflections on Christian discipleship, composed in the face of mounting tyranny and published in 1937, contain one of the clearest and most beautiful elucidations of the worldliness of Christianity in the modern age, a worldliness that Luther had impelled. Bonhoeffer's account reminds us that despite the troubling obstacles that cause us to stumble as we make our way through Luther's life, from today's perspective the reformer merits our attention not as the hero of the Germans or as founder of an 'improved' church, but as a historic actor who in an age of upheaval and transformation decisively shaped both public and private lives. Bonhoeffer recorded:

> When the Reformation came, the providence of God raised Martin Luther to restore the gospel of pure, costly grace. Luther passed through the cloister...
> Luther had to leave the cloister and go back to the world, not because the world in itself was good and holy, but because even the cloister was only a part of the world.
> Luther's return from the cloister to the world was the worst blow the world had suffered since the days of early Christianity. The renunciation he made

when he became a monk was child's play compared with that which he had to make when he returned to the world. Now came the frontal assault. The only way to follow Jesus was by living in the world. Hitherto the Christian life had been the achievement of a few choice spirits under the exceptionally favourable conditions of monasticism; now it is a duty laid on every Christian living in the world. The commandment of Jesus must be accorded perfect obedience in one's daily vocation of life. The conflict between the life of the Christian and the life of the world was thus thrown into the sharpest possible relief. It was a hand-to-hand conflict between the Christian and the world.[13]

Notes

PROLOGUE

1. In Johann Wolfgang von Goethe, *West-East Divan: The Poems, with 'Notes and Essays'*; *Goethe's Intercultural Dialogues*, trans. with introduction and commentary by Martin Bidney (Albany, NY, 2010), p. 244.
2. Research in recent decades into confessionalization has demonstrated that the new concentration on religion and confession contained impulses for change and 'modernization'; confessionalization should not be viewed, therefore, as a reversal of the advances of humanism and the Renaissance.
3. First quotation: Peter Laslett, *The World We Have Lost* (London, 1965); second quotation: Heiko A. Oberman, *Luther: Man between God and the Devil*, trans. Eileen Walliser-Schwarzbart (New Haven, CT, 1989).
4. See translator's note, p. xvii.
5. Research in recent years into personal testimonies and ego documents has proved less productive for Luther, who understood himself not in light of his implicit or explicit being but as an instrument of God in the history of salvation.

PART ONE. CHAPTER I

1. On the change of name, see p. 139.
2. LW 75, Church Postil 1, Epistle for Christmas Day, pp. 187–208; 'Day of Christ's Ascension into Heaven. Second Sermon. Mark 16:14–20' in *Writings of Martin Luther*, vol. 12, trans. John Nicholas Lenker (Minneapolis, MN, 1907), pp. 195–208, with cited text on p. 201.
3. See WW 53, p. 169.
4. *Dux Cliviae est papa in territoriis suis*, Wilhelm Janssen, 'Landesherrschaft und Kirche am Niederrhein im späten Mittelalter', in J. F. G. Goeters and J. Prieur, eds., *Der Niederrhein zwischen Mittelalter und Neuzeit* (Wesel, 1986), p. 31.
5. Erasmus von Rotterdam, *Complaint of Peace* (1517), cited from 'A Complaint of Peace Spurned and Rejected by the Whole World', trans. Betty Radice, in *Collected Works of Erasmus*, vol. 27 (Toronto, 1986), pp. 305, 315.
6. Wilhelm Abel, 'Landwirtschaft 1500–1648', in Hermann Aubin and Wolfgang Zorn, eds., *Handbuch der deutschen Wirtschafts- und Sozialgeschichte*, vol. 1 (Stuttgart, 1971), p. 386.

7. Immanuel Wallerstein, *The Modern World-System,* vol. 1: *Capitalist Agriculture and the Origins of the European World-Economy in the Sixteenth Century* (New York, 1974); in place of this suggestive terminology, it seems to me more meaningful to speak of a Baltic–northwest-European–Atlantic economic system.
8. Thomas DaCosta Kaufmann, *Court, Cloister, and City: The Art and Culture of Central Europe, 1450–1800* (London, 1995).
9. Erich Meuthen, 'Reiche, Kirchen und Kurie im späten Mittelalter', *Historische Zeitschrift* 265 (1997), pp. 597–637.
10. A well-known saying found in Hutten's letter to Willibald Pirckheimer, a Nuremberg patrician, of 25 October 1518; see Ulrich von Hutten, *Deutsche Schriften,* ed. Peter Ukena (Munich, 1970), p. 340.
11. Carl Theodor Gemeiner, *Regensburgische Chronik, Nachdruck der Ausgabe Regensburg 1800–1824,* 4 vols. (Munich, 1971), 4:383.

PART ONE. CHAPTER II

1. WT 5, no. 5362, p. 95.
2. WW 47, p. 379, ll. 7ff.; p. 340, ll. 7ff.
3. WT 3, no. 2888, p. 51.
4. See the title of the work by American psychologist Erik H. Erikson, *Young Man Luther: A Study in Psychoanalysis and History* (New York, 1958).
5. LW 54, Table Talk, no. 1559, p. 157; no. 3556A, p. 235.
6. LW 48, Letters 1, to George Spalatin, 11 November 1521, p. 326.
7. WW 54, pp. 195–299.
8. LW 54, Table Talk, no. 5557, p. 452.
9. Erich Kleineidam, *Universitas studii Erffordensis. Überblick über die Geschichte der Universität Erfurt,* vol. 2 (Leipzig, 1969).
10. WW 6, p. 195, ll. 4–5.
11. LW 59, Prefaces 1, Preface to Philip Melanchthon, 'Exposition of Colossians, Translated into German by Justus Jonas', p. 250.

PART ONE. CHAPTER III

1. WT 1, no. 134, similar are nos. 320, 349; WT 6, no. 6944, p. 702.
2. LW 54, Table Talk, no. 149, p. 22.
3. See WW 40/2, p. 283.
4. LW 48, Letters 1, to Hans Luther, 21 November 1521, p. 331.
5. WT 4, no. 4707, p. 440 with n. 5; further instances: WT 1, no. 116; WT 5, no. 5373.
6. WW 8, pp. 564–669, here pp. 573–6.
7. The sense of being compelled was emphasized by Luther in both his letter of dedication of 1521 and a Table Talk recollection of 1539, see WW 8, p. 573, ll. 31ff.; WT 4, no. 4707, l. 9.

8. WW 36, p. 388, 22 December 1532.

9. WT 4, no. 4707.

10. LW 54, Table Talk, no. 116, p. 14.

11. Letter of 1530 from Hieronymus Dungersheim of Ochsenfurt to Luther, cited in Reinhold Weijenborg, 'Neuentdeckte Dokumente im Zusammenhang mit Luthers Romreise', *Antonianum* 32 (1957), p. 187, n. 1.

12. WW 8, p. 574, l. 2.

13. LW 48, Letters 1, to Hans Luther, 21 November 1521, p. 333.

14. Luther Bornkamm, *Luther, Gestalt und Wirkungen* (Gütersloh, 1975), p. 13.

15. Martin Brecht, *Martin Luther*, vol. 1: *His Road to Reformation, 1483–1521*, trans. James L. Schaaf (Philadelphia, PA, 1985), p. 49.

16. WT 4, no. 4707.

17. Kaspar Elm, 'Mendikanten und Humanisten im Florenz des Tre- und Quattrocento. Zum Problem der Legitimierung humanistischer Studien in den Bettelorden', in Otto Herding and Reinhard Stupperich, eds., *Die Humanisten in ihrer politischen und sozialen Umwelt* (Bonn, 1976), p. 58.

18. LW 49, Letters 2, to John von Staupitz, 17 September 1523, p. 48.

19. Helmar Junghans, *Der junge Luther und die Humanisten* (Weimar, 1984), p. 320.

20. WW 6, p. 591, ll. 17ff; WT 2, no. 2288; Greffenstein is surely also the individual referenced in WB 9, no. 3493, p. 133, ll. 40f.

21. WT 1, no. 261; WT 2, no. 1294.

22. Luther frequently made reference to his time in the monastery, but always retrospectively and therefore in light of the Reformation's fundamental rejection of monastic life; see WW 45, p. 681, ll. 4ff.; WW 17/1, p. 112, ll. 3ff.; WT 1, no. 518, esp. p. 240, ll. 10ff.; WW 17/1, p. 112, ll. 9ff.; WW 41, p. 695, ll. 1ff.; WW 45, p. 681, ll. 4ff.

23. LW 54, Table Talk, no. 518, p. 94; WT 2, nos. 1288, 2283.

24. See WT 2, no. 2283, p. 403, ll. 19f.

25. Both quotations: LW 24, Sermons on the Gospel of Saint John Chapters 14–16, p. 24.

26. LW 48, Letters 1, to John Braun, 22 April 1507, p. 3.

27. LW 54, Table Talk, no. 1558, p. 156.

28. See WW 6, p. 591, l. 20.

29. For citations see WT 1, no. 137; WB 11, no. 4088, p. 67, ll. 5ff.; see also, for example, WB 3, no. 659, p. 155, ll. 5f.; WT 1, no. 526.

30. From Lothar Graf zu Dohna and Richard Wetzel, eds., *Johann von Staupitz. Sämtliche Schriften*, vol. 5 (Berlin, 2001), p. 194.

31. WT 5, no. 5346, p. 76, ll. 6f.; WT 5, no. 5374.

32. WT 2, no. 1552; WT 4, no. 4692; WT 5, no. 5346.

33. WB 2, no. 510, pp. 563f., ll. 1ff.; WW 38, p. 105, ll. 8ff.

34. WW 48, p. 241; see also the account recorded by Johannes Aurifaber, WT 5, no. 5468.

35. WT 5, nos. 5375, 6039.

36. Weijenborg, 'Neuentdeckte Dokumente', pp. 154, 157.
37. Weijenborg, 'Neuentdeckte Dokumente', pp. 192, 194.
38. LW 14, Selected Psalms 3, Psalm 117, p. 6.
39. WW 31/1, p. 226, ll. 9–17; similar is WW 1, p. 390, ll. 1–4.
40. See WW 2, p. 72, ll. 30ff. (1519).
41. Weijenborg, 'Neuentdeckte Dokumente', pp. 186f.
42. Weijenborg, 'Neuentdeckte Dokumente', p. 201.
43. Weijenborg, 'Neuentdeckte Dokumente', pp. 201f.
44. See letters of Luther to Melchior Dressel, Augustinian prior in Neustadt an der Orla, 23 June 1516 and 25 September 1516, WB 1, nos. 17 and 22.
45. WT 1, no. 137 (end of 1531).

PART TWO. CHAPTER 1

1. For the term '*in termino civilitatis*' see Karlheinz Blaschke, *Wittenberg, die Lutherstadt* (Leipzig, 1977), p. 13.
2. Melanchthon to Kilian Goldstein, 20 November 1544, *Melanchthons Briefwechsel*, vol. T13 (Stuttgart-Bad Cannstatt, 2012), no. 3736.
3. Fritz Bellmann, Marie-Luise Harksen, and Roland Werner, eds., *Die Denkmale der Lutherstadt Wittenberg* (Weimar, 1979), p. 33.
4. WT 2, no. 2540a.
5. WT 5, no. 5552, p. 232.
6. For 'a song of fearlessness' (*Lied der Furchtlosigkeit*), see Gottfried Maron, 'Eine feste Burg ist unser Gott', in *Die ganze Christenheit auf Erden. Gesammelte Aufsätze* (Göttingen, 1993); for 'a song of redemption in Christ' (*heilsgeschichtliches Christuslied*), see Martin Brecht, 'Zum Verständnis von Luthers Lied "Ein feste Burg"', *Archiv für Reformationsgeschichte* 70 (1979), p. 120.
7. For 'Marseillaise of the Reformation' (*Marseiller Hymne der Reformation*), see Heinrich Heine, *Zur Geschichte der Religion und Philosophie in Deutschland*, ed. Manfred Windfuhr, vol. 8 (Hamburg, 1981), pp. 41–2.
8. WB 1, no. 53, November 1517; WT 5, no. 5343; on Luther's salary and income, see WB 12, no. 4223 (with receipts).
9. WB 3, no. 600; WT 4, no. 5151.
10. Bellmann, Harksen, and Werner, eds., *Die Denkmale der Lutherstadt Wittenberg*, p. 33.
11. He described the town as a '*Schindleiche*', the place where animals were flayed, as cited in Bellmann, Harksen, and Werner, eds., *Die Denkmale der Lutherstadt Wittenberg*, p. 33.
12. See letters of 14 December 1516 to Spalatin and 6 November 1517 to Elector Frederick, WB 1, nos. 30, 51.
13. LW 48, Letters 1, to Elector Frederick, about 6 November 1517, p. 51.
14. WB 1, no. 51; see also WB 2, no. 455, 5 March 1522, for example.

15. WB 1, no. 7; see also nos. 27 and 120, 14 December 1518, to Reuchlin, on the occasion of the successful outcome of the legal process.
16. Letters of 19 October and 31 December 1516 to Spalatin, WB 1, nos. 27, 31.
17. Letters of 15 and 22 February 1518, WB 1, nos. 59, 61.
18. WT 3, no. 3722.
19. WB 1, no. 63.
20. First citation from a letter to Reuchlin, Melanchthon's uncle, WB 1, no. 120, 14 December 1518; second citation from LW 48, Letters 1, no. 47, to John Lang, 18 December 1519, p. 136.
21. Melanchthon, *Corpus Reformatorum* 6, no. 880, April 1548, to Christoph von Carlowitz.
22. Gustav Bauch, 'Die Einführung des Hebräischen in Wittenberg', *Monatsschrift für Geschichte und Wissenschaft des Judentums* (1904), pp. 159f.
23. Luther had voiced his support for Aurogallus in a number of letters; see, for example, correspondence sent to Spalatin in February and March 1521, WB 2, nos. 377 and 389.
24. WB 1, no. 192, ll. 41–45; WB 2, no. 266, ll. 16–18.
25. WB 12, no. 4215.
26. WB 10, no. 4021.

PART TWO. CHAPTER II

1. LW 39, Church and Ministry 1, Answer to the Hyperchristian, Hyperspiritual, and Hyperlearned Book by Goat Emser in Leipzig, p. 164.
2. As found both in a preface addressed to Staupitz in 1518, WW 1, pp. 525–7, and in his personal testimonial of 1545, WW 54, pp. 179–87.
3. First citation WT 2, no. 1681, p. 177; second citation LW 54, Table Talk, no. 3232c, p. 194.
4. LW 34, Career of the Reformer 4, Preface to the Complete Edition of Luther's Latin Writings, 1545, pp. 334, 337–8.
5. See the preface in the form of a letter to his mentor Staupitz, WW 1, pp. 525–7.
6. Preface to the Prophet Daniel, in *Die gantze Heilige Schrift deudsch, Wittenberg 1545*, ed. Hans Volz (Munich, 1972), 2:1530.
7. See WW 2, pp. 145–52.
8. LW 34, Career of the Reformer 4, Preface to the Complete Edition of Luther's Latin Writings, 1545, p. 337.
9. Citations throughout this paragraph are from LW 48, Letters 1, to John von Staupitz, 30 May 1518, pp. 64–70.
10. The reference is to Psalm 120:4.
11. *Die gantze Heilige Schrift deudsch, Wittenberg 1545*, ed. Volz, 2:2270.
12. LW 34, Career of the Reformer 4, Preface to the Complete Edition of Luther's Latin Writings, 1545, p. 334.

13. This possible connection is yet to be explored by historians of Luther and of the Reformation but appears all the more plausible, and in need of examination, in light of recent work on the legal and cultural history of clemency in medieval law.

14. Cited in Heinz Kühn, *Lexikon der Päpste Päpste. Von Petrus bis Johannes XXIII.* (Frankfurt am Main, 1960), p. 126.

15. See Wilhelm Ernst Winterhager, 'Ablaßkritik als Indikator historischen Wandels vor 1517. Ein Beitrag zu Voraussetzungen und Einordnung der Reformation', *Archiv für Reformationsgeschichte* 90 (1999), p. 17.

16. Friedrich Myconius, *Geschichte der Reformation*, ed. Otto Clemen (Leipzig, 1914).

17. WT 5, no. 5349, p. 77, ll. 14–19.

18. See WB 1, no. 26, October 1516.

19. See WB 1, no. 62, 5 March 1518, to Christoph Scheurl.

20. WB 1, no. 62, 5 March 1518.

21. WB 1, no. 48; the letter to Bishop Schulz has not been preserved.

22. See WW 1, 277, ll, 19f.; WB 1, nos. 64, 74.

23. WT 4, no. 4763 (1537), p. 477.

24. Letter from Albrecht Dürer to Georg Spalatin, early 1520, in Albrecht Dürer, *Tagebücher und Briefe* (Munich, 1969), p. 165. In 1518 Luther had already thanked Dürer for a gift, WB 1, no. 62, 5 March 1518, to Christoph Scheurl in Nuremberg.

25. WB 1, no. 62, 5 March 1518.

26. See WB 1, no. 111, letter of 22 January 1518.

27. WB 1, no. 62, 5 March 1518.

28. Both citations, WB 1, no. 52.

29. WB 1, no. 62, 5 March 1518.

30. WB 1, no. 62, 5 March 1518.

31. From the preface by Protestant church historians Karin Bornkamm and Gerhard Ebeling for their edited work *Martin Luther, Ausgewählte Schriften*, 6 vols. (Frankfurt am Main, 1982), 1:vif.

32. 10 May 1521, Erasmus to Justus Jonas, in *Collected Works of Erasmus*, vol. 8: *Letters 1122 to 1251, 1520 to 1521*, trans. R. A. B. Mynors (Toronto, 1988), p. 203.

33. LW 34, Career of the Reformer 4, Preface to the Complete Edition of Luther's Latin Writings, 1545, pp. 328, 334.

34. Citation is from LW 48, Letters 1, to John von Staupitz, 30 May 1518, p. 69.

35. First quotation: WB 2, no. 327, 18 August 1520, to Johannes Lang; similar is WB 2, no. 341; second quotation: WB 2, no. 377, 17 February 1521, to Spalatin.

36. First quotation, preface to the Prophet Daniel, 1530, in *Die gantze Heilige Schrift deudsch, Wittenberg 1545*, ed. Volz, 2:1517, ll. 225ff.; second quotation LW 41, Church and Ministry 3, Against Hanswurst, p. 237.

37. As in the preface to the Prophet Daniel, 1530, in *Die gantze Heilige Schrift deudsch, Wittenberg 1545*, ed. Volz, 2:1530, 1523, 1841f.

38. 'The Small Catechism', in *The Book of Concord: The Confessions of the Evangelical Lutheran Church*, ed. Robert Kolb and Timothy J. Wengert (Minneapolis, MN, 2000), p. 360.
39. 'Concerning Christian Liberty', in *Luther's Primary Works Together with His Shorter and Larger Catechisms*, ed. Henry Wace and C. A. Buchheim (London, 1896), p. 266.
40. LW 48, Letters 1, to Philip Melanchthon, 1 August 1521, p. 282.
41. LW 38, Word and Sacrament 4, Admonition concerning the Sacrament of the Body and Blood of our Lord, p. 129.

PART TWO. CHAPTER III

1. WT 3, no. 3846.
2. Letters to Spalatin and Frederick the Wise from October, November, and December 1518, WB 1, nos. 105–18, quotations are from letters of 31 October and 9 December.
3. See letter of 10 October 1518 to Spalatin, WB 1, no. 97.
4. See letters of 31 October and 9 December 1518, WB 1.
5. WB 1, nos. 74, 75.
6. All citations from LW 48, Letters 1, to George Spalatin, 31 October 1518.
7. LW 31, Career of the Reformer 1, Proceedings at Augsburg 1518, pp. 259–92.
8. Letter of 9 December 1518, WB 1, no. 118.
9. The citations here and below are from LW 31, Career of the Reformer 1, Letter from Luther to Spalatin concerning the Leipzig Debate, 20 July 1519, pp. 318–25.
10. LW 51, Sermons 1, Sermon Preached in the Castle at Leipzig on the Day of St. Peter and St. Paul, Matt. 16:13–19, 29 June 1519, pp. 56, 59.
11. On the accusation about his background, see LW 48, Letters 1, to George Spalatin, 4 January 1520, pp. 143–8, citation p. 146.
12. LW 48, Letters 1, to George Spalatin, 4 January 1520, pp. 146, 144.
13. LW 31, Career of the Reformer 1, Letter from Luther to Spalatin concerning the Leipzig Debate, 20 July 1519, p. 325.
14. WB 2, no. 255, letter to Spalatin, mid-February 1520.
15. LW 48, Letters 1, to George Spalatin, about 14 February 1520, p. 153.
16. WB 2, no. 271, 25 March 1520, to Spalatin.
17. The term 'golden year' comes from Heiko A. Oberman.
18. LW 44, The Christian in Society 1, To the Christian Nobility of the German Nation concerning the Reform of the Christian Estate, p. 123.
19. WB 2, no. 327, 18 August 1520, to Johannes Lang.
20. 11 October 1520 to Spalatin, WB 2, no. 341.
21. See, also for the quotation that follows, LW 48, Letters 1, to George Spalatin, 12 October 1520, pp. 179–81.

22. A phrase used in his letter of 18 August 1520 to his fellow Augustinian Johannes Lang, WB 2, no. 327.
23. See WW 7, pp. 1ff., 39ff.
24. LW 31, Career of the Reformer, 1, An Open Letter to Leo X, p. 336 (first two quotations), p. 343 (final quotation).
25. LW 48, Letters 1, to George Spalatin, 12 October 1520, p. 181.
26. LW 31, Career of the Reformer 1, Martin Luther's Treatise on Christian Liberty, p. 344.
27. Else Hocks, *Der letzte deutsche Papst. Adrian VI. 1522–1523* (Freiburg, 1939), p. 108.
28. WW 6, pp. 597ff.; text pp. 614–29.
29. WW 7, p. 183.
30. LW 48, Letters 1, to John von Staupitz, 14 January 1521, p. 192.
31. See WB 2, no. 361.
32. WW 7, pp. 152–82, 184–6.
33. Adolf Wrede, ed., *Deutsche Reichstagsakten unter Kaiser Karl V.,* N.S, vol. 2: *Der Reichstag zu Worms 1521* (1896; rept. Gotha, 1962), [hereafter Wrede, RTA, vol. 2] p. 476, n. 3, according to a letter from Aleander; letter printed as WB 2, no. 332.
34. Wrede, RTA, vol. 2, no. 59A (Louvain, Liège), no. 63, p. 473, n. 1 (Cologne, Mainz), no. 67, p. 498, n. 2 (Louvain, Cologne).
35. Wrede, RTA, vol. 2, pp. 517, 670ff.
36. Wrede, RTA, vol. 2, no. 69; WT 3, no. 3357a, p. 282.
37. See Wrede, RTA, vol. 2, no. 60, pp. 462–8.
38. Wrede, RTA, vol. 2, no. 61 (agreement of 28 November), no. 62 (cancellation of 17 December), and no. 63 (letter from Electoral Saxony to the Emperor, 20 December), citation p. 471.
39. Wrede, RTA, vol. 2, no. 66, pp. 477–94; according to Martin Brecht, *Martin Luther*, 3 vols. (Stuttgart, 1981–1987), 2:416, the January date is plausible.
40. See Wrede, RTA, vol. 2, no. 69. pp. 514–17.
41. Wrede, RTA, vol. 2, no. 210, p. 891.
42. Wrede, RTA, vol. 2, no. 368, l. 25.
43. Wrede, RTA, vol. 2, no. 361.
44. Wrede, RTA, vol. 2, no. 368.
45. Wrede, RTA, vol. 2, no. 332; WW 6, pp. 474–83, for draft WW 9, pp. 301–4.
46. WB 3, no. 349.
47. See letter to Staupitz, 14 January 1521, WB 2, no. 366; to Spalatin, 16 January 1521, WB 2, no. 368; Wrede, RTA, vol. 2, p. 476, n. 1.
48. Letter to the Emperor, WB 2, no. 332, and Wrede, RTA, vol. 2, p. 476, n. 3, with an extensive source-based account of the somewhat complicated course of events.
49. Letter of 11 October 1520 to Spalatin, WB 2, no. 341.
50. LW 48, Letters 1, to Elector Frederick, January 1521, p. 195.

51. See pp. 412–17.
52. Letter of 16 January 1521 to Spalatin, WB 2, no. 368.
53. Letter of 16 January 1521 to Spalatin, WB 2, no. 368.
54. For example, on 29 December 1520 to Spalatin, WB 2, no. 365; according to Wrede, RTA, vol. 2, p. 476, n. 1.
55. In the letter he sent to the Emperor after their encounter, Luther indicated that his fear had been justified, Kurt Aland, ed., *Luther Deutsch*, 10 vols. (4th ed.; Göttingen, 1991), 10:88.
56. WT 3, no. 3357a, p. 282, l. 8.
57. LW 48, Letters 1, to John von Staupitz, 14 January 1521, pp. 191–4.
58. Letter of 11 October 1520, to Spalatin, WB 2, no. 341.
59. LW 48, Letters 1, to Cardinal Albrecht, 1 December 1521, p. 342.
60. This citation and below, LW 48, Letters 1, to Elector Frederick, 25 January 1521, p. 196.
61. LW 48, Letters 1, to George Spalatin, 14 April 1521, p. 197; for the saying, see p. 197, n. 4; see also WT 3, no. 3357 a, b; WT 5, no. 5342, p. 65.
62. LW 53, Liturgy and Hymns, 'Our God He Is a Castle Strong', p. 285.
63. Wrede, RTA, vol. 2, p. 628.
64. LW 48, Letters 1, to George Spalatin, 14 April 1521, p. 198.
65. LW 48, Letters 1, to Philip Melanchthon, 12 May 1531, p. 217.
66. LW 48, Letters 1, to George Spalatin, 10 June 1521, p. 255.
67. LW 50, Letters 3, to Mrs Martin Luther, 1 February 1546, p. 291.
68. Detailed report to Duke John of Saxony, see Wrede, RTA, vol. 2, no. 190, pp. 850f.
69. See Wrede, RTA, vol. 2, p. 863.
70. Several accounts of the events at Worms provided by both the Saxon and Imperial/papal parties provide us with a comprehensive picture. See Wrede, RTA, vol. 2, especially nos. 79–88; Luther himself repeatedly provided retrospective reflection in his Table Talk, see WT 3, no. 3357 a, b (1533); WT 5, no. 5342 (1540).
71. LW 48, Letters 1, to John Cuspinian, 17 April 1521, p. 200.
72. See Wrede, RTA, vol. 2, p. 863; WT 3, no. 3357 a, b; WT 5, no. 5342.
73. The renowned thesis of Herbert Schöffler.
74. For both quotations see Wrede, RTA, vol. 2, no. 7, proposition, 27/28 January 1521, p. 154.
75. See Wrede, RTA, vol. 2, pp. 540–86, 599–611; for Vehus' report, no. 86, pp. 611–24; see also the section entitled 'Korrespondenz', nos. 113ff., pp. 767–953.
76. Wrede, RTA, vol. 2, p. 574.
77. Wrede, RTA, vol. 2, no. 81, pp. 588–94.
78. Wrede, RTA, vol. 2, p. 547, n. 11.
79. Wrede, RTA, vol. 2, no. 191, p. 851.
80. Wrede, RTA, vol. 2, no. 191, p. 851.

81. See Wrede, RTA, vol. 2, no. 194, p. 862.

82. The speech is well preserved in both Latin and German. See Wrede, RTA, vol. 2, nos. 79, 80, with information on its various publications.

83. All direct citations from Luther's speech here and below are from LW 32, Career of the Reformer 2, Luther at the Diet of Worms, pp. 109–14.

84. Wrede, RTA, vol. 2, p. 550.

85. 'Ich kann nicht anders / hier stehe ich / Gott helfe mir / Amen.' Wrede, RTA, vol. 2, p. 582, n.c., p. 571.

86. First the French original was read, then the German translation; see Wrede, RTA, vol. 2, no. 82, pp. 594–6 and n. 1.

87. Translation based on author's translation of original French. See, with sources, Heinz Schilling, 'Karl V. und die Religion. Das Ringen um Reinheit und Einheit des Christentums', in Karl V. und seine Zeit, 1500–1558, ed. Hugo Soly (Cologne, 2000), pp. 285–363.

88. According to Bernd Moeller.

89. Wrede, RTA, vol. 2, no. 85, p. 601.

90. Wrede, RTA, p. 559, n. 1; WT 5, no. 5302a.

91. According to the report of the Spanish observer, Wrede, RTA, vol. 2, no. 88, p. 636, ll. 24–26.

92. See Wrede, RTA, vol. 2, no. 88, p. 559, n. 2.

93. Wrede, RTA, vol. 2, no. 85, pp. 599–611.

94. Wrede, RTA, vol. 2, no. 85, p. 603.

95. Wrede, RTA, vol. 2, no. 85, p. 603.

96. LW 32, Career of the Reformer 2, Luther at the Diet of Worms, p. 118.

97. See Wrede, RTA, vol. 2, no. 85, p. 607; Luther: WT 3, no. 3357 a, p. 283.

98. Wrede, RTA, vol. 2, no. 85, p. 610f.

99. LW 32, Career of the Reformer 2, Luther at the Diet of Worms, p. 123.

100. Wrede, RTA, vol. 2, no. 92, pp. 640–59; with an outline of the course of its production, p. 453.

101. Wrede, RTA, vol. 2, p. 640, nn. 1, 2.

102. Wrede, RTA, vol. 2, p. 453, l. 44.

103. Theodor Brieger, Aleander und Luther 1521. Die vervollständigten Aleander-Depeschen (Gotha, 1884), 1:47ff.

104. Citations are from LW 48, Letters 1, to Emperor Charles V, 28 April 1521, pp. 204–9.

105. From a Table Talk of 1532, WT 2, no. 2640b, p. 572.

PART TWO. CHAPTER IV

1. The expression 'Wegscheide der Weltgeschichte' draws on Gottfried Schramm, Fünf Wegscheiden der Weltgeschichte [Five Crossroads in World History] (Göttingen, 2004) and is also an homage to Gottfried Schramm, my teacher in Freiburg almost half a century ago.

2. Wrede, RTA, no. 85, p. 610, l. 10.

3. LW 48, Letters 1, to Philip Melanchthon, 12 May 1521, p. 215.

4. Letter of 4 February 1523 to Electoral Saxon councillor Hans von der Planitz, WB 3, no. 581, pp. 27f., ll. 24–29.

5. LW 48, Letters 1, to Lucas Cranach, 28 April 1521, pp. 201, 202.

6. Dürer, *Tagebücher und Briefe*, pp. 83–87.

7. WB 1, no. 146, pp. 332f.

8. Martin Warnke, *Cranachs Luther. Entwürfe für ein Image* (Frankfurt am Main, 1994), p. 2; see the refutation by Ruth Slenczka, 'Dürers, Holbeins und Cranachs Melanchthon: Künstlerischer Austausch und innovative Medien in der Porträtkunst um 1530', in Franz Fuchs, ed., *Der frühe Melanchthon und der Humanismus* (Wiesbaden, 2011), pp. 95–134, which I follow here.

9. Dürer, *Tagebücher und Briefe*, p. 165, letter to Spalatin, early 1520.

10. 4 June 1520, WB 2, no. 295, p. 117, ll. 29f.

11.
> Und nehmen stets von Teutschen Geld,
> Dahin ihr Prattik ist gestellt.
> Und finden täglich neuwe Weg,
> Daß Geld man in den Kasten leg.
> Do kummen Teutschen umb ihr Gut.
> Ist niemand, den das reuen tut?
>
> . . .
>
> Und daß die Summ ich red darvon,
> die Bullen, so von Rom hergohn,
> verkehren Sitten weit und breit,
> dardurch würd böser Som gespreit.
> Dieweil es nun ist so gestalt,
> so ist vonnöten mit Gewalt
> den Sachen bringen Hilf und Rat,
> herwider an der Lugen Statt
> die göttlich Wahrheit führen ein,
> die hat gelitten Schmach und Pein,
> den falschen Simon treiben aus,
> daß halt Sankt Peter wieder Haus.
> Ich habs gewagt.

Ulrich von Hutten, *Deutsche Schriften*, ed. Peter Ukena (Munich, 1970), pp. 61, 134–5.

12. Cited in Heinz Schilling, *Aufbruch und Krise. Deutschland 1517–1618* (Berlin, 1988), p. 131.

13.
> Wach auff es nahend gen dem tag,
> Ich hör singen im grünen Hag
> Ein wunnigkliche Nachtigal,
> Ihr stimb durchklinget Berg und Thal,

Die Nacht neugt sich gen Occident,
Der Tag geht auff von Orient.
Und sind auch nachgefolget ihm,
der sie geführt hat mit liste
Gantz weit abwegs tieff in die Wüste...
Da sie der Löw dann fand verstricket
Zuriß er sie, danach verschlicket.

Hans Sachs, 'Die wittenbergisch Nachtigall, die man jetzt höret überall', in Hans Sachs, *Werke in der Reihenfolge ihrer Entstehung*, ed. Wolfgang F. Michael and Roger A. Crockett (Berne, 1996), p. 28, ll. 1–6, 20–2, 27–8.

14. 'The German Reformation was an urban event', Arthur Geoffrey Dickens, *The German Nation and Martin Luther* (Glasgow, 1974), p. 182.
15. LW 48, Letters 1, to Philip Melanchthon, 26 May 1521, p. 233.
16. LW 48, Letters 1, to Philip Melanchthon, 26 May 1521, p. 233.
17. WB 3, no. 581, p. 27, ll. 20–22.
18. LW 48, letters 1, to Philip Melanchthon, 13 July 1521, p. 258.
19. WB 2, no. 408, 12 May 1521; see also no. 410, 14 May, to Spalatin.
20. LW 48, Letters 1, to George Spalatin, 14 May 1521, p. 228.
21. LW 48, Letters 1, to Nicholas von Amsdorf, 12 May 1521, p. 219.
22. WB 2, no. 426.
23. LW 48, Letters 1, to George Spalatin, 15 August 1521, pp. 294, 295.
24. LW 48, Letters 1, to George Spalatin, 15 August 1521, p. 295.
25. LW 48, Letters 1, to George Spalatin, 14 May 1521, p. 225.
26. LW 48, Letters 1, to Philip Melanchthon, 13 July 1521, p. 257.
27. LW 48, Letters 1, to George Spalatin, 14 May 1521, p. 225.
28. LW 48, Letters 1, to George Spalatin, 10 June 1521, p. 255.
29. LW 48, Letters 1, to George Spalatin, 14 May 1521, p. 228; to Philip Melanchthon, 26 May 1521, p. 236; to George Spalatin, 10 June 1521, p. 256.
30. LW 48, Letters 1, to Philip Melanchthon, 26 May 1521, p. 234.
31. LW 48, Letters 1, to Philip Melanchthon, 26 May 1521, p. 232.
32. WB 2, no. 417, 10 June 1521; no. 438, 11 November 1521; no. 441, 22 November 1521, all to Georg Spalatin.
33. Wolfgang Simon, *Die Messopfertheologie Martin Luthers: Voraussetzungen, Genese, Gestalt und Rezeption* (Tübingen, 2003), p. 327, with n. 262.
34. LW 48, Letters 1, to Philip Melanchthon, 9 September 1521, p. 297.
35. See WW 7, pp. 538–60.
36. LW 21, The Sermon on the Mount (Sermons) and the Magnificat, The Magnificat, p. 344.
37. *Rationis Latomianae Confutatio*, WW 8, pp. 36ff.
38. LW 48, Letters 1, to George Spalatin, 11 November 1521, p. 326.
39. WB 2, no. 442.

40. The citations in this paragraph are from LW 48, Letters 1, to Cardinal Albrecht, Archbishop of Mainz, 1 December 1521, pp. 339–43.

41. WB 2, no. 448, p. 421, ll. 8–12.

42. WB 2, nos. 438, 441.

43. WB 2, pp. 391–2.

44. See WW 8, pp. 398ff., 477ff.

45. For concise juxtaposition: WW 8, p. 469, ll. 27ff. (Latin); p. 554, ll. 9ff. (German).

46. For the citation see Simon, *Die Messopfertheologie Martin Luthers*, p. 346.

47. Letters of 6 and 15 August 1521 to Spalatin, WB 2, nos. 426, 427.

48. LW 48, Letters 1, to Philip Melanchthon, 26 May 1521, p. 235.

49. As he wrote to his fellow Augustinian Wenzeslaus Linck, cited in WW 8, p. 565.

50. LW 48, Letters 1, to Hans Luther, 21 November 1521, p. 334.

51. See WW 8, pp. 313–35.

52. LW 48, Letters 1, to Philip Melanchthon, 9 September 1521, citations are on p. 297.

53. See WW 8, pp. 564–669.

54. LW 48, Letters 1, to Philip Melanchthon, 9 September 1521, p. 302.

55. From Romans 14:23; WW 8, p. 591.

56. Cited in WW 8, p. 317.

57. See WW 8, pp. 566–9.

58. See WW 10, pp. 1–555.

59. LW 53, Liturgy and Hymns, The German Mass and Order of Service, p. 78. Luther's description of these problematic sermons translates literally as 'sermons on blue ducks'.

60. *Germanis meis natus sum, quibus et serviam*, see LW 48, Letters 1, to Nicholas Gerbel, 1 November 1521, p. 320; LW 47, The Christian in Society IV, Luther's Warning to his Dear German People, p. 29.

61. None of the German-language collections of Kurt Aland, Günther Wartenberg, and Johannes Schilling includes this letter; Martin Brecht gives it only passing reference, see Brecht, *Martin Luther*, 3 vols. (Stuttgart, 1981–1987), 2:25.

62. WT 5, no. 5982, p. 415.

63. Albert Gerhards, 'Ein Reformprojekt am Vorabend der Reformation: Der Libellus ad Leonem X (1513)', in Johannes Laudage, ed., *Frömmigkeitsformen in Mittelalter und Renaissance* (Düsseldorf, 2004), pp. 399f.

64. WB 2, no. 445, to Johann Lang; no. 446, to Wenzeslaus Linck.

65. WT 1, no. 961, p. 487, supplement 2.

66. One characteristic example: where an anonymous translator from around Nuremberg at the end of the fifteenth century rendered Psalm 23 as 'Der herr der richt mich und mir gebrast nit, und an der stat der weyde do satzt er mich. Er fuortte mich ob dem wasser der widerbringung', the Wittenberg translation of 1531 has 'Der Herr ist mein Hirte, mir wird nichts mangeln.

Er läßt mich weiden da viel Gras steht, und führet mich zum Wasser, das mich erkühlet.' Polished by the revision commission, the final rendering, which would be the accepted version for almost the next 500 years, read, 'Der Herr ist mein Hirte, mir wird nichts mangeln. Er weidet mich auf einer grünen Aue und führet mich zum frischen Wasser.' Millions of Christians carried the memory of these words of pastoral consolation until in our own time Luther's nurturing shepherd proved too shocking and the Bible translation 'in unbiased language' produced a detached and flattened wording: 'Adonaj weidet mich, mir fehlt es an nichts. Auf grüner Wiese läßt Gott mich lagern, zu Wassern der Ruhe leitet Gott mich sanft. Meine Lebendigkeit kehrt zurück.'

67. The price of the Bible is based on Martin Volz, *Luthers deutsche Bibel. Entstehung und Geschichte der Lutherbibel* (Leipzig, 1981), p. 155; the worker's salary on Helmut Bräuer, *Gesellen im sächsischen Zunfthandwerk des 15. und 16. Jahrhunderts* (Weimar, 1989), pp. 52ff.

68. LW 35, Word and Sacrament 1, Preface to the Old Testament 1545 (1523), p. 249.

PART TWO. CHAPTER V

1. LW 48, Letters 1, about 5 December 1521, to George Spalatin, p. 351.
2. LW 45, The Christian in Society 2, Sincere Admonition by Martin Luther to All Christians to Guard against Insurrection and Rebellion, pp. 60, 59.
3. LW 48, Letters 1, to Elector Frederick, 5 March 1522, p. 390.
4. LW 45, The Christian in Society 2, Sincere Admonition by Martin Luther to All Christians to Guard against Insurrection and Rebellion, pp. 70, 71.
5. For the following discussion see the letters to, from, and about Luther at WB 2, pp. 448–73.
6. Printed in WB 2, no. 458, supplement, pp. 449–52.
7. For the citations from the letter see LW 48, Letters 1, 5 March 1522, to Elector Frederick, pp. 389–93.
8. Printed in WB 2, no. 458, supplement, pp. 449–52.
9. LW 48, Letters 1, 17 March 1522, to Nicholas Hausmann, p. 401.
10. WB 2, no. 458, supplement, p. 472.
11. WB 2, nos. 456–458 including supplements.
12. See WB 4, no. 984, letter of 9 March 1526 to Amsdorf; WT 2, no 2667b; also WB 3, no. 796 with n. 4; WB 4, no. 985.
13. See letter of 18 December 1521 to Wenzeslaus Linck, WB 2, no. 446.
14. See letters of 13 January 1522 from the Wartburg to Amsdorf and Melanchthon, WB 2, nos. 449, 450.
15. LW 48, Letters 1, 13 January 1522, to Philip Melanchthon, pp. 366, 372.
16. The term used by Luther himself, as for example in the Schmalkaldic Articles of 1537, WW 50, p. 194.

17. LW 48, Letters 1, 13 January 1522, to Philip Melanchthon, pp. 371–2.
18. Table Talk 1531, WT 2, no. 2060; also no. 2837; WT 1, no. 362.
19. WT 1, no. 362.
20. 12 April 1522 to Johannes Lang, WB 2, no. 473; also WT 1, no. 362. Further locations: WB 2, nos. 450, 472, 535; WT 3, no. 2837, WT 5, no. 5568.
21. *Iudicium meum de Lutero 1523*, in Franz Hipler, ed., *Nikolaus Kopernikus und Martin Luther. Nach ermländischen Archivalien* (Brunswick, 1868).
22. Citations from the Twelve Articles that follow here are taken from LW 46, The Christian in Society 3, The Twelve Articles, pp. 8–16.
23. Günther Franz, ed., *Quellen zur Geschichte des deutschen Bauernstandes in der Neuzeit* (Darmstadt, 1963), p. 193; extracts from Kessler's Chronicle found in Klaus Kaczerowsky, ed., *Flugschriften des Bauernkriegs* (Hamburg, 1970), pp. 224ff.
24. LW 46, The Christian in Society 3, Admonition to Peace, A Reply to the Twelve Articles of the Peasants in Swabia 1525, pp. 19, 22, 32.
25. LW 46, The Christian in Society 3, Admonition to Peace, A Reply to the Twelve Articles of the Peasants in Swabia 1525, p. 43.
26. Ludwig Fischer, ed., Die lutherischen Pamphlete gegen Thomas Müntzer (Tübingen, 1976), pp. 1–12, here pp. 5, 11.
27. Citations are from Thomas Müntzer, *Kritische Gesamtausgabe, im Auftrag der Sächsische Akademie der Wissenschaften*, ed. Helmar Junghans and Armin Kohnle, vol. 2, *Briefwechsel*, ed. Siegfried Bräuer and Manfred Kobuch (Leipzig, 2010), letter no. 135, p. 449 (Mühlhausen, 9 May 1525); letter no. 114, p. 415, to former members of the Allstedt union (Mühlhausen, 26 May 1525).
28. See WB 3, no. 840, p. 453, ll. 8–10.
29. WB 3, no. 874, p. 508, l. 27; 23 May to Johannes Rühel.
30. LW 49, Letters 2, 4 May 1525, to John Rühel, p. 108.
31. WB 3, no. 874, p. 508, ll. 29–31; 23 May to Johannes Rühel.
32. WB 3, no. 859.
33. WW 18, pp. 357–61.
34. LW 46, The Christian in Society 3, Against the Robbing and Murdering Hordes of Peasants, pp. 54–5.
35. LW 46, The Christian in Society 3, Against the Robbing and Murdering Hordes of Peasants, p. 53.
36. 'Müntzer to the people of Allstedt. 1525 (c. 26, 27 April)', in *The Collected Works of Thomas Müntzer*, ed. and trans. Peter Matheson (Edinburgh, 1988), p. 142.
37. 'Müntzer to the people of Mühlhausen, Heldrungen, 17 May 1525', in *The Collected Works of Thomas Müntzer*, ed. and trans. Matheson, pp. 160–1.
38. First citation, WB 3, no. 874; second citation, LW 49, Letters 2, 30 May 1525, to Nicholas von Amsdorf, p. 114.
39. WW 17:1, pp. 265–7, citation, p. 267, ll. 28–29.
40. LW 46, The Christian in Society 3, An Open Letter on the Harsh Book against the Peasants, p. 63.

41. LW 46, The Christian in Society 3, An Open Letter on the Harsh Book against the Peasants, pp. 70, 76, 84, 63.
42. See WB 3, no. 900, 21 June 1525, to Amsdorf.
43. See p. 415, on his text *Warnung D. Martin Luthers an seine lieben Deutschen*, of 1531.
44. LW 49, Letters 2, 21 June 1525, to Nicholas von Amsdorf, pp. 118–19.
45. WB 3, no. 905, p. 547, ll. 11–31.
46. Both citations are from letters to Johannes Rühel, WB 3, no. 877, p. 516, ll. 34f., of 30 May; and no. 874, p. 507, ll. 6f., of 23 May 1525.
47. WT 1, no. 446, p. 195, ll. 18–20.

PART TWO. CHAPTER VI

1. Marguerite Yourcenar, *The Abyss*, trans. Grace Frick (New York, 1976), p. 90; just one randomly selected example.
2. LW 28, Commentaries on 1 Corinthians 7, 1 Corinthians 15; Lectures on 1 Timothy, 1 Corinthians 7, p. 40.
3. LW 49, Letters 2, to George Spalatin, 30 November 1524, p. 93.
4. An express instruction given by Luther's novice master at Erfurt, see WT 2, no. 2288.
5. Spring 1524 to Bucer in Strasburg, WB 12, no. 4225a, p. 60, ll. 6f.; similarly, WB 3, no. 626, p. 97, and no. 633, p. 109.
6. See WW 11, pp. 394–400, for citations see pp. 394, 400.
7. WW 15, pp. 79–93.
8. WB 3, no. 782, p. 358.
9. WT 4, no. 4786.
10. Both citations are from the account by Nikolaus von Amsdorff, who reported in detail on the events running up to the marriage, printed in Ernst Kroker, 'Luthers Werbung um Katharina von Bora. Eine Untersuchung über die Quelle einer alten Überlieferung', in *Lutherstudien zur 4. Jahrhundertfeier der Reformation* (Weimar, 1917), pp. 140–50.
11. On 10 April 1525, WB 3, no. 857.
12. See WT 4, no. 4786.
13. Both citations LW 49, Letters 2, to John Rühel, 4 May 1525, p. 111.
14. 15 June 1525 to Mansfeld friends, WB 3, no. 890, p. 531, ll. 5 and 9f.
15. See WB 3, p. 531, l. 14, also no. 900, p. 541, p. 5, letter of 21 June 1525 to Amsdorf.
16. LW 49, Letters 2, to George Spalatin, 16 April 1525, pp. 104–5.
17. See WT 3, no. 3179b; WT 2, no. 1657.
18. *Luther's Correspondence and Other Contemporary Letters*, vol. 2: *1521–1530*, trans. and ed. Preserved Smith and Charles M. Jacobs (Philadelphia, PA, 1918), letter 692, p. 325.

19. 16 June 1525, letter of invitation to Spalatin, WB 3, no. 892.
20. 15 June 1525, WB 3, no. 890, p. 531, ll. 20, 27.
21. LW 49, Letters 2, to Nicholas von Amsdorf, 21 June 1525.
22. 13 March 1526, to François Dubois, in *Collected Works of Erasmus*, vol. 12: *Letters 1658 to 1801, January 1526–March 1527*, trans. Alexander Dalzell (Toronto, 2003), p. 79.
23. *Luther's Correspondence and Other Contemporary Letters*, vol. 2: *1521–1530*, trans. and ed. Preserved Smith and Charles M. Jacobs, letter 692, p. 325.
24. 10 October 1525, Erasmus to Daniel Mauch, in *Collected Works of Erasmus*, p. 12:325.
25. *Collected Works of Erasmus*, vol. 12: *Letters 1658 to 1801, January 1526–March 1527*, trans. Alexander Dalzell, p. 79.
26. Siegfried Bräuer, 'Katharina von Bora, die Lutherin—im Urteil der Zeit', in Peter Freybeu, ed., *Mönchshure und Morgenstern, 'Katharina von Bora, die Lutherin'* (Wittenberg, 1999), p. 24; also WB 4, no. 1305, supplement, p. 527.
27. *Collected Works of Erasmus*, p. 12:79.
28. WT 2, no. 1656.
29. LW 54, Table Talk, no 3178a, p. 191.
30. LW 49, Letters 2, to Nicholas von Amsdorf, 21 June 1525, p. 117.
31. Letter to three nuns, 6 August 1524, WB 3, no. 766.
32. Preface to Justus Menius, *Oeconomia Christiana*, LW 59, Prefaces 1, p. 245.
33. LW 54, Table Talk, no. 3510, p. 218.
34. See WT 2, no. 1647: Question: 'Many lawyers say that [extramarital] carnal desire should not be punished...'
35. WW 6, p. 467, An den Christlichen Adel; letter of 3 September 1540, to Hieronymus Weller, WB 9, no. 3532; WT 6, no. 6924, pp. 272f.
36. WT 4, no. 4857.
37. WW 34:1, pp. 69ff., sermon on Hebrews 13:4; WT 3, no. 3508; WB 12, no. 4274, Letter of 1534 to unknown addressee; WT 3, no. 3182a, ll. 25f., no. 3182b, l. 32.
38. LW 7, Lectures on Genesis, chapters 38–44, p. 21.
39. WT 6, no. 6909.
40. WT 4, no. 4786.
41. See WB 8, no. 3140, 27 February 1537, to his wife; no. 3141 with supplement.
42. LW 50, Letters 3, to Mrs Martin Luther, 10 February 1546, pp. 305–6 (stone); 7 February 1546, p. 302.
43. WB 9, no. 3455, letter of 19 March 1540 to Jonas, Bugenhagen, Cruciger, and Melanchthon with n. 2, suspension of the journey by the elector, Gustav Kawerau, ed., *Der Briefwechsel des Justus Jonas*, part 1 (Hildesheim, 1884/1885; rept. 1964), no. 481.
44. WW 10/2, p. 301; WT 4, no. 4709; WW 53, pp. 203f.
45. See WB 9, no. 3509, p. 169, n. 1.
46. The report, made orally by Nikolaus von Amsdorff and recorded in writing shortly before the death of Katharina von Bora, is edited in Kroker, 'Luthers

Werbung um Katharina von Bora', with the cited material on pp. 143 and 145.

47. See pp. 99.

48. 'Ich armer man so halt ich haus: / Wo ich mein gelt sol geben aus, / Da durft ichs wol an sieben ort, / Und fleyet mit allweg hie und dort', WB 9, no. 3699, supplement 4, p. 585, ll. 206–209.

49. WT 4, no. 4783, pp. 500f.

50. LW 34, Career of the Reformer 4, Luther's Will, 6 January 1542, pp. 296, 295.

51. For a useful and vivid overview see Antje Heling, *Zu Haus bei Martin Luther: ein alltagsgeschichtlicher Rundgang* (Wittenberg, 2003), with the quoted passage on p. 11.

52. WB 10, no. 3727a.

53. LW 50, Letters 3, to Mrs Martin Luther, 2 July 1540, p. 209.

54. See WB 5, no. 1476.

55. LW 50, Letters 3, to Mrs Martin Luther, 1 February 1546, p. 290.

56. See WT 4, nos. 4860, 5567.

57. Theodor Kolde, ed., *Analecta Lutheriana* (Gotha, 1883), p. 378.

58. LW 54, Table Talk, no. 148, p. 21.

59. WB 6, p. 271.

60. WB 5, p. 379.

61. WB 5, no. 1595.

62. WT 3, no. 3456.

63. LW 45, Christian in Society 2, The Estate of Marriage, pp. 40–1.

64. WB 4, p. 269, ll. 26–28; WT 2, no. 1712.

65. LW 49, Letters 2, to Mrs Martin Luther, 5 June 1530, pp. 312–14. It would be interesting to know whether Luther really did only discuss such household matters with Argula von Grumbach, who was well versed and knowledgeable in both theology and politics.

66. See 15 September 1538 to Jakob Probst, WB 8, no. 3259, p. 292, ll. 35f.

67. WB 4, no. 1310, p. 541, ll. 9f.

68. LW 50, Letters 3, to Marcus Crodel, 6 (16?) September 1543, p. 235.

69. LW 54, Table Talk, no. 5494, p. 430.

70. See WT 3, no. 3777.

71. LW 50, Letters 3, to John Luther, 27 January 1537, p. 153.

72. LW 50, Letters 3, to Marcus Crodel, 28 August 1542, p. 233.

73. See WB 10, no. 3785; WT 5, no. 6192.

74. LW 54, Table Talk, no. 1422, pp. 150–1.

75. Volker Leppin, *Luther privat—Sohn, Vater, Ehemann* (Darmstadt, 2006), p. 29.

PART THREE. CHAPTER I

1. LW 46, The Christian in Society 3, An Open Letter on the Harsh Book, p. 84.

2. The citation is taken from the first two lines of a dedicatory text composed in summer 1545 that accompanied a woodcut depicting Wittenberg on the Elbe. See WW 35, p. 594. The dedication reads:

> Wittenberg, die kleine arme Stadt,
> Einen großen Nahmen itzund hat
> Von Gottes Wort, das heraus leucht
> Und viel Seelen zum Himmel zeucht.
> Damit sie ein Glied wird genannt,
> Der Stadt Jerusalem verwand.
> Gott geb ihr, dass sie danckbar sei
> Und ewig bleibe dabey,
> Und so gnug thu ihrem Namen,
> Daß sie selig werde, Amen

3. See WT 2, no. 2247.
4. LW 50, Letters 3, to Elector John, 16 June 1531, p. 24.
5. LW 54, Table Talk, no. 1646, p. 159.
6. LW 50, Letters 3, to Elector John, 16 June 1531, p. 24.
7. LW 50, Letters 3, to Elector John, 16 June 1531, p. 24.
8. WB 6, no. 1826.
9. LW 50, Letters 3, to Elector John, 16 June 1531, pp. 25, 26.
10. WT 5, no. 6425.
11. See Nikolaus Müller, 'Die Kirchen- und Schulvisitationen im Kreis Belzig', *Jahrbuch für Brandenburgische Kirchengeschichte* 1 (1904), pp. 64–5, n. 4.
12. LW 50, Letters 3, to Elector John, 16 June 1531, p. 24.
13. See p. 184.
14. LW 54, Table Talk, no. 1647, p. 160.
15. The term 'interdict' is used in WB 6, 21 June 1531, to Nikolaus Hausmann.
16. See Roth's letter to Luther, WB 6, no. 1802; in Luther's letter to the preachers of Zwickau, WB 6, no. 1827, 21 June 1531, Roth and his party are described as a 'frenzied fury'.
17. See p. 115.
18. The surviving letters are listed chronologically in Ute Mennecke-Haustein, *Luthers Trostbriefe* (Gütersloh, 1988), pp. 278–81.
19. WB 9, no. 3501, 18 June 1540.
20. See WT 2, no. 2266b, August 1531.
21. Bernhard Lohse, *Evangelium in der Geschichte* (Göttingen, 1988), p. 169.
22. Both citations are from Gustav Pfizer, *Martin Luthers Leben* (Stuttgart, 1836), pp. 833, 827.
23. WW 8, pp. 477ff.
24. LW 36, Word and Sacrament 2, The Misuse of the Mass, pp. 148, 152.
25. LW 36, Word and Sacrament 2, The Misuse of the Mass, p. 151.
26. See, for example, the lectures on the lesser prophets, WW 13.

27. LW 30, Sermons on the First Epistle of St. Peter, Foreword, pp. 3–4.

28. WW 12, p. 438, ll. 8 ff.

29. *Eyn Sermon von Stärke und Zunehmen des Glaubens und der Liebe*, WW 17/1, pp. 428ff.

30. WW 29, pp. 83f.

31. Elector John to Luther, 18 January 1530, WB 5, no. 1521.

32. See p. 286.

33. See WW 52.

34. 20 June 1529, WB 5, no. 1456.

35. Letter of July or August 1544, WB 10, no. 4013, p. 614, ll. 13–18.

36. Letter of August 1544, WB 10, no. 4014.

37. Letter to Lauterbach, July or August 1544, WB 10, no. 4013, p. 614, l. 20.

38. WB 5, no. 1394.

39. WB 5, no. 1397 (1 March 1529), no. 1418 (10 May 1529), no. 1510 (21 December 1529).

40. LW 14, Selected Psalms 3, Psalm 147, Preface, p. 110.

41. LW 14, Selected Psalms 3, Psalm 147, pp. 109–28.

42. See WW 31/1, pp. 426–556; see also WB 6, no. 1889, 16 December 1531, to Hans von Löser.

43. Citations here and below are from LW 50, Letters 3, no. 312, to Mrs Martin Luther, 28 July 1545, pp. 277–81.

44. Brück's report is published at WB 11, pp. 160f., as a supplement to the letter from Elector John Frederick to Luther of 5 August 1545.

45. Supplements to the letter from Elector John Frederick to Luther of 5 August 1545, WB 11, no. 4143, p. 164.

46. WB 11, no. 4143, p. 162, 9 July (so shortly before his flight), to Amsdorf; WB 11, no. 4132.

47. See pp. 214–15.

48. A comprehensive account of this process is a mighty task that cannot be achieved within the framework of this study and would require preliminary work, yet to be undertaken, which would provide an overview of early controversial theology and analyse the early modern theologies that subsequently developed in parallel.

49. Cited in the introduction to *De Servo Arbitrio* of 1525, WW 18, p. 582.

50. For detailed evidence for the discussion that follows, see the introduction to *De Servo Arbitrio* of 1525, WW 18, pp. 551ff., see also pp. 554ff.

51. See p. 142.

52. LW 49, Letters 2, to Erasmus of Rotterdam, about 18 April 1524, pp. 77–81.

53. See, for example, Martin Brecht, *Martin Luther*, 3 vols. (Stuttgart, 1981–7), 2:216.

54. *Luther and Erasmus, Free Will and Salvation*, ed. E. Gordon Rupp and Philip Saville (Philadelphia, PA, 1969), p. 47.

55. Heinz Scheible, *Melanchthon. Eine Biographie* (Munich, 1997), p. 151.

56. WT 4, no. 5069.

57. 28 September 1525 to Georg Spalatin, WB 3, p. 583, ll. 14–16.

58. WW 18, pp. 600–789; introduction on the sources, pp. 551–99.

59. LW 33, Career of the Reformer 3, The Bondage of the Will, pp. 15, 17, 16.

60. LW 33, Career of the Reformer 3, The Bondage of the Will, pp. 190–1.

61. LW 50, Letters 3, to Wolfgang Capito, 9 July 1537, pp. 172–3.

62. See pp. 157–8.

63. 'Handbook, The Small Catechism [of Dr. Martin Luther] for Ordinary Pastors and Preachers', in *The Book of Concord: The Confessions of the Evangelical Lutheran Church*, ed. Robert Kolb and Timothy J. Wengert (Minneapolis, MN, 2000), p. 359.

64. According to Elector John Frederick in a letter of 25 May 1536, WB 7, no. 3027.

65. LW 37, Word and Sacrament 3, Confession concerning Christ's Supper, pp. 360, 372.

66. WB 10, p. 615.

67. Letter of August 1544, WB 10, no. 4014, pp. 617f.

68. Letter of August 1544, WB 10, no. 4014, p. 616.

69. WW 54, pp. 141–67, also introduction, pp. 119–35, see also pp. 133f.

70. In particular in Gerhard Ebeling, *Lutherstudien*, 3 vols. (Tübingen, 1971–89), vols. 2 and 3.

71. *De homine*: no. 27, in Reinhard Schwarz, 'Disputationen', in Albrecht Beutel, ed., *Luther Handbuch* (Tübingen, 2005), p. 336; the translation of theses 11, 13, 17, 20 and the two last theses, 39 and 40, is based, in turn, on the translation by Gerhard Ebeling, in Karin Bornkamm and Gerhard Ebeling, eds., *Martin Luther, Ausgewählte Schriften*, 6 vols. (Frankfurt am Main, 1982), 2:294–7.

72. See pp. 387–99.

73. LW 49, Letters 2, to Lazarus Spengler, 8 July 1530, pp. 358–9.

74. LW 21, The Sermon on the Mount and the Magnificat, The Magnificat, p. 298.

75. LW 21, The Sermon on the Mount and the Magnificat, The Magnificat, p. 298.

76. WW 37, no. 23 and no. 24, pp. 91–9, quotation p. 97; similar on Mary: 1539, WW 50, pp. 488–653; WT nos. 494, 579, 4435, 5554, 5839.

77. As proposed in Martin Ohst, review of Burger, *Marias Lied*, in *Theologische Rundschau* 74 (May 2009), p. 237.

78. See pp. 142–3.

79. LW 31, Career of the Reformer 1, The Freedom of a Christian, p. 356.

80. LW 39, Church and Ministry 1, That a Christian Assembly of Congregation Has the Right and Power to Judge All Teaching and to Call, Appoint, and Dismiss Teachers, Established and Proven by Scripture, 1523, p. 309.

81. LW 45, The Christian in Society 2, Ordinance of a Common Chest, p. 172.

82. LW 46, The Christian in Society 3, The Twelve Articles, p. 10.

83. WW 12, p. 15.

84. See the introduction at WW 12, pp. 6, 8.

85. LW 49, Letters 2, to Elector John, 31 October 1525, p. 135.

86. LW 41, Church and Ministry 3, On the Councils and the Church, 1539, p. 144.

87. 22 November 1526, to Elector Johann, WB 4, no. 1052.

88. LW 49, Letters 2, to Elector John, 31 October 1525, p. 135.

89. Letters of 30 November 1525 and 22 November 1526, WB 3, no. 950; WB 4, no. 1052.

90. 22 November 1526, to Elector Johann, WB 4, no. 1052.

91. 30 November 1525, to Elector Johann, WB 3, no. 950.

92. 22 November 1526, to Elector Johann, WB 4, no. 1052.

93. WW 26, pp. 195–201.

94. LW 40, Church and Ministry 2, Instructions for the Visitors of Parish Pastors, 1528, pp. 271, 272.

95. WB 2, no. 483, p. 515, ll. 21f., 12 May 1522, to Spalatin.

96. Letter of 11 November 1525 to Spalatin, WB 3, no. 946, pp. 615f.

97. Cited in Hans-Walter Krumwiede, *Zur Entstehung des landesherrlichen Kirchenregimentes in Kursachsen und Braunschweig-Wolfenbüttel* (Göttingen, 1967), p. 9.

98. Letter of 22 November 1526, WB 4, no. 1052.

99. WW 15, pp. 9–53; pp. 15ff. provide an overview of the many editions up until recent times.

100. WW 15, p. 28.

101. LW 45, The Christian in Society 2, To the Councilmen of All Cities in Germany That They Establish and Maintain Christian Schools, 1524, p. 350.

102. LW 45, The Christian in Society 2, To the Councilmen of All Cities in Germany That They Establish and Maintain Christian Schools, 1524, pp. 359, 358.

103. LW 46, The Christian in Society 3, A Sermon on Keeping Children in School, 1530, pp. 257, 257–8.

104. LW 46, The Christian in Society 3, A Sermon on Keeping Children in School, 1530, p. 219.

105. LW 45, The Christian in Society 2, The Estate of Marriage, 1522, pp. 35, 49.

106. LW 45, The Christian in Society 2, The Estate of Marriage, 1522, pp. 37, 25; see also WW 12, p. 126.

107. WW 26, p. 185.

108. LW 40, Church and Ministry 2, Instructions for the Visitors of Parish Pastors, 1528, p. 301.

109. 'Handbook, The Small Catechism [of Dr. Martin Luther]', ed. Kolb and Wengert, p. 347.

110. LW 53, Liturgy and Hymns, Martin Luther's Preface to the German Mass and Order of Service, pp. 65, 67.

111. 'Handbook, The Small Catechism [of Dr. Martin Luther]', ed. Kolb and Wengert, p. 348.
112. 'Handbook, The Small Catechism [of Dr. Martin Luther]', ed. Kolb and Wengert, pp. 348–9.
113. 'Handbook, The Small Catechism [of Dr. Martin Luther]', ed. Kolb and Wengert, p. 367.
114. WW 27, p. 444.
115. 'Handbook, The Small Catechism [of Dr. Martin Luther]', ed. Kolb and Wengert, pp. 361–2.
116. WW 15, pp. 11–12.

PART THREE. CHAPTER II

1. Announcement of the Imperial diet, 21 January 1530, cited in Alfred Kohler, ed., *Quellen zur Geschichte Karls V.* (Darmstadt, 1990), p. 163, n. 2.
2. Volker Leppin, *Martin Luther* (Darmstadt, 2006); earlier Paul Joachimsen, *Die Reformation als Epoche der deutschen Geschichte* (Munich, 1950), p. 281.
3. For these quotations, see LW 49, Letters 2, to George Spalatin, 24 April 1530, pp. 292–5.
4. LW 49, Letters 2, to Philip Melanchthon, 24 April 1530, pp. 288–9.
5. WW 50, pp. 452–60; the manuscript of Luther's edition of Aesop's fables was uncovered in the Vatican Library in 1887; its nine pages contain the outline and the first draft of the fables, along with corrections and additions.
6. WW 32, individual sermons were also published immediately (for example in 1531 by Lufft in Wittenberg); the collection of Coburg sermons was published in 1730 by Korte in Altona.
7. 'We have finally arrived at our Sinai . . . , but we shall make a Zion out of this Sinai', LW 49, Letters 2, to Philip Melanchthon, 24 April 1530, p. 288.
8. WW 30/2, pp. 236–356.
9. For the citations WW 30/2, pp. 399–400, 412.
10. LW 49, Letters 2, to Philip Melanchthon, 24 April 1530, p. 289.
11. As recorded in the marginal notes to the translation of the prophets in the complete Wittenberg Bible of 1545: *Die gantze Heilige Schrift deudsch, Wittenberg 1545*, ed. Volz, 2:1474, 1475.
12. 29 June 1530, WB 5, no. 1609.
13. 15 June 1530, WB 5, no. 1584.
14. LW 24, Sermons on the Gospel of St. John Chapters 14–16, p. 394.
15. 12 May 1530, WB 5, no. 1566.
16. LW 48, Letters 1, to Landgrave Philip of Hesse, 20 May 1530, pp. 297–8.
17. LW 48, Letters 1, to Philip Melanchthon, 3 July 1530, p. 343.
18. WB 5, nos. 1605ff.
19. 26 August 1530, WB 5, no. 1698; 20 September 1530, WB 5, no. 1722.

20. Heinz Scheible, *Melanchthon. Eine Biographie* (Munich, 1997), p. 156.
21. LW 49, Letters 2, to Philip Melanchthon, 29 June 1530, p. 333.
22. WB 5, no. 1707.
23. According to a history of the Reformation published in 1566 in Nuremberg by eyewitness Johannes Mathesius; cited in Christian Peters, 'Er hats immer wollen besser machen ... Melanchthons fortgesetzte Arbeit am Text der lateinischen Apologie auf und nach dem Augsburger Reichstag von 1530', in Herbert Immenkötter and Gunter Wenz, eds., *Im Schatten der Confessio Augustana* (Münster, 1997), p. 113.
24. Eike Wolgast, ed., *Deutsche Reichstagsakten*, new series, vol. 10, pt. 4: *Der Reichstag zu Augsburg 1555* (Munich, 2009), no. 390, Abschied des Augsburger Reichstages 1555, § 25, p. 3112.
25. WB 7, no. 2093, pp. 27–40.
26. 11 January 1541, WB 11, no. 4185.
27. WB 9, no. 3554, also nos. 3561, 3600, 3602 from April 1541 to Regensburg.
28. WB 9, no. 3616, 10 or 11 May 1541, pp. 407 and 409.
29. WW 50, pp. 488–653, text from p. 509.
30. LW 41, Church and Ministry 3, On the Councils and the Church, p. 16.
31. LW 50, Letters 3, to Nicholas von Amsdorf, 9 July 1545, pp. 266–7.
32. In the seventeenth century the ring became part of the Wettin treasury, now in the Grünes Gewölbe Dresden, inv. no. VIII 97.
33. LW 49, Letters 2, to Mrs Martin Luther, 24 September 1530, p. 424.
34. Letters of Saturday, 15 October, and Tuesday, 18 October 1530, WB 5, nos. 1735 and 1736; also no. 1737, letter from Philip of Hesse to Luther.
35. WT 1, no. 154.
36. WW 11, pp. 230–44, editor's introduction.
37. LW 45, The Christian in Society 2, Temporal Authority: To What Extent It Should Be Obeyed, p. 81.
38. Citations are from LW 45, The Christian in Society 2, Temporal Authority: To What Extent It Should Be Obeyed, pp. 85–6, 88, 91, 94.
39. WW 19, pp. 616–62.
40. LW 45, The Christian in Society 2, Temporal Authority: To What Extent It Should Be Obeyed, pp. 120, 121.
41. For quotations, LW 45, The Christian in Society 2, Temporal Authority: To What Extent It Should Be Obeyed, pp. 104, 105, 106.
42. LW 45, The Christian in Society 2, Temporal Authority: To What Extent It Should Be Obeyed, pp. 121, 124.
43. LW 45, The Christian in Society 2, Temporal Authority: To What Extent It Should Be Obeyed, p. 108.
44. For Luther's report of March 1530, from which the citations are drawn, see Heinz Scheible, ed., *Das Widerstandsrecht als Problem der deutschen Protestanten 1523–1546* (Gütersloh, 1969), pp. 154–65.

45. The various positions are documented particularly well in the source collection Scheible, ed., *Das Widerstandsrecht*.
46. WB 5, no. 1737, quotation p. 654.
47. Scheible, ed., *Das Widerstandsrecht*, no. 16, p. 67.
48. Eike Wolgast, *Die Wittenberger Theologie und die Politik der evangelischen Stände. Studien zu Luthers Gutachten in politischen Fragen* (Gütersloh, 1977), p. 173.
49. LW 47, The Christian in Society 4, Luther's Warning to His Dear German People, p. 30.
50. LW 47, The Christian in Society 4, Luther's Warning to His Dear German People, p. 18.
51. WW 51, pp. 462–572, 1541.
52. WB 7, no. 2151.
53. WW 37.
54. WW 38, pp. 336–40.
55. WW 50, pp. 6–15.
56. WB 7, no. 3026, letter of 24 May 1536; response of the Wittenberg theologians from 5 June 1536, no. 3033.
57. LW 54, Table Talk, no. 3504, p. 216.
58. Scheible, ed., *Das Widerstandsrecht*, no. 20, pp. 89, 92.
59. WW 50, pp. 160–254; citations here are from 'Smalcald Articles', in *The Book of Concord: The Confessions of the Evangelical Lutheran Church*, ed. Robert Kolb and Timothy J. Wengert (Minneapolis, MN, 2000), pp. 297–328.
60. 'Smalcald Articles', p. 326. [The editors of the English translation note that the spelling 'Melanthon' in this instance is correct, RJ].
61. 'Smalcald Articles', pp. 297, 298.
62. A detailed account of the course of events was given by Luther himself in a letter of 10 June 1540 to Elector John Frederick, WB 9, no. 3493.
63. For the nineteenth and early twentieth centuries see Luther biographers Protestant Julius Köstlin and Jesuit Hans Wolters. For the present see the Marburg legal historian Stephan Buchholz, as well as church historian Wolfgang Breul-Kunkel's '"Mit gutem Gewissen": zum religiösen Hintergrund der Doppelehe Landgraf Philipps von Hessen', *Zeitschrift für Kirchengeschichte* 119 (2008), pp. 149–77, and his inaugural lecture at Marburg, 'Das Ende der Doppelmoral. Zum religiösen Hintergrund der Doppelehe Landgraf Philipps von Hessen'.
64. WB 8, no. 3423, pp. 628–37, introductory comments and excerpts from the sources.
65. LW 41, Church and Ministry 3, Against Hanswurst, pp. 239, 241.
66. WW 50, p. 423, n. 2.
67. See p. 177.
68. LW 54, Table Talk, between 21 May and 11 June 1540, no. 5038, p. 380.
69. WB 9, no. 3493, p. 133.
70. WB 8, no. 3423, text, pp. 638–44.
71. WB 9, no. 3488, 2 June 1540, pp. 123ff.

72. LW 54, Table Talk, 18 June 1540, no. 5096, p. 387; between 21 May and 11 June 1540, no. 5046, p. 382; during these months the guests around the table at the Luther House returned repeatedly, and in detail, to the theme of the double marriage and its consequences; see also nos. 5038 and 5088b.

73. WB 9, no. 3493.

74. LW 54, Table Talk, nos. 5096, 5045, 5088b.

75. Martin Brecht, *Martin Luther*, vol. 3: *The Preservation of the Church, 1532–1546* (Minneapolis, MN, 1993), p. 206.

76. Hermann Barge, *Luther und der Frühkapitalismus* (Gütersloh, 1951), p. 47; Hermann Lehman, 'Luthers Platz in der Geschichte der politischen Ökonomie', in Günter Vogler, ed., *Martin Luther. Leben—Werk—Wirkung* (Berlin, 1983), pp. 279–94. In the 1970s and 1980s Luther's comments on the economy, and on usury in particular, were also discussed in non-Marxist scholarship.

77. WW 6, pp. 1–35, 36–60; WW 15, pp. 279–322.

78. WB 3, no. 861, pp. 483f., with the report, from which the citations come, on pp. 484–6.

79. Both citations, LW 45, The Christian in Society, Trade and Usury, 1524, p. 310.

80. Citations in this paragraph are from LW 45, The Christian in Society, Trade and Usury, 1524, pp. 269–71.

81. WW 47, pp. 558f; similar is WW 51, p. 417.

82. Words spoken from the pulpit in 1542, see WW 53, p. 212.

83. WB 8, no. 3319, p. 405, with the reference to Cranach and the Table Talk. See also WB 12, no. 2704.

84. WW 51, p. 336.

85. Letter of Luther, Jonas, Bugenhagen, and Melanchthon of January 1540 to Elector Joachim II of Brandenburg, WB 9, no. 3430, pp. 6–8.

86. WT 4, no. 4496, p. 345.

87. Written during the crisis of autumn 1539 and available in published form in early 1540, WW 51, pp. 325–424; text, based on Luther's manuscript and the original publication, is on pp. 331–424, citations pp. 353f., 423; for examples of the damage caused by a debtor's failure to pay on time, see pp. 543ff.

88. For this and the following citations see WT 4, no. 4805, pp. 524, 525; WW 51, pp. 423, ll. 12ff.

89. WT 4, no. 4805, p. 525, l. 22.

90. All citations from LW 37, Word and Sacrament 3, Confession concerning Christ's Supper, 1528, p. 364. See also WW 39/2, circular disputation, 9 May 1539, on Matthew 19:21; WW 42, Lectures on Genesis, 1535–45.

91. LW 37, Word and Sacrament 3, Confession concerning Christ's Supper, 1528, p. 365.

92. For a flavour of Luther's own words, 1 Corinthians 7:20–2 in his own translation reads 'Ein iglicher bleibe in dem ruff, darinnen er beruffen ist. Bistu ein Knecht beruffen, sorge dir nicht. . . . Denn wer ein Knecht breruffen ist in dem herrn, der ist ein Gefreiter des Herrn'; *Die gantze Heilige Schrift deudsch, Wittenberg 1545*, ed. Volz, 2:2309.

93. LW 75, Church Postil 1, Gospel for St. John's Day, John 21:19–24, p. 355.
94. '*Unser Leben, . . . wens köstlich gewesen ist, so ists Mühe und Erbeit gewesen*', *Die gantze Heilige Schrift deudsch, Wittenberg 1545*, ed. Volz, 2:1045.
95. In Weber's famous treatment, *The Protestant Ethic and the Spirit of Capitalism*, first published, in German, in 1905.
96. Balthasar Bekker, *De betoverde weereld*, 4 vols. (Amsterdam, 1691–3).
97. WT 2, nos. 2540a, 2540b.
98. LW 75, Church Postil 1, Gospel for St. John's Day, John 21:19–24, p. 354.
99. WT 4, no. 3979, p. 51.
100. WT 6, no. 6592, p. 62.
101. A particularly memorable example is provided by the castle church at the small Thuringian administrative town and residence of Eisenberg, where in a series of pictures and statues the Saxe-Altenburg minor branch of the family had Christ and the princes appear almost as equals.
102. Thomas Kaufmann, *Geschichte der Reformation* (Frankfurt am Main, 2009), p. 716.

PART THREE. CHAPTER III

1. LW 13, Selected Psalms 2, Psalm 90, pp. 120, 123.
2. As Luther had already written to Duke George of Saxony on 21 December 1525, WB 3, no. 954.
3. *Die gantze Heilige Schrift deudsch, Wittenberg 1545*, ed. Volz, 1:7.
4. Christof Schubart, *Die Berichte über Luthers Tod und Begräbnis* (Weimar, 1917), no. 18, p. 20.
5. LW 34, Career of the Reformer 4, Preface to the Complete Edition of Luther's Latin Writings (1545), p. 338.
6. The Smalcald Articles (1537), preface, in *Concordia: The Lutheran Confessions; A Reader's Edition of the Book of Concord*, ed. Paul Timothy McCain (2nd ed., St Louis, MO, 2006), p. 261.
7. Vermanung Doctoris Martini Lutheri, In abwesenheit Doctoris Pomerani, WW 53, pp. 211–12.
8. LW 50, Letters 3, to Mrs Martin Luther, 25 January 1546, p. 286; 1 February 1546, p. 290; 6 February 1546, p. 300.
9. LW 51, Sermons 1, Eight Sermons at Wittenberg, 1522, Fourth Sermon, 12 March 1522, Wednesday after Invocavit, p. 86.
10. LW 40, Church and Ministry 2, Against the Heavenly Prophets in the Matter of Images and Sacraments, p. 88.
11. LW 37, Word and Sacrament 3, Confession concerning Christ's Supper (1528), p. 371.
12. WW 19, p. 42; WW 11, pp. 371, 373; WW 54, pp. 195–228; WB 2, no. 385, p. 283; 'das Kühnste, was der lange und erbitterte Kampf zwischen Rom und der Reformation hervorbrachte', E. Fuchs, *Die Karikatur der europäischen Völker,*

vol. 1 (Berlin, 1902), p. 72, cited in Christoph Weimer, *Luther, Cranach und die Bilder. Gesetz und Evangelium—Schlüssel zum reformatorischen Bildgebrauch* (Stuttgart, 1999), p. 68.

13. LW 54, Table Talk, no. 3528, between 14 and 31 January 1537, p. 222.

14. I thank Professor Silvana Seidel-Menchi of the University of Pisa for this information.

15. The original citation can be found in Veit-Jakobus Dieterich, *Martin Luther. Sein Leben und seine Zeit* (Munich, 2008), p. 153; see for the figures p. 165.

16. WT 5, no. 6143, p. 510; WT 2, no. 2758b, pp. 639f.

17. For example *Bluttgeld, fewreyffer, fridfertig, gastfrey, menschenfischer, morgenland, nachjagen, plappern, schaffskleyder, schedelstett, wetterwendisch, kleingläubig, Nächstenliebe.*

18. 'The Small Catechism', in *The Book of Concord: The Confessions of the Evangelical Lutheran Church*, ed. Robert Kolb and Timothy J. Wengert (Minneapolis, MN, 2000), p. 354.

19. For example, 'Lasst euer Licht Leuchten vor den Leuten' from the Sermon on the Mount (Matthew 5:16); 'Ihr werdet finden das Kind in Windeln gewickelt und in einer Krippe liegen' from the Christmas story (Luke 2:12).

20. LW 54, Table Talk, 18 June 1540, p. 389.

21. WW 37, pp. 296f.

22. LW 15, Notes on Ecclesiastes; Lectures on the Song of Solomon; Treatise on the Last Words of David, Treatise on the Last Words of David, p. 322.

23. LW 29, Lectures on Titus, Philemon, and Hebrews, Titus, p. 31.

24. WT 3, no. 3579, p. 428.

25. WW 50, p. 452.

26. See WW 50, pp. 452–60, citation pp. 454f.

27. WW 50, pp. 454 and 457. Luther's text reads: 'Es lief ein Hund durch ein Wasserstrom, und hatte ein stück Fleisch im Maule. Als er aber den schemen [also das Spiegelbild] vom Fleisch im Wasser sihet, wehnet er, es were auch Fleisch, und schnappet girig darnach. Da er aber das Maul auffthet, empfiel im das stück Fleisch, und das Wasser fürets weg. Also verlor er beide, das Fleisch und schemen. – Lere: Man sol sich benügen lassen an dem, das Gott gibt. Wem das wenige verschmähet, dem wird das Grössere nicht. Wer zu viel haben wil, der behelt zu letzt nichts. Mancher verleuret das gewisse uber dem ungewissen.'

28. Letter of 2 March 1535 to Linck, WB 7, no. 2181.

29. Erasmus' *Adagia*, which contained Greek and Latin proverbs, appeared first in 1500 and in its final, much-extended form in 1535.

30. Preface to his Fables of Aesop, WW 50, p. 452.

31. WW 51, pp. 634–62, proverbs begin on p. 645.

32. Was were dreck, wenn er nicht stüncke; wie Ochsen am berge stehen; der katzen spiel ist der meuse tod; Hunde seer bellen/die beissen nicht; viel hände machen leicht erbeit; Speck ym nacken; Feuer im arse; auf rosen gehen; er nympt kein blat furs maul; Horner auff setzen; die gelerten, die verkereten; Ein offenbar lug ist keiner antwort wert; was nicht dein ist, das las ligen; es

schmeckt nach dem Fasse; wer was eigens hat, greift drein wie eine saltzmeste; Trew erbeiter beten zwifeltig; from WW 51, pp. 645, 646, 647, 648, 651, 657, 659, 662 [As the language is paramount here, the proverbs have been translated literally. RJ].

33. LW 49, Letters 2, to Louis Senfl, 4 October 1530, pp. 428, 427.

34. As cited in Robin A. Leaver, *Luther's Liturgical Music: Principles and Implications* (Grand Rapids, MI, 2007), p. 86.

35. See WB 2, no. 281, p. 91; Johannes Schilling, 'Musik', in Albrecht Beutel, ed., *Luther Handbuch* (Tübingen, 2005), p. 238; WW 9, p. 518; WW 10/3, p. 433; WW 44, p. 548; WB 5, no. 1727, p. 639; WT 1, no. 522, pp. 243f.; WT 4, no. 4795, pp. 517f.

36. See WT 5, no 6428, p. 657.

37. Markus Jenny, 'Kirchenlied, Gesangbuch und Kirchenmusik', in Gerhard Bott, ed., *Martin Luther und die Reformation in Deutschland. Ausstellung zum 500. Geburtstag Martin Luthers* (Frankfurt am Main, 1983), p. 313.

38. *'velut Orpheus quidam'*, Cochläus' report is cited in Schilling, 'Musik', p. 238.

39. Citation from Schilling, 'Musik', p. 239.

40. Cited in Willibald Gurlitt, 'Johannes Walter und die Musik der Reformations-zeit', in *Luther-Jahrbuch* 15 (1933), p. 98.

41. WT 4, no. 4192, p. 191.

42. LW 53, Liturgy and Hymns, Preface to the Babst Hymnal (1545), p. 333.

43. Citations are from LW 49, Letters 2, to George Spalatin, end 1523, pp. 68, 69.

44. The songs are found in WW 35; with a supplemental revision by Markus Jenny in *Archiv zur Weimarer Ausgabe* 4 (1985), pp. 3–52; the oldest extant edition of the songbook, for which Luther added his own works for festivals of the church year to the initial grouping, is dated to 1533. The edition of 1535 includes Luther's Christmas songs for children, although in an earlier version than the established form of 1539.

45. Albert Becker, 'Gestalt und Gehalt in Wort und Ton. Von der Wortkunst und Musik zur Volkskunde', *Germanisch-romanische Monatsschrift* 34 (1953), p. 24.

46. WT 5, no. 6247, p. 557.

47. 'Du sollst deins Nächsten Weib und Haus / Begehren nicht, noch etwas draus; / Du sollst ihm wünschen alles Gut' / Wie dir dein Herze selber tut. / Kyrieleis'.

48. 'Nun bitten wir den heilgen Geist / Um den rechten Glauben allermeist, / dass er uns behüte an unserm Ende, / wenn wir heimfahrn aus diesem Elende. / Kyrieleis'.

49. 'Aus tiefer Not schrei ich zu dir, / Herr Gott, erhör mein Rufen. / Dein gnädig Ohren wend zu mir / Und meiner Bitt sie öffne. / . . . / Bei dir gilt nichts denn Gnad und Gunst, / die Sünden zu vergeben. / Es ist doch unser Tun umsunst, / auch in dem besten Leben. / Vor dir niemand sich rühmen kann; / des muss sich fürchten jedermann / und deiner Gnade leben.'

50. 'Verleih uns Frieden gnädiglich, / Herr Gott, zu unsern Zeiten. / Es ist doch ja kein andrer nicht, / der für uns könnte streiten, / denn du, unser Gott, alleine.'

51. LW 76, Church Postil 2, Gospel for the Second Sunday after Epiphany, John 2:1–11, p. 242.

52. Gottfried Herder, *Von Deutscher Art und Kunst. Einige fliegende Blätter* (Hamburg, 1773), p. 65.

53. Nietzsche to Peter Gast, 5 October 1879, in *Selected Letters of Friedrich Nietzsche*, ed. and trans. Christopher Middleton (Chicago, 1969), p. 168, second citation, 'Mitten wir im Leben sind mit dem Tod umfangen', Nietzsche to Peter Gast, 11 September 1879, Friedrich Nietzsche, *Briefe, ausgewählt und herausgegeben von Richard Oehler* (Leipzig, 1917), p. 220.

54. WW 35, pp. 467f.

55. LW 49, Letters 2, to Philip Melanchthon, 24 April 1530, p. 289.

56. LW 60, Prefaces 2, Preface to Brother Richard, 'Refutation of the Koran', pp. 255, 255–6.

57. LW 31, Career of the Reformer 1, Explanations of the Ninety-Five Theses, pp. 91, 92.

58. The context is also evident from two fundamental texts from this period, 'Sermon on Double Justification' (*Predigt zur doppelten Gerechtigkeit*) and 'On the New Meaning of Penance' (*Vom neuen Sinn der Buße*) with a letter to his mentor Staupitz as the preface; see also p. 122.

59. LW 46, The Christian in Society 3, On War Against the Turk, p. 170.

60. LW 46, The Christian in Society 3, On War Against the Turk, p. 175, 171, 185, 184.

61. As in Heiko A. Oberman, *Two Reformations: The Journey from the Last Days to the New World* (New Haven, CT, 2003), chapter 5, 'From Luther to Hitler', the work of an outstanding historian of the Reformation who in 1981 had published an insightful account of Luther's image of the Jews. The cited material was edited posthumously.

62. 'Güte und Milde . . . suchen wir . . . vergebens. Er hat Haß und Vernichtung der Menschenwürde gepredigt', Marianne Awerbuch, 'Humanismus—Reformation und Judentum', *Jahrbuch for Berlin-Brandenburgische Kirchengeschichte* 55 (1985), p. 35, cited in Peter von der Osten-Sacken, *Martin Luther und die Juden. Neu untersucht anhand von Anton Margarithas 'Der gantz Jüdisch glaub' (1530/31)* (Stuttgart, 2002), p. 300.

63. 'Letter to the Baptized Jew, Bernard (1523)', in Brooks Schramm and Kirsi I. Stjerna, *Martin Luther, the Bible, and the Jewish People: A Reader* (Minneapolis, MN, 2012), p. 86.

64. So WB 7, no. 2223, p. 233.

65. LW 47, The Christian in Society 4, On the Jews and Their Lies, pp. 191–2.

66. Citations of 'Letter to Josel of Rosheim', in Schramm and Stjerna, *Martin Luther, the Bible, and the Jewish People*, pp. 127–8.

67. The mandate is published in Carl August Hugo Burkhardt, 'Die Judenverfolgung im Kurfürstentum Sachsen von 1536 an', *Theologische Studien und Kritiken* 70 (1897), pp. 596–8, citation from p. 597.

68. Paul Reiter, *Martin Luthers Umwelt, Charakter und Psychose. Eine historisch psychiatrische Studie*, 2 vols. (Copenhagen, 1941), 2:210.

69. 'That Jesus Christ was born a Jew', in Schramm and Stjerna, *Martin Luther, the Bible, and the Jewish People*, p. 78.

70. 'Letter to the Baptized Jew, Bernard (1523)', in Schramm and Stjerna, *Martin Luther, the Bible, and the Jewish People*, p. 86.

71. 'That Jesus Christ was born a Jew', in Schramm and Stjerna, *Martin Luther, the Bible, and the Jewish People*, pp. 78, 83.

72. 'That Jesus Christ was born a Jew', in Schramm and Stjerna, *Martin Luther, the Bible, and the Jewish People*, p. 79.

73. 'Letter to Josel of Rosheim', in Schramm and Stjerna, *Martin Luther, the Bible, and the Jewish People*, p. 128.

74. The original German title is 'Der ganz Jüdisch Glaub mitsamt einer gründlichen und wahrhaften Anzeigung aller Satzungen, Ceremonien, Gebete, heimlichen und öffentlichen Gebräuche, deren sich die Juden halten durch das ganze Jahr'.

75. Citations from 'On the Jews and their Lies (January 1543)', in Schramm and Stjerna, *Martin Luther, the Bible, and the Jewish People*, p. 167.

76. LW 47, The Christian in Society 4, On the Jews and their Lies, p. 192.

77. LW 47, The Christian in Society 4, On the Jews and their Lies, pp. 276, 217, 284, 170, 217.

78. LW 47, The Christian in Society 4, On the Jews and their Lies, pp. 217, 218.

79. LW 47, The Christian in Society 4, On the Jews and their Lies, pp. 268–72.

80. LW 58, Sermon on the Gospel for the Fourth Sunday after Epiphany, Matthew 8, January 31, 1546. p. 419.

81. LW 58, Sermons 5, Admonition against the Jews, p. 458.

82. 'An Admonition against the Jews (1546)', in Schramm and Stjerna, *Martin Luther, the Bible, and the Jewish People*, p. 201; see also LW 58, Sermons 5, Admonition against the Jews, p. 458.

83. LW 47, The Christian in Society 4, On the Jews and their Lies, p. 306.

84. LW 58, Sermons 5, Admonition against the Jews, p. 458.

85. Cited in Leaver, *Luther's Liturgical Music*, p. 107.

86. See Mark U. Edwards Jr, *Luther's Last Battles: Politics and Polemics, 1531–46* (Ithaca, NY, 1983).

87. WW 30/2, p. 180.

88. LW 46, The Christian in Society 3, On War against the Turk, pp. 198, 199.

PART THREE. CHAPTER IV

1. WB 11, no. 4188, 17 January 1546.

2. 'Lutherportrait von 1543', in Christian von Mechel, ed., *Stammbuch, enthaltend die in Miniatur gemalte . . . Bildnisse der vorzüglichsten Fürsten und Gelehrten aus der Reformations-Geschichte* (Berlin, 1814; copy in Staatsbibliothek Berlin), p. 5 with image in the appendix.

3. Von Mechel, ed., *Stammbuch*, p. 5, a reproduction of the image with the handwritten note is in the appendix.

4. LW 50, Letters 3, to Mrs Martin Luther, 10 February 1546, p. 306.

5. Eisleben, 14 February 1546, WB 11, no. 4208.

6. Christof Schubart, *Die Berichte über Luthers Tod und Begräbnis* (Weimar, 1917), no. 12, p. 16.

7. As he wrote on 3 March 1541 to the Mansfeld court preacher, WB 9, no. 3579.

8. LW 50, Letters 3, to Caspar Müller, 19 January 1536, p. 128.

9. WB 9, no. 3481, 24 May 1540; no. 3579, 19 March 1541.

10. WB 9, no. 3716, p. 628.

11. 7 October 1545, WB 11, no. 4157.

12. LW 50, Letters 3, to Mrs Martin Luther, 25 January 1546, pp. 286, 287.

13. LW 58, Sermons 5, On the Conversion of St. Paul, Against the Monks, etc. From the Ninth Chapter of Acts, Given at Halle on 26 January 1546, pp. 372, 374, 375.

14. The building in which Luther died was some three or four houses below the house that now serves as a memorial site; in the nineteenth century this latter building was declared to be where the reformer had died.

15. WT 6, nos. 7030, 7031.

16. LW 50, Letters 3, to Mrs Martin Luther, 6 February 1546, p. 300.

17. Both citations, LW 50, Letters 3, to Mrs Martin Luther, 7 February 1546, p. 303.

18. LW 50, Letters 3, to Philip Melanchthon, 6 February 1646, p. 298.

19. The agreements are printed in WB 12, nos. 4300 and 4301 (excerpt).

20. LW 58, Sermons 5, The Third Sermon. For the Fifth Sunday after Epiphany. The Gospel, Matthew 13, Preached in Eisleben, 7 February 1546, pp. 446, 451.

21. LW 51, Sermons 1, The Last Sermon, Preached in Eisleben, Matt. 11:25–30, 15 February 1546, p. 392.

22. LW 50, Letters 3, to Mrs Martin Luther, 1 February 1546, pp. 291, 290.

23. WW 51, pp. 195–6. See WB 11, no. 4195, 1 February 1546, p. 276, n. 7; no. 4201, 7 February 1546, p. 288, n. 15.

24. LW 58, Sermons 5, An Admonition against the Jews, p. 458.

25. LW 50, Letters 3, to Mrs Martin Luther, 7 February 1546, p. 303.

26. 'An Admonition against the Jews (1546)', in Brooks Schramm and Kirsi I. Stjerna, *Martin Luther, the Bible, and the Jewish People: A Reader* (Minneapolis, MN, 2012), p. 201; see also LW 58, Sermons 5, An Admonition against the Jews, p. 458.

27. LW 50, Letters 3, to Mrs Martin Luther, 14 February 1546, p. 311.

28. The numerous reports of Luther's death and burial have been collected in Schubart, *Die Berichte über Luthers Tod und Begräbnis*, with the 'original' report, made by Justus Jonas in the early hours of 18 February, the morning on which Luther died, number one in that collection; on the cause of death see nos. 22 and 26b, by Melanchthon.

29. WW 48, p. 241.

30. Heinrich Bornkamm, *Luthers geistige Welt* (3rd ed.; Gütersloh, 1959), p. 17.

31. LW 34, Career of the Reformer 4, An Italian Lie concerning Dr Martin Luther's Death, 1545, p. 366.

32. LW 50, Letters 3, to Justus Jonas, 16 February 1542, p. 228.

33. WB 10, no. 3848, p. 262.

34. Schubart, *Die Berichte über Luthers Tod und Begräbnis*, no. 69, pp. 59–67; the sources for the discussion below are also in Schubart.

35. Paul Majunke, *Luthers Lebensende. Eine historische Untersuchung* (3rd ed.; Mainz, 1890); a remarkable three editions appeared in 1889/90; for a Catholic refutation, although still polemically charged, see Nikolaus Paulus, *Luthers Lebensende. Eine kritische Untersuchung* (Freiburg i. Br., 1898).

36. Schubart, *Die Berichte über Luthers Tod und Begräbnis*, no. 15, p. 18.

37. Schubart, *Die Berichte über Luthers Tod und Begräbnis*, no. 12, p. 16 with n. 1.

38. Schubart, *Die Berichte über Luthers Tod und Begräbnis*, no. 78, pp. 74ff.

39. Recorded, as is the material that follows, in Schubart, *Die Berichte über Luthers Tod und Begräbnis*, no. 69, pp. 67ff.; no. 80, pp. 81ff.

40. LW 50, Letters 3, to Mrs Martin Luther, 14 February 1546, p. 312.

41. From the only surviving personal letter from Katharina, dictated on 25 April 1546, cited in Volkmar Joestel and Friedrich Schorlemmer, eds., *Die Nonne heiratet den Mönch. Luthers Hochzeit als Scandalon: Eine Textsammlung* (Wittenberg, 1999), p. 37.

42. LW 50, Letters 3, to Mrs Martin Luther, 14 February 1546, pp. 312–13.

43. The English citation of Melanchthon's funeral oration for Luther is taken from James William Richard, *Philip Melanchthon the Protestant Preceptor of Germany, 1497–1560* (1898), cited in *The Protestant Reformation*, ed. Lewis W. Spitz (Englewood Cliffs, NJ, 1966), pp. 68–76.

44. Such artefacts, found not just in central Germany, are currently being researched by archaeologists under the auspices of the state of Saxony.

45. Charles' visit to Luther's grave appears first in sources from the second half of the sixteenth century, but there is still good evidence that the encounter did take place. See Helmar Junghans, 'Kaiser Karl V. am Grabe Martin Luthers in der Schloßkirche zu Wittenberg', *Lutherjahrbuch* 54 (1987), pp. 100–13.

46. See p. 379.

47. The German, 'Das Interim, das Interim, der Teufel, der steckt hinter im', contains a neat wordplay—RJ.

EPILOGUE

1. Adolf von Harnack, 'Die Reformation und ihre Vorstellung', in his *Erforschtes und Erlebtes* (Giessen, 1923), p. 110.

2. See Jean Bodin, *Les six livres de la République* (1576).

3. An expression drawn, as previously noted, from Gottfried Schramm and his *Fünf Wegscheiden der Weltgeschichte* [Five Crossroads in World History] (Göttingen, 2004).

4. LW 59, Prefaces 1, Preface to Philip Melanchthon, Exposition of Colossians, Translated into German by Justus Jonas, p. 251.

5. This verdict, which diverges from the position taken in older work on ecclesiastical history and the sociology of religion, is a product of the confessionalization paradigm.

6. Louis Châtellier, *The Europe of the Devout: The Catholic Reformation and the Formation of a New Society*, trans. Jean Birrell (Cambridge, 1987), pp. 135, 111.

7. For 'delayed nation', Helmuth Plessner, *Die verspätete Nation* (Stuttgart, 1959); for 'long road West', Heinrich August Winkler, *Der lange Weg nach Westen*, 2 vols. (5th ed.; Munich, 2012/2009), English translation, 'Germany: The Long Road West', trans. Alexander J. Sager, 2 vols. (Oxford, 2000).

8. I thank theologians Michael Beintker and Dorothea Wendebourg for discussions that helped me craft the following paragraphs.

9. LW 40, Church and Ministry 2, Letter to the Princes of Saxony concerning the Rebellious Spirit, p. 56.

10. See p. 142.

11. LW 44, The Christian in Society 1, Treatise on Good Works, p. 66.

12. LW 51, Sermons 1, Sermon at the Dedication of Castle Church, Torgau, 1544, p. 337.

13. Dietrich Bonhoeffer, *The Cost of Discipleship* (1937), trans. R. H. Fuller (Bury St. Edmunds, 2001), pp. 7–8.

Index

Note: For books of the Bible, *see under* Bible; for published works, *see under* author's name; for works of art, *see under* artist's name

Maps

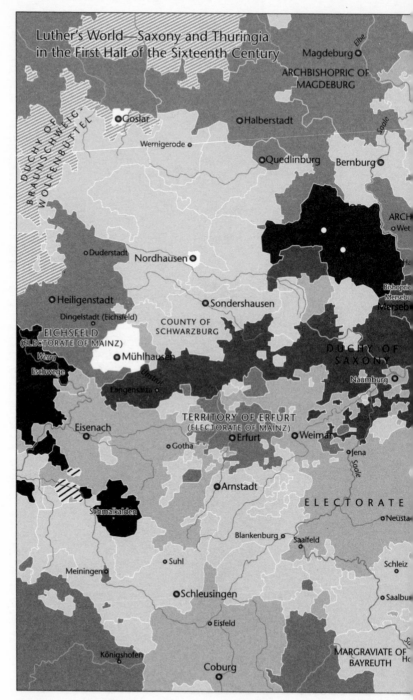

Map 3. Luther's World—Saxony and Thuringia in the First Half of the Sixte
Century.

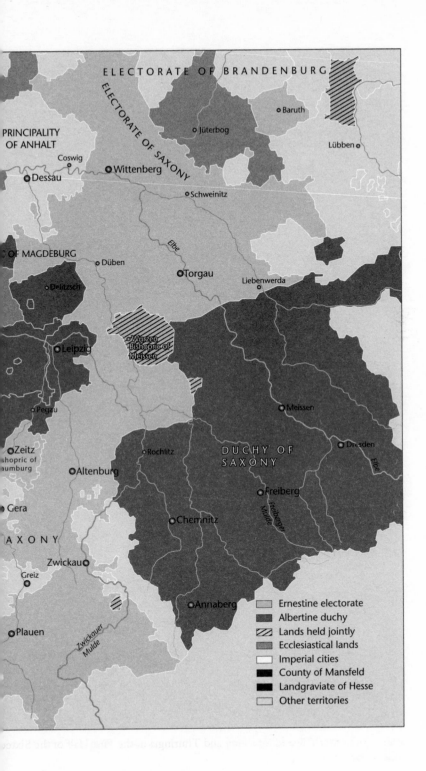

ELECTORATE OF BRANDENBURG

PRINCIPALITY
OF ANHALT

○ Baruth

○ Jüterbog

Lübben ○

Coswig

○ Wittenberg

○ Dessau

ELECTORATE OF SAXONY

○ Schweinitz

Elbe

OF MAGDEBURG

○ Düben

○ Torgau

Liebenwerda
○

○ Delitzsch

Wurzen
Bishopric of
Meissen

○ Leipzig

○ Meissen

○ Pegau

○ Zeitz

○ Rochlitz

DUCHY OF
SAXONY

○ Dresden

Elbe

shopric of
aumburg

○ Altenburg

○ Freiberg

Freiberger
Mulde

○ Gera

○ Chemnitz

AXONY

Zwickau ○

Greiz

○ Annaberg

Ernestine electorate

Albertine duchy

Lands held jointly

Ecclesiastical lands

Imperial cities

County of Mansfeld

Landgraviate of Hesse

Other territories

○ Plauen

Zwickauer
Mulde

Map 4. Towns, Villages, and Hamlets in Saxony and Thuringia with Which Luther Had Ties.

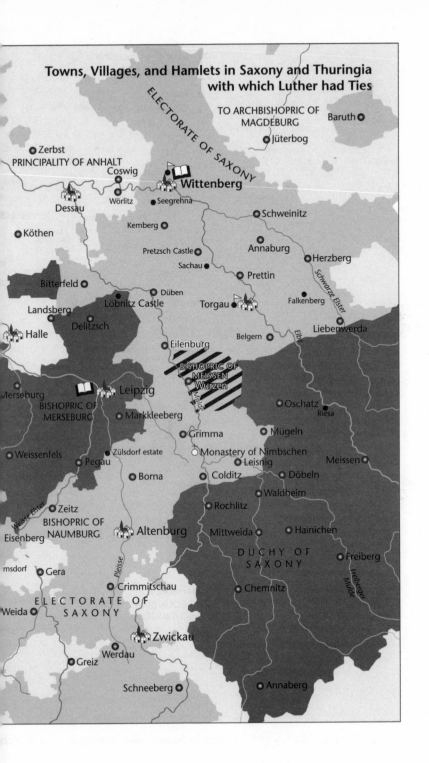

Towns, Villages, and Hamlets in Saxony and Thuringia with which Luther had Ties

ELECTORATE OF SAXONY

TO ARCHBISHOPRIC OF MAGDEBURG

Baruth

Jüterbog

Zerbst

PRINCIPALITY OF ANHALT

Coswig

Wittenberg

Wörlitz

Seegrehna

Dessau

Schweinitz

Kemberg

Köthen

Annaburg

Pretzsch Castle

Herzberg

Sachau

Prettin

Bitterfeld

Düben

Falkenberg

Landsberg

Löbnitz Castle

Torgau

Halle

Delitzsch

Belgern

Liebenwerda

Eilenburg

BISHOPRIC OF MEISSEN

Wurzen

Merseburg

Leipzig

Oschatz

BISHOPRIC OF MERSEBURG

Riesa

Markkleeberg

Mügeln

Weissenfels

Zülsdorf estate

Monastery of Nimbschen

Meissen

Pegau

Leisnig

Borna

Colditz

Döbeln

Zeitz

Waldheim

BISHOPRIC OF NAUMBURG

Rochlitz

Eisenberg

Altenburg

Mittweida

Hainichen

msdorf

Gera

DUCHY OF SAXONY

Freiberg

Crimmitschau

Chemnitz

ELECTORATE OF SAXONY

Weida

Zwickau

Greiz

Werdau

Schneeberg

Annaberg

Schwarze Elster

Elbe

Mulde

Weisse Elster

Pleisse

Freiberger Mulde